WSUA Core SDK

Windows® via C/C++

Fifth Edition

Jeffrey Richter (Wintellect)
Christophe Nasarre

PUBLISHED BY
Microsoft Press
A Division of Microsoft Corporation
One Microsoft Way
Redmond, Washington 98052-6399

Library of Congress Control Number: 2007939306

Printed and bound in the United States of America.

1 2 3 4 5 6 7 8 9   QWT   2 1 0 9 8 7

Distributed in Canada by H.B. Fenn and Company Ltd.

A CIP catalogue record for this book is available from the British Library.

Microsoft Press books are available through booksellers and distributors worldwide. For further information about international editions, contact your local Microsoft Corporation office or contact Microsoft Press International directly at fax (425) 936-7329. Visit our Web site at www.microsoft.com/mspress. Send comments to mspinput@microsoft.com.

Microsoft, ActiveX, Developer Studio, Intellisense, Internet Explorer, Microsoft Press, MSDN, MS-DOS, PowerPoint, SQL Server, SuperFetch, Visual Basic, Visual C++, Visual Studio, Win32, Win32s, Windows, Windows Media, Windows NT, Windows Server, and Windows Vista are either registered trademarks or trademarks of Microsoft Corporation in the United States and/or other countries. <possible third-party trademark info>. Other product and company names mentioned herein may be the trademarks of their respective owners.

The example companies, organizations, products, domain names, e-mail addresses, logos, people, places, and events depicted herein are fictitious. No association with any real company, organization, product, domain name, e-mail address, logo, person, place, or event is intended or should be inferred.

This book expresses the author's views and opinions. The information contained in this book is provided without any express, statutory, or implied warranties. Neither the authors, Microsoft Corporation, nor its resellers, or distributors will be held liable for any damages caused or alleged to be caused either directly or indirectly by this book.

Acquisitions Editor: Ben Ryan
Developmental and Project Editor: Lynn Finnel
Editorial Production: Publishing.com
Technical Reviewer: Scott Seely; Technical Review services provided by Content Master, a member of CM Group, Ltd.

Body Part No. X14-25709

Dedication

To Kristin, words cannot express how I feel about our life together.
I cherish our family and all our adventures.
I'm filled each day with love for you.

To Aidan, you have been an inspiration to me and have taught me
to play and have fun. Watching you grow up has been so rewarding
and enjoyable for me. I feel lucky to be able to
partake in your life; it has made me a better person.

To My New Baby Boy (shipping Q1 2008),
you have been wanted for so long it's hard to believe
that you're almost here. You bring completeness and balance
to our family. I look forward to playing with you,
learning who you are, and enjoying our time together.

– Jeffrey Richter

To my wife Florence, au moins cette fois c'est écrit: je t'aime Flo.

To my parents who cannot believe that learning English
with Dungeons & Dragons rules could have been so efficient.

– Christophe Nasarre

Contents at a Glance

Table of Contents

What do you think of this book? We want to hear from you!

Microsoft is interested in hearing your feedback so we can continually improve our books and learning resources for you. To participate in a brief online survey, please visit:

www.microsoft.com/learning/booksurvey/

Part VI **Appendixes**

A   **The Build Environment. 761**

What do you think of this book? We want to hear from you!

Microsoft is interested in hearing your feedback so we can continually improve our books and learning resources for you. To participate in a brief online survey, please visit:

www.microsoft.com/learning/booksurvey/

Acknowledgments

We could not have written this book without the help and technical assistance of several people. In particular, we'd like to thank the following people:

Jeffrey's Family

Jeffrey would like to thank Kristin (his wife) and Aidan (his son) for their never ending love and support.

Christophe's Family

Christophe would not have been able to write the fifth edition of this book without the love and support of Florence (his wife), the never ending curiosity of Celia (his daughter), and the purring sneak attacks of Canelle and Nougat (his cats). Now, I don't have any good excuse to not take care of you!

Technical Assistance

For writing a book like this one, personal research is not enough. We were owe great thanks to various Microsoft employees who helped us. Specifically, we'd like to thank Arun Kishan, who was able to either instantly answer weird and complicated questions or find the right person on the Windows team to provide more detailed explanations. We would also like to thank Kinshuman Kinshumann, Stephan Doll, Wedson Almeida Filho, Eric Li, Jean-Yves Poublan, Sandeep Ranade, Alan Chan, Ale Contenti, Kang Su Gatlin, Kai Hsu, Mehmet Iyigun, Ken Jung, Pavel Lebedynskiy, Paul Sliwowicz, and Landy Wang. In addition, there are those who listened to questions posted on Microsoft internal forums and shared their extensive knowledge, such as Raymond Chen, Sunggook Chue, Chris Corio, Larry Osterman, Richard Russell, Mark Russinovich, Mike Sheldon, Damien Watkins, and Junfeng Zhang. Last but not least, we would like to warmly thank John "Bugslayer" Robbins and Kenny Kerr who were kind enough to provide great feedback on chapters of this book.

Microsoft Press Editorial Team

We would like to thank Ben Ryan (acquisitions editor) for trusting a crazy French guy like Christophe, managers Lynn Finnel and Curtis Philips for their patience, Scott Seely for his constant search for technical accuracy, Roger LeBlanc for his talent in transforming Christophe's French-like English into something understandable, and Andrea Fox for her meticulous proofreading. In addition to the Redmond team, Joyanta Sen spent a lot of his personal time supporting us.

Mutual Admiration

Christophe sincerely thanks Jeffrey Richter for trusting him not to spoil the fifth edition of Jeff's book.

Jeffrey also thanks Christophe for his tireless efforts in researching, reorganizing, rewriting, and reworking the content in an attempt to reach Jeff's idea of perfection.

Introduction

Microsoft Windows is a complex operating system. It offers so many features and does so much that it's impossible for any one person to fully understand the entire system. This complexity also makes it difficult for someone to decide where to start concentrating the learning effort. Well, I always like to start at the lowest level by gaining a solid understanding of the system's basic building blocks. Once you understand the basics, it's easy to incrementally add any higher-level aspects of the system to your knowledge. So this book focuses on Windows' basic building blocks and the fundamental concepts that you must know when architecting and implementing software targeting the Windows operating system. In short, this book teaches the reader about various Windows features and how to access them via the C and C++ programming languages.

Although this book does not cover some Windows concepts—such as the Component Object Model (COM)—COM is built on top of basic building blocks such as processes, threads, memory management, DLLs, thread local storage, Unicode, and so on. If you know these basic building blocks, understanding COM is just a matter of understanding how the building blocks are used. I have great sympathy for people who attempt to jump ahead in learning COM's architecture. They have a long road ahead and are bound to have gaping holes in their knowledge, which is bound to negatively affect their code and their software development schedules.

The Microsoft .NET Framework's common language runtime (CLR) is another technology not specifically addressed in this book. (However, it is addressed in my other book: *CLR via C#,* Jeffrey Richter, Microsoft Press, 2006). However, the CLR is implemented as a COM object in a dynamic-link library (DLL) that loads in a process and uses threads to execute code that manipulates Unicode strings that are managed in memory. So again, the basic building blocks presented in this book will help developers writing managed code. In addition, by way of the CLR's Platform Invocation (P/Invoke) technology, you can call into the various Windows' APIs presented throughout this book.

So that's what this book is all about: the basic Windows building blocks that every Windows developer (at least in my opinion) should be intimately aware of. As each block is discussed, I also describe how the system uses these blocks and how your own applications can best take advantage of these blocks. In many chapters, I show you how to create building blocks of your own. These building blocks, typically implemented as generic functions or C++ classes, group a set of Windows building blocks together to create a whole that is much greater than the sum of its parts.

64-Bit Windows

Microsoft has been shipping 32-bit versions of Windows that support the *x86* CPU architecture for many years. Today, Microsoft also offers 64-bit versions of Windows that support the *x64* and IA-64 CPU architectures. Machines based on these 64-bit CPU architectures are fast gaining acceptance. In fact, in the very near future, it is expected that all desktop and server machines will contain 64-bit CPUs. Because of this, Microsoft has stated that Windows Server 2008 will be the last 32-bit version of Windows ever! For developers, now is the time to focus on making sure your applications run correctly on 64-bit Windows. To this end, this book includes solid coverage of what you need to know to have your applications run on 64-bit Windows (as well as 32-bit Windows).

The biggest advantage your application gets from a 64-bit address space is the ability to easily manipulate large amounts of data, because your process is no longer constrained to a 2-GB usable address space. Even if your application doesn't need all this address space, Windows itself takes advantage of the significantly larger address space (about 8 terabytes), allowing it to run faster.

Here is a quick look at what you need to know about 64-bit Windows:

- The 64-bit Windows kernel is a port of the 32-bit Windows kernel. This means that all the details and intricacies that you've learned about 32-bit Windows still apply in the 64-bit world. In fact, Microsoft has modified the 32-bit Windows source code so that it can be compiled to produce a 32-bit or a 64-bit system. They have just one source-code base, so new features and bug fixes are simultaneously applied to both systems.

- Because the kernels use the same code and underlying concepts, the Windows API is identical on both platforms. This means that you do not have to redesign or reimplement your application to work on 64-bit Windows. You can simply make slight modifications to your source code and then rebuild.

- For backward compatibility, 64-bit Windows can execute 32-bit applications. However, your application's performance will improve if the application is built as a true 64-bit application.

- Because it is so easy to port 32-bit code, there are already device drivers, tools, and applications available for 64-bit Windows. Unfortunately, Visual Studio is a native 32-bit application and Microsoft seems to be in no hurry to port it to be a native 64-bit application. However, the good news is that 32-bit Visual Studio does run quite well on 64-bit Windows; it just has a limited address space for its own data structures. And Visual Studio does allow you to debug a 64-bit application.

- There is little new for you to learn. You'll be happy to know that most data types remain 32 bits wide. These include **int**s, **DWORD**s, **LONG**s, **BOOL**s, and so on. In fact, you mostly just need to worry about pointers and handles, since they are now 64-bit values.

Because Microsoft offers so much information on how to modify your existing source code to be 64-bit ready, I will not go into those details in this book. However, I thought about 64-bit Windows as I wrote each chapter. Where appropriate, I have included information specific to 64-bit Windows. In addition, I have compiled and tested all the sample applications in this book for 64-bit Windows. So, if you follow the sample applications in this book and do as I've done, you should have no trouble creating a single source-code base that you can easily compile for 32-bit or 64-bit Windows.

What's New in the Fifth Edition

In the past, this book has been titled *Advanced Windows NT*, *Advanced Windows*, and *Programming Applications for Microsoft Windows*. In keeping with tradition, this edition of the book has gotten a new title: *Windows via C/C++*. This new title indicates that the book is for C and C++ programmers wanting to understand Windows. This new edition covers more than 170 new functions and Windows features that have been introduced in Windows XP, Windows Vista, and Windows Server 2008.

Some chapters have been completely rewritten—such as Chapter 11, which explains how the new thread pool API should be used. Existing chapters have been greatly enhanced to present new features. For example, Chapter 4 now includes coverage of User Account Control and Chapter 8 now covers new synchronization mechanisms (Interlocked Singly-Linked List, Slim Reader-Writer Locks, and condition variables).

I also give much more coverage of how the C/C++ run-time library interacts with the operating system—particularly on enhancing security as well as exception handling. Last but not least, two new chapters have been added to explain how I/O operations work and to dig into the new Windows Error Reporting system that changes the way you must think about application error reporting and application recovery.

In addition to the new organization and greater depth, I added a ton of new content. Here is a partial list of enhancements made for this edition:

New Windows Vista and Windows Server 2008 features   Of course, the book would not be a true revision unless it covered new features offered in Windows XP, Windows Vista, Windows Server 2008, and the C/C++ run-time library. This edition has new information on the secure string functions, the kernel object changes (such as namespaces and boundary descriptors), thread and process attribute lists, thread and I/O priority scheduling, synchronous I/O cancellation, vectored exception handling, and more.

64-bit Windows support   The text addresses 64-bit Windows-specific issues; all sample applications have been built and tested on 64-bit Windows.

Use of C++   The sample applications use C++ and require fewer lines of code, and their logic is easier to follow and understand.

Reusable code   Whenever possible, I created the source code to be generic and reusable. This should allow you to take individual functions or entire C++ classes and drop them into your own applications with little or no modification. The use of C++ made reusability much easier.

The ProcessInfo utility   This particular sample application from the earlier editions has been enhanced to show the process owner, command line, and UAC-related details.

The LockCop utility   This sample application is new. It shows which processes are running on the system. Once you select a process, this utility lists the threads of the process and, for each, on which kind of synchronization mechanism it is blocked—with deadlocks explicitly pointed out.

API hooking   I present updated C++ classes that make it trivial to hook APIs in one or all modules of a process. My code even traps run-time calls to **LoadLibrary** and **GetProcAddress** so that your API hooks are enforced.

Structured exception handling improvements   I have rewritten and reorganized much of the structured exception handling material. I have more information on unhandled exceptions, and I've added coverage on customizing Windows Error Reporting to fulfill your needs.

Code Samples and System Requirements

The sample applications presented throughout this book can be downloaded from the book's companion content Web page at

http://www.Wintellect.com/Books.aspx

To build the applications, you'll need Visual Studio 2005 (or later), the Microsoft Platform SDK for Windows Vista and Windows Server 2008 (which comes with some versions of Visual Studio). In addition, to run the applications, you'll need a computer (or virtual machine) with Windows Vista (or later) installed.

Support for This Book

Every effort has been made to ensure the accuracy of this book and the companion content. As corrections or changes are collected, they will be added to an Errata document downloadable at the following Web site:

http://www.Wintellect.com/Books.aspx

Questions and Comments

If you have comments, questions, or ideas regarding the book or the companion content, or questions that are not answered by visiting the site just mentioned, please send them to Microsoft Press via e-mail to

mspinput@microsoft.com

Or via postal mail to

Microsoft Press
Attn: *Windows via C/C++* Editor
One Microsoft Way
Redmond, WA 98052-6399

Please note that Microsoft software product support is not offered through the above addresses.

Part I
Required Reading

Chapter 1
Error Handling

Before we jump in and start examining the many features that Microsoft Windows has to offer, you should understand how the various Windows functions perform their error handling.

When you call a Windows function, it validates the parameters that you pass to it and then attempts to perform its duty. If you pass an invalid parameter or if for some other reason the action cannot be performed, the function's return value indicates that the function failed in some way. Table 1-1 shows the return value data types that most Windows functions use.

Table 1-1   Common Return Types for Windows Functions

Data Type	Value to Indicate Failure
VOID	This function cannot possibly fail. Very few Windows functions have a return type of **VOID**.
BOOL	If the function fails, the return value is 0; otherwise, the return value is non-zero. Avoid testing the return value to see if it is **TRUE**: it is always best to test this return value to see if it is different from **FALSE**.
HANDLE	If the function fails, the return value is usually **NULL**; otherwise, the **HANDLE** identifies an object that you can manipulate. Be careful with this one because some functions return a handle value of **INVALID_HANDLE_VALUE**, which is defined as −1. The Platform SDK documentation for the function will clearly state whether the function returns **NULL** or **INVALID_HANDLE_VALUE** to indicate failure.
PVOID	If the function fails, the return value is **NULL**; otherwise, **PVOID** identifies the memory address of a data block.
LONG/DWORD	This is a tough one. Functions that return counts usually return a **LONG** or **DWORD**. If for some reason the function can't count the thing you want counted, the function usually returns 0 or −1 (depending on the function). If you are calling a function that returns a **LONG/DWORD**, please read the Platform SDK documentation carefully to ensure that you are properly checking for potential errors.

When a Windows function returns with an error code, it's frequently useful to understand why the function failed. Microsoft has compiled a list of all possible error codes and has assigned each error code a 32-bit number.

Internally, when a Windows function detects an error, it uses a mechanism called thread-local storage to associate the appropriate error-code number with the calling thread. (Thread-local storage is discussed in Chapter 21, "Thread-Local Storage.") This mechanism allows threads to run independently of each other without affecting each other's error codes. When the function returns to you, its return value indicates that an error has occurred. To see exactly which error this is, call the **GetLastError** function:

```
DWORD GetLastError();
```

This function simply returns the thread's 32-bit error code set by the last function call.

Now that you have the 32-bit error code number, you need to translate that number into something more useful. The WinError.h header file contains the list of Microsoft-defined error codes. I'll reproduce some of it here so that you can see what it looks like:

```
// MessageId: ERROR_SUCCESS
//
// MessageText:
//
//  The operation completed successfully.
//
#define ERROR_SUCCESS                   0L

#define NO_ERROR 0L                            // dderror
#define SEC_E_OK                        ((HRESULT)0x00000000L)


//
// MessageId: ERROR_INVALID_FUNCTION
//
// MessageText:
//
//  Incorrect function.
//
#define ERROR_INVALID_FUNCTION          1L    // dderror


//
// MessageId: ERROR_FILE_NOT_FOUND
//
// MessageText:
//
//  The system cannot find the file specified.
//
#define ERROR_FILE_NOT_FOUND            2L


//
// MessageId: ERROR_PATH_NOT_FOUND
//
// MessageText:
//
//  The system cannot find the path specified.
//
#define ERROR_PATH_NOT_FOUND            3L
```

```
//
// MessageId: ERROR_TOO_MANY_OPEN_FILES
//
// MessageText:
//
//  The system cannot open the file.
//
#define ERROR_TOO_MANY_OPEN_FILES      4L


//
// MessageId: ERROR_ACCESS_DENIED
//
// MessageText:
//
//  Access is denied.
//
#define ERROR_ACCESS_DENIED            5L
```

As you can see, each error has three representations: a message ID (a macro that you can use in your source code to compare against the return value of **GetLastError**), message text (an English text description of the error), and a number (which you should avoid using and instead use the message ID). Keep in mind that I selected only a very tiny portion of the WinError.h header file to show you; the complete file is more than 39,000 lines long!

When a Windows function fails, you should call **GetLastError** right away because the value is very likely to be overwritten if you call another Windows function. Notice that a Windows function that succeeds might overwrite this value with **ERROR_SUCCESS**.

Some Windows functions can succeed for several reasons. For example, attempting to create a named event kernel object can succeed either because you actually create the object or because an event kernel object with the same name already exists. Your application might need to know the reason for success. To return this information to you, Microsoft chose to use the last error-code mechanism. So when certain functions succeed, you can determine additional information by calling **GetLastError**. For functions with this behavior, the Platform SDK documentation clearly states that **GetLastError** can be used this way. See the documentation for the **CreateEvent** function for an example where **ERROR_ALREADY_EXISTS** is returned when a named event already exists.

While debugging, I find it extremely useful to monitor the thread's last error code. In Microsoft Visual Studio, Microsoft's debugger supports a useful feature—you can configure the Watch window to always show you the thread's last error code number and the text description of the error. This is done by selecting a row in the Watch window and typing **$err,hr**. Examine Figure 1-1. You'll see that I've called the **CreateFile** function. This function returned a **HANDLE** of **INVALID_HANDLE_VALUE** (−1), indicating that it failed to open the specified file. But the Watch window shows us that the last error code (the error code that would be returned by the **Get-LastError** function if I called it) is 0x00000002. Thanks to the **,hr** qualifier, the Watch window further indicates that error code 2 is "The system cannot find the file specified." You'll notice that this is the same string mentioned in the WinError.h header file for error code number 2.

```
(Global Scope)                                              ▼  ⚙ WinMain(HINSTANCE hInstanceExe, HINSTANCE, PTSTR pszCmdl ▼
    9
   10 ⊟ int WINAPI _tWinMain(HINSTANCE hInstanceExe, HINSTANCE, PTSTR pszCmdLine, int) {
   11
   12       HANDLE hFile = CreateFile(TEXT("c:\\Jeff"), 0, 0, NULL, OPEN_EXISTING, 0, NULL);
   13       return(0);
   14 }
   15
```

```
Autos                          ▾ 🗗 ✕    Watch 1                                                   ▾ 🗗 ✕
Name        Value       Type           Name        Value                                          Type
  ◆ hFile   0xffffffff  void *           ◆ $err,hr  0x00000002 The system cannot find the file specified.  unsigned
```

Figure 1-1   Using **$err,hr** in Visual Studio's Watch window to view the current thread's last error code

Visual Studio also ships with a small utility called Error Lookup. You can use Error Lookup to convert an error code number into its textual description.

If I detect an error in an application I've written, I might want to show the text description to the user. Windows offers a function that converts an error code into its text description. This function is called **FormatMessage**:

```
DWORD FormatMessage(
    DWORD dwFlags,
    LPCVOID pSource,
    DWORD dwMessageId,
    DWORD dwLanguageId,
    PTSTR pszBuffer,
    DWORD nSize,
    va_list *Arguments);
```

FormatMessage is actually quite rich in functionality and is the preferred way of constructing strings that are to be shown to the user. One reason for this function's usefulness is that it works easily with multiple languages. This function takes a language identifier as a parameter and returns the appropriate text. Of course, first you must translate the strings yourself and embed the translated message table resource inside your .exe or DLL module, but then the function will select the correct one. The ErrorShow sample application (shown later in this chapter) demonstrates how to call this function to convert a Microsoft-defined error code number into its text description.

Every now and then, someone asks me if Microsoft produces a master list indicating all the possible error codes that can be returned from every Windows function. The answer, unfortunately, is no. What's more, Microsoft will never produce this list—it's just too difficult to construct and maintain as new versions of the system are created.

The problem with assembling such a list is that you can call one Windows function, but internally that function might call another function, and so on. Any of these functions could fail, for lots of different reasons. Sometimes when a function fails, the higher-level function can recover and still perform what you want it to. To create this master list, Microsoft would have to trace the path of every function and build the list of all possible error codes. This is difficult. And as new versions of the system were created, these function-execution paths would change.

Defining Your Own Error Codes

OK, I've shown you how Windows functions indicate errors to their callers. Microsoft also makes this mechanism available to you for use in your own functions. Let's say you're writing a function that you expect others to call. Your function might fail for one reason or another and you need to indicate that failure back to your caller.

To indicate failure, simply set the thread's last error code and then have your function return **FALSE**, **INVALID_HANDLE_VALUE**, **NULL**, or whatever is appropriate. To set the thread's last error code, you simply call

```
VOID SetLastError(DWORD dwErrCode);
```

passing into the function whatever 32-bit number you think is appropriate. I try to use codes that already exist in WinError.h–as long as the code maps well to the error I'm trying to report. If you don't think that any of the codes in WinError.h accurately reflect the error, you can create your own code. The error code is a 32-bit number that is divided into the fields shown in Table 1-2.

Table 1-2 Error Code Fields

Bits:	31–30	29	28	27–16	15–0
Contents	Severity	Microsoft/ customer	Reserved	Facility code	Exception code
Meaning	0 = Success 1 = Informational 2 = Warning 3 = Error	0 = Microsoft-defined code 1 = customer-defined code	Must be 0	The first 256 values are reserved by Microsoft	Microsoft/ customer-defined code

These fields are discussed in detail in Chapter 24, "Exception Handlers and Software Exceptions." For now, the only important field you need to be aware of is in bit 29. Microsoft promises that all error codes it produces will have a 0 in this bit. If you create your own error codes, you must put a 1 in this bit. This way, you're guaranteed that your error code will never conflict with a Microsoft-defined error code that currently exists or is created in the future. Note that the Facility field is large enough to hold 4096 possible values. Of these, the first 256 values are reserved for Microsoft; the remaining values can be defined by your own application.

The ErrorShow Sample Application

The ErrorShow application, 01-ErrorShow.exe, demonstrates how to get the text description for an error code. The source code and resource files for the application are in the 01-ErrorShow directory on this book's companion content Web page, which is located at *http://wintellect.com/Books.aspx*.

Basically, this application shows how the debugger's Watch window and Error Lookup programs do their things. When you start the program, the following window appears.

You can type any error number into the edit control. When you click the Look Up button, the error's text description is displayed in the scrollable window at the bottom. The only interesting feature of this application is how to call **FormatMessage**. Here's how I use this function:

```
// Get the error code
DWORD dwError = GetDlgItemInt(hwnd, IDC_ERRORCODE, NULL, FALSE);

HLOCAL hlocal = NULL;   // Buffer that gets the error message string

// Use the default system locale since we look for Windows messages
// Note: this MAKELANGID combination has a value of 0
DWORD systemLocale = MAKELANGID(LANG_NEUTRAL, SUBLANG_NEUTRAL);

// Get the error code's textual description
BOOL fOk = FormatMessage(
   FORMAT_MESSAGE_FROM_SYSTEM | FORMAT_MESSAGE_IGNORE_INSERTS |
   FORMAT_MESSAGE_ALLOCATE_BUFFER,
   NULL, dwError, systemLocale,
   (PTSTR) &hlocal, 0, NULL);

if (!fOk) {
   // Is it a network-related error?
   HMODULE hDll = LoadLibraryEx(TEXT("netmsg.dll"), NULL,
      DONT_RESOLVE_DLL_REFERENCES);

   if (hDll != NULL) {
      fOk = FormatMessage(
         FORMAT_MESSAGE_FROM_HMODULE | FORMAT_MESSAGE_IGNORE_INSERTS |
         FORMAT_MESSAGE_ALLOCATE_BUFFER,
         hDll, dwError, systemLocale,
         (PTSTR) &hlocal, 0, NULL);
      FreeLibrary(hDll);
   }
}

if (fOk && (hlocal != NULL)) {
   SetDlgItemText(hwnd, IDC_ERRORTEXT, (PCTSTR) LocalLock(hlocal));
   LocalFree(hlocal);
} else {
   SetDlgItemText(hwnd, IDC_ERRORTEXT,
      TEXT("No text found for this error number."));
```

The first line retrieves the error code number out of the edit control. Then a handle to a memory block is instantiated and initialized to **NULL**. The **FormatMessage** function internally allocates the block of memory and returns its handle back to us.

When calling **FormatMessage**, I pass the **FORMAT_MESSAGE_FROM_SYSTEM** flag. This flag tells **FormatMessage** that we want the string for a system-defined error code. I also pass the **FORMAT_MESSAGE_ALLOCATE_BUFFER** flag to tell the function to allocate a block of memory large enough for the error's text description. The handle to this block will be returned in the **hlocal** variable. The **FORMAT_MESSAGE_IGNORE_INSERTS** flag lets you get messages with % placeholders for parameters that are used by Windows to provide more contextual information, as shown by the following screen shot:

If you don't pass this flag, you have to provide the values for these placeholders in the **Arguments** parameter; but this is not possible for Error Show because the content of the messages is not known in advance.

The third parameter indicates the error number we want looked up. The fourth parameter indicates what language we want the text description in. Because we are interested in messages provided by Windows itself, the language identifier is built based on the two specific constants whose association ends up being to the 0 value—meaning the default language of the operating system. This is a case where you can't hardcode a specific language because you don't know in advance what the operating system installation language will be.

If **FormatMessage** returns success, the text description is in the memory block and I copy it to the scrollable window at the bottom of the dialog box. If **FormatMessage** fails, I try to look up the message code in the NetMsg.dll module to see if the error is network related (look at Chapter 20, "DLL Advanced Techniques," for details about how DLLs are searched on the disk). Using the handle of the NetMsg.dll module, I again call **FormatMessage**. You see, each DLL (or .exe) can have its own set of error codes that you can add to the module by using the Message Compiler (MC.exe) and adding a resource to the module. This is what Visual Studio's Error Lookup tool allows you to do using the Modules dialog box.

Chapter 2
Working with Characters and Strings

With Microsoft Windows becoming more and more popular around the world, it is increasingly important that we, as developers, target the various international markets. It was once common for U.S. versions of software to ship as much as six months prior to the shipping of international versions. But increasing international support for the operating system is making it easier to produce applications for international markets and therefore is reducing the time lag between distribution of the U.S. and international versions of our software.

Windows has always offered support to help developers localize their applications. An application can get country-specific information from various functions and can examine Control Panel settings to determine the user's preferences. Windows even supports different fonts for our applications. Last but not least, in Windows Vista, Unicode 5.0 is now supported. (Read "Extend The Global Reach Of Your Applications With Unicode 5.0" at *http://msdn.microsoft.com/msdnmag/ issues/07/01/Unicode/default.aspx* for a high-level presentation of Unicode 5.0.)

Buffer overrun errors (which are typical when manipulating character strings) have become a vector for security attacks against applications and even against parts of the operating system. In previous years, Microsoft put forth a lot of internal and external efforts to raise the security bar in the Windows world. The second part of this chapter presents new functions provided by Microsoft in the C run-time library. You should use these new functions to protect your code against buffer overruns when manipulating strings.

I decided to present this chapter early in the book because I highly recommend that your application always use Unicode strings and that you always manipulate these strings via the new secure string functions. As you'll see, issues regarding the secure use of Unicode strings are discussed in just about every chapter and in all the sample applications presented in this book. If you have a code base that is non-Unicode, you'll be best served by moving that code base to Unicode, as this will improve your application's execution performance as well as prepare it for localization. It will also help when interoperating with COM and the .NET Framework.

Character Encodings

The real problem with localization has always been manipulating different character sets. For years, most of us have been coding text strings as a series of single-byte characters with a zero at the end. This is second nature to us. When we call **strlen**, it returns the number of characters in a zero-terminated array of ANSI single-byte characters.

The problem is that some languages and writing systems (Japanese kanji being a classic example) have so many symbols in their character sets that a single byte, which offers no more than 256 different symbols at best, is just not enough. So double-byte character sets (DBCSs) were created to support these languages and writing systems. In a double-byte character set, each character in a string consists of either 1 or 2 bytes. With kanji, for example, if the first character is between 0x81 and 0x9F or between 0xE0 and 0xFC, you must look at the next byte to determine the full character in the string. Working with double-byte character sets is a programmer's nightmare because some characters are 1 byte wide and some are 2 bytes wide. Fortunately, you can forget about DBCS and take advantage of the support of Unicode strings supported by Windows functions and the C run-time library functions.

Unicode is a standard founded by Apple and Xerox in 1988. In 1991, a consortium was created to develop and promote Unicode. The consortium consists of companies such as Apple, Compaq, Hewlett-Packard, IBM, Microsoft, Oracle, Silicon Graphics, Sybase, Unisys, and Xerox. (A complete and updated list of consortium members is available at *http://www.Unicode.org.*) This group of companies is responsible for maintaining the Unicode standard. The full description of Unicode can be found in *The Unicode Standard*, published by Addison-Wesley. (This book is available through *http://www.Unicode.org.*)

In Windows Vista, each Unicode character is encoded using UTF-16 (where *UTF* is an acronym for *Unicode Transformation Format*). UTF-16 encodes each character as 2 bytes (or 16 bits). In this book, when we talk about Unicode, we are always referring to UTF-16 encoding unless we state otherwise. Windows uses UTF-16 because characters from most languages used throughout the world can easily be represented via a 16-bit value, allowing programs to easily traverse a string and calculate its length. However, 16-bits is not enough to represent all characters from certain languages. For these languages, UTF-16 supports surrogates, which are a way of using 32 bits (or 4 bytes) to represent a single character. Because few applications need to represent the characters of these languages, UTF-16 is a good compromise between saving space and providing ease of coding. Note that the .NET Framework always encodes all characters and strings using UTF-16, so using UTF-16 in your Windows application will improve performance and reduce memory consumption if you need to pass characters or strings between native and managed code.

There are other UTF standards for representing characters, including the following ones:

UTF-8   UTF-8 encodes some characters as 1 byte, some characters as 2 bytes, some characters as 3 bytes, and some characters as 4 bytes. Characters with a value below 0x0080 are compressed to 1 byte, which works very well for characters used in the United States. Characters between 0x0080 and 0x07FF are converted to 2 bytes, which works well for European and Middle Eastern languages. Characters of 0x0800 and above are converted to 3 bytes, which works well for East Asian languages. Finally, surrogate pairs are written out as 4 bytes. UTF-8 is an extremely popular encoding format, but it's less efficient than UTF-16 if you encode many characters with values of 0x0800 or above.

UTF-32   UTF-32 encodes every character as 4 bytes. This encoding is useful when you want to write a simple algorithm to traverse characters (used in any language) and you don't want to have to deal with characters taking a variable number of bytes. For example, with UTF-32, you do not need to think about surrogates because every character is 4 bytes. Obviously, UTF-32 is not an efficient encoding format in terms of memory usage. Therefore, it's rarely used for saving or transmitting strings to a file or network. This encoding format is typically used inside the program itself.

Currently, Unicode code points[1] are defined for the Arabic, Chinese bopomofo, Cyrillic (Russian), Greek, Hebrew, Japanese kana, Korean hangul, and Latin (English) alphabets—called scripts—and more. Each version of Unicode brings new characters in existing scripts and even new scripts such as Phoenician (an ancient Mediterranean alphabet). A large number of punctuation marks, mathematical symbols, technical symbols, arrows, dingbats, diacritics, and other characters are also included in the character sets.

These 65,536 characters are divided into regions. Table 2-1 shows some of the regions and the characters that are assigned to them.

Table 2-1   Unicode Character Sets and Alphabets

16-Bit Code	Characters	16-Bit Code	Alphabet/Scripts
0000–007F	ASCII	0300–036F	Generic diacritical marks
0080–00FF	Latin1 characters	0400–04FF	Cyrillic
0100–017F	European Latin	0530–058F	Armenian
0180–01FF	Extended Latin	0590–05FF	Hebrew
0250–02AF	Standard phonetic	0600–06FF	Arabic
02B0–02FF	Modified letters	0900–097F	Devanagari

ANSI and Unicode Character and String Data Types

I'm sure you're aware that the C language uses the **char** data type to represent an 8-bit ANSI character. By default, when you declare a literal string in your source code, the C compiler turns the string's characters into an array of 8-bit **char** data types:

```
// An 8-bit character
char c = 'A';

// An array of 99 8-bit characters and an 8-bit terminating zero.
char szBuffer[100] = "A String";
```

Microsoft's C/C++ compiler defines a built-in data type, **wchar_t**, which represents a 16-bit Unicode (UTF-16) character. Because earlier versions of Microsoft's compiler did not offer this built-in data type, the compiler defines this data type only when the **/Zc:wchar_t** compiler switch is specified. By default, when you create a C++ project in Microsoft Visual Studio, this compiler switch is specified. We recommend that you always specify this compiler switch, as it is better to work with Unicode characters by way of the built-in primitive type understood intrinsically by the compiler.

---

1 A code point is the position of a symbol in a character set.

> **Note** Prior to the built-in compiler support, a C header file defined a **wchar_t** data type as follows:
>
> ```
> typedef unsigned short wchar_t;
> ```

Here is how you declare a Unicode character and string:

```
// A 16-bit character
wchar_t c = L'A';

// An array up to 99 16-bit characters and a 16-bit terminating zero.
wchar_t szBuffer[100] = L"A String";
```

An uppercase **L** before a literal string informs the compiler that the string should be compiled as a Unicode string. When the compiler places the string in the program's data section, it encodes each character using UTF16, interspersing zero bytes between every ASCII character in this simple case.

The Windows team at Microsoft wants to define its own data types to isolate itself a little bit from the C language. And so, the Windows header file, WinNT.h, defines the following data types:

```
typedef char    CHAR;   // An 8-bit character
```

```
typedef wchar_t WCHAR;   // A 16-bit character
```

Furthermore, the WinNT.h header file defines a bunch of convenience data types for working with pointers to characters and pointers to strings:

```
// Pointer to 8-bit character(s)
typedef CHAR *PCHAR;
typedef CHAR *PSTR;
typedef CONST CHAR *PCSTR
```

```
// Pointer to 16-bit character(s)
typedef WCHAR *PWCHAR;
typedef WCHAR *PWSTR;
typedef CONST WCHAR *PCWSTR;
```

> **Note** If you take a look at WinNT.h, you'll find the following definition:
>
> ```
> typedef __nullterminated WCHAR *NWPSTR, *LPWSTR, *PWSTR;
> ```
>
> The **__nullterminated** prefix is a *header annotation* that describes how types are expected to be used as function parameters and return values. In the Enterprise version of Visual Studio, you can set the Code Analysis option in the project properties. This adds the **/analyze** switch to the command line of the compiler that detects when your code calls functions in a way that breaks the semantic defined by the annotations. Notice that only Enterprise versions of the compiler support this **/analyze** switch. To keep the code more readable in this book, the header annotations are removed. You should read the "Header Annotations" documentation on MSDN at *http://msdn2.microsoft.com/En-US/library/aa383701.aspx* for more details about the header annotations language.

In your own source code, it doesn't matter which data type you use, but I'd recommend you try to be consistent to improve maintainability in your code. Personally, as a Windows programmer, I always use the Windows data types because the data types match up with the MSDN documentation, making things easier for everyone reading the code.

It is possible to write your source code so that it can be compiled using ANSI or Unicode characters and strings. In the WinNT.h header file, the following types and macros are defined:

```
#ifdef UNICODE

typedef WCHAR TCHAR, *PTCHAR, PTSTR;
typedef CONST WCHAR *PCTSTR;
#define __TEXT(quote) quote          // r_winnt

#define __TEXT(quote) L##quote

#else

typedef CHAR TCHAR, *PTCHAR, PTSTR;
typedef CONST CHAR *PCTSTR;
#define __TEXT(quote) quote

#endif

#define   TEXT(quote) __TEXT(quote)
```

These types and macros (plus a few less commonly used ones that I do not show here) are used to create source code that can be compiled using either ANSI or Unicode chacters and strings, for example:

```
// If UNICODE defined, a 16-bit character; else an 8-bit character
TCHAR c = TEXT('A');

// If UNICODE defined, an array of 16-bit characters; else 8-bit characters
TCHAR szBuffer[100] = TEXT("A String");
```

Unicode and ANSI Functions in Windows

Since Windows NT, all Windows versions are built from the ground up using Unicode. That is, all the core functions for creating windows, displaying text, performing string manipulations, and so forth require Unicode strings. If you call any Windows function passing it an ANSI string (a string of 1-byte characters), the function first converts the string to Unicode and then passes the Unicode string to the operating system. If you are expecting ANSI strings back from a function, the system converts the Unicode string to an ANSI string before returning to your application. All these conversions occur invisibly to you. Of course, there is time and memory overhead involved for the system to carry out all these string conversions.

When Windows exposes a function that takes a string as a parameter, two versions of the same function are usually provided–for example, a **CreateWindowEx** that accepts Unicode strings and a second **CreateWindowEx** that accepts ANSI strings. This is true, but the two functions are actually prototyped as follows:

```
HWND WINAPI CreateWindowExW(
    DWORD dwExStyle,
    PCWSTR pClassName,     // A Unicode string
    PCWSTR pWindowName,    // A Unicode string
    DWORD dwStyle,
    int X,
    int Y,
    int nWidth,
    int nHeight,
    HWND hWndParent,
    HMENU hMenu,
    HINSTANCE hInstance,
    PVOID pParam);

HWND WINAPI CreateWindowExA(
    DWORD dwExStyle,
    PCSTR pClassName,      // An ANSI string
    PCSTR pWindowName,     // An ANSI string
    DWORD dwStyle,
    int X,
    int Y,
    int nWidth,
    int nHeight,
    HWND hWndParent,
    HMENU hMenu,
    HINSTANCE hInstance,
    PVOID pParam);
```

CreateWindowExW is the version that accepts Unicode strings. The uppercase *W* at the end of the function name stands for *wide*. Unicode characters are 16 bits wide, so they are frequently referred to as wide characters. The uppercase *A* at the end of **CreateWindowExA** indicates that the function accepts ANSI character strings.

But usually we just include a call to **CreateWindowEx** in our code and don't directly call either **CreateWindowExW** or **CreateWindowExA**. In WinUser.h, **CreateWindowEx** is actually a macro defined as

```
#ifdef UNICODE
#define CreateWindowEx CreateWindowExW
#else
#define CreateWindowEx CreateWindowExA
#endif
```

Whether or not **UNICODE** is defined when you compile your source code module determines which version of **CreateWindowEx** is called. When you create a new project with Visual Studio, it defines **UNICODE** by default. So, by default, any calls you make to **CreateWindowEx** expand the macro to call **CreateWindowExW**—the Unicode version of **CreateWindowEx**.

Under Windows Vista, Microsoft's source code for **CreateWindowExA** is simply a translation layer that allocates memory to convert ANSI strings to Unicode strings; the code then calls **Create-WindowExW**, passing the converted strings. When **CreateWindowExW** returns, **CreateWindowExA** frees its memory buffers and returns the window handle to you. So, for functions that fill buffers with strings, the system must convert from Unicode to non-Unicode equivalents before your application can process the string. Because the system must perform all these conversions, your application requires more memory and runs slower. You can make your application perform more efficiently by developing your application using Unicode from the start. Also, Windows has been known to have some bugs in these translation functions, so avoiding them also eliminates some potential bugs.

If you're creating dynamic-link libraries (DLLs) that other software developers will use, consider using this technique: supply two exported functions in the DLL—an ANSI version and a Unicode version. In the ANSI version, simply allocate memory, perform the necessary string conversions, and call the Unicode version of the function. I'll demonstrate this process later in this chapter in "Exporting ANSI and Unicode DLL Functions" on page 29.

Certain functions in the Windows API, such as **WinExec** and **OpenFile**, exist solely for backward compatibility with 16-bit Windows programs that supported only ANSI strings. These methods should be avoided by today's programs. You should replace any calls to **WinExec** and **OpenFile** with calls to the **CreateProcess** and **CreateFile** functions. Internally, the old functions call the new functions anyway. The big problem with the old functions is that they don't accept Unicode strings and they typically offer fewer features. When you call these functions, you must pass ANSI strings. On Windows Vista, most non-obsolete functions have both Unicode and ANSI versions. However, Microsoft has started to get into the habit of producing some functions offering only Unicode versions—for example, **ReadDirectoryChangesW** and **CreateProcessWithLogonW**.

When Microsoft was porting COM from 16-bit Windows to Win32, an executive decision was made that all COM interface methods requiring a string would accept only Unicode strings. This was a great decision because COM is typically used to allow different components to talk to each other and Unicode is the richest way to pass strings around. Using Unicode throughout your application makes interacting with COM easier too.

Finally, when the resource compiler compiles all your resources, the output file is a binary representation of the resources. String values in your resources (string tables, dialog box templates, menus, and so on) are always written as Unicode strings. Under Windows Vista, the system performs internal conversions if your application doesn't define the **UNICODE** macro. For example, if **UNICODE** is not defined when you compile your source module, a call to **LoadString** will actually call the **LoadStringA** function. **LoadStringA** will then read the Unicode string from your resources and convert the string to ANSI. The ANSI representation of the string will be returned from the function to your application.

Unicode and ANSI Functions in the C Run-Time Library

Like the Windows functions, the C run-time library offers one set of functions to manipulate ANSI characters and strings and another set of functions to manipulate Unicode characters and strings. However, unlike Windows, the ANSI functions do the work; they do not translate the strings to Unicode and then call the Unicode version of the functions internally. And, of course, the Unicode versions do the work themselves too; they do not internally call the ANSI versions.

An example of a C run-time function that returns the length of an ANSI string is **strlen**, and an example of an equivalent C run-time function that returns the length of a Unicode string is **wcslen**.

Both of these functions are prototyped in String.h. To write source code that can be compiled for either ANSI or Unicode, you must also include TChar.h, which defines the following macro:

```
#ifdef _UNICODE
#define _tcslen      wcslen
#else
#define _tcslen      strlen
#endif
```

Now, in your code, you should call **_tcslen**. If **_UNICODE** is defined, it expands to **wcslen**; otherwise, it expands to **strlen**. By default, when you create a new C++ project in Visual Studio, **_UNICODE** is defined (just like **UNICODE** is defined). The C run-time library always prefixes identifiers that are not part of the C++ standard with underscores, while the Windows team does not do this. So, in your applications you'll want to make sure that both **UNICODE** and **_UNICODE** are defined or that neither is defined. Appendix A, "The Build Environment," will describe the details of the CmnHdr.h header file used by all the code samples of this book to avoid this kind of problem.

Secure String Functions in the C Run-Time Library

Any function that modifies a string exposes a potential danger: if the destination string buffer is not large enough to contain the resulting string, memory corruption occurs. Here is an example:

```
// The following puts 4 characters in a
// 3-character buffer, resulting in memory corruption
WCHAR szBuffer[3] = L"";
wcscpy(szBuffer, L"abc"); // The terminating 0 is a character too!
```

The problem with the **strcpy** and **wcscpy** functions (and most other string manipulation functions) is that they do not accept an argument specifying the maximum size of the buffer, and therefore, the function doesn't know that it is corrupting memory. Because the function doesn't know that it is corrupting memory, it can't report an error back to your code, and therefore, you have no way of knowing that memory was corrupted. And, of course, it would be best if the function just failed without corrupting any memory at all.

This kind of misbehavior has been heavily exploited by malware in the past. Microsoft is now providing a set of new functions that replace the unsafe string manipulation functions (such as **wcscat**, which was shown earlier) provided by the C run-time library that many of us have grown to know and love over the years. To write safe code, you should no longer use any of the familiar C run-time functions that modify a string. (Functions such as **strlen**, **wcslen**, and **_tcslen** are OK, however, because they do not attempt to modify the string passed to them even though they assume that the string is **0** terminated, which might not be the case.) Instead, you should take advantage of the new secure string functions defined by Microsoft's StrSafe.h file.

Note   Internally, Microsoft has retrofitted its ATL and MFC class libraries to use the new safe string functions, and therefore, if you use these libraries, rebuilding your application to the new versions is all you have to do to make your application more secure.

Because this book is not dedicated to C/C++ programming, for a detailed usage of this library, you should take a look at the following sources of information:

- The MSDN Magazine article "Repel Attacks on Your Code with the Visual Studio 2005 Safe C and C++ Libraries" by Martyn Lovell, located at *http://msdn.microsoft.com/msdnmag/ issues/05/05/SafeCandC/default.aspx*

- The Martyn Lovell video presentation on Channel9, located at *http://channel9.msdn.com/ Showpost.aspx?postid=186406*

- The secure strings topic on MSDN Online, located at *http://msdn2.microsoft.com/en-us/ library/ms647466.aspx*

- The list of all C run-time secured replacement functions on MSDN Online, which you can find at *http://msdn2.microsoft.com/en-us/library/wd3wzwts(VS.80).aspx*

However, it is worth discussing a couple of details in this chapter. I'll start by describing the patterns employed by the new functions. Next, I'll mention the pitfalls you might encounter if you are following the migration path from legacy functions to their corresponding secure versions, like using **_tcscpy_s** instead of **_tcscpy**. Then I'll show you in which case it might be more interesting to call the new **StringC*** functions instead.

Introducing the New Secure String Functions

When you include StrSafe.h, String.h is also included and the existing string manipulation functions of the C run-time library, such as those behind the **_tcscpy** macro, are flagged with obsolete warnings during compilation. Note that the inclusion of StrSafe.h must appear after all other include files in your source code. I recommend that you use the compilation warnings to explicitly replace all the occurrences of the deprecated functions by their safer substitutes—thinking each time about possible buffer overflow and, if it is not possible to recover, how to gracefully terminate the application.

Each existing function, like **_tcscpy** or **_tcscat**, has a corresponding new function that starts with the same name that ends with the **_s** (for *secure*) suffix. All these new functions share common characteristics that require explanation. Let's start by examining their prototypes in the following code snippet, which shows the side-by-side definitions of two usual string functions:

```
PTSTR   _tcscpy (PTSTR strDestination, PCTSTR strSource);
errno_t _tcscpy_s(PTSTR strDestination, size_t numberOfCharacters,
   PCTSTR strSource);

PTSTR   _tcscat (PTSTR strDestination, PCTSTR strSource);
errno_t _tcscat_s(PTSTR strDestination, size_t numberOfcharacters,
   PCTSTR strSource);
```

When a writable buffer is passed as a parameter, its size must also be provided. This value is expected in the character count, which is easily computed by using the **_countof** macro (defined in stdlib.h) on your buffer.

All of the secure (**_s**) functions validate their arguments as the first thing they do. Checks are performed to make sure that pointers are not **NULL**, that integers are within a valid range, that enumeration values are valid, and that buffers are large enough to hold the resulting data. If any of these checks fail, the functions set the thread-local C run-time variable **errno** and the function returns an **errno_t** value to indicate success or failure. However, these functions don't actually return; instead, in a debug build, they display a user-unfriendly assertion dialog box similar to that shown in Figure 2-1. Then your application is terminated. The release builds directly auto-terminate.

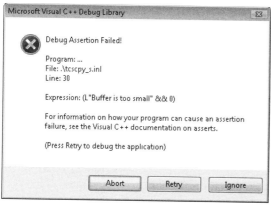

Figure 2-1   Assertion dialog box displayed when an error occurs

The C run time actually allows you to provide a function of your own, which it will call when it detects an invalid parameter. Then, in this function, you can log the failure, attach a debugger, or do whatever you like. To enable this, you must first define a function that matches the following prototype:

```
void InvalidParameterHandler(PCTSTR expression, PCTSTR function,
    PCTSTR file, unsigned int line, uintptr_t /*pReserved*/);
```

The **expression** parameter describes the failed expectation in the C run-time implementation code, such as **(L"Buffer is too small" && 0)**. As you can see, this is not very user friendly and should not be shown to the end user. This comment also applies to the next three parameters because **function**, **file**, and **line** describe the function name, the source code file, and the source code line number where the error occurred, respectively.

> **Note**   All these arguments will have a value of **NULL** if **DEBUG** is not defined. So this handler is valuable for logging errors only when testing debug builds. In a release build, you could replace the assertion dialog box with a more user-friendly message explaining that an unexpected error occurred that requires the application to shut down—maybe with specific logging behavior or an application restart. If its memory state is corrupted, your application execution should stop. However, it is recommended that you wait for the **errno_t** check to decide whether the error is recoverable or not.

The next step is to register this handler by calling **_set_invalid_parameter_handler**. However, this step is not enough because the assertion dialog box will still appear. You need to call **_CrtSetReportMode(_CRT_ASSERT, 0);** at the beginning of your application, disabling all assertion dialog boxes that could be triggered by the C run time.

Now, when you call one of the legacy replacement functions defined in String.h, you are able to check the returned **errno_t** value to understand what happened. Only the value **S_OK** means that the call was successful. The other possible return values found in errno.h, such as **EINVAL**, are for invalid arguments such as **NULL** pointers.

Let's take an example of a string that is copied into a buffer that is too small for one character:

```
TCHAR szBefore[5] = {
    TEXT('B'), TEXT('B'), TEXT('B'), TEXT('B'), '\0'
};

TCHAR szBuffer[10] = {
    TEXT('-'), TEXT('-'), TEXT('-'), TEXT('-'), TEXT('-'),
    TEXT('-'), TEXT('-'), TEXT('-'), TEXT('-'), '\0'
};

TCHAR szAfter[5] = {
    TEXT('A'), TEXT('A'), TEXT('A'), TEXT('A'), '\0'
};

errno_t result = _tcscpy_s(szBuffer, _countof(szBuffer),
    TEXT("0123456789"));
```

Just before the call to **_tcscpy_s**, each variable has the content shown in Figure 2-2.

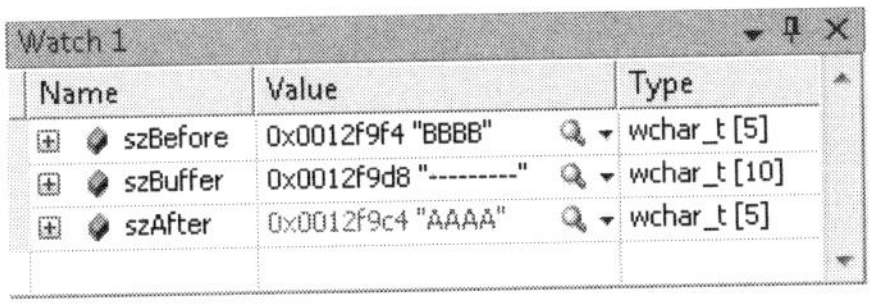

Figure 2-2   Variable state before the _tcscpy_s call

Because the "1234567890" string to be copied into **szBuffer** has exactly the same 10-character size as the buffer, there is not enough room to copy the terminating **'\0'** character. You might expect that the value of **result** is now **STRUNCATE** and the last character **'9'** has not been copied, but this is not the case. **ERANGE** is returned, and the state of each variable is shown in Figure 2-3.

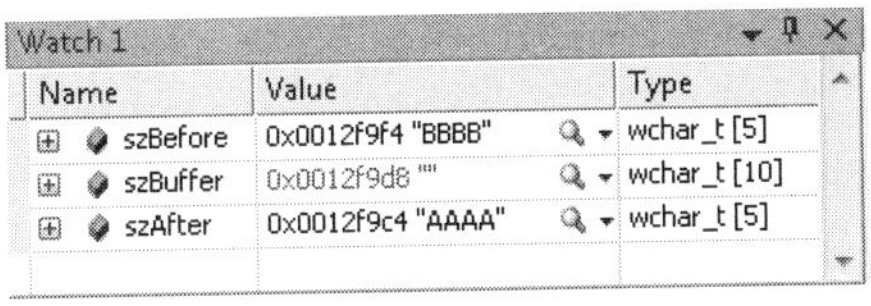

Figure 2-3   Variable state after the _tcscpy_s call

There is one side effect that you don't see unless you take a look at the memory behind **szBuffer**, as shown in Figure 2-4.

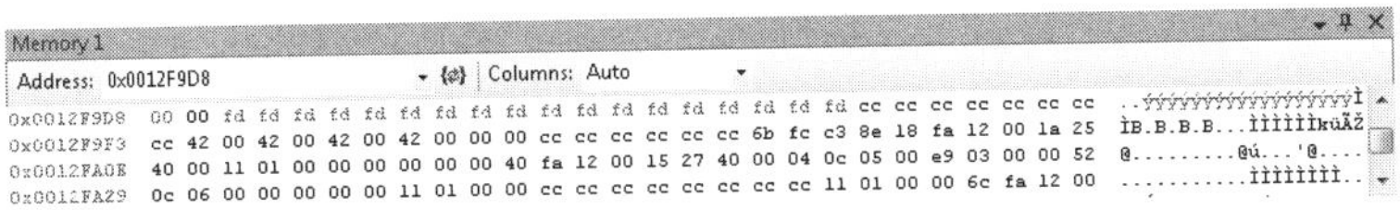

Figure 2-4   Content of *szBuffer* memory after a failed call

The first character of **szBuffer** has been set to **'\0'**, and all other bytes now contain the value **0xfd**. So the resulting string has been truncated to an empty string and the remaining bytes of the buffer have been set to a filler value (**0xfd**).

> **Note**   If you wonder why the memory after all the variables have been defined is filled up
> with the **0xcc** value in Figure 2-4, the answer is in the result of the compiler implementation
> of the run-time checks (**/RTCs**, **/RTCu**, or **/RTC1**) that automatically detect buffer overrun at
> run time. If you compile your code without these **/RTCx** flags, the memory view will show all
> **sz*** variables side by side. But remember that your builds should always be compiled with
> these run-time checks to detect any remaining buffer overrun early in the development cycle.

How to Get More Control When Performing String Operations

In addition to the new secure string functions, the C run-time library has some new functions that
provide more control when performing string manipulations. For example, you can control the
filler values or how truncation is performed. Naturally, the C run time offers both ANSI (A) versions of the functions as well as Unicode (W) versions of the functions. Here are the prototypes for
some of these functions (and many more exist that are not shown here):

```
HRESULT StringCchCat(PTSTR pszDest, size_t cchDest, PCTSTR pszSrc);
HRESULT StringCchCatEx(PTSTR pszDest, size_t cchDest, PCTSTR pszSrc,
   PTSTR *ppszDestEnd, size_t *pcchRemaining, DWORD dwFlags);

HRESULT StringCchCopy(PTSTR pszDest, size_t cchDest, PCTSTR pszSrc);
HRESULT StringCchCopyEx(PTSTR pszDest, size_t cchDest, PCTSTR pszSrc,
   PTSTR *ppszDestEnd, size_t *pcchRemaining, DWORD dwFlags);

HRESULT StringCchPrintf(PTSTR pszDest, size_t cchDest,
   PCTSTR pszFormat, ...);
HRESULT StringCchPrintfEx(PTSTR pszDest, size_t cchDest,
   PTSTR *ppszDestEnd, size_t *pcchRemaining, DWORD dwFlags,
   PCTSTR pszFormat,...);
```

You'll notice that all the methods shown have "Cch" in their name. This stands for *Count of characters*, and you'll typically use the **_countof** macro to get this value. There is also a set of functions
that have "Cb" in their name, such as **StringCbCat(Ex)**, **StringCbCopy(Ex)**, and **StringCb-
Printf(Ex)**. These functions expect that the size argument is in count of bytes instead of count of
characters. You'll typically use the **sizeof** operator to get this value.

All these functions return an **HRESULT** with one of the values shown in Table 2-2.

Table 2-2   HRESULT Values for Safe String Functions

HRESULT Value	Description
S_OK	Success. The destination buffer contains the source string and is terminated by **'\0'**.
STRSAFE_E_INVALID_PARAMETER	Failure. The **NULL** value has been passed as a parameter.
STRSAFE_E_INSUFFICIENT_BUFFER	Failure. The given destination buffer was too small to contain the entire source string.

Unlike the secure (**_s** suffixed) functions, when a buffer is too small, these functions do perform
truncation. You can detect such a situation when **STRSAFE_E_INSUFFICIENT_BUFFER** is returned.
As you can see in StrSafe.h, the value of this code is **0x8007007a** and is treated as a failure by

SUCCEEDED/FAILED macros. However, in that case, the part of the source buffer that could fit into the destination writable buffer has been copied and the last available character is set to **'\0'**. So, in the previous example, **szBuffer** would contain the string "012345678" if **StringCchCopy** is used instead of **_tcscpy_s**. Notice that the truncation feature might or might not be what you need, depending on what you are trying to achieve, and this is why it is treated as a failure (by default). For example, in the case of a path that you are building by concatenating different pieces of information, a truncated result is unusable. If you are building a message for user feedback, this could be acceptable. It's up to you to decide how to handle a truncated result.

Last but not least, you'll notice that an extended (**Ex**) version exists for many of the functions shown earlier. These extended versions take three additional parameters, which are described in Table 2-3.

Table 2-3   Extended Version Parameters

Parameters and Values	Description
`size_t* pcchRemaining`	Pointer to a variable that indicates the number of unused characters in the destination buffer. The copied terminating **'\0'** character is not counted. For example, if one character is copied into a buffer that is 10 characters wide, 9 is returned even though you won't be able to use more than 8 characters without truncation. If **pcchRemaining** is **NULL**, the count is not returned.
`LPTSTR* ppszDestEnd`	If **ppszDestEnd** is non-**NULL**, it points to the terminating **'\0'** character at the end of the string contained by the destination buffer.
`DWORD dwFlags`	One or more of the following values separated by '|'.
`STRSAFE_FILL_BEHIND_NULL`	If the function succeeds, the low byte of **dwFlags** is used to fill the rest of the destination buffer, just after the terminating **'\0'** character. (See the comment about **STRSAFE_FILL_BYTE** just after this table for more details.)
`STRSAFE_IGNORE_NULLS`	Treats **NULL** string pointers like empty strings **(TEXT(""))**.
`STRSAFE_FILL_ON_FAILURE`	If the function fails, the low byte of **dwFlags** is used to fill the entire destination buffer except the first **'\0'** character used to set an empty string result. (See the comment about **STRSAFE_FILL_BYTE** just after this table for more details.) In the case of a **STRSAFE_E_INSUFFICIENT_BUFFER** failure, any character in the string being returned is replaced by the filler byte value.
`STRSAFE_NULL_ON_FAILURE`	If the function fails, the first character of the destination buffer is set to **'\0'** to define an empty string **(TEXT(""))**. In the case of a **STRSAFE_E_INSUFFICIENT_BUFFER** failure, any truncated string is overwritten.
`STRSAFE_NO_TRUNCATION`	As in the case of **STRSAFE_NULL_ON_FAILURE**, if the function fails, the destination buffer is set to an empty string **(TEXT(""))**. In the case of a **STRSAFE_E_INSUFFICIENT_BUFFER** failure, any truncated string is overwritten.

> **Note** Even if **STRSAFE_NO_TRUNCATION** is used as a flag, the characters of the source string are still copied, up to the last available character of the destination buffer. Then both the first and the last characters of the destination buffer are set to **'\0'**. This is not really important except if, for security purposes, you don't want to keep garbage data.

There is a last detail to mention that is related to the remark that you read at the bottom of page 21. In Figure 2-4, the **0xfd** value is used to replace all the characters after the **'\0'**, up to the end of the destination buffer. With the **Ex** version of these functions, you can choose whether you want this expensive filling operation (especially if the destination buffer is large) to occur and with which byte value. If you add **STRSAFE_FILL_BEHIND_NULL** to **dwFlag**, the remaining characters are set to **'\0'**. When you replace **STRSAFE_FILL_BEHIND_NULL** with the **STRSAFE_FILL_BYTE** macro, the given byte value is used to fill up the remaining values of the destination buffer.

Windows String Functions

Windows also offers various functions for manipulating strings. Many of these functions, such as **lstrcat** and **lstrcpy**, are now deprecated because they do not detect buffer overrun problems. Also, the ShlwApi.h file defines a number of handy string functions that format operating system–related numeric values, such as **StrFormatKBSize** and **StrFormatByteSize**. See *http://msdn2.microsoft.com/en-us/library/ms538658.aspx* for a description of shell string handling functions.

It is common to want to compare strings for equality or for sorting. The best functions to use for this are **CompareString(Ex)** and **CompareStringOrdinal**. You use **CompareString(Ex)** to compare strings that will be presented to the user in a linguistically correct manner. Here is the prototype of the **CompareString** function:

```
int CompareString(
   LCID locale,
   DWORD dwCmdFlags,
   PCTSTR pString1,
   int cch1,
   PCTSTR pString2,
   int cch2);
```

This function compares two strings. The first parameter to **CompareString** specifies a locale ID (LCID), a 32-bit value that identifies a particular language. **CompareString** uses this LCID to compare the two strings by checking the meaning of the characters as they apply to a particular language. A linguistically correct comparison produces results much more meaningful to an end user. However, this type of comparison is slower than doing an ordinal comparison. You can get the locale ID of the calling thread by calling the Windows **GetThreadLocale** function:

```
LCID GetThreadLocale();
```

The second parameter of **CompareString** identifies flags that modify the method used by the function to compare the two strings. Table 2-4 shows the possible flags.

Table 2-4 Flags Used by the CompareString Function

Flag	Meaning
NORM_IGNORECASE LINGUISTIC_IGNORECASE	Ignore case difference.
NORM_IGNOREKANATYPE	Do not differentiate between hiragana and katakana characters.
NORM_IGNORENONSPACE LINGUISTIC_IGNOREDIACRITIC	Ignore nonspacing characters.
NORM_IGNORESYMBOLS	Ignore symbols.
NORM_IGNOREWIDTH	Do not differentiate between a single-byte character and the same character as a double-byte character.
SORT_STRINGSORT	Treat punctuation the same as symbols.

The remaining four parameters of **CompareString** specify the two strings and their respective lengths in characters (not in bytes). If you pass negative values for the **cch1** parameter, the function assumes that the **pString1** string is zero-terminated and calculates the length of the string. This also is true for the **cch2** parameter with respect to the **pString2** string. If you need more advanced linguistic options, you should take a look at the **CompareStringEx** functions.

To compare strings that are used for programmatic strings (such as pathnames, registry keys/values, XML elements/attributes, and so on), use **CompareStringOrdinal**:

```
int CompareStringOrdinal(
  PCWSTR pString1,
  int cchCount1,
  PCWSTR pString2,
  int cchCount2,
  BOOL bIgnoreCase);
```

This function performs a code-point comparison without regard to the locale, and therefore it is fast. And because programmatic strings are not typically shown to an end user, this function makes the most sense. Notice that only Unicode strings are expected by this function.

The **CompareString** and **CompareStringOrdinal** functions' return values are unlike the return values you get back from the C run-time library's ***cmp** string comparison functions. **Compare-String(Ordinal)** returns **0** to indicate failure, **CSTR_LESS_THAN** (defined as **1**) to indicate that **pString1** is less than **pString2**, **CSTR_EQUAL** (defined as **2**) to indicate that **pString1** is equal to **pString2**, and **CSTR_GREATER_THAN** (defined as **3**) to indicate that **pString1** is greater than **pString2**. To make things slightly more convenient, if the functions succeed, you can subtract **2** from the return value to make the result consistent with the result of the C run-time library functions (**-1**, **0**, and **+1**).

Why You Should Use Unicode

When developing an application, we highly recommend that you use Unicode characters and strings. Here are some of the reasons why:

- Unicode makes it easy for you to localize your application to world markets.

- Unicode allows you to distribute a single binary (.exe or DLL) file that supports all languages.

- Unicode improves the efficiency of your application because the code performs faster and uses less memory. Windows internally does everything with Unicode characters and strings, so when you pass an ANSI character or string, Windows must allocate memory and convert the ANSI character or string to its Unicode equivalent.

- Using Unicode ensures that your application can easily call all nondeprecated Windows functions, as some Windows functions offer versions that operate only on Unicode characters and strings.

- Using Unicode ensures that your code easily integrates with COM (which requires the use of Unicode characters and strings).

- Using Unicode ensures that your code easily integrates with the .NET Framework (which also requires the use of Unicode characters and strings).

- Using Unicode ensures that your code easily manipulates your own resources (where strings are always persisted as Unicode).

How We Recommend Working with Characters and Strings

Based on what you've read in this chapter, the first part of this section summarizes what you should always keep in mind when developing your code. The second part of the section provides tips and tricks for better Unicode and ANSI string manipulations. It's a good idea to start converting your application to be Unicode-ready even if you don't plan to use Unicode right away. Here are the basic guidelines you should follow:

- Start thinking of text strings as arrays of characters, not as arrays of **chars** or arrays of bytes.

- Use generic data types (such as **TCHAR/PTSTR**) for text characters and strings.

- Use explicit data types (such as **BYTE** and **PBYTE**) for bytes, byte pointers, and data buffers.

- Use the **TEXT** or **_T** macro for literal characters and strings, but avoid mixing both for the sake of consistency and for better readability.

- Perform global replaces. (For example, replace **PSTR** with **PTSTR**.)

- Modify string arithmetic problems. For example, functions usually expect you to pass a buffer's size in characters, not bytes. This means you should pass **_countof(szBuffer)** instead of **sizeof(szBuffer)**. Also, if you need to allocate a block of memory for a string and you have the number of characters in the string, remember that you allocate memory in bytes. This means that you must call **malloc(nCharacters * sizeof(TCHAR))** and not call **malloc(nCharacters)**. Of all the guidelines I've just listed, this is the most difficult one to remember, and the compiler offers no warnings or errors if you make a mistake. This is a good opportunity to define your own macros, such as the following:

```
#define chmalloc(nCharacters)  (TCHAR*)malloc(nCharacters * sizeof(TCHAR)).
```

- Avoid **printf** family functions, especially by using **%s** and **%S** field types to convert ANSI to Unicode strings and vice versa. Use **MultiByteToWideChar** and **WideCharToMultiByte** instead, as shown in "Translating Strings Between Unicode and ANSI" below.

- Always specify both **UNICODE** and **_UNICODE** symbols or neither of them.

In terms of string manipulation functions, here are the basic guidelines that you should follow:

- Always work with safe string manipulation functions such as those suffixed with **_s** or prefixed with **StringCch**. Use the latter for explicit truncation handling, but prefer the former otherwise.

- Don't use the unsafe C run-time library string manipulation functions. (See the previous recommendation.) In a more general way, don't use or implement any buffer manipulation routine that would not take the size of the destination buffer as a parameter. The C run-time library provides a replacement for buffer manipulation functions such as **memcpy_s**, **memmove_s**, **wmemcpy_s**, or **wmemmove_s**. All these methods are available when the **__STDC_WANT_SECURE_LIB__** symbol is defined, which is the case by default in CrtDefs.h. So don't undefine **__STDC_WANT_SECURE_LIB__**.

- Take advantage of the **/GS** (*http://msdn2.microsoft.com/en-us/library/aa290051(VS.71).aspx*) and **/RTCs** compiler flags to automatically detect buffer overruns.

- Don't use Kernel32 methods for string manipulation such as **lstrcat** and **lstrcpy**.

- There are two kinds of strings that we compare in our code. Programmatic strings are file names, paths, XML elements and attributes, and registry keys/values. For these, use **CompareStringOrdinal**, as it is very fast and does not take the user's locale into account. This is good because these strings remain the same no matter where your application is running in the world. User strings are typically strings that appear in the user interface. For these, call **CompareString(Ex)**, as it takes the locale into account when comparing strings.

You don't have a choice: as a professional developer, you can't write code based on unsafe buffer manipulation functions. And this is the reason why all the code in this book relies on these safer functions from the C run-time library.

Translating Strings Between Unicode and ANSI

You use the Windows function **MultiByteToWideChar** to convert multibyte-character strings to wide-character strings. **MultiByteToWideChar** is shown here:

```
int MultiByteToWideChar(
   UINT uCodePage,
   DWORD dwFlags,
   PCSTR pMultiByteStr,
   int cbMultiByte,
   PWSTR pWideCharStr,
   int cchWideChar);
```

The **uCodePage** parameter identifies a code page number that is associated with the multibyte string. The **dwFlags** parameter allows you to specify an additional control that affects characters with diacritical marks such as accents. Usually the flags aren't used, and **0** is passed in the **dwFlags** parameter (For more details about the possible values for this flag, read the MSDN online help at *http://msdn2.microsoft.com/en-us/library/ms776413.aspx*.) The **pMultiByteStr** parameter specifies the string to be converted, and the **cbMultiByte** parameter indicates the length (in bytes) of the string. The function automatically determines the length of the source string if you pass −1 for the **cbMultiByte** parameter.

The Unicode version of the string resulting from the conversion is written to the buffer located in memory at the address specified by the **pWideCharStr** parameter. You must specify the maximum size of this buffer (in characters) in the **cchWideChar** parameter. If you call **MultiByteToWide-Char**, passing **0** for the **cchWideChar** parameter, the function doesn't perform the conversion and instead returns the number of wide characters (including the terminating **'\0'** character) that the buffer must provide for the conversion to succeed. Typically, you convert a multibyte-character string to its Unicode equivalent by performing the following steps:

1. Call **MultiByteToWideChar**, passing **NULL** for the **pWideCharStr** parameter and **0** for the **cchWideChar** parameter and −1 for the **cbMultiByte** parameter.

2. Allocate a block of memory large enough to hold the converted Unicode string. This size is computed based on the value returned by the previous call to **MultiByteToWideChar** multiplied by **sizeof(wchar_t)**.

3. Call **MultiByteToWideChar** again, this time passing the address of the buffer as the **pWideCharStr** parameter and passing the size computed based on the value returned by the first call to **MultiByteToWideChar** multiplied by **sizeof(wchar_t)** as the **cchWideChar** parameter.

4. Use the converted string.

5. Free the memory block occupying the Unicode string.

The function **WideCharToMultiByte** converts a wide-character string to its multibyte-string equivalent, as shown here:

```
int WideCharToMultiByte(
   UINT uCodePage,
   DWORD dwFlags,
   PCWSTR pWideCharStr,
   int cchWideChar,
   PSTR pMultiByteStr,
   int cbMultiByte,
   PCSTR pDefaultChar,
   PBOOL pfUsedDefaultChar);
```

This function is similar to the **MultiByteToWideChar** function. Again, the **uCodePage** parameter identifies the code page to be associated with the newly converted string. The **dwFlags** parameter allows you to specify additional control over the conversion. The flags affect characters with diacritical marks and characters that the system is unable to convert. Usually, you won't need this degree of control over the conversion, and you'll pass **0** for the **dwFlags** parameter.

The **pWideCharStr** parameter specifies the address in memory of the string to be converted, and the **cchWideChar** parameter indicates the length (in characters) of this string. The function determines the length of the source string if you pass −1 for the **cchWideChar** parameter.

The multibyte version of the string resulting from the conversion is written to the buffer indicated by the **pMultiByteStr** parameter. You must specify the maximum size of this buffer (in bytes) in the **cbMultiByte** parameter. Passing **0** as the **cbMultiByte** parameter of the **WideCharToMulti-Byte** function causes the function to return the size required by the destination buffer. You'll typically convert a wide-character string to a multibyte-character string using a sequence of events similar to those discussed when converting a multibyte string to a wide-character string, except that the return value is directly the number of bytes required for the conversion to succeed.

You'll notice that the **WideCharToMultiByte** function accepts two parameters more than the **MultiByteToWideChar** function: **pDefaultChar** and **pfUsedDefaultChar**. These parameters are used by the **WideCharToMultiByte** function only if it comes across a wide character that doesn't have a representation in the code page identified by the **uCodePage** parameter. If the wide character cannot be converted, the function uses the character pointed to by the **pDefaultChar** parameter. If this parameter is **NULL**, which is most common, the function uses a system default character. This default character is usually a question mark. This is dangerous for filenames because the question mark is a wildcard character.

The **pfUsedDefaultChar** parameter points to a Boolean variable that the function sets to **TRUE** if at least one character in the wide-character string could not be converted to its multibyte equivalent. The function sets the variable to **FALSE** if all the characters convert successfully. You can test this variable after the function returns to check whether the wide-character string was converted successfully. Again, you usually pass **NULL** for this parameter.

For a more complete description of how to use these functions, please refer to the Platform SDK documentation.

Exporting ANSI and Unicode DLL Functions

You could use these two functions to easily create both Unicode and ANSI versions of functions. For example, you might have a dynamic-link library containing a function that reverses all the characters in a string. You could write the Unicode version of the function as shown here:

```
BOOL StringReverseW(PWSTR pWideCharStr, DWORD cchLength) {

   // Get a pointer to the last character in the string.
   PWSTR pEndOfStr = pWideCharStr + wcsnlen_s(pWideCharStr , cchLength) - 1;
   wchar_t cCharT;
   // Repeat until we reach the center character in the string.
   while (pWideCharStr < pEndOfStr) {
      // Save a character in a temporary variable.
      cCharT = *pWideCharStr;

      // Put the last character in the first character.
      *pWideCharStr = *pEndOfStr;

      // Put the temporary character in the last character.
      *pEndOfStr = cCharT;

      // Move in one character from the left.
      pWideCharStr++;

      // Move in one character from the right.
      pEndOfStr--;
   }

   // The string is reversed; return success.
   return(TRUE);
}
```

And you could write the ANSI version of the function so that it doesn't perform the actual work of reversing the string at all. Instead, you could write the ANSI version so that it converts the ANSI string to Unicode, passes the Unicode string to the **StringReverseW** function, and then converts the reversed string back to ANSI. The function would look like this:

```
BOOL StringReverseA(PSTR pMultiByteStr, DWORD cchLength) {
    PWSTR pWideCharStr;
    int nLenOfWideCharStr;
    BOOL fOk = FALSE;

    // Calculate the number of characters needed to hold
    // the wide-character version of the string.
    nLenOfWideCharStr = MultiByteToWideChar(CP_ACP, 0,
        pMultiByteStr, cchLength, NULL, 0);

    // Allocate memory from the process' default heap to
    // accommodate the size of the wide-character string.
    // Don't forget that MultiByteToWideChar returns the
    // number of characters, not the number of bytes, so
    // you must multiply by the size of a wide character.
    pWideCharStr = (PWSTR)HeapAlloc(GetProcessHeap(), 0,
        nLenOfWideCharStr * sizeof(wchar_t));

    if (pWideCharStr == NULL)
        return(fOk);

    // Convert the multibyte string to a wide-character string.
    MultiByteToWideChar(CP_ACP, 0, pMultiByteStr, cchLength,
        pWideCharStr, nLenOfWideCharStr);

    // Call the wide-character version of this
    // function to do the actual work.
    fOk = StringReverseW(pWideCharStr, cchLength);

    if (fOk) {
        // Convert the wide-character string back
        // to a multibyte string.
        WideCharToMultiByte(CP_ACP, 0, pWideCharStr, cchLength,
            pMultiByteStr, (int)strlen(pMultiByteStr), NULL, NULL);
    }

    // Free the memory containing the wide-character string.
    HeapFree(GetProcessHeap(), 0, pWideCharStr);

    return(fOk);
}
```

Finally, in the header file that you distribute with the dynamic-link library, you prototype the two functions as follows:

```
BOOL StringReverseW(PWSTR pWideCharStr, DWORD cchLength);
BOOL StringReverseA(PSTR pMultiByteStr, DWORD cchLength);

#ifdef UNICODE
#define StringReverse StringReverseW
#else
#define StringReverse StringReverseA
#endif // !UNICODE
```

Determining If Text Is ANSI or Unicode

The Windows Notepad application allows you to open both Unicode and ANSI files as well as create them. In fact, Figure 2-5 shows Notepad's File Save As dialog box. Notice the different ways that you can save a text file.

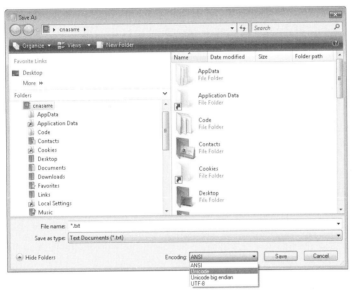

Figure 2-5   The Windows Vista Notepad File Save As dialog box

For many applications that open text files and process them, such as compilers, it would be convenient if, after opening a file, the application could determine whether the text file contained ANSI characters or Unicode characters. The **IsTextUnicode** function exported by AdvApi32.dll and declared in WinBase.h can help make this distinction:

```
BOOL IsTextUnicode(CONST PVOID pvBuffer, int cb, PINT pResult);
```

The problem with text files is that there are no hard and fast rules as to their content. This makes it extremely difficult to determine whether the file contains ANSI or Unicode characters. **IsText-Unicode** uses a series of statistical and deterministic methods to guess at the content of the buffer. Because this is not an exact science, it is possible that **IsTextUnicode** will return an incorrect result.

The first parameter, **pvBuffer**, identifies the address of a buffer that you want to test. The data is a void pointer because you don't know whether you have an array of ANSI characters or an array of Unicode characters.

The second parameter, **cb**, specifies the number of bytes that **pvBuffer** points to. Again, because you don't know what's in the buffer, **cb** is a count of bytes rather than a count of characters. Note that you do not have to specify the entire length of the buffer. Of course, the more bytes **IsText-Unicode** can test, the more accurate a response you're likely to get.

The third parameter, **pResult**, is the address of an integer that you must initialize before calling **IsTextUnicode**. You initialize this integer to indicate which tests you want **IsTextUnicode** to perform. You can also pass **NULL** for this parameter, in which case **IsTextUnicode** will perform every test it can. (See the Platform SDK documentation for more details.)

If **IsTextUnicode** thinks that the buffer contains Unicode text, **TRUE** is returned; otherwise, **FALSE** is returned. If specific tests were requested in the integer pointed to by the **pResult** parameter, the function sets the bits in the integer before returning to reflect the results of each test.

The FileRev sample application presented in Chapter 17, "Memory-Mapped Files," demonstrates the use of the **IsTextUnicode** function.

Chapter 3
Kernel Objects

We begin our understanding of the Microsoft Windows application programming interface (API) by examining kernel objects and their handles. This chapter covers relatively abstract concepts— I'm not going to discuss the particulars of any specific kernel object. Instead, I'm going to discuss features that apply to all kernel objects.

I would have preferred to start off with a more concrete topic, but a solid understanding of kernel objects is critical to becoming a proficient Windows software developer. Kernel objects are used by the system and by the applications we write to manage numerous resources such as processes, threads, and files (to name just a few). The concepts presented in this chapter will appear throughout most of the remaining chapters in this book. However, I do realize that some of the material covered in this chapter won't sink in until you start manipulating kernel objects using actual functions. So, as you read various other chapters in this book, you'll probably want to refer back to this chapter from time to time.

What Is a Kernel Object?

As a Windows software developer, you create, open, and manipulate kernel objects regularly. The system creates and manipulates several types of kernel objects, such as access token objects, event objects, file objects, file-mapping objects, I/O completion port objects, job objects, mailslot objects, mutex objects, pipe objects, process objects, semaphore objects, thread objects, waitable timer objects, and thread pool worker factory objects. The free WinObj tool from Sysinternals (located at *http://www.microsoft.com/technet/sysinternals/utilities/winobj.mspx*) allows you to see the list of all the kernel object types. Notice that you have to run it as Administrator through Windows Explorer to be able to see the list on the next page.

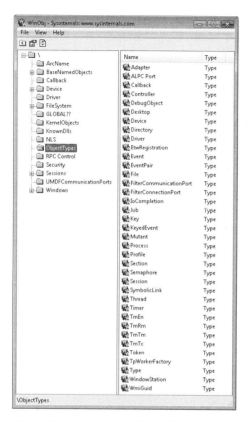

These objects are created by calling various functions with names that don't necessarily map to the type of the objects used at kernel level. For example, the **CreateFileMapping** function causes the system to create a file mapping that corresponds to a **Section** object, as you can see in WinObj. Each kernel object is simply a memory block allocated by the kernel and is accessible only by the kernel. This memory block is a data structure whose members maintain information about the object. Some members (security descriptor, usage count, and so on) are the same across all object types, but most are specific to a particular object type. For example, a process object has a process ID, a base priority, and an exit code, whereas a file object has a byte offset, a sharing mode, and an open mode.

Because the kernel object data structures are accessible only by the kernel, it is impossible for an application to locate these data structures in memory and directly alter their contents. Microsoft enforces this restriction deliberately to ensure that the kernel object structures maintain a consistent state. This restriction also allows Microsoft to add, remove, or change the members in these structures without breaking any applications.

If we cannot alter these structures directly, how do our applications manipulate these kernel objects? The answer is that Windows offers a set of functions that manipulate these structures in well-defined ways. These kernel objects are always accessible via these functions. When you call a function that creates a kernel object, the function returns a handle that identifies the object. Think of this handle as an opaque value that can be used by any thread in your process. A handle is a

32-bit value in a 32-bit Windows process and a 64-bit value in a 64-bit Windows process. You pass this handle to the various Windows functions so that the system knows which kernel object you want to manipulate. I'll talk a lot more about these handles later in this chapter.

To make the operating system robust, these handle values are process-relative. So if you were to pass this handle value to a thread in another process (using some form of interprocess communication), the calls that this other process would make using your process' handle value might fail or, even worse, they will create a reference to a totally different kernel object at the same index in your process handle table. In "Sharing Kernel Objects Across Process Boundaries" on page 43, we'll look at three mechanisms that allow multiple processes to successfully share a single kernel object.

Usage Counting

Kernel objects are owned by the kernel, not by a process. In other words, if your process calls a function that creates a kernel object and then your process terminates, the kernel object is not necessarily destroyed. Under most circumstances, the object will be destroyed; but if another process is using the kernel object your process created, the kernel knows not to destroy the object until the other process has stopped using it. The important thing to remember is that a kernel object can outlive the process that created it.

The kernel knows how many processes are using a particular kernel object because each object contains a usage count. The usage count is one of the data members common to all kernel object types. When an object is first created, its usage count is set to 1. When another process gains access to an existing kernel object, the usage count is incremented. When a process terminates, the kernel automatically decrements the usage count for all the kernel objects the process still has open. If the object's usage count goes to 0, the kernel destroys the object. This ensures that no kernel object will remain in the system if no processes are referencing the object.

Security

Kernel objects can be protected with a security descriptor. A security descriptor describes who owns the object (usually its creator), which group and users can gain access to or use the object, and which group and users are denied access to the object. Security descriptors are usually used when writing server applications. However, with Microsoft Windows Vista, this feature becomes more visible for client-side applications with private namespaces, as you will see later in this chapter and in "When Administrator Runs as a Standard User" on page 110.

Almost all functions that create kernel objects have a pointer to a **SECURITY_ATTRIBUTES** structure as an argument, as shown here with the **CreateFileMapping** function:

```
HANDLE CreateFileMapping(
    HANDLE hFile,
    PSECURITY_ATTRIBUTES psa,
    DWORD flProtect,
    DWORD dwMaximumSizeHigh,
    DWORD dwMaximumSizeLow,
    PCTSTR pszName);
```

Most applications simply pass **NULL** for this argument so that the object is created with a default security build based on the current process security token. However, you can allocate a

SECURITY_ATTRIBUTES structure, initialize it, and pass the address of the structure for this parameter. A **SECURITY_ATTRIBUTES** structure looks like this:

```
typedef struct _SECURITY_ATTRIBUTES {
   DWORD nLength;
   LPVOID lpSecurityDescriptor;
   BOOL bInheritHandle;
} SECURITY_ATTRIBUTES;
```

Even though this structure is called **SECURITY_ATTRIBUTES**, it really includes only one member that has anything to do with security: **lpSecurityDescriptor**. If you want to restrict access to a kernel object you create, you must create a security descriptor and then initialize the **SECURITY_ATTRIBUTES** structure as follows:

```
SECURITY_ATTRIBUTES sa;
sa.nLength = sizeof(sa);           // Used for versioning
sa.lpSecurityDescriptor = pSD;     // Address of an initialized SD
sa.bInheritHandle = FALSE;         // Discussed later
HANDLE hFileMapping = CreateFileMapping(INVALID_HANDLE_VALUE, &sa,
   PAGE_READWRITE, 0, 1024, TEXT("MyFileMapping"));
```

Because this member has nothing to do with security, I'll postpone discussing the **bInherit-Handle** member until "Using Object Handle Inheritance" on page 43.

When you want to gain access to an existing kernel object (rather than create a new one), you must specify the operations you intend to perform on the object. For example, if I want to gain access to an existing file-mapping kernel object so that I could read data from it, I call **OpenFileMapping** as follows:

```
HANDLE hFileMapping = OpenFileMapping(FILE_MAP_READ, FALSE,
   TEXT("MyFileMapping"));
```

By passing **FILE_MAP_READ** as the first parameter to **OpenFileMapping**, I am indicating that I intend to read from this file mapping after I gain access to it. The **OpenFileMapping** function performs a security check first, before it returns a valid handle value. If I (the logged-on user) am allowed access to the existing file-mapping kernel object, **OpenFileMapping** returns a valid handle. However, if I am denied this access, **OpenFileMapping** returns **NULL** and a call to **GetLastError** will return a value of 5 (**ERROR_ACCESS_DENIED**). Don't forget that if the returned handle is used to call an API that requires a right different from **FILE_MAP_READ**, the same "access denied" error occurs. Again, most applications do not use security, so I won't go into this issue any further.

Although many applications do not need to be concerned about security, many Windows functions require that you pass desired security access information. Several applications designed for previous versions of Windows do not work properly on Windows Vista because security was not given enough consideration when the application was implemented.

For example, imagine an application that, when started, reads some data from a registry subkey. To do this properly, your code should call **RegOpenKeyEx**, passing **KEY_QUERY_VALUE** for the desired access.

However, many applications were originally developed for pre–Windows 2000 operating systems without any consideration for security. Some software developers could have called

RegOpenKeyEx, passing **KEY_ALL_ACCESS** as the desired access. Developers used this approach because it was a simpler solution and didn't require the developer to really think about what access was required. The problem is that the registry subkey, such as HKLM, might be readable, but not writable, to a user who is not an administrator. So, when such an application runs on Windows Vista, the call to **RegOpenKeyEx** with **KEY_ALL_ACCESS** fails, and without proper error checking, the application could run with totally unpredictable results.

If the developer had thought about security just a little and changed **KEY_ALL_ACCESS** to **KEY_QUERY_VALUE** (which is all that is necessary in this example), the product would work on all operating system platforms.

Neglecting proper security access flags is one of the biggest mistakes that developers make. Using the correct flags will certainly make it much easier to port an application between Windows versions. However, you also need to realize that each new version of Windows brings a new set of constraints that did not exist in the previous versions. For example, in Windows Vista, you need to take care of the User Account Control (UAC) feature. By default, UAC forces applications to run in a restricted context for security safety even though the current user is part of the Administrators group. We'll look at UAC more in Chapter 4, "Processes."

In addition to using kernel objects, your application might use other types of objects, such as menus, windows, mouse cursors, brushes, and fonts. These objects are User objects or Graphical Device Interface (GDI) objects, not kernel objects. When you first start programming for Windows, you might be confused when you try to differentiate a User object or a GDI object from a kernel object. For example, is an icon a User object or a kernel object? The easiest way to determine whether an object is a kernel object is to examine the function that creates the object. Almost all functions that create kernel objects have a parameter that allows you to specify security attribute information, as did the **CreateFileMapping** function shown earlier.

None of the functions that create User or GDI objects have a **PSECURITY_ATTRIBUTES** parameter. For example, take a look at the **CreateIcon** function:

```
HICON CreateIcon(
   HINSTANCE hinst,
   int nWidth,
   int nHeight,
   BYTE cPlanes,
   BYTE cBitsPixel,
   CONST BYTE *pbANDbits,
   CONST BYTE *pbXORbits);
```

The MSDN article *http://msdn.microsoft.com/msdnmag/issues/03/01/GDILeaks* provides plenty of details about GDI and User objects and how to track them.

A Process' Kernel Object Handle Table

When a process is initialized, the system allocates a handle table for it. This handle table is used only for kernel objects, not for User objects or GDI objects. The details of how the handle table is structured and managed are undocumented. Normally, I would refrain from discussing undocumented parts of the operating system. In this case, however, I'm making an exception because I believe that a competent Windows programmer must understand how a process' handle table is managed. Because this information is undocumented, I will not get all the details completely correct, and the internal implementation is certainly different among various versions of Windows. So read the following discussion to improve your understanding, not to learn how the system really does it.

Table 3-1 shows what a process' handle table looks like. As you can see, it is simply an array of data structures. Each structure contains a pointer to a kernel object, an access mask, and some flags.

Table 3-1   The Structure of a Process' Handle Table

Index	Pointer to Kernel Object Memory Block	Access Mask (DWORD of Flag Bits)	Flags
1	0x????????	0x????????	0x????????
2	0x????????	0x????????	0x????????
...	...	...	...

Creating a Kernel Object

When a process first initializes, its handle table is empty. When a thread in the process calls a function that creates a kernel object, such as **CreateFileMapping**, the kernel allocates a block of memory for the object and initializes it. The kernel then scans the process' handle table for an empty entry. Because the handle table in Table 3-1 is empty, the kernel finds the structure at index 1 and initializes it. The pointer member will be set to the internal memory address of the kernel object's data structure, the access mask will be set to full access, and the flags will be set. (I'll discuss the flags in "Using Object Handle Inheritance" on page 43.

Here are some of the functions that create kernel objects (but this is in no way a complete list):

```
HANDLE CreateThread(
    PSECURITY_ATTRIBUTES psa,
    size_t dwStackSize,
    LPTHREAD_START_ROUTINE pfnStartAddress,
    PVOID pvParam,
    DWORD dwCreationFlags,
    PDWORD pdwThreadId);

HANDLE CreateFile(
    PCTSTR pszFileName,
    DWORD dwDesiredAccess,
    DWORD dwShareMode,
    PSECURITY_ATTRIBUTES psa,
    DWORD dwCreationDisposition,
    DWORD dwFlagsAndAttributes,
    HANDLE hTemplateFile);

HANDLE CreateFileMapping(
    HANDLE hFile,
    PSECURITY_ATTRIBUTES psa,
    DWORD flProtect,
    DWORD dwMaximumSizeHigh,
    DWORD dwMaximumSizeLow,
    PCTSTR pszName);
```

```
HANDLE CreateSemaphore(
   PSECURITY_ATTRIBUTES psa,
   LONG lInitialCount,
   LONG lMaximumCount,
   PCTSTR pszName);
```

All functions that create kernel objects return process-relative handles that can be used success-fully by any and all threads that are running in the same process. This handle value should actually be divided by 4 (or shifted right two bits to ignore the last two bits that are used internally by Windows) to obtain the real index into the process' handle table that identifies where the kernel object's information is stored. So when you debug an application and examine the actual value of a kernel object handle, you'll see small values such as 4, 8, and so on. Remember that the meaning of the handle is undocumented and is subject to change.

Whenever you call a function that accepts a kernel object handle as an argument, you pass the value returned by one of the **Create*** functions. Internally, the function looks in your process' handle table to get the address of the kernel object you want to manipulate and then manipulates the object's data structure in a well-defined fashion.

If you pass an invalid handle, the function returns failure and **GetLastError** returns 6 (**ERROR_INVALID_HANDLE**). Because handle values are actually used as indexes into the process' handle table, these handles are process-relative and cannot be used successfully from other processes. And if you ever tried to do so, you would simply reference the kernel object stored at the same index into the other process' handle table, without any idea of what this object would be.

If you call a function to create a kernel object and the call fails, the handle value returned is usually 0 (**NULL**), and this is why the first valid handle value is 4. The system would have to be very low on memory or encountering a security problem for this to happen. Unfortunately, a few functions return a handle value of –1 (**INVALID_HANDLE_VALUE** defined in WinBase.h) when they fail. For example, if **CreateFile** fails to open the specified file, it returns **INVALID_HANDLE_VALUE** instead of **NULL**. You must be very careful when checking the return value of a function that creates a kernel object. Specifically, you can compare the value with **INVALID_HANDLE_VALUE** only when you call **CreateFile**. The following code is incorrect:

```
HANDLE hMutex = CreateMutex(...);
if (hMutex == INVALID_HANDLE_VALUE) {
   // We will never execute this code because
   // CreateMutex returns NULL if it fails.
}
```

Likewise, the following code is also incorrect:

```
HANDLE hFile = CreateFile(...);
if (hFile == NULL) {
   // We will never execute this code because CreateFile
   // returns INVALID_HANDLE_VALUE (-1) if it fails.
}
```

Closing a Kernel Object

Regardless of how you create a kernel object, you indicate to the system that you are done manip-ulating the object by calling **CloseHandle**:

```
BOOL CloseHandle(HANDLE hobject);
```

Internally, this function first checks the calling process' handle table to ensure that the handle value passed to it identifies an object that the process does in fact have access to. If the handle is valid, the system gets the address of the kernel object's data structure and decrements the usage count member in the structure. If the count is zero, the kernel object is destroyed and removed from memory.

If an invalid handle is passed to **CloseHandle**, one of two things might happen. If your process is running normally, **CloseHandle** returns **FALSE** and **GetLastError** returns **ERROR_INVALID_ HANDLE**. Or, if your process is being debugged, the system throws the exception 0xC0000008 ("An invalid handle was specified") so that you can debug the error.

Right before **CloseHandle** returns, it clears out the entry in the process' handle table—this handle is now invalid for your process, and you should not attempt to use it. The clearing happens whether or not the kernel object has been destroyed! After you call **CloseHandle**, you no longer have access to the kernel object; however, if the object's count did not decrement to zero, the object has not been destroyed. This is OK; it just means that one or more other processes are still using the object. When the other processes stop using the object (by calling **CloseHandle**), the object will be destroyed.

> **Note**   Usually, when you create a kernel object, you store the corresponding handle in a variable. After you call **CloseHandle** with this variable as a parameter, you should also reset the variable to **NULL**. If, by mistake, you reuse this variable to call a Win32 function, two unexpected situations might occur. Because the handle table slot referenced by the variable has been cleared, Windows receives an invalid parameter and you get an error. But another situation that is harder to debug is also possible. When you create a new kernel object, Windows looks for a free slot in the handle table. So, if new kernel objects have been constructed in your application workflows, the handle table slot referenced by the variable will certainly contain one of these new kernel objects. Thus, the call might target a kernel object of the wrong type or, even worse, a kernel object of the same type as the closed one. Your application state then becomes corrupted without any chance to recover.

Let's say that you forget to call **CloseHandle**—will there be an object leak? Well, yes and no. It is possible for a process to leak resources (such as kernel objects) while the process runs. However, when the process terminates, the operating system ensures that all resources used by the process are freed—this is guaranteed. For kernel objects, the system performs the following actions: When your process terminates, the system automatically scans the process' handle table. If the table has any valid entries (objects that you didn't close before terminating), the system closes these object handles for you. If the usage count of any of these objects goes to zero, the kernel destroys the object.

So your application can leak kernel objects while it runs, but when your process terminates, the system guarantees that everything is cleaned up properly. By the way, this is true for *all* objects, resources such as GDI objects, and memory blocks—when a process terminates, the system ensures that your process leaves nothing behind. An easy way to detect whether kernel objects leak while your application is running is simply to use Windows Task Manager. First, as shown in Figure 3-1, you need to force the corresponding Handles column to appear on the Processes tab from the Select Process Page Columns dialog box that is accessible through the View/Select Columns menu item.

Figure 3-1   Selecting the Handles column in the Select Process Page Columns dialog box

Then you can monitor the number of kernel objects used by any application, as shown in Figure 3-2.

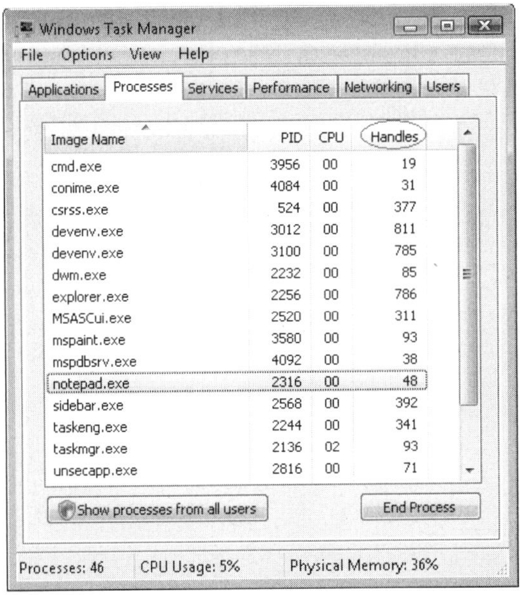

Figure 3-2   Counting handles in Windows Task Manager

If the number in the Handles column grows continuously, the next step to identifying which kernel objects are not closed is to take advantage of the free Process Explorer tool from Sysinternals (available at *http://www.microsoft.com/technet/sysinternals/ProcessesAndThreads/ProcessExplorer.mspx*). First, right-click in the header of the lower Handles pane. Then, in the Select Columns dialog box shown in Figure 3-3, select all the columns.

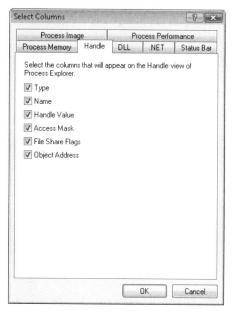

Figure 3-3   Selecting details for the Handle view in Process Explorer

Once this is done, change the Update Speed to Paused on the View menu. Select your process in the upper pane, and press F5 to get the up-to-date list of kernel objects. Execute the workflow you need to validate with your application, and once it is finished, press F5 again in Process Explorer. Each new kernel object is displayed in green, which you see represented as a darker gray in Figure 3-4.

Type	Name	Handle	Access	Object Address
IoCompletion		0x1E0	0x001F0003	0x83354350
IoCompletion		0x208	0x001F0003	0x833CB570
Key	HKLM	0x1C	0x00020019	0x97D6F1E0
Key	HKLM\SYSTEM\ControlSet001\Control\Session Manager	0x24	0x00000001	0x9B73A3C8
Key	HKCU	0xA8	0x000F003F	0xA36CC438
Key	HKLM\SYSTEM\ControlSet001\Control\Nls\Locale\Alternate Sorts	0xAC	0x00020019	0x9B64F8D0
Key	HKLM\SYSTEM\ControlSet001\Control\Nls\Locale	0xB0	0x00020019	0x9FBAB988
Key	HKLM\SYSTEM\ControlSet001\Control\Nls\Language Groups	0xB4	0x00020019	0x9FB403C0
Key	HKCU\Software\Classes	0xC8	0x000F003F	0x9FA66850
Key	HKCU\Software\Microsoft\Windows\CurrentVersion\Explorer	0xD0	0x00000001	0x95359CB0
Key	HKCU\Software\Microsoft\Windows\CurrentVersion\Explorer\ComDlg3...	0xDC	0x00002001F	0x95C29AC0
Key	HKLM\SOFTWARE\Microsoft\Windows\CurrentVersion\explorer	0x130	0x00020019	0xA683E568
Key	HKCU\Software\Classes	0x138	0x000F003F	0x9991230B

CPU Usage: 8.20%   Commit Charge: 30.54%   Processes: 48   Paused

Figure 3-4   Detecting new kernel objects in Process Explorer

Note that the first column gives you the type of the kernel object that is not closed. To enhance your chances of finding where the leaks are, the second column provides the name of the kernel object. As you'll see in the next section, the string you give as a name to a kernel object allows you to share this object among processes. Obviously, it also helps you to figure out much more easily which object is not closed based on its type (first column) and its name (second column). If you are leaking lots of objects, they are probably not named because you can create only one instance of a named object—other attempts just open it.

Sharing Kernel Objects Across Process Boundaries

Frequently, threads running in different processes need to share kernel objects. Here are some of the reasons why:

- File-mapping objects allow you to share blocks of data between two processes running on a single machine.
- Mailslots and named pipes allow applications to send blocks of data between processes running on different machines connected to the network.
- Mutexes, semaphores, and events allow threads in different processes to synchronize their continued execution, as in the case of an application that needs to notify another application when it has completed some task.

Because kernel object handles are process-relative, performing these tasks is difficult. However, Microsoft had several good reasons for designing the handles to be process-relative. The most important reason was robustness. If kernel object handles were systemwide values, one process could easily obtain the handle to an object that another process was using and wreak havoc on that process. Another reason for process-relative handles is security. Kernel objects are protected with security, and a process must request permission to manipulate an object before attempting to manipulate it. The creator of the object can prevent an unauthorized user from touching the object simply by denying access to it.

In the following section, we'll look at the three different mechanisms that allow processes to share kernel objects: using object handle inheritance, naming objects, and duplicating object handles.

Using Object Handle Inheritance

Object handle inheritance can be used only when processes have a parent-child relationship. In this scenario, one or more kernel object handles are available to the parent process, and the parent decides to spawn a child process, giving the child access to the parent's kernel objects. For this type of inheritance to work, the parent process must perform several steps.

First, when the parent process creates a kernel object, the parent must indicate to the system that it wants the object's handle to be inheritable. Sometimes I hear people use the term *object inheritance*. However, there is no such thing as object inheritance; Windows supports *object handle inheritance*. In other words, it is the handles that are inheritable, not the objects themselves.

To create an inheritable handle, the parent process must allocate and initialize a **SECURITY_ATTRIBUTES** structure and pass the structure's address to the specific **Create** function. The following code creates a mutex object and returns an inheritable handle to it:

```
SECURITY_ATTRIBUTES sa;
sa.nLength = sizeof(sa);
sa.lpSecurityDescriptor = NULL;
sa.bInheritHandle = TRUE;   // Make the returned handle inheritable.

HANDLE hMutex = CreateMutex(&sa, FALSE, NULL);
```

This code initializes a **SECURITY_ATTRIBUTES** structure indicating that the object should be created using default security and that the returned handle should be inheritable.

Now we come to the flags that are stored in a process' handle table entry. Each handle table entry has a flag bit indicating whether the handle is inheritable. If you pass **NULL** as the **PSECURITY_ATTRIBUTES** parameter when you create a kernel object, the handle returned is not inheritable and this bit is zero. Setting the **bInheritHandle** member to **TRUE** causes this flag bit to be set to 1.

Imagine a process' handle table that looks like the one shown in Table 3-2.

Table 3-2   Process' Handle Table Containing Two Valid Entries

Index	Pointer to Kernel Object Memory Block	Access Mask (DWORD of Flag Bits)	Flags
1	0xF0000000	0x????????	0x00000000
2	0x00000000	(N/A)	(N/A)
3	0xF0000010	0x????????	0x00000001

Table 3-2 indicates that this process has access to two kernel objects (handles 1 and 3). Handle 1 is not inheritable, and handle 3 is inheritable.

The next step to perform when using object handle inheritance is for the parent process to spawn the child process. This is done using the **CreateProcess** function:

```
BOOL CreateProcess(
   PCTSTR pszApplicationName,
   PTSTR pszCommandLine,
   PSECURITY_ATTRIBUTES psaProcess,
   PSECURITY_ATTRIBUTES psaThread,
   BOOL bInheritHandles,
   DWORD dwCreationFlags,
   PVOID pvEnvironment,
   PCTSTR pszCurrentDirectory,
   LPSTARTUPINFO pStartupInfo,
   PPROCESS_INFORMATION pProcessInformation);
```

We'll examine this function in detail in the next chapter, but for now I want to draw your attention to the **bInheritHandles** parameter. Usually, when you spawn a process, you pass **FALSE** for this parameter. This value tells the system that you do not want the child process to inherit the inheritable handles that are in the parent process' handle table.

If you pass **TRUE** for this parameter, however, the child inherits the parent's inheritable handle values. When you pass **TRUE**, the operating system creates the new child process but does not allow the child process to begin executing its code right away. Of course, the system creates a new, empty process handle table for the child process–just as it would for any new process. But because you passed **TRUE** to **CreateProcess**' **bInheritHandles** parameter, the system does one more thing: it walks the parent process' handle table, and for each entry it finds that contains a valid inheritable handle, the system copies the entry exactly into the child process' handle table. The entry is copied to the exact same position in the child process' handle table as in the parent's handle table. This fact is important because it means that the handle value that identifies a kernel object is identical in both the parent and child processes.

In addition to copying the handle table entry, the system increments the usage count of the kernel object because two processes are now using the object. For the kernel object to be destroyed, both the parent process and the child process must either call **CloseHandle** on the object or terminate. The child does not have to terminate first–but neither does the parent. In fact, the parent process can close its handle to the object immediately after the **CreateProcess** function returns without affecting the child's ability to manipulate the object.

Table 3-3 shows the child process' handle table immediately before the process is allowed to begin execution. You can see that entries 1 and 2 are not initialized and are therefore invalid handles for the child process to use. However, index 3 does identify a kernel object. In fact, it identifies the kernel object at address 0xF0000010–the same object as in the parent process' handle table.

Table 3-3   A Child Process' Handle Table After Inheriting the Parent Process' Inheritable Handle

Index	Pointer to Kernel Object Memory Block	Access Mask (DWORD of Flag Bits)	Flags
1	0x00000000	(N/A)	(N/A)
2	0x00000000	(N/A)	(N/A)
3	0xF0000010	0x????????	0x00000001

As you will see in Chapter 13, "Windows Memory Architecture," the content of kernel objects is stored in the kernel address space that is shared by all processes running on the system. For 32-bit systems, this is in memory between the following memory addresses: 0x80000000 and 0xFFFFFFFF. For 64-bit systems, this is in memory between the following memory addresses: 0x00000400'00000000 and 0xFFFFFFFF'FFFFFFFF. The access mask is identical to the mask in the parent, and the flags are also identical. This means that if the child process were to spawn its own child process (a grandchild process of the parent) with the same **bInheritHandles** parameter of **CreateProcess** set to **TRUE**, this grandchild process would also inherit this kernel object handle with the same handle value, same access, and same flags, and the usage count on the object would again be incremented.

Be aware that object handle inheritance applies only at the time the child process is spawned. If the parent process were to create any new kernel objects with inheritable handles, an already-running child process would not inherit these new handles.

Object handle inheritance has one very strange characteristic: when you use it, the child has no idea that it has inherited any handles. Kernel object handle inheritance is useful only when the child process documents the fact that it expects to be given access to a kernel object when spawned from another process. Usually, the parent and child applications are written by the same company; however, a different company can write the child application if that company documents what the child application expects.

By far, the most common way for a child process to determine the handle value of the kernel object that it's expecting is to have the handle value passed as a command-line argument to the child process. The child process' initialization code parses the command line (usually by calling **_stscanf_s**) and extracts the handle value. Once the child has the handle value, it has the same access to the object as its parent. Note that the only reason handle inheritance works is because the handle value of the shared kernel object is identical in both the parent process and the child process. This is why the parent process is able to pass the handle value as a command-line argument.

Of course, you can use other forms of interprocess communication to transfer an inherited kernel object handle value from the parent process into the child process. One technique is for the parent to wait for the child to complete initialization (using the **WaitForInputIdle** function discussed in Chapter 9, "Thread Synchronization with Kernel Objects"); then the parent can send or post a message to a window created by a thread in the child process.

Another technique is for the parent process to add an environment variable to its environment block. The variable's name would be something that the child process knows to look for, and the variable's value would be the handle value of the kernel object to be inherited. Then when the parent spawns the child process, the child process inherits the parent's environment variables and can easily call **GetEnvironmentVariable** to obtain the inherited object's handle value. This approach is excellent if the child process is going to spawn another child process, because the environment variables can be inherited again. The special case of a child process inheriting its parent console is detailed in the Microsoft Knowledge Base at *http://support.microsoft.com/kb/190351*.

Changing a Handle's Flags

Occasionally, you might encounter a situation in which a parent process creates a kernel object retrieving an inheritable handle and then spawns two child processes. The parent process wants only one child to inherit the kernel object handle. In other words, you might at times want to control which child processes inherit kernel object handles. To alter the inheritance flag of a kernel object handle, you can call the **SetHandleInformation** function:

```
BOOL SetHandleInformation(
   HANDLE hObject,
   DWORD dwMask,
   DWORD dwFlags);
```

As you can see, this function takes three parameters. The first, **hObject**, identifies a valid handle. The second parameter, **dwMask**, tells the function which flag or flags you want to change. Currently, two flags are associated with each handle:

```
#define HANDLE_FLAG_INHERIT            0x00000001
#define HANDLE_FLAG_PROTECT_FROM_CLOSE 0x00000002
```

You can perform a bitwise OR on both of these flags together if you want to change each object's flags simultaneously. **SetHandleInformation**'s third parameter, **dwFlags**, indicates what you want to set the flags to. For example, to turn on the inheritance flag for a kernel object handle, do the following:

```
SetHandleInformation(hObj, HANDLE_FLAG_INHERIT, HANDLE_FLAG_INHERIT);
```

To turn off this flag, do this:

```
SetHandleInformation(hObj, HANDLE_FLAG_INHERIT, 0);
```

The **HANDLE_FLAG_PROTECT_FROM_CLOSE** flag tells the system that this handle should not be allowed to be closed:

```
SetHandleInformation(hObj, HANDLE_FLAG_PROTECT_FROM_CLOSE,
   HANDLE_FLAG_PROTECT_FROM_CLOSE);
CloseHandle(hObj);    // Exception is raised
```

When running under a debugger, if a thread attempts to close a protected handle, **CloseHandle** raises an exception. Outside the control of a debugger, **CloseHandle** simply returns **FALSE**. You rarely want to protect a handle from being closed. However, this flag might be useful if you had a process that spawned a child that in turn spawned a grandchild process. The parent process might be expecting the grandchild to inherit the object handle given to the immediate child. It is possible, however, that the immediate child might close the handle before spawning the grandchild. If this were to happen, the parent might not be able to communicate with the grandchild because the grandchild did not inherit the kernel object. By marking the handle as "protected from close," the grandchild has a better chance to inherit a handle to a valid and live object.

This approach has one flaw, however. The immediate child process might call the following code to turn off the **HANDLE_FLAG_PROTECT_FROM_CLOSE** flag and then close the handle:

```
SetHandleInformation(hobj, HANDLE_FLAG_PROTECT_FROM_CLOSE, 0);
CloseHandle(hObj);
```

The parent process is gambling that the child process will not execute this code. Of course, the parent is also gambling that the child process will spawn the grandchild, so this bet is not that risky.

For the sake of completeness, I'll also mention the **GetHandleInformation** function:

```
BOOL GetHandleInformation(
   HANDLE hObject,
   PDWORD pdwFlags);
```

This function returns the current flag settings for the specified handle in the DWORD pointed to by **pdwFlags**. To see if a handle is inheritable, do the following:

```
DWORD dwFlags;
GetHandleInformation(hObj, &dwFlags);
BOOL fHandleIsInheritable = (0 != (dwFlags & HANDLE_FLAG_INHERIT));
```

Naming Objects

The second method available for sharing kernel objects across process boundaries is to name the objects. Many—though not all—kernel objects can be named. For example, all of the following functions create named kernel objects:

```
HANDLE CreateMutex(
    PSECURITY_ATTRIBUTES psa,
    BOOL bInitialOwner,
    PCTSTR pszName);

HANDLE CreateEvent(
    PSECURITY_ATTRIBUTES psa,
    BOOL bManualReset,
    BOOL bInitialState,
    PCTSTR pszName);

HANDLE CreateSemaphore(
    PSECURITY_ATTRIBUTES psa,
    LONG lInitialCount,
    LONG lMaximumCount,
    PCTSTR pszName);

HANDLE CreateWaitableTimer(
    PSECURITY_ATTRIBUTES psa,
    BOOL bManualReset,
    PCTSTR pszName);

HANDLE CreateFileMapping(
    HANDLE hFile,
    PSECURITY_ATTRIBUTES psa,
    DWORD flProtect,
    DWORD dwMaximumSizeHigh,
    DWORD dwMaximumSizeLow,
    PCTSTR pszName);

HANDLE CreateJobObject(
    PSECURITY_ATTRIBUTES psa,
    PCTSTR pszName);
```

All these functions have a common last parameter, **pszName**. When you pass **NULL** for this parameter, you are indicating to the system that you want to create an unnamed (anonymous) kernel object. When you create an unnamed object, you can share the object across processes by using either inheritance (as discussed in the previous section) or **DuplicateHandle** (discussed in the next section). To share an object by name, you must give the object a name.

If you don't pass **NULL** for the **pszName** parameter, you should pass the address of a zero-terminated string name. This name can be up to **MAX_PATH** characters long (defined as 260). Unfortunately, Microsoft offers no guidance for assigning names to kernel objects. For example, if you attempt to create an object called "JeffObj," there's no guarantee that an object called "JeffObj" doesn't already exist. To make matters worse, all these objects share a single namespace even though they don't share the same type. Because of this, the following call to **CreateSemaphore** always returns **NULL**—because a mutex already exists with the same name:

```
HANDLE hMutex = CreateMutex(NULL, FALSE, TEXT("JeffObj"));
HANDLE hSem = CreateSemaphore(NULL, 1, 1, TEXT("JeffObj"));
DWORD dwErrorCode = GetLastError();
```

If you examine the value of **dwErrorCode** after executing the preceding code, you'll see a return code of 6 (**ERROR_INVALID_HANDLE**). This error code is not very descriptive, but what can you do?

Now that you know how to name an object, let's see how to share objects this way. Let's say that Process A starts up and calls the following function:

```
HANDLE hMutexProcessA = CreateMutex(NULL, FALSE, TEXT("JeffMutex"));
```

This function call creates a new mutex kernel object and assigns it the name "JeffMutex". Notice that in Process A's handle, **hMutexProcessA** is not an inheritable handle—and it doesn't have to be when you're only naming objects.

Some time later, some process spawns Process B. Process B does not have to be a child of Process A; it might be spawned from Windows Explorer or any other application. The fact that Process B need not be a child of Process A is an advantage of using named objects instead of inheritance. When Process B starts executing, it executes the following code:

```
HANDLE hMutexProcessB = CreateMutex(NULL, FALSE, TEXT("JeffMutex"));
```

When Process B's call to **CreateMutex** is made, the system first checks to find out whether a kernel object with the name "JeffMutex" already exists. Because an object with this name does exist, the kernel then checks the object type. Because we are attempting to create a mutex and the object with the name "JeffMutex" is also a mutex, the system then makes a security check to see whether the caller has full access to the object. If it does, the system locates an empty entry in Process B's handle table and initializes the entry to point to the existing kernel object. If the object types don't match or if the caller is denied access, **CreateMutex** fails (returns **NULL**).

> **Note** Kernel object creation functions (such as **CreateSemaphore**) always return handles with a full access right. If you want to restrict the available access rights for a handle, you can take advantage of the extended versions of kernel object creation functions (with an **Ex** postfix) that accept an additional DWORD **dwDesiredAccess** parameter. For example, you can allow or disallow **ReleaseSemaphore** to be called on a semaphore handle by using or not **SEMAPHORE_MODIFY_STATE** in the call to **CreateSemaphoreEx**. Read the Windows SDK documentation for the details of the specific rights corresponding to each kind of kernel object at *http://msdn2.microsoft.com/en-us/library/ms686670.aspx*.

When Process B's call to **CreateMutex** is successful, a mutex is not actually created. Instead, Process B is simply assigned a process-relative handle value that identifies the existing mutex object in the kernel. Of course, because a new entry in Process B's handle table references this object, the mutex object's usage count is incremented. The object will not be destroyed until both Process A and Process B have closed their handles to the object. Notice that the handle values in the two processes are most likely going to be different values. This is OK. Process A will use its handle value, and Process B will use its own handle value to manipulate the one mutex kernel object.

> **Note** When you have kernel objects sharing names, be aware of one extremely important detail. When Process B calls **CreateMutex**, it passes security attribute information and a second parameter to the function. These parameters are ignored if an object with the specified name already exists! An application can determine whether it did, in fact, create a new kernel object rather than simply open an existing object by calling **GetLastError** immediately after the call to the **Create*** function:
>
> ```
> HANDLE hMutex = CreateMutex(&sa, FALSE, TEXT("JeffObj"));
> if (GetLastError() == ERROR_ALREADY_EXISTS) {
>     // Opened a handle to an existing object.
>     // sa.lpSecurityDescriptor and the second parameter
>     // (FALSE) are ignored.
> } else {
>     // Created a brand new objcct.
>     // sa.lpSecurityDescriptor and the second parameter
>     // (FALSE) are used to construct the object.
> }
> ```

An alternative method exists for sharing objects by name. Instead of calling a **Create*** function, a process can call one of the **Open*** functions shown here:

```
HANDLE OpenMutex(
    DWORD dwDesiredAccess,
    BOOL bInheritHandle,
    PCTSTR pszName);

HANDLE OpenEvent(
    DWORD dwDesiredAccess,
    BOOL bInheritHandle,
    PCTSTR pszName);

HANDLE OpenSemaphore(
    DWORD dwDesiredAccess,
    BOOL bInheritHandle,
    PCTSTR pszName);

HANDLE OpenWaitableTimer(
    DWORD dwDesiredAccess,
    BOOL bInheritHandle,
    PCTSTR pszName);

HANDLE OpenFileMapping(
    DWORD dwDesiredAccess,
    BOOL bInheritHandle,
    PCTSTR pszName);

HANDLE OpenJobObject(
    DWORD dwDesiredAccess,
    BOOL bInheritHandle,
    PCTSTR pszName);
```

Notice that all these functions have the same prototype. The last parameter, **pszName**, indicates the name of a kernel object. You cannot pass **NULL** for this parameter; you must pass the address of a zero-terminated string. These functions search the single namespace of kernel objects attempting to find a match. If no kernel object with the specified name exists, the functions return **NULL** and **GetLastError** returns 2 (**ERROR_FILE_NOT_FOUND**). However, if a kernel object with the specified name does exist, but it has a different type, the functions return **NULL** and **GetLastError** returns 6 (**ERROR_INVALID_HANDLE**). And if it is the same type of object, the system then checks to see whether the requested access (via the **dwDesiredAccess** parameter) is allowed. If it is, the calling process' handle table is updated and the object's usage count is incremented. The returned handle will be inheritable if you pass **TRUE** for the **bInheritHandle** parameter.

The main difference between calling a **Create*** function versus calling an **Open*** function is that if the object doesn't already exist, the **Create*** function will create it, whereas the **Open*** function will simply fail.

As I mentioned earlier, Microsoft offers no real guidelines on how to create unique object names. In other words, it would be a problem if a user attempted to run two programs from different companies and each program attempted to create an object called "MyObject." For uniqueness, I recommend that you create a GUID and use the string representation of the GUID for your object names. You will see another way to ensure name uniqueness in "Private Namespaces" on page 53.

Named objects are commonly used to prevent multiple instances of an application from running. To do this, simply call a **Create*** function in your **_tmain** or **_tWinMain** function to create a named object. (It doesn't matter what type of object you create.) When the **Create*** function returns, call **GetLastError**. If **GetLastError** returns **ERROR_ALREADY_EXISTS**, another instance of your application is running and the new instance can exit. Here's some code that illustrates this:

```
int WINAPI _tWinMain(HINSTANCE hInstExe, HINSTANCE, PTSTR pszCmdLine,
   int nCmdShow) {
   HANDLE h = CreateMutex(NULL, FALSE,
      TEXT("{FA531CC1-0497-11d3-A180-00105A276C3E}"));
   if (GetLastError() == ERROR_ALREADY_EXISTS) {
      // There is already an instance of this application running.
      // Close the object and immediately return.
      CloseHandle(h);
      return(0);
   }

   // This is the first instance of this application running.
   ...
   // Before exiting, close the object.
   CloseHandle(h);
   return(0);
}
```

Terminal Services Namespaces

Note that Terminal Services changes the preceding scenario a little bit. A machine running Terminal Services has multiple namespaces for kernel objects. There is one global namespace, which is used by kernel objects that are meant to be accessible by all client sessions. This namespace is mostly used by services. In addition, each client session has its own namespace. This arrangement keeps two or more sessions that are running the same application from trampling over each other—one session cannot access another session's objects even though the objects share the same name.

These scenarios are not just related to server machines because Remote Desktop and Fast User Switching features are also implemented by taking advantage of Terminal Services sessions.

> **Note**   Before any user logs in, the services are starting in the first session, which is noninterative. In Windows Vista, unlike previous version of Windows, as soon as a user logs in, the applications are started in a new session—different from Session 0, which is dedicated to services. That way, these core components of the system, which are usually running with high privileges, are more isolated from any malware started by an unfortunate user.
>
> For service developers, necessarily running in a session different from their client application affects the naming convention for shared kernel objects. It is now mandatory to create objects to be shared with user applications in the global namespace. This is the same kind of issue that you face when you need to write a service that is supposed to communicate with applications that might run when different users are logged in to different sessions through Fast User Switching—the service can't assume that it is running in the same session as the user application. For more details on Session 0 isolation and the impact it has on service developers, you should read "Impact of Session 0 Isolation on Services and Drivers in Windows Vista," which is located at *http://www.microsoft.com/whdc/system/vista/services.mspx*.

If you have to know in which Terminal Services session your process is running, the **ProcessId-ToSessionId** function (exported by kernel32.dll and declared in WinBase.h) is what you need, as shown in the following example:

```
DWORD processID = GetCurrentProcessId();
DWORD sessionID;
if (ProcessIdToSessionId(processID, &sessionID)) {
   tprintf(
      TEXT("Process '%u' runs in Terminal Services session '%u'"),
      processID, sessionID);
} else {
   // ProcessIdToSessionId might fail if you don't have enough rights
   // to access the process for which you pass the ID as parameter.
   // Notice that it is not the case here because we're using our own process ID.
   tprintf(
      TEXT("Unable to get Terminal Services session ID for process '%u'"),
      processID);
}
```

A service's named kernel objects always go in the global namespace. By default, in Terminal Services, an application's named kernel object goes in the session's namespace. However, it is possible to force the named object to go into the global namespace by prefixing the name with "Global\", as in the following example:

```
HANDLE h = CreateEvent(NULL, FALSE, FALSE, TEXT("Global\\MyName"));
```

You can also explicitly state that you want a kernel object to go in the current session's namespace by prefixing the name with "Local\", as in the following example:

```
HANDLE h = CreateEvent(NULL, FALSE, FALSE, TEXT("Local\\MyName"));
```

Microsoft considers *Global* and *Local* to be reserved keywords that you should not use in object names except to force a particular namespace. Microsoft also considers *Session* to be a reserved keyword. So, for example, you could use Session\<*current session ID*>\. However, it is not possible to create an object with a name in another session with the *Session* prefix—the function call fails, and **GetLastError** returns **ERROR_ACCESS_DENIED**.

> **Note**   All these reserved keywords are case sensitive.

Private Namespaces

When you create a kernel object, you can protect the access to it by passing a pointer to a **SECURITY_ATTRIBUTES** structure. However, prior to the release of Windows Vista, it was not possible to protect the name of a shared object against hijacking. Any process, even with the lowest privileges, is able to create an object with a given name. If you take the previous example where an application is using a named mutex to detect whether or not it is already started, you could very easily write another application that creates a kernel object with the same name. If it gets started before the singleton application, this application becomes a "none-gleton" because it will start and then always immediately exit, thinking that another instance of itself is already running. This is the base mechanism behind a couple of attacks known as Denial of Service (DoS) attacks. Notice that unnamed kernel objects are not subject to DoS attacks, and it is quite common for an application to use unnamed objects, even though they can't be shared between processes.

If you want to ensure that the kernel object names created by your own applications never conflict with any other application's names or are the subject of hijack attacks, you can define a custom prefix and use it as a private namespace as you do with *Global* and *Local*. The server process responsible for creating the kernel object defines a *boundary descriptor* that protects the namespace name itself.

The Singleton application 03-Singleton.exe (with the corresponding Singleton.cpp source code listed a bit later in the chapter) shows how to use private namespaces to implement the same singleton pattern presented earlier but in a more secure way. When you start the program, the window shown in Figure 3-5 appears.

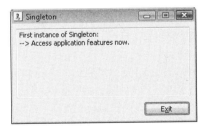

Figure 3-5   First instance of Singleton running

If you start the same program with the first one still running, the window shown in Figure 3-6 explains that the previous instance has been detected.

Figure 3-6   Second instance of Singleton when started while the first one is still running

The **CheckInstances** function in the following source code shows how to create a boundary, associate a *security identifier* (or SID) corresponding to the Local Administrators group with it, and create or open the private namespace whose name is used as a prefix by the mutex kernel object. The boundary descriptor gets a name, but more importantly, it gets a SID of a privileged user group that is associated with it. That way, Windows ensures that only the applications running under the context of a user that is a part of this privileged group is able to create the same namespace in the same boundary and thereby access the kernel objects created within this boundary that are prefixed with the private namespace name.

If a low-privileged malware application creates the same boundary descriptor because the name and the SID have been stolen, for example, when it tries to create or open the private namespace protected with a high-privileged account, the corresponding calls fail, with **GetLastError** returning **ERROR_ACCESS_DENIED**. If the malware application has enough privileges to create or open the namespace, worrying about this is not important because the malware application has enough control that it can cause much more damage than simply hijacking a kernel object name.

Singleton.cpp
```
/******************************************************************************
Module:  Singleton.cpp
Notices: Copyright (c) 2008 Jeffrey Richter & Christophe Nasarre
******************************************************************************/
//


#include "stdafx.h"
#include "resource.h"


#include "..\CommonFiles\CmnHdr.h"      /* See Appendix A. */
#include <windowsx.h>
#include <Sddl.h>            // for SID management
#include <tchar.h>
#include <strsafe.h>



///////////////////////////////////////////////////////////////////////////////


// Main dialog
HWND     g_hDlg;
```

```
// Mutex, boundary and namespace used to detect previous running instance
HANDLE    g_hSingleton = NULL;
HANDLE    g_hBoundary = NULL;
HANDLE    g_hNamespace = NULL;

// Keep track whether or not the namespace was created or open for clean-up
BOOL      g_bNamespaceOpened = FALSE;

// Names of boundary and private namespace
PCTSTR    g_szBoundary = TEXT("3-Boundary");
PCTSTR    g_szNamespace = TEXT("3-Namespace");


#define DETAILS_CTRL GetDlgItem(g_hDlg, IDC_EDIT_DETAILS)


///////////////////////////////////////////////////////////////////////////////


// Adds a string to the "Details" edit control
void AddText(PCTSTR pszFormat, ...) {

   va_list argList;
   va_start(argList, pszFormat);

   TCHAR sz[20 * 1024];

   Edit_GetText(DETAILS_CTRL, sz, _countof(sz));
   _vstprintf_s(
      _tcschr(sz, TEXT('\0')), _countof(sz) - _tcslen(sz),
      pszFormat, argList);
   Edit_SetText(DETAILS_CTRL, sz);
   va_end(argList);
}


///////////////////////////////////////////////////////////////////////////////


void Dlg_OnCommand(HWND hwnd, int id, HWND hwndCtl, UINT codeNotify) {

   switch (id) {
      case IDOK:
      case IDCANCEL:
         // User has clicked on the Exit button
         // or dismissed the dialog with ESCAPE
         EndDialog(hwnd, id);
         break;
   }
}


///////////////////////////////////////////////////////////////////////////////
```

```
void CheckInstances() {

  // Create the boundary descriptor
  g_hBoundary = CreateBoundaryDescriptor(g_szBoundary, 0);

  // Create a SID corresponding to the Local Administrator group
  BYTE localAdminSID[SECURITY_MAX_SID_SIZE];
  PSID pLocalAdminSID = &localAdminSID;
  DWORD cbSID = sizeof(localAdminSID);
  if (!CreateWellKnownSid(
    WinBuiltinAdministratorsSid, NULL, pLocalAdminSID, &cbSID)) {
    AddText(TEXT("AddSIDToBoundaryDescriptor failed: %u\r\n"),
      GetLastError());
    return;
  }

  // Associate the Local Admin SID to the boundary descriptor
  // --> only applications running under an administrator user
  //     will be able to access the kernel objects in the same namespace
  if (!AddSIDToBoundaryDescriptor(&g_hBoundary, pLocalAdminSID)) {
    AddText(TEXT("AddSIDToBoundaryDescriptor failed: %u\r\n"),
      GetLastError());
    return;
  }

  // Create the namespace for Local Administrators only
  SECURITY_ATTRIBUTES sa;
  sa.nLength = sizeof(sa);
  sa.bInheritHandle = FALSE;
  if (!ConvertStringSecurityDescriptorToSecurityDescriptor(
    TEXT("D:(A;;GA;;;BA)"),
    SDDL_REVISION_1, &sa.lpSecurityDescriptor, NULL)) {
    AddText(TEXT("Security Descriptor creation failed: %u\r\n"), GetLastError());
    return;
  }

  g_hNamespace =
    CreatePrivateNamespace(&sa, g_hBoundary, g_szNamespace);

  // Don't forget to release memory for the security descriptor
  LocalFree(sa.lpSecurityDescriptor);


  // Check the private namespace creation result
  DWORD dwLastError = GetLastError();
  if (g_hNamespace == NULL) {
    // Nothing to do if access is denied
    // --> this code must run under a Local Administrator account
    if (dwLastError == ERROR_ACCESS_DENIED) {
      AddText(TEXT("Access denied when creating the namespace.\r\n"));
      AddText(TEXT("  You must be running as Administrator.\r\n\r\n"));
      return;
```

```
      } else {
         if (dwLastError == ERROR_ALREADY_EXISTS) {
            // If another instance has already created the namespace,
            // we need to open it instead.
               AddText(TEXT("CreatePrivateNamespace failed: %u\r\n"), dwLastError);
               g_hNamespace = OpenPrivateNamespace(g_hBoundary, g_szNamespace);
               if (g_hNamespace == NULL) {
                  AddText(TEXT("   and OpenPrivateNamespace failed: %u\r\n"),
                     dwLastError);
                  return;
               } else {
                  g_bNamespaceOpened = TRUE;
                  AddText(TEXT("   but OpenPrivateNamespace succeeded\r\n\r\n"));
               }
         } else {
            AddText(TEXT("Unexpected error occurred: %u\r\n\r\n"),
               dwLastError);
            return;
         }
      }
   }

   // Try to create the mutex object with a name
   // based on the private namespace
   TCHAR szMutexName[64];
   StringCchPrintf(szMutexName, _countof(szMutexName), TEXT("%s\\%s"),
      g_szNamespace, TEXT("Singleton"));

   g_hSingleton = CreateMutex(NULL, FALSE, szMutexName);
   if (GetLastError() == ERROR_ALREADY_EXISTS) {
      // There is already an instance of this Singleton object
      AddText(TEXT("Another instance of Singleton is running:\r\n"));
      AddText(TEXT("--> Impossible to access application features.\r\n"));
   } else {
      // First time the Singleton object is created
      AddText(TEXT("First instance of Singleton:\r\n"));
      AddText(TEXT("--> Access application features now.\r\n"));
   }
}


///////////////////////////////////////////////////////////////////////////////


BOOL Dlg_OnInitDialog(HWND hwnd, HWND hwndFocus, LPARAM lParam) {

   chSETDLGICONS(hwnd, IDI_SINGLETON);

   // Keep track of the main dialog window handle
   g_hDlg = hwnd;

   // Check whether another instance is already running
   CheckInstances();

   return(TRUE);
}
```

```
///////////////////////////////////////////////////////////////////////////

INT_PTR WINAPI Dlg_Proc(HWND hwnd, UINT uMsg, WPARAM wParam, LPARAM lParam) {

   switch (uMsg) {
      chHANDLE_DLGMSG(hwnd, WM_COMMAND,    Dlg_OnCommand);
      chHANDLE_DLGMSG(hwnd, WM_INITDIALOG, Dlg_OnInitDialog);
   }

   return(FALSE);
}


///////////////////////////////////////////////////////////////////////////


int APIENTRY _tWinMain(HINSTANCE hInstance,
                       HINSTANCE hPrevInstance,
                       LPTSTR    lpCmdLine,
                       int       nCmdShow)
{
   UNREFERENCED_PARAMETER(hPrevInstance);
   UNREFERENCED_PARAMETER(lpCmdLine);

   // Show main window
   DialogBox(hInstance, MAKEINTRESOURCE(IDD_SINGLETON), NULL, Dlg_Proc);

   // Don't forget to clean up and release kernel resources
   if (g_hSingleton != NULL) {
      CloseHandle(g_hSingleton);
   }

   if (g_hNamespace != NULL) {
      if (g_bNamespaceOpened) {  // Open namespace
         ClosePrivateNamespace(g_hNamespace, 0);
      } else { // Created namespace
         ClosePrivateNamespace(g_hNamespace, PRIVATE_NAMESPACE_FLAG_DESTROY);
      }
   }

   if (g_hBoundary != NULL) {
      DeleteBoundaryDescriptor(g_hBoundary);
   }

   return(0);
}

////////////////////////////// End of File //////////////////////////////////
```

Let's examine the different steps of the **CheckInstances** function. First, the creation of a boundary descriptor requires a string identifier to name the scope where the private namespace will be defined. This name is passed as the first parameter of the following function:

```
HANDLE CreateBoundaryDescriptor(
    PCTSTR pszName,
    DWORD dwFlags);
```

Current versions of Windows do not use the second parameter, and therefore you should pass 0 for it. Note that the function signature implies that the return value is a kernel object handle; however, it is not. The return value is a pointer to a user-mode structure containing the definition of the boundary. For this reason, you should never pass the returned handle value to **CloseHandle**; you should pass it to **DeleteBoundaryDescriptor** instead.

The next step is to associate the SID of a privileged group of users that the client applications are supposed to run under with the boundary descriptor by calling the following function:

```
BOOL AddSIDToBoundaryDescriptor(
    HANDLE* phBoundaryDescriptor,
    PSID pRequiredSid);
```

In the Singleton example, the SID of the Local Administrator group is created by calling **AllocateAndInitializeSid** with **SECURITY_BUILTIN_DOMAIN_RID** and **DOMAIN_ALIAS_RID_ADMINS** as parameters that describe the group. The list of all well-known groups is defined in the WinNT.h header file.

This boundary descriptor handle is passed as the second parameter when you call the following function to create the private namespace:

```
HANDLE CreatePrivateNamespace(
    PSECURITY_ATTRIBUTES psa,
    PVOID pvBoundaryDescriptor,
    PCTSTR pszAliasPrefix);
```

The **SECURITY_ATTRIBUTES** that you pass as the first parameter to this function is used by Windows to allow or not allow an application calling **OpenPrivateNamespace** to access the namespace and open or create objects within that namespace. You have exactly the same options as within a file system directory. This is the level of filter that you provide for opening the namespace. The SID you added to the boundary descriptor is used to define who is able to enter the boundary and create the namespace. In the Singleton example, the **SECURITY_ATTRIBUTE** is constructed by calling the **ConvertStringSecurityDescriptorToSecurityDescriptor** function that takes a string with a complicated syntax as the first parameter. The security descriptor string syntax is documented at *http://msdn2.microsoft.com/en-us/library/aa374928.aspx* and *http://msdn2.microsoft.com/en-us/library/aa379602.aspx.*

The type of **pvBoundaryDescriptor** is **PVOID**, even though **CreateBoundaryDescriptor** returns a **HANDLE**—even at Microsoft it is seen as a pseudohandle. The string prefix you want to use to create your kernel objects is given as the third parameter. If you try to create a private namespace that already exists, **CreatePrivateNamespace** returns **NULL** and **GetLastError** returns **ERROR_ALREADY_EXISTS**. In this case, you need to open the existing private namespace using the following function:

```
HANDLE OpenPrivateNamespace(
   PVOID pvBoundaryDescriptor,
   PCTSTR pszAliasPrefix);
```

Note that the **HANDLE**s returned by **CreatePrivateNamespace** and **OpenPrivateNamespace** are not kernel object handles; you close any of these pseudohandles by calling **ClosePrivate-Namespace**:

```
BOOLEAN ClosePrivateNamespace(
   HANDLE hNamespace,
   DWORD dwFlags);
```

If you created the namespace and you don't want it to be visible after you close it, you should pass **PRIVATE_NAMESPACE_FLAG_DESTROY** as the second parameter and pass 0 otherwise. The boundary is closed either when the process ends or if you call the **DeleteBoundaryDescriptor** function with the boundary pseudohandle as the only parameter. The namespace must not be closed while the kernel object is used. If you close the namespace while an object exists inside it, it becomes possible to create another kernel object with the same name in the same re-created namespace in the same boundary, thus enabling DoS attacks once more.

To sum up, a private namespace is just a directory where you create kernel objects. Like other directories, a private namespace has a security descriptor associated with it that is set when you call **CreatePrivateNamespace**. However, unlike file system directories, this namespace does not have a parent or a name—the boundary descriptor is used as a name to refer to it. This is the reason why the kernel objects created with a prefix based on a private namespace appear in Process Explorer from Sysinternals with a "...\" prefix instead of the expected "*namespace name*\". The "...\" prefix hides information, thereby granting more protection against potential hackers. The name that you give to a private namespace is an alias visible only within the process. Other processes (and even the same process) can open the very same private namespace and give it a different alias.

To create regular directories, an access check is performed against the parent to determine whether or not a subdirectory can be created. To create namespaces, a boundary test is performed—the token of the current thread must include all the SIDs that are part of the boundary.

Duplicating Object Handles

The last technique for sharing kernel objects across process boundaries requires the use of the **DuplicateHandle** function:

```
BOOL DuplicateHandle(
   HANDLE hSourceProcessHandle,
   HANDLE hSourceHandle,
   HANDLE hTargetProcessHandle,
   PHANDLE phTargetHandle,
   DWORD dwDesiredAccess,
   BOOL bInheritHandle,
   DWORD dwOptions);
```

Simply stated, this function takes an entry in one process' handle table and makes a copy of the entry into another process' handle table. **DuplicateHandle** takes several parameters but is actually quite straightforward. The most general usage of the **DuplicateHandle** function could involve three different processes that are running in the system.

When you call **DuplicateHandle**, the first and third parameters—**hSourceProcessHandle** and **hTargetProcessHandle**—are kernel object handles. The handles themselves must be relative to the process that is calling the **DuplicateHandle** function. In addition, these two parameters must identify process kernel objects; the function fails if you pass handles to any other type of kernel object. We'll discuss process kernel objects in more detail in Chapter 4; for now, all you need to know is that a process kernel object is created whenever a new process is invoked in the system.

The second parameter, **hSourceHandle**, is a handle to any type of kernel object. However, the handle value is not relative to the process that calls **DuplicateHandle**. Instead, this handle must be relative to the process identified by the **hSourceProcessHandle** handle. The fourth parameter, **phTargetHandle**, is the address of a **HANDLE** variable that receives as its value the **HANDLE** of the entry in the handle table of the process identified by **hTargetProcessHandle**, where the source's handle information gets copied.

DuplicateHandle's last three parameters allow you to indicate the value of the access mask and the inheritance flag that should be used in the target's entry for this kernel object handle. The **dwOptions** parameter can be 0 (zero) or any combination of the following two flags: **DUPLICATE_SAME_ACCESS** and **DUPLICATE_CLOSE_SOURCE**.

Specifying **DUPLICATE_SAME_ACCESS** tells **DuplicateHandle** that you want the target's handle to have the same access mask as the source process' handle. Using this flag causes **DuplicateHandle** to ignore its **dwDesiredAccess** parameter.

Specifying **DUPLICATE_CLOSE_SOURCE** has the effect of closing the handle in the source process. This flag makes it easy for one process to hand a kernel object over to another process. When this flag is used, the usage count of the kernel object is not affected.

I'll use an example to show you how **DuplicateHandle** works. For this demonstration, Process S is the source process that currently has access to some kernel object and Process T is the target process that will gain access to this kernel object. Process C is the catalyst process that will execute the call to **DuplicateHandle**. In this example, I use hard-coded numbers for handle values only to demonstrate how the function operates. In real applications, you would have the various handle values in variables and pass the variables as arguments to the function.

Process C's handle table (Table 3-4) contains two handle values, 1 and 2. Handle value 1 identifies Process S's process kernel object, and handle value 2 identifies Process T's process kernel object.

Table 3-4   Process C's Handle Table

Index	Pointer to Kernel Object Memory Block	Access Mask (DWORD of Flag Bits)	Flags
1	0xF0000000 (Process S's kernel object)	0x????????	0x00000000
2	0xF0000010 (Process T's kernel object)	0x????????	0x00000000

Table 3-5 is Process S's handle table, which contains a single entry with a handle value of 2. This handle can identify any type of kernel object—it doesn't have to be a process kernel object.

Table 3-5   Process S's Handle Table

Index	Pointer to Kernel Object Memory Block	Access Mask (DWORD of Flag Bits)	Flags
1	0x00000000	(N/A)	(N/A)
2	0xF0000020 (any kernel object)	0x????????	0x00000000

Table 3-6 shows what Process T's handle table contains before Process C calls the **DuplicateHandle** function. As you can see, Process T's handle table contains only a single entry with a handle value of 2; handle entry 1 is currently unused.

Table 3-6   Process T's Handle Table Before Calling DuplicateHandle

Index	Pointer to Kernel Object Memory Block	Access Mask (DWORD of Flag Bits)	Flags
1	0x00000000	(N/A)	(N/A)
2	0xF0000030 (any kernel object)	0x????????	0x00000000

If Process C now calls **DuplicateHandle** using the following code, only Process T's handle table has changed, as shown in Table 3-7:

```
DuplicateHandle(1, 2, 2, &hObj, 0, TRUE, DUPLICATE_SAME_ACCESS);
```

Table 3-7   Process T's Handle Table After Calling DuplicateHandle

Index	Pointer to Kernel Object Memory Block	Access Mask (DWORD of Flag Bits)	Flags
1	0xF0000020	0x????????	0x00000001
2	0xF0000030 (any kernel object)	0x????????	0x00000000

The second entry in Process S's handle table has been copied to the first entry in Process T's handle table. **DuplicateHandle** has also filled in Process C's **hObj** variable with a value of 1, which is the index in process T's handle table in which the new entry was placed.

Because the **DUPLICATE_SAME_ACCESS** flag was passed to **DuplicateHandle**, the access mask for this handle in Process T's table is identical to the access mask in Process S's table entry. Also, passing the **DUPLICATE_SAME_ACCESS** flag causes **DuplicateHandle** to ignore its **dwDesiredAccess** parameter. Finally, notice that the inheritance bit flag has been turned on because **TRUE** was passed for **DuplicateHandle**'s **bInheritHandle** parameter.

As with inheritance, one of the odd things about the **DuplicateHandle** function is that the target process is not given any notification that a new kernel object is now accessible to it. So Process C must somehow notify Process T that it now has access to a kernel object, and it must use some form of interprocess communication to pass the handle value in **hObj** to Process T. Obviously, using a command-line argument or changing Process T's environment variables is out of the question because the process is already up and running. A window message or some other interprocess communication (IPC) mechanism must be used.

What I have just explained is the most general usage of **DuplicateHandle**. As you can see, it is a very flexible function. However, it is rarely used when three different processes are involved (partly because it is unlikely that Process C would know the handle value of an object in use by Process S). Usually, **DuplicateHandle** is called when only two processes are involved. Imagine a situation in which one process has access to an object that another process wants access to, or a case in which one process wants to give access to a kernel object to another process. For example, let's say that Process S has access to a kernel object and wants to give Process T access to this object. To do this, you call **DuplicateHandle** as follows:

```
// All of the following code is executed by Process S.

// Create a mutex object accessible by Process S.
HANDLE hObjInProcessS = CreateMutex(NULL, FALSE, NULL);

// Get a handle to Process T's kernel object.
HANDLE hProcessT = OpenProcess(PROCESS_ALL_ACCESS, FALSE,
   dwProcessIdT);

HANDLE hObjInProcessT;   // An uninitialized handle relative to Process T.

// Give Process T access to our mutex object.
DuplicateHandle(GetCurrentProcess(), hObjInProcessS, hProcessT,
   &hObjInProcessT, 0, FALSE, DUPLICATE_SAME_ACCESS);

// Use some IPC mechanism to get the handle value of hObjInProcessS into Process T.
...
// We no longer need to communicate with Process T.
CloseHandle(hProcessT);
...
// When Process S no longer needs to use the mutex, it should close it.
CloseHandle(hObjInProcessS);
```

The call to **GetCurrentProcess** returns a pseudohandle that always identifies the calling process—Process S in this example. Once **DuplicateHandle** returns, **hObjInProcessT** is a handle relative to Process T that identifies the same object that the handle for **hObjInProcessS** does when referenced by code in Process S. Process S should never execute the following code:

```
// Process S should never attempt to close the duplicated handle.
CloseHandle(hObjInProcessT);
```

If Process S executed this code, the call might or might not fail. But this is not the problem. The call would succeed if Process S happened to have access to a kernel object with the same handle value as **hObjInProcessT**. This call would have the unexpected effect of closing some random kernel object so that the next time Process S tried to access it, it would certainly cause the application to behave undesirably (to put it nicely).

Here is another way to use **DuplicateHandle**: Suppose that a process has read and write access to a file-mapping object. At some point, a function is called that is supposed to access the file-mapping object by only reading it. To make our application more robust, we can use **Duplicate-Handle** to create a new handle for the existing object and ensure that this new handle has read-only access on it. We would then pass this read-only handle to the function; this way, the code in the function would never be able to accidentally write to the file-mapping object. The following code illustrates this example:

```
int WINAPI _tWinMain(HINSTANCE hInstExe, HINSTANCE,
    LPTSTR szCmdLine, int nCmdShow) {

    // Create a file-mapping object; the handle has read/write access.
    HANDLE hFileMapRW = CreateFileMapping(INVALID_HANDLE_VALUE,
        NULL, PAGE_READWRITE, 0, 10240, NULL);

    // Create another handle to the file-mapping object;
    // the handle has read-only access.
    HANDLE hFileMapRO;
    DuplicateHandle(GetCurrentProcess(), hFileMapRW, GetCurrentProcess(),
        &hFileMapRO, FILE_MAP_READ, FALSE, 0);

    // Call the function that should only read from the file mapping.
    ReadFromTheFileMapping(hFileMapRO);

    // Close the read-only file-mapping object.
    CloseHandle(hFileMapRO);

    // We can still read/write the file-mapping object using hFileMapRW.
    ...
    // When the main code doesn't access the file mapping anymore,
    // close it.
    CloseHandle(hFileMapRW);
}
```

Part II
Getting Work Done

Chapter 4
Processes

This chapter discusses how the system manages all of the running applications. I'll begin by explaining what a process is and how the system creates a process kernel object to manage each process. I'll then show you how to manipulate a process using its associated kernel object. Following that, I'll discuss the various attributes, or properties, of a process as well as several functions for querying and changing these properties. I'll also examine the functions that allow you to create or spawn additional processes in the system. And, of course, no discussion of processes would be complete without an in-depth look at how they terminate. OK, let's begin.

A process is usually defined as an instance of a running program and consists of two components:

- A kernel object that the operating system uses to manage the process. The kernel object is also where the system keeps statistical information about the process.
- An address space that contains all the executable or dynamic-link library (DLL) module's code and data. It also contains dynamic memory allocations such as thread stacks and heap allocations.

Processes are inert. For a process to accomplish anything, it must have a thread that runs in its context; this thread is responsible for executing the code contained in the process' address space. In fact, a single process might contain several threads, all of them executing code "simultaneously" in the process' address space. To do this, each thread has its own set of CPU registers and its own stack. Each process has at least one thread that executes code in the process' address space. When a process is created, the system automatically creates its first thread, called the *primary thread*. This thread can then create additional threads, and these can in turn create even more threads. If there were no threads executing code in the process' address space, there would be no reason for the process to continue to exist, and the system would automatically destroy the process and its address space.

For all of these threads to run, the operating system schedules some CPU time for each thread. It creates the illusion that all the threads run concurrently by offering time slices (called *quantums*) to the threads in a round-robin fashion. Figure 4-1 shows how this works on a machine with a single CPU.

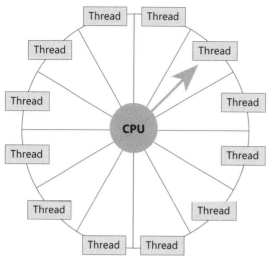

Figure 4-1   The operating system offers quantums to individual threads in a round-robin fashion on a single-CPU machine

If the machine has multiple CPUs, the operating system's algorithm for load balancing the threads over the CPUs is much more complex. Microsoft Windows can schedule different threads on each CPU simultaneously so that multiple threads do truly run concurrently. The Windows kernel handles all the management and scheduling of threads on this type of system. You do not have to do anything special in your code to gain the advantages offered by a multiprocessor machine. However, there are things you can do in your application's algorithms to better take advantage of these CPUs.

Writing Your First Windows Application

Windows supports two types of applications: those based on a graphical user interface (GUI) and those based on a console user interface (CUI). A GUI-based application has a graphical front end. It can create windows, have menus, interact with the user via dialog boxes, and use all the standard "Windowsy" stuff. Almost all the accessory applications that ship with Windows (such as Notepad, Calculator, and WordPad) are GUI-based applications. Console-based applications are text-based. They don't usually create windows or process messages, and they don't require a graphical user interface. Although CUI-based applications are contained within a window on the screen, the window contains only text. The command prompt—CMD.EXE (for Windows Vista)—is a typical example of CUI-based applications.

The line between these two types of applications is very fuzzy. It is possible to create CUI-based applications that display dialog boxes. For example, the command shell could have a special command that causes it to display a graphical dialog box, in which you can select the command you want to execute instead of having to remember the various commands supported by the shell. You can also create a GUI-based application that outputs text strings to a console window. I frequently create GUI-based applications that create a console window in which I can view debugging information as the application executes. You are certainly encouraged to use a GUI in your applications instead of the old-fashioned character interface, which is much less user friendly.

When you use Microsoft Visual Studio to create an application project, the integrated environment sets up various linker switches so that the linker embeds the proper type of subsystem in the resulting executable. This linker switch is **/SUBSYSTEM:CONSOLE** for CUI applications and **/SUB-SYSTEM:WINDOWS** for GUI applications. When the user runs an application, the operating system's loader looks inside the executable image's header and grabs this subsystem value. If the value indicates a CUI-based application, the loader automatically ensures that a text console window is available for the application—such as when the application is started from a command prompt—and, if needed, another one is created—such as when the same CUI-based application is started from Windows Explorer. If the value indicates a GUI-based application, the loader doesn't create the console window and just loads the application. Once the application starts running, the operating system doesn't care what type of UI your application has.

Your Windows application must have an entry-point function that is called when the application starts running. As a C/C++ developer, there are two possible entry-point functions you can use:

```
int WINAPI _tWinMain(
   HINSTANCE hInstanceExe,
   HINSTANCE,
   PTSTR pszCmdLine,
   int nCmdShow);

int _tmain(
   int argc,
   TCHAR *argv[],
   TCHAR *envp[]);
```

Notice that the exact symbol depends on whether you are using Unicode strings or not. The operating system doesn't actually call the entry-point function you write. Instead, it calls a C/C++ run-time startup function implemented by the C/C++ run time and set at link time with the **-entry:** command-line option. This function initializes the C/C++ run-time library so that you can call functions such as **malloc** and **free**. It also ensures that any global and static C++ objects that you have declared are constructed properly before your code executes. Table 4-1 tells you which entry point to implement in your source code and when.

Table 4-1   Application Types and Corresponding Entry Points

Application Type	Entry Point	Startup Function Embedded in Your Executable
GUI application that wants ANSI characters and strings	`_tWinMain (WinMain)`	`WinMainCRTStartup`
GUI application that wants Unicode characters and strings	`_tWinMain (wWinMain)`	`wWinMainCRTStartup`
CUI application that wants ANSI characters and strings	`_tmain (Main)`	`mainCRTStartup`
CUI application that wants Unicode characters and strings	`_tmain (Wmain)`	`wmainCRTStartup`

The linker is responsible for choosing the proper C/C++ run-time startup function when it links your executable. If the **/SUBSYSTEM:WINDOWS** linker switch is specified, the linker expects to find either a **WinMain** or **wWinMain** function. If neither of these functions is present, the linker returns an "unresolved external symbol" error; otherwise, it chooses to call either the **WinMainCRT-Startup** or **wWinMainCRTStartup** function, respectively.

Likewise, if the **/SUBSYSTEM:CONSOLE** linker switch is specified, the linker expects to find either a **main** or **wmain** function and chooses to call either the **mainCRTStartup** or **wmainCRTStartup** function, respectively. Again, if neither **main** nor **wmain** exist, the linker returns an "unresolved external symbol" error.

However, it is a little-known fact that you can remove the **/SUBSYSTEM** linker switch from your project altogether. When you do this, the linker automatically determines which subsystem your application should be set to. When linking, the linker checks to see which of the four functions (**WinMain**, **wWinMain**, **main**, or **wmain**) is present in your code and then infers which subsystem your executable should be and which C/C++ startup function should be embedded in your executable.

One mistake that new Windows/Visual C++ developers commonly make is to accidentally select the wrong project type when they create a new project. For example, a developer might create a new Win32 Application project but create an entry-point function of **main**. When building the application, the developer will get a linker error because a Win32 Application project sets the **/SUBSYSTEM:WINDOWS** linker switch but no **WinMain** or **wWinMain** function exists. At this point, the developer has four options:

- Change the **main** function to **WinMain**. This is usually not the best choice because the developer probably wants to create a console application.

- Create a new Win32 Console Application in Visual C++, and add the existing source code modules to the new project. This option is tedious because it feels like you're starting over and you have to delete the original project file.

- Click on the Link tab of the project properties dialog box, and change the **/SUBSYSTEM:WINDOWS** switch to **/SUBSYSTEM :CONSOLE** in the Configuration Properties/Linker/System/Sub-System option, as shown in Figure 4-2. This is an easy way to fix the problem; few people are aware that this is all they have to do.

- Click on the Link tab of the project properties dialog box, and delete the **/SUBSYSTEM:WINDOWS** switch entirely. This is my favorite choice because it gives you the most flexibility. Now the linker will simply do the right thing based on which function you implement in your source code. I have no idea why this isn't the default when you create a new Win32 Application or Win32 Console Application project with Visual Studio.

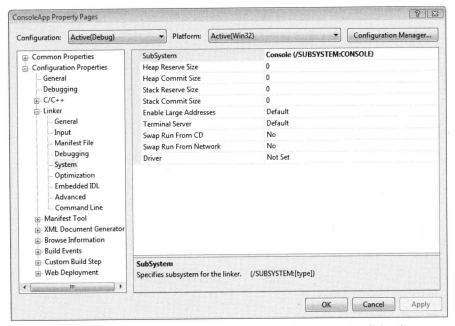

Figure 4-2   Selecting a CUI subsystem for a project in the properties dialog box

All of the C/C++ run-time startup functions do basically the same thing. The difference is in whether they process ANSI or Unicode strings and which entry-point function they call after they initialize the C run-time library. Visual C++ ships with the source code to the C run-time library. You can find the code for the four startup functions in the crtexe.c file. Here's a summary of what the startup functions do:

- Retrieve a pointer to the new process' full command line.

- Retrieve a pointer to the new process' environment variables.

- Initialize the C/C++ run time's global variables. Your code can access these variables if you include StdLib.h. The variables are listed in Table 4-2.

- Initialize the heap used by the C run-time memory allocation functions (**malloc** and **calloc**) and other low-level input/output routines.

- Call constructors for all global and static C++ class objects.

After all of this initialization, the C/C++ startup function calls your application's entry-point function. If you wrote a **_tWinMain** function with **_UNICODE** defined, it is called as follows:

```
GetStartupInfo(&StartupInfo);
int nMainRetVal = wWinMain((HINSTANCE)&__ImageBase, NULL, pszCommandLineUnicode,
   (StartupInfo.dwFlags & STARTF_USESHOWWINDOW)
      ? StartupInfo.wShowWindow : SW_SHOWDEFAULT);
```

And it is called as follows without **_UNICODE** defined:

```
GetStartupInfo(&StartupInfo);
int nMainRetVal = WinMain((HINSTANCE)&__ImageBase, NULL, pszCommandLineAnsi,
    (StartupInfo.dwFlags & STARTF_USESHOWWINDOW)
        ? StartupInfo.wShowWindow : SW_SHOWDEFAULT);
```

Notice that **_ImageBase** is a linker defined pseudo-variable that shows where the executable file is mapped into the application memory. More details will be provided later in "A Process Instance Handle" on the next page.

If you wrote a **_tmain** function, it is called as follows when **_UNICODE** is defined:

```
int nMainRetVal = wmain(argc, argv, envp);
```

And it is called as follows when **_UNICODE** is not defined:

```
int nMainRetVal = main(argc, argv, envp);
```

Notice that when you generate your application through Visual Studio wizards, the third parameter (environment variable block) is not defined in your CUI-application entry point, as shown next:

```
int _tmain(int argc, TCHAR* argv[]);
```

If you need to access the environment variables of the process, simply replace the previous definition with the following:

```
int _tmain(int argc, TCHAR* argv[], TCHAR* env[])
```

This **env** parameter points to an array that contains all the environment variables followed by their value and separated by the equal sign (=) character. A detailed explanation of the environment variables is provided in "A Process' Environment Variables" on page 77.

When your entry-point function returns, the startup function calls the C run-time **exit** function, passing it your return value (**nMainRetVal**). The **exit** function does the following:

- It calls any functions registered by calls to the **_onexit** function.
- It calls destructors for all global and static C++ class objects.
- In **DEBUG** builds, leaks in the C/C++ run-time memory management are listed by a call to the **_CrtDumpMemoryLeaks** function if the **_CRTDBG_LEAK_CHECK_DF** flag has been set.
- It calls the operating system's **ExitProcess** function, passing it **nMainRetVal**. This causes the operating system to kill your process and set its exit code.

Notice that all these variables have been deprecated for security's sake because the code that is using them might be running before the C run-time library has the chance to initialize them. This is why you should rather directly call the corresponding functions of the Windows API.

Table 4-2   The C/C++ Run-Time Global Variables Available to Your Programs

Variable Name	Type	Description and Recommended Windows Function Replacement
_osver	unsigned int	The build version of the operating system. For example, Windows Vista RTM was build 6000. Thus, **_osver** has a value of 6000. Use **GetVersionEx** instead.
_winmajor	unsigned int	A major version of Windows in hexadecimal notation. For Windows Vista, the value is 6. Use **GetVersionEx** instead.
_winminor	unsigned int	A minor version of Windows in hexadecimal notation. For Windows Vista, the value is 0. Use **GetVersionEx** instead.
_winver	unsigned int	(**_winmajor** << 8) + **_winminor**. Use **GetVersionEx** instead.
__argc	unsigned int	The number of arguments passed on the command line. Use **GetCommandLine** instead.
__argv **__wargv**	char wchar_t	An array of size **__argc** with pointers to ANSI/Unicode strings. Each array entry points to a command-line argument. Notice that **__argv** is **NULL** if _UNICODE is defined and **__wargv** is **NULL** if it is not defined. Use **GetCommandLine** instead.
_environ **_wenviron**	char wchar_t	An array of pointers to ANSI/Unicode strings. Each array entry points to an environment string. Notice that **_wenviron** is **NULL** if **_UNICODE** is not defined and **_environ** is **NULL** if **_UNICODE** is defined. Use **GetEnvironmentStrings** or **GetEnvironment-Variable** instead.
_pgmptr **_wpgmptr**	char wchar_t	The ANSI/Unicode full path and name of the running program. Notice that **_pgmptr** is **NULL** if **_UNICODE** is defined and **_wpgmptr** is **NULL** if it is not defined. Use **GetModuleFileName**, passing **NULL** as the first parameter, instead.

A Process Instance Handle

Every executable or DLL file loaded into a process' address space is assigned a unique instance handle. Your executable file's instance is passed as **(w)WinMain**'s first parameter, **hInstanceExe**. The handle's value is typically needed for calls that load resources. For example, to load an icon resource from the executable file's image, you need to call this function:

```
HICON LoadIcon(
   HINSTANCE hInstance,
   PCTSTR pszIcon);
```

The first parameter to **LoadIcon** indicates which file (executable or DLL) contains the resource you want to load. Many applications save **(w)WinMain**'s **hInstanceExe** parameter in a global variable so that it is easily accessible to all the executable file's code.

The Platform SDK documentation states that some functions require a parameter of the type **HMODULE**. An example is the **GetModuleFileName** function, which is shown here:

```
DWORD GetModuleFileName(
    HMODULE hInstModule,
    PTSTR pszPath,
    DWORD cchPath);
```

Note   As it turns out, **HMODULE**s and **HINSTANCE**s are exactly the same thing. If the documentation for a function indicates that an **HMODULE** is required, you can pass an **HINSTANCE**, and vice versa. There are two data types because in 16-bit Windows **HMODULE**s and **HINSTANCE**s identified different things.

The actual value of **(w)WinMain**'s **hInstanceExe** parameter is the base memory address where the system loaded the executable file's image into the process' address space. For example, if the system opens the executable file and loads its contents at address 0x00400000, **(w)WinMain**'s **hInstanceExe** parameter has a value of 0x00400000.

The base address where an executable file's image loads is determined by the linker. Different linkers can use different default base addresses. The Visual Studio linker uses a default base address of 0x00400000 for a historical reason: this is the lowest address an executable file image can load to when you run Windows 98. You can change the base address that your application loads to by using the **/BASE:address** linker switch for Microsoft's linker.

The **GetModuleHandle** function, shown next, returns the handle/base address where an executable or DLL file is loaded in the process' address space:

```
HMODULE GetModuleHandle(PCTSTR pszModule);
```

When you call this function, you pass a zero-terminated string that specifies the name of an executable or DLL file loaded into the calling process' address space. If the system finds the specified executable or DLL name, **GetModuleHandle** returns the base address where that executable or DLL's file image is loaded. The system returns **NULL** if it cannot find the file. You can also call **GetModuleHandle**, passing **NULL** for the **pszModule** parameter; **GetModuleHandle** returns the calling executable file's base address. If your code is in a DLL, you have two ways to know in which module your code is running. First, you can take advantage of the pseudo-variable **__ImageBase** provided by the linker that points to the base address of the current running module. This is what the C run-time startup code does when it calls your **(w)WinMain** function, as discussed previously.

The other option is to call the **GetModuleHandleEx** function with **GET_MODULE_HANDLE_EX_FLAG_FROM_ADDRESS** as the first parameter and the address of the current method as the second parameter. The pointer to an **HMODULE** passed as the last parameter will be filled in by **GetModuleHandleEx**, with the corresponding base address of the DLL containing the passed-in function. The following code presents both options:

```
extern "C" const IMAGE_DOS_HEADER __ImageBase;

void DumpModule() {
   // Get the base address of the running application.
   // Can be different from the running module if this code is in a DLL.
   HMODULE hModule = GetModuleHandle(NULL);
   _tprintf(TEXT("with GetModuleHandle(NULL) = 0x%x\r\n"), hModule);


   // Use the pseudo-variable __ImageBase to get
   // the address of the current module hModule/hInstance.
   _tprintf(TEXT("with __ImageBase = 0x%x\r\n"), (HINSTANCE)&__ImageBase);


   // Pass the address of the current method DumpModule
   // as parameter to GetModuleHandleEx to get the address
   // of the current module hModule/hInstance.
   hModule = NULL;
   GetModuleHandleEx(
      GET_MODULE_HANDLE_EX_FLAG_FROM_ADDRESS,
      (PCTSTR)DumpModule,
      &hModule);
   _tprintf(TEXT("with GetModuleHandleEx = 0x%x\r\n"), hModule);
}

int _tmain(int argc, TCHAR* argv[]) {
   DumpModule();
   return(0);
}
```

Keep in mind two important characteristics of the **GetModuleHandle** function. First, it examines only the calling process' address space. If the calling process does not use any common dialog functions, calling **GetModuleHandle** and passing it *ComDlg32* causes **NULL** to be returned even though ComDlg32.dll is probably loaded into the address spaces of other processes. Second, calling **GetModuleHandle** and passing a value of **NULL** returns the base address of the executable file in the process' address space. So even if you call **GetModuleHandle(NULL)** from code that is contained inside a DLL, the value returned is the executable file's base address—not the DLL file's base address.

A Process' Previous Instance Handle

As noted earlier, the C/C++ run-time startup code always passes **NULL** to **(w)WinMain**'s **hPrevInstance** parameter. This parameter was used in 16-bit Windows and remains a parameter to **(w)WinMain** solely to ease porting of 16-bit Windows applications. You should never reference this parameter inside your code. For this reason, I always write my **(w)WinMain** functions as follows:

```
int WINAPI _tWinMain(
   HINSTANCE hInstanceExe,
   HINSTANCE,
   PSTR pszCmdLine,
   int nCmdShow);
```

Because no parameter name is given for the second parameter, the compiler does not issue a "parameter not referenced" warning. Visual Studio has chosen a different solution: the wizard-generated C++ GUI projects defined take advantage of the **UNREFERENCED_PARAMETER** macro to remove these warnings, as shown in the following code snippet:

```
int APIENTRY _tWinMain(HINSTANCE hInstance,
                       HINSTANCE hPrevInstance,
                       LPTSTR    lpCmdLine,
                       int       nCmdShow) {
    UNREFERENCED_PARAMETER(hPrevInstance);
    UNREFERENCED_PARAMETER(lpCmdLine);
    ...
}
```

A Process' Command Line

When a new process is created, it is passed a command line. The command line is almost never blank; at the very least, the name of the executable file used to create the new process is the first token on the command line. However, as you'll see later when we discuss the **CreateProcess** function, a process can receive a command line that consists of a single character: the string-terminating zero. When the C run time's startup code begins executing a GUI application, it retrieves the process' complete command line by calling the **GetCommandLine** Windows function, skips over the executable file's name, and passes a pointer to the remainder of the command line to **WinMain**'s **pszCmdLine** parameter.

An application can parse and interpret the command-line string any way it chooses. You can actually write to the memory buffer pointed to by the **pszCmdLine** parameter—but you should not, under any circumstances, write beyond the end of the buffer. Personally, I always consider this a read-only buffer. If I want to make changes to the command line, I first copy the command-line buffer to a local buffer in my application, and then I modify my local buffer.

Following the example of the C run time, you can also obtain a pointer to your process' complete command line by calling the **GetCommandLine** function:

```
PTSTR GetCommandLine();
```

This function returns a pointer to a buffer containing the full command line, including the full pathname of the executed file. Be aware that **GetCommandLine** always returns the address of the same buffer. This is another reason why you should not write into **pszCmdLine**: it points to the same buffer, and after you modify it, there is no way for you to know what the original command line was.

Many applications prefer to have the command line parsed into its separate tokens. An application can gain access to the command line's individual components by using the global **__argc** and **__argv** (or **__wargv**) variables even though they have been deprecated. The following function declared in ShellAPI.h and exported by Shell32.dll, **CommandLineToArgvW**, separates any Unicode string into its separate tokens:

```
PWSTR* CommandLineToArgvW(
   PWSTR pszCmdLine,
   int* pNumArgs);
```

As the *W* at the end of the function name implies, this function exists in a Unicode version only. (The *W* stands for *wide*.) The first parameter, **pszCmdLine**, points to a command-line string. This is usually the return value from an earlier call to **GetCommandLineW**. The **pNumArgs** parameter is the address of an integer; the integer is set to the number of arguments in the command line. **CommandLineToArgvW** returns the address to an array of Unicode string pointers.

CommandLineToArgvW allocates memory internally. Most applications do not free this memory—they count on the operating system to free it when the process terminates. This is totally acceptable. However, if you want to free the memory yourself, the proper way to do so is by calling **Heap-Free** as follows:

```
int nNumArgs;
PWSTR *ppArgv = CommandLineToArgvW(GetCommandLineW(), &nNumArgs);

// Use the arguments…
if (*ppArgv[1] == L'x') {
   ...
}
// Free the memory block
HeapFree(GetProcessHeap(), 0, ppArgv);
```

A Process' Environment Variables

Every process has an environment block associated with it. An environment block is a block of memory allocated within the process' address space that contains a set of strings with the following appearance:

```
=::=::\ ...
VarName1=VarValue1\0
VarName2=VarValue2\0
VarName3=VarValue3\0 ...
VarNameX=VarValueX\0
\0
```

The first part of each string is the name of an environment variable. This is followed by an equal sign, which is followed by the value you want to assign to the variable. Notice that, in addition to the first `=::=::\`string, some other strings in the block might start with the = character. In that case, these strings are not used as environment variables, as you'll soon see in "A Process' Current Directories" on page 84.

The two ways of getting access to the environment block have been introduced already, but each one provides a different output with a different parsing. The first way retrieves the complete environment block by calling the **GetEnvironmentStrings** function. The format is exactly as described in the previous paragraph. The following code shows how to extract the environment variables and their content in that case:

```
void DumpEnvStrings() {
   PTSTR pEnvBlock = GetEnvironmentStrings();

   // Parse the block with the following format:
   //    =::=::\
   //    =...
   //    var=value\0
```

```
//    ...
//    var=value\0\0
// Note that some other strings might begin with '='.
// Here is an example when the application is started from a network share.
//    [0] =::=::\
//    [1] =C:=C:\Windows\System32
//    [2] =ExitCode=00000000
//
TCHAR szName[MAX_PATH];
TCHAR szValue[MAX_PATH];
PTSTR pszCurrent = pEnvBlock;
HRESULT hr = S_OK;
PCTSTR pszPos = NULL;
int current = 0;

while (pszCurrent != NULL) {
   // Skip the meaningless strings like:
   // "=::=::\"
   if (*pszCurrent != TEXT('=')) {
      // Look for '=' separator.
      pszPos = _tcschr(pszCurrent, TEXT('='));

      // Point now to the first character of the value.
      pszPos++;

      // Copy the variable name.
      size_t cbNameLength =    //               Without the' ='
         (size_t)pszPos - (size_t)pszCurrent - sizeof(TCHAR);
      hr = StringCbCopyN(szName, MAX_PATH, pszCurrent, cbNameLength);
      if (FAILED(hr)) {
         break;
      }

      // Copy the variable value with the last NULL character
      // and allow truncation because this is for UI only.
      hr = StringCchCopyN(szValue, MAX_PATH, pszPos, _tcslen(pszPos)+1);
      if (SUCCEEDED(hr)) {
         _tprintf(TEXT("[%u] %s=%s\r\n"), current, szName, szValue);
      } else   // something wrong happened; check for truncation.
      if (hr == STRSAFE_E_INSUFFICIENT_BUFFER) {
         _tprintf(TEXT("[%u] %s=%s...\r\n"), current, szName, szValue);
      } else { // This should never occur.
         _tprintf(
            TEXT("[%u] %s=???\r\n"), current, szName
            );
         break;
      }
   } else {
      _tprintf(TEXT("[%u] %s\r\n"), current, pszCurrent);
   }

   // Next variable please.
   current++;
```

```
        // Move to the end of the string.
        while (*pszCurrent != TEXT('\0'))
            pszCurrent++;
        pszCurrent++;

        // Check if it was not the last string.
        if (*pszCurrent == TEXT('\0'))
            break;
    };

    // Don't forget to free the memory.
    FreeEnvironmentStrings(pEnvBlock);
}
```

The invalid strings starting with the = character are skipped. Each other valid string is parsed one by one—the = character is used as a separator between the name and the value. When you no longer need the block of memory returned by **GetEnvironmentStrings**, you should free it by calling **FreeEnvironmentStrings**:

```
BOOL FreeEnvironmentStrings(PTSTR pszEnvironmentBlock);
```

Note that safe string functions of the C run time are used in this code snippet to take advantage of the size calculation in bytes with **StringCbCopyN** and the truncation with **StringCchCopyN** when the value is too long for the copy buffer.

The second way of accessing the environment variables is available only for CUI applications through the **TCHAR* env[]** parameter received by your **main** entry point. Unlike what is returned by **GetEnvironmentStrings**, **env** is an array of string pointers, each one pointing to a different environment variable definition with the usual "name=value" format. A **NULL** pointer appears after the pointer to the last variable string as shown in the following listing:

```
void DumpEnvVariables(PTSTR pEnvBlock[]) {
    int current = 0;
    PTSTR* pElement = (PTSTR*)pEnvBlock;
    PTSTR pCurrent = NULL;
    while (pElement != NULL) {
        pCurrent = (PTSTR)(*pElement);
        if (pCurrent == NULL) {
            // No more environment variable.
            pElement = NULL;
        } else {
            _tprintf(TEXT("[%u] %s\r\n"), current, pCurrent);
            current++;
            pElement++;
        }
    }
}
```

Notice that the weird strings starting with the = character are removed before you receive **env**, so you don't have to process them yourself.

Because the equal sign is used to separate the name from the value, an equal sign cannot be part of the name. Also, spaces are significant. For example, if you declare the following two variables and then compare the value of *XYZ* with the value of *ABC*, the system will report that the two variables are different because any white space that appears immediately before or after the equal sign is taken into account:

```
XYZ= Windows   (Notice the space after the equal sign.)
ABC=Windows
```

For example, if you were to add the following two strings to the environment block, the environment variable *XYZ* with a space after it would contain *Home* and the environment variable *XYZ* without the space would contain *Work*.

```
XYZ =Home   (Notice the space before the equal sign.)
XYZ=Work
```

When a user logs on to Windows, the system creates the shell process and associates a set of environment strings with it. The system obtains the initial set of environment strings by examining two keys in the registry.

The first key contains the list of all environment variables that apply to the system:

```
HKEY_LOCAL_MACHINE\SYSTEM\CurrentControlSet\Control\
    Session Manager\Environment
```

The second key contains the list of all environment variables that apply to the user currently logged on:

```
HKEY_CURRENT_USER\Environment
```

A user can add, delete, or change any of these entries by selecting System in Control Panel, clicking the Advanced System Settings link on the left, and clicking the Environment Variables button to bring up the following dialog box:

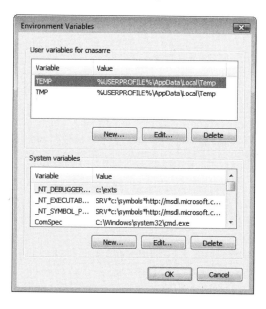

Only a user who has Administrator privileges can alter the variables contained in the System Variables list.

Your application can also use the various registry functions to modify these registry entries. However, for the changes to take effect for all applications, the user must log off and then log back on. Some applications—such as Explorer, Task Manager, and Control Panel—can update their environment block with the new registry entries when their main windows receive a **WM_SETTINGCHANGE** message. For example, if you update the registry entries and want to have the interested applications update their environment blocks, you can make the following call:

```
SendMessage(HWND_BROADCAST, WM_SETTINGCHANGE, 0, (LPARAM) TEXT("Environment"));
```

Normally, a child process inherits a set of environment variables that are the same as those of its parent process. However, the parent process can control what environment variables a child inherits, as you'll see later when we discuss the **CreateProcess** function. By *inherit*, I mean that the child process gets its own copy of the parent's environment block; the child and parent do not share the same block. This means that a child process can add, delete, or modify a variable in its block and the change will not be reflected in the parent's block.

An application usually uses environment variables to let the user fine-tune its behavior. The user creates an environment variable and initializes it. Then, when the user invokes the application, the application examines the environment block for the variable. If it finds the variable, it parses the value of the variable and adjusts its own behavior.

The problem with environment variables is that they are not easy for users to set or to understand. Users need to spell variable names correctly, and they must also know the exact syntax expected of the variable's value. Most (if not all) graphical applications, on the other hand, allow users to fine-tune an application's behavior using dialog boxes. This approach is far more user friendly.

If you still want to use environment variables, there are a few functions that your applications can call. The **GetEnvironmentVariable** function allows you to determine the existence and value of an environment variable:

```
DWORD GetEnvironmentVariable(
    PCTSTR pszName,
    PTSTR pszValue,
    DWORD cchValue);
```

When calling **GetEnvironmentVariable**, **pszName** points to the desired variable name, **pszValue** points to the buffer that will hold the variable's value, and **cchValue** indicates the size of the buffer in characters. The function returns either the number of characters copied into the buffer or **0** if the variable name cannot be found in the environment. However, because you don't know how many characters are needed to store the value of an environment variable, **GetEnvironmentVariable** returns the number of characters plus the final **NULL** character when **0** is passed to the **cchValue** parameter. The following code demonstrates how to safely use this function:

```
void PrintEnvironmentVariable(PCTSTR pszVariableName) {
    PTSTR pszValue = NULL;
    // Get the size of the buffer that is required to store the value
    DWORD dwResult = GetEnvironmentVariable(pszVariableName, pszValue, 0);
```

```
    if (dwResult != 0) {
        // Allocate the buffer to store the environment variable value
        DWORD size = dwResult * sizeof(TCHAR);
        pszValue = (PTSTR)malloc(size);
        GetEnvironmentVariable(pszVariableName, pszValue, size);
        _tprintf(TEXT("%s=%s\n"), pszVariableName, pszValue);
        free(pszValue);
    } else {
        _tprintf(TEXT("'%s'=<unknown value>\n"), pszVariableName);
    }
}
```

Many strings contain replaceable strings within them. For example, I found this string somewhere in the registry:

```
%USERPROFILE%\Documents
```

The portion that appears in between percent signs (%) indicates a replaceable string. In this case, the value of the environment variable, **USERPROFILE**, should be placed in the string. On my machine, the value of my **USERPROFILE** environment variable is

```
C:\Users\jrichter
```

So, after performing the string replacement, the resulting string becomes

```
C:\Users\jrichter\Documents
```

Because this type of string replacement is common, Windows offers the **ExpandEnvironment-Strings** function:

```
DWORD ExpandEnvironmentStrings(
    PTCSTR pszSrc,
    PTSTR pszDst,
    DWORD chSize);
```

When you call this function, the **pszSrc** parameter is the address of the string that contains replaceable environment variable strings. The **pszDst** parameter is the address of the buffer that will receive the expanded string, and the **chSize** parameter is the maximum size of this buffer, in characters. The returned value is the size in characters of the buffer needed to store the expanded string. If the **chSize** parameter is less than this value, the **%%** variables are not expanded but replaced by empty strings. So you usually call **ExpandEnvironmentStrings** twice as shown in the following code snippet:

```
DWORD chValue =
    ExpandEnvironmentStrings(TEXT("PATH='%PATH%'"), NULL, 0);
PTSTR pszBuffer = new TCHAR[chValue];
chValue = ExpandEnvironmentStrings(TEXT("PATH='%PATH%'"), pszBuffer, chValue);
_tprintf(TEXT("%s\r\n"), pszBuffer);
delete[] pszBuffer;
```

Finally, you can use the **SetEnvironmentVariable** function to add a variable, delete a variable, or modify a variable's value:

```
BOOL SetEnvironmentVariable(
   PCTSTR pszName,
   PCTSTR pszValue);
```

This function sets the variable identified by the **pszName** parameter to the value identified by the **pszValue** parameter. If a variable with the specified name already exists, **SetEnvironment-Variable** modifies the value. If the specified variable doesn't exist, the variable is added and, if **pszValue** is **NULL**, the variable is deleted from the environment block.

You should always use these functions for manipulating your process' environment block.

A Process' Affinity

Normally, threads within a process can execute on any of the CPUs in the host machine. However, a process' threads can be forced to run on a subset of the available CPUs. This is called *processor affinity* and is discussed in detail in Chapter 7, "Thread Scheduling, Priorities, and Affinities." Child processes inherit the affinity of their parent processes.

A Process' Error Mode

Associated with each process is a set of flags that tells the system how the process should respond to serious errors, which include disk media failures, unhandled exceptions, file-find failures, and data misalignment. A process can tell the system how to handle each of these errors by calling the **SetErrorMode** function:

```
UINT SetErrorMode(UINT fuErrorMode);
```

The **fuErrorMode** parameter is a combination of any of the flags shown in Table 4-3 bitwise **OR**ed together.

Table 4-3   Flags for SetErrorMode

Flag	Description
SEM_FAILCRITICALERRORS	The system does not display the critical-error-handler message box and returns the error to the calling process.
SEM_NOGPFAULTERRORBOX	The system does not display the general-protection-fault message box. This flag should be set only by debugging applications that handle general protection (GP) faults themselves with an exception handler.
SEM_NOOPENFILEERRORBOX	The system does not display a message box when it fails to find a file.
SEM_NOALIGNMENTFAULTEXCEPT	The system automatically fixes memory alignment faults and makes them invisible to the application. This flag has no effect on *x86/x64* processors.

By default, a child process inherits the error mode flags of its parent. In other words, if a process has the **SEM_NOGPFAULTERRORBOX** flag turned on and then spawns a child process, the child process will also have this flag turned on. However, the child process is not notified of this, and it might not have been written to handle GP fault errors. If a GP fault occurs in one of the child's threads, the child process might terminate without notifying the user. A parent process can prevent a child process from inheriting its error mode by specifying the **CREATE_DEFAULT_ERROR_MODE** flag when calling **CreateProcess**. (We'll discuss **CreateProcess** later in this chapter.)

A Process' Current Drive and Directory

When full pathnames are not supplied, the various Windows functions look for files and directories in the current directory of the current drive. For example, if a thread in a process calls **Create-File** to open a file (without specifying a full pathname), the system looks for the file in the current drive and directory.

The system keeps track of a process' current drive and directory internally. Because this information is maintained on a per-process basis, a thread in the process that changes the current drive or directory changes this information for all the threads in the process.

A thread can obtain and set its process' current drive and directory by calling the following two functions:

```
DWORD GetCurrentDirectory(
    DWORD cchCurDir,
    PTSTR pszCurDir);
BOOL SetCurrentDirectory(PCTSTR pszCurDir);
```

If the buffer you provide is not large enough, **GetCurrentDirectory** returns the number of characters required to store this folder, including the final '\0' character, and copies nothing into the provided buffer, which can be set to **NULL** in that case. When the call is successful, the length of the string in characters is returned, without counting the terminating '\0' character.

> **Note**   The **MAX_PATH** constant defined in WinDef.h as 260 is the maximum number of characters for a directory name or a filename. So it is safe to pass a buffer of **MAX_PATH** elements of the **TCHAR** type when you call **GetCurrentDirectory**.

A Process' Current Directories

The system keeps track of the process' current drive and directory, but it does not keep track of the current directory for every drive. However, there is some operating system support for handling current directories for multiple drives. This support is offered via the process' environment strings. For example, a process can have two environment variables, as shown here:

```
=C:=C:\Utility\Bin
=D:=D:\Program Files
```

These variables indicate that the process' current directory for drive C is \Utility\Bin and that its current directory for drive D is \Program Files.

If you call a function, passing a drive-qualified name indicating a drive that is not the current drive, the system looks in the process' environment block for the variable associated with the specified drive letter. If the variable for the drive exists, the system uses the variable's value as the current directory. If the variable does not exist, the system assumes that the current directory for the specified drive is its root directory.

For example, if your process' current directory is C:\Utility\Bin and you call **CreateFile** to open D:ReadMe.Txt, the system looks up the environment variable **=D:**. Because the **=D:** variable exists, the system attempts to open the ReadMe.Txt file from the D:\Program Files directory. If the **=D:** variable did not exist, the system would attempt to open the ReadMe.Txt file from the root directory of drive D. The Windows file functions never add or change a drive-letter environment variable—they only read the variables.

> **Note**   You can use the C run-time function **_chdir** instead of the Windows **SetCurrentDirectory** function to change the current directory. The **_chdir** function calls **SetCurrentDirectory** internally, but **_chdir** also adds or modifies the environment variables by calling **SetEnvironmentVariable** so that the current directory of different drives is preserved.

If a parent process creates an environment block that it wants to pass to a child process, the child's environment block does not automatically inherit the parent process' current directories. Instead, the child process' current directories default to the root directory of every drive. If you want the child process to inherit the parent's current directories, the parent process must create these drive-letter environment variables and add them to the environment block before spawning the child process. The parent process can obtain its current directories by calling **GetFullPathName**:

```
DWORD GetFullPathName(
    PCTSTR pszFile,
    DWORD cchPath,
    PTSTR pszPath,
    PTSTR *ppszFilePart);
```

For example, to get the current directory for drive C, you call **GetFullPathName** as follows:

```
TCHAR szCurDir[MAX_PATH];
DWORD cchLength = GetFullPathName(TEXT("C:"), MAX_PATH, szCurDir, NULL);
```

As a result, the drive-letter environment variables usually must be placed at the beginning of the environment block.

The System Version

Frequently, an application needs to determine which version of Windows the user is running. For example, an application might take advantage of the Windows transacted file system feature by calling the special functions such as **CreateFileTransacted**. However, these functions are fully implemented only on Windows Vista.

For as long as I can remember, the Windows application programming interface (API) has had a **GetVersion** function:

```
DWORD GetVersion();
```

This function has quite a history behind it. It was first one designed for 16-bit Windows. The idea was simple—to return the MS-DOS version number in the high word and return the Windows version number in the low word. For each word, the high byte would represent the major version number and the low byte would represent the minor version number.

Unfortunately, the programmer who wrote this code made a small mistake, coding the function so that the Windows version numbers were reversed—the major version number was in the low byte and the minor number was in the high byte. Because many programmers had already started using this function, Microsoft was forced to leave the function as it was and change the documentation to reflect the mistake.

Because of all the confusion surrounding **GetVersion**, Microsoft added a new function, **GetVersionEx**:

```
BOOL GetVersionEx(POSVERSIONINFOEX pVersionInformation);
```

This function requires you to allocate an **OSVERSIONINFOEX** structure in your application and pass the structure's address to **GetVersionEx**. The **OSVERSIONINFOEX** structure is shown here:

```
typedef struct {
   DWORD dwOSVersionInfoSize;
   DWORD dwMajorVersion;
   DWORD dwMinorVersion;
   DWORD dwBuildNumber;
   DWORD dwPlatformId;
   TCHAR szCSDVersion[128];
   WORD  wServicePackMajor;
   WORD  wServicePackMinor;
   WORD  wSuiteMask;
   BYTE  wProductType;
   BYTE  wReserved;
} OSVERSIONINFOEX, *POSVERSIONINFOEX;
```

The **OSVERSIONINFOEX** structure has been available since Windows 2000. Other versions of Windows use the older **OSVERSIONINFO** structure, which does not have the service pack, suite mask, product type, and reserved members.

Notice that the structure has different members for each component of the system's version number. This was done so that programmers would not have to bother with extracting low words, high words, low bytes, and high bytes, which should make it much easier for applications to compare their expected version number with the host system's version number. Table 4-4 describes the **OSVERSIONINFOEX** structure's members.

The "Getting the System Version" page on the MSDN Web site (*http://msdn2.microsoft.com/en-gb/library/ms724429.aspx*) provides a very detailed code sample based on **OSVERSIONINFOEX** that shows you how to decipher each field of this structure.

To make things even easier, Windows Vista offers the function **VerifyVersionInfo**, which compares the host system's version with the version your application requires:

```
BOOL VerifyVersionInfo(
   POSVERSIONINFOEX pVersionInformation,
   DWORD dwTypeMask,
   DWORDLONG dwlConditionMask);
```

Table 4-4   The OSVERSIONINFOEX Structure's Members

Member	Description
dwOSVersionInfoSize	Must be set to **sizeof(OSVERSIONINFO)** or **sizeof(OSVERSION-INFOEX)** prior to calling the **GetVersionEx** function.
dwMajorVersion	Major version number of the host system.
dwMinorVersion	Minor version number of the host system.
dwBuildNumber	Build number of the current system.
dwPlatformId	Identifies the platform supported by the current system. This can be **VER_PLATFORM_WIN32s** (Win32s), **VER_PLATFORM_WIN32_WINDOWS** (Windows 95/Windows 98), or **VER_PLATFORM_WIN32_NT** (Windows NT/Windows 2000, Windows XP, Windows Server 2003, and Windows Vista).
szCSDVersion	This field contains additional text that provides further information about the installed operating system.
wServicePackMajor	Major version number of latest installed service pack.
wServicePackMinor	Minor version number of latest installed service pack.
wSuiteMask	Identifies which suite or suites are available on the system (**VER_SUITE_SMALLBUSINESS, VER_SUITE_ENTERPRISE, VER_SUITE_BACKOFFICE, VER_SUITE_COMMUNICATIONS, VER_SUITE_TERMINAL, VER_SUITE_SMALLBUSINESS_RESTRICTED, VER_SUITE_EMBEDDEDNT, VER_SUITE_DATACENTER, VER_SUITE_SINGLEUSERTS** (for single terminal services session per user), **VER_SUITE_PERSONAL** (to make the difference between Home and Professional editions of Vista), **VER_SUITE_BLADE, VER_SUITE_EMBEDDED_RESTRICTED, VER_SUITE_SECURITY_APPLIANCE, VER_SUITE_STORAGE_SERVER,** and **VER_SUITE_COMPUTE_SERVER**).
wProductType	Identifies which one of the following operating system products is installed: **VER_NT_WORKSTATION, VER_NT_SERVER,** or **VER_NT_DOMAIN_CONTROLLER**.
wReserved	Reserved for future use.

To use this function, you must allocate an **OSVERSIONINFOEX** structure, initialize its **dwOSVersion-InfoSize** member to the size of the structure, and then initialize any other members of the structure that are important to your application. When you call **VerifyVersionInfo**, the **dwTypeMask** parameter indicates which members of the structure you have initialized. The **dwTypeMask** parameter is any of the following flags ORed together: **VER_MINORVERSION, VER_MAJORVERSION, VER_BUILDNUMBER, VER_PLATFORMID, VER_SERVICEPACKMINOR, VER_SERVICEPACKMAJOR, VER_SUITENAME,** and **VER_PRODUCT_TYPE**. The last parameter, **dwlConditionMask**, is a 64-bit value that controls how the function compares the system's version information to your desired information.

The **dwlConditionMask** describes the comparison using a complex set of bit combinations. To create the desired bit combination, you use the **VER_SET_CONDITION** macro:

```
VER_SET_CONDITION(
    DWORDLONG dwlConditionMask,
    ULONG dwTypeBitMask,
    ULONG dwConditionMask)
```

The first parameter, **dwlConditionMask**, identifies the variable whose bits you are manipulating. Note that you do not pass the address of this variable because **VER_SET_CONDITION** is a macro, not a function. The **dwTypeBitMask** parameter indicates a single member in the **OSVERSIONINFOEX** structure that you want to compare. To compare multiple members, you must call **VER_SET_CONDITION** multiple times, once for each member. The flags you pass to **VerifyVersionInfo**'s **dwTypeMask** parameter (**VER_MINORVERSION**, **VER_BUILDNUMBER**, and so on) are the same flags that you use for **VER_SET_CONDITION**'s **dwTypeBitMask** parameter.

VER_SET_CONDITION's last parameter, **dwConditionMask**, indicates how you want the comparison made. This can be one of the following values: **VER_EQUAL**, **VER_GREATER**, **VER_GREATER_EQUAL**, **VER_LESS**, or **VER_LESS_EQUAL**. Note that you can use these values when comparing **VER_PRODUCT_TYPE** information. For example, **VER_NT_WORKSTATION** is less than **VER_NT_SERVER**. However, for the **VER_SUITENAME** information, you cannot use these test values. Instead, you must use **VER_AND** (all suite products must be installed) or **VER_OR** (at least one of the suite products must be installed).

After you build up the set of conditions, you call **VerifyVersionInfo** and it returns a nonzero value if successful (if the host system meets all of your application's requirements). If **VerifyVersionInfo** returns 0, the host system does not meet your requirements or you called the function improperly. You can determine why the function returned 0 by calling **GetLastError**. If **GetLastError** returns **ERROR_OLD_WIN_VERSION**, you called the function correctly but the system doesn't meet your requirements.

Here is an example of how to test whether the host system is exactly Windows Vista:

```
// Prepare the OSVERSIONINFOEX structure to indicate Windows Vista.
OSVERSIONINFOEX osver = { 0 };
osver.dwOSVersionInfoSize = sizeof(osver);
osver.dwMajorVersion = 6;
osver.dwMinorVersion = 0;
osver.dwPlatformId = VER_PLATFORM_WIN32_NT;

// Prepare the condition mask.
DWORDLONG dwlConditionMask = 0;// You MUST initialize this to 0.
VER_SET_CONDITION(dwlConditionMask, VER_MAJORVERSION, VER_EQUAL);
VER_SET_CONDITION(dwlConditionMask, VER_MINORVERSION, VER_EQUAL);
VER_SET_CONDITION(dwlConditionMask, VER_PLATFORMID, VER_EQUAL);

// Perform the version test.
if (VerifyVersionInfo(&osver, VER_MAJORVERSION  | VER_MINORVERSION | VER_PLATFORMID,
   dwlConditionMask)) {
   // The host system is Windows Vista exactly.
} else {
   // The host system is NOT Windows Vista.
}
```

The *CreateProcess* Function

You create a process with the **CreateProcess** function:

```
BOOL CreateProcess(
    PCTSTR pszApplicationName,
    PTSTR pszCommandLine,
    PSECURITY_ATTRIBUTES psaProcess,
    PSECURITY_ATTRIBUTES psaThread,
    BOOL bInheritHandles,
    DWORD fdwCreate,
    PVOID pvEnvironment,
    PCTSTR pszCurDir,
    PSTARTUPINFO psiStartInfo,
    PPROCESS_INFORMATION ppiProcInfo);
```

When a thread calls **CreateProcess**, the system creates a process kernel object with an initial usage count of **1**. This process kernel object is not the process itself but a small data structure that the operating system uses to manage the process—you can think of the process kernel object as a small data structure that consists of statistical information about the process. The system then creates a virtual address space for the new process and loads the code and data for the executable file and any required DLLs into the process' address space.

The system then creates a thread kernel object (with a usage count of **1**) for the new process' primary thread. Like the process kernel object, the thread kernel object is a small data structure that the operating system uses to manage the thread. This primary thread begins by executing the application entry point set by the linker as the C/C++ run-time startup code, which eventually calls your **WinMain**, **wWinMain**, **main**, or **wmain** function. If the system successfully creates the new process and primary thread, **CreateProcess** returns **TRUE**.

> **Note** **CreateProcess** returns **TRUE** before the process has fully initialized. This means that the operating system loader has not attempted to locate all the required DLLs yet. If a DLL can't be located or fails to initialize correctly, the process is terminated. Because **CreateProcess** returned **TRUE**, the parent process is not aware of any initialization problems.

OK, that's the broad overview. The following sections dissect each of **CreateProcess**' parameters.

pszApplicationName and *pszCommandLine*

The **pszApplicationName** and **pszCommandLine** parameters specify the name of the executable file the new process will use and the command-line string that will be passed to the new process, respectively. Let's talk about the **pszCommandLine** parameter first.

Notice that the **pszCommandLine** parameter is prototyped as a **PTSTR**. This means that **CreateProcess** expects that you are passing the address of a non-constant string. Internally, **CreateProcess** actually does modify the command-line string that you pass to it. But before **CreateProcess** returns, it restores the string to its original form.

This is important because an access violation will occur if your command-line string is contained in a read-only portion of your file image. For example, the following code causes an access violation because Microsoft's C/C++ compiler places the "NOTEPAD" string in read-only memory:

```
STARTUPINFO si = { sizeof(si) };
PROCESS_INFORMATION pi;
CreateProcess(NULL, TEXT("NOTEPAD"), NULL, NULL,
    FALSE, 0, NULL, NULL, &si, &pi);
```

When **CreateProcess** attempts to modify the string, an access violation occurs. (Earlier versions of Microsoft's C/C++ compiler placed the string in read/write memory, so calls to **CreateProcess** did not cause access violations.)

The best way to solve this problem is to copy the constant string to a temporary buffer before calling **CreateProcess** as follows:

```
STARTUPINFO si = { sizeof(si) };
PROCESS_INFORMATION pi;
TCHAR szCommandLine[] = TEXT("NOTEPAD");
CreateProcess(NULL, szCommandLine, NULL, NULL,
    FALSE, 0, NULL, NULL, &si, &pi);
```

You might also look into using Microsoft C++'s **/Gf** and **/GF** compiler switches, which control the elimination of duplicate strings and determine whether those strings are placed in a read-only section. (Also note that the **/ZI** switch, which allows the use of Visual Studio's Edit & Continue debugging feature, implies the **/GF** switch.) The best thing you can do is to use the **/GF** compiler switch and a temporary buffer. The best thing Microsoft can do is fix **CreateProcess** so that it takes over the responsibility of making a temporary copy of the string so that we don't have to do it. Maybe this will happen in a future version of Windows.

By the way, if you are calling the ANSI version of **CreateProcess** on Windows Vista, you will not get an access violation because a temporary copy of the command-line string is made. (For more information about this, see Chapter 2, "Working with Characters and Strings.")

You use the **pszCommandLine** parameter to specify a complete command line that **CreateProcess** uses to create the new process. When **CreateProcess** parses the **pszCommandLine** string, it examines the first token in the string and assumes that this token is the name of the executable file you want to run. If the executable file's name does not have an extension, an .exe extension is assumed. **CreateProcess** also searches for the executable in the following order:

1. The directory containing the .exe file of the calling process
2. The current directory of the calling process
3. The Windows system directory—that is, the System32 subfolder as returned by **GetSystem-Directory**
4. The Windows directory
5. The directories listed in the **PATH** environment variable

Of course, if the filename includes a full path, the system looks for the executable using the full path and does not search the directories. If the system finds the executable file, it creates a new process and maps the executable's code and data into the new process's address space. The system then calls the C/C++ run-time startup routine set by the linker as the application entry point. As noted earlier, the C/C++ run-time startup routine examines the process' command line and passes the address to the first argument after the executable file's name as **(w)WinMain**'s **pszCmdLine** parameter.

All of this happens as long as the **pszApplicationName** parameter is **NULL** (which should be the case more than 99 percent of the time). Instead of passing **NULL**, you can pass the address to a string containing the name of the executable file you want to run in the **pszApplicationName** parameter. Note that you must specify the file's extension; the system will not automatically assume that the filename has an .exe extension. **CreateProcess** assumes that the file is in the current directory unless a path precedes the filename. If the file can't be found in the current directory, **CreateProcess** doesn't look for the file in any other directory—it simply fails.

Even if you specify a filename in the **pszApplicationName** parameter, however, **CreateProcess** passes the contents of the **pszCommandLine** parameter to the new process as its command line. For example, say that you call **CreateProcess** like this:

```
// Make sure that the path is in a read/write section of memory.
TCHAR szPath[] = TEXT("WORDPAD README.TXT");

// Spawn the new process.
CreateProcess(TEXT("C:\\WINDOWS\\SYSTEM32\\NOTEPAD.EXE"),szPath,...);
```

The system invokes the Notepad application, but Notepad's command line is WORDPAD README.TXT. This quirk is certainly a little strange, but that's how **CreateProcess** works. This capability provided by the **pszApplicationName** parameter was actually added to **Create-Process** to support Windows's POSIX subsystem.

psaProcess, psaThread, and bInheritHandles

To create a new process, the system must create a process kernel object and a thread kernel object (for the process' primary thread). Because these are kernel objects, the parent process gets the opportunity to associate security attributes with these two objects. You use the **psaProcess** and **psaThread** parameters to specify the desired security for the process object and the thread object, respectively. You can pass **NULL** for these parameters, in which case the system gives these objects default security descriptors. Or you can allocate and initialize two **SECURITY_ATTRIBUTES** structures to create and assign your own security privileges to the process and thread objects.

Another reason to use **SECURITY_ATTRIBUTES** structures for the **psaProcess** and **psaThread** parameters is if you want either of these two object handles to be inheritable by any child processes spawned in the future by this parent process. (I discussed the theory behind kernel object handle inheritance in Chapter 3, "Kernel Objects.")

Inherit.cpp, shown next, is a short program that demonstrates kernel object handle inheritance. Let's say that Process A creates Process B by calling **CreateProcess** and passing the address of a **SECURITY_ATTRIBUTES** structure for the **psaProcess** parameter in which the **bInheritHandle** member is set to **TRUE**. In this same call, the **psaThread** parameter points to another **SECURITY_ATTRIBUTES** structure in which its **bInheritHandle** member is set to **FALSE**.

When the system creates Process B, it allocates both a process kernel object and a thread kernel object and returns handles back to Process A in the structure pointed to by the **ppiProcInfo** parameter (discussed shortly). Process A can now manipulate the newly created process object and thread object by using these handles.

Now let's say that Process A will call **CreateProcess** a second time to create Process C. Process A can decide whether to grant Process C the ability to manipulate some of the kernel objects that Process A has access to. The **bInheritHandles** parameter is used for this purpose. If **bInherit-Handles** is set to **TRUE**, the system causes Process C to inherit any inheritable handles in Process A. In this case, the handle to Process B's process object is inheritable. The handle to Process B's primary thread object is not inherited no matter what the value of the **bInheritHandles** parameter to **CreateProcess** is. Also, if Process A calls **CreateProcess**, passing **FALSE** for the **bInherit-Handles** parameter, Process C does not inherit any of the handles currently used by Process A.

```
Inherit.cpp
/******************************************************************
Module name: Inherit.cpp
Notices: Copyright (c) 2008 Jeffrey Richter & Christophe Nasarre
******************************************************************/


#include <Windows.h>


int WINAPI _tWinMain (HINSTANCE hInstanceExe, HINSTANCE,
   PTSTR pszCmdLine, int nCmdShow) {

   // Prepare a STARTUPINFO structure for spawning processes.
   STARTUPINFO si = { sizeof(si) };
   SECURITY_ATTRIBUTES saProcess, saThread;
   PROCESS_INFORMATION piProcessB, piProcessC;
   TCHAR szPath[MAX_PATH];

   // Prepare to spawn Process B from Process A.
   // The handle identifying the new process
   // object should be inheritable.
   saProcess.nLength = sizeof(saProcess);
   saProcess.lpSecurityDescriptor = NULL;
   saProcess.bInheritHandle = TRUE;

   // The handle identifying the new thread
   // object should NOT be inheritable.
   saThread.nLength = sizeof(saThread);
   saThread.lpSecurityDescriptor = NULL;
   saThread.bInheritHandle = FALSE;

   // Spawn Process B.
   _tcscpy_s(szPath, _countof(szPath), TEXT("ProcessB"));
   CreateProcess(NULL, szPath, &saProcess, &saThread,
      FALSE, 0, NULL, NULL, &si, &piProcessB);

   // The pi structure contains two handles
   // relative to Process A:
   // hProcess, which identifies Process B's process
   // object and is inheritable; and hThread, which identifies
   // Process B's primary thread object and is NOT inheritable.
```

```
// Prepare to spawn Process C from Process A.
// Since NULL is passed for the psaProcess and psaThread
// parameters, the handles to Process C's process and
// primary thread objects default to "noninheritable."

// If Process A were to spawn another process, this new
// process would NOT inherit handles to Process C's process
// and thread objects.

// Because TRUE is passed for the bInheritHandles parameter,
// Process C will inherit the handle that identifies Process
// B's process object but will not inherit a handle to
// Process B's primary thread object.
_tcscpy_s(szPath, _countof(szPath), TEXT("ProcessC"));
CreateProcess(NULL, szPath, NULL, NULL,
    TRUE, 0, NULL, NULL, &si, &piProcessC);

return(0);
}
```

fdwCreate

The **fdwCreate** parameter identifies flags that affect how the new process is created. You can specify multiple flags if you combine them with the bitwise **OR** operator. Following is a list of the available flags:

- The **DEBUG_PROCESS** flag tells the system that the parent process wants to debug the child
  process and any processes spawned by the child process in the future. This flag tells the system to notify the parent process (now the debugger) when certain events occur in any of the
  child processes (the debuggees).

- The **DEBUG_ONLY_THIS_PROCESS** flag is similar to **DEBUG_PROCESS** except that the debugger
  is notified only of special events occurring in the immediate child process. If the child process
  spawns any additional processes, the debugger is not notified of events in these processes.
  Read the "Escape from DLL Hell with Custom Debugging and Instrumentation Tools and
  Utilities, Part 2" article on MSDN (*http://msdn.microsoft.com/msdnmag/issues/02/08/
  EscapefromDLLHell/*) for more details about using these two flags to write a debugger and get
  live information about DLLs and threads from a running debuggee application.

- The **CREATE_SUSPENDED** flag causes the new process to be created, but its primary thread is
  suspended. This allows the parent process to modify memory in the child process' address
  space, alter the child process' primary thread's priority, or add the process to a job before the
  process has had a chance to execute any code. Once the parent process has modified the
  child process, the parent process allows the child process to execute code by calling the
  ResumeThread function (discussed in Chapter 7).

- The **DETACHED_PROCESS** flag blocks a CUI-based process' access to its parent's console window and tells the system to send its output to a new console window. If a CUI-based process
  is created by another CUI-based process, the new process will, by default, use the parent's
  console window. (When you run the C++ compiler from the command shell, a new console

window isn't created; the output is simply appended to the bottom of the existing console window.) By specifying this flag, the new process will have to create its own console itself by calling the **AllocConsole** function if it needs to send its output to a new console window.

■ The **CREATE_NEW_CONSOLE** flag tells the system to create a new console window for the new process. Specifying both the **CREATE_NEW_CONSOLE** and **DETACHED_PROCESS** flags results in an error.

■ The **CREATE_NO_WINDOW** flag tells the system not to create any console window for the application. You can use this flag to execute a console application without a user interface.

■ The **CREATE_NEW_PROCESS_GROUP** flag modifies the list of processes that are notified when the user presses the Ctrl+C or Ctrl+Break keys. If you have several CUI-based processes running when the user presses one of these key combinations, the system notifies all the processes in a process group that the user wants to break out of the current operation. By specifying this flag when creating a new CUI-based process, you create a new process group. If the user presses Ctrl+C or Ctrl+Break while a process in this group is active, the system notifies only processes in this group of the user's request.

■ The **CREATE_DEFAULT_ERROR_MODE** flag tells the system that the new process should not inherit the error mode used by the parent process. (See the **SetErrorMode** function discussion earlier in this chapter.)

■ The **CREATE_SEPARATE_WOW_VDM** flag is useful only when you invoke a 16-bit Windows application on Windows. It tells the system to create a separate Virtual DOS Machine (VDM) and run the 16-bit Windows application in this VDM. By default, all 16-bit Windows applications execute in a single shared VDM. The advantage of running an application in a separate VDM is that if the application crashes, it kills only the single VDM; any other programs running in distinct VDMs continue to function normally. Also, 16-bit Windows applications that run in separate VDMs have separate input queues. This means that if one application hangs momentarily, applications in separate VDMs continue to receive input. The disadvantage of running multiple VDMs is that each VDM consumes a significant amount of physical storage. Windows 98 runs all 16-bit Windows applications in a single virtual machine—you cannot override this.

■ The **CREATE_SHARED_WOW_VDM** flag is useful only when you invoke a 16-bit Windows application on Windows. By default, all 16-bit Windows applications run in a single VDM unless the **CREATE_SEPARATE_WOW_VDM** flag is specified. However, you can override this default behavior by setting the **DefaultSeparate** VDM value in the registry under HKEY_LOCAL_MACHINE\System\CurrentControlSet\Control\WOW to yes. The **CREATE_SHARED_WOW_VDM** flag then runs the 16-bit Windows application in the system's shared VDM. (You must reboot after changing this registry setting.) Notice that an application is able to detect that a 32-bit process is running under a 64-bit operating system by calling the **IsWow64Process** function, passing the process handle as first parameter and a pointer to a Boolean that will be set to **TRUE** in that case.

■ The **CREATE_UNICODE_ENVIRONMENT** flag tells the system that the child process' environment block should contain Unicode characters. By default, a process' environment block contains ANSI strings.

■ The **CREATE_FORCEDOS** flag forces the system to run the MS-DOS application that is embedded inside a 16-bit OS/2 application.

- The **CREATE_BREAKAWAY_FROM_JOB** flag allows a process in a job to spawn a new process that is disassociated from the job. (See Chapter 5, "Jobs," for more information.)
- The **EXTENDED_STARTUPINFO_PRESENT** flag tells the operating system that a **STARTUP-INFOEX** structure is passed to the **psiStartInfo** parameter.

The **fdwCreate** parameter also allows you to specify a priority class. However, you don't have to do this, and for most applications you shouldn't—the system will assign a default priority class to the new process. Table 4-5 shows the possible priority classes.

Table 4-5   Priority Classes Set by the fdwCreate Parameter

Priority Class	Flag Identifier
Idle	`IDLE_PRIORITY_CLASS`
Below normal	`BELOW_NORMAL_PRIORITY_CLASS`
Normal	`NORMAL_PRIORITY_CLASS`
Above normal	`ABOVE_NORMAL_PRIORITY_CLASS`
High	`HIGH_PRIORITY_CLASS`
Realtime	`REALTIME_PRIORITY_CLASS`

These priority classes affect how the threads contained within the process are scheduled with respect to other processes' threads. See "An Abstract View of Priorities" on page 188 for more information.

pvEnvironment

The **pvEnvironment** parameter points to a block of memory that contains environment strings that the new process will use. Most of the time, **NULL** is passed for this parameter, causing the child process to inherit the set of environment strings that its parent is using. Alternatively, you can use the **GetEnvironmentStrings** function:

```
PVOID GetEnvironmentStrings();
```

This function gets the address of the environment string data block that the calling process is using. You can use the address returned by this function as the **pvEnvironment** parameter of **CreateProcess**. This is exactly what **CreateProcess** does if you pass **NULL** for the **pvEnvironment** parameter. When you no longer need this block of memory, you should free it by calling **FreeEnvironmentStrings**:

```
BOOL FreeEnvironmentStrings(PTSTR pszEnvironmentBlock);
```

pszCurDir

The **pszCurDir** parameter allows the parent process to set the child process' current drive and directory. If this parameter is **NULL**, the new process' working directory will be the same as that of the application spawning the new process. If this parameter is not **NULL**, **pszCurDir** must point to a zero-terminated string containing the desired working drive and directory. Notice that you must specify a drive letter in the path.

psiStartInfo

The **psiStartInfo** parameter points either to a **STARTUPINFO** or **STARTUPINFOEX** structure:

```
typedef struct _STARTUPINFO {
    DWORD cb;
    PSTR lpReserved;
    PSTR lpDesktop;
    PSTR lpTitle;
    DWORD dwX;
    DWORD dwY;
    DWORD dwXSize;
    DWORD dwYSize;
    DWORD dwXCountChars;
    DWORD dwYCountChars;
    DWORD dwFillAttribute;
    DWORD dwFlags;
    WORD wShowWindow;
    WORD cbReserved2;
    PBYTE lpReserved2;
    HANDLE hStdInput;
    HANDLE hStdOutput;
    HANDLE hStdError;
} STARTUPINFO, *LPSTARTUPINFO;

typedef struct _STARTUPINFOEX {
    STARTUPINFO StartupInfo;
    struct _PROC_THREAD_ATTRIBUTE_LIST *lpAttributeList;
} STARTUPINFOEX, *LPSTARTUPINFOEX;
```

Windows uses the members of this structure when it creates the new process. Most applications will want the spawned application simply to use default values. At a minimum, you should initialize all the members in this structure to zero and then set the *cb* member to the size of the structure:

```
STARTUPINFO si = { sizeof(si) };
CreateProcess(..., &si, ...);
```

If you fail to zero the contents of the structure, the members will contain whatever garbage is on the calling thread's stack. Passing this garbage to **CreateProcess** means that sometimes the new process will be created and sometimes it won't, depending on the garbage. It is important to set the unused members of this structure to zero so that **CreateProcess** will work consistently. Failing to do so is one of the most common mistakes I see developers make.

Now, if you want to initialize some of the members of the structure, you simply do so before the call to **CreateProcess**. We'll discuss each member in turn. Some members are meaningful only if the child application creates an overlapped window; others are meaningful only if the child performs CUI-based input and output. Table 4-6 describes the usefulness of each member.

Table 4-6   Members of STARTUPINFO and STARTUPINFOEX Structures

Member	Window, Console, or Both	Purpose
cb	Both	Contains the number of bytes in the **STARTUPINFO** structure. Acts as a version control in case Microsoft expands this structure in the future as it has been done with **STARTUPINFOEX**. Your application must initialize **cb** to `sizeof(STARTUPINFO)` or `sizeof(STARTUPINFOEX)`.
lpReserved	Both	Reserved. Must be initialized to **NULL**.
lpDesktop	Both	Identifies the name of the desktop on which to start the application. If the desktop exists, the new process is associated with the specified desktop. If the desktop does not exist, a desktop with default attributes is created with the specified name for the new process. If **lpDesktop** is **NULL** (which is most common), the process is associated with the current desktop.
lpTitle	Console	Specifies the window title for a console window. If **lpTitle** is **NULL**, the name of the executable file is used as the window title.
dwX **dwY**	Both	Specify the x and y coordinates (in pixels) of the location where the application's window should be placed on the screen. These coordinates are used only if the child process creates its first overlapped window with **CW_USEDEFAULT** as the x parameter of **CreateWindow**. For applications that create console windows, these members indicate the upper-left corner of the console window.
dwXSize **dwYSize**	Both	Specify the width and height (in pixels) of an application's window. These values are used only if the child process creates its first overlapped window with **CW_USEDEFAULT** as the **nWidth** parameter of **CreateWindow**. For applications that create console windows, these members indicate the width and height of the console window.
dwXCountChars **dwYCountChars**	Console	Specify the width and height (in characters) of a child's console windows.
dwFill-Attribute	Console	Specifies the text and background colors used by a child's console window.
dwFlags	Both	See the following section and the next table.
wShowWindow	Window	Specifies how the application's main window should appear. The value of **wShowWindow** will be used by the first call to **ShowWindow** instead of the **nCmdShow** value passed as a parameter. On subsequent calls, **wShowWindow** value is used only when **SW_SHOWDEFAULT** is passed to **ShowWindow**. Note that **dwFlags** must have the **STARTF_USESHOWWINDOW** flag set for **wShowWindow** to be taken into account.

Table 4-6   Members of STARTUPINFO and STARTUPINFOEX Structures

Member	Window, Console, or Both	Purpose
cbReserved2	Both	Reserved. Must be initialized to 0.
lpReserved2	Both	Reserved. Must be initialized to **NULL**. **cbReserved2** and **lpReserved2** are used by the C run time to pass informa-tion when **_dospawn** is used to start an application. Take a look at dospawn.c and ioinit.c in the VC\crt\src\ subfolder of the Visual Studio directory for the imple-mentation details.
hStdInput hStdOutput hStdError	Console	Specify handles to buffers for console input and output. By default, **hStdInput** identifies a keyboard buffer; **hStdOutput** and **hStdError** identify a console window's buffer. These fields are used when you need to redirect the input/output of the child process as explained in the "How to spawn console processes with redirected standard handles" MSDN page (*http://support.microsoft.com/kb/190351*).

Now, as promised, I'll discuss the **dwFlags** member. This member contains a set of flags that modify how the child process is to be created. Most of the flags simply tell **CreateProcess** whether other members of the **STARTUPINFO** structure contain useful information or whether some of the members should be ignored. Table 4-7 shows the list of possible flags and their meanings.

Table 4-7   Flags for dwFlags

Flag	Meaning
STARTF_USESIZE	Use the **dwXSize** and **dwYSize** members.
STARTF_USESHOWWINDOW	Use the **wShowWindow** member.
STARTF_USEPOSITION	Use the **dwX** and **dwY** members.
STARTF_USECOUNTCHARS	Use the **dwXCountChars** and **dwYCountChars** members.
STARTF_USEFILLATTRIBUTE	Use the **dwFillAttribute** member.
STARTF_USESTDHANDLES	Use the **hStdInput**, **hStdOutput**, and **hStdError** members.
STARTF_RUNFULLSCREEN	Forces a console application running on an *x*86 computer to start in full-screen mode.

Two additional flags, **STARTF_FORCEONFEEDBACK** and **STARTF_FORCEOFFFEEDBACK**, give you control over the mouse cursor when you invoke a new process. Because Windows supports true preemptive multitasking, you can invoke an application and, while the process is initializing, use another program. To give visual feedback to the user, **CreateProcess** temporarily changes the system's arrow cursor to a dedicated cursor:

This cursor indicates that you can wait for something to happen or you can continue to use the system. The **CreateProcess** function gives you more control over the cursor when invoking another process. When you specify the **STARTF_FORCEOFFFEEDBACK** flag, **CreateProcess** does not change the cursor into the start glass.

STARTF_FORCEONFEEDBACK causes **CreateProcess** to monitor the new process' initialization and to alter the cursor based on the result. When **CreateProcess** is called with this flag, the cursor changes into the start glass. If, after two seconds, the new process does not make a GUI call, **CreateProcess** resets the cursor to an arrow.

If the process makes a GUI call within two seconds, **CreateProcess** waits for the application to show a window. This must occur within five seconds after the process makes the GUI call. If a window is not displayed, **CreateProcess** resets the cursor. If a window is displayed, **CreateProcess** keeps the start glass cursor on for another five seconds. If at any time the application calls the **GetMessage** function, indicating that it is finished initializing, **CreateProcess** immediately resets the cursor and stops monitoring the new process.

You initialize the **wShowWindow** member to the value that is passed to **(w)WinMain**'s last parameter, **nCmdShow**. This member indicates the value you want passed to the new process' **(w)WinMain** function's last parameter, **nCmdShow**. It is one of the identifiers that can be passed to the **Show-Window** function. Usually, **nCmdShow**'s value is either **SW_SHOWNORMAL** or **SW_SHOWMINNOACTIVE**. However, it can sometimes be **SW_SHOWDEFAULT**.

When you invoke an application from Windows Explorer, the application's **(w)WinMain** function is called with **SW_SHOWNORMAL** passed as the **nCmdShow** parameter. If you create a shortcut for the application, you can use the shortcut's property page to tell the system how the application's window should first appear. Figure 4-3 shows the property page for a shortcut that runs Notepad. Notice that the Run option's combo box allows you to specify how Notepad's window is displayed.

When you use Windows Explorer to invoke this shortcut, Windows Explorer prepares the **STARTUPINFO** structure properly and calls **CreateProcess**. Notepad executes and its **(w)WinMain** function is passed **SW_SHOWMINNOACTIVE** for the **nCmdShow** parameter.

In this way, the user can easily start an application with its main window showing in the normal state, minimized state, or maximized state.

Before concluding this section, I'd like to mention the role of the **STARTUPINFOEX** structure. The **CreateProcess** signature has not changed since the availability of Win32. Microsoft has decided to allow more extensibility but without changing the function signature or creating a **Create-ProcessEx**, then **CreateProcess2**, and so on. So, in addition to the expected **StartupInfo** field, the **STARTUPINFOEX** structure contains one field, **lpAttributeList**, which is used to pass additional parameters called *attributes*:

```
typedef struct _STARTUPINFOEXA {
    STARTUPINFOA StartupInfo;
    struct _PROC_THREAD_ATTRIBUTE_LIST *lpAttributeList;
} STARTUPINFOEXA, *LPSTARTUPINFOEXA;
typedef struct _STARTUPINFOEXW {
    STARTUPINFOW StartupInfo;
    struct _PROC_THREAD_ATTRIBUTE_LIST *lpAttributeList;
} STARTUPINFOEXW, *LPSTARTUPINFOEXW;
```

Figure 4-3   The property page for a shortcut that runs Notepad

The attribute list contains a series of key/value pairs, one for each attribute. Currently, only two attribute keys are documented:

- The **PROC_THREAD_ATTRIBUTE_HANDLE_LIST** attribute key tells **CreateProcess** exactly which kernel object handles the child process should inherit. These object handles must be created as inheritable with **SECURITY_ATTRIBUTES** containing a **bInheritHandle** field set to **TRUE**, as explained in "*psaProcess, psaThread,* and *bInheritHandles*" on page 91. However, it is not required to pass **TRUE** for **CreateProcess**' **bInheritHandles** parameter. Using this attribute, only a chosen subset of handles are inherited by a child process instead of all the inheritable handles. This is particularly important when a process creates multiple child processes in different security contexts, and thus, each child shouldn't inherit all of the handles from the parent because that could be a security issue.

- The **PROC_THREAD_ATTRIBUTE_PARENT_PROCESS** attribute key expects a process handle as a value. The specified process (with its inheritable handles, processor affinity, priority class, quotas, user token, and attached job) will be used as the parent process instead of the current process calling **CreateProcess**. Notice that this re-parenting does not change the way a debugger process, creating a debuggee process, will still be responsible for receiving the debugging notifications and managing the debuggee life. The ToolHelp API presented in "Enumerating the Processes Running in the System" on page 118 shows the process given for this attribute as the parent of the created process.

Because the attribute list is opaque, you need to call the following function twice to create an empty attribute list:

```
BOOL InitializeProcThreadAttributeList(
   PPROC_THREAD_ATTRIBUTE_LIST pAttributeList,
   DWORD dwAttributeCount,
   DWORD dwFlags,
   PSIZE_T pSize);
```

Notice that the **dwFlags** parameter is reserved and you should always pass 0 for it. The first call is required to know the size of the memory block used by Windows to store the attributes:

```
SIZE_T cbAttributeListSize = 0;
BOOL bReturn = InitializeProcThreadAttributeList(
   NULL, 1, 0, &cbAttributeListSize);
// bReturn is FALSE but GetLastError() returns ERROR_INSUFFICIENT_BUFFER
```

The **SIZE_T** variable pointed to by **pSize** will receive the size of the memory block that you need to allocate based on the number of attributes to pass given by the **dwAttributeCount**:

```
pAttributeList = (PPROC_THREAD_ATTRIBUTE_LIST)
   HeapAlloc(GetProcessHeap(), 0, cbAttributeListSize);
```

After the memory is allocated for the attribute list, **InitializeProcThreadAttributeList** is called again to initialize its opaque content:

```
bReturn = InitializeProcThreadAttributeList(
   pAttributeList, 1, 0, &cbAttributeListSize);
```

Once the attribute list is allocated and initialized, you add the key/value pair you need with the following function:

```
BOOL UpdateProcThreadAttribute(
   PPROC_THREAD_ATTRIBUTE_LIST pAttributeList,
   DWORD dwFlags,
   DWORD_PTR Attribute,
   PVOID pValue,
   SIZE_T cbSize,
   PVOID pPreviousValue,
   PSIZE_T pReturnSize);
```

The **pAttributeList** parameter is the attribute list previously allocated and initialized in which this function will add a new key/value pair. The **Attribute** parameter is the key part of the pair and accepts either **PROC_THREAD_ATTRIBUTE_PARENT_PROCESS** or **PROC_THREAD_ATTRIBUTE_ HANDLE_LIST**. For the former, the **pValue** parameter must point to a variable containing the handle of the new parent process and **cbSize** should have **sizeof(HANDLE)** as its value. For the latter, **pValue** points to the start of an array containing the inheritable kernel object handles made accessible to the child process and **cbSize** should be equal to **sizeof(HANDLE)** multiplied by the number of handles. The **dwFlags**, **pPreviousValue**, and **pReturnSize** parameters are reserved and must be set to **0**, **NULL**, and **NULL**, respectively.

> **Caution**   If you need to pass the two attributes at the same time, don't forget that the handles associated with **PROC_THREAD_ATTRIBUTE_HANDLE_LIST** must be valid in the new parent process associated with **PROC_THREAD_ATTRIBUTE_PARENT_PROCESS** because they will be inherited from this process, not the current process calling **CreateProcess**.

Before calling **CreateProcess** with **EXTENDED_STARTUPINFO_PRESENT** in **dwCreationFlags**, you need to define a **STARTUPINFOEX** variable (with the **pAttributeList** field set to the attribute list you've just initialized) that will be used as the **pStartupInfo** parameter:

```
STARTUPINFOEX esi = { sizeof(STARTUPINFOEX) };
esi.lpAttributeList = pAttributeList;
bReturn = CreateProcess(
   ..., EXTENDED_STARTUPINFO_PRESENT, ...
   &esi.StartupInfo, ...);
```

When you don't need the parameters anymore, you need to clean up the opaque attribute list with the following method before releasing the corresponding allocated memory:

```
VOID DeleteProcThreadAttributeList(
   PPROC_THREAD_ATTRIBUTE_LIST pAttributeList);
```

Finally, an application can call the following function to obtain a copy of the **STARTUPINFO** structure that was initialized by the parent process. The child process can examine this structure and alter its behavior based on the values of the structure's members:

```
VOID GetStartupInfo(LPSTARTUPINFO pStartupInfo);
```

This function always fills up a **STARTUPINFO** structure even in a child process started through a call to **CreateProcess** with **STARTUPINFOEX**—the attributes are meaningful only in the parent process address space where the memory has been allocated for the attribute list. So, as explained previously, you need to find another way to pass the values of the inherited handles, such as through the command line.

ppiProcInfo

The **ppiProcInfo** parameter points to a **PROCESS_INFORMATION** structure that you must allocate; **CreateProcess** initializes the members of this structure before it returns. The structure appears as follows:

```
typedef struct _PROCESS_INFORMATION {
   HANDLE hProcess;
   HANDLE hThread;
   DWORD  dwProcessId;
   DWORD  dwThreadId;
} PROCESS_INFORMATION;
```

As already mentioned, creating a new process causes the system to create a process kernel object and a thread kernel object. At creation time, the system gives each object an initial usage count of 1. Then, just before **CreateProcess** returns, the function opens with full access to the process object and the thread object, and it places the process-relative handles for each in the **hProcess** and **hThread** members of the **PROCESS_INFORMATION** structure. When **CreateProcess** opens these objects internally, the usage count for each becomes 2.

This means that before the system can free the process object, the process must terminate (decrementing the usage count by 1) and the parent process must call **CloseHandle** (decrementing the usage count again by 1, making it 0). Similarly, to free the thread object, the thread must terminate and the parent process must close the handle to the thread object. (See "Child Processes" on page 108 for more information about freeing thread objects.)

Note You must close the handles to the child process and its primary thread to avoid resource leaks while your application is running. Of course, the system will clean up these leaks automatically when your process terminates, but well-written software explicitly closes these handles (by calling the **CloseHandle** function) when the process no longer needs to access the child process and its primary thread. Failure to close these handles is one of the most common mistakes developers make.

For some reason, many developers believe that closing the handle to a process or thread forces the system to kill that process or thread. This is absolutely not true. Closing the handle simply tells the system that you are not interested in the process or thread's statistical data. The process or thread will continue to execute until it terminates on its own.

When a process kernel object is created, the system assigns the object a unique identifier; no other process kernel object in the system will have the same ID number. The same is true for thread kernel objects. When a thread kernel object is created, the object is assigned a unique, systemwide ID number. Process IDs and thread IDs share the same number pool. This means that it is impossible for a process and a thread to have the same ID. In addition, an object is never assigned an ID of 0. Notice that Windows Task Manager associates a process ID of 0 to the "System Idle Process" as shown next. However, there is really no such thing as the "System Idle Process." Task Manager creates this fictitious process as a placeholder for the Idle thread that runs when nothing else is running. The number of threads in the System Idle Process is always equal to the number of CPUs in the machine. As such, it always represents the percentage of CPU usage that is not being used by real processes.

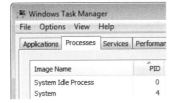

Before **CreateProcess** returns, it fills the **dwProcessId** and **dwThreadId** members of the **PROCESS_INFORMATION** structure with these IDs. IDs simply make it easy for you to identify the processes and threads in the system. IDs are mostly used by utility applications (such as Task Manager) and rarely by productivity applications. For this reason, most applications ignore IDs altogether.

If your application uses IDs to track processes and threads, you must be aware that the system reuses process and thread IDs immediately. For example, let's say that when a process is created, the system allocates a process object and assigns it the ID value 124. If a new process object is created, the system doesn't assign the same ID number. However, if the first process object is freed, the system might assign 124 to the next process object created. Keep this in mind so that you avoid writing code that references an incorrect process object or thread. It's easy to acquire a process ID and save the ID; but the next thing you know, the process identified by the ID is freed and a new process is created and given the same ID. When you use the saved process ID, you end up manipulating the new process, not the process whose ID you originally acquired.

You can discover the ID of the current process by using **GetCurrentProcessId** and the ID of the running thread by calling **GetCurrentThreadId**. You can also get the ID of a process given its handle by using **GetProcessId** and the ID of a thread given its handle by using **GetThreadId**. Last but not least, from a thread handle, you can determine the ID of its owning process by calling **GetProcessIdOfThread**.

Occasionally, you'll work on an application that wants to determine its parent process. The first thing you should know is that a parent-child relationship exists between processes only at the time when the child is spawned. Just before the child process begins executing code, Windows does not consider a parent-child relationship to exist anymore. The ToolHelp functions allow a process to query its parent process via the **PROCESSENTRY32** structure. Inside this structure is a **th32Parent-ProcessID** member that the documentation claims will return the ID of the process' parent.

The system does remember the ID of each process' parent process, but because IDs are immediately reused, by the time you get your parent process' ID, that ID might identify a completely different process running in the system. Your parent process will probably have terminated. If your application needs to communicate with its "creator," you are better off not using IDs. Instead, you should define a more persistent mechanism to communicate—kernel objects, window handles, and so forth.

The only way to guarantee that a process or thread ID isn't reused is to make sure that the process or thread kernel object doesn't get destroyed. If you have just created a new process or thread, you can do this simply by not closing the handles to these objects. Then, once your application has finished using the ID, call **CloseHandle** to release the kernel object or objects, and remember that it is no longer safe for you to use or rely on the process ID. If you are the child process, you can do nothing to ensure the validity of your parent's process or thread IDs unless the parent process duplicates handles for its own process or thread objects and allows you, the child process, to inherit these handles.

Terminating a Process

A process can be terminated in four ways:

- The primary thread's entry-point function returns. (This is highly recommended.)
- One thread in the process calls the **ExitProcess** function. (Avoid this method.)
- A thread in another process calls the **TerminateProcess** function. (Avoid this method.)
- All the threads in the process just die on their own. (This hardly ever happens.)

This section discusses all four methods and describes what actually happens when a process ends.

The Primary Thread's Entry-Point Function Returns

You should always design an application so that its process terminates only when your primary thread's entry-point function returns. This is the only way to guarantee that all your primary thread's resources are cleaned up properly.

Having your primary thread's entry-point function return ensures the following:

- Any C++ objects created by this thread will be destroyed properly using their destructors.
- The operating system will properly free the memory used by the thread's stack.

- The system will set the process' exit code (maintained in the process kernel object) to your entry-point function's return value.
- The system will decrement the process kernel object's usage count.

The *ExitProcess* Function

A process terminates when one of the threads in the process calls **ExitProcess**:

```
VOID ExitProcess(UINT fuExitCode);
```

This function terminates the process and sets the exit code of the process to **fuExitCode**. **Exit-Process** doesn't return a value because the process has terminated. If you include any code following the call to **ExitProcess**, that code will never execute.

When your primary thread's entry-point function (**WinMain**, **wWinMain**, **main**, or **wmain**) returns, it returns to the C/C++ run-time startup code, which properly cleans up all the C run-time resources used by the process. After the C run-time resources have been freed, the C run-time startup code explicitly calls **ExitProcess**, passing it the value returned from your entry-point function. This explains why simply returning from your primary thread's entry-point function terminates the entire process. Note that any other threads running in the process terminate along with the process.

The Windows Platform SDK documentation states that a process does not terminate until all its threads terminate. As far as the operating system goes, this statement is true. However, the C/C++ run time imposes a different policy on an application: the C/C++ run-time startup code ensures that the process terminates when your application's primary thread returns from its entry-point function—whether or not other threads are running in the process—by calling **ExitProcess**. However, if you call **ExitThread** in your entry-point function instead of calling **ExitProcess** or simply returning, the primary thread for your application will stop executing but the process will not terminate if at least one other thread in the process is still running.

Note that calling **ExitProcess** or **ExitThread** causes a process or thread to die while inside a function. As far the operating system is concerned, this is fine and all of the process' or thread's operating system resources will be cleaned up perfectly. However, a C/C++ application should avoid calling these functions because the C/C++ run time might not be able to clean up properly. Examine the following code:

```
#include <windows.h>
#include <stdio.h>

class CSomeObj {
public:
   CSomeObj()  { printf("Constructor\r\n"); }
   ~CSomeObj() { printf("Destructor\r\n"); }
};


CSomeObj g_GlobalObj;
```

```
void main () {
  CSomeObj LocalObj;
  ExitProcess(0);     // This shouldn't be here

  // At the end of this function, the compiler automatically added
  // the code necessary to call LocalObj's destructor.
  // ExitProcess prevents it from executing.
}
```

When the preceding code executes, you'll see the following:

```
Constructor
Constructor
```

Two objects are being constructed: a global object and a local object. However, you'll never see the word *Destructor* appear. The C++ objects are not properly destructed because **ExitProcess** forces the process to die on the spot: the C/C++ run time is not given a chance to clean up.

As I said, you should never call **ExitProcess** explicitly. If I remove the call to **ExitProcess** in the preceding code, running the program yields this:

```
Constructor
Constructor
Destructor
Destructor
```

By simply allowing the primary thread's entry-point function to return, the C/C++ run time can perform its cleanup and properly destruct all C++ objects. By the way, this discussion does not apply only to C++ objects. The C/C++ run time does many things on behalf of your process; it is best to allow the run time to clean it up properly.

> **Note** Making explicit calls to **ExitProcess** and **ExitThread** is a common problem that causes an application to not clean itself up properly. In the case of **ExitThread**, the process continues to run but can leak memory or other resources.

The *TerminateProcess* Function

A call to **TerminateProcess** also ends a process:

```
BOOL TerminateProcess(
  HANDLE hProcess,
  UINT fuExitCode);
```

This function is different from **ExitProcess** in one major way: any thread can call **Terminate-Process** to terminate another process or its own process. The **hProcess** parameter identifies the handle of the process to be terminated. When the process terminates, its exit code becomes the value you passed as the **fuExitCode** parameter.

You should use **TerminateProcess** only if you can't force a process to exit by using another method. The process being terminated is given absolutely no notification that it is dying—the application cannot clean up properly and cannot prevent itself from being killed (except by normal security mechanisms). For example, the process cannot flush any information it might have in memory out to disk.

Although it is true that the process will not have a chance to do its own cleanup, the operating system does clean up completely after the process so that no operating system resources remain. This means that all memory used by the process is freed, any open files are closed, all kernel objects have their usage counts decremented, and all User and GDI objects are destroyed.

Once a process terminates (no matter how), the system guarantees that the process will not leave any parts of itself behind. There is absolutely no way of knowing whether that process had ever run. *A process will leak absolutely nothing once it has terminated.* I hope that this is clear.

> **Note**   The **TerminateProcess** function is asynchronous—that is, it tells the system that you want the process to terminate but the process is not guaranteed to be killed by the time the function returns. So you might want to call **WaitForSingleObject** (described in Chapter 9, "Thread Synchronization with Kernel Objects") or a similar function, passing the handle of the process if you need to know for sure that the process has terminated.

When All the Threads in the Process Die

If all the threads in a process die (either because they've all called **ExitThread** or because they've been terminated with **TerminateThread**), the operating system assumes that there is no reason to keep the process' address space around. This is a fair assumption because there are no more threads executing any code in the address space. When the system detects that no threads are running any more, it terminates the process. When this happens, the process' exit code is set to the same exit code as the last thread that died.

When a Process Terminates

When a process terminates, the following actions are set in motion:

1. Any remaining threads in the process are terminated.
2. All the User and GDI objects allocated by the process are freed, and all the kernel objects are closed. (These kernel objects are destroyed if no other process has open handles to them. However, the kernel objects are not destroyed if other processes do have open handles to them.)
3. The process' exit code changes from **STILL_ACTIVE** to the code passed to **ExitProcess** or **TerminateProcess**.
4. The process kernel object's status becomes signaled. (See Chapter 9 for more information about signaling.) This is why other threads in the system can suspend themselves until the process is terminated.
5. The process kernel object's usage count is decremented by 1.

Note that a process' kernel object always lives at least as long as the process itself. However, the process kernel object might live well beyond its process. When a process terminates, the system automatically decrements the usage count of its kernel object. If the count goes to 0, no other process has an open handle to the object and the object is destroyed when the process is destroyed.

However, the process kernel object's count will not go to 0 if another process in the system has an open handle to the dying process' kernel object. This usually happens when parent processes forget to close their handle to a child process. This is a feature, not a bug. Remember that the process kernel object maintains statistical information about the process. This information can be useful even after the process has terminated. For example, you might want to know how much CPU time the process required. Or, more likely, you might want to obtain the now-defunct process' exit code by calling **GetExitCodeProcess**:

```
BOOL GetExitCodeProcess(
    HANDLE hProcess,
    PDWORD pdwExitCode);
```

This function looks into the process kernel object (identified by the **hProcess** parameter) and extracts the member within the kernel object's data structure that identifies the process' exit code. The exit code value is returned in the **DWORD** pointed to by the **pdwExitCode** parameter.

You can call this function at any time. If the process hasn't terminated when **GetExitCode-Process** is called, the function fills the **DWORD** with the **STILL_ACTIVE** identifier (defined as 0x103). If the process has terminated, the actual exit code value is returned.

You might think that you can write code to determine whether a process has terminated by calling **GetExitCodeProcess** periodically and checking the exit code. This would work in many situations, but it would be inefficient. I'll explain the proper way to determine when a process has terminated in the next section.

Once again, let me remind you that you should tell the system when you are no longer interested in a process' statistical data by calling **CloseHandle**. If the process has already terminated, **Close-Handle** will decrement the count on the kernel object and free it.

Child Processes

When you design an application, you might encounter situations in which you want another block of code to perform work. You assign work like this all the time by calling functions or subroutines. When you call a function, your code cannot continue processing until the function has returned. And in many situations, this single-tasking synchronization is needed. An alternative way to have another block of code perform work is to create a new thread within your process and have it help with the processing. This lets your code continue processing while the other thread performs the work you requested. This technique is useful, but it creates synchronization problems when your thread needs to see the results of the new thread.

Another approach is to spawn off a new process—a child process—to help with the work. Let's say that the work you need to do is pretty complex. To process the work, you simply create a new thread within the same process. You write some code, test it, and get some incorrect results. You might have an error in your algorithm, or maybe you dereferenced something incorrectly and accidentally overwrote something important in your address space. One way to protect your address space while having the work processed is to have a new process perform the work. You can then wait for the new process to terminate before continuing with your own work, or you can continue working while the new process works.

Unfortunately, the new process probably needs to perform operations on data contained in your address space. In this case, it might be a good idea to have the process run in its own address space and simply give it access to the relevant data contained in the parent process' address space, thus protecting all the data not relevant to the task at hand. Windows offers several methods for transferring data between different processes: Dynamic Data Exchange (DDE), OLE, pipes, mailslots, and so on. One of the most convenient ways to share the data is to use memory-mapped files. (See Chapter 17, "Memory-Mapped Files," for a detailed discussion of them.)

If you want to create a new process, have it do some work, and wait for the result, you can use code similar to the following:

```
PROCESS_INFORMATION pi;
DWORD dwExitCode;

// Spawn the child process.
BOOL fSuccess = CreateProcess(..., &pi);
if (fSuccess) {

    // Close the thread handle as soon as it is no longer needed!
    CloseHandle(pi.hThread);

    // Suspend our execution until the child has terminated.
    WaitForSingleObject(pi.hProcess, INFINITE);

    // The child process terminated; get its exit code.
    GetExitCodeProcess(pi.hProcess, &dwExitCode);

    // Close the process handle as soon as it is no longer needed.
    CloseHandle(pi.hProcess);
}
```

In the preceding code fragment, you create the new process and, if it is successful, you call the **WaitForSingleObject** function:

```
DWORD WaitForSingleObject(HANDLE hObject, DWORD dwTimeout);
```

I'll discuss the **WaitForSingleObject** function exhaustively in Chapter 9. For now, all you need to know is that it waits until the object identified by the **hObject** parameter becomes *signaled*. Process objects become signaled when they terminate. So the call to **WaitForSingleObject** suspends the parent's thread until the child process terminates. After **WaitForSingleObject** returns, you can get the exit code of the child process by calling **GetExitCodeProcess**.

The calls to **CloseHandle** in the preceding code fragment cause the system to decrement the usage count for the thread and process objects to 0, allowing the objects' memories to be freed.

You'll notice that in the code fragment, we close the handle to the child process' primary thread kernel object immediately after **CreateProcess** returns. This does not cause the child's primary thread to terminate—it simply decrements the usage count of the child's primary thread object. Here's why this practice is a good idea: Suppose that the child process' primary thread spawns off another thread and then the primary thread terminates. At this point, the system can free the child's primary thread object from its memory if the parent process doesn't have an outstanding handle to this thread object. But if the parent process does have a handle to the child's thread object, the system can't free the object until the parent process closes the handle.

Running Detached Child Processes

Most of the time, an application starts another process as a *detached process*. This means that after the process is created and executing, the parent process doesn't need to communicate with the new process or doesn't require it to complete its work before the parent process continues. This is how Windows Explorer works. After Windows Explorer creates a new process for the user, it doesn't care whether that process continues to live or whether the user terminates it.

To give up all ties to the child process, Windows Explorer must close its handles to the new process and its primary thread by calling **CloseHandle**. The following code example shows how to create a new process and how to let it run detached:

```
PROCESS_INFORMATION pi;

// Spawn the child process.
BOOL fSuccess = CreateProcess(..., &pi);
if (fSuccess) {

    // Allow the system to destroy the process & thread kernel
    // objects as soon as the child process terminates.
    CloseHandle(pi.hThread);
    CloseHandle(pi.hProcess);
}
```

When Administrator Runs as a Standard User

Windows Vista raises the security bar for the end user thanks to a set of new technologies. For application developers, the technology with the most impact is certainly the User Account Control (UAC).

Microsoft observed that most users were logging on to Windows with an Administrator account, which gave them access to vital system resources with almost no restriction because high privileges are granted to this account. Once the user logged on to a pre-Vista Windows system with such a privileged account, a security token was created and used thereafter by the operating system each time a piece of code tried to access a securable resource. This token was associated to newly created processes, starting with Windows Explorer, which then gave it to all its children processes and so on. In this configuration, if a malware application downloaded from the Internet or a script in an e-mail message ran, it inherited the high privileges of an Administrator under which the hosting application was running—so it was free to change whatever it wanted on the machine or even to start another process that inherited the same high privileges.

With Windows Vista, if a user logs on to the system with an account that grants high privileges such as Administrator, in addition to the security token corresponding to this privileged account, a filtered token is also created but granted only with the privileges of a Standard User. This filtered token is then associated to each new process launched by the system on behalf of the end user, starting with Windows Explorer. But wait.... If all applications are running with a Standard User set of privileges, how can restricted resources be accessed? The short answer is: there is no way for a privilege-restricted process to access secured resources that require higher privileges. It is now time to give the long answer and the rest of this section is dedicated to explain how you, as a developer, should take advantage of UAC.

First, you can ask the operating system to elevate the privileges, but only on a process boundary. What does this mean? By default, when a process is started, it gets associated with the filtered token of the logged-on user. If you want to give more privileges to a process, you need to tell Windows to kindly ask the end user for his acknowledgement *before* the process is started. As an end user, you can use the Run As Administrator command on the context menu displayed by Windows Explorer when you right-click on an application.

If you are logged on as an Administrator, a confirmation dialog box will appear in a secure Windows desktop for you to validate the elevation of privileges up to the level of the nonfiltered security token. Three types of dialog boxes can be shown to the user at this point. If the application is part of the system, the following security confirmation will appear on your screen with a blue banner:

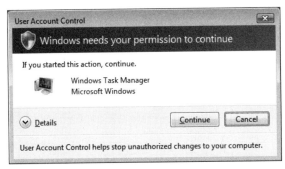

If the application is signed, you get the prompt with a less confident gray banner:

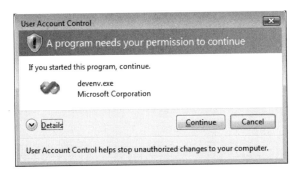

And finally, if the application is not signed, you are asked to be more cautious in answering the dialog box with the orange banner:

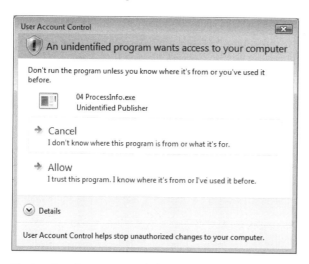

Notice that if you are simply logged on as a Standard User, another dialog box will prompt you for the credentials of an elevated account, which allows an Administrator to help a Standard User logged on the machine to execute tasks requiring high privileges. This is called an over-the-shoulder logon.

> **Note**   Many people ask why Windows Vista doesn't just ask once and then let the user's desire to run a specific application as Administrator be stored in the system so that Windows Vista never asks the user again. Windows Vista doesn't offer this because it would have to store the data somewhere (like in the registry or in some other file), and if this store ever got compromised, an application could modify the store so that its malware always ran elevated without the user being prompted.

In addition to the Run As Administrator command that is available from the context menu of Windows Explorer, I'm sure you have noticed that a new *shield* icon is displayed close to a couple of links or the button responsible for administration tasks in Windows Vista. This user interface hint tells the user that she should expect an elevation confirmation prompt to pop up. The Process Information sample code presented at the end of this chapter shows how easy it is to display the shield icon in a button of your application.

Let's take a simple example. When you start the Task Manager available from the context menu of the taskbar, the shield icon is visible in the Show Processes From All Users button.

Take a look at the process ID of the Task Manager before clicking the button. After accepting the privileges elevation, the Task Manager is not visible for half a second and then it reappears but with a check box in place of the shield button.

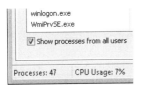

If you take a look at the process ID of the Task Manager, you'll notice that it is not the same as the one you remember from before the privileges elevation prompt. Does it mean that Task Manager had to spawn another instance of itself to get elevated? Yes. Always the same answer: Windows allows privileges elevation only on a process boundary. Once a process is started, it is too late to ask for more privileges. However, an unelevated process can spawn another elevated process that contains a COM server in it and keep it alive so that it can do IPC calls to the elevated process without the need to start a new instance and then terminate itself.

> **Note**   In a video and Microsoft Office PowerPoint presentation available at *http://www. microsoft.com/emea/itsshowtime/sessionh.aspx?videoid=360*, Mark Russinovich presents the inner mechanisms of UAC with other details, such as the virtualization of system resources provided by Windows that allows better compatibility for applications that are unaware of the new Administrator privileges restrictions.

Elevating a Process Automatically

If your application always requires Administrator privileges, such as during an installation step, the operating system can automatically prompt the user for privileges elevation each time your application is invoked. How do the UAC components of Windows decide what to do when a new process is spawned?

If a specific kind of resource (**RT_MANIFEST**) is found embedded within the application executable, the system looks for the **<trustInfo>** section and parses its contents. Here is an example of this section in the manifest file:

```
...
<trustInfo xmlns="urn:schemas-microsoft-com:asm.v2">
   <security>
      <requestedPrivileges>
         <requestedExecutionLevel
            level="requireAdministrator"
         />
      </requestedPrivileges>
   </security>
</trustInfo>
...
```

Three different values are possible for the **level** attribute, as shown in Table 4-8.

Table 4-8   Values for the level Attribute

Value	Description
requireAdministrator	The application must be started with Administrator privileges; it won't run otherwise.
highestAvailable	The application is started with the highest possible privileges.
	If the user is logged on with an Administrator account, an elevation prompt appears.
	If the user is a Standard User, the application is started (without any elevation prompt) with these standard privileges.
asInvoker	The application is started with the same privileges as the calling application.

Instead of embedding the manifest into the resources of an executable, it is possible to store the manifest in the same folder as the executable file with the exact same, but additional, *.manifest* suffix.

An external manifest might not be taken into account immediately, especially if you have already launched the executable before the manifest file was present. In that case, you need to log off and re-log on before the external manifest file is taken into account by Windows. In all cases, if the executable file contains an embedded manifest, the external file has no effect.

In addition to the explicit requirement set through an XML manifest, the operating system also follows a special set of compatibility rules to determine that a program is recognized as a setup application, which requires automatic privileges elevation prompting, for example. For other applications, without any manifest or setup-like behavior, the end user can decide to start the process as an Administrator by selecting the corresponding check box on the Compatibility tab of the executable file properties dialog box as shown on the next page.

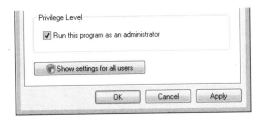

Note   The features related to application compatibility are beyond the scope of this book, but the white paper about how to develop UAC-compliant applications for Windows Vista at *http://www.microsoft.com/downloads/details.aspx?FamilyID=ba73b169-a648-49af-bc5e-a2eebb74c16b&DisplayLang=en* provides additional details.

Elevating a Process by Hand

If you read the detailed description of the **CreateProcess** function earlier in this chapter, you certainly noticed that no special flag or parameter was presented to require this privileges elevation. Instead, you call the **ShellExecuteEx** function:

```
BOOL ShellExecuteEx(LPSHELLEXECUTEINFO pExecInfo);

typedef struct _SHELLEXECUTEINFO {
    DWORD cbSize;
    ULONG fMask;
    HWND hwnd;
    PCTSTR lpVerb;
    PCTSTR lpFile;
    PCTSTR lpParameters;
    PCTSTR lpDirectory;
    int nShow;
    HINSTANCE hInstApp;
    PVOID lpIDList;
    PCTSTR lpClass;
    HKEY hkeyClass;
    DWORD dwHotKey;
    union {
        HANDLE hIcon;
        HANDLE hMonitor;
    } DUMMYUNIONNAME;
    HANDLE hProcess;
} SHELLEXECUTEINFO, *LPSHELLEXECUTEINFO;
```

The only interesting fields of the **SHELLEXECUTEINFO** structure are **lpVerb**, which must be set to *"runas"*, and **lpFile**, which must contain the path of the executable to be started with elevated privileges, as shown in the following code snippet:

```
// Initialize the structure.
SHELLEXECUTEINFO sei = { sizeof(SHELLEXECUTEINFO) };

// Ask for privileges elevation.
sei.lpVerb = TEXT("runas");
```

```
// Create a Command Prompt from which you will be able to start
// other elevated applications.
sei.lpFile = TEXT("cmd.exe");

// Don't forget this parameter; otherwise, the window will be hidden.
sei.nShow = SW_SHOWNORMAL;

if (!ShellExecuteEx(&sei)) {
   DWORD dwStatus = GetLastError();

   if (dwStatus == ERROR_CANCELLED) {
      // The user refused to allow privileges elevation.
   }
   else
   if (dwStatus == ERROR_FILE_NOT_FOUND) {
      // The file defined by lpFile was not found and
      // an error message popped up.
   }
}
```

If the user refuses to elevate privileges, **ShellExecuteEx** returns **FALSE** and **GetLastError** identifies this situation by using an **ERROR_CANCELLED** value.

Notice that when a process is started with elevated privileges, each time it spawns another process with **CreateProcess**, this child process gets the same elevated privileges as its parent—there's no need to call **ShellExecuteEx** in that case. If, from an application running with a filtered token, you try to spawn an executable that requires privileges elevation by calling **CreateProcess**, it fails and **GetLastError** returns **ERROR_ELEVATION_REQUIRED**.

To sum up, in order to be a good citizen in Windows Vista, your application should be able to run as a Standard User most of the time, and when it requires more privileges, the user interface should explicitly show the shield icon close to the user interface element (button, link, or menu item) corresponding to this administrative task. (An example is given in the Process Information example later in this chapter.) Because the administrative tasks must be executed by another process or a COM server in another process, you should gather all the tasks requiring Administrator privileges inside a second application and elevate it by calling **ShellExecuteEx** with **"runas"** in **lpVerb**, and then pass the privileged action to be executed as a parameter on the command line of the new process with the **lpParameters** field of **SHELLEXECUTEINFO**.

Tip   Debugging elevated/filtered processes can be frustrating, but the golden rule to follow is very simple: start Visual Studio with the same privileges you want your debuggee to inherit.

If you need to debug a filtered process running as a Standard User, you must start Visual Studio as a Standard User, like what you get when you click on the default shortcut or through the Start menu. Otherwise, the debuggee will inherit the elevated privileges from a Visual Studio instance started as an Administrator, and this is not what you want.

In the case of debugging a process that needs to run as Administrator—as described by its manifest, for example—the instance of Visual Studio must have been started as an Administrator too. Otherwise, you will get an error message explaining that "the requested operation requires elevation" and the debuggee will not be started at all.

What Is the Current Privileges Context?

If you remember the example of the Task Manager, which displays either a shield icon or a check box depending on how it was spawned, two pieces of information have not been unveiled yet. You need to determine whether or not your application is running as Administrator and, more importantly, whether or not it has been elevated back to Administrator privileges or is simply running with the filtered token.

The following **GetProcessElevation** helper function returns both the elevation type and a Boolean value indicating whether you are running as Administrator or not:

```
BOOL GetProcessElevation(TOKEN_ELEVATION_TYPE* pElevationType, BOOL* pIsAdmin) {
   HANDLE hToken = NULL;
   DWORD dwSize;

   // Get current process token
   if (!OpenProcessToken(GetCurrentProcess(), TOKEN_QUERY, &hToken))
      return(FALSE);

   BOOL bResult = FALSE;

   // Retrieve elevation type information
   if (GetTokenInformation(hToken, TokenElevationType,
      pElevationType, sizeof(TOKEN_ELEVATION_TYPE), &dwSize)) {
      // Create the SID corresponding to the Administrators group
      BYTE adminSID[SECURITY_MAX_SID_SIZE];
      dwSize = sizeof(adminSID);
      CreateWellKnownSid(WinBuiltinAdministratorsSid, NULL, &adminSID,
         &dwSize);

      if (*pElevationType == TokenElevationTypeLimited) {
         // Get handle to linked token (will have one if we are lua)
         HANDLE hUnfilteredToken = NULL;
         GetTokenInformation(hToken, TokenLinkedToken, (VOID*)
            &hUnfilteredToken, sizeof(HANDLE), &dwSize);

         // Check if this original token contains admin SID
         if (CheckTokenMembership(hUnfilteredToken, &adminSID, pIsAdmin)) {
            bResult = TRUE;
         }

         // Don't forget to close the unfiltered token
         CloseHandle(hUnfilteredToken);
      } else {
         *pIsAdmin = IsUserAnAdmin();
         bResult = TRUE;
      }
   }

   // Don't forget to close the process token
   CloseHandle(hToken);

   return(bResult);
}
```

Notice that **GetTokenInformation** is called with the token associated with the process and the **TokenElevationType** parameter to get the elevation type, which can have the values defined by the **TOKEN_ELEVATION_TYPE** enumeration listed in Table 4-9.

Table 4-9   TOKEN_ELEVATION_TYPE Values

Value	Description
TokenElevationTypeDefault	Process is running as default user or UAC is disabled.
TokenElevationTypeFull	Process has been successfully elevated, and the token is not filtered.
TokenElevationTypeLimited	Process is running with limited privileges corresponding to a filtered token.

These values let you know if you are running with a filtered token or not. The next step is to discover whether or not the user is an Administrator. If the token is not filtered, **IsUserAnAdmin** is the perfect function to use to know whether or not you are running as Administrator. In the other case of a filtered token, you need to grab the nonfiltered token (by passing **TokenLinkedToken** to **GetTokenInformation**) and check whether or not the Administrator SID (with the help of **CreateWellKnownSid** and **CheckTokenMembership**) is present.

As an example, the Process Information sample application detailed in the next section is using this helper function in the **WM_INITDIALOG** message-handling code to prefix the title with the elevation details and show or hide a shield icon.

> **Tip**   Notice that the **Button_SetElevationRequiredState** macro (defined in Comm-Ctrl.h) is used to show or hide the shield icon in a button. You can also get the shield directly as an icon by calling **SHGetStockIconInfo** with **SIID_SHIELD** as a parameter; both are defined in shellapi.h. For other types of controls supporting the shield metaphor, you should take a look at the corresponding MSDN online help at *http://msdn2.microsoft.com/en-us/library/aa480150.aspx*.

Enumerating the Processes Running in the System

Many software developers try to write tools or utilities for Windows that require the set of running processes to be enumerated. The Windows API originally had no functions that enumerated the running processes. However, Windows NT has a constantly updating database called the Performance Data database. This database contains a ton of information and is available through registry functions such as **RegQueryValueEx** with the **HKEY_PERFORMANCE_DATA** root key. Few Windows programmers know about the performance database for these reasons:

- It has no functions that are specific to it; it simply uses existing registry functions.
- It was not available on Windows 95 and Windows 98.
- The layout of information in the database is complex; many developers avoid using it. This prevents knowledge of its existence from spreading by word of mouth.

To make working with this database easier, Microsoft created a Performance Data Helper set of functions (contained in PDH.dll). For more information about this library, search for Performance Data Helper in the Platform SDK documentation.

As I mentioned, Windows 95 and 98 do not offer this performance database. Instead, they have their own set of functions to enumerate processes and information about them. These are in the ToolHelp API. For more information, search for the **Process32First** and **Process32Next** functions in the Platform SDK documentation.

To make things more fun, Microsoft's Windows NT team, which doesn't like the ToolHelp functions, did not add them to Windows NT. Instead, they produced their own Process Status functions to enumerate processes (contained in PSAPI.dll). For more information, search for the **EnumProcesses** function in the Platform SDK documentation.

Microsoft might appear to be making life difficult for tool and utility developers, but it has added the ToolHelp functions to Windows since Windows 2000. Finally, developers have a way to write tools and utilities that have common source code for Windows 95, Windows 98, and up to Windows Vista!

The Process Information Sample Application

The ProcessInfo application 04-ProcessInfo.exe shows how to use the ToolHelp functions to produce a very useful utility. The source code and resource files for the application are in the 04-ProcessInfo directory on this book's companion content Web page. When you start the program, the window shown in Figure 4-4 appears.

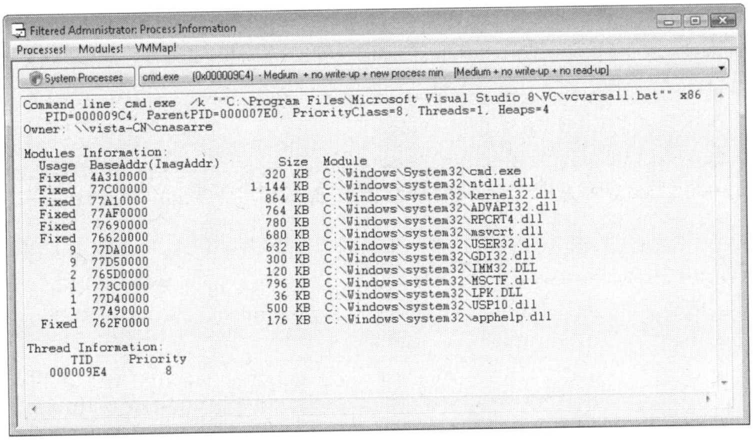

Figure 4-4   ProcessInfo in action

ProcessInfo first enumerates the set of processes currently running and places each process' name and ID in the top combo box. Then the first process is selected and information about that process is shown in the large read-only edit control. As you can see, the process' ID is shown along with its command line, owner, parent process' ID, the priority class of the process, and the number of threads currently running in the context of the process. Much of the information is beyond the scope of this chapter but will be discussed in later chapters.

When you look at the process list, the VMMap menu item is available. (This item is disabled when you look at the module information.) Selecting the VMMap menu item causes the VMMap sample application (discussed in Chapter 14, "Exploring Virtual Memory") to run. This application walks the address space of the selected process.

The module information portion shows the list of modules (executables and DLLs) that are mapped into the process' address space. A fixed module is one that was implicitly loaded when the process initialized. For explicitly loaded DLLs, the DLL's usage count is shown. The second field shows the memory address where the module is mapped. If the module is not mapped at its preferred base address, the preferred base address also appears in parentheses. The third field shows the size of the module formatted in kilobytes, and finally, the full pathname of the module is displayed. The thread information portion shows the set of threads currently running in the context of this process. Each thread's ID and priority is shown.

In addition to the process information, you can choose the Modules! menu item. This causes ProcessInfo to enumerate the set of modules currently loaded throughout the system and places each module's name in the top combo box. Then ProcessInfo selects the first module and displays information about it, as Figure 4-5 shows.

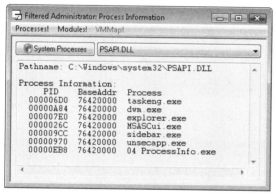

Figure 4-5   ProcessInfo showing all processes that have Psapi.dll loaded in their address space

When you use the ProcessInfo utility in this way, you can easily determine which processes are using a particular module. As you can see, the module's full pathname is shown at the top. The Process Information section then shows the list of processes that contain the module. In addition to each process' ID and name, the address where the module is loaded in each process is shown.

Basically, all the information displayed by the ProcessInfo application is produced by calling the various ToolHelp functions. To make working with the ToolHelp functions a little easier, I created a CToolhelp C++ class (contained in the Toolhelp.h file). This C++ class encapsulates a ToolHelp snapshot and makes calling the other ToolHelp functions a bit easier.

The **GetModulePreferredBaseAddr** function inside ProcessInfo.cpp is particularly interesting:

```
PVOID GetModulePreferredBaseAddr(
   DWORD dwProcessId,
   PVOID pvModuleRemote);
```

This function accepts a process ID and the address of a module in that process. It then looks in that process' address space, locates that module, and reads the module's header information to determine the module's preferred base address. A module should always load at its preferred base address; otherwise, applications that use the module require more memory and take a performance hit while initializing. Because this is such a horrible situation, I added this function and I show when a module doesn't load at its preferred base address. You'll see more on preferred base addresses and this time/memory performance hit in "Rebasing Modules" on page 586.

There is no direct way to get the command line of a process. As it has been explained in the "Escape from DLL Hell with Custom Debugging and Instrumentation Tools and Utilities, Part 2" article of MSDN Magazine (*http://msdn.microsoft.com/msdnmag/issues/02/08/EscapefromDLLHell/*), you need to dig into the *Process Environment Block (PEB)* of the remote process to find the command line. However, a couple of things have changed since Windows XP that deserve explanations. First, the command to use in WinDbg (downloadable at *http://www.microsoft.com/whdc/devtools/debugging/default.mspx*) to get the details of a structure of the kernel-like Process Environment Block has changed. Instead of **"strct"** implemented by the kdex2x86 extension, you simply call the **"dt"** command. For example **"dt nt! PEB"** lists the following definition for a Process Environment Block:

```
+0x000 InheritedAddressSpace : UChar
+0x001 ReadImageFileExecOptions : UChar
+0x002 BeingDebugged     : UChar
+0x003 BitField          : UChar
+0x003 ImageUsesLargePages : Pos 0, 1 Bit
+0x003 IsProtectedProcess : Pos 1, 1 Bit
+0x003 IsLegacyProcess   : Pos 2, 1 Bit
+0x003 IsImageDynamicallyRelocated : Pos 3, 1 Bit
+0x003 SpareBits         : Pos 4, 4 Bits
+0x004 Mutant            : Ptr32 Void
+0x008 ImageBaseAddress  : Ptr32 Void
+0x00c Ldr               : Ptr32 _PEB_LDR_DATA
+0x010 ProcessParameters : Ptr32 _RTL_USER_PROCESS_PARAMETERS
+0x014 SubSystemData     : Ptr32 Void
+0x018 ProcessHeap       : Ptr32 Void
...
```

And the **RTL_USER_PROCESS_PARAMETERS** structure has the following definition listed by the **"dt nt!_RTL_USER_PROCESS_PARAMETERS"** command in WinDbg:

```
+0x000 MaximumLength     : Uint4B
+0x004 Length            : Uint4B
+0x008 Flags             : Uint4B
+0x00c DebugFlags        : Uint4B
+0x010 ConsoleHandle     : Ptr32 Void
+0x014 ConsoleFlags      : Uint4B
+0x018 StandardInput     : Ptr32 Void
+0x01c StandardOutput    : Ptr32 Void
+0x020 StandardError     : Ptr32 Void
+0x024 CurrentDirectory  : _CURDIR
+0x030 DllPath           : _UNICODE_STRING
+0x038 ImagePathName     : _UNICODE_STRING
+0x040 CommandLine       : _UNICODE_STRING
+0x048 Environment       : Ptr32 Void
...
```

And this is how the following internal structures are computed to help in reaching the command line:

```
typedef struct
{
    DWORD Filler[4];
    DWORD InfoBlockAddress;
} __PEB;

typedef struct
{
    DWORD Filler[17];
    DWORD wszCmdLineAddress;
} __INFOBLOCK;
```

Second, as you will learn in Chapter 14, in Windows Vista the system DLLs are loaded at a random address in a process address space. So, instead of hardcoding the address of the PEB to 0x7ffdf000 as was the case in Windows XP, you need to call **NtQueryInformationProcess** with **ProcessBasicInformation** as the parameter. Don't forget that the undocumented details that you have discovered for a version of Windows might change in the next version.

Last but not least, when using the Process Information application, you might notice that some processes are listed in the combo box but no details such as loaded DLLs are available. For example, audiodg.exe ("Windows Audio Device Graph Isolation") is a *protected process*. Windows Vista introduces this new type of process to provide more isolation for DRM applications, for example. And it is not surprising that the right, for a remote process, to access to the virtual memory of a protected process has been removed. So, because this is required to list the loaded DLLs, the ToolHelp API fails to return these details. You can download the white paper about protected processes at *http://www.microsoft.com/whdc/system/vista/process_Vista.mspx*.

There is another reason why the Process Information application might not be able to retrieve all the details of a running process. If this tool is started without being elevated, it might not be able to access—and certainly will be unable to modify—processes started with privileges elevation. In fact, the limitations go beyond that simplistic view. Windows Vista implements another security mechanism called *Windows Integrity Mechanism* (or previously known as Mandatory Integrity Control).

In addition to the well-known security descriptors and access control lists, an *integrity level* is assigned to securable resources through a new access control entry (ACE) called a *mandatory label* in the *system access control list (SACL)*. Securable objects without such an ACE are treated by the operating system as implicitly having an integrity level of Medium. Each process also has an integrity level based on its security token that corresponds to the level of trust that the system grants to it as shown in Table 4-10.

Table 4-10   Levels of Trust

Level	Example of Applications
Low	Internet Explorer in Protected Mode is running with Low level of trust to deny downloaded code the right to modify the other applications and the Windows environment.
Medium	By default, all applications are started in Medium level of trust and run with a filtered token.
High	When an application is started with privileges elevation, it runs with High level of trust.
System	Only processes running as Local System or Local Service gain this level of trust.

When a piece of code tries to access a kernel object, the system compares the integrity level of the calling process with the integrity level associated to the kernel object. If the latter is higher than the former, modify and delete actions are denied. Notice that this comparison is done before checking ACLs. So, even though the process would have the right privileges to access the resource, the fact that it runs with an integrity level lower than the one required by the resource denies the requested access to the object. This is particularly important with applications that run code or scripts downloaded from the Web, and Internet Explorer 7 on Windows Vista takes advantage of this mechanism to run at Low integrity level. That way, downloaded code is not able to change the state of any other applications because these processes are, by default, running at Medium integrity level.

Tip   The Process Explorer tool from Sysinternals (*http://www.microsoft.com/technet/ sysinternals/ProcessesAndThreads/ProcessExplorer.mspx*) allows you to see the integrity level of processes if you select the column with the same name on the Process Image tab of the Select Columns dialog box.

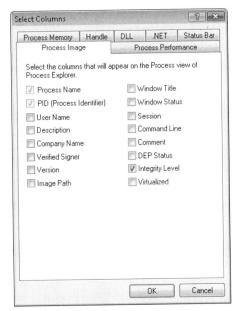

The **GetProcessIntegrityLevel** function found in the source code demonstrates the programmatic way to retrieve the same detail and much more. The console mode AccessChk tool from Sysinternals (*http://www.microsoft.com/technet/sysinternals/utilities/accesschk.mspx*) lists the integrity levels required for accessing resources such as files, folders, and registry keys when you are using the **-i** or **-e** command switches. Last but not least, the icacls.exe Vista console mode tool provides a **/setintegritylevel** command-line switch to set the integrity level of a file system resource.

Once the integrity levels of the token of a process and the kernel object it is trying to access are known, the system checks what kind of action is possible based on a code *policy* stored in both the token and the resource. First, **GetTokenInformation** is called, passing it **TokenMandatoryPolicy** and the process' security token handle. **GetTokenInformation** then returns a **DWORD** value containing a bitwise mask, which details the policies that apply. Table 4-11 lists the possible policies.

Table 4-11   Code Policies

TOKEN_MANDATORY_* constant from WinNT.h	Description
POLICY_NO_WRITE_UP	The code running under this security token cannot write into a resource with a higher integrity level.
POLICY_NEW_PROCESS_MIN	When the code running under this security token starts a new process, this child process inherits a lowest possible priority level between the one of the parent and the one described in the manifest (or Medium if there is no manifest).

Two other constants are defined for you to easily detect either no policy (**TOKEN_MANDATORY_POLICY_OFF** as **0**) or a bitwise mask (**TOKEN_MANDATORY_POLICY_VALID_MASK**) to validate a policy value as shown in ProcessInfo.cpp.

Second, the resource policy is set on the bitwise mask of the Label ACE attached to the kernel object. (See the **GetProcessIntegrityLevel** function in ProcessInfo.cpp for implementation details.) Two *resource policies* are available to decide what kind of access to allow or deny on the resource. The default one is **SYSTEM_MANDATORY_LABEL_NO_WRITE_UP**, which indicates that it is possible for a lower integrity process to read but not to write or delete a higher integrity resource. The **SYSTEM_MANDATORY_LABEL_NO_READ_UP** resource policy is even more restrictive because it does not allow a lower integrity process to read a higher integrity resource.

> **Note**   In the case of a high-integrity process kernel object, even if "No-Read-Up" is set, another lower integrity process will be able to read inside the higher integrity address space if the Debug privilege is granted. This is the reason why the Process Information tool is able to read the command line of System integrity level processes when you run it as Administrator, which is required to grant ourselves the Debug privilege.

Beyond securing the accesses to kernel objects between processes, the integrity level is also used by the windowing system to deny Low integrity level processes to access and update the user interfaces of processes with a higher integrity level. This mechanism is called *User Interface Privilege Isolation* (UIPI). The operating system blocks posted (via **PostMessage**), sent (via **SendMessage**), or intercepted (via Windows hooks) Windows messages from lower integrity processes to prevent information retrieval or fake input injection to a window owned by a higher integrity level process. This is particularly visible if you are trying to use the WindowDump utility (*http://download.microsoft.com/download/8/3/f/83f69587-47f1-48e2-86a6-aab14f01f1fe/EscapeFromDLLHell.exe*). To get the text displayed by each item of a list box, WindowDump is calling **SendMessage** with **LB_GETCOUNT** as a parameter to get the number of elements whose text content will be retrieved later by calling **SendMessage** with **LB_GETTEXT** as a parameter. However, if it is running with a lower integrity level than the processes owning the list box, the first **SendMessage** call succeeds but returns 0 as the elements count. You can observe the same filtered behavior with Spy++ started with a Medium integrity level that tries to get messages from a window created by a higher integrity level process: it will fail.

Chapter 5
Jobs

You often need to treat a group of processes as a single entity. For example, when you tell Microsoft Visual Studio to build a C++ project, it spawns Cl.exe, which might have to spawn additional processes (such as the individual passes of the compiler). But if the user wants to prematurely stop the build, Visual Studio must somehow be able to terminate Cl.exe and all its child processes. Solving this simple (and common) problem in Microsoft Windows has been notoriously difficult because Windows doesn't maintain a parent/child relationship between processes. In particular, child processes continue to execute even after their parent process has been terminated.

When you design a server, you must also treat a set of processes as a single group. For instance, a client might request that a server execute an application (which might spawn children of its own) and return the results back to the client. Because many clients might connect to this server, it would be nice if the server could somehow restrict what a client can request to prevent any single client from monopolizing all of its resources. These restrictions might include maximum CPU time that can be allocated to the client's request, minimum and maximum working set sizes, preventing the client's application from shutting down the computer, and security restrictions.

Microsoft Windows offers a job kernel object that lets you group processes together and create a "sandbox" that restricts what the processes can do. It is best to think of a job object as a container of processes. However, it is also useful to create jobs that contain a single process because you can place restrictions on that process that you normally cannot.

My **StartRestrictedProcess** function places a process in a job that restricts the process' ability to do certain things:

```
void StartRestrictedProcess() {
   // Check if we are not already associated with a job.
   // If this is the case, there is no way to switch to
   // another job.
   BOOL bInJob = FALSE;
   IsProcessInJob(GetCurrentProcess(), NULL, &bInJob);
   if (bInJob) {
      MessageBox(NULL, TEXT("Process already in a job"),
         TEXT(""), MB_ICONINFORMATION | MB_OK);
      return;
   }
```

```
// Create a job kernel object.
HANDLE hjob = CreateJobObject(NULL,
   TEXT("Wintellect_RestrictedProcessJob"));

// Place some restrictions on processes in the job.

// First, set some basic restrictions.
JOBOBJECT_BASIC_LIMIT_INFORMATION jobli = { 0 };

// The process always runs in the idle priority class.
jobli.PriorityClass = IDLE_PRIORITY_CLASS;

// The job cannot use more than 1 second of CPU time.
jobli.PerJobUserTimeLimit.QuadPart = 10000; // 1 sec in 100-ns intervals

// These are the only 2 restrictions I want placed on the job (process).
jobli.LimitFlags = JOB_OBJECT_LIMIT_PRIORITY_CLASS
   | JOB_OBJECT_LIMIT_JOB_TIME;
SetInformationJobObject(hjob, JobObjectBasicLimitInformation, &jobli,
   sizeof(jobli));

// Second, set some UI restrictions.
JOBOBJECT_BASIC_UI_RESTRICTIONS jobuir;
jobuir.UIRestrictionsClass = JOB_OBJECT_UILIMIT_NONE;    // A fancy zero

// The process can't log off the system.
jobuir.UIRestrictionsClass |= JOB_OBJECT_UILIMIT_EXITWINDOWS;

// The process can't access USER objects (such as other windows)
// in the system.
jobuir.UIRestrictionsClass |= JOB_OBJECT_UILIMIT_HANDLES;

SetInformationJobObject(hjob, JobObjectBasicUIRestrictions, &jobuir,
   sizeof(jobuir));

// Spawn the process that is to be in the job.
// Note: You must first spawn the process and then place the process in
//       the job. This means that the process' thread must be initially
//       suspended so that it can't execute any code outside of the job's
//       restrictions.
STARTUPINFO si = { sizeof(si) };
PROCESS_INFORMATION pi;
TCHAR szCmdLine[8];
_tcscpy_s(szCmdLine, _countof(szCmdLine), TEXT("CMD"));
BOOL bResult =
   CreateProcess(
      NULL, szCmdLine, NULL, NULL, FALSE,
      CREATE_SUSPENDED | CREATE_NEW_CONSOLE, NULL, NULL, &si, &pi);
// Place the process in the job.
// Note: If this process spawns any children, the children are
//       automatically part of the same job.
AssignProcessToJobObject(hjob, pi.hProcess);
```

```
    // Now we can allow the child process' thread to execute code.
    ResumeThread(pi.hThread);
    CloseHandle(pi.hThread);

    // Wait for the process to terminate or
    // for all the job's allotted CPU time to be used.
    HANDLE h[2];
    h[0] = pi.hProcess;
    h[1] = hjob;
    DWORD dw = WaitForMultipleObjects(2, h, FALSE, INFINITE);
    switch (dw - WAIT_OBJECT_0) {
        case 0:
            // The process has terminated...
            break;
        case 1:
            // All of the job's allotted CPU time was used...
            break;
    }

    FILETIME CreationTime;
    FILETIME ExitTime;
    FILETIME KernelTime;
    FILETIME UserTime;
    TCHAR szInfo[MAX_PATH];
    GetProcessTimes(pi.hProcess, &CreationTime, &ExitTime,
        &KernelTime, &UserTime);
    StringCchPrintf(szInfo, _countof(szInfo), TEXT("Kernel = %u  |  User = %u\n"),
        KernelTime.dwLowDateTime / 10000, UserTime.dwLowDateTime / 10000);
    MessageBox(GetActiveWindow(), szInfo, TEXT("Restricted Process times"),
        MB_ICONINFORMATION | MB_OK);

    // Clean up properly.
    CloseHandle(pi.hProcess);
    CloseHandle(hjob);
}
```

Now, let me explain how **StartRestrictedProcess** works. Before anything else, I first check whether or not the current process is running under the control of an existing job by passing **NULL** as the second parameter to the following function:

```
BOOL IsProcessInJob(
    HANDLE hProcess,
    HANDLE hJob,
    PBOOL pbInJob);
```

If the process is already associated with a job, there is no way to move away from it: both for the current process or any other spawn process. This is a security feature to ensure that you can't escape from the restrictions set for you.

> **Caution**   By default, when you start an application through Windows Explorer, the process gets automatically associated to a dedicated job, whose name is prefixed by the "PCA" string. As you will see in "Job Notifications" on page 140, it is possible to receive a notification when a process in a job exits. So, when a legacy application started by Windows Explorer appears to fail, the Program Compatibility Assistant is triggered.
>
> If your application needs to create a job like the Job Lab program presented at the end of this chapter, you are out of luck because this creation will fail because of the "PCA"-prefixed job object that is already associated with your process.
>
> This feature is provided by Windows Vista only to detect compatibility issues. So, if you have defined a manifest for your application as explained in Chapter 4, "Processes," Windows Explorer won't attach your process to the "PCA"-prefixed job, assuming that you have already fixed any possible compatibility problem.
>
> However, when you need to debug your application, if the debugger has been started from Windows Explorer, even with a manifest, your application will inherit the "PCA"-prefixed job from the debugger. One easy solution is to start the debugger from a command shell instead of from Windows Explorer. In that case, the job association does not occur.

Then I create a new job kernel object by calling the following:

```
HANDLE CreateJobObject(
   PSECURITY_ATTRIBUTES psa,
   PCTSTR pszName);
```

Like all kernel objects, the first parameter associates security information with the new job object and tells the system whether you want the returned handle to be inheritable. The last parameter names the job object so that it can be accessed by another process via the **OpenJobObject** function shown later in the chapter.

```
HANDLE OpenJobObject(
   DWORD dwDesiredAccess,
   BOOL bInheritHandle,
   PCTSTR pszName);
```

As always, if you know that you will no longer access the job object in your code, you must close its handle by calling **CloseHandle**. You can see this at the end of my **StartRestrictedProcess** function. Be aware that closing a job object does not force all the processes in the job to be terminated. The job object is actually marked for deletion and is destroyed automatically only after all the processes within the job have been terminated.

Note that closing the job's handle causes the job to be inaccessible to all processes even though the job still exists, as shown in the following code:

```
// Create a named job object.
HANDLE hJob = CreateJobObject(NULL, TEXT("Jeff"));

// Put our own process in the job.
AssignProcessToJobObject(hJob, GetCurrentProcess());
```

```
// Closing the job does not kill our process or the job.
// But the name ("Jeff") is immediately disassociated with the job.
CloseHandle(hJob);

// Try to open the existing job.
hJob = OpenJobObject(JOB_OBJECT_ALL_ACCESS, FALSE, TEXT("Jeff"));
// OpenJobObject fails and returns NULL here because the name ("Jeff")
// was disassociated from the job when CloseHandle was called.
// There is no way to get a handle to this job now.
```

Placing Restrictions on a Job's Processes

After creating a job, you will typically want to set up the sandbox (set restrictions) on what processes within the job can do. You can place several different types of restrictions on a job:

- The basic limit and extended basic limit prevent processes within a job from monopolizing the system's resources.
- Basic UI restrictions prevent processes within a job from altering the user interface.
- Security limits prevent processes within a job from accessing secure resources (files, registry subkeys, and so on).

You place restrictions on a job by calling the following:

```
BOOL SetInformationJobObject(
   HANDLE hJob,
   JOBOBJECTINFOCLASS JobObjectInformationClass,
   PVOID pJobObjectInformation,
   DWORD cbJobObjectInformationSize);
```

The first parameter identifies the job you want to restrict. The second parameter is an enumerated type and indicates the type of restriction you want to apply. The third parameter is the address of a data structure containing the restriction settings, and the fourth parameter indicates the size of this structure (used for versioning). Table 5-1 summarizes how to set restrictions.

Table 5-1 Restriction Types

Limit Type	Value of Second Parameter	Structure of Third Parameter
Basic limit	JobObjectBasicLimit-Information	JOBOBJECT_BASIC_LIMIT_INFORMATION
Extended basic limit	JobObjectExtendedLimit-Information	JOBOBJECT_EXTENDED_LIMIT_INFORMATION
Basic UI restrictions	JobObjectBasicUI-Restrictions	JOBOBJECT_BASIC_UI_RESTRICTIONS
Security limit	JobObjectSecurityLimit-Information	JOBOBJECT_SECURITY_LIMIT_INFORMATION

In my **StartRestrictedProcess** function, I set only some basic restrictions on the job. I allocated a **JOBOBJECT_BASIC_LIMIT_INFORMATION** structure, initialized it, and then called

SetInformationJobObject. A **JOBOBJECT_BASIC_LIMIT_INFORMATION** structure looks like this:

```
typedef struct _JOBOBJECT_BASIC_LIMIT_INFORMATION {
   LARGE_INTEGER PerProcessUserTimeLimit;
   LARGE_INTEGER PerJobUserTimeLimit;
   DWORD         LimitFlags;
   DWORD         MinimumWorkingSetSize;
   DWORD         MaximumWorkingSetSize;
   DWORD         ActiveProcessLimit;
   DWORD_PTR     Affinity;
   DWORD         PriorityClass;
   DWORD         SchedulingClass;
} JOBOBJECT_BASIC_LIMIT_INFORMATION, *PJOBOBJECT_BASIC_LIMIT_INFORMATION;
```

Table 5-2 briefly describes the members.

I'd like to explain a few things about this structure that I don't think are clear in the Platform SDK documentation. You set bits in the **LimitFlags** member to indicate the restrictions you want applied to the job. For example, in my **StartRestrictedProcess** function, I set the **JOB_OBJECT_LIMIT_PRIORITY_CLASS** and **JOB_OBJECT_LIMIT_JOB_TIME** bits. This means that these are the only two restrictions that I place on the job. I impose no restrictions on CPU affinity, working set size, per-process CPU time, and so on.

As the job runs, it maintains accounting information—such as how much CPU time the processes in the job have used. Each time you set the basic limit using the **JOB_OBJECT_LIMIT_JOB_TIME** flag, the job subtracts the CPU time accounting information for processes that have terminated. This shows you how much CPU time is used by the currently active processes. However, what if you want to change the affinity of the job but not reset the CPU time accounting information? To do this, you have to set a new basic limit using the **JOB_OBJECT_LIMIT_AFFINITY** flag, and you have to leave off the **JOB_OBJECT_LIMIT_JOB_TIME** flag. But by doing this, you tell the job that you no longer want to enforce a CPU time restriction. This is not what you want.

What you want is to change the affinity restriction and keep the existing CPU time restriction; you just don't want the CPU time accounting information for the terminated processes to be subtracted. To solve this problem, use a special flag: **JOB_OBJECT_LIMIT_PRESERVE_JOB_TIME**. This flag and the **JOB_OBJECT_LIMIT_JOB_TIME** flag are mutually exclusive. The **JOB_OBJECT_LIMIT_PRESERVE_JOB_TIME** flag indicates that you want to change the restrictions without subtracting the CPU time accounting information for the terminated processes.

We should also talk about the **JOBOBJECT_BASIC_LIMIT_INFORMATION** structure's **SchedulingClass** member. Imagine that you have two jobs running and you set the priority class of both jobs to **NORMAL_PRIORITY_CLASS**. But you also want processes in one job to get more CPU time than processes in the other job. You can use the **SchedulingClass** member to change the relative scheduling of jobs that have the same priority class. You can set a value between 0 and 9, inclusive; 5 is the default. On Windows Vista, a higher value tells the system to give a longer time quantum to threads in processes in a particular job; a lower value reduces the threads' time quantum.

Table 5-2 JOBOBJECT_BASIC_LIMIT_INFORMATION Members

Member	Description	Notes
PerProcess-UserTimeLimit	Specifies the maximum user mode time allotted to each process (in 100-nanosecond intervals).	The system automatically terminates any process that uses more than its allotted time. To set this limit, specify the **JOB_OBJECT_LIMIT_PROCESS_TIME** flag in the **LimitFlags** member.
PerJobUser-TimeLimit	Specifies how much more user mode time the processes in this job can use (in 100-nanosecond intervals).	By default, the system automatically terminates all processes when this time limit is reached. You can change this value periodically as the job runs. To set this limit, specify the **JOB_OBJECT_LIMIT_JOB_TIME** flag in the **LimitFlags** member.
LimitFlags	Indicates which restrictions to apply to the job.	See the section that follows this table for more information.
MinimumWork-ingSetSize **MaximumWork-ingSetSize**	Specifies the minimum and maximum working set size for each process (not for all processes within the job).	Normally, a process' working set can grow above its maximum; setting **MaximumWorkingSetSize** forces a hard limit. Once the process' working set reaches this limit, the process pages against itself. Calls to **SetProcessWorkingSetSize** by an individual process are ignored unless the process is just trying to empty its working set. To set this limit, specify the **JOB_OBJECT_LIMIT_WORK-INGSET** flag in the **LimitFlags** member.
ActiveProcess-Limit	Specifies the maximum number of processes that can run concurrently in the job.	Any attempt to go over this limit causes the new process to be terminated with a "not enough quota" error. To set this limit, specify the **JOB_OBJECT_LIMIT_ACTIVE_PROCESS** flag in the **LimitFlags** member.
Affinity	Specifies the subset of the CPU(s) that can run the processes.	Individual processes can limit this even further. To set this limit, specify the **JOB_OBJECT_LIMIT_AFFINITY** flag in the **LimitFlags** member.
PriorityClass	Specifies the priority class used by all processes.	If a process calls **SetPriorityClass**, the call returns successfully even though it actually fails. If the process calls **GetPriorityClass**, the function returns what the process has set the priority class to even though this might not be the process' actual priority class. In addition, **SetThreadPriority** fails to raise threads above normal priority but can be used to lower a thread's priority. To set this limit, specify the **JOB_OBJECT_LIMIT_PRIORITY_CLASS** flag in the **LimitFlags** member.
Scheduling-Class	Specifies a relative time quantum difference assigned to threads in the job.	Value can be from 0 to 9 inclusive; 5 is the default. See the text after this table for more information. To set this limit, specify the **JOB_OBJECT_LIMIT_SCHEDULING_CLASS** flag in the **LimitFlags** member.

For example, let's say that I have two normal priority class jobs. Each job contains one process, and each process has just one (normal priority) thread. Under ordinary circumstances, these two threads would be scheduled in a round-robin fashion and each would get the same time quantum. However, if we set the **SchedulingClass** member of the first job to 3, when threads in this job are scheduled CPU time, their quantum is shorter than for threads that are in the second job.

If you use the **SchedulingClass** member, you should avoid using large numbers and hence larger time quantums because larger time quantums reduce the overall responsiveness of the other jobs, processes, and threads in the system.

One last limit that deserves special mention is the **JOB_OBJECT_LIMIT_DIE_ON_UNHANDLED_ EXCEPTION** limit flag. This limit causes the system to turn off the "unhandled exception" dialog box for each process associated with the job. The system does this by calling the **SetErrorMode** function, passing it the **SEM_NOGPFAULTERRORBOX** flag for each process in the job. A process in a job that raises an unhandled exception is immediately terminated without any user interface being displayed. This is a useful limit flag for services and other batch-oriented jobs. Without it, a process in a job can raise an exception and never terminate, thereby wasting system resources.

In addition to the basic limits, you can set extended limits on a job using the **JOBOBJECT_ EXTENDED_LIMIT_INFORMATION** structure:

```
typedef struct _JOBOBJECT_EXTENDED_LIMIT_INFORMATION {
    JOBOBJECT_BASIC_LIMIT_INFORMATION BasicLimitInformation;
    IO_COUNTERS IoInfo;
    SIZE_T ProcessMemoryLimit;
    SIZE_T JobMemoryLimit;
    SIZE_T PeakProcessMemoryUsed;
    SIZE_T PeakJobMemoryUsed;
} JOBOBJECT_EXTENDED_LIMIT_INFORMATION, *PJOBOBJECT_EXTENDED_LIMIT_INFORMATION;
```

As you can see, this structure contains a **JOBOBJECT_BASIC_LIMIT_INFORMATION** structure, which makes it a superset of the basic limits. This structure is a little strange because it includes members that have nothing to do with setting limits on a job. First, the **IoInfo** member is reserved; you should not access it in any way. I'll discuss how you can query I/O counter information later in the chapter. In addition, the **PeakProcessMemoryUsed** and **PeakJobMemoryUsed** members are read-only and tell you the maximum amount of committed storage that has been required for any one process and for all processes within the job, respectively.

The two remaining members, **ProcessMemoryLimit** and **JobMemoryLimit**, restrict the amount of committed storage used by any one process or by all processes in the job, respectively. To set either of these limits, you specify the **JOB_OBJECT_LIMIT_JOB_MEMORY** and **JOB_OBJECT_LIMIT_ PROCESS_MEMORY** flags in the **LimitFlags** member, respectively.

Now let's turn our attention back to other restrictions that you can place on a job. A **JOBOBJECT_ BASIC_UI_RESTRICTIONS** structure looks like this:

```
typedef struct _JOBOBJECT_BASIC_UI_RESTRICTIONS {
    DWORD UIRestrictionsClass;
} JOBOBJECT_BASIC_UI_RESTRICTIONS, *PJOBOBJECT_BASIC_UI_RESTRICTIONS;
```

This structure has only one data member, **UIRestrictionsClass**, which holds a set of bit flags briefly described in Table 5-3.

Table 5-3   Bit Flags for Basic User-Interface Restrictions for a Job Object

Flag	Description
JOB_OBJECT_UILIMIT_EXITWINDOWS	Prevents processes from logging off, shutting down, rebooting, or powering off the system via the **ExitWindowsEx** function
JOB_OBJECT_UILIMIT_READCLIPBOARD	Prevents processes from reading the Clipboard
JOB_OBJECT_UILIMIT_WRITECLIPBOARD	Prevents processes from erasing the Clipboard
JOB_OBJECT_UILIMIT_SYSTEMPARAMETERS	Prevents processes from changing system parameters via the **SystemParameters-Info** function
JOB_OBJECT_UILIMIT_DISPLAYSETTINGS	Prevents processes from changing the display settings via the **ChangeDisplay-Settings** function
JOB_OBJECT_UILIMIT_GLOBALATOMS	Gives the job its own global atom table, and restricts processes in the job to accessing only the job's table
JOB_OBJECT_UILIMIT_DESKTOP	Prevents processes from creating or switching desktops using the **CreateDesktop** or **SwitchDesktop** function
JOB_OBJECT_UILIMIT_HANDLES	Prevents processes in a job from using **USER** objects (such as **HWNDs**) created by processes outside the same job

The last flag, **JOB_OBJECT_UILIMIT_HANDLES**, is particularly interesting. This restriction means that no processes in the job can access **USER** objects created by processes outside the job. So if you try to run Microsoft Spy++ inside a job, you won't see any windows except the windows that Spy++ itself creates. Figure 5-1 shows Spy++ with two MDI child windows open.

Notice that the Threads 1 window contains a list of threads in the system. Only one of those threads, 00000AA8 SPYXX, seems to have created any windows. This is because I ran Spy++ in its own job and restricted its use of UI handles. In the same window, you can see the **EXPLORER** and **DEVENV** threads, but it appears that they have not created any windows. I assure you that these threads have definitely created windows, but Spy++ cannot access them. On the right side, you see the Windows 1 window, in which Spy++ shows the hierarchy of all windows existing on the desktop. Notice that there is only one entry, 00000000. Spy++ must just put this here as a placeholder.

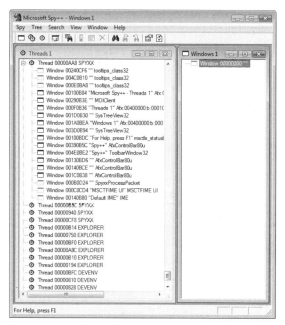

Figure 5-1   Microsoft Spy++ running in a job that restricts access to UI handles

Note that this UI restriction is only one-way. That is, processes outside of a job can see **USER** objects created by processes within a job. For example, if I run Notepad in a job and Spy++ outside of a job, Spy++ can see Notepad's window even if the job that Notepad is in specifies the **JOB_OBJECT_UILIMIT_HANDLES** flag. Also, if Spy++ is in its own job, it can also see Notepad's window unless the job has the **JOB_OBJECT_UILIMIT_HANDLES** flag specified.

The restricting of UI handles is awesome if you want to create a really secure sandbox for your job's processes to play in. However, it is useful to have a process that is part of a job communicate with a process outside of the job.

One easy way to accomplish this is to use window messages. However, if the job's processes can't access UI handles, a process in the job can't send or post a window message to a window created by a process outside the job. Fortunately, you can solve this problem using another function:

```
BOOL UserHandleGrantAccess(
   HANDLE hUserObj,
   HANDLE hJob,
   BOOL bGrant);
```

The **hUserObj** parameter indicates a single **USER** object whose access you want to grant or deny to processes within the job. This is almost always a window handle, but it can be another **USER** object, such as a desktop, hook, icon, or menu. The last two parameters, **hJob** and **bGrant**, indicate which job you are granting or denying access to. Note that this function fails if it is called from a process within the job identified by **hJob**—this prevents a process within a job from simply granting itself access to an object.

The last type of restriction that you place on a job is related to security. (Note that once applied, security restrictions cannot be revoked.) A **JOBOBJECT_SECURITY_LIMIT_INFORMATION** structure looks like this:

```
typedef struct _JOBOBJECT_SECURITY_LIMIT_INFORMATION {
   DWORD SecurityLimitFlags;
   HANDLE JobToken;
   PTOKEN_GROUPS SidsToDisable;
   PTOKEN_PRIVILEGES PrivilegesToDelete;
   PTOKEN_GROUPS RestrictedSids;
} JOBOBJECT_SECURITY_LIMIT_INFORMATION, *PJOBOBJECT_SECURITY_LIMIT_INFORMATION;
```

Table 5-4 briefly describes the members.

Table 5-4 Members of JOBOBJECT_SECURITY_LIMIT_INFORMATION

Member	Description
SecurityLimitFlags	Indicates whether to disallow administrator access, disallow unrestricted token access, force a specific access token, or disable certain security identifiers (SIDs) and privileges
JobToken	Access token to be used by all processes in the job
SidsToDisable	Indicates which SIDs to disable for access checking
PrivilegesToDelete	Indicates which privileges to delete from the access token
RestrictedSids	Indicates a set of deny-only SIDs that should be added to the access token

Naturally, once you have placed restrictions on a job, you might want to query those restrictions. You can do so easily by calling

```
BOOL QueryInformationJobObject(
   HANDLE hJob,
   JOBOBJECTINFOCLASS JobObjectInformationClass,
   PVOID pvJobObjectInformation,
   DWORD cbJobObjectInformationSize,
   PDWORD pdwReturnSize);
```

You pass this function the handle of the job (like you do with **SetInformationJobObject**)—an enumerated type that indicates what restriction information you want, the address of the data structure to be initialized by the function, and the size of the data block containing that structure. The last parameter, **pdwReturnSize**, points to a **DWORD** that is filled in by the function, which tells you how many bytes were placed in the buffer. You can (and usually will) pass **NULL** for this parameter if you don't care.

> **Note** A process in a job can call **QueryInformationJobObject** to obtain information about the job to which it belongs by passing **NULL** for the job handle parameter. This can be very useful because it allows a process to see what restrictions have been placed on it. However, the **SetInformationJobObject** function fails if you pass **NULL** for the job handle parameter because this allows a process to remove restrictions placed on it.

Placing a Process in a Job

OK, that's it for setting and querying restrictions. Now let's get back to my **StartRestricted-Process** function. After I place some restrictions on the job, I spawn the process that I intend to place in the job by calling **CreateProcess**. However, notice that I use the **CREATE_SUSPENDED** flag when calling **CreateProcess**. This creates the new process but doesn't allow it to execute any code. Because the **StartRestrictedProcess** function is being executed from a process that is not part of a job, the child process will also not be part of a job. If I were to allow the child process to immediately start executing code, it would run out of my sandbox and could successfully do things that I want to restrict it from doing. So after I create the child process and before I allow it to start running, I must explicitly place the process in my newly created job by calling the following:

```
BOOL AssignProcessToJobObject(
    HANDLE hJob,
    HANDLE hProcess);
```

This function tells the system to treat the process (identified by **hProcess**) as part of an existing job (identified by **hJob**). Note that this function allows only a process that is not assigned to any job to be assigned to a job, and you can check this by using the already presented **IsProcess-InJob** function. Once a process is part of a job, it cannot be moved to another job and it cannot become jobless (so to speak). Also note that when a process that is part of a job spawns another process, the new process is automatically made part of the parent's job. However, you can alter this behavior in the following ways:

- Turn on the **JOB_OBJECT_LIMIT_BREAKAWAY_OK** flag in **JOBOBJECT_BASIC_LIMIT_INFORMATION**'s **LimitFlags** member to tell the system that a newly spawned process can execute outside the job. To make this happen, you must call **CreateProcess** with the new **CREATE_BREAKAWAY_FROM_JOB** flag. If you call **CreateProcess** with the **CREATE_BREAK-AWAY_FROM_JOB** flag but the job does not have the **JOB_OBJECT_LIMIT_BREAKAWAY_OK** limit flag turned on, **CreateProcess** fails. This mechanism is useful if the newly spawned process also controls jobs.

- Turn on the **JOB_OBJECT_LIMIT_SILENT_BREAKAWAY_OK** flag in the **JOBOBJECT_BASIC_LIMIT_INFORMATION**'s **LimitFlags** member. This flag also tells the system that newly spawned processes should not be part of the job. However, there is no need to pass any additional flags to **CreateProcess**. In fact, this flag forces new processes to not be part of the job. This flag is useful for processes that were originally designed knowing nothing about job objects.

As for my **StartRestrictedProcess** function, after I call **AssignProcessToJobObject**, my new process is part of my restricted job. I then call **ResumeThread** so that the process' thread can execute code under the job's restrictions. At this point, I also close the handle to the thread because I no longer need it.

Terminating All Processes in a Job

Well, certainly one of the most popular things that you will want to do with a job is kill all the processes within it. At the beginning of this chapter, I mentioned that Visual Studio doesn't have an easy way to stop a build that is in progress because it would have to know which processes were spawned from the first process that it spawned. (This is very tricky. I explain how Developer Studio accomplished this in my Win32 Q & A column in the June 1998 issue of Microsoft Systems Journal, readable at *http://www.microsoft.com/msj/0698/win320698.aspx.*) Maybe future versions of Visual Studio will use jobs instead because the code is a lot easier to write and you can do much more with it.

To kill all the processes within a job, you simply call

```
BOOL TerminateJobObject(
   HANDLE hJob,
   UINT uExitCode);
```

This is similar to calling **TerminateProcess** for every process contained within the job, setting all their exit codes to **uExitCode**.

Querying Job Statistics

We've already discussed how to use the **QueryInformationJobObject** function to get the current restrictions on a job. You can also use it to get statistical information about a job. For example, to get basic accounting information, you call **QueryInformationJobObject**, passing **JobObjectBasicAccountingInformation** for the second parameter and the address of a **JOBOBJECT_BASIC_ACCOUNTING_INFORMATION** structure:

```
typedef struct _JOBOBJECT_BASIC_ACCOUNTING_INFORMATION {
   LARGE_INTEGER TotalUserTime;
   LARGE_INTEGER TotalKernelTime;
   LARGE_INTEGER ThisPeriodTotalUserTime;
   LARGE_INTEGER ThisPeriodTotalKernelTime;
   DWORD TotalPageFaultCount;
   DWORD TotalProcesses;
   DWORD ActiveProcesses;
   DWORD TotalTerminatedProcesses;
} JOBOBJECT_BASIC_ACCOUNTING_INFORMATION,
   *PJOBOBJECT_BASIC_ACCOUNTING_INFORMATION;
```

Table 5-5 briefly describes the members.

Table 5-5   Members of the JOBOBJECT_BASIC_ACCOUNTING_INFORMATION Structure

Member	Description
TotalUserTime	Specifies how much user-mode CPU time the processes in the job have used
TotalKernelTime	Specifies how much kernel-mode CPU time the processes in the job have used
ThisPeriodTotalUserTime	Like **TotalUserTime**, except this value is reset to 0 when **SetInformationJobObject** is called to change basic limit information and the **JOB_OBJECT_LIMIT_PRESERVE_JOB_TIME** limit flag is not used
ThisPeriodTotalKernelTime	Like **ThisPeriodTotalUserTime**, except this value shows kernel-mode time
TotalPageFaultCount	Specifies the total number of page faults that processes in the job have accrued

Table 5-5   Members of the JOBOBJECT_BASIC_ACCOUNTING_INFORMATION Structure

Member	Description
TotalProcesses	Specifies the total number of processes that have ever been part of the job
ActiveProcesses	Specifies the number of processes that are currently part of the job
TotalTerminatedProcesses	Specifies the number of processes that have been killed because they have exceeded their allotted CPU time limit

As you can see at the end of the **StartRestrictedProcess** function implementation, it is possible to obtain CPU time consumption information for any process, even if it does not belong to a job, by calling the **GetProcessTimes** function, which will be detailed in Chapter 7, "Thread Scheduling, Priorities, and Affinities."

In addition to querying this basic accounting information, you can make a single call to query both basic accounting and I/O accounting information. To do this, you pass **JobObjectBasicAndIo-AccountingInformation** for the second parameter and the address of a **JOBOBJECT_BASIC_AND_IO_ACCOUNTING_INFORMATION** structure:

```
typedef struct JOBOBJECT_BASIC_AND_IO_ACCOUNTING_INFORMATION {
    JOBOBJECT_BASIC_ACCOUNTING_INFORMATION BasicInfo;
    IO_COUNTERS IoInfo;
} JOBOBJECT_BASIC_AND_IO_ACCOUNTING_INFORMATION,
    *PJOBOBJECT_BASIC_AND_IO_ACCOUNTING_INFORMATION;
```

As you can see, this structure simply returns **JOBOBJECT_BASIC_ACCOUNTING_INFORMATION** and an **IO_COUNTERS** structure:

```
typedef struct _IO_COUNTERS {
    ULONGLONG ReadOperationCount;
    ULONGLONG WriteOperationCount;
    ULONGLONG OtherOperationCount;
    ULONGLONG ReadTransferCount;
    ULONGLONG WriteTransferCount;
    ULONGLONG OtherTransferCount;
} IO_COUNTERS, *PIO_COUNTERS;
```

This structure tells you the number of read, write, and non-read/write operations (as well as total bytes transferred during those operations) that have been performed by processes in the job. By the way, you can use the **GetProcessIoCounters** function to obtain this information for processes that are not in jobs:

```
BOOL GetProcessIoCounters(
    HANDLE hProcess,
    PIO_COUNTERS pIoCounters);
```

You can also call **QueryInformationJobObject** at any time to get the set of process IDs for processes that are currently running in the job. To do this, you must first guess how many processes you expect to see in the job, and then you have to allocate a block of memory large enough to hold an array of these process IDs plus the size of a **JOBOBJECT_BASIC_PROCESS_ID_LIST** structure:

```
typedef struct _JOBOBJECT_BASIC_PROCESS_ID_LIST {
   DWORD NumberOfAssignedProcesses;
   DWORD NumberOfProcessIdsInList;
   DWORD ProcessIdList[1];
} JOBOBJECT_BASIC_PROCESS_ID_LIST, *PJOBOBJECT_BASIC_PROCESS_ID_LIST;
```

So, to get the set of process IDs currently in a job, you must execute code similar to the following:

```
void EnumProcessIdsInJob(HANDLE hjob) {

   // I assume that there will never be more
   // than 10 processes in this job.
   #define MAX_PROCESS_IDS   10

   // Calculate the number of bytes needed for structure & process IDs.
   DWORD cb = sizeof(JOBOBJECT_BASIC_PROCESS_ID_LIST) +
      (MAX_PROCESS_IDS - 1) * sizeof(DWORD);

   // Allocate the block of memory.
   PJOBOBJECT_BASIC_PROCESS_ID_LIST pjobpil =
      (PJOBOBJECT_BASIC_PROCESS_ID_LIST)_alloca(cb);

   // Tell the function the maximum number of processes
   // that we allocated space for.
   pjobpil->NumberOfAssignedProcesses = MAX_PROCESS_IDS;

   // Request the current set of process IDs.
   QueryInformationJobObject(hjob, JobObjectBasicProcessIdList,
      pjobpil, cb, &cb);

   // Enumerate the process IDs.
   for (DWORD x = 0; x < pjobpil->NumberOfProcessIdsInList; x++) {
      // Use pjobpil->ProcessIdList[x]...
   }

   // Since _alloca was used to allocate the memory,
   // we don't need to free it here.
}
```

This is all the information you get using these functions, but the operating system actually keeps a lot more information about jobs. It does this using performance counters; you can retrieve the information using the functions in the Performance Data Helper function library (PDH.dll). You can also use the Reliability and Performance Monitor (from Administrative Tools) to view the job information, but only globally named job objects are visible. However, Process Explorer from Sysinternals (*http://www.microsoft.com/technet/sysinternals/ProcessesAndThreads/ProcessExplorer.mspx*) is a very useful tool when the time comes to consider jobs. By default, processes under the restrictions of jobs are highlighted in brown.

But even better, for such a process, the Job tab of the property dialog box lists the job name if there is any and the restrictions, as shown in Figure 5-2.

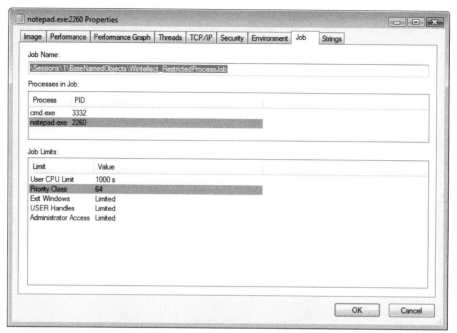

Figure 5-2 Details of the restrictions on the Job tab of Process Explorer

 Warning The only misinterpreted piece of information is the "User CPU Limit" that you should read in milliseconds instead of seconds, as presented, but this should be fixed in a forthcoming update.

Job Notifications

At this point, you certainly know the basics about job objects; the only thing left to cover is notifications. For example, wouldn't you like to know when all the processes in the job terminate or if all the allotted CPU time has expired? Or maybe you'd like to know when a new process is spawned within a job or when a process in the job terminates? If you don't care about these notifications—and many applications won't care—working with jobs is as easy as what I've already described. If you do care about these events, you have a little more to do.

If all you care about is whether all the allotted CPU time has expired, you can easily get this notification. Job objects are nonsignaled while the processes in the job have not used up the allotted CPU time. Once all the allotted CPU time has been used, Windows forcibly kills all the processes in the job and signals the job object. You can easily trap this event by calling **WaitForSingle-Object** (or a similar function). Incidentally, you can reset the job object back to the nonsignaled state later by calling **SetInformationJobObject** and granting the job more CPU time.

When I first started working with jobs, it seemed to me that the job object should be signaled when no processes are running within it. After all, process and thread objects are signaled when they stop running; so it seemed that a job should be signaled when it stops running. In this way, you could easily determine when a job had run to completion. However, Microsoft chose to signal the job when the allotted time expires because that signals an error condition. Because many jobs start with one parent process that hangs around until all its children are done, you can simply wait on the parent process' handle to know when the entire job is finished. My **StartRestrictedProcess** function shows how to determine when the job's allotted time has expired or when the parent process in the job has terminated.

Well, I've described how to get some simple notifications, but I haven't explained what you need to do to get more "advanced" notifications such as process creation/termination. If you want these additional notifications, you must put a lot more infrastructure into your application. In particular, you must create an I/O completion port kernel object and associate your job object or objects with the completion port. Then you must have one or more threads that wait on the completion port for job notifications to arrive so that they can be processed.

Once you create the I/O completion port, you associate a job with it by calling **SetInformation-JobObject**, as follows:

```
JOBOBJECT_ASSOCIATE_COMPLETION_PORT joacp;
joacp.CompletionKey  = 1;    // Any value to uniquely identify this job
joacp.CompletionPort = hIOCP;   // Handle of completion port that
                                // receives notifications
SetInformationJobObject(hJob, JobObjectAssociateCompletionPortInformation,
   &joacp,  sizeof(jaocp));
```

After the preceding code executes, the system monitors the job, and as events occur it posts them to the I/O completion port. (By the way, you can call **QueryInformationJobObject** to retrieve the completion key and completion port handle, but it is rare that you ever have to do this.) Threads usually monitor an I/O completion port by calling **GetQueuedCompletionStatus**:

```
BOOL GetQueuedCompletionStatus(
   HANDLE hIOCP,
   PDWORD pNumBytesTransferred,
   PULONG_PTR pCompletionKey,
   POVERLAPPED *pOverlapped,
   DWORD dwMilliseconds);
```

When this function returns a job event notification, **pCompletionKey** contains the completion key value set when **SetInformationJobObject** was called to associate the job with the completion port. This lets you know which job had an event. The value in **pNumBytesTransferred** indicates which event occurred. (See Table 5-6.) Depending on the event, instead of being an address, the value in **pOverlapped** will indicate a process ID.

Table 5-6   Job Event Notifications That the System Can Send to a Job's Associated Completion Port

Event	Description
JOB_OBJECT_MSG_ACTIVE_PROCESS_ZERO	Posted when no processes are running in the job.
JOB_OBJECT_MSG_END_OF_PROCESS_TIME	Posted when a process' allotted CPU time is exceeded. The process is terminated, and the process' ID is given.
JOB_OBJECT_MSG_ACTIVE_PROCESS_LIMIT	Posted when attempting to exceed the number of active processes in the job.
JOB_OBJECT_MSG_PROCESS_MEMORY_LIMIT	Posted when a process attempts to commit storage over the process' limit. The process' ID is given.
JOB_OBJECT_MSG_JOB_MEMORY_LIMIT	Posted when a process attempts to commit storage over the job's limit. The process' ID is given.
JOB_OBJECT_MSG_NEW_PROCESS	Posted when a process is added to a job. The process' ID is given.
JOB_OBJECT_MSG_EXIT_PROCESS	Posted when a process terminates. The process' ID is given.
JOB_OBJECT_MSG_ABNORMAL_EXIT_PROCESS	Posted when a process terminates because of an unhandled exception. The process' ID is given.
JOB_OBJECT_MSG_END_OF_JOB_TIME	Posted when the job's allotted CPU time is exceeded. The processes are not terminated. You can allow them to continue running, set a new time limit, or call **TerminateJobObject** yourself.

Just one last note: by default, a job object is configured so that when the job's allotted CPU time expires, all the job's processes are automatically terminated and the **JOB_OBJECT_MSG_END_OF_JOB_TIME** notification does not get posted. If you want to prevent the job object from killing the processes and instead just notify you that the time has been exceeded, you must execute code like this:

```
// Create a JOBOBJECT_END_OF_JOB_TIME_INFORMATION structure
// and initialize its only member.
JOBOBJECT_END_OF_JOB_TIME_INFORMATION joeojti;
joeojti.EndOfJobTimeAction = JOB_OBJECT_POST_AT_END_OF_JOB;

// Tell the job object what we want it to do when the job time is
// exceeded.
SetInformationJobObject(hJob, JobObjectEndOfJobTimeInformation,
   &joeojti, sizeof(joeojti));
```

The only other value you can specify for an end-of-job-time action is **JOB_OBJECT_TERMINATE_AT_END_OF_JOB**, which is the default when jobs are created anyway.

The Job Lab Sample Application

The Job Lab application, 05-JobLab.exe, allows you to easily experiment with jobs. The source code and resource files for the application are in the 05-JobLab directory on the companion content Web page. When you start the program, the window shown in Figure 5-3 appears.

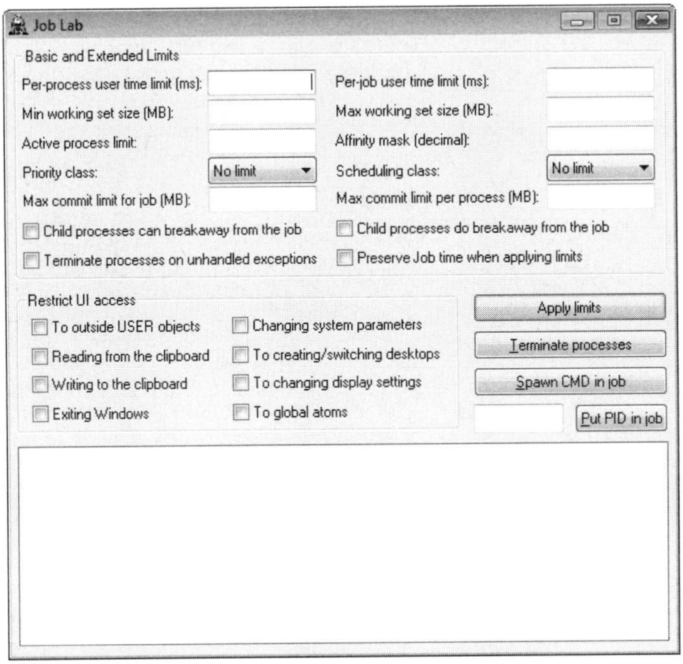

Figure 5-3   Job Lab sample application

When the process initializes, it creates a job object. I created this job object with the name JobLab so that you can use the MMC Performance Monitor Snap-in to see it and monitor its performance. The application also creates an I/O completion port and associates the job object with it. This allows notifications from the job to be monitored and displayed in the list box at the bottom of the window.

Initially, the job has no processes and no limits or restrictions. The fields at the top set basic and extended limits on the job object. All you do is fill them in with valid values and click the Apply Limits button. If you leave a field empty, that limit will not be applied. Besides the basic and extended limits, you can turn various UI restrictions on and off. Note that the Preserve Job Time When Applying Limits check box does not set a limit; it simply allows you to change the job's limits without resetting the **ThisPeriodTotalUserTime** and **ThisPeriodTotalKernelTime** members when querying the basic accounting information. This check box is disabled when you apply a per-job time limit.The remaining buttons let you manipulate the job in other ways. The Terminate Processes button kills all the processes in the job. The Spawn CMD In Job button spawns a command shell process that is associated with the job. From this command shell, you can spawn additional child processes and see how they behave as part of the job. I found this very useful for experimenting. The last button, Put PID In Job, lets you associate an existing jobless process with the job.

The list box at the bottom of the window shows updated status information about the job. Every 10 seconds, this window shows the basic and I/O accounting information as well as the peak process/job memory usage. The process ID and full pathname for each process currently in the job are also shown.

> **Caution**   Notice how you could be tempted to take advantage of functions from psapi.h, such as **GetModuleFileNameEx** and **GetProcessImageFileName**, to obtain the full pathname of a process given its process ID. However, the former fails when the job is notified that a new process is created under its constraints because the address space is not fully initialized: the modules are not yet mapped into it. The case of **GetProcessImageFileName** is interesting because it is able to retrieve the full pathname in that extreme condition, but the obtained syntax is closer to what you see in kernel mode rather than in user mode—for example, \Device\HarddiskVolume1\Windows\System32\notepad.exe instead of C:\Windows\System32\notepad.exe. This is why you should rely on the new **QueryFull-ProcessImageName** function, which returns the expected full pathname in all situations.

In addition to all this statistical information, the list box displays any notifications that come from the job to the application's I/O completion port. Whenever a notification is posted to the list box, the status information at that time is also displayed.

One last note: if you modify the source code and create the job kernel object without a name, you can run multiple copies of this application to create two or more job objects on the same machine and perform more experiments that way.

As far as the source code goes, there isn't anything special to discuss because the source code is well annotated. I did, however, create a Job.h file that defines a CJob C++ class that encapsulates the operating system's job object. This made things a little easier to work with because I didn't have to pass around the job's handle. This class also reduces the amount of casting that I would ordinarily need to do when calling the **QueryInformationJobObject** and **SetInformationJobObject** functions.

Chapter 6
Thread Basics

It is critical that you understand threads because every process requires at least one thread. In this chapter, I'll go into much more detail about threads. In particular, I'll explain how processes and threads differ and what responsibility each has. I'll also explain how the system uses thread kernel objects to manage the threads. Like process kernel objects, thread kernel objects have properties, and we'll examine many of the functions that are available for querying and changing these properties. I'll also examine the functions you can use to create or spawn additional threads in a process.

In Chapter 4, "Processes," we discussed how a process actually consists of two components: a process kernel object and an address space. Similarly, a thread consists of two components:

- A kernel object that the operating system uses to manage the thread. The kernel object is also where the system keeps statistical information about the thread.

- A thread stack that maintains all the function parameters and local variables required as the thread executes code. (In Chapter 16, "A Thread's Stack," I'll go into detail about how the system manages a thread's stack.)

I said in Chapter 4 that processes are inert. A process never executes anything; it is simply a container for threads. Threads are always created in the context of some process and live their entire life within that process. What this really means is that the thread executes code and manipulates data within its process' address space. So if you have two or more threads running in the context of a single process, the threads share a single address space. The threads can execute the same code and manipulate the same data. Threads can also share kernel object handles because the handle table exists for each process, not each thread.

As you can see, processes use a lot more system resources than threads do. The reason for this is the address space. Creating a virtual address space for a process requires a lot of system resources. A lot of record keeping takes place in the system, and this requires a lot of memory. Also, because .exe and .dll files get loaded into an address space, file resources are required as well. A thread, on the other hand, uses significantly fewer system resources. In fact, a thread has just a kernel object and a stack; little record keeping is involved, and little memory is required.

Because threads require less overhead than processes, you should always try to solve your programming problems using additional threads and avoid creating new processes. However, don't take this recommendation as law. Many designs are better implemented using multiple processes. You should be aware of the tradeoffs, and experience will guide you.

Before we get into the nitty-gritty details of threads, let's spend a little time discussing how to appropriately use threads in your application's architecture.

When to Create a Thread

A thread describes a path of execution within a process. Every time a process is initialized, the system creates a primary thread. For applications built with the Microsoft C/C++ compiler, this thread begins executing with the C/C++ run-time library's startup code, which in turn calls your entry-point function (**_tmain**, or **_tWinMain**) and continues executing until the entry-point function returns to the C/C++ run-time library's startup code that ends up calling **ExitProcess**. For many applications, this primary thread is the only thread the application requires. However, processes can create additional threads to help them do their work.

Every computer has an extremely powerful resource: the CPU. There is absolutely no reason in the world why a CPU should be idle (if you ignore power conservation and possibly heat dissipation issues). To keep the CPU busy, you give it varied tasks to perform. Here are a few examples:

■   Windows Indexing Services in the operating system creates a low-priority thread that periodically wakes up and indexes the contents of the files on certain areas of your disk drives. The Windows indexing service improves performance greatly because each search doesn't have to open, scan, and close every file on your disk drives. By taking advantage of this indexing, Microsoft Windows Vista comes with advanced searching features. You have two ways to locate a file. First, you click the Start button and, as you type in the Search text field at the bottom, the list on the left displays both the programs and the files or folders that fit the currently typed text based on the index, as shown next.

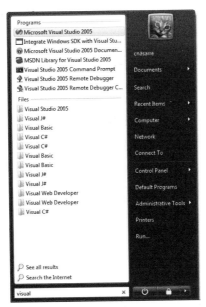

Second, you invoke the Search window (by right-clicking the Start button and then selecting Search from the context menu) and enter your search criteria in the Search text field. The index is searched only if Indexed Locations is selected in the Location combo box (which is the default) as shown here.

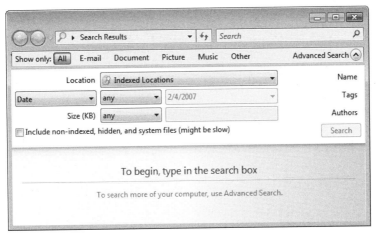

- You can use the disk defragmenting software that ships with the operating system. Normally, this type of utility has many administrative options that the average user can't understand, such as how often the utility should run and when. Using lower priority threads, you can run the utility in the background and defragment the drive when the system is otherwise idle.

- The Microsoft Visual Studio IDE automatically compiles your C# and Microsoft Visual Basic .NET source code file whenever you pause typing. In the editor window, the invalid expressions are underlined and you get the corresponding warnings and errors when the cursor is hovered over them.

- Spreadsheet applications can perform recalculations in the background.

- Word processor applications can perform repagination, spelling and grammar checking, and printing in the background.

- Files can be copied to other media in the background.

- Web browsers can communicate with their servers in the background. A user can thus resize the browser's window or go to another Web site before the results from the current Web site have come in.

One important thing that you should notice about many of these examples is that multithreading allows the application's user interface to be simplified. If the compiler builds your application whenever you stop typing, there is no need to offer a Build menu option. The word processor application doesn't need Check Spelling and Check Grammar menu options.

In the Web browser example, notice that using a separate thread for I/O (be it network, file, or other) allows the application's user interface to stay responsive. You can imagine an application that sorts the records of a database, prints a document, or copies files. By using a separate thread for this I/O-bound task, a user can continue to use your application's interface to cancel the operation while in progress.

Designing an application to be multithreaded allows that application to scale. As we'll see in the next chapter, each thread is assigned a CPU. So if you have two CPUs in your computer and two threads in your application, both CPUs will be busy. In effect, you get two tasks done in the time it would take for one.

Every process has at least one thread in it. So if you do nothing special in your application, you already get a lot of benefit just from running on a multithreaded operating system. For example, you can build an application and use the word processor at the same time (something I do a lot). If the computer has two CPUs, the build executes on one processor while the other processor handles a document. In other words, the user notices no degradation in performance and there's no glitch in the user interface as he types. Also, if the compiler has a bug that causes its thread to enter an infinite loop, you can still use other processes. (This is not true of 16-bit Windows and MS-DOS applications.)

When Not to Create a Thread

So far, I've been singing the praises of multithreaded applications. Although there are a lot of great things about multithreaded applications, there are also some not-so-nice things. Some developers believe that the way to solve *any* problem is to divide it into threads. They could not be more wrong!

Threads are incredibly useful and have a place, but when you use threads you can create new problems while trying to solve the old ones. For example, let's say you're developing a word processing application and want to allow the printing function to run as its own thread. This sounds like a good idea because the user can immediately go back and start editing the document while it's printing. But wait—this means that the data in the document might be changed while the document is printing. Maybe it would be best not to have the printing take place in its own thread, but this "solution" seems a bit drastic. How about if you let the user edit another document but lock the printing document so that it can't be modified until the printing has been completed? Or here's a third idea: copy the document to a temporary file, print the contents of the temporary file, and let the user modify the original. When the temporary file containing the document has finished printing, delete the temporary file.

As you can see, threads can solve some problems while creating new ones. Another common misuse of threads can arise during the development of an application's user interface. In almost all applications, all the user interface components (windows) should share the same thread. A single thread should definitely create all of a window's child windows. Sometimes creating different windows on different threads is useful, but these occasions are rare indeed.

Usually, an application has one user interface thread that creates all windows and has a **Get-Message** loop. Any other threads in the process are worker threads that are compute-bound or I/O-bound—these threads never create windows. Also, the one user interface thread usually has a higher priority than the worker threads, so the user interface is responsive to the user.

Although it is unusual for a single process to have multiple user interface threads, there are some valid uses for this. Windows Explorer creates a separate thread for each folder's window. This allows you to copy files from one folder to another and still explore other folders on your system. Also, if Windows Explorer has a bug in it, the thread handling one folder might crash, but you can still manipulate other folders—at least until you do the thing that causes the other folder to crash too.

The moral of this story is that you should use multiple threads judiciously. Don't use them just because you can. You can still write many useful and powerful applications using nothing more than the primary thread assigned to the process.

Writing Your First Thread Function

Every thread must have an entry-point function where it begins execution. We already discussed this entry-point function for your primary thread: **_tmain** or **_tWinMain**. If you want to create a secondary thread in your process, it must also have an entry-point function, which should look something like this:

```
DWORD WINAPI ThreadFunc(PVOID pvParam){
   DWORD dwResult = 0;
   ...
   return(dwResult);
}
```

Your thread function can perform any task you want it to. Ultimately, your thread function will come to an end and return. At this point, your thread stops running, the memory for its stack is freed, and the usage count of your thread's kernel object is decremented. If the usage count becomes **0**, the thread kernel object is destroyed. Like process kernel objects, thread kernel objects always live at least as long as the thread they are associated with, but the object might live well beyond the lifetime of the thread itself.

Let me point out a few things about thread functions:

- Unlike a primary thread's entry-point function, which by default must be named **main**, **wmain**, **WinMain**, or **wWinMain** (except when the **/ENTRY:** linker option is used to select another of your functions as the entry point), a thread function can have any name. In fact, if you have multiple thread functions in your application, you have to give them different names or the compiler/linker will think that you've created multiple implementations for a single function.

- Because your primary thread's entry-point function is passed string parameters, ANSI/Unicode versions of the entry-point functions are available: **main**/**wmain** and **WinMain**/**wWinMain**. Thread functions are passed a single parameter whose meaning is defined by you, not the operating system. Therefore, you do not have to worry about ANSI/Unicode issues.

- Your thread function must return a value, which becomes the thread's exit code. This is analogous to the C/C++ run-time library's policy of making your primary thread's exit code your process' exit code.

- Your thread function (and really all your functions) should try to use function parameters and local variables as much as possible. When you use static and global variables, multiple threads can access the variables at the same time, potentially corrupting the variables' contents. However, parameters and local variables are created on the thread's stack and are therefore far less likely to be corrupted by another thread.

Now that you know how to implement a thread function, let's talk about how to actually get the operating system to create a thread that executes your thread function.

The *CreateThread* Function

We've already discussed how a process' primary thread comes into being when **CreateProcess** is called. If you want to create one or more secondary threads, you simply have an already running thread call **CreateThread**:

```
HANDLE CreateThread(
    PSECURITY_ATTRIBUTES psa,
    DWORD cbStackSize,
    PTHREAD_START_ROUTINE pfnStartAddr,
    PVOID pvParam,
    DWORD dwCreateFlags,
    PDWORD pdwThreadID);
```

When **CreateThread** is called, the system creates a thread kernel object. This thread kernel object is not the thread itself but a small data structure that the operating system uses to manage the thread. You can think of the thread kernel object as a small data structure that consists of statistical information about the thread. This is identical to the way processes and process kernel objects relate to each other.

The system allocates memory out of the process' address space for use by the thread's stack. The new thread runs in the same process context as the creating thread. The new thread therefore has access to all of the process' kernel object handles, all of the memory in the process, and the stacks of all other threads that are in this same process. This makes it really easy for multiple threads in a single process to communicate with each other.

> **Note**   The **CreateThread** function is the Windows function that creates a thread. However, if you are writing C/C++ code, you should never call **CreateThread**. Instead, you should use the Microsoft C++ run-time library function **_beginthreadex**. If you do not use Microsoft's C++ compiler, your compiler vendor will have its own alternative to **Create-Thread**. Whatever this alternative is, you must use it. Later in this chapter, I'll explain what **_beginthreadex** does and why it is so important.

OK, that's the broad overview. The following sections explain each of **CreateThread**'s parameters.

psa

The **psa** parameter is a pointer to a **SECURITY_ATTRIBUTES** structure. You can (and usually will) pass **NULL** if you want the default security attributes for the thread kernel object. If you want any child processes to be able to inherit a handle to this thread object, you must specify a **SECURITY_ATTRIBUTES** structure, whose **bInheritHandle** member is initialized to **TRUE**. See Chapter 3, "Kernel Objects," for more information.

cbStackSize

The **cbStackSize** parameter specifies how much address space the thread can use for its own stack. Every thread owns its own stack. When **CreateProcess** starts a process, it internally calls **CreateThread** to initialize the process' primary thread. For the **cbStackSize** parameter, **CreateProcess** uses a value stored inside the executable file. You can control this value using the linker's **/STACK** switch:

```
/STACK:[reserve] [,commit]
```

The **reserve** argument sets the amount of address space the system should reserve for the thread's stack. The default is 1 MB. The **commit** argument specifies the amount of physical storage that should be initially committed to the stack's reserved region. The default is one page. As the code in your thread executes, you might require more than one page of storage. When your thread overflows its stack, an exception is generated. (See Chapter 16 for more information about a thread's stack and stack overflow exceptions; see Chapter 23, "Termination Handlers," for more information about general exception handling.) The system catches the exception and commits another page (or whatever you specified for the **commit** argument) to the reserved space, which allows a thread's stack to grow dynamically as needed.

When you call **CreateThread**, passing a value other than 0 causes the function to reserve and commit all storage for the thread's stack. Because all the storage is committed up front, the thread is guaranteed to have the specified amount of stack storage available. The amount of reserved space is either the amount specified by the **/STACK** linker switch or the value of **cbStack**, whichever is larger. The amount of storage committed matches the value you passed for **cbStack**. If you pass **0** to the **cbStack** parameter, **CreateThread** reserves a region and commits the amount of storage indicated by the **/STACK** linker switch information embedded in the .exe file by the linker.

The reserve amount sets an upper limit for the stack so that you can catch endless recursion bugs in your code. For example, let's say that you're writing a function that calls itself recursively. This function also has a bug that causes endless recursion. Every time the function calls itself, a new stack frame is created on the stack. If the system didn't set a maximum limit on the stack size, the recursive function would never stop calling itself. All of the process' address space would be allocated, and enormous amounts of physical storage would be committed to the stack. By setting a stack limit, you prevent your application from using up enormous amounts of physical storage, and you also know much sooner when a bug exists in your program. (The Summation sample application on page 457 shows how to trap and handle stack overflows in your application.)

pfnStartAddr and *pvParam*

The **pfnStartAddr** parameter indicates the address of the thread function that you want the new thread to execute. A thread function's **pvParam** parameter is the same as the **pvParam** parameter that you originally passed to **CreateThread**. **CreateThread** does nothing with this parameter except pass it on to the thread function when the thread starts executing. This parameter provides a way to pass an initialization value to the thread function. This initialization data can be either a numeric value or a pointer to a data structure that contains additional information.

It is perfectly legal and actually quite useful to create multiple threads that have the same function address as their starting point. For example, you can implement a Web server that creates a new thread to handle each client's request. Each thread knows which client it is processing because you pass a different **pvParam** value as you create each thread.

Remember that Windows is a preemptive multithreading system, which means that the new thread and the thread that called **CreateThread** can execute simultaneously. Because the threads run simultaneously, problems can occur. Watch out for code like this:

```
DWORD WINAPI FirstThread(PVOID pvParam) {
   // Initialize a stack-based variable
   int x = 0;
   DWORD dwThreadID;

   // Create a new thread.
   HANDLE hThread = CreateThread(NULL, 0, SecondThread, (PVOID) &x,
      0, &dwThreadID);

   // We don't reference the new thread anymore,
   // so close our handle to it.
   CloseHandle(hThread);

   // Our thread is done.
   // BUG: our stack will be destroyed, but
   //      SecondThread might try to access it.
   return(0);
}


DWORD WINAPI SecondThread(PVOID pvParam) {
   // Do some lengthy processing here. ...    //
 Attempt to access the variable on FirstThread's stack.
   // NOTE: This may cause an access violation - it depends on timing!
   * ((int *) pvParam) = 5; ...      return(0);
}
```

In the preceding code, **FirstThread** might finish its work before **SecondThread** assigns **5** to **FirstThread**'s *x*. If this happens, **SecondThread** won't know that **FirstThread** no longer exists and will attempt to change the contents of what is now an invalid address. This causes **SecondThread** to raise an access violation because **FirstThread**'s stack is destroyed when **FirstThread** terminates. One way to solve this problem is to declare *x* as a static variable so that the compiler will create a storage area for *x* in the application's data section rather than on the stack.

However, this makes the function nonreentrant. In other words, you can't create two threads that execute the same function because the static variable would be shared between the two threads. Another way to solve this problem (and its more complex variations) is to use proper thread synchronization techniques (discussed in Chapter 8, "Thread Synchronization in User Mode," and Chapter 9, "Thread Synchronization with Kernel Objects").

dwCreateFlags

The **dwCreateFlags** parameter specifies additional flags that control the creation of the thread. It can be one of two values. If the value is **0**, the thread is schedulable immediately after it is created. If the value is **CREATE_SUSPENDED**, the system fully creates and initializes the thread but suspends the thread so that it is not schedulable.

The **CREATE_SUSPENDED** flag allows an application to alter some properties of a thread before it has a chance to execute any code. Because this is rarely necessary, this flag is not commonly used. The Job Lab application presented on page 143 demonstrates a correct use of this flag with **CreateProcess**.

pdwThreadID

The last parameter of **CreateThread**, **pdwThreadID**, must be a valid address of a **DWORD** in which **CreateThread** stores the ID that the system assigns to the new thread. (Process and thread IDs were discussed in Chapter 4.) You can (and usually do) pass **NULL** for this parameter. This tells the function that you're not interested in the thread's ID.

Terminating a Thread

A thread can be terminated in four ways:

- The thread function returns. (This is highly recommended.)
- The thread kills itself by calling the **ExitThread** function. (Avoid this method.)
- A thread in the same process or in another one calls the **TerminateThread** function. (Avoid this method.)
- The process containing the thread terminates. (Avoid this method.)

This section discusses all four methods for terminating a thread and describes what happens when a thread ends.

The Thread Function Returns

You should always design your thread functions so that they return when you want the thread to terminate. This is the only way to guarantee that all your thread's resources are cleaned up properly.

Having your thread function return ensures the following:

- All C++ objects created in your thread function will be destroyed properly via their destructors.

- The operating system will properly free the memory used by the thread's stack.

- The system will set the thread's exit code (maintained in the thread's kernel object) to your thread function's return value.

- The system will decrement the usage count of the thread's kernel object.

The *ExitThread* Function

You can force your thread to terminate by having it call **ExitThread**:

```
VOID ExitThread(DWORD dwExitCode);
```

This function terminates the thread and causes the operating system to clean up all the operating system resources that were used by the thread. However, your C/C++ resources (such as C++ class objects) will not be destroyed. For this reason, it is much better to simply return from your thread function instead of calling **ExitThread** yourself. (For more information, see "The *ExitProcess* Function" on page 105.)

Of course, you use **ExitThread**'s **dwExitCode** parameter to tell the system what to set the thread's exit code to. The **ExitThread** function does not return a value because the thread has terminated and cannot execute any more code.

> **Note**   The recommended way to have a thread terminate is by having its thread function simply return (as described in the previous section). However, if you use the method described in this section, be aware that the **ExitThread** function is the Windows function that kills a thread. If you are writing C/C++ code, you should never call **ExitThread**. Instead, you should use the C++ run-time library function **_endthreadex**. If you do not use Microsoft's C++ compiler, your compiler vendor will have its own alternative to **ExitThread**. Whatever this alternative is, you must use it. Later in this chapter, I will explain what **_endthreadex** does and why it is so important.

The *TerminateThread* Function

A call to **TerminateThread** also kills a thread:

```
BOOL TerminateThread(
   HANDLE hThread,
   DWORD dwExitCode);
```

Unlike **ExitThread**, which always kills the calling thread, **TerminateThread** can kill any thread. The **hThread** parameter identifies the handle of the thread to be terminated. When the thread terminates, its exit code becomes the value you passed as the **dwExitCode** parameter. Also, the thread's kernel object has its usage count decremented.

> **Note**   The **TerminateThread** function is asynchronous. That is, it tells the system that you want the thread to terminate but the thread is not guaranteed to be killed by the time the function returns. If you need to know for sure that the thread has terminated, you might want to call **WaitForSingleObject** (described in Chapter 9) or a similar function, passing the handle of the thread.

A well-designed application never uses this function because the thread being terminated receives no notification that it is dying. The thread cannot clean up properly, and it cannot prevent itself from being killed.

> **Note**   When a thread dies by returning or calling **ExitThread**, the stack for the thread is destroyed. However, if **TerminateThread** is used, the system does not destroy the thread's stack until the process that owned the thread terminates. Microsoft purposely implemented **TerminateThread** in this way. If other still-executing threads were to reference values on the forcibly killed thread's stack, these other threads would raise access violations. By leaving the killed thread's stack in memory, other threads can continue to execute just fine.
>
> In addition, dynamic-link libraries (DLLs) usually receive notifications when a thread is terminating. If a thread is forcibly killed with **TerminateThread**, however, the DLLs do not receive this notification, which can prevent proper cleanup. (See Chapter 20, "DLL Advanced Techniques," for more information.)

When a Process Terminates

The **ExitProcess** and **TerminateProcess** functions discussed in Chapter 4 also terminate threads. The difference is that these functions terminate all the threads contained in the process being terminated. Also, because the entire process is being shut down, all resources in use by the process are guaranteed to be cleaned up. This certainly includes all thread stacks. These two functions cause the remaining threads in the process to be forcibly killed, as if **TerminateThread** were called for each remaining thread. Obviously, this means that proper application cleanup does not occur: C++ object destructors aren't called, data isn't flushed to disk, and so on. As I explained at the beginning of this chapter, when the application entry point returns, the C/C++ run-time library's startup code calls **ExitProcess**. So, if several threads run concurrently in your application, you need to explicitly handle how each one stops before the main thread returns. Otherwise, all other running threads will die abruptly and silently.

When a Thread Terminates

The following actions occur when a thread terminates:

- All User object handles owned by the thread are freed. In Windows, most objects are owned by the process containing the thread that creates the objects. However, a thread owns two

User objects: windows and hooks. When a thread dies, the system automatically destroys any windows and uninstalls any hooks that were created or installed by the thread. Other objects are destroyed only when the owning process terminates.

- The thread's exit code changes from **STILL_ACTIVE** to the code passed to **ExitThread** or **TerminateThread**.

- The state of the thread kernel object becomes signaled.

- If the thread is the last active thread in the process, the system considers the process terminated as well.

- The thread kernel object's usage count is decremented by 1.

When a thread terminates, its associated thread kernel object doesn't automatically become freed until all the outstanding references to the object are closed.

Once a thread is no longer running, there isn't much any other thread in the system can do with the thread's handle. However, these other threads can call **GetExitCodeThread** to check whether the thread identified by **hThread** has terminated and, if it has, determine its exit code:

```
BOOL GetExitCodeThread(
   HANDLE hThread,
   PDWORD pdwExitCode);
```

The exit code value is returned in the **DWORD** pointed to by **pdwExitCode**. If the thread hasn't terminated when **GetExitCodeThread** is called, the function fills the **DWORD** with the **STILL_ACTIVE** identifier (defined as 0x103). If the function is successful, **TRUE** is returned. (Chapter 9 has more information about using the thread's handle to determine when the thread has terminated.)

Some Thread Internals

So far, I've explained how to implement a thread function and how to have the system create a thread to execute that function. In this section, we'll look at how the system pulls this off.

Figure 6-1 shows what the system must do to create and initialize a thread.

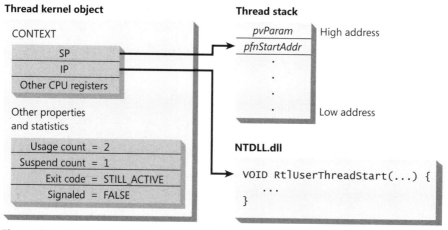

Figure 6-1 How a thread is created and initialized

Let's look closely at this figure to understand exactly what's going on. A call to **CreateThread** causes the system to create a thread kernel object. This object has an initial usage count of **2**. (The thread kernel object is not destroyed until the thread stops running *and* the handle returned from **CreateThread** is closed.) Other properties of the thread's kernel object are also initialized: the suspension count is set to **1**, the exit code is set to **STILL_ACTIVE** (0x103), and the object is set to the nonsignaled state.

Once the kernel object has been created, the system allocates memory, which is used for the thread's stack. This memory is allocated from the process' address space because threads don't have an address space of their own. The system then writes two values to the upper end of the new thread's stack. (Thread stacks always build from high memory addresses to low memory addresses.) The first value written to the stack is the value of the **pvParam** parameter that you passed to **CreateThread**. Immediately below it is the **pfnStartAddr** value that you also passed to **CreateThread**.

Each thread has its own set of CPU registers, called the thread's *context*. The context reflects the state of the thread's CPU registers when the thread last executed. The set of CPU registers for the thread is saved in a **CONTEXT** structure (defined in the WinNT.h header file). The **CONTEXT** structure is itself contained in the thread's kernel object.

The instruction pointer and stack pointer registers are the two most important registers in the thread's context. Remember that threads always run in the context of a process. So both these addresses identify memory in the owning process' address space. When the thread's kernel object is initialized, the **CONTEXT** structure's stack pointer register is set to the address of where **pfnStartAddr** was placed on the thread's stack. The instruction pointer register is set to the address of an undocumented function called **RtlUserThreadStart**, which is exported by the NTDLL.dll module. Figure 6-1 shows all of this.

Here is what **RtlUserThreadStart** basically does:

```
VOID RtlUserThreadStart(PTHREAD_START_ROUTINE pfnStartAddr, PVOID pvParam) {
    __try {
        ExitThread((pfnStartAddr)(pvParam));
    }
    __except(UnhandledExceptionFilter(GetExceptionInformation())) {
        ExitProcess(GetExceptionCode());
    }
    // NOTE: We never get here.
}
```

After the thread has completely initialized, the system checks to see whether the **CREATE_SUSPENDED** flag was passed to **CreateThread**. If this flag was not passed, the system decrements the thread's suspend count to **0** and the thread can be scheduled to a processor. The system then loads the actual CPU registers with the values that were last saved in the thread's context. The thread can now execute code and manipulate data in its process' address space.

Because a new thread's instruction pointer is set to **RtlUserThreadStart**, this function is really where the thread begins execution. **RtlUserThreadStart**'s prototype makes you think that the function receives two parameters, but this implies that the function is called from another function, which is not true. The new thread simply comes into existence and starts executing here. **Rtl-UserThreadStart** believes that it was called from another function because it has access to two parameters. But access to these parameters works because the operating system explicitly wrote the values to the thread's stack (which is how parameters are normally passed to a function). Note that some CPU architectures pass parameters using CPU registers instead of the stack. For these architectures, the system initializes the proper registers correctly before allowing the thread to execute the **RtlUserThreadStart** function.

When the new thread executes the **RtlUserThreadStart** function, the following things happen:

■ A structured exception handling (SEH) frame is set up around your thread function so that any exceptions raised while your thread executes get some default handling by the system. (See Chapter 23, "Termination Handlers," Chapter 24, "Exception Handlers and Software Exceptions," and Chapter 25, "Unhandled Exceptions, Vectored Exception Handling, and C++ Exceptions," for more information about structured exception handling.)

■ The system calls your thread function, passing it the **pvParam** parameter that you passed to the **CreateThread** function.

■ When your thread function returns, **RtlUserThreadStart** calls **ExitThread**, passing it your thread function's return value. The thread kernel object's usage count is decremented and the thread stops executing.

■ If your thread raises an exception that is not handled, the SEH frame set up by the **RtlUser-ThreadStart** function handles the exception. Usually, this means that a message box is presented to the user and that when the user dismisses the message box, **RtlUserThreadStart** calls **ExitProcess** to terminate the entire process, not just the offending thread.

Notice that within **RtlUserThreadStart**, the thread calls either **ExitThread** or **ExitProcess**. This means that the thread cannot ever exit this function; it always dies inside it. This is why **Rtl-UserThreadStart** is prototyped as returning **VOID**—it never returns.

Also, your thread function can return when it's done processing because of **RtlUserThread-Start**. When **RtlUserThreadStart** calls your thread function, it pushes its return address on the stack so that your thread function knows where to return. But **RtlUserThreadStart** is not allowed to return. If it didn't forcibly kill the thread and simply tried to return, an access violation would almost definitely be raised because there is no function return address on the thread's stack and **RtlUserThreadStart** would try to return to some random memory location.

When a process' primary thread is initialized, its instruction pointer is set to the same undocumented function, **RtlUserThreadStart**.

When **RtlUserThreadStart** begins executing, it calls the C/C++ run-time library's startup code, which initializes and then calls your **_tmain** or **_tWinMain** function. When your entry-point function returns, the C/C++ run-time library startup code calls **ExitProcess**. So for a C/C++ application, the primary thread never returns to the **RtlUserThreadStart** function.

C/C++ Run-Time Library Considerations

Four native C/C++ run-time libraries and two targeting the managed world of Microsoft .NET ship with Visual Studio. Notice that all these libraries support multithreaded development: there is no longer a C/C++ library specifically designed to target only single-threaded development. Table 6-1 describes the libraries.

Table 6-1   C/C++ Libraries that Ship with Microsoft Visual Studio

Library Name	Description
LibCMt.lib	Statically linked release version of the library.
LibCMtD.lib	Statically linked debug version of the library.
MSVCRt.lib	Import library for dynamically linking the release version of the MSVCR80.dll library. (This is the default library when you create a new project.)
MSVCRtD.lib	Import library for dynamically linking the debug version of the MSVCR80D.dll library.
MSVCMRt.lib	Import library used for mixed managed/native code.
MSVCURt.lib	Import library compiled as 100-percent pure MSIL code.

When you implement any type of project, you must know which library you're linking your project with. You select a library using the project properties dialog box, shown below. On the Configuration Properties, C/C++, Code Generation tab, in the Runtime Library category, select one of the four available options from the Use Run-Time Library combo box.

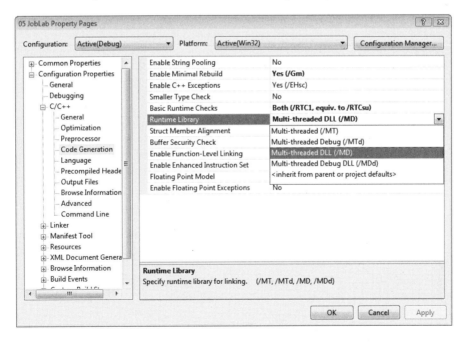

Let's go back for a second to the ancient time when there was one library for single-threaded applications and another library for multithreaded applications. The reason this setup existed is that the standard C run-time library was invented around 1970, long before threads were available on any operating system. The inventors of the library didn't consider the problems of using the C run-time library with multithreaded applications. Let's take an example that shows you in which kind of details the devil could hide.

Consider the standard C run-time global variable **errno**. Some functions set this variable when an error occurs. Let's say you have the following code fragment:

```
BOOL fFailure = (system("NOTEPAD.EXE README.TXT") == -1);

if (fFailure) {
   switch (errno) {
   case E2BIG:   // Argument list or environment too big
      break;
   case ENOENT:  // Command interpreter cannot be found
      break;
   case ENOEXEC: // Command interpreter has bad format
      break;
   case ENOMEM:  // Insufficient memory to run command
      break;
   }
}
```

Now let's say that the thread executing the code just shown is interrupted after the call to the **system** function and before the **if** statement. And imagine that the thread is being interrupted to allow a second thread in the same process to execute and that this new thread will execute another C run-time function that sets the global variable **errno**. When the CPU is later assigned back to the first thread, the value of **errno** no longer reflects the proper error code for the call to **system** in the preceding code. To solve this problem, each thread requires its own **errno** variable. In addition, there must be some mechanism that allows a thread to reference its own **errno** variable but not touch another thread's **errno** variable.

This is only one example of how the standard C/C++ run-time library was not originally designed for multithreaded applications. The C/C++ run-time library variables and functions that have problems in multithreaded environments include **errno**, **_doserrno**, **strtok**, **_wcstok**, **strerror**, **_strerror**, **tmpnam**, **tmpfile**, **asctime**, **_wasctime**, **gmtime**, **_ecvt**, and **_fcvt**—to name just a few.

For multithreaded C and C++ programs to work properly, a data structure must be created and associated with each thread that uses C/C++ run-time library functions. Then, when you make C/C++ run-time library calls, those functions must know to look in the calling thread's data block so that no other thread is adversely affected.

So how does the system know to allocate this data block when a new thread is created? The answer is that it doesn't. The system has no idea that your application is written in C/C++ and that you are calling functions that are not natively thread-safe. The onus is on you to do everything correctly. To create a new thread, you must not call the operating system's **CreateThread** function—you must call the C/C++ run-time library function **_beginthreadex**:

```
unsigned long _beginthreadex(
   void *security,
   unsigned stack_size,
   unsigned (*start_address)(void *),
   void *arglist,
   unsigned initflag,
   unsigned *thrdaddr);
```

The **_beginthreadex** function has the same parameter list as the **CreateThread** function, but the parameter names and types are not exactly the same. This is because Microsoft's C/C++ run-time library group believes that C/C++ run-time library functions should not have any dependencies on Windows data types. The **_beginthreadex** function also returns the handle of the newly created thread, just like **CreateThread** does. So, if you've been calling **CreateThread** in your source code, it is fairly easy to globally replace all these calls with calls to **_beginthreadex**. However, because the data types are not quite the same, you might have to perform some casting to make the compiler happy. To make things easier, I've created a macro, **chBEGINTHREADEX**, to use in my source code:

```
typedef unsigned (__stdcall *PTHREAD_START) (void *);

#define chBEGINTHREADEX(psa, cbStack, pfnStartAddr, \
   pvParam, fdwCreate, pdwThreadID)                 \
      ((HANDLE) _beginthreadex(                      \
         (void *) (psa),                             \
         (unsigned) (cbStackSize),                   \
         (PTHREAD_START) (pfnStartAddr),             \
         (void *) (pvParam),                         \
         (unsigned) (dwCreateFlags),                 \
         (unsigned *) (pdwThreadID)))
```

Because Microsoft ships the source code to the C/C++ run-time library, it's easy to determine exactly what **_beginthreadex** does that **CreateThread** doesn't do. In fact, I searched the Visual Studio installation folders and found the source code for **_beginthreadex** in <Program Files>\ Microsoft Visual Studio 8\VC\crt\src\Threadex.c. Rather than reprint the source code for it here, I'll give you a pseudocode version of it and highlight the interesting points:

```
uintptr_t __cdecl _beginthreadex (
   void *psa,
   unsigned cbStackSize,
   unsigned (__stdcall * pfnStartAddr) (void *),
   void * pvParam,
   unsigned dwCreateFlags,
   unsigned *pdwThreadID) {

   _ptiddata ptd;        // Pointer to thread's data block
   uintptr_t thdl;       // Thread's handle
```

```
    // Allocate data block for the new thread.
    if ((ptd = (_ptiddata)_calloc_crt(1, sizeof(struct _tiddata))) == NULL)
        goto error_return;

    // Initialize the data block.
    initptd(ptd);

    // Save the desired thread function and the parameter
    // we want it to get in the data block.
    ptd->_initaddr = (void *) pfnStartAddr;
    ptd->_initarg = pvParam;
    ptd->_thandle = (uintptr_t)(-1);

    // Create the new thread.
    thdl = (uintptr_t) CreateThread((LPSECURITY_ATTRIBUTES)psa, cbStackSize,
        _threadstartex, (PVOID) ptd,  dwCreateFlags, pdwThreadID);
    if (thdl == 0) {
        // Thread couldn't be created, cleanup and return failure.
        goto error_return;
    }

    // Thread created OK, return the handle as unsigned long.
    return(thdl);

error_return:
    // Error: data block or thread couldn't be created.
    // GetLastError() is mapped into errno corresponding values
    // if something wrong happened in CreateThread.

    _free_crt(ptd);
    return((uintptr_t)0L);
}
```

Here are the important things to note about **_beginthreadex**:

- Each thread gets its very own **_tiddata** memory block allocated from the C/C++ run-time library's heap.

- The address of the thread function passed to **_beginthreadex** is saved in the **_tiddata** memory block. (The **_tiddata** structure is in the C++ source code in the Mtdll.h file). Just for fun, I'll reproduce the structure below. The parameter to be passed to this function is also saved in this data block.

- **_beginthreadex** does call **CreateThread** internally because this is the only way that the operating system knows how to create a new thread.

- When **CreateThread** is called, it is told to start executing the new thread with a function called **_threadstartex**, not **pfnStartAddr**. Also, note that the parameter passed to the thread function is the address of the **_tiddata** structure, not **pvParam**.

- If all goes well, the thread handle is returned just like **CreateThread**. If any operation fails, **0** is returned.

```
struct _tiddata {
   unsigned long   _tid;         /* thread ID */

   unsigned long   _thandle;     /* thread handle */

   int     _terrno;              /* errno value */
   unsigned long   _tdoserrno;   /* _doserrno value */
   unsigned int    _fpds;        /* Floating Point data segment */
   unsigned long   _holdrand;    /* rand() seed value */
   char*           _token;       /* ptr to strtok() token */
   wchar_t*        _wtoken;      /* ptr to wcstok() token */
   unsigned char*  _mtoken;      /* ptr to _mbstok() token */

   /* following pointers get malloc'd at runtime */
   char*       _errmsg;          /* ptr to strerror()/_strerror() buff */
   wchar_t*    _werrmsg;         /* ptr to _wcserror()/__wcserror() buff */
   char*       _namebuf0;        /* ptr to tmpnam() buffer */
   wchar_t*    _wnamebuf0;       /* ptr to _wtmpnam() buffer */
   char*       _namebuf1;        /* ptr to tmpfile() buffer */
   wchar_t*    _wnamebuf1;       /* ptr to _wtmpfile() buffer */
   char*       _asctimebuf;      /* ptr to asctime() buffer */
   wchar_t*    _wasctimebuf;     /* ptr to _wasctime() buffer */
   void*       _gmtimebuf;       /* ptr to gmtime() structure */
   char*       _cvtbuf;          /* ptr to ecvt()/fcvt buffer */

   unsigned char _con_ch_buf[MB_LEN_MAX];
                                 /* ptr to putch() buffer */
   unsigned short _ch_buf_used;  /* if the _con_ch_buf is used */

   /* following fields are needed by _beginthread code */
   void*       _initaddr;        /* initial user thread address */
   void*       _initarg;         /* initial user thread argument */

   /* following three fields are needed to support signal handling and runtime errors */
   void*       _pxcptacttab;     /* ptr to exception-action table */
   void*       _tpxcptinfoptrs;  /* ptr to exception info pointers */
   int         _tfpecode;        /* float point exception code */

   /* pointer to the copy of the multibyte character information used by the thread */
   pthreadmbcinfo  ptmbcinfo;

   /* pointer to the copy of the locale information used by the thread */
   pthreadlocinfo  ptlocinfo;
   int         _ownlocale;       /* if 1, this thread owns its own locale */

   /* following field is needed by NLG routines */
   unsigned long   _NLG_dwCode;

   /*
    * Per-Thread data needed by C++ Exception Handling
    */
   void*       _terminate;       /* terminate() routine */
```

```
    void*       _unexpected;    /* unexpected() routine */
    void*       _translator;    /* S.E. translator */
    void*       _purecall;      /* called when pure virtual happens */
    void*       _curexception;  /* current exception */
    void*       _curcontext;    /* current exception context */
    int         _ProcessingThrow; /* for uncaught_exception */
    void*       _curexcspec;    /* for handling exceptions thrown from std::unexpected */

#if defined (_M_IA64) || defined (_M_AMD64)
    void*       _pExitContext;
    void*       _pUnwindContext;
    void*       _pFrameInfoChain;
    unsigned __int64  _ImageBase;
#if defined (_M_IA64)
    unsigned __int64  TargetGp;
#endif  /* defined (_M_IA64) */
    unsigned __int64   _ThrowImageBase;
    void*       _pForeignException;
#elif defined (_M_IX86)
    void*       _pFrameInfoChain;
#endif  /* defined (_M_IX86) */
    _setloc_struct _setloc_data;

    void*       _encode_ptr;    /* EncodePointer() routine */
    void*       _decode_ptr;    /* DecodePointer() routine */

    void*       _reserved1;     /* nothing */
    void*       _reserved2;     /* nothing */
    void*       _reserved3;     /* nothing */

    int _        cxxReThrow;    /* Set to True if it's a rethrown C++ Exception */

    unsigned long __initDomain;    /* initial domain used by _beginthread[ex] for managed
function */
};

typedef struct _tiddata * _ptiddata;
```

So now that a **_tiddata** structure has been allocated and initialized for the new thread, we need to see how this structure is associated with the thread. Let's take a look at the **_threadstartex** function (which is also in the C/C++ run-time library's Threadex.c file). Here is my pseudocode version of this function with its helper function **__callthreadstartex**:

```
static unsigned long WINAPI _threadstartex (void* ptd) {
    // Note: ptd is the address of this thread's tiddata block.

    // Associate the tiddata block with this thread so
    // _getptd() will be able to find it in _callthreadstartex.
    TlsSetValue(__tlsindex, ptd);

    // Save this thread ID in the _tiddata block.
    ((_ptiddata) ptd)->_tid = GetCurrentThreadId();

    // Initialize floating-point support (code not shown).
```

```
    // call helper function.
    _callthreadstartex();

    // We never get here; the thread dies in _callthreadstartex.
    return(0L);
}

static void _callthreadstartex(void) {
    _ptiddata ptd; /* pointer to thread's _tiddata struct */

    // get the pointer to thread data from TLS
    ptd = _getptd();

    // Wrap desired thread function in SEH frame to
    // handle run-time errors and signal support.
    __try {
        // Call desired thread function, passing it the desired parameter.
        // Pass thread's exit code value to _endthreadex.
        _endthreadex(
            ( (unsigned (WINAPI *)(void *))(((_ptiddata)ptd)->_initaddr) )
                ( ((_ptiddata)ptd)->_initarg ) ) ;
    }
    __except(_XcptFilter(GetExceptionCode(), GetExceptionInformation())){
        // The C run-time's exception handler deals with run-time errors
        // and signal support; we should never get it here.
        _exit(GetExceptionCode());
    }
}
```

Here are the important things to note about **_threadstartex**:

- The new thread begins executing with **RtlUserThreadStart** (in NTDLL.dll) and then jumps to **_threadstartex**.

- **_threadstartex** is passed the address to this new thread's **_tiddata** block as its only parameter.

- **TlsSetValue** is an operating system function that associates a value with the calling thread. This is called Thread Local Storage (TLS) and is discussed in Chapter 21, "Thread-Local Storage." The **_threadstartex** function associates the **_tiddata** block with the new thread.

- In the helper parameterless function **_callthreadstartex**, an SEH frame is placed around the desired thread function. This frame handles many things related to the run-time library—for example, run-time errors (such as throwing C++ exceptions that are not caught) and the C/C++ run-time library's **signal** function. This is critically important. If you were to create a thread using **CreateThread** and then call the C/C++ run-time library's **signal** function, the function would not work correctly.

- The desired thread function is called and passed the desired parameter. Recall that the address of the function and the parameter were saved in the **_tiddata** block saved in TLS by **_beginthreadex** and retrieved from TLS in **_callthreadstartex**.

- The return value from the desired thread function is supposed to be the thread's exit code. Note that **_callthreadstartex** does not simply return back to **_threadstartex** and then to **RtlUserThreadStart**. If it were to do that, the thread would die and its exit code would be set correctly but the thread's **_tiddata** memory block would not be destroyed. This would cause a leak in your application. To prevent this leak, another C/C++ run-time library function, **_endthreadex**, is called and passed the exit code.

The last function that we need to look at is **_endthreadex** (which is also in the C run-time library's Threadex.c file). Here is my pseudocode version of this function:

```
void __cdecl _endthreadex (unsigned retcode) {
   _ptiddata ptd;          // Pointer to thread's data block

   // Clean up floating-point support (code not shown).

   // Get the address of this thread's tiddata block.
   ptd = _getptd_noexit ();

   // Free the tiddata block.
   if (ptd != NULL)
      _freeptd(ptd);

   // Terminate the thread.
   ExitThread(retcode);
}
```

Here are the important things to note about **_endthreadex**:

■ The C run-time library's **_getptd_noexit** function internally calls the operating system's **TlsGetValue** function, which retrieves the address of the calling thread's **tiddata** memory block.

■ This data block is then freed, and the operating system's **ExitThread** function is called to truly destroy the thread. Of course, the exit code is passed and set correctly.

Earlier in this chapter, I said that you should always try to avoid using the **ExitThread** function. This is true, and I'm not going to contradict myself now. I said that it kills the calling thread and doesn't allow it to return from the currently executing function. Because the function doesn't return, any C++ objects you can construct will not be destructed. Here's another reason not to call **ExitThread**: it prevents the thread's **_tiddata** memory block from being freed, so your application will leak memory (until the whole process is terminated).

Microsoft's C++ team realizes that developers like to call **ExitThread** anyway, so they have made this possible without forcing your application to leak memory. If you really want to forcibly kill your thread, you can have it call **_endthreadex** (instead of **ExitThread**) to free the thread's **_tiddata** block and then exit. Still, I discourage you from calling **_endthreadex**.

By now you should understand why the C/C++ run-time library's functions need a separate data block for each thread created, and you should also see how calling **_beginthreadex** allocates, initializes, and associates this data block with the newly created thread. You should also understand how the **_endthreadex** function frees the data block when the thread terminates.

Once this data block is initialized and associated with the thread, any C/C++ run-time library functions the thread calls that require per-thread instance data can easily retrieve the address to the calling thread's data block (via **TlsGetValue**) and manipulate the thread's data. This is fine for functions, but you might wonder how this works for a global variable such as **errno**. Well, **errno** is defined in the standard C headers, like this:

```
_CRTIMP extern int * __cdecl _errno(void);
#define errno    (*_errno())

int* __cdecl _errno(void) {
   _ptiddata ptd = _getptd_noexit();
   if (!ptd) {
      return &ErrnoNoMem;
   } else {
      return (&ptd->_terrno);
   }
}
```

Then, whenever you reference **errno**, you actually make a call to the internal C/C++ run-time library function **_errno**. This function returns the address to the **errno** data member in the calling thread's associated data block. You'll notice that the **errno** macro is defined as taking the contents of this address. This definition is necessary because it's possible to write code like this:

```
int *p = &errno;
if (*p == ENOMEM) {
   ...
}
```

If the internal **_errno** function simply returned the value of **errno**, the preceding code wouldn't compile.

The C/C++ run-time library also places synchronization primitives around certain functions. For example, if two threads simultaneously call **malloc**, the heap can become corrupted. The C/C++ run-time library prevents two threads from allocating memory from the heap at the same time. It does this by making the second thread wait until the first has returned from **malloc**. Then the second thread is allowed to enter. (Thread synchronization is discussed in more detail in Chapters 8 and 9.) Obviously, all this additional work affects the performance of the multithreaded version of the C/C++ run-time library.

The dynamically linked version of the C/C++ run-time library was written to be generic so that it can be shared by all running applications and DLLs using the C/C++ run-time library functions. For this reason, the library exists only in a multithreaded version. Because the C/C++ run-time library is supplied in a DLL, applications (.exe files) and DLLs don't need to include the code for the C/C++ run-time library function and are smaller as a result. Also, if Microsoft fixes a bug in the C/C++ run-time library DLL, applications automatically gain the fix as well.

As you might expect, the C/C++ run-time library's startup code allocates and initializes a data block for your application's primary thread. This allows the primary thread to safely call any of the C/C++ run-time functions. When your primary thread returns from its entry-point function, the C/C++ run-time library frees the associated data block. In addition, the startup code sets up the proper structured exception handling code so that the primary thread can successfully call the C/C++ run-time library's **signal** function.

Oops—I Called *CreateThread* Instead of *_beginthreadex* by Mistake

You might wonder what happens if you create your new threads by calling **CreateThread** instead of the C/C++ run-time library's **_beginthreadex** function. When a thread calls a C/C++ run-time library function that requires the **_tiddata** structure, here is what happens. (Most C/C++ run-time library functions are thread-safe and do not require this structure.) First, the C/C++ run-time function attempts to get the address of the thread's data block (by calling **TlsGetValue**). If **NULL** is returned as the address of the **_tiddata** block, the calling thread doesn't have a **_tiddata** block associated with it. At this point, the C/C++ run-time function allocates and initializes a **_tiddata** block for the calling thread right on the spot. The block is then associated with the thread (via **TlsSetValue**) and this block stays with the thread for as long as the thread continues to run. The C/C++ run-time function can now use the thread's **_tiddata** block, and so can any C/C++ run-time functions that are called in the future.

This, of course, is fantastic because your thread runs without a hitch (almost). Well, actually there are a few problems. First, if the thread uses the C/C++ run-time library's **signal** function, the entire process terminates because the structured exception handling frame has not been prepared. Second, if the thread terminates without calling **_endthreadex**, the data block cannot be destroyed and a memory leak occurs. (And who would call **_endthreadex** for a thread created with **CreateThread**?)

> **Note** When your module links to the DLL version of the C/C++ run-time library, the library receives a **DLL_THREAD_DETACH** notification when the thread terminates and frees the **_tiddata** block (if allocated). Even though this prevents the leaking of the **_tiddata** block, I strongly recommend that you create your threads using **_beginthreadex** instead of **CreateThread**.

C/C++ Run-Time Library Functions That You Should Never Call

The C/C++ run-time library also contains two other functions:

```
unsigned long _beginthread(
    void (__cdecl *start_address)(void *),
    unsigned stack_size,
    void *arglist);
```

and

```
void _endthread(void);
```

These two functions were originally created to do the work of the new **_beginthreadex** and **_endthreadex** functions, respectively. However, as you can see, the **_beginthread** function has fewer parameters and is therefore more limited than the full-featured **_beginthreadex** function. For example, if you use **_beginthread**, you cannot create the new thread with security attributes, you cannot create the thread suspended, and you cannot obtain the thread's ID value. The **_endthread** function has a similar story: it takes no parameters, which means that the thread's exit code is hardcoded to 0.

The **_endthread** function has another significant problem that you can't see. Just before **_endthread** calls **ExitThread**, it calls **CloseHandle**, passing the handle of the new thread. To see why this is a problem, examine the following code:

```
DWORD dwExitCode;
HANDLE hThread = _beginthread(...);
GetExitCodeThread(hThread, &dwExitCode);
CloseHandle(hThread);
```

The newly created thread might execute, return, and terminate before the first thread can call **GetExitCodeThread**. If this happens, the value in **hThread** will be invalid because **_endthread** has closed the new thread's handle. Needless to say, the call to **CloseHandle** will also fail for the same reason.

The new **_endthreadex** function does not close the thread's handle, so the preceding code fragment will work correctly if we replace the call to **_beginthread** with a call to **_beginthreadex**. Remember that when your thread function returns, **_beginthreadex** calls **_endthreadex**, while **_beginthread** calls **_endthread**.

Gaining a Sense of One's Own Identity

As threads execute, they frequently want to call Windows functions that change their execution environment. For example, a thread might want to alter its priority or its process' priority. (Priorities are discussed in Chapter 7, "Thread Scheduling, Priorities, and Affinities.") Because it is common for a thread to alter its (or its process') environment, Windows offers functions that make it easy for a thread to refer to its process kernel object or to its own thread kernel object:

```
HANDLE GetCurrentProcess();
HANDLE GetCurrentThread();
```

Both of these functions return a pseudohandle to the calling thread's process or thread kernel object. These functions do not create new handles in the calling process' handle table. Also, calling these functions has no effect on the usage count of the process or thread kernel object. If you call **CloseHandle**, passing a pseudohandle as the parameter, **CloseHandle** simply ignores the call and returns **FALSE**; **GetLastError** returns **ERROR_INVALID_HANDLE** in that case.

When you call a Windows function that requires a handle to a process or thread, you can pass a pseudohandle, which causes the function to perform its action on the calling process or thread. For example, a thread can query its process' time usage by calling **GetProcessTimes** as follows:

```
FILETIME ftCreationTime, ftExitTime, ftKernelTime, ftUserTime;
GetProcessTimes(GetCurrentProcess(),
   &ftCreationTime, &ftExitTime, &ftKernelTime, &ftUserTime);
```

Likewise, a thread can query its own thread times by calling **GetThreadTimes**:

```
FILETIME ftCreationTime, ftExitTime, ftKernelTime, ftUserTime;
GetThreadTimes(GetCurrentThread(),
   &ftCreationTime, &ftExitTime, &ftKernelTime, &ftUserTime);
```

A few Windows functions allow you to identify a specific process or thread by its unique system-wide ID. The following functions allow a thread to query its process' unique ID or its own unique ID:

```
DWORD GetCurrentProcessId();
DWORD GetCurrentThreadId();
```

These functions are generally not as useful as the functions that return pseudohandles, but occasionally they come in handy.

Converting a Pseudohandle to a Real Handle

Sometimes you might need to acquire a real handle to a thread instead of a pseudohandle. By "real," I mean a handle that unambiguously identifies a unique thread. Examine the following code:

```
DWORD WINAPI ParentThread(PVOID pvParam) {
   HANDLE hThreadParent = GetCurrentThread();
   CreateThread(NULL, 0, ChildThread, (PVOID) hThreadParent, 0, NULL);
   // Function continues...
}

DWORD WINAPI ChildThread(PVOID pvParam) {
   HANDLE hThreadParent = (HANDLE) pvParam;
   FILETIME ftCreationTime, ftExitTime, ftKernelTime, ftUserTime;
   GetThreadTimes(hThreadParent,
      &ftCreationTime, &ftExitTime, &ftKernelTime, &ftUserTime);
   // Function continues...
}
```

Can you see the problem with this code fragment? The idea is to have the parent thread pass to the child thread a thread handle that identifies the parent thread. However, the parent thread passes a pseudohandle, not a real handle. When the child thread begins executing, it passes the pseudohandle to the **GetThreadTimes** function, which causes the child thread to get its own CPU times, not the parent thread's CPU times. This happens because a thread pseudohandle is a handle to the current thread—that is, a handle to whichever thread is making the function call.

To fix this code, we must turn the pseudohandle into a real handle. The **DuplicateHandle** function (discussed in Chapter 3) can do this transformation:

```
BOOL DuplicateHandle(
   HANDLE hSourceProcess,
   HANDLE hSource,
   HANDLE hTargetProcess,
   PHANDLE phTarget,
   DWORD dwDesiredAccess,
   BOOL bInheritHandle,
   DWORD dwOptions);
```

Usually, you use this function to create a new process-relative handle from a kernel object handle that is relative to another process. However, we can use it in an unusual way to correct the code fragment discussed earlier. The corrected code fragment is as follows:

```
DWORD WINAPI ParentThread(PVOID pvParam) {
   HANDLE hThreadParent;

   DuplicateHandle(
      GetCurrentProcess(),      // Handle of process that thread
                                // pseudohandle is relative to
      GetCurrentThread(),       // Parent thread's pseudohandle
      GetCurrentProcess(),      // Handle of process that the new, real,
                                // thread handle is relative to
      &hThreadParent,           // Will receive the new, real, handle
                                // identifying the parent thread
      0,                        // Ignored due to DUPLICATE_SAME_ACCESS
      FALSE,                    // New thread handle is not inheritable
      DUPLICATE_SAME_ACCESS);   // New thread handle has same
                                // access as pseudohandle

   CreateThread(NULL, 0, ChildThread, (PVOID) hThreadParent, 0, NULL);
   // Function continues...
}
DWORD WINAPI ChildThread(PVOID pvParam) {
   HANDLE hThreadParent = (HANDLE) pvParam;
   FILETIME ftCreationTime, ftExitTime, ftKernelTime, ftUserTime;
   GetThreadTimes(hThreadParent,
      &ftCreationTime, &ftExitTime, &ftKernelTime, &ftUserTime);
   CloseHandle(hThreadParent);
   // Function continues...
}
```

Now when the parent thread executes, it converts the ambiguous pseudohandle identifying the parent thread to a new, real handle that unambiguously identifies the parent thread, and it passes this real handle to **CreateThread**. When the child thread starts executing, its **pvParam** parameter contains the real thread handle. Any calls to functions passing this handle will affect the parent thread, not the child thread.

Because **DuplicateHandle** increments the usage count of the specified kernel object, it is important to decrement the object's usage count by passing the target handle to **CloseHandle** when you finish using the duplicated object handle. This is shown in the preceding code fragment. Immediately after the call to **GetThreadTimes**, the child thread calls **CloseHandle** to decrement the parent thread object's usage count. In this code fragment, I assumed that the child thread would not call any other functions using this handle. If other functions are to be called passing the parent thread's handle, the call to **CloseHandle** should not be made until the child thread no longer requires the handle.

I should also point out that the **DuplicateHandle** function can be used to convert a pseudo-handle for a process to a real process handle as follows:

```
HANDLE hProcess;
DuplicateHandle(
   GetCurrentProcess(),    // Handle of process that the process
                           // pseudohandle is relative to
   GetCurrentProcess(),    // Process' pseudohandle
   GetCurrentProcess(),    // Handle of process that the new, real,
                           // process handle is relative to
   &hProcess,              // Will receive the new, real
                           // handle identifying the process
   0,                      // Ignored because of DUPLICATE_SAME_ACCESS
   FALSE,                  // New process handle is not inheritable
   DUPLICATE_SAME_ACCESS); // New process handle has same
                           // access as pseudohandle
```

Chapter 7
Thread Scheduling, Priorities, and Affinities

A preemptive operating system must use some algorithm to determine which threads should be scheduled when and for how long. In this chapter, we'll look at the algorithms that Microsoft Windows Vista uses.

In Chapter 6, "Thread Basics," we discussed how every thread has a context structure, which is maintained inside the thread's kernel object. This context structure reflects the state of the thread's CPU registers when the thread was last executing. Every 20 milliseconds or so (as returned by the second parameter of the **GetSystemTimeAdjustment** function), Windows looks at all the thread kernel objects currently in existence. Of these objects, only some are considered schedulable. Windows selects one of the schedulable thread kernel objects and loads the CPU's registers with the values that were last saved in the thread's context. This action is called a *context switch*. Windows actually keeps a record of how many times each thread gets a chance to run. You can see this when using a tool such as Microsoft Spy++. The following figure shows the properties for a thread. Notice that this thread has been scheduled 182,524 times.

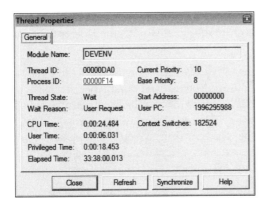

At this point, the thread is executing code and manipulating data in its process' address space. After another 20 milliseconds or so, Windows saves the CPU's registers back into the thread's context. The thread is no longer running. The system again examines the remaining schedulable thread kernel objects, selects another thread's kernel object, loads this thread's context into the CPU's registers, and continues. This operation of loading a thread's context, letting the thread run, saving the context, and repeating the operation begins when the system boots and continues until the system is shut down.

That, in short, is how the system schedules multiple threads. We'll discuss more details later, but that is basically it. Simple, isn't it? Windows is called a *preemptive multithreaded operating system* because a thread can be stopped at any time and another thread can be scheduled. As you'll see, you have some control over this, but not much. Just remember that you cannot guarantee that your thread will always be running, that your thread will get the whole processor, that no other thread will be allowed to run, and so on.

> **Note**   Developers frequently ask me how they can guarantee that their thread will start running within some time period of some event—for example, how can you ensure that a particular thread will start running within 1 millisecond of data coming from the serial port? I have an easy answer: You can't.
>
> Real-time operating systems can make these promises, but Windows is not a real-time operating system. A real-time operating system requires intimate knowledge of the hardware it is running on so that it knows the latency associated with its hard disk controllers, keyboards, and so on. Microsoft's goal with Windows is to make it work on a wide variety of hardware: different CPUs, different drives, different networks, and so forth. In short, Windows is not designed to be a real-time operating system even though new extended mechanisms are now available in Windows Vista—such as the Thread Ordering service (which you can read about at *http://msdn2.microsoft.com/en-us/library/ms686752.aspx*) or the Multimedia Class Scheduler service (which you can read about at *http://msdn2.microsoft.com/en-us/library/ms684247.aspx*) for multimedia applications such as Windows Media Player 11.

I stress the idea that the system schedules only schedulable threads, but as it turns out, most of the threads in the system are not schedulable. For example, some thread objects might have a suspend count greater than 0. This means that the thread is suspended and should not be scheduled any CPU time. You can create a suspended thread by calling **CreateProcess** or **CreateThread** using the **CREATE_SUSPENDED** flag. (Later in this chapter, I'll also discuss the **SuspendThread** and **ResumeThread** functions.)

In addition to suspended threads, many other threads are not schedulable because they are waiting for something to happen. For example, if you run Notepad and don't type, Notepad's thread has nothing to do. The system does not assign CPU time to threads that have nothing to do. When you move Notepad's window, or if Notepad's window needs to repaint its contents, or if you type into Notepad, the system automatically makes Notepad's thread schedulable. This does not mean that Notepad's thread gets CPU time immediately. It's just that Notepad's thread has something to do and the system will get around to scheduling it at some time—in the near future, we hope.

Suspending and Resuming a Thread

Inside a thread kernel object is a value that indicates the thread's suspend count. When you call **CreateProcess** or **CreateThread**, the thread kernel object is created and the suspend count is initialized to **1**. This prevents the thread from being scheduled to a CPU. This is, of course, desirable because it takes time for the thread to be initialized and you don't want the system to start executing the thread before it is fully ready.

After the thread is fully initialized, **CreateProcess** or **CreateThread** checks to see whether you've passed the **CREATE_SUSPENDED** flag. If you have, the functions return and the new thread is left in the suspended state. If you have not, the function decrements the thread's suspend count to **0**. When a thread's suspend count is **0**, the thread is schedulable unless it is waiting for something else to happen (such as keyboard input).

Creating a thread in the suspended state allows you to alter the thread's environment (such as priority, discussed later in the chapter) before the thread has a chance to execute any code. Once you alter the thread's environment, you must make the thread schedulable. You do this by calling **ResumeThread** and passing it the thread handle returned by the call to **CreateThread** (or the thread handle from the structure pointed to by the **ppiProcInfo** parameter passed to **CreateProcess**):

```
DWORD ResumeThread(HANDLE hThread);
```

If **ResumeThread** is successful, it returns the thread's previous suspend count; otherwise, it returns 0xFFFFFFFF.

A single thread can be suspended several times. If a thread is suspended three times, it must be resumed three times before it is eligible for assignment to a CPU. In addition to using the **CREATE_SUSPENDED** flag when you create a thread, you can suspend a thread by calling **SuspendThread**:

```
DWORD SuspendThread(HANDLE hThread);
```

Any thread can call this function to suspend another thread (as long as you have the thread's handle). It goes without saying (but I'll say it anyway) that a thread can suspend itself but cannot resume itself. Like **ResumeThread**, **SuspendThread** returns the thread's previous suspend count. A thread can be suspended as many as **MAXIMUM_SUSPEND_COUNT** times (defined as 127 in WinNT.h). Note that **SuspendThread** is asynchronous with respect to kernel-mode execution, but user-mode execution does not occur until the thread is resumed.

In real life, an application must be careful when it calls **SuspendThread** because you have no idea what the thread might be doing when you attempt to suspend it. If the thread is attempting to allocate memory from a heap, for example, the thread will have a lock on the heap. As other threads attempt to access the heap, their execution will be halted until the first thread is resumed. **SuspendThread** is safe only if you know exactly what the target thread is (or might be doing) and you take extreme measures to avoid problems or deadlocks caused by suspending the thread. (Deadlocking and other thread synchronization issues are discussed in Chapter 8, "Thread Synchronization in User Mode," Chapter 9, "Thread Synchronization with Kernel Objects," and Chapter 10, "Synchronous and Asynchronous Device I/O.")

Suspending and Resuming a Process

The concept of suspending or resuming a process doesn't exist for Windows because processes are never scheduled CPU time. However, I have been asked numerous times how to suspend all the threads in a process. In the special case of a debugger handling a debug event returned by **WaitForDebugEvent**, Windows freezes all the threads in the debuggee process until the debugger calls **ContinueDebugEvent**. You can also use the "Suspend Process" feature of Process Explorer from Sysinternals (*http://www.microsoft.com/technet/sysinternals/ProcessesAndThreads/ ProcessExplorer.mspx*) to achieve the same effect: all the threads in the process are suspended.

Windows doesn't offer any other way to suspend all threads in a process because of race conditions. For example, while the threads are suspended, a new thread might be created. Somehow the system must suspend any new threads during this window of time. Microsoft has integrated this functionality into the debugging mechanism of the system.

Although you cannot create an absolutely perfect **SuspendProcess** function, you can create an implementation of this function that works well in many situations. Here is my implementation of a **SuspendProcess** function:

```
VOID SuspendProcess(DWORD dwProcessID, BOOL fSuspend) {

   // Get the list of threads in the system.
   HANDLE hSnapshot = CreateToolhelp32Snapshot(
      TH32CS_SNAPTHREAD, dwProcessID);

   if (hSnapshot != INVALID_HANDLE_VALUE) {

      // Walk the list of threads.
      THREADENTRY32 te = { sizeof(te) };
      BOOL fOk = Thread32First(hSnapshot, &te);
      for (; fOk; fOk = Thread32Next(hSnapshot, &te)) {

         // Is this thread in the desired process?
         if (te.th32OwnerProcessID == dwProcessID) {

            // Attempt to convert the thread ID into a handle.
            HANDLE hThread = OpenThread(THREAD_SUSPEND_RESUME,
               FALSE, te.th32ThreadID);

            if (hThread != NULL) {

               // Suspend or resume the thread.
               if (fSuspend)
                  SuspendThread(hThread);
               else
                  ResumeThread(hThread);
            }
            CloseHandle(hThread);
         }
      }
      CloseHandle(hSnapshot);
   }
}
```

My **SuspendProcess** function uses the ToolHelp functions (discussed in Chapter 4, "Processes") to enumerate the list of threads in the system. As I locate threads that are part of the specified process, I call **OpenThread**:

```
HANDLE OpenThread(
   DWORD dwDesiredAccess,
   BOOL bInheritHandle,
   DWORD dwThreadID);
```

This function locates the thread kernel object with the matching thread ID, increments the kernel object's usage count, and returns a handle to the object. With this handle, I call **SuspendThread** (or **ResumeThread**).

You probably understand why **SuspendProcess** does not work 100 percent of the time: while enumerating the set of threads, new threads can be created and destroyed. So after I call **Create-Toolhelp32Snapshot**, a new thread might appear in the target process, which my function will not suspend. Later, when you call **SuspendProcess** to resume the threads, it will resume a thread that it never suspended. Even worse, while it is enumerating the thread IDs, an existing thread might be destroyed and a new thread might be created, and both of these threads might have the same ID. This would cause the function to suspend some arbitrary thread (probably in a process other than the target process).

Of course, these situations are unlikely, and if you have intimate knowledge of how the target process operates, these issues might not be problems at all. I offer you this function to use at your own risk.

Sleeping

A thread can also tell the system that it does not want to be schedulable for a certain amount of time. This is accomplished by calling **Sleep**:

```
VOID Sleep(DWORD dwMilliseconds);
```

This function causes the thread to suspend itself until **dwMilliseconds** have elapsed. There are a few important things to notice about **Sleep**:

- Calling **Sleep** allows the thread to voluntarily give up the remainder of its time slice.
- The system makes the thread not schedulable for *approximately* the number of milliseconds specified. That's right—if you tell the system you want to sleep for 100 milliseconds, you will sleep approximately that long, but possibly several seconds or minutes more. Remember that Windows is not a real-time operating system. Your thread will probably wake up at the right time, but whether it does depends on what else is going on in the system.
- You can call **Sleep** and pass **INFINITE** for the **dwMilliseconds** parameter. This tells the system to never schedule the thread. This is not a useful thing to do. It is much better to have the thread exit and to recover its stack and kernel object.
- You can pass **0** to **Sleep**. This tells the system that the calling thread relinquishes the remainder of its time slice, and it forces the system to schedule another thread. However, the system can reschedule the thread that just called **Sleep**. This will happen if there are no more schedulable threads at the same priority or higher.

Switching to Another Thread

The system offers a function called **SwitchToThread** that allows another schedulable thread to run if one exists:

```
BOOL SwitchToThread();
```

When you call this function, the system checks to see whether there is a thread that is being starved of CPU time. If no thread is starving, **SwitchToThread** returns immediately. If there is a starving thread, **SwitchToThread** schedules that thread (which might have a lower priority than the thread calling **SwitchToThread**). The starving thread is allowed to run for one time quantum and then the system scheduler operates as usual.

This function allows a thread that wants a resource to force a lower-priority thread that might currently own the resource to relinquish the resource. If no other thread can run when **SwitchTo-Thread** is called, the function returns **FALSE**; otherwise, it returns a nonzero value.

Calling **SwitchToThread** is similar to calling **Sleep** and passing it a timeout of **0** milliseconds. The difference is that **SwitchToThread** allows lower-priority threads to execute. **Sleep** reschedules the calling thread immediately even if lower-priority threads are being starved.

Switching to Another Thread on a Hyper-Threaded CPU

Hyper-threading is a technology available on some Xeon, Pentium 4, and later CPUs. A hyper-threaded processor chip has multiple "logical" CPUs, and each can run a thread. Each thread has its own architectural state (set of registers), but all threads share main execution resources such as the CPU cache. When one thread is paused, the CPU automatically executes another thread; this happens without operating system intervention. A pause is a cache miss, branch misprediction, waiting for results of a previous instruction, and so on. Intel reports that hyper-threaded CPUs improve throughput somewhere between 10 percent to 30 percent, depending on the application and how it is using memory. For more information about hyper-threaded CPUs, see *http://www.microsoft.com/whdc/system/CEC/HT-Windows.mspx.*

When executing spin loops on hyper-threaded CPUs, you need to force the current thread to pause so that the other thread has access to the chip's resources. The *x86* architecture supports the PAUSE assembly language instruction. The PAUSE instruction ensures that a memory order violation is avoided, improving performance. In addition, the instruction reduces power consumption by placing a hiccup into what would be a very hot, tight loop. On *x86*, the PAUSE instruction is equivalent to a REP NOP instruction, which makes it compatible on earlier IA-32 CPUs that do not support hyper-threading. PAUSE causes a finite delay (0 on some CPUs). In the Win32 API, the *x86* PAUSE instruction is emitted by calling the **YieldProcessor** macro defined in WinNT.h. This macro exists so that you can write code in a way that is CPU architecture independent. Also, use of the macro expands the code inline, avoiding the overhead of a function call.

A Thread's Execution Times

Sometimes you want to time how long it takes a thread to perform a particular task. What many people do is write code similar to the following, taking advantage of the new **GetTickCount64** function:

```
// Get the current time (start time).
ULONGLONG qwStartTime = GetTickCount64();

// Perform complex algorithm here.

// Subtract start time from current time to get duration.
ULONGLONG qwElapsedTime = GetTickCount64() - qwStartTime;
```

This code makes a simple assumption: it won't be interrupted. However, in a preemptive operating system, you never know when your thread will be scheduled CPU time. When CPU time is taken away from your thread, it becomes more difficult to time how long it takes your thread to perform various tasks. What we need is a function that returns the amount of CPU time that the thread has received. Fortunately, prior to Windows Vista, the operating system offers a function called **GetThreadTimes** that returns this information:

```
BOOL GetThreadTimes(
    HANDLE hThread,
    PFILETIME pftCreationTime,
    PFILETIME pftExitTime,
    PFILETIME pftKernelTime,
    PFILETIME pftUserTime);
```

GetThreadTimes returns four different time values, as shown in Table 7-1.

Table 7-1   Time Details Returned by GetThreadTime

Time Value	Meaning
Creation time	An absolute value expressed in 100-nanosecond intervals past midnight on January 1, 1601, at Greenwich, England, indicating when the thread was created.
Exit time	An absolute value expressed in 100-nanosecond intervals past midnight on January 1, 1601, at Greenwich, England, indicating when the thread exited. If the thread is still running, the exit time is undefined.
Kernel time	A relative value indicating how many 100-nanosecond intervals of CPU time the thread has spent executing operating system code in kernel mode.
User time	A relative value indicating how many 100-nanosecond intervals of CPU time the thread has spent executing application code.

Using this function, you can determine the amount of time needed to execute a complex algorithm by using code such as the following.

```
__int64 FileTimeToQuadWord (PFILETIME pft) {
   return(Int64ShllMod32(pft->dwHighDateTime, 32) | pft->dwLowDateTime);
}


void PerformLongOperation () {

   FILETIME ftKernelTimeStart, ftKernelTimeEnd;
   FILETIME ftUserTimeStart,   ftUserTimeEnd;
   FILETIME ftDummy;
   __int64 qwKernelTimeElapsed, qwUserTimeElapsed,
      qwTotalTimeElapsed;

   // Get starting times.
   GetThreadTimes(GetCurrentThread(), &ftDummy, &ftDummy,
      &ftKernelTimeStart, &ftUserTimeStart);


   // Perform complex algorithm here.


   // Get ending times.
   GetThreadTimes(GetCurrentThread(), &ftDummy, &ftDummy,
      &ftKernelTimeEnd, &ftUserTimeEnd);

   // Get the elapsed kernel and user times by converting the start
   // and end times from FILETIMEs to quad words, and then subtract
   // the start times from the end times.
   qwKernelTimeElapsed = FileTimeToQuadWord(&ftKernelTimeEnd) -
      FileTimeToQuadWord(&ftKernelTimeStart);

   qwUserTimeElapsed = FileTimeToQuadWord(&ftUserTimeEnd) -
      FileTimeToQuadWord(&ftUserTimeStart);

   // Get total time duration by adding the kernel and user times.
   qwTotalTimeElapsed = qwKernelTimeElapsed + qwUserTimeElapsed;

   // The total elapsed time is in qwTotalTimeElapsed.
}
```

Note that **GetProcessTimes**, a function similar to **GetThreadTimes**, applies to all the threads in a process:

```
BOOL GetProcessTimes(
   HANDLE hProcess,
   PFILETIME pftCreationTime,
   PFILETIME pftExitTime,
   PFILETIME pftKernelTime,
   PFILETIME pftUserTime);
```

GetProcessTimes returns times that apply to all the threads in a specified process (even threads that have terminated). For example, the kernel time returned is the sum of all the elapsed times that all the process' threads have spent in kernel mode.

In Windows Vista, the way the CPU time is charged for a thread has changed. Instead of relying on the interval clock timer, which is about 10 to 15 milliseconds long (read *http://www.microsoft.com/ technet/sysinternals/information/highresolutiontimers.mspx* for more details and the ClockRes tool used to measure it), the operating system is now using the 64-bit *Time Stamp Counter* (TSC) of the processor, which counts the number of cycles since the machine started. With our gigahertz machines, you can imagine how much more accurate this value could be compared to milliseconds.

When a thread is stopped by the scheduler, the difference between the value of the TSC and the value of the TSC when the thread started its execution quantum is computed and added to the execution time of the thread, without counting the interrupt time, as was the case before Windows Vista. The **QueryThreadCycleTime** and **QueryProcessCycleTime** functions return the number of cycles charged for a given thread or all the threads of a given process, respectively. If you want to replace **GetTickCount64** in your code with something more accurate, you should get the current value of the TSC by calling the **ReadTimeStampCounter** macro defined in WinNT.h that points to the **__rdtsc** intrinsic function provided by the C++ compiler.

For high-resolution profiling, the **GetThreadTimes** function is not good enough. Windows does offer these high-resolution performance functions:

```
BOOL QueryPerformanceFrequency(LARGE_INTEGER* pliFrequency);

BOOL QueryPerformanceCounter(LARGE_INTEGER* pliCount);
```

These functions assume that the executing thread does not get preempted, but most high-resolution profiling is done for short-lived blocks of code anyway. To make working with these functions a little easier, I have created the following C++ class:

```
class CStopwatch {
public:
   CStopwatch() { QueryPerformanceFrequency(&m_liPerfFreq); Start(); }

   void Start() { QueryPerformanceCounter(&m_liPerfStart); }

   __int64 Now() const {    // Returns # of milliseconds since Start was called
      LARGE_INTEGER liPerfNow;
      QueryPerformanceCounter(&liPerfNow);
      return(((liPerfNow.QuadPart - m_liPerfStart.QuadPart) * 1000)
         / m_liPerfFreq.QuadPart);
   }

   __int64 NowInMicro() const {   // Returns # of microseconds
                                  // since Start was called
      LARGE_INTEGER liPerfNow;
      QueryPerformanceCounter(&liPerfNow);
      return(((liPerfNow.QuadPart - m_liPerfStart.QuadPart) * 1000000)
         / m_liPerfFreq.QuadPart);
   }

private:
   LARGE_INTEGER m_liPerfFreq;   // Counts per second
   LARGE_INTEGER m_liPerfStart;  // Starting count
};
```

I use this class as follows:

```
// Create a stopwatch timer (which defaults to the current time).
CStopwatch stopwatch;

// Execute the code I want to profile here.

// Get how much time has elapsed up to now.
__int64 qwElapsedTime = stopwatch.Now();

// qwElapsedTime indicates how long the profiled code
// executed in milliseconds.
```

The high-resolution timer functions will be useful to transform the numbers returned by the new **Get*CycleTime** functions. Because the measured cycles are dependent on the processor frequency, you need to find out what this frequency is so that you can transform the cycle numbers into more meaningful timing values. For example, with a 2-GHz processor, 2,000,000,000 cycles occur in 1 second and 800,000 cycles represent 0.4 millisecond, but it represents 0.8 millisecond on a slower 1-GHz processor. Here is the implementation of the **GetCPUFrequencyInMHz** function:

```
DWORD GetCPUFrequencyInMHz() {
   // change the priority to ensure the thread will have more chances
   // to be scheduled when Sleep() ends
   int currentPriority = GetThreadPriority(GetCurrentThread());
   SetThreadPriority(GetCurrentThread(), THREAD_PRIORITY_HIGHEST);

   // keep track of the elapsed time with the other timer
   __int64 elapsedTime = 0;

   // Create a stopwatch timer (which defaults to the current time).
   CStopwatch stopwatch;
   __int64 perfCountStart = stopwatch.NowInMicro();

   // get the current number of cycles
   unsigned __int64 cyclesOnStart = ReadTimeStampCounter();

   // wait for ~1 second
   Sleep(1000);

   // get the number of cycles after ~1 second
   unsigned __int64 numberOfCycles = ReadTimeStampCounter() - cyclesOnStart;

   // Get how much time has elapsed with greater precision
   elapsedTime = stopwatch.NowInMicro() - perfCountStart;

   // Restore the thread priority
   SetThreadPriority(GetCurrentThread(), currentPriority);

   // Compute the frequency in MHz
   DWORD dwCPUFrequency = (DWORD)(numberOfCycles / elapsedTime);
   return(dwCPUFrequency);
}
```

When you need the number of milliseconds corresponding to the cycle count returned by **QueryProcessCycleTime**, you simply divide this cycle count by **GetCPUFrequencyInMHz** and multiply the result by 1000. Even if this computation is very simple arithmetic, the result might be totally incorrect. The frequency of a processor might vary in time, depending on the settings chosen by the end user or whether or not the computer is connected to a power supply. Last but not least, on a multiprocessor machine, a thread can be scheduled on different processors with little differences in terms of frequency.

Putting the *CONTEXT* in Context

By now, you should understand the important role that the **CONTEXT** structure plays in thread scheduling. The **CONTEXT** structure allows the system to remember a thread's state so that the thread can pick up where it left off the next time it has a CPU to run on.

You might be surprised to learn that such a low-level data structure is completely documented in the Platform SDK. However, if you look up the **CONTEXT** structure in the documentation, all you'll see is this:

> *"A CONTEXT structure contains processor-specific register data. The system uses CONTEXT structures to perform various internal operations. Refer to the header file WinNT.h for definitions of these structures."*

The documentation does not show you the structure's members and does not describe the members in any way whatsoever because the members depend on which CPU Windows is running on. In fact, of all the data structures Windows defines, the **CONTEXT** structure is the only data structure that is CPU-specific.

So what's in the **CONTEXT** structure? Well, it contains a data member for each register on the host CPU. On an *x86* machine, the members are **Eax**, **Ebx**, **Ecx**, **Edx**, and so on. The following code fragment shows the complete **CONTEXT** structure for an *x86* CPU:

```
typedef struct _CONTEXT {

    //
    // The flag values within this flag control the contents of
    // a CONTEXT record.
    //
    // If the context record is used as an input parameter, then
    // for each portion of the context record controlled by a flag
    // whose value is set, it is assumed that that portion of the
    // context record contains valid context. If the context record
    // is being used to modify a thread's context,  only that
    // portion of the thread's context will be modified.
    //
    // If the context record is used as an IN OUT parameter to capture
    // the context of a thread, only those portions of the thread's
    // context corresponding to set flags will be returned.
    //
    // The context record is never used as an OUT only parameter.
    //

    DWORD ContextFlags;
```

```
    //
    // This section is specified/returned if CONTEXT_DEBUG_REGISTERS is
    // set in ContextFlags. Note that CONTEXT_DEBUG_REGISTERS is NOT
    // included in CONTEXT_FULL.
    //

    DWORD    Dr0;
    DWORD    Dr1;
    DWORD    Dr2;
    DWORD    Dr3;
    DWORD    Dr6;
    DWORD    Dr7;


    //
    // This section is specified/returned if the
    // ContextFlags word contains the flag CONTEXT_FLOATING_POINT.
    //

    FLOATING_SAVE_AREA FloatSave;

    //
    // This section is specified/returned if the
    // ContextFlags word contains the flag CONTEXT_SEGMENTS.
    //

    DWORD    SegGs;
    DWORD    SegFs;
    DWORD    SegEs;
    DWORD    SegDs;

    //
    // This section is specified/returned if the
    // ContextFlags word contains the flag CONTEXT_INTEGER.
    //

    DWORD    Edi;
    DWORD    Esi;
    DWORD    Ebx;
    DWORD    Edx;
    DWORD    Ecx;
    DWORD    Eax;

    //
    // This section is specified/returned if the
    // ContextFlags word contains the flag CONTEXT_CONTROL.
    //

    DWORD    Ebp;
    DWORD    Eip;
    DWORD    SegCs;               // MUST BE SANITIZED
    DWORD    EFlags;              // MUST BE SANITIZED
    DWORD    Esp;
    DWORD    SegSs;
```

```
   //
   // This section is specified/returned if the ContextFlags word
   // contains the flag CONTEXT_EXTENDED_REGISTERS.
   // The format and contexts are processor specific
   //

   BYTE      ExtendedRegisters[MAXIMUM_SUPPORTED_EXTENSION];

} CONTEXT;
```

A **CONTEXT** structure has several sections. **CONTEXT_CONTROL** contains the control registers of the CPU, such as the instruction pointer, stack pointer, flags, and function return address. **CONTEXT_INTEGER** identifies the CPU's integer registers; **CONTEXT_FLOATING_POINT** identifies the CPU's floating-point registers; **CONTEXT_SEGMENTS** identifies the CPU's segment registers; **CONTEXT_DEBUG_REGISTERS** identifies the CPU's debug registers; and **CONTEXT_EXTENDED_REGISTERS** identifies the CPU's extended registers.

Windows actually lets you look inside a thread's kernel object and grab its current set of CPU registers. To do this, you simply call **GetThreadContext**:

```
BOOL GetThreadContext(
   HANDLE hThread,
   PCONTEXT pContext);
```

To call this function, just allocate a **CONTEXT** structure, initialize some flags (the structure's **ContextFlags** member) indicating which registers you want to get back, and pass the address of the structure to **GetThreadContext**. The function then fills in the members you've requested.

You should call **SuspendThread** before calling **GetThreadContext**; otherwise, the thread might be scheduled and the thread's context might be different from what you get back. A thread actually has two contexts: user mode and kernel mode. **GetThreadContext** can return only the user-mode context of a thread. If you call **SuspendThread** to stop a thread but that thread is currently executing in kernel mode, its user-mode context is stable even though **SuspendThread** hasn't actually suspended the thread yet. But the thread cannot execute any more user-mode code until it is resumed, so you can safely consider the thread suspended and **GetThreadContext** will work.

The **CONTEXT** structure's **ContextFlags** member does not correspond to any CPU registers. The **ContextFlags** member indicates to the **GetThreadContext** function which registers you want to retrieve. For example, if you want to get the control registers for a thread, you can write something like this:

```
// Create a CONTEXT structure.
CONTEXT Context;

// Tell the system that we are interested in only the
// control registers.
Context.ContextFlags = CONTEXT_CONTROL;

// Tell the system to get the registers associated with a thread.
GetThreadContext(hThread, &Context);

// The control register members in the CONTEXT structure
// reflect the thread's control registers. The other members
// are undefined.
```

Notice that you must first initialize the **ContextFlags** member in the **CONTEXT** structure before calling **GetThreadContext**. If you want to get a thread's control and integer registers, you should initialize **ContextFlags** as follows:

```
// Tell the system that we are interested
// in the control and integer registers.
Context.ContextFlags = CONTEXT_CONTROL | CONTEXT_INTEGER;
```

Here is the identifier you can use to get all of the thread's important registers (that is, the ones Microsoft deems to be most commonly used):

```
// Tell the system we are interested in the important registers.
Context.ContextFlags = CONTEXT_FULL;
```

CONTEXT_FULL is defined in WinNT.h as **CONTEXT_CONTROL | CONTEXT_INTEGER | CONTEXT_ SEGMENTS**.

When **GetThreadContext** returns, you can easily examine any of the thread's register values, but remember that this means writing CPU-dependent code. For example, for an *x86* CPU type, the **Eip** field stores the Instruction Pointer and the **Esp** field stores the Stack Pointer.

It's amazing how much power Windows offers the developer! But, if you think that's cool, you're gonna love this: Windows lets you change the members in the **CONTEXT** structure and then place the new register values back into the thread's kernel object by calling **SetThreadContext**:

```
BOOL SetThreadContext(
   HANDLE hThread,
   CONST CONTEXT *pContext);
```

Again, the thread whose context you're changing should be suspended first or the results will be unpredictable.

Before calling **SetThreadContext**, you must initialize the **ContextFlags** member of **CONTEXT** again, as shown here:

```
CONTEXT Context;

// Stop the thread from running.
SuspendThread(hThread);

// Get the thread's context registers.
Context.ContextFlags = CONTEXT_CONTROL;
GetThreadContext(hThread, &Context);

// Make the instruction pointer point to the address of your choice.
// Here I've arbitrarily set the address instruction pointer to
// 0x00010000.
Context.Eip = 0x00010000;

// Set the thread's registers to reflect the changed values.
// It's not really necessary to reset the ContextFlags member
// because it was set earlier.
Context.ContextFlags = CONTEXT_CONTROL;
SetThreadContext(hThread, &Context);
```

```
// Resuming the thread will cause it to begin execution
// at address 0x00010000.
ResumeThread(hThread);
```

This will probably cause an access violation in the remote thread; the unhandled exception message box will be presented to the user, and the remote process will be terminated. That's right—the remote process will be terminated, not your process. You will have successfully crashed another process while yours continues to execute just fine!

The **GetThreadContext** and **SetThreadContext** functions give you a lot of control over threads, but you should use them with caution. In fact, few applications ever call these functions at all. The functions were added to help debuggers and other tools implementing advanced features such as Set Next Statement. But any application can call them.

I'll talk about the **CONTEXT** structure more in Chapter 24, "Exception Handlers and Software Exceptions."

Thread Priorities

At the beginning of this chapter, I explained how a CPU can run a thread for only about 20 milliseconds before the scheduler assigns another schedulable thread to that CPU. This happens if all the threads have the same priority, but in reality threads are assigned a lot of different priorities and this affects which thread the scheduler picks as the next thread to run.

Every thread is assigned a priority number ranging from 0 (the lowest) to 31 (the highest). When the system decides which thread to assign to a CPU, it examines the priority 31 threads first and schedules them in a round-robin fashion. If a priority 31 thread is schedulable, it is assigned to a CPU. At the end of this thread's time slice, the system checks to see whether there is another priority 31 thread that can run; if so, it allows that thread to be assigned to a CPU.

As long as a priority 31 thread is schedulable, the system never assigns any thread with a priority of 0 through 30 to a CPU. This condition is called *starvation*. Starvation occurs when higher-priority threads use so much CPU time that they prevent lower-priority threads from executing. Starvation is much less likely to occur on a multiprocessor machine because on such a machine a priority 31 thread and a priority 30 thread can run simultaneously. The system always tries to keep the CPUs busy, and CPUs sit idle only if no threads are schedulable.

You might assume that lower-priority threads never get a chance to run in a system designed like this. But as I've pointed out, at any one time most threads in the system are not schedulable. For example, if your process' primary thread calls **GetMessage** and the system sees that no messages are pending, the system suspends your process' thread, relinquishes the remainder of the thread's time slice, and immediately assigns the CPU to another, waiting, thread.

If no messages show up for **GetMessage** to retrieve, the process' primary thread stays suspended and is never assigned to a CPU. However, when a message is placed in the thread's queue, the system knows that the thread should no longer be suspended and assigns the thread to a CPU if no higher-priority threads need to execute.

Let me point out another issue. Higher-priority threads always preempt lower-priority threads, regardless of what the lower-priority threads are executing. For example, if a priority 5 thread is running and the system determines that a higher-priority thread is ready to run, the system immediately suspends the lower-priority thread (even if it's in the middle of its time slice) and assigns the CPU to the higher-priority thread, which gets a full time slice.

By the way, when the system boots, it creates a special thread called the *zero page thread*. This thread is assigned priority 0 and is the only thread in the entire system that runs at priority 0. The zero page thread is responsible for zeroing any free pages of RAM in the system when there are no other threads that need to perform work.

An Abstract View of Priorities

When Microsoft developers designed the thread scheduler, they realized that it would not fit everyone's needs all the time. They also realized that the "purpose" of the computer would change over time. When Windows NT first came out, object linking and embedding (OLE) applications were just starting to be written. Now, OLE applications are commonplace. Game and multimedia software is much more prevalent, and certainly the Internet wasn't discussed much in the early days of Windows.

The scheduling algorithm has a significant effect on the types of applications that users run. From the beginning, Microsoft developers realized that they would need to modify the scheduling algorithm over time as the purpose of the system changed. But software developers need to write software today, and Microsoft guarantees that your software will run on future versions of the system. How can Microsoft change the way the system works and still keep your software running? Here are a few answers:

- Microsoft doesn't fully document the behavior of the scheduler.
- Microsoft doesn't let applications take full advantage of the scheduler's features.
- Microsoft tells you that the scheduler's algorithm is subject to change so that you can code defensively.

The Windows API exposes an abstract layer over the system's scheduler, so you never talk to the scheduler directly. Instead, you call Windows functions that "interpret" your parameters depending on the version of the system you're running on. So, in this chapter, I'll be discussing this abstract layer.

When you design an application, you should think about what other applications your user might run along with your application. Then you should choose a priority class based on how responsive you need the threads in your application to be. I know that this sounds vague; it's supposed to. Microsoft doesn't want to make any promises that will break your code in the future.

Windows supports six priority classes: idle, below normal, normal, above normal, high, and real-time. Of course, normal is the most common priority class and is used by 99 percent of the applications out there. Table 7-2 describes the priority classes.

The idle priority class is perfect for applications that run when the system is all but doing nothing. A computer that is not being used interactively might still be busy (acting as a file server, for example) and should not have to compete for CPU time with a screen saver. Statistics-tracking applications that periodically update some state about the system usually should not interfere with more critical tasks.

You should use the high-priority class only when absolutely necessary. You should avoid the real-time priority class if possible. In fact, the early betas of Windows NT 3.1 did not expose this priority class to applications even though the operating system supported it. Real-time priority is extremely high and can interfere with operating system tasks because most operating system threads execute at a lower priority. So real-time threads can prevent required disk I/O and network traffic from occurring. In addition, keyboard and mouse input are not processed in a timely manner; the user might think that the system is hung. Basically, you should have a good reason for using real-time priority—such as the need to respond to hardware events with short latency or to perform some short-lived task that just can't be interrupted.

Table 7-2   Process Priority Classes

Priority Class	Description
Real-time	The threads in this process must respond immediately to events to execute time-critical tasks. Threads in this process also preempt operating system components. Use this priority class with extreme caution.
High	The threads in this process must respond immediately to events to execute time-critical tasks. The Task Manager runs at this class so that a user can kill runaway processes.
Above normal	The threads in this process run between the normal and high-priority classes.
Normal	The threads in this process have no special scheduling needs.
Below normal	The threads in this process run between the normal and idle priority classes.
Idle	The threads in this process run when the system is otherwise idle. This process is typically used by screen savers or background utility and statistics-gathering software.

Note   A process cannot run in the real-time priority class unless the user has the Increase Scheduling Priority privilege. Any user designated as an administrator or a power user has this privilege by default.

Of course, most processes are part of the normal priority class. In Windows 2000, Microsoft added two other priority classes, below normal and above normal, because several companies complained that the existing priority classes didn't offer enough flexibility.

Once you select a priority class, you should stop thinking about how your application interrelates with other applications and just concentrate on the threads within your application. Windows supports seven relative thread priorities: idle, lowest, below normal, normal, above normal, highest, and time-critical. These priorities are relative to the process' priority class. Again, most threads use the normal thread priority. Table 7-3 describes the relative thread priorities.

So, to summarize, your process is part of a priority class and you assign the threads within the process relative thread priorities. You'll notice that I haven't said anything about priority levels 0 through 31. Application developers never work with priority levels. Instead, the system maps the process' priority class and a thread's relative priority to a priority level. It is precisely this mapping that Microsoft does not want to commit to. In fact, this mapping has changed between versions of the system.

Table 7-3   Relative Thread Priorities

Relative Thread Priority	Description
Time-critical	Thread runs at 31 for the real-time priority class and at 15 for all other priority classes.
Highest	Thread runs two levels above normal.
Above normal	Thread runs one level above normal.
Normal	Thread runs normally for the process' priority class.
Below normal	Thread runs one level below normal.
Lowest	Thread runs two levels below normal.
Idle	Thread runs at 16 for the real-time priority class and at 1 for all other priority classes.

Table 7-4 shows how this mapping works for Windows Vista, but be aware that earlier versions of Windows NT and certainly Windows 95 and Windows 98 have slightly different mappings. Also be aware that the mapping will change in future versions of Windows.

For example, a normal thread in a normal process is assigned a priority level of 8. Because most processes are of the normal priority class and most threads are of normal thread priority, most threads in the system have a priority level of 8.

If you have a normal thread in a high-priority process, the thread will have a priority level of 13. If you change the process' priority class to idle, the thread's priority level becomes 4. Remember that thread priorities are relative to the process' priority class. If you change a process' priority class, the thread's relative priority will not change but its priority level will.

Table 7-4   How Process Priority Class and Relative Thread Priorities Map to Priority Values

Relative Thread Priority	Process Priority Class					
	Idle	Below Normal	Normal	Above Normal	High	Real-Time
Time-critical	15	15	15	15	15	31
Highest	6	8	10	12	15	26
Above normal	5	7	9	11	14	25
Normal	4	6	8	10	13	24
Below normal	3	5	7	9	12	23
Lowest	2	4	6	8	11	22
Idle	1	1	1	1	1	16

Notice that the table does not show any way for a thread to have a priority level of 0. This is because the 0 priority is reserved for the zero page thread and the system does not allow any other thread to have a priority of 0. Also, the following priority levels are not obtainable: 17, 18, 19, 20, 21, 27, 28, 29, or 30. If you are writing a device driver that runs in kernel mode, you can obtain these levels; a user-mode application cannot. Also note that a thread in the real-time priority class can't be below priority level 16. Likewise, a thread in a non-real-time priority class cannot be above 15.

Note   The concept of a process priority class confuses some people. They think that this somehow means that processes are scheduled. Processes are never scheduled; only threads are scheduled. The process priority class is an abstract concept that Microsoft created to help isolate you from the internal workings of the scheduler; it serves no other purpose.

Note   In general, a thread with a high priority level should not be schedulable most of the time. When the thread has something to do, it quickly gets CPU time. At this point, the thread should execute as few CPU instructions as possible and go back to sleep, waiting to be schedulable again. In contrast, a thread with a low priority level can remain schedulable and execute a lot of CPU instructions to do its work. If you follow these rules, the entire operating system will be responsive to its users.

Programming Priorities

So how is a process assigned a priority class? Well, when you call **CreateProcess**, you can pass the desired priority class in the **fdwCreate** parameter. Table 7-5 shows the priority class identifiers.

Table 7-5   Process Priority Classes

Priority Class	Symbolic Identifiers
Real-time	**REALTIME_PRIORITY_CLASS**
High	**HIGH_PRIORITY_CLASS**
Above normal	**ABOVE_NORMAL_PRIORITY_CLASS**
Normal	**NORMAL_PRIORITY_CLASS**
Below normal	**BELOW_NORMAL_PRIORITY_CLASS**
Idle	**IDLE_PRIORITY_CLASS**

It might seem odd that the process that creates a child process chooses the priority class at which the child process runs. Let's consider Windows Explorer as an example. When you use Windows Explorer to run an application, the new process runs at normal priority. Windows Explorer has no idea what the process does or how often its threads need to be scheduled. However, once the child process is running, it can change its own priority class by calling **SetPriorityClass**:

```
BOOL SetPriorityClass(
   HANDLE hProcess,
   DWORD fdwPriority);
```

This function changes the priority class identified by **hProcess** to the value specified in the **fdwPriority** parameter. The **fdwPriority** parameter can be one of the identifiers shown in the preceding table. Because this function takes a process handle, you can alter the priority class of any process running in the system as long as you have a handle to it and sufficient access.

Normally, a process will attempt to alter its own priority class. Here is an example of how to have a process set its own priority class to idle:

```
BOOL SetPriorityClass(
   GetCurrentProcess(),
   IDLE_PRIORITY_CLASS);
```

Here is the complementary function used to retrieve the priority class of a process:

```
DWORD GetPriorityClass(HANDLE hProcess);
```

As you might expect, this function returns one of the identifiers listed in Table 7-5.

When you invoke a program using the command shell, the program's starting priority is normal. However, if you invoke the program using the **START** command, you can use a switch to specify the starting priority of the application. For example, the following command entered at the command shell causes the system to invoke the Calculator and initially run it at idle priority:

```
C:\>START /LOW CALC.EXE
```

The **START** command also recognizes the **/BELOWNORMAL**, **/NORMAL**, **/ABOVENORMAL**, **/HIGH**, and **/REALTIME** switches to start executing an application at their respective priority classes. Of course, once an application starts executing, it can call **SetPriorityClass** to alter its own priority to whatever it chooses.

The Windows Task Manager allows the user to change the priority class of a process. The following figure shows the Task Manager's Processes tab, which shows all the processes currently running. The Base Pri column shows each process' priority class. You can alter a process' priority class by selecting a process and then selecting an option from the context menu's Set Priority submenu.

When a thread is first created, its relative thread priority is always set to normal. It has always seemed odd to me that **CreateThread** doesn't offer a way for the caller to set the new thread's relative priority. To set and get a thread's relative priority, you must call these functions:

```
BOOL SetThreadPriority(
   HANDLE hThread,
   int nPriority);
```

Of course, the **hThread** parameter identifies the single thread whose priority you want to change, and the **nPriority** parameter is one of the seven identifiers listed in Table 7-6.

Table 7-6   Relative Thread Priorities

Relative Thread Priority	Symbolic Constant
Time-critical	THREAD_PRIORITY_TIME_CRITICAL
Highest	THREAD_PRIORITY_HIGHEST
Above normal	THREAD_PRIORITY_ABOVE_NORMAL
Normal	THREAD_PRIORITY_NORMAL
Below normal	THREAD_PRIORITY_BELOW_NORMAL
Lowest	THREAD_PRIORITY_LOWEST
Idle	THREAD_PRIORITY_IDLE

Here is the complementary function for retrieving a thread's relative priority:

```
int GetThreadPriority(HANDLE hThread);
```

This function returns one of the identifiers listed in the preceding table.

To create a thread with an idle relative thread priority, you execute code similar to the following:

```
DWORD dwThreadID;
HANDLE hThread = CreateThread(NULL, 0, ThreadFunc, NULL,
   CREATE_SUSPENDED, &dwThreadID);
SetThreadPriority(hThread, THREAD_PRIORITY_IDLE);
ResumeThread(hThread);
CloseHandle(hThread);
```

Note that **CreateThread** always creates a new thread with a normal relative thread priority. To have the thread execute using idle priority, you pass the **CREATE_SUSPENDED** flag to **CreateThread**; this prevents the thread from executing any code at all. Then you call **SetThreadPriority** to change the thread to an idle relative thread priority. You then call **ResumeThread** so that the thread can be schedulable. You don't know when the thread will get CPU time, but the scheduler takes into account the fact that this thread has an idle thread priority. Finally, you close the handle to the new thread so that the kernel object can be destroyed as soon as the thread terminates.

> **Note**   Windows does not offer a function that returns a thread's priority level. This omission is deliberate. Remember that Microsoft reserves the right to change the scheduling algorithm at any time. You should not design an application that requires specific knowledge of the scheduling algorithm. If you stick with process priority classes and relative thread priorities, your application should run well today and on future versions of the system.

Dynamically Boosting Thread Priority Levels

The system determines the thread's priority level by combining a thread's relative priority with the priority class of the thread's process. This is sometimes referred to as the thread's *base priority level*. Occasionally, the system boosts the priority level of a thread—usually in response to some I/O event such as a window message or a disk read.

For example, a thread with a normal thread priority in a high-priority class process has a base priority level of 13. If the user presses a key, the system places a **WM_KEYDOWN** message in the thread's queue. Because a message has appeared in the thread's queue, the thread is schedulable. In addition, the keyboard device driver can tell the system to temporarily boost the thread's level. So the thread might be boosted by 2 and have a current priority level of 15.

The thread is scheduled for one time slice at priority 15. Once that time slice expires, the system drops the thread's priority by 1 to 14 for the next time slice. The thread's third time slice is executed with a priority level of 13. Any additional time slices required by the thread are executed at priority level 13, the thread's base priority level.

Note that a thread's current priority level never goes below the thread's base priority level. Also note that the device driver that causes the thread to be schedulable determines the amount of the boost. Again, Microsoft does not document how much boost a thread will get by any individual device driver. This allows Microsoft to continuously fine-tune the dynamic boosts to determine the best overall responsiveness.

The system boosts only threads that have a base priority level between 1 and 15. In fact, this is why this range is referred to as the *dynamic priority range*. In addition, the system never boosts a thread into the real-time range (above 15). Because threads in the real-time range perform most operating system functions, enforcing a cap on the boost prevents an application from interfering with the operating system. Also, the system never dynamically boosts threads in the real-time range (16 through 31).

Some developers complained that the system's dynamic boosts had an adverse affect on their threads' performance, so Microsoft added the following two functions to let you disable the system's dynamic boosting of thread priority levels:

```
BOOL SetProcessPriorityBoost(
   HANDLE hProcess,
   BOOL bDisablePriorityBoost);
BOOL SetThreadPriorityBoost(
   HANDLE hThread,
   BOOL bDisablePriorityBoost);
```

SetProcessPriorityBoost tells the system to enable or disable priority boosting for all threads within a process; **SetThreadPriorityBoost** lets you enable or disable priority boosting for individual threads. These two functions have counterparts that allow you to determine whether priority boosting is enabled or disabled:

```
BOOL GetProcessPriorityBoost(
   HANDLE hProcess,
   PBOOL pbDisablePriorityBoost);
BOOL GetThreadPriorityBoost(
   HANDLE hThread,
   PBOOL pbDisablePriorityBoost);
```

To each of these functions, you pass the handle of the process or thread that you want to query along with the address of a BOOL that will be set by the function.

Another situation causes the system to dynamically boost a thread's priority level. Imagine a priority 4 thread that is ready to run but cannot because a priority 8 thread is constantly schedulable. In this scenario, the priority 4 thread is being starved of CPU time. When the system detects that a thread has been starved of CPU time for about three to four seconds, it dynamically boosts the starving thread's priority to 15 and allows that thread to run for twice its time quantum. When the double time quantum expires, the thread's priority immediately returns to its base priority.

Tweaking the Scheduler for the Foreground Process

When the user works with windows of a process, that process is said to be the *foreground process* and all other processes are *background processes*. Certainly, a user would prefer the process that he or she is using to behave more responsively than the background processes. To improve the responsiveness of the foreground process, Windows tweaks the scheduling algorithm for threads in the foreground process. The system gives foreground process threads a larger time quantum than they would usually receive. This tweak is performed only if the foreground process is of the normal priority class. If it is of any other priority class, no tweaking is performed.

Windows Vista actually allows a user to configure this tweaking. On the Advanced tab of the System Properties dialog box, the user can click the Settings button of the Performance section to pop up the Performance Options dialog box and finally select the Advanced tab.

If the user chooses to optimize performance for programs (which is the default in Windows Vista), the system performs the tweaking. If the user chooses to optimize performance for background services, no tweaking is performed.

Scheduling I/O Request Priorities

Setting thread priorities affects how threads are scheduled CPU resources. However, threads also perform I/O requests to read and write data from disk files. If a low-priority thread gets CPU time, it could easily queue hundreds or thousands of I/O requests in a very short time. Because I/O requests typically require time to process, it is possible that a low-priority thread could significantly affect the responsiveness of the system by suspending high-priority threads, which prevents them from getting their work done. Because of this, you can see a machine become less responsive when executing long-running low-priority services such as disk defragmenters, virus scanners, content indexers, and so on.

Starting with Windows Vista, it is now possible for a thread to specify a priority when making I/O requests. You can tell Windows that a thread should issue low-priority I/O requests by calling **SetThreadPriority** passing **THREAD_MODE_BACKGROUND_BEGIN**. Note, this also lowers the CPU scheduling priority of the thread. You can return the thread to making normal priority I/O requests (and normal CPU scheduling priority) by calling **SetThreadPriority**, again passing **THREAD_MODE_BACKGROUND_END**. When you call **SetThreadPriority** passing either of these flags, you must pass the handle to the calling thread (returned by calling **GetCurrentThread**); a thread is not allowed to change the I/O priority of another thread.

If you want all threads in a process to make low-priority I/O requests and have low CPU scheduling, you can call **SetPriorityClass** passing **PROCESS_MODE_BACKGROUND_BEGIN**. You can reverse this action by calling **SetPriorityClass** passing **PROCESS_MODE_BACKGROUND_END**. When you call **SetPriorityClass** passing either of these flags, you must pass the handle to the calling process (returned by calling **GetCurrentProcess**); a thread is not allowed to change the I/O priority of threads in another process.

At an even finer grain, a normal-priority thread can perform background-priority I/Os on a specific file as shown in the following code snippet:

```
FILE_IO_PRIORITY_HINT_INFO phi;
phi.PriorityHint = IoPriorityHintLow;
SetFileInformationByHandle(
    hFile, FileIoPriorityHintInfo, &phi, sizeof(PriorityHint));
```

The priority set by **SetFileInformationByHandle** overrides the priority set at the process or thread level by **SetPriorityClass** or **SetThreadPriority**, respectively.

As a developer, it is your responsibility to use these new background priorities to allow the foreground applications to be more responsive, taking care to avoid *priority inversion*. In the presence of intense normal-priority I/Os, a thread running at background priority can be delayed for *seconds* before getting the result of its I/O requests. If a low-priority thread has grabbed a lock for which the normal-priority thread is waiting, the normal-priority threads might end up waiting for the background-priority thread until the low-priority I/O requests are completed. Your background-priority thread does not even have to submit I/Os for the problem to happen. So using shared synchronization objects between normal and background-priority threads should be minimized (or eliminated if possible) to avoid these priority inversions where normal-priority threads are blocked on locks owned by background-priority threads.

> **Note**   Notice that SuperFetch is taking advantage of these new background priorities. For more details about priority I/O, refer to the white paper on *http://www.microsoft.com/whdc/ driver/priorityio.mspx*.

The Scheduling Lab Sample Application

Using the Scheduling Lab application, 07-SchedLab.exe (listed on the next page), you can experiment with process priority classes and relative thread priorities to see their effect on the system's overall performance. The source code and resource files for the application are in the 07-SchedLab directory on the companion content Web page. When you start the program, the window shown here appears.

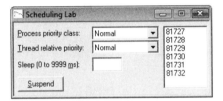

Initially, the primary thread is always busy, so your CPU usage immediately jumps to 100 percent. The primary thread constantly increments a number and adds it to the list box on the right. The number doesn't have any meaning—it simply shows that the thread is busy doing something. To get a feel for how thread scheduling actually affects the system, I recommend that you run at least two instances of this sample application simultaneously to see how changing the priorities of one instance affects the other instances. You can also run Task Manager and monitor the CPU usage of all instances.

When you perform these tests, the CPU usage will initially go to 100 percent and all instances of the application will get about equal CPU time. (Task Manager should show about the same percentage of CPU usage for all instances.) If you change one instance's priority class to above normal or high, you should see it get the bulk of the CPU usage. The scrolling of numbers in the other instances will become erratic. However, the other instances do not stop scrolling completely because of the dynamic boosting that the system automatically performs for starving threads. Anyway, you can play with the priority class and relative thread priorities to see how they affect the other instances. I purposely coded the Scheduling Lab application so that it doesn't allow you to change the process to the real-time priority class because this prevents operating system threads from performing properly. If you want to experiment with real-time priority, you must modify the source code yourself.

You can use the Sleep field to stop the primary thread from being schedulable for any number of milliseconds from 0 to 9999. Experiment with this and see how much CPU processing time you recover by passing a sleep value of just 1 millisecond. On my 2.2-GHz Pentium notebook computer, I gain back 99 percent—quite a drop!

Clicking the Suspend button causes the primary thread to spawn a secondary thread. This secondary thread suspends the primary thread and displays the following message box.

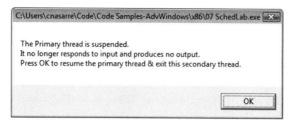

While this message box is displayed, the primary thread is completely suspended and uses no CPU time. The secondary thread also does not use any CPU time because it is simply waiting for the user to do something. While the message box is displayed, you can move it over the application's main window and then move it away so that you can see the main window. Because the primary thread is suspended, the main window will not handle any window messages (including **WM_PAINT**). This is proof positive that the thread is suspended. When you dismiss the message box, the primary thread is resumed and the CPU usage goes back up to 100 percent.

For one more test, display the Performance Options dialog box discussed in the previous section, and change the setting from Application to Background Services or vice versa. Then take multiple instances of the SchedLab program, set them all to the normal priority class, and activate one of them to make it the foreground process. You'll see what effect the performance setting has on the foreground/background processes.

```
SchedLab.cpp
/******************************************************************************
Module:  SchedLab.cpp
Notices: Copyright (c) 2008 Jeffrey Richter & Christophe Nasarre
******************************************************************************/


#include "..\CommonFiles\CmnHdr.h"      /* See Appendix A. */
#include <windowsx.h>
#include <tchar.h>
#include "Resource.h"
#include <StrSafe.h>


///////////////////////////////////////////////////////////////////////////////


DWORD WINAPI ThreadFunc(PVOID pvParam) {

   HANDLE hThreadPrimary = (HANDLE) pvParam;
   SuspendThread(hThreadPrimary);
   chMB(
      "The Primary thread is suspended.\n"
      "It no longer responds to input and produces no output.\n"
      "Press OK to resume the primary thread & exit this secondary thread.\n");
   ResumeThread(hThreadPrimary);
   CloseHandle(hThreadPrimary);
```

```
   // To avoid deadlock, call EnableWindow after ResumeThread.
   EnableWindow(
      GetDlgItem(FindWindow(NULL, TEXT("Scheduling Lab")), IDC_SUSPEND),
      TRUE);
   return(0);
}


//////////////////////////////////////////////////////////////////////////


BOOL Dlg_OnInitDialog (HWND hWnd, HWND hWndFocus, LPARAM lParam) {

   chSETDLGICONS(hWnd, IDI_SCHEDLAB);

   // Initialize process priority classes
   HWND hWndCtl = GetDlgItem(hWnd, IDC_PROCESSPRIORITYCLASS);

   int n = ComboBox_AddString(hWndCtl, TEXT("High"));
   ComboBox_SetItemData(hWndCtl, n, HIGH_PRIORITY_CLASS);

   // Save our current priority class
   DWORD dwpc = GetPriorityClass(GetCurrentProcess());

   if (SetPriorityClass(GetCurrentProcess(), BELOW_NORMAL_PRIORITY_CLASS)) {

      // This system supports the BELOW_NORMAL_PRIORITY_CLASS class

      // Restore our original priority class
      SetPriorityClass(GetCurrentProcess(), dwpc);

      // Add the Above Normal priority class
      n = ComboBox_AddString(hWndCtl, TEXT("Above normal"));
      ComboBox_SetItemData(hWndCtl, n, ABOVE_NORMAL_PRIORITY_CLASS);

      dwpc = 0;  // Remember that this system supports below normal
   }

   int nNormal = n = ComboBox_AddString(hWndCtl, TEXT("Normal"));
   ComboBox_SetItemData(hWndCtl, n, NORMAL_PRIORITY_CLASS);

   if (dwpc == 0) {

      // This system supports the BELOW_NORMAL_PRIORITY_CLASS class

      // Add the Below Normal priority class
      n = ComboBox_AddString(hWndCtl, TEXT("Below normal"));
      ComboBox_SetItemData(hWndCtl, n, BELOW_NORMAL_PRIORITY_CLASS);
   }

   n = ComboBox_AddString(hWndCtl, TEXT("Idle"));
   ComboBox_SetItemData(hWndCtl, n, IDLE_PRIORITY_CLASS);

   ComboBox_SetCurSel(hWndCtl, nNormal);
```

```
      // Initialize thread relative priorities
      hWndCtl = GetDlgItem(hWnd, IDC_THREADRELATIVEPRIORITY);

      n = ComboBox_AddString(hWndCtl, TEXT("Time critical"));
      ComboBox_SetItemData(hWndCtl, n, THREAD_PRIORITY_TIME_CRITICAL);

      n = ComboBox_AddString(hWndCtl, TEXT("Highest"));
      ComboBox_SetItemData(hWndCtl, n, THREAD_PRIORITY_HIGHEST);

      n = ComboBox_AddString(hWndCtl, TEXT("Above normal"));
      ComboBox_SetItemData(hWndCtl, n, THREAD_PRIORITY_ABOVE_NORMAL);

      nNormal = n = ComboBox_AddString(hWndCtl, TEXT("Normal"));
      ComboBox_SetItemData(hWndCtl, n, THREAD_PRIORITY_NORMAL);

      n = ComboBox_AddString(hWndCtl, TEXT("Below normal"));
      ComboBox_SetItemData(hWndCtl, n, THREAD_PRIORITY_BELOW_NORMAL);

      n = ComboBox_AddString(hWndCtl, TEXT("Lowest"));
      ComboBox_SetItemData(hWndCtl, n, THREAD_PRIORITY_LOWEST);

      n = ComboBox_AddString(hWndCtl, TEXT("Idle"));
      ComboBox_SetItemData(hWndCtl, n, THREAD_PRIORITY_IDLE);

      ComboBox_SetCurSel(hWndCtl, nNormal);

      Edit_LimitText(GetDlgItem(hWnd, IDC_SLEEPTIME), 4);   // Maximum of 9999
      return(TRUE);
}


///////////////////////////////////////////////////////////////////////////////


void Dlg_OnCommand (HWND hWnd, int id, HWND hWndCtl, UINT codeNotify) {

   switch (id) {
      case IDCANCEL:
         PostQuitMessage(0);
         break;

      case IDC_PROCESSPRIORITYCLASS:
         if (codeNotify == CBN_SELCHANGE) {
            SetPriorityClass(GetCurrentProcess(), (DWORD)
               ComboBox_GetItemData(hWndCtl, ComboBox_GetCurSel(hWndCtl)));
         }
         break;

      case IDC_THREADRELATIVEPRIORITY:
         if (codeNotify == CBN_SELCHANGE) {
            SetThreadPriority(GetCurrentThread(), (DWORD)
               ComboBox_GetItemData(hWndCtl, ComboBox_GetCurSel(hWndCtl)));
         }
         break;
```

```
        case IDC_SUSPEND:
            // To avoid deadlock, call EnableWindow before creating
            // the thread that calls SuspendThread.
            EnableWindow(hWndCtl, FALSE);

            HANDLE hThreadPrimary;
            DuplicateHandle(GetCurrentProcess(), GetCurrentThread(),
                GetCurrentProcess(), &hThreadPrimary,
                THREAD_SUSPEND_RESUME, FALSE, DUPLICATE_SAME_ACCESS);
            DWORD dwThreadID;
            CloseHandle(chBEGINTHREADEX(NULL, 0, ThreadFunc,
                hThreadPrimary, 0, &dwThreadID));
            break;
    }
}


/////////////////////////////////////////////////////////////////////////////


INT_PTR WINAPI Dlg_Proc(HWND hWnd, UINT uMsg, WPARAM wParam, LPARAM lParam) {

   switch (uMsg) {
      chHANDLE_DLGMSG(hWnd, WM_INITDIALOG, Dlg_OnInitDialog);
      chHANDLE_DLGMSG(hWnd, WM_COMMAND,    Dlg_OnCommand);
   }

   return(FALSE);
}


/////////////////////////////////////////////////////////////////////////////


class CStopwatch {
public:
   CStopwatch() { QueryPerformanceFrequency(&m_liPerfFreq); Start(); }

   void Start() { QueryPerformanceCounter(&m_liPerfStart); }

   __int64 Now() const {   // Returns # of milliseconds since Start was called
      LARGE_INTEGER liPerfNow;
      QueryPerformanceCounter(&liPerfNow);
      return(((liPerfNow.QuadPart - m_liPerfStart.QuadPart) * 1000)
         / m_liPerfFreq.QuadPart);
   }

private:
   LARGE_INTEGER m_liPerfFreq;   // Counts per second
   LARGE_INTEGER m_liPerfStart;  // Starting count
};
```

```
__int64 FileTimeToQuadWord (PFILETIME pft) {
   return(Int64Sh11Mod32(pft->dwHighDateTime, 32) | pft->dwLowDateTime);
}



int WINAPI _tWinMain(HINSTANCE hInstExe, HINSTANCE, PTSTR pszCmdLine, int) {

   HWND hWnd =
      CreateDialog(hInstExe, MAKEINTRESOURCE(IDD_SCHEDLAB), NULL, Dlg_Proc);
   BOOL fQuit = FALSE;

   while (!fQuit) {
      MSG msg;
      if (PeekMessage(&msg, NULL, 0, 0, PM_REMOVE)) {

         // IsDialogMessage allows keyboard navigation to work properly.
         if (!IsDialogMessage(hWnd, &msg)) {

            if (msg.message == WM_QUIT) {
               fQuit = TRUE;  // For WM_QUIT, terminate the loop.
            } else {
               // Not a WM_QUIT message. Translate it and dispatch it.
               TranslateMessage(&msg);
               DispatchMessage(&msg);
            }
         } // if (!IsDialogMessage())
      } else {

         // Add a number to the listbox
         static int s_n = -1;
         TCHAR sz[20];
         StringCChPrintf(sz, _countof(sz), TEXT("%u"), ++s_n);
         HWND hWndWork = GetDlgItem(hWnd, IDC_WORK);
         ListBox_SetCurSel(hWndWork, ListBox_AddString(hWndWork, sz));

         // Remove some strings if there are too many entries
         while (ListBox_GetCount(hWndWork) > 100)
            ListBox_DeleteString(hWndWork, 0);

         // How long should the thread sleep
         int nSleep = GetDlgItemInt(hWnd, IDC_SLEEPTIME, NULL, FALSE);
         if (chINRANGE(1, nSleep, 9999))
            Sleep(nSleep);
      }
   }

   DestroyWindow(hWnd);
   return(0);
}


////////////////////////////// End of File //////////////////////////////
```

Affinities

By default, Windows Vista uses *soft affinity* when assigning threads to processors. This means that if all other factors are equal, it tries to run the thread on the processor it ran on last. Having a thread stay on a single processor helps reuse data that is still in the processor's memory cache.

There is a computer architecture called NUMA (Non-Uniform Memory Access) in which a machine consists of several boards. Each board has its own CPUs and its own bank of memory. The following figure shows a machine with three boards in it, with each board having 4 CPUs, making 12 CPUs available so that any single thread can run on any of the 12 CPUs.

NUMA Machine

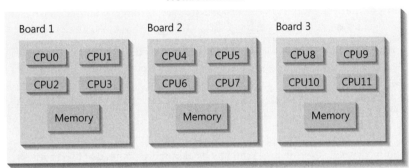

A NUMA system performs best when a CPU accesses the memory that is on its own board. If the CPU needs to touch memory that is on another board, an enormous performance hit is incurred. In such an environment, it is desirable to have threads from one process run on CPUs 0 through 3 and have threads in another process run on CPUs 4 through 7, and so on. To accommodate such machine architectures, Windows Vista allows you to set process and thread affinities. In other words, you can control which CPUs can run certain threads. This is called *hard affinity*.

The system determines how many CPUs are available in the machine at boot time. An application can query the number of CPUs on the machine by calling **GetSystemInfo** (discussed in Chapter 14, "Exploring Virtual Memory"). By default, any thread can be scheduled to any of these CPUs. To limit threads in a single process to run on a subset of the available CPUs, you can call **Set-ProcessAffinityMask**:

```
BOOL SetProcessAffinityMask(
    HANDLE hProcess,
    DWORD_PTR dwProcessAffinityMask);
```

The first parameter, **hProcess**, indicates which process to affect. The second parameter, **dwProcessAffinityMask**, is a bitmask indicating which CPUs the threads can run on. For example, passing 0x00000005 means that threads in this process can run on CPU 0 and CPU 2 but not on CPU 1 and CPUs 3 through 31.

Note that child processes inherit process affinity. So if a process has an affinity mask of 0x00000005, any threads in its child processes have the same mask and share the same CPUs. In addition, you can use the job kernel object (discussed in Chapter 5, "Jobs") to restrict a set of processes to a desired set of CPUs.

Of course, there is also a function that returns a process' affinity mask, **GetProcessAffinityMask**:

```
BOOL GetProcessAffinityMask(
    HANDLE hProcess,
    PDWORD_PTR pdwProcessAffinityMask,
    PDWORD_PTR pdwSystemAffinityMask);
```

Here, you also pass the handle of the process whose affinity mask you want and the function fills in the variable pointed to by **pdwProcessAffinityMask**. This function also returns the system's affinity mask (in the variable pointed to by **pdwSystemAffinityMask**). The system's affinity mask indicates which of the system's CPUs can process threads. A process' affinity mask is always a proper subset of the system's affinity mask.

So far, we've discussed how to limit the threads of a process to a set of CPUs. Sometimes you might want to limit a thread within a process to a set of CPUs. For example, you might have a process containing four threads running on a machine with four CPUs. If one of these threads is doing important work and you want to increase the likelihood that a CPU will always be available for it, you limit the other three threads so that they cannot run on CPU 0 and can run only on CPUs 1, 2, and 3.

You can set affinity masks for individual threads by calling **SetThreadAffinityMask**:

```
DWORD_PTR SetThreadAffinityMask(
    HANDLE hThread,
    DWORD_PTR dwThreadAffinityMask);
```

The **hThread** parameter indicates which thread to limit, and the **dwThreadAffinityMask** indicates which CPUs the thread can run on. The **dwThreadAffinityMask** must be a proper subset of the process' affinity mask. The return value is the thread's previous affinity mask. So, to limit three threads to CPUs 1, 2, and 3, you do this:

```
// Thread 0 can only run on CPU 0.
SetThreadAffinityMask(hThread0, 0x00000001);

// Threads 1, 2, 3 run on CPUs 1, 2, 3.
SetThreadAffinityMask(hThread1, 0x0000000E);
SetThreadAffinityMask(hThread2, 0x0000000E);
SetThreadAffinityMask(hThread3, 0x0000000E);
```

When an *x86* system boots, the system executes code that detects which CPUs on the host machine experience the famous Pentium floating-point bug. The system must test this for each CPU by setting a thread's affinity to the first CPU, performing the potentially faulty divide operation, and comparing the result with the known correct answer. Then this sequence is attempted again for the next CPU, and so on.

> **Note** In most environments, altering thread affinities interferes with the scheduler's ability to effectively migrate threads across CPUs that make the most efficient use of CPU time. The following table shows an example.
>
> | Thread | Priority | Affinity Mask | Result |
> |--------|----------|---------------|--------|
> | A | 4 | 0x00000001 | CPU 0 |
> | B | 8 | 0x00000003 | CPU 1 |
> | C | 6 | 0x00000002 | Can't run |
>
> When Thread A wakes, the scheduler sees that the thread can run on CPU 0 and it is assigned to CPU 0. Thread B then wakes, and the scheduler sees that the thread can be assigned to CPU 0 or 1, but because CPU 0 is in use, the scheduler assigns it to CPU 1. So far, so good.
>
> Now Thread C wakes, and the scheduler sees that it can run only on CPU 1. But CPU 1 is in use by Thread B, a priority 8 thread. Because Thread C is a priority 6 thread, it can't preempt Thread B. Thread C can preempt Thread A, a priority 4 thread, but the scheduler will not preempt Thread A because Thread C can't run on CPU 0.
>
> This demonstrates how setting hard affinities for threads can interfere with the scheduler's priority scheme.

Sometimes forcing a thread to a specific CPU is not the best idea. For example, you might have three threads all limited to CPU 0, but CPUs 1, 2, and 3 might be sitting idle. It would be better if you could tell the system that you want a thread to run on a particular CPU but allow the thread to migrate to another CPU if one is available.

To set an ideal CPU for a thread, you call **SetThreadIdealProcessor**:

```
DWORD SetThreadIdealProcessor(
   HANDLE hThread,
   DWORD dwIdealProcessor);
```

The **hThread** parameter indicates which thread to set a preferred CPU for. However, unlike all the other functions we've been discussing, the **dwIdealProcessor** is not a bitmask; it is an integer from 0 through 31/63 that indicates the preferred CPU for the thread. You can pass a value of **MAXIMUM_PROCESSORS** (defined either as 32 for 32-bit operating systems or as 64 for 64-bit operating systems in WinNT.h) to indicate that the thread has no ideal CPU. The function returns the previous ideal CPU or **MAXIMUM_PROCESSORS** if the thread doesn't have an ideal CPU set for it.

You can also set processor affinity in the header of an executable file. Oddly, there doesn't seem to be a linker switch for this, but you can use code similar to this that takes advantage of functions declared in ImageHlp.h:

```
// Load the EXE into memory.
PLOADED_IMAGE pLoadedImage = ImageLoad(szExeName, NULL);

// Get the current load configuration information for the EXE.
IMAGE_LOAD_CONFIG_DIRECTORY ilcd;
GetImageConfigInformation(pLoadedImage, &ilcd);
```

```
// Change the processor affinity mask.
ilcd.ProcessAffinityMask = 0x00000003; // I desire CPUs 0 and 1

// Save the new load configuration information.
SetImageConfigInformation(pLoadedImage, &ilcd);

// Unload the EXE from memory
ImageUnload(pLoadedImage);
```

I won't bother to explain all these functions in detail; you can look them up in the Platform SDK documentation if you're interested.

Finally, the Windows Task Manager allows a user to alter a process' CPU affinity by selecting a process and displaying its context menu. If you run on a multiprocessor machine, you see a Set Affinity menu item. (This menu item is not available on uniprocessor machines.) When you choose this menu item, you see the following dialog box, in which you can select which CPUs the threads in the chosen process can run on.

When Windows Vista boots on an *x86* machine, you can limit the number of CPUs that the system will use. During the boot cycle, the system examines the *boot configuration data (BCD)*, which is a data store that replaces the old boot.ini text file and provides an abstraction level above the hardware and firmware of the machine. A very detailed white paper about BCD is available at *http://www.microsoft.com/whdc/system/platform/firmware/bcd.mspx*.

The programmatic configuration of the BCD is done through Windows Management Instrumentation (WMI), but you have access to some of the most common parameters through a graphical user interface. For limiting the number of CPUs used by Windows, you need to open Control Panel and select System Configuration from Administrative Tools. On the Boot tab, you click the Advanced button to be able to choose the Number Of Processors check box and select the number you want.

Chapter 8
Thread Synchronization in User Mode

Microsoft Windows runs best when all the threads can go about their business without having to communicate with each other. However, a thread can rarely act independently all the time. Usually, threads are spawned to handle some task. When the task is complete, another thread will probably want to know about it.

All threads in the system must have access to system resources, such as heaps, serial ports, files, windows, and countless others. If one thread requests exclusive access to a resource, other threads cannot get their work done. On the flip side, you can't just let any thread touch any resource at any time. Imagine a thread writing to a memory block while another thread reads from the same memory block. This is analogous to reading a book while someone is changing the text on the page. The thoughts on the page are all jumbled, and nothing useful comes of it.

Threads need to communicate with each other in two basic situations:

- When you have multiple threads accessing a shared resource in such a way that the resource does not become corrupt
- When one thread needs to notify one or more other threads that a specific task has been completed

Thread synchronization has many aspects, which I'll discuss over the next few chapters. The good news is that Microsoft Windows offers many facilities to make thread synchronization easy. The bad news is that anticipating what a bunch of threads might attempt to do at any time is extremely difficult. Our minds just don't work asynchronously; we like to think things through in an orderly fashion, one step at a time. But that's not how a multithreaded environment works.

I first started working with multiple threads around 1992. At first, I made many programming mistakes and actually published book chapters and magazine articles that had thread synchronization–related bugs in them. Today, I'm much more skilled, but hardly perfect, and I truly believe that everything in this book is bug free (even though I should know better by now). The only way to get good at thread synchronization is by doing it. In these chapters, I'll explain how the system works and show you how to properly synchronize threads. But you should face the music now: you'll make mistakes as you gain experience.

Atomic Access: The Interlocked Family of Functions

A big part of thread synchronization has to do with *atomic access*—a thread's ability to access a resource with the guarantee that no other thread will access that same resource at the same time. Let's look at a simple example:

```
// Define a global variable.
long g_x = 0;

DWORD WINAPI ThreadFunc1(PVOID pvParam) {
    g_x++;
    return(0);
}

DWORD WINAPI ThreadFunc2(PVOID pvParam) {
    g_x++;
    return(0);
}
```

I've declared a global variable, **g_x**, and initialized it to **0**. Now let's say that I create two threads: one thread executes **ThreadFunc1**, and the other thread executes **ThreadFunc2**. The code in these two functions is identical: they both add 1 to the global variable **g_x**. So when both threads stop running, you might expect to see the value **2** in **g_x**. But do you? The answer is ... maybe. The way the code is written, you can't tell what **g_x** will ultimately contain. Here's why. Let's say that the compiler generates the following code for the line that increments **g_x** by 1:

```
MOV EAX, [g_x]      ; Move the value in g_x into a register.
INC EAX             ; Increment the value in the register.
MOV [g_x], EAX      ; Store the new value back in g_x.
```

Both threads are unlikely to execute this code at exactly the same time. So if one thread executes this code followed by another thread, here is what effectively executes:

```
MOV EAX, [g_x]      ; Thread 1: Move 0 into a register.
INC EAX             ; Thread 1: Increment the register to 1.
MOV [g_x], EAX      ; Thread 1: Store 1 back in g_x.

MOV EAX, [g_x]      ; Thread 2: Move 1 into a register.
INC EAX             ; Thread 2: Increment the register to 2.
MOV [g_x], EAX      ; Thread 2: Store 2 back in g_x.
```

After both threads are done incrementing **g_x**, the value in **g_x** is **2**. This is great and is exactly what we expect: take zero (0), increment it by 1 twice, and the answer is 2. Beautiful. But wait—Windows is a preemptive, multithreaded environment. So a thread can be switched away from at any time and another thread might continue executing at any time. So the preceding code might not execute exactly as I've written it. Instead, it might execute as follows:

```
MOV EAX, [g_x]        ; Thread 1: Move 0 into a register.
INC EAX               ; Thread 1: Increment the register to 1.

MOV EAX, [g_x]        ; Thread 2: Move 0 into a register.
INC EAX               ; Thread 2: Increment the register to 1.
MOV [g_x], EAX        ; Thread 2: Store 1 back in g_x.

MOV [g_x], EAX        ; Thread 1: Store 1 back in g_x.
```

If the code executes this way, the final value in **g_x** is **1**—not **2** as you expect! This is pretty scary, especially because you have so little control over the scheduler. In fact, if you have 100 threads executing similar thread functions, after all of them exit, the value in **g_x** might still be **1**! Obviously, software developers can't work in an environment like this. We expect that incrementing 0 twice results in 2 all the time. Also, let's not forget that the results might be different depending on how the compiler generates code, what CPU is executing the code, and how many CPUs are installed in the host computer. This is how the environment works, and there is nothing we can do about that. But Windows does offer some functions that, when used correctly, guarantee the outcome of our application's code.

To solve the problem just presented, we need something simple. We need a way to guarantee that the incrementing of the value is done atomically—that is, without interruption. The interlocked family of functions provides the solution we need. The interlocked functions are awesome and underused by most software developers, even though they are incredibly helpful and easy to understand. All the functions manipulate a value atomically. Take a look at **Interlocked-ExchangeAdd** and its sibling **InterlockedExchangeAdd64** that works on **LONGLONG** values:

```
LONG InterlockedExchangeAdd(
    PLONG volatile plAddend,
    LONG lIncrement);

LONGLONG InterlockedExchangeAdd64(
    PLONGLONG volatile pllAddend,
    LONGLONG llIncrement );
```

What could be simpler? You call this function, passing the address of a long variable and indicating by how much to increment this value. But this function guarantees that the adding of the value is accomplished atomically. So we can rewrite the code presented earlier as follows:

```
// Define a global variable.
long g_x = 0;

DWORD WINAPI ThreadFunc1(PVOID pvParam) {
    InterlockedExchangeAdd(&g_x, 1);
    return(0);
}

DWORD WINAPI ThreadFunc2(PVOID pvParam) {
    InterlockedExchangeAdd(&g_x, 1);
    return(0);
}
```

By making this small change, **g_x** is incremented atomically and therefore you are guaranteed that the final value in **g_x** will be **2**. Notice that you can also use the **InterlockedIncrement** function when you simply need to atomically increment a value by 1. Don't you feel better already? Note that all the threads should attempt to modify the shared long variable by calling these functions; no thread should ever attempt to modify the shared variable by using simple C++ statements:

```
// The long variable shared by many threads
LONG g_x; ...

// Incorrect way to increment the long
g_x++; ...

// Correct way to increment the long
InterlockedExchangeAdd(&g_x, 1);
```

How do the interlocked functions work? The answer depends on the CPU platform that you're running on. For the x86 family of CPUs, interlocked functions assert a hardware signal on the bus that prevents another CPU from accessing the same memory address.

You need not understand exactly how the interlocked functions work. What's important to know is that they guarantee that a value will be modified atomically, no matter how the compiler generates code and no matter how many CPUs are installed in the host machine. You must also ensure that the variable addresses that you pass to these functions are properly aligned or the functions might fail. (I'll discuss data alignment in Chapter 13, "Windows Memory Architecture.")

> **Note**   The C run-time library offers an **_aligned_malloc** function that you can use to allocate a block of memory that is properly aligned. Its prototype is as follows:
>
> ```
> void * _aligned_malloc(size_t size, size_t alignment);
> ```
>
> The **size** argument identifies the number of bytes you want to allocate, and the **alignment** argument indicates the byte boundary that you want the block aligned on. The value you pass for the **alignment** argument must be an integer power of 2.

Another important thing to know about the interlocked functions is that they execute extremely quickly. A call to an interlocked function usually causes just a few CPU cycles (usually less than 50) to execute, and there is no transition from user mode to kernel mode (which usually requires more than 1000 cycles to execute).

Of course, you can use **InterlockedExchangeAdd** to subtract a value—you simply pass a negative value for the second parameter. **InterlockedExchangeAdd** returns the original value that was in ***plAddend**.

Here are three more interlocked functions:

```
LONG InterlockedExchange(
   PLONG volatile plTarget,
   LONG lValue);

LONGLONG InterlockedExchange64(
   PLONGLONG volatile plTarget,
   LONGLONG lValue);
```

```
PVOID InterlockedExchangePointer(
   PVOID* volatile ppvTarget,
   PVOID pvValue);
```

InterlockedExchange and **InterlockedExchangePointer** atomically replace the current value whose address is passed in the first parameter with a value passed in the second parameter. For a 32-bit application, both functions replace a 32-bit value with another 32-bit value. But for a 64-bit application, **InterlockedExchange** replaces a 32-bit value while **InterlockedExchange-Pointer** replaces a 64-bit value. Both functions return the original value. **InterlockedExchange** is extremely useful when you implement a spinlock:

```
// Global variable indicating whether a shared resource is in use or not
BOOL g_fResourceInUse = FALSE; ...
void Func1() {
   // Wait to access the resource.
   while (InterlockedExchange (&g_fResourceInUse, TRUE) == TRUE)
      Sleep(0);

   // Access the resource.
   ...

   // We no longer need to access the resource.
   InterlockedExchange(&g_fResourceInUse, FALSE);
}
```

The **while** loop spins repeatedly, changing the value in **g_fResourceInUse** to **TRUE** and checking its previous value to see if it was **TRUE**. If the value was previously **FALSE**, the resource was not in use but the calling thread just set it to "in use" and exits the loop. If the previous value was **TRUE**, the resource was in use by another thread and the **while** loop continues to spin.

If another thread were to execute similar code, it would spin in its **while** loop until **g_fResource-InUse** was changed back to **FALSE**. The call to **InterlockedExchange** at the end of the function shows how **g_fResourceInUse** should be set back to **FALSE**.

You must take extreme care when using this technique because a spinlock wastes CPU time. The CPU must constantly compare two values until one "magically" changes because of another thread. Also, this code assumes that all threads using the spinlock run at the same priority level. You might also want to disable thread priority boosting (by calling **SetProcessPriorityBoost** or **SetThreadPriorityBoost**) for threads that execute spinlocks.

In addition, you should ensure that the lock variable and the data that the lock protects are maintained in different cache lines (discussed later in this chapter). If the lock variable and data share the same cache line, a CPU using the resource will contend with any CPUs attempting access of the resource. This hurts performance.

You should avoid using spinlocks on single-CPU machines. If a thread is spinning, it's wasting precious CPU time, which prevents the other thread from changing the value. My use of **Sleep** in the **while** loop shown earlier improves this situation somewhat. If you use **Sleep**, you might want to sleep a random amount of time, and each time the request to access the resource is denied, you might want to increase the sleep time even more. This prevents threads from simply wasting CPU time. Depending on your situation, it might be better to remove the call to **Sleep** altogether. Or you might want to replace it with a call to **SwitchToThread**. I hate to say it, but trial and error might be your best approach.

Spinlocks assume that the protected resource is always accessed for short periods of time. This makes it more efficient to spin and then transition to kernel mode and wait. Many developers spin some number of times (say 4000), and if access to the resource is still denied, the thread transitions to kernel mode, where it waits (consuming no CPU time) until the resource becomes available. This is how critical sections are implemented.

Spinlocks are useful on multiprocessor machines because one thread can spin while the other thread runs on another CPU. However, even in this scenario, you must be careful. You do not want a thread to spin for a long time, or you'll waste more CPU time. We'll discuss spinlocks further later in this chapter.

Here are the last interlocked exchange functions:

```
PVOID InterlockedCompareExchange(
    PLONG plDestination,
    LONG lExchange,
    LONG lComparand);


PVOID InterlockedCompareExchangePointer(
    PVOID* ppvDestination,
    PVOID pvExchange,
    PVOID pvComparand);
```

These two functions perform an atomic test and set operation: for a 32-bit application, both functions operate on 32-bit values, but in a 64-bit application, **InterlockedCompareExchange** operates on 32-bit values while **InterlockedCompareExchangePointer** operates on 64-bit values. In pseudocode, here is what happens:

```
LONG InterlockedCompareExchange(PLONG plDestination,
    LONG lExchange, LONG lComparand) {

    LONG lRet = *plDestination;   // Original value

    if (*plDestination == lComparand)
       *plDestination = lExchange;
    return(lRet);
}
```

The function compares the current value (pointed to by the **plDestination** parameter) with the value passed in the **lComparand** parameter. If the values are the same, ***plDestination** is changed to the value of the **lExchange** parameter. If what is in ***plDestination** doesn't match the value of **lComparand**, ***plDestination** is not changed. The function returns the original value in ***plDestination**. Remember that all these operations are performed as one atomic unit of execution. Notice that a version working on aligned 64-bit values is now available:

```
LONGLONG InterlockedCompareExchange64(
    LONGLONG pllDestination,
    LONGLONG llExchange,
    LONGLONG llComparand);
```

There is no interlocked function that simply reads a value (without changing it) because no such function is necessary. If a thread simply attempts to read the contents of a value that is always modified with an interlocked function, the value read is always a good value. You don't know if you'll read the original value or the updated value, but you know that it will be one of them. For most applications, this is sufficient. In addition, the interlocked functions might be used by threads in multiple processes when you're synchronizing access to a value that is in a shared memory section such as a memory-mapped file. (Chapter 9, "Thread Synchronization with Kernel Objects," includes a few sample applications that show how to properly use the interlocked functions.)

Windows offers a few other interlocked functions, but the functions I've described do everything that the other functions do and more. Here are two other functions:

```
LONG InterlockedIncrement(PLONG plAddend);
```

```
LONG InterlockedDecrement(PLONG plAddend);
```

InterlockedExchangeAdd replaces both of these older functions. The new function can add or subtract any value; the old functions are limited to adding or subtracting 1. A set of **OR**, **AND**, and **XOR** interlocked helper functions based on **InterlockedCompareExchange64** are available. Their implementation is visible in WinBase.h and uses the same kind of spinlocks presented earlier, as shown in the following code snippet:

```
LONGLONG InterlockedAnd64(
   LONGLONG* Destination,
   LONGLONG Value) {
   LONGLONG Old;

   do {
      Old = *Destination;
   } while (InterlockedCompareExchange64(Destination, Old & Value, Old) != Old);

   return Old;
}
```

Since Windows XP, in addition to these atomic manipulations of integer or Boolean values, you have access to a series of functions that allow you to easily manipulate a stack called an *Interlocked Singly Linked List*. Each operation, such as pushing or popping an element, is assured to be executed in an atomic way. Table 8-1 lists the functions found in the Interlocked Singly Linked List.

Table 8-1 Interlocked Singly Linked List Functions

Function	Description
InitializeSListHead	Creates an empty stack
InterlockedPushEntrySList	Adds an element on top of the stack
InterlockedPopEntrySList	Removes the top element of the stack and returns it
InterlockedFlushSList	Empties the stack
QueryDepthSList	Returns the number of elements stored in the stack

Cache Lines

If you want to build a high-performance application that runs on multiprocessor machines, you must be aware of CPU cache lines. When a CPU reads a byte from memory, it does not just fetch the single byte; it fetches enough bytes to fill a cache line. Cache lines consist of 32 (for older CPUs), 64, or even 128 bytes (depending on the CPU), and they are always aligned on 32-byte, 64-byte, or 128-byte boundaries, respectively. Cache lines exist to improve performance. Usually, an application manipulates a set of adjacent bytes. If these bytes are in the cache, the CPU does not have to access the memory bus, which requires much more time.

However, cache lines make memory updates more difficult in a multiprocessor environment, as you can see in this example:

1. CPU1 reads a byte, causing this byte and its adjacent bytes to be read into CPU1's cache line.
2. CPU2 reads the same byte, which causes the same bytes in step 1 to be read into CPU2's cache line.
3. CPU1 changes the byte in memory, causing the byte to be written to CPU1's cache line. But the information is not yet written to RAM.
4. CPU2 reads the same byte again. Because this byte was already in CPU2's cache line, it doesn't have to access memory. But CPU2 will not see the new value of the byte in memory.

This scenario would be disastrous. Of course, chip designers are well aware of this problem and design their CPUs to handle this. Specifically, when a CPU changes bytes in a cache line, the other CPUs in the machine are made aware of this and their cache lines are invalidated. So in the scenario just shown, CPU2's cache is invalidated when CPU1 changes the value of the byte. In step 4, CPU1 has to flush its cache to RAM and CPU2 has to access memory again to refill its cache line. As you can see, the cache lines can help performance, but they can also be a detriment on multiprocessor machines.

What all this means is that you should group your application's data together in cache line–size chunks and on cache-line boundaries. The goal is to make sure that different CPUs access different memory addresses separated by at least a cache-line boundary. Also, you should separate your read-only data (or infrequently read data) from read-write data. And you should group together pieces of data that are accessed around the same time.

Here is an example of a poorly designed data structure:

```
struct CUSTINFO {
   DWORD    dwCustomerID;      // Mostly read-only
   int      nBalanceDue;       // Read-write
   wchar_t  szName[100];       // Mostly read-only
   FILETIME ftLastOrderDate;   // Read-write
};
```

The easiest way to determine the cache line size of a CPU is by calling Win32's **GetLogical-ProcessorInformation** function. This functions returns an array of **SYSTEM_LOGICAL_PROCESSOR_INFORMATION** structures. You can examine a structure's **Cache** field, which refers to a **CACHE_DESCRIPTOR** structure that contains a **LineSize** field indicating the CPU's cache line size. Once you have this information, you can use the C/C++ compiler's **__declspec(align(#))** directive to control field alignment. Here is an improved version of this structure:

```
#define CACHE_ALIGN  64

// Force each structure to be in a different cache line.
struct __declspec(align(CACHE_ALIGN)) CUSTINFO {
    DWORD    dwCustomerID;     // Mostly read-only
    wchar_t  szName[100];      // Mostly read-only

    // Force the following members to be in a different cache line.
    __declspec(align(CACHE_ALIGN))
    int nBalanceDue;           // Read-write
    FILETIME ftLastOrderDate;  // Read-write
};
```

For more information on using **__declspec(align(#))**, read *http://msdn2.microsoft.com/en-us/ library/83ythb65.aspx.*

> **Note**   It is best for data to be always accessed by a single thread (function parameters and local variables are the easiest way to ensure this) or for the data to be always accessed by a single CPU (using thread affinity). If you do either of these, you avoid cache-line issues entirely.

Advanced Thread Synchronization

The interlocked family of functions is great when you need to atomically modify a single value. You should definitely try them first. But most real-life programming problems deal with data structures that are far more complex than a single 32-bit or 64-bit value. To get "atomic" access of more sophisticated data structures, you must leave the interlocked functions behind and use some other features offered by Windows.

In the previous section, I stressed that you should not use spinlocks on uniprocessor machines and you should use them cautiously even on multiprocessor machines. Again, the reason is that CPU time is a terrible thing to waste. So we need a mechanism that allows our thread to not waste CPU time while waiting to access a shared resource.

When a thread wants to access a shared resource or be notified of some "special event," the thread must call an operating system function, passing it parameters that indicate what the thread is waiting for. If the operating system detects that the resource is available or that the special event has occurred, the function returns and the thread remains schedulable. (The thread might not execute right away; it is schedulable and will be assigned to a CPU using the rules described in the previous chapter.)

If the resource is unavailable or the special event hasn't yet occurred, the system places the thread in a wait state, making the thread unschedulable. This prevents the thread from wasting any CPU time. While your thread is waiting, the system acts as an agent on your thread's behalf. The system remembers what your thread wants and automatically takes it out of the wait state when the resource becomes available—the thread's execution is synchronized with the special event.

As it turns out, most threads are almost always in a wait state. And the system's power management kicks in when the system detects that all threads are in a wait state for several minutes.

A Technique to Avoid

Without synchronization objects and the operating system's ability to watch for special events, a thread would be forced to synchronize itself with special events by using the technique that I am about to demonstrate. However, because the operating system has built-in support for thread synchronization, you should never use this technique.

In this technique, one thread synchronizes itself with the completion of a task in another thread by continuously polling the state of a variable that is shared by or accessible to multiple threads. The following code fragment illustrates this:

```
volatile BOOL g_fFinishedCalculation = FALSE;

int WINAPI _tWinMain(...) {
   CreateThread(..., RecalcFunc, ...);
   ...
   // Wait for the recalculation to complete.
   while (!g_fFinishedCalculation)
      ;
   ...
}

DWORD WINAPI RecalcFunc(PVOID pvParam) {
   // Perform the recalculation.
   ...    g_fFinishedCalculation = TRUE;
   return(0);
}
```

As you can see, the primary thread (executing **_tWinMain**) doesn't put itself to sleep when it needs to synchronize itself with the completion of the **RecalcFunc** function. Because the primary thread does not sleep, it is continuously scheduled CPU time by the operating system. This takes precious time cycles away from other threads.

Another problem with the polling method used in the previous code fragment is that the **BOOL** variable **g_fFinishedCalculation** might never be set to **TRUE**. This can happen if the primary thread has a higher priority than the thread executing the **RecalcFunc** function. In this case, the system never assigns any time slices to the **RecalcFunc** thread, which never executes the statement that sets **g_fFinishedCalculation** to **TRUE**. If the thread executing the **_tWinMain** function is put to sleep instead of polling, it is not scheduled time and the system can schedule time to lower-priority threads, such as the **RecalcFunc** thread, allowing them to execute.

I'll admit that sometimes polling comes in handy. After all, this is what a spinlock does. But there are proper ways to do this and improper ways to do this. As a general rule, you should not use spinlocks and you should not poll. Instead, you should call the functions that place your thread into a wait state until what your thread wants is available. I'll explain a proper way in the next section.

First, let me point out one more thing: At the top of the previous code fragment, you'll notice the use of **volatile**. For this code fragment to even come close to working, the **volatile** type qualifier must be there. This tells the compiler that the variable can be modified by something outside of the application itself, such as the operating system, hardware, or a concurrently executing thread. Specifically, the **volatile** qualifier tells the compiler to exclude the variable from any optimizations and always reload the value from the variable's memory location. Let's say that the compiler has generated the following pseudocode for the **while** statement shown in the previous code fragment:

```
MOV   Reg0, [g_fFinishedCalculation]   ; Copy the value into a register
Label: TEST  Reg0, 0                    ; Is the value 0?
JMP   Reg0 == 0, Label                  ; The register is 0, try again
...                                     ; The register is not 0 (end of loop)
```

Without making the Boolean variable **volatile**, it's possible that the compiler might optimize your C++ code as shown here. For this optimization, the compiler loads the value of the **BOOL** variable into a CPU register just once. Then it repeatedly performs tests against the CPU register. This certainly yields better performance than constantly rereading the value in a memory address and retesting it; therefore, an optimizing compiler might write code like that just shown. However, if the compiler does this, the thread enters an infinite loop and never wakes up. By the way, making a structure **volatile** ensures that all of its members are volatile and are always read from memory when referenced.

You might wonder whether my spinlock variable, **g_fResourceInUse** (used in the spinlock code shown on page 211), should be declared as **volatile**. The answer is no because we are passing the address of this variable to the various interlocked functions and not the variable's value itself. When you pass a variable's address to a function, the function must read the value from memory. The optimizer cannot affect this.

Critical Sections

A *critical section* is a small section of code that requires exclusive access to some shared resource before the code can execute. This is a way to have several lines of code "atomically" manipulate a resource. By *atomic*, I mean that the code knows that no other thread will access the resource. Of course, the system can still preempt your thread and schedule other threads. However, it will not schedule any other threads that want to access the same resource until your thread leaves the critical section.

Here is some problematic code that demonstrates what happens without the use of a critical section:

```
const int COUNT = 1000;
int    g_nSum = 0;

DWORD WINAPI FirstThread(PVOID pvParam) {
   g_nSum = 0;
   for (int n = 1; n <= COUNT; n++) {
      g_nSum += n;
   }
   return(g_nSum);
}


DWORD WINAPI SecondThread(PVOID pvParam) {
   g_nSum = 0;
   for (int n = 1; n <= COUNT; n++) {
      g_nSum += n;
   }
   return(g_nSum);
}
```

Taken independently, both thread functions are supposed to produce the same result (especially because each is coded identically). If the **FirstThread** function were to run by itself, it would sum up all the numbers between 0 and **COUNT**. The same thing would happen if the **SecondThread** function were to run by itself. However, because both threads access a shared variable (**g_nSum**), if the two threads execute at the same time (perhaps on different CPUs), each thread is modifying **g_nSum** behind the other thread's back, causing unpredictable results.

I'll admit that this example is a bit contrived (especially because the sum could easily be calculated without a loop by using **g_nSum = COUNT * (COUNT + 1) / 2**. It's difficult to come up with a real-life example that doesn't require several pages of source code. However, you can see how this problem could extend to real-life examples. Consider the case of managing a linked list of objects. If access to the linked list is not synchronized, one thread can add an item to the list while another thread is trying to search for an item in the list. The situation can become more chaotic if the two threads add items to the list at the same time. By using critical sections, you can ensure that access to the data structures is coordinated among threads.

Now that you see all the problems, let's correct the code using a critical section:

```
const int COUNT = 10;
int g_nSum = 0;
CRITICAL_SECTION g_cs;

DWORD WINAPI FirstThread(PVOID pvParam) {
   EnterCriticalSection(&g_cs);
   g_nSum = 0;
   for (int n = 1; n <= COUNT; n++) {
      g_nSum += n;
   }
   LeaveCriticalSection(&g_cs);
   return(g_nSum);
}


DWORD WINAPI SecondThread(PVOID pvParam) {
   EnterCriticalSection(&g_cs);
   g_nSum = 0;
   for (int n = 1; n <= COUNT; n++) {
      g_nSum += n;
   }
   LeaveCriticalSection(&g_cs);
   return(g_nSum);
}
```

I allocated a **CRITICAL_SECTION** data structure, **g_cs**, and then I wrapped any code that touches the shared resource (**g_nSum** in this example) inside calls to **EnterCriticalSection** and **LeaveCriticalSection**. Notice that I passed the address of **g_cs** in all calls to **EnterCritical-Section** and **LeaveCriticalSection**.

What are the key points to remember? When you have a resource that is accessed by multiple threads, you should create a **CRITICAL_SECTION** structure. Since I'm writing this on an airplane flight, let me draw the following analogy. A **CRITICAL_SECTION** structure is like an airplane's lavatory, and the toilet is the data that you want protected. Because the lavatory is small, only one person (thread) at a time can be inside the lavatory (critical section) using the toilet (protected resource).

If you have multiple resources that are always used together, you can place them all in a single lavatory: create just one **CRITICAL_SECTION** structure to guard them all.

If you have multiple resources that are not always used together—for example, threads 1 and 2 access one resource and threads 1 and 3 access another resource—you should create a separate lavatory, or **CRITICAL_SECTION** structure, for each resource.

Now, wherever you have code that touches a resource, you must place a call to **EnterCritical-Section**, passing it the address of the **CRITICAL_SECTION** structure that identifies the resource. This is like saying that when a thread wants to access a resource, it must first check the Occupied sign on the lavatory door. The **CRITICAL_SECTION** structure identifies which lavatory the thread wants to enter, and the **EnterCriticalSection** function is what the thread uses to check the Occupied sign.

If **EnterCriticalSection** sees that no other thread is in the lavatory (the door shows Unoccupied), the calling thread is allowed to use it. If **EnterCriticalSection** sees that another thread is in the lavatory, the calling thread must wait outside the lavatory door until the other thread in the lavatory leaves.

When a thread no longer executes code that touches the resource, it should call **LeaveCritical-Section**. This is how the thread tells the system that it has left the lavatory containing the resource. If you forget to call **LeaveCriticalSection**, the system will think that the resource is still in the lavatory and will not allow any waiting threads in. This is similar to leaving the lavatory without changing the sign on the door back to Unoccupied.

> **Note**   The hardest thing to remember is that any code you write that touches a shared resource must be wrapped inside **EnterCriticalSection** and **LeaveCriticalSection** functions. If you forget to wrap your code in just one place, the shared resource will be subject to corruption. For instance, if I remove **FirstThread**'s calls to **EnterCriticalSection** and **LeaveCriticalSection**, the **g_nSum** variable becomes corrupted. This happens even though **SecondThread** still calls **EnterCriticalSection** and **LeaveCriticalSection** properly.
>
> Forgetting calls to **EnterCriticalSection** and **LeaveCriticalSection** is like not requesting permission to enter the lavatory. The thread just muscles its way in and manipulates the resource. As you can imagine, if just one thread exhibits this rather rude behavior, the resource is corrupted.

When you can't solve your synchronization problem with interlocked functions, you should try using critical sections. The great thing about critical sections is that they are easy to use and they use the interlocked functions internally, so they execute quickly. The major disadvantage of critical sections is that you cannot use them to synchronize threads in multiple processes.

Critical Sections: The Fine Print

By now, you have the theory behind critical sections—why they're useful and how they allow "atomic" access to a shared resource. Now let's look more closely at how critical sections tick. We'll start with the **CRITICAL_SECTION** data structure. If you look up this structure in the Platform SDK documentation, you won't even find an entry for it. What's this all about?

It's not that the **CRITICAL_SECTION** structure is undocumented; it's just that Microsoft doesn't think you need to understand what this structure is all about—and rightly so. To us, this structure is opaque—the structure is documented, but the member variables within it are not. Of course, because this is just a data structure, you can look it up in the Windows header files and see the data members. (**CRITICAL_SECTION** is defined in WinBase.h as **RTL_CRITICAL_SECTION**; the **RTL_ CRITICAL_SECTION** structure is typedefed in WinNT.h.) But you should never write code that references these members.

To manipulate a **CRITICAL_SECTION** structure, you *always* call a Windows function, passing it the address of the structure. The function knows how to manipulate the members and guarantees that the structure's state is always consistent. So now, let's turn our attention to these functions.

Normally, **CRITICAL_SECTION** structures are allocated as global variables to allow all threads in the process an easy way to reference the structure—by variable name. However, **CRITICAL_ SECTION** structures can be allocated as local variables or dynamically allocated from a heap; and it is common to allocate them as private fields of a class definition. There are just two requirements. The first is that all threads that want to access the resource must know the address of the **CRITICAL_SECTION** structure that protects the resource. You can get this address to these threads using any mechanism you like. The second requirement is that the members within the **CRITICAL_SECTION** structure be initialized before any threads attempt to access the protected resource. The structure is initialized via a call to

```
VOID InitializeCriticalSection(PCRITICAL_SECTION pcs);
```

This function initializes the members of a **CRITICAL_SECTION** structure (pointed to by **pcs**). Because this function simply sets some member variables, it cannot fail and is therefore prototyped with a return value of **VOID**. This function must be called before any thread calls **EnterCritical- Section**. The Platform SDK documentation clearly states that the results are undefined if a thread attempts to enter an uninitialized **CRITICAL_SECTION**.

When you know that your process' threads will no longer attempt to access the shared resource, you should clean up the **CRITICAL_SECTION** structure by calling this function:

```
VOID DeleteCriticalSection(PCRITICAL_SECTION pcs);
```

DeleteCriticalSection resets the member variables inside the structure. Naturally, you should not delete a critical section if any threads are still using it. Again, the Platform SDK documentation clearly states that the results are undefined if you do.

When you write code that touches a shared resource, you must prefix that code with a call to

```
VOID EnterCriticalSection(PCRITICAL_SECTION pcs);
```

EnterCriticalSection examines the member variables inside the structure. The variables indicate which thread, if any, is currently accessing the resource. **EnterCriticalSection** performs the following tests:

- If no thread is accessing the resource, **EnterCriticalSection** updates the member variables to indicate that the calling thread has been granted access and returns immediately, allowing the thread to continue executing (accessing the resource).

- If the member variables indicate that the calling thread was already granted access to the resource, **EnterCriticalSection** updates the variables to indicate how many times the calling thread was granted access and returns immediately, allowing the thread to continue executing. This situation is rare and occurs only if the thread calls **EnterCriticalSection** twice in a row without an intervening call to **LeaveCriticalSection**.

- If the member variables indicate that a thread (other than the calling thread) was granted access to the resource, **EnterCriticalSection** places the calling thread in a wait state by using an event kernel object (described in the next chapter). This is terrific because the waiting thread does not waste any CPU time! The system remembers that the thread wants access to the resource, automatically updates the **CRITICAL_SECTION**'s member variables, and allows the thread to be schedulable as soon as the thread currently accessing the resource calls **LeaveCriticalSection**.

EnterCriticalSection isn't too complicated internally; it performs just a few simple tests. What makes this function so valuable is that it can perform all these tests atomically. If two threads call **EnterCriticalSection** at exactly the same time on a multiprocessor machine, the function still behaves correctly: one thread is granted access to the resource, and the other thread is placed in a wait state.

If **EnterCriticalSection** places a thread in a wait state, the thread might not be scheduled again for a long time. In fact, in a poorly written application, the thread might never be scheduled CPU time again. If this happens, the thread is said to be *starved*.

> **Note**   In reality, threads waiting for a critical section never starve. Calls to **Enter-CriticalSection** eventually time out, causing an exception to be raised. You can then attach a debugger to your application to determine what went wrong. The amount of time that must expire is determined by the **CriticalSectionTimeout** data value contained in the following registry subkey:
>
> HKEY_LOCAL_MACHINE\System\CurrentControlSet\Control\Session Manager
>
> This value is in seconds and defaults to 2,592,000 seconds, or about 30 days. Do not set this value too low (below 3 seconds, for example) or you will adversely affect threads in the system and other applications that normally wait more than 3 seconds for a critical section.

You can use this function instead of **EnterCriticalSection**:

```
BOOL TryEnterCriticalSection(PCRITICAL_SECTION pcs);
```

TryEnterCriticalSection never allows the calling thread to enter a wait state. Instead, its return value indicates whether the calling thread was able to gain access to the resource. So if **TryEnterCriticalSection** sees that the resource is being accessed by another thread, it returns **FALSE**. In all other cases, it returns **TRUE**.

With this function, a thread can quickly check to see if it can access a certain shared resource and, if not, continue doing something else instead of waiting. If **TryEnterCriticalSection** does return **TRUE**, the **CRITICAL_SECTION**'s member variables have been updated to reflect that the thread is accessing the resource. Therefore, every call to **TryEnterCriticalSection** that returns **TRUE** must be matched with a call to **LeaveCriticalSection**.

At the end of your code that touches the shared resource, you must call this function:

```
VOID LeaveCriticalSection(PCRITICAL_SECTION pcs);
```

LeaveCriticalSection examines the member variables inside the structure. The function decrements by 1 a counter that indicates how many times the calling thread was granted access to the shared resource. If the counter is greater than 0, **LeaveCriticalSection** does nothing else and simply returns.

If the counter becomes 0, **LeaveCriticalSection** updates the member variables to indicate that no thread is accessing the resource and it checks to see whether any other threads are waiting in a call to **EnterCriticalSection**. If at least one thread is waiting, it updates the member variables and makes one of the waiting threads (selected "fairly") schedulable again. Like **EnterCritical-Section**, **LeaveCriticalSection** performs all these tests and updates atomically. However, **LeaveCriticalSection** never places a thread in a wait state; it always returns immediately.

Critical Sections and Spinlocks

When a thread attempts to enter a critical section owned by another thread, the calling thread is placed immediately into a wait state. This means that the thread must transition from user mode to kernel mode (about 1000 CPU cycles). This transition is very expensive. On a multiprocessor machine, the thread that currently owns the resource might execute on a different processor and might relinquish control of the resource shortly. In fact, the thread that owns the resource might release it before the other thread has completed executing its transition into kernel mode. If this happens, a lot of CPU time is wasted.

To improve the performance of critical sections, Microsoft has incorporated spinlocks into them. So when **EnterCriticalSection** is called, it loops using a spinlock to try to acquire the resource some number of times. Only if all the attempts fail does the thread transition to kernel mode to enter a wait state.

To use a spinlock with a critical section, you should initialize the critical section by calling this function:

```
BOOL InitializeCriticalSectionAndSpinCount(
   PCRITICAL_SECTION pcs,
   DWORD dwSpinCount);
```

As in **InitializeCriticalSection**, the first parameter of **InitializeCriticalSection-AndSpinCount** is the address of the critical section structure. But in the second parameter, **dwSpinCount**, you pass the number of times you want the spinlock loop to iterate as it tries to acquire the resource before making the thread wait. This value can be any number from 0 through 0x00FFFFFF. If you call this function while running on a single-processor machine, the **dwSpinCount** parameter is ignored and the count is always set to 0. This is good because setting a spin count on a single-processor machine is useless: the thread owning the resource can't relinquish it if another thread is spinning.

You can change a critical section's spin count by calling this function:

```
DWORD SetCriticalSectionSpinCount(
   PCRITICAL_SECTION pcs,
   DWORD dwSpinCount);
```

Again, the **dwSpinCount** value is ignored if the host machine has just one processor.

In my opinion, you should always use spinlocks with critical sections because you have nothing to lose. The hard part is determining what value to pass for the **dwSpinCount** parameters. For the best performance, you simply have to play with numbers until you're happy with the performance results. As a guide, the critical section that guards access to your process' heap uses a spin count of roughly 4000.

Critical Sections and Error Handling

There is a small chance that the **InitializeCriticalSection** function can fail. Microsoft didn't really think about this when it originally designed the function, which is why the function is proto-typed as returning **VOID**. The function might fail because it allocates a block of memory so that the system can have some internal debugging information. If this memory allocation fails, a **STATUS_ NO_MEMORY** exception is raised. You can trap this in your code using structured exception handling (discussed in Chapter 23, "Termination Handlers," Chapter 24, "Exception Handlers and Software Exceptions," and Chapter 25, "Unhandled Exceptions, Vectored Exception Handling, and C++ Exceptions").

You can more easily trap this problem using the **InitializeCriticalSectionAndSpinCount** function. This function also allocates the memory block for debugging information but returns **FALSE** if the memory could not be allocated.

Another problem can arise when you use critical sections. Internally, critical sections use an event kernel object if two or more threads contend for the critical section at the same time. Because contention is rare, the system does not create the event kernel object until the first time it is required. This saves a lot of system resources because most critical sections never have contention. By the way, this event kernel object is only released when you call **DeleteCriticalSection**; so you should never forget to call this function when you're done with the critical section.

Before Windows XP, in a low-memory situation, a critical section might have contention, and the system might be unable to create the required event kernel object. The **EnterCriticalSection** function will then raise an **EXCEPTION_INVALID_HANDLE** exception. Most developers simply ignore this potential error and have no special handling in their code because this error is extremely rare. However, if you want to be prepared for this situation, you do have two options.

You can use structured exception handling and trap the error. When the error occurs, you can either not access the resource protected with the critical section or wait for some memory to become available and then call **EnterCriticalSection** again.

Your other option is to create the critical section using **InitializeCriticalSectionAndSpin-Count**, making sure that you set the high bit of the **dwSpinCount** parameter. When this function sees that the high bit is set, it creates the event kernel object and associates it with the critical section at initialization time. If the event cannot be created, the function returns **FALSE** and you can handle this more gracefully in your code. If the event is created successfully, you know that **Enter-CriticalSection** will always work and never raise an exception. (Always preallocating the event kernel objects can waste system resources. You should do this only if your code cannot tolerate **EnterCriticalSection** failing, if you are sure that contention will occur, or if you expect the process to be run in very low-memory environments.)

Since Windows XP, the new *keyed event* type of kernel objects has been introduced to help to solve this event creation issue under low resource conditions. One keyed event is always created by the operating system when a process is created, and you can easily find this instance (named \KernelObjects\CritSecOutOfMemoryEvent) by using the Process Explorer tool from Sysinternals (*http://www.microsoft.com/technet/sysinternals/utilities/ProcessExplorer.mspx*). This undocumented kernel object behaves like an event except that one instance is able to synchronize different sets of threads, each one identified and blocked on a simple pointer-size key. In the case of the critical section, when memory is low enough, making it impossible to create an event, the address of the critical section is used as a key. The threads that are trying to enter this particular critical section will be synchronized and, if needed, blocked on this keyed event by using the address of the critical section as a key.

Slim Reader-Writer Locks

An **SRWLock** has the same purpose as a simple critical section: to protect a single resource against access made by different threads. However, unlike a critical section, an **SRWLock** allows you to distinguish between threads that simply want to read the value of the resource (the readers) and other threads that are trying to update this value (the writers). It should be possible for all readers to access the shared resource at the same time because there is no risk of data corruption if you only read the value of a resource. The need for synchronization begins when a writer thread wants to update the resource. In that case, the access should be exclusive: no other thread, neither a reader nor a writer, should be allowed to access the resource. This is exactly what an **SRWLock** allows you to do in your code and in a very explicit way.

First, you allocate an **SRWLOCK** structure and initialize it with the **InitializeSRWLock** function:

```
VOID InitializeSRWLock(PSRWLOCK SRWLock);
```

The **SRWLOCK** structure is typedefed as **RTL_SRWLOCK** in WinBase.h. This structure, defined in WinNT.h, only contains a pointer that refers to something else. However, what it refers to is completely undocumented, and therefore you cannot write code to access it (unlike the fields of a **CRITICAL_SECTION**).

```
typedef struct _RTL_SRWLOCK {
    PVOID Ptr;
} RTL_SRWLOCK, *PRTL_SRWLOCK;
```

Once an **SRWLock** is initialized, a writer thread can try to acquire an exclusive access to the resource protected by the **SRWLock** by calling **AcquireSRWLockExclusive** with the address of the **SRWLOCK** object as its parameter:

```
VOID AcquireSRWLockExclusive(PSRWLOCK SRWLock);
```

When the resource has been updated, the lock is released by calling **ReleaseSRWLockExclusive** with the address of the **SRWLOCK** object as its parameter:

```
VOID ReleaseSRWLockExclusive(PSRWLOCK SRWLock);
```

For a reader thread, the same two-step scenario occurs but with the following two new functions:

```
VOID AcquireSRWLockShared(PSRWLOCK SRWLock);
VOID ReleaseSRWLockShared(PSRWLOCK SRWLock);
```

And that's it. There is no function to delete or destroy an **SRWLOCK**, as the system is able to do it automatically.

Compared to a critical section, an **SRWLock** is missing some features:

- There is no **TryEnter(Shared/Exclusive)SRWLock**: your calls to the **AcquireSRWLock (Shared/Exclusive)** functions block the calling thread if the lock is already owned.
- It is not possible to recursively acquire an **SRWLOCK**; that is, a single thread cannot acquire the lock for writing multiple times and then release it with a corresponding number of **ReleaseSRWLock*** calls.

However, if you can live with these limitations, you will get a real performance and scalability boost by using an **SRWLock** instead of a critical section. If you need to be convinced of the difference in terms of performance between these two synchronization mechanisms, you should execute on your multiprocessor machine the project 08-UserSyncCompare from the companion content Web page of this book.

This simple benchmark spawns one, two, and four threads that execute the same task repeatedly using different thread synchronization primitives. Each task was run on my dual-processor machine, and the elapsed time was recorded. The results are shown in Table 8-2.

Table 8-2   Comparison of Synchronization Mechanism Performance

Threads\ milliseconds	Volatile Read	Volatile Write	Interlocked Increment	Critical Section	SRWLock Shared	SRWLock Exclusive	Mutex
1	8	8	35	66	66	67	1060
2	8	76	153	268	134	148	11082
4	9	145	361	768	244	307	23785

Each cell of Table 8-2 contains the elapsed time in milliseconds (measured thanks to the **StopWatch** class presented in Chapter 7, "Thread Scheduling, Priorities, and Affinities") between the start of the threads and the time when the last thread has finished the execution of the 1000000 iterations of the following tasks:

- Read a volatile long value:

  ```
  LONG lValue = gv_value;
  ```

  Volatile read is fast because no synchronization is required and the CPU caches stay independent. Basically, the time stays uniform regardless of the number of CPUs or threads.

- Write into a volatile long value:

  ```
  gv_value = 0;
  ```

  With one thread, the time is just 8 milliseconds (ms). You would think that performing this operation with two threads would simply double the time, but the time is much worse (76 ms) on a dual-CPU machine because the CPUs have to communicate with each other to maintain cache coherency. Using four threads makes it take about twice as long (145 ms) simply because the amount of work is doubled. However, the time isn't substantially worse because the data is being manipulated by just two CPUs. If my machine had more CPUs in it, performance would decrease, as more CPU communication would be necessary to keep all the CPU caches coherent.

■ Use **InterlockedIncrement** to safely increment a volatile long value:

```
InterlockedIncrement(&gv_value);
```

InterlockedIncrement is slower than volatile read/write because the CPUs have to lock the memory. As a result, only one CPU at a time can access it. Using two threads makes it much slower because of Ping-Ponging the data between the two CPUs for cache coherency. Four threads makes it slower because of doubling the work, but again, the work is being done by two CPUs. Performance would probably be worse on a four-CPU machine because data would have to Ping-Pong between four CPUs.

■ Use a critical section to read a volatile long value:

```
EnterCriticalSection(&g_cs);
gv_value = 0;
LeaveCriticalSection(&g_cs);
```

Critical sections are slower still because you must enter and leave them (two operations). Also, entering and leaving modifies multiple fields in the **CRITICAL_SECTION** structure. Critical sections are much slower when contention occurs, as you can see from the numbers in Table 8-2. For example, four threads takes 768 milliseconds, which is more than double 268 (two threads) as a result of context switching increasing the likelihood of contention.

■ Use an **SRWLock** to read a volatile long value:

```
AcquireSRWLockShared/Exclusive(&g_srwLock);
gv_value = 0;
ReleaseSRWLockShared/Exclusive(&g_srwLock);
```

The **SRWLock** performs about the same when reading or writing when just one thread is using it. The **SRWLock** has slightly better performance with two threads when reading compared to writing because the two threads can read concurrently, while writers are mutually exclusive. With four threads, the **SRWLock** performs better when reading than writing for the same reason: multiple readers are allowed simultaneously. You might expect the results to be better than what is shown in Table 8-2, but this simple code isn't doing very much once the lock is held. Also, because the lock's fields and the data modified by the lock are being written to constantly by multiple threads, the CPUs have to Ping-Pong the data back and forth between their caches.

■ Use a synchronization kernel object mutex (described in Chapter 9) to safely read a volatile long value:

```
WaitForSingleObject(g_hMutex, INFINITE);
gv_value = 0;
ReleaseMutex(g_hMutex);
```

Mutexes are by far the worst performing because waiting on a mutex and later releasing it requires that the thread perform a user-mode to kernel-mode transition (and back) with each iteration. These transitions are very expensive in terms of CPU time. Add in contention (which occurs when the sample runs with two and four threads) and the time gets substantially worse.

The performance of the **SRWLock** is quite comparable to the performance of a critical section. In fact, from these results, the **SRWLock** outperforms the critical section in many of our tests. So I'd recommended using the **SRWLock** instead of the critical section. The **SRWLock** is faster and allows multiple concurrent readers, increasing throughput and scalability for threads that just want to read a shared resource (a common case in many applications).

To summarize, if you want to get the best performance in an application, you should try to use non-shared data first and then use volatile reads, volatile writes, interlocked APIs, **SRWLocks**, critical sections. And if all of these won't work for your situation, then and only then, use kernel objects (the topic of our next chapter).

Condition Variables

You have seen that an **SRWLock** is used when you want to allow producer and consumer threads access to the same resource either in exclusive or shared mode. In these kinds of situations, if there is nothing to consume for a reader thread, it should release the lock and wait until there is something new produced by a writer thread. If the data structure used to receive the items produced by a writer thread becomes full, the lock should also be released and the writer thread put to sleep until reader threads have emptied the data structure.

Condition variables are designed to simplify your life when implementing synchronization scenarios where a thread has to atomically release a lock on a resource and blocks until a condition is met through the **SleepConditionVariableCS** or **SleepConditionVariableSRW** functions:

```
BOOL SleepConditionVariableCS(
   PCONDITION_VARIABLE pConditionVariable,
   PCRITICAL_SECTION pCriticalSection,
   DWORD dwMilliseconds);

BOOL SleepConditionVariableSRW(
   PCONDITION_VARIABLE pConditionVariable,
   PSRWLOCK pSRWLock,
   DWORD dwMilliseconds,
   ULONG Flags);
```

The **pConditionVariable** parameter is a pointer to an initialized condition variable the calling thread will wait for. The second parameter is a pointer to either a critical section or an **SRWLock** that is used to synchronize the access to a shared resource. The **dwMilliseconds** parameter indicates how long (and the setting can be **INFINITE**) you want the calling thread to wait for the condition variable to be signaled. The **Flags** parameter in the second function details how you want the lock to be acquired once the condition variable is signaled: you should pass **0** for acquiring the lock in an exclusive way for a writer thread, and you should pass **CONDITION_VARIABLE_LOCKMODE_SHARED** for acquiring the lock in a shared way for a reader thread. These functions return **FALSE** when the timeout expires before the condition variable gets signaled, or they return **TRUE** otherwise. Notice that the lock or the critical section is obviously not acquired when **FALSE** is returned.

A thread blocked inside these **Sleep*** functions is awakened when **WakeConditionVariable** or **WakeAllConditionVariable** is called by another thread that detects that the right condition is satisfied, such as the presence of an element to consume for a reader thread or enough room to insert a produced element for a writer thread. The difference between these two signaling functions is not obvious:

```
VOID WakeConditionVariable(
    PCONDITION_VARIABLE ConditionVariable);

VOID WakeAllConditionVariable(
    PCONDITION_VARIABLE ConditionVariable);
```

When you call **WakeConditionVariable**, one thread waiting for the same condition variable to be signaled inside a **SleepConditionVariable*** function will return with the lock acquired. When this thread releases the same lock, no other thread waiting on the same condition variable will be awakened. When you call **WakeAllConditionVariable**, one or several threads waiting for the same condition variable inside a **SleepConditionVariable*** function might wake up and return. Having multiple threads wake up is OK because you are assured that the lock can be acquired by only one writer thread at a time if you requested an exclusive lock or by several reader threads if you passed **CONDITION_VARIABLE_LOCKMODE_SHARED** to the **Flag** parameter. So, sometimes, all reader threads will wake up, or one reader and then one writer, and so on until each blocked thread has acquired the lock. If you work with the Microsoft .NET Framework, you might find similarities between the **Monitor** class and a condition variable. Both provide synchronized access through **SleepConditionVariable** / **Wait** and a signal feature with **Wake*ConditionVariable** / **Pulse(All)**. You can find more details about the **Monitor** class in the page dedicated to that topic on MSDN (*http://msdn2.microsoft.com/en-us/library/hf5de04k.aspx*) or in my book *CLR via C#, Second Edition* (Microsoft Press, 2006).

The Queue Sample Application

A condition variable always works in conjunction with a lock: either a critical section or an **SRWLock**. The Queue (08-Queue.exe) application uses an **SRWLock** and two condition variables to control a queue of request elements. The source code and resource files for the application are in the 08-Queue directory on the companion content Web page mentioned earlier. When you run the application and click the Stop button, after a while the following dialog box appears:

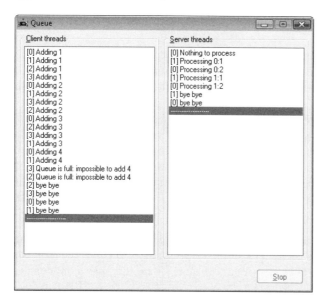

When Queue initializes, it creates four client threads (writers) and two server threads (readers). Each client thread appends a request element to a queue before sleeping for a period of time, and then it tries to add a request again. As an element is queued, the Client Threads list box is updated. Each entry indicates which client thread added the request element with its number. For example, the first entry in the list box indicates that client thread 0 appended its first request. Then client threads 1, 2, and 3 appended their first requests, followed by client thread 0 appending its second request, and so on.

Each server thread is responsible for processing requests—represented by an even number for thread 0 and an odd number for thread 1—but both have nothing to do until at least one element appears in the queue. When an element appears, a server thread wakes up to process the request. If the request number is even or odd as expected, the server thread processes the request, marks it as read, notifies the client's threads that it is possible for them to add a new request into the queue, and finally goes back to sleep until a new request is available. If there is no compatible request element to process, it goes back to sleep until there is something to read.

The Server Threads list box shows the status of the server threads. The first entry shows that server thread 0 is trying to find a request with an even number in the queue but does not find any. The second entry shows that server thread 1 is processing the first request from client thread 0. The third entry shows server thread 0 processing client thread 0's second request, and so on. The Stop button has been clicked, so the threads are notified to stop their processing and say "bye bye" in their related list box.

In this example, the server threads cannot process the client's requests quickly enough and the queue fills to maximum capacity. I initialized the queue data structure so that it can hold no more than 10 elements at a time; this causes the queue to fill quickly. Plus, there are four client threads and only two server threads. We see that the queue is full when client threads 3 and 2 attempt to append their fourth request to the queue without success.

The Queue Implementation Details

OK, so that's what you see—what's more interesting is how it works. The queue is managed by a C++ class, **CQueue**:

```
class CQueue
{
public:
   struct ELEMENT {
      int   m_nThreadNum;
      int   m_nRequestNum;
      // Other element data should go here
   };
   typedef ELEMENT* PELEMENT;

private:
   struct INNER_ELEMENT {
      int      m_nStamp;  // 0 means empty
      ELEMENT  m_element;
   };
   typedef INNER_ELEMENT* PINNER_ELEMENT;
```

```
private:
   PINNER_ELEMENT m_pElements;       // Array of elements to be processed
   int            m_nMaxElements;    // Maximum # of elements in the array
   int            m_nCurrentStamp;   // Keep track of the # of added elements

private:
   int GetFreeSlot();
   int GetNextSlot(int nThreadNum);

public:
   CQueue(int nMaxElements);
   ~CQueue();
   BOOL IsFull();
   BOOL IsEmpty(int nThreadNum);
   void AddElement(ELEMENT e);
   BOOL GetNewElement(int nThreadNum, ELEMENT& e);
};
```

The public **ELEMENT** structure inside this class defines what a queue data element looks like. The actual content is not particularly important. For this sample application, clients store their client thread number and their request number in this request element so that the servers can display this information in their list box when they process the retrieved even or odd request element. A real-life application generally does not require this information. This **ELEMENT** structure is wrapped by an **INNER_ELEMENT** structure that keeps track of the insertion order through the **m_nStamp** field, which is incremented each time an element is added.

For the other private members, we have **m_pElements**, which points to a fixed-size array of **INNER_ELEMENT** structures. This is the data that needs to be protected from the multiple client/server threads accesses. The **m_nMaxElements** member indicates how large this array is initialized to when the **CQueue** object is constructed. The next member, **m_nCurrentStamp**, is an integer that is incremented each time a new element is added to the queue. The **GetFreeSlot** private function returns the index of the first **INNER_ELEMENT** of **m_pElements** with an **m_nStamp** of **0** (meaning its content has been already read or is empty). If no such element is found, **–1** is returned.

```
int CQueue::GetFreeSlot() {

   // Look for the first element with a 0 stamp
   for (int current = 0; current < m_nMaxElements; current++) {
      if (m_pElements[current].m_nStamp == 0)
         return(current);
   }

   // No free slot was found
   return(-1);
}
```

The **GetNextSlot** private helper functions return the index in **m_pElements** of the **INNER_ELEMENT** with the lowest stamp (which means that it was added first) but different from 0 (which means free or read). If all elements have been read (their stamp is equal to 0), **−1** is returned.

```
int CQueue::GetNextSlot(int nThreadNum) {

   // By default, there is no slot for this thread
   int firstSlot = -1;

   // The element can't have a stamp higher than the last added
   int firstStamp = m_nCurrentStamp+1;

   // Look for the even (thread 0) / odd (thread 1) element that is not free
   for (int current = 0; current < m_nMaxElements; current++) {

      // Keep track of the first added (lowest stamp) in the queue
      // --> so that "first in first out" behavior is ensured
      if ((m_pElements[current].m_nStamp != 0) && // free element
          ((m_pElements[current].m_element.m_nRequestNum % 2) == nThreadNum) &&
          (m_pElements[current].m_nStamp < firstStamp)) {

         firstStamp = m_pElements[current].m_nStamp;
         firstSlot = current;
      }
   }

   return(firstSlot);
}
```

You should now have no trouble understanding **CQueue**'s constructor, destructor, and **IsFull** and **IsEmpty** methods, so let's turn our attention to the **AddElement** function, which is called by client threads to add a request element into the queue:

```
void CQueue::AddElement(ELEMENT e) {

   // Do nothing if the queue is full
   int nFreeSlot = GetFreeSlot();
   if (nFreeSlot == -1)
      return;

   // Copy the content of the element
   m_pElements[nFreeSlot].m_element = e;

   // Mark the element with the new stamp
   m_pElements[nFreeSlot].m_nStamp = ++m_nCurrentStamp;
}
```

If there is a free slot in **m_pElements**, it is used to store the **ELEMENT** passed as a parameter and the current stamp is incremented to count the number of added request elements. When a server thread wants to process a request, it calls **GetNewElement**, passing the thread number (0 or 1) and the **ELEMENT** to be filled with the details of a corresponding new request:

```
BOOL CQueue::GetNewElement(int nThreadNum, ELEMENT& e) {

   int nNewSlot = GetNextSlot(nThreadNum);
   if (nNewSlot == -1)
      return(FALSE);

   // Copy the content of the element
   e = m_pElements[nNewSlot].m_element;

   // Mark the element as read
   m_pElements[nNewSlot].m_nStamp = 0;

   return(TRUE);
}
```

The **GetNextSlot** helper function does most of the job of finding the first element corresponding to the given reader thread. If there is one in the queue, **GetNewElement** copies this request's details back to the caller before stamping it as read with an **m_nStamp** value of **0**.

There is nothing really complicated here, and you must be thinking that the **CQueue** is not thread safe. You're right. In Chapter 9, I explain how other synchronization kernel objects can be used to build a thread-safe version of a queue. However, in the 08-Queue.exe application, it is the responsibility of the client and server thread to synchronize their access to the global instance of the queue:

```
CQueue                g_q(10);     // The shared queue
```

In the 08-Queue.exe application, three global variables are used to let client (writer) threads and server (reader) threads work in harmony, without corrupting the queue:

```
SRWLOCK               g_srwLock; // Reader/writer lock to protect the queue
CONDITION_VARIABLE    g_cvReadyToConsume;  // Signaled by writers
CONDITION_VARIABLE    g_cvReadyToProduce;  // Signaled by readers
```

Each time a thread wants access to the queue, the **SRWLock** must be acquired, either in share mode by the server (reader) threads or in exclusive mode by the client (writer) threads.

The Client Thread Is the *WriterThread*

Let's see the client thread implementation:

```
DWORD WINAPI WriterThread(PVOID pvParam) {

   int nThreadNum = PtrToUlong(pvParam);
   HWND hWndLB = GetDlgItem(g_hWnd, IDC_CLIENTS);

   for (int nRequestNum = 1; !g_fShutdown; nRequestNum++) {

      CQueue::ELEMENT e = { nThreadNum, nRequestNum };
```

```
      // Require access for writing
      AcquireSRWLockExclusive(&g_srwLock);

      // If the queue is full, fall asleep as long as the condition variable
      // is not signaled
      // Note: During the wait for acquiring the lock,
      //       a stop might have been received
      if (g_q.IsFull() & !g_fShutdown) {
         // No more room in the queue
         AddText(hWndLB, TEXT("[%d] Queue is full: impossible to add %d"),
            nThreadNum, nRequestNum);

         // --> Need to wait for a reader to empty a slot before acquiring
         //     the lock again
         SleepConditionVariableSRW(&g_cvReadyToProduce, &g_srwLock,
            INFINITE, 0);
      }

      // Other writer threads might still be blocked on the lock
      // --> Release the lock and notify the remaining writer threads to quit
      if (g_fShutdown) {
         // Show that the current thread is exiting
         AddText(hWndLB, TEXT("[%d] bye bye"), nThreadNum);

         // No need to keep the lock any longer
         ReleaseSRWLockExclusive(&g_srwLock);

         // Signal other blocked writer threads that it is time to exit
         WakeAllConditionVariable(&g_cvReadyToProduce);

         // Bye bye
         return(0);
      } else {
         // Add the new ELEMENT into the queue
         g_q.AddElement(e);

         // Show result of processing element
         AddText(hWndLB, TEXT("[%d] Adding %d"), nThreadNum, nRequestNum);

         // No need to keep the lock any longer
         ReleaseSRWLockExclusive(&g_srwLock);

         // Signal reader threads that there is an element to consume
         WakeAllConditionVariable(&g_cvReadyToConsume);

         // Wait before adding a new element
         Sleep(1500);
      }
   }

   // Show that the current thread is exiting
   AddText(hWndLB, TEXT("[%d] bye bye"), nThreadNum);

   return(0);
}
```

The **for** loop increments the counter of requests this thread produces, and it ends if the **g_fShutdown** Boolean variable is set to **TRUE** when the application main window is dismissed or the Stop button is clicked. I'll come back to this topic later when discussing the issue related to stopping the background client/server threads from the user interface thread.

Before trying to add a new request element, the **SRWLock** is acquired in exclusive mode with **AcquireSRWLockExclusive**. If the lock is already acquired, either by a server or client thread, the thread blocks in **AcquireSRWLockExclusive**, waiting for the lock to be released. When the function returns, the lock is acquired but there is still a condition to be met before being allowed to add the request: the queue must not be full. If the queue is full, we have to sleep until a reader consumes one request and frees a slot to receive our request element. But the lock must be released before falling asleep or we will enter a deadlock: no reader thread would empty the queue since the access will be denied because the lock is still acquired. This is exactly what **SleepCondition-VariableSRW** does: it releases the **g_srwLock** passed as a parameter and puts the calling thread in a sleeping state until the **g_cvReadyToProduce** condition variable gets signaled through a call to **WakeConditionVariable**, which is done by a server thread when an empty slot is ready.

When **SleepConditionVariableSRW** returns, two conditions are met: the lock is acquired again, and another thread has signaled the condition variable to let a client thread know that an empty slot is available in the queue. At that time, the thread is ready to add a new request element into the queue. However, it first checks whether it was asked to end the processing while it was sleeping. If this is not the case, the new request element is placed into the queue, a message is sent to the client list box to show the processing status, and the lock is released with a call to **Release-SRWLockExclusive**. Before going to the next loop iteration, **WakeAllConditionVariable** is called with **&g_cvReadyToConsume** as a parameter to signal all server threads that there is something for them to consume.

Consuming Requests by the Server Threads

Two different server threads are spawned with the same callback function. Each one is consuming either even or odd request elements by calling the **ConsumeElement** function in a loop until **g_fShutdown** is set to **TRUE**. This helper function returns **TRUE** when a request has been processed and **FALSE** if it detects that **g_fShutdown** has been set to **TRUE**.

```
BOOL ConsumeElement(int nThreadNum, int nRequestNum, HWND hWndLB) {

    // Get access to the queue to consume a new element
    AcquireSRWLockShared(&g_srwLock);

    // Fall asleep until there is something to read.
    // Check if, while it was asleep,
    // it was not decided that the thread should stop
    while (g_q.IsEmpty(nThreadNum) && !g_fShutdown) {
        // There was not a readable element
        AddText(hWndLB, TEXT("[%d] Nothing to process"), nThreadNum);

        // The queue is empty
        // --> Wait until a writer adds a new element to read
        //     and come back with the lock acquired in shared mode
        SleepConditionVariableSRW(&g_cvReadyToConsume, &g_srwLock,
            INFINITE, CONDITION_VARIABLE_LOCKMODE_SHARED);
    }
```

```c
    // When thread is exiting, the lock should be released for writer
    // and readers should be signaled through the condition variable
    if (g_fShutdown) {
        // Show that the current thread is exiting
        AddText(hWndLB, TEXT("[%d] bye bye"), nThreadNum);

        // Another writer thread might still be blocked on the lock
        // --> release it before exiting
        ReleaseSRWLockShared(&g_srwLock);

        // Notify other readers that it is time to exit
        // --> release readers
        WakeConditionVariable(&g_cvReadyToConsume);

        return(FALSE);
    }


    // Get the first new element
    CQueue::ELEMENT e;
    // Note: No need to test the return value since IsEmpty
    //       returned FALSE
    g_q.GetNewElement(nThreadNum, e);

    // No need to keep the lock any longer
    ReleaseSRWLockShared(&g_srwLock);

    // Show result of consuming the element
    AddText(hWndLB, TEXT("[%d] Processing %d:%d"),
        nThreadNum, e.m_nThreadNum, e.m_nRequestNum);

    // A free slot is now available for writer threads to produce
    // --> wake up a writer thread
    WakeConditionVariable(&g_cvReadyToProduce);

    return(TRUE);
}


DWORD WINAPI ReaderThread(PVOID pvParam) {

    int nThreadNum = PtrToUlong(pvParam);
    HWND hWndLB = GetDlgItem(g_hWnd, IDC_SERVERS);

    for (int nRequestNum = 1; !g_fShutdown; nRequestNum++) {

        if (!ConsumeElement(nThreadNum, nRequestNum, hWndLB))
            return(0);

        Sleep(2500);   // Wait before reading another element
    }

    // g_fShutdown has been set during Sleep
    // --> Show that the current thread is exiting
    AddText(hWndLB, TEXT("[%d] bye bye"), nThreadNum);

    return(0);
}
```

Before processing a request, **srwLock** is acquired in shared mode by calling **AcquireSRWLock-Shared**. If the lock has already been acquired in exclusive mode by a client thread, the call is blocked. If the lock is already acquired in shared mode by another server thread, the call immediately returns, allowing a request to be processed. Even if the lock is acquired, the queue might not contain any new request element corresponding to the given thread—for example, a request with an odd number is available, but thread 0 looks for a request with an even number. In that case, a message is sent to the server list box and the thread blocks on **SleepConditionVariableSRW** until the **g_cvReadyToConsume** condition variable is signaled by a client thread when a new request element is available for consumption. When **SleepConditionVariableSRW** returns, **g_srwLock** has been acquired and a new request element is available in the queue. Again, its number might not be the expected one: this is why the **SleepConditionVariableSRW** call appears in a loop and checks that there is a request element available with the right number. Notice that two condition variables could have been used instead of only **cvReadyToConsume**: one for even requests and one for odd requests. Doing so would have avoided the situation where a server thread is woken up for nothing if the new request does not have the right number. In the current implementation, each thread acquires the lock in shared mode even though the queue content is updated when **GetNewElement** is called because the **m_nStamp** field of the request element is set to 0 to mark it as having been read. This is not a problem because each server thread never updates the same request elements: thread 0 processes even ones and thread 1 processes odd ones.

When a request with the right number is found, it is extracted from the queue, and **Release-SRWLockShared** is called before sending a message to the server list box. It is now time to signal client threads by calling **WakeConditionVariable** with **&g_cvReadyToProduce** as a parameter and inform them that a new empty slot is available in the queue.

Deadlock Issues When Stopping Threads

When I first added the Stop button in the dialog box, I did not think that it would end in a deadlock situation. The code to stop the client/server threads is straightforward:

```
void StopProcessing() {

    if (!g_fShutdown) {
        // Ask all threads to end
        InterlockedExchangePointer((PLONG*) &g_fShutdown, (LONG) TRUE);

        // Free all threads waiting on condition variables
        WakeAllConditionVariable(&g_cvReadyToConsume);
        WakeAllConditionVariable(&g_cvReadyToProduce);

        // Wait for all the threads to terminate & then clean up
        WaitForMultipleObjects(g_nNumThreads, g_hThreads, TRUE, INFINITE);

        // Don't forget to clean up kernel resources
        // Note: This is not really mandatory since the process is exiting
        while (g_nNumThreads--)
            CloseHandle(g_hThreads[g_nNumThreads]);

        // Close each list box
        AddText(GetDlgItem(g_hWnd, IDC_SERVERS), TEXT("--------------------"));
        AddText(GetDlgItem(g_hWnd, IDC_CLIENTS), TEXT("--------------------"));
    }
}
```

The **g_fShutdown** flag is set to **TRUE**, and the two condition variables are signaled by calling **WakeAllConditionVariable**. Then I just have to call **WaitForMultipleObjects** with an array containing the handles of the running threads as a parameter. After **WaitForMultipleObjects** returns, the thread handles are closed and a final line is added to the list boxes.

On the client/server side, once unblocked from their **SleepConditionVariableSRW** calls thanks to **WakeAllConditionVariable**, these threads are supposed to listen to the **g_fShutdown** flag and simply exit after writing "bye bye" in their list box. And this is exactly when a thread sends a message to the list box that a deadlock might occur. If the code executing the **StopProcessing** function is in a **WM_COMMAND** message handler, the user interface thread responsible for handling the messages is blocked inside **WaitForMultipleObjects**. So, when one of the clients or servers calls **ListBox_SetCurSel** and **ListBox_AddString** to add a new entry in the list box, the user interface thread is not able to answer, and ... deadlock. The solution I've chosen is to gray the button in the **Stop** command message handler before spawning another thread that will call the **StopProcessing** function without any risk of deadlock because the message handler has immediately returned:

```
DWORD WINAPI StoppingThread(PVOID pvParam) {

    StopProcessing();
    return(0);
}


void Dlg_OnCommand(HWND hWnd, int id, HWND hWndCtl, UINT codeNotify) {

    switch (id) {
        case IDCANCEL:
            EndDialog(hWnd, id);
            break;

        case IDC_BTN_STOP:
        {
            // StopProcessing can't be called from the UI thread
            // or a deadlock will occur: SendMessage() is used
            // to fill up the list boxes
            // --> Another thread is required
            DWORD dwThreadID;
            CloseHandle(chBEGINTHREADEX(NULL, 0, StoppingThread,
                NULL, 0, &dwThreadID));

            // This button can't be pushed twice
            Button_Enable(hWndCtl, FALSE);
        }
        break;
    }
}
```

Don't forget that you are facing the same deadlock dangers when you are synchronizing the content of the user interface from another thread with blocking actions, such as when you are synchronizing the access to a shared resource. The following section provides a couple of tips and techniques that illustrate how to avoid deadlocks.

Last but not least, the strings are appended into the list boxes through the **AddText** helper function, which takes advantage of a new secure string **_vstprintf_s** function:

```
void AddText(HWND hWndLB, PCTSTR pszFormat, ...) {

    va_list argList;
    va_start(argList, pszFormat);

    TCHAR sz[20 * 1024];
    _vstprintf_s(sz, _countof(sz), pszFormat, argList);
    ListBox_SetCurSel(hWndLB, ListBox_AddString(hWndLB, sz));

    va_end(argList);
}
```

Useful Tips and Techniques

When you use locks such as a critical section or a reader-writer lock, there are some good habits to get into and some things to avoid. Here are several tips and techniques to help you when you use a lock. These techniques also apply to kernel synchronization objects (discussed in the next chapter).

Use One Lock per Atomically-Manipulated Object Set

It is common to have several objects that, together, make up a single "logical" resource. For example, it could be that whenever you add an element to a collection, you also need to update a counter too. To accomplish this, you should have just one lock that you take whenever you want to read or write to this logical resource.

Each logical resource in your application should have its own lock that is used to synchronize access to any and all parts of the logical resource. You should not have a single lock for all logical resources, as this reduces scalability if multiple threads are accessing different logical resources: only one thread will be allowed to execute at any one time.

Accessing Multiple Logical Resources Simultaneously

Sometimes you'll need to access two (or more) logical resources simultaneously. For example, your application might need to lock one resource to extract an item and lock another resource to add the item. If each resource has its own lock, you have to use both locks to do all of this atomically. Here is an example:

```
DWORD WINAPI ThreadFunc(PVOID pvParam) {

    EnterCriticalSection(&g_csResource1);
    EnterCriticalSection(&g_csResource2);

    // Extract the item from Resource1
    // Insert the item into Resource2
    LeaveCriticalSection(&g_csResource2);
    LeaveCriticalSection(&g_csResource1);
    return(0);
}
```

Suppose another thread in the process, written as follows, also requires access to the two resources:

```
DWORD WINAPI OtherThreadFunc(PVOID pvParam) {

   EnterCriticalSection(&g_csResource2);
   EnterCriticalSection(&g_csResource1);

   // Extract the item from Resource1
   // Insert the item into Resource2
   LeaveCriticalSection(&g_csResource2);
   LeaveCriticalSection(&g_csResource1);
   return(0);
}
```

All I did in the preceding function was switch the order of the calls to **EnterCriticalSection** and **LeaveCriticalSection**. But because the two functions are written the way they are, a deadlock might occur. Suppose that **ThreadFunc** begins executing and gains ownership of the **g_csResource1** critical section. Then the thread executing the **OtherThreadFunc** function is given some CPU time and gains ownership of the **g_csResource2** critical section. Now you have a deadlock situation. When either **ThreadFunc** or **OtherThreadFunc** tries to continue executing, neither function can gain ownership of the other critical section it requires.

To solve this problem, you must always enter resource locks in exactly the same order everywhere in your code. Notice that order does not matter when you call **LeaveCriticalSection** because this function never causes a thread to enter a wait state.

Don't Hold a Lock for a Long Time

When a lock is held for a long time, other threads might enter wait states, which will hurt your application's performance. Here is a technique you can use to minimize the time spent inside a critical section. The following code prevents other threads from changing the value in **g_s** before the **WM_SOMEMSG** message is sent to a window:

```
SOMESTRUCT g_s;
CRITICAL_SECTION g_cs;

DWORD WINAPI SomeThread(PVOID pvParam) {
   EnterCriticalSection(&g_cs);

   // Send a message to a window.
   SendMessage(hWndSomeWnd, WM_SOMEMSG, &g_s, 0);

   LeaveCriticalSection(&g_cs);
   return(0);
}
```

It's impossible to tell how much time the window procedure requires for processing the **WM_SOMEMSG** message—it might be a few milliseconds or a few years. During that time, no other threads can gain access to the **g_s** structure. It's better to write the code as follows:

```
SOMESTRUCT g_s;
CRITICAL_SECTION g_cs;

DWORD WINAPI SomeThread(PVOID pvParam) {

    EnterCriticalSection(&g_cs);
    SOMESTRUCT sTemp = g_s;
    LeaveCriticalSection(&g_cs);

    // Send a message to a window.
    SendMessage(hWndSomeWnd, WM_SOMEMSG, &sTemp, 0);
    return(0);
}
```

This code saves the value in **sTemp**, a temporary variable. You can probably guess how long the CPU requires to execute this line—only a few CPU cycles. Immediately after the temporary variable is saved, **LeaveCriticalSection** is called because the global structure no longer needs to be protected. This second implementation is much better than the first because other threads are stopped from using the **g_s** structure for only a few CPU cycles instead of for an unknown amount of time. Of course, this technique assumes that the "snapshot" of the structure is good enough for the window procedure to read. It also assumes that the window procedure doesn't need to change the members in the structure.

Chapter 9
Thread Synchronization with Kernel Objects

In the last chapter, we discussed how to synchronize threads using mechanisms that allow your threads to remain in user mode. The wonderful thing about user-mode synchronization is that it is very fast. If you are concerned about your thread's performance, you should first determine whether a user-mode thread synchronization mechanism will work for you.

Although user-mode thread synchronization mechanisms offer great performance, they do have limitations, and for many applications they simply do not work. For example, the interlocked family of functions operates only on single values and never places a thread into a wait state. You can use critical sections to place a thread in a wait state, but you can use them only to synchronize threads contained within a single process. Also, you can easily get into deadlock situations with critical sections because you cannot specify a timeout value while waiting to enter the critical section.

In this chapter, we'll discuss how to use kernel objects to synchronize threads. As you'll see, kernel objects are far more versatile than the user-mode mechanisms. In fact, the only bad side to kernel objects is their performance. When you call any of the new functions mentioned in this chapter, the calling thread must transition from user mode to kernel mode. This transition is costly: it takes about 200 CPU cycles on the x86 platform for an empty system call—and this, of course, does not include the execution of the kernel-mode code that actually implements the function your thread is calling. But what takes several orders of magnitude more is the overhead of scheduling a new thread with all the cache flushes/misses it entails. Here we're talking about tens of thousands of cycles.

Throughout this book, we've discussed several kernel objects, including processes, threads, and jobs. You can use almost all of these kernel objects for synchronization purposes. For thread synchronization, each of these kernel objects is said to be in a *signaled* or *nonsignaled* state. The toggling of this state is determined by rules that Microsoft has created for each object. For example, process kernel objects are always created in the nonsignaled state. When the process terminates, the operating system automatically makes the process kernel object signaled. Once a process kernel object is signaled, it remains that way forever; its state never changes back to nonsignaled.

Inside a process kernel object is a Boolean value that is initialized to **FALSE** (nonsignaled) when the object is created. When the process terminates, the operating system automatically changes the corresponding object's Boolean value to **TRUE**, indicating that the object is signaled.

If you want to write code that checks whether a process is still running, all you do is call a function that asks the operating system to check the process object's Boolean value. That's easy enough. You might also want to tell the system to put your thread in a wait state and wake it up automatically when the Boolean value changes from **FALSE** to **TRUE**. This way, you can write code in which a thread in a parent process that needs to wait for the child process to terminate can simply put itself to sleep until the kernel object identifying the child process becomes signaled. As you'll see, Microsoft Windows offers functions that accomplish all this easily.

I've just described the rules that Microsoft has defined for a process kernel object. As it turns out, thread kernel objects follow the same rules. That is, thread kernel objects are always created in the nonsignaled state. When the thread terminates, the operating system automatically changes the thread object's state to signaled. Therefore, you can use the same technique in your application to determine whether a thread is no longer executing. Just like process kernel objects, thread kernel objects never return to the nonsignaled state.

The following kernel objects can be in a signaled or nonsignaled state:

- Processes
- Threads
- Jobs
- File and console standard input/output/error streams
- Events
- Waitable timers
- Semaphores
- Mutexes

Threads can put themselves into a wait state until an object becomes signaled. Note that the rules that govern the signaled/nonsignaled state of each object depend on the type of object. I've already mentioned the rules for process and thread objects. I discuss the rules for jobs in Chapter 5, "Jobs."

In this chapter, we'll look at the functions that allow a thread to wait for a specific kernel object to become signaled. Then we'll look at the kernel objects that Windows offers specifically to help you synchronize threads: events, waitable timers, semaphores, and mutexes.

When I was first learning this stuff, it helped if I imagined that kernel objects contained a flag (the wave-in-the-air kind, not the bit kind). When the object was signaled, the flag was raised; when the object was nonsignaled, the flag was lowered.

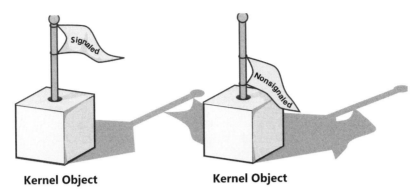

Kernel Object   **Kernel Object**

Threads are not schedulable when the objects they are waiting for are nonsignaled (the flag is low-ered). However, as soon as the object becomes signaled (the flag goes up), the thread sees the flag, becomes schedulable, and shortly resumes execution.

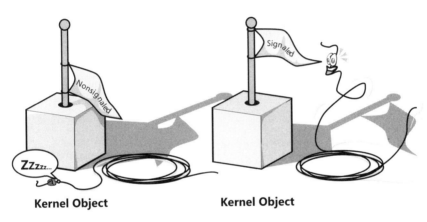

Kernel Object   **Kernel Object**

Wait Functions

Wait functions cause a thread to voluntarily place itself into a wait state until a specific kernel object becomes signaled. Notice that the thread is not placed into a wait state if the kernel object is signaled when a Wait function is called. By far, the most common of these functions is **WaitForSingleObject**:

```
DWORD WaitForSingleObject(
   HANDLE hObject,
   DWORD dwMilliseconds);
```

When a thread calls this function, the first parameter, **hObject**, identifies a kernel object that sup-ports being signaled/nonsignaled. (Any object mentioned in the list on the previous page works just great.) The second parameter, **dwMilliseconds**, allows the thread to indicate how long it is willing to wait for the object to become signaled.

The following function call tells the system that the calling thread wants to wait until the process identified by the **hProcess** handle terminates:

```
WaitForSingleObject(hProcess, INFINITE);
```

The second parameter tells the system that the calling thread is willing to wait forever (an infinite amount of time) or until this process terminates.

Usually, **INFINITE** is passed as the second parameter to **WaitForSingleObject**, but you can pass any value (in milliseconds). By the way, **INFINITE** is defined as 0xFFFFFFFF (or −1). Of course, passing **INFINITE** can be a little dangerous. If the object never becomes signaled, the calling thread never wakes up—it is forever blocked but, fortunately, not wasting precious CPU time.

Here's an example of how to call **WaitForSingleObject** with a timeout value other than **INFINITE**:

```
DWORD dw = WaitForSingleObject(hProcess, 5000);
switch (dw) {

   case WAIT_OBJECT_0:
      // The process terminated.
      break;

   case WAIT_TIMEOUT:
      // The process did not terminate within 5000 milliseconds.
      break;

   case WAIT_FAILED:
      // Bad call to function (invalid handle?)
      break;
}
```

The preceding code tells the system that the calling thread should not be schedulable until either the specified process has terminated or 5000 milliseconds have expired, whichever comes first. So this call returns in less than 5000 milliseconds if the process terminates, and it returns in about 5000 milliseconds if the process hasn't terminated. Note that you can pass **0** for the **dwMilliseconds** parameter. If you do this, **WaitForSingleObject** always returns immediately, even if the wait condition hasn't been satisfied.

WaitForSingleObject's return value indicates why the calling thread became schedulable again. If the object the thread is waiting on became signaled, the return value is **WAIT_OBJECT_0**; if the timeout expires, the return value is **WAIT_TIMEOUT**. If you pass a bad parameter (such as an invalid handle) to **WaitForSingleObject**, the return value is **WAIT_FAILED** (call **GetLastError** for more information).

The following function, **WaitForMultipleObjects**, is similar to **WaitForSingleObject** except that it allows the calling thread to check the signaled state of several kernel objects simultaneously:

```
DWORD WaitForMultipleObjects(
   DWORD dwCount,
   CONST HANDLE* phObjects,
   BOOL bWaitAll,
   DWORD dwMilliseconds);
```

The **dwCount** parameter indicates the number of kernel objects you want the function to check. This value must be between 1 and **MAXIMUM_WAIT_OBJECTS** (defined as **64** in the WinNT.h header file). The **phObjects** parameter is a pointer to an array of kernel object handles.

You can use **WaitForMultipleObjects** in two different ways—to allow a thread to enter a wait state until any one of the specified kernel objects becomes signaled, or to allow a thread to wait until all the specified kernel objects become signaled. The **bWaitAll** parameter tells the function which way you want it to work. If you pass **TRUE** for this parameter, the function does not allow the calling thread to execute until all the objects have become signaled.

The **dwMilliseconds** parameter works exactly as it does for **WaitForSingleObject**. If, while waiting, the specified time expires, the function returns anyway. Again, **INFINITE** is usually passed for this parameter, but you should write your code carefully to avoid the possibility of being forever blocked.

The **WaitForMultipleObjects** function's return value tells the caller why it got rescheduled. The possible return values are **WAIT_FAILED** and **WAIT_TIMEOUT**, which are self-explanatory. If you pass **TRUE** for **bWaitAll** and all the objects become signaled, the return value is **WAIT_OBJECT_0**. If you pass **FALSE** for **bWaitAll**, the function returns as soon as any of the objects becomes signaled. In this case, you probably want to know which object became signaled. The return value is a value between **WAIT_OBJECT_0** and (**WAIT_OBJECT_0** + **dwCount** - **1**). In other words, if the return value is not **WAIT_TIMEOUT** and is not **WAIT_FAILED**, you should subtract **WAIT_OBJECT_0** from the return value. The resulting number is an index into the array of handles that you passed as the second parameter to **WaitForMultipleObjects**. The index tells you which object became signaled.

Here's some sample code to make this clear:

```
HANDLE3];
h[0] = hProcess1;
h[1] = hProcess2;
h[2] = hProcess3;
DWORD dw = WaitForMultipleObjects(3, h, FALSE, 5000);
switch (dw) {
   case WAIT_FAILED:
      // Bad call to function (invalid handle?)
      break;

   case WAIT_TIMEOUT:
      // None of the objects became signaled within 5000 milliseconds.
      break;

   case WAIT_OBJECT_0 + 0:
      // The process identified by h[0] (hProcess1) terminated.
      break;

   case WAIT_OBJECT_0 + 1:
      // The process identified by h[1] (hProcess2) terminated.
      break;

   case WAIT_OBJECT_0 + 2:
      // The process identified by h[2] (hProcess3) terminated.
      break;
}
```

If you pass **FALSE** for the **bWaitAll** parameter, **WaitForMultipleObjects** scans the handle array from index 0 on up, and the first object that is signaled satisfies the wait. This can have some undesirable ramifications. For example, your thread might be waiting for three child processes to terminate by passing three process handles to this function. If the process at index 0 in the array terminates, **WaitForMultipleObjects** returns. Now the thread can do whatever it needs to and then loop back around, waiting for another process to terminate. If the thread passes the same three handles, the function returns immediately with **WAIT_OBJECT_0** again. Unless you remove the handles that you've already received notifications from, your code will not work correctly.

Successful Wait Side Effects

For some kernel objects, a successful call to **WaitForSingleObject** or **WaitForMultiple-Objects** actually alters the state of the object. A successful call is one in which the function sees that the object was signaled and returns a value relative to **WAIT_OBJECT_0**. A call is unsuccessful if the function returns **WAIT_TIMEOUT** or **WAIT_FAILED**. Objects never have their state altered for unsuccessful calls.

When an object has its state altered, I call this a *successful wait side effect*. For example, let's say that a thread is waiting on an auto-reset event object (discussed later in this chapter). When the event object becomes signaled, the function detects this and can return **WAIT_OBJECT_0** to the calling thread. However, just before the function returns, the event is set to the nonsignaled state—the side effect of the successful wait.

This side effect is applied to auto-reset event kernel objects because it is one of the rules that Microsoft has defined for this type of object. Other objects have different side effects, and some objects have no side effects at all. Process and thread kernel objects have no side effects at all—that is, waiting on one of these objects never alters the object's state. As we discuss various kernel objects in this chapter, we'll go into detail about their successful wait side effects.

What makes **WaitForMultipleObjects** so useful is that it performs all of its operations atomically. When a thread calls **WaitForMultipleObjects**, the function can test the signaled state of all the objects and perform the required side effects all as a single operation.

Let's look at an example. Two threads call **WaitForMultipleObjects** in exactly the same way:

```
HANDLE h[2];
h[0] = hAutoResetEvent1;   // Initially nonsignaled
h[1] = hAutoResetEvent2;   // Initially nonsignaled
WaitForMultipleObjects(2, h, TRUE, INFINITE);
```

When **WaitForMultipleObjects** is called, both event objects are nonsignaled; this forces both threads to enter a wait state. Then the **hAutoResetEvent1** object becomes signaled. Both threads see that the event has become signaled, but neither can wake up because the **hAutoResetEvent2** object is still nonsignaled. Because neither thread has successfully waited yet, no side effect happens to the **hAutoResetEvent1** object.

Next, the **hAutoResetEvent2** object becomes signaled. At this point, one of the two threads detects that both objects it is waiting for have become signaled. The wait is successful, both event objects are set to the nonsignaled state, and the thread is schedulable. But what about the other thread? It continues to wait until it sees that both event objects are signaled. Even though it originally detected that **hAutoResetEvent1** was signaled, it now sees this object as nonsignaled.

As I mentioned, it's important to note that **WaitForMultipleObjects** works atomically. When it checks the state of the kernel objects, no other thread can alter any object's state behind its back. This prevents deadlock situations. Imagine what would happen if one thread saw that **hAuto-ResetEvent1** was signaled and reset the event to nonsignaled, and then the other thread saw that **hAutoResetEvent2** was signaled and reset this event to nonsignaled. Both threads would be frozen: one thread would wait for an object that another thread had gotten, and vice versa. **WaitFor-MultipleObjects** ensures that this never happens.

This brings up an interesting question: If multiple threads wait for a single kernel object, which thread does the system decide to wake up when the object becomes signaled? Microsoft's official response to this question is, "The algorithm is fair." Microsoft doesn't want to commit to the internal algorithm used by the system. All it says is that the algorithm is fair, which means that if multiple threads are waiting, each should get its own chance to wake up each time the object becomes signaled.

This means that thread priority has no effect: the highest-priority thread does not necessarily get the object. It also means that the thread waiting the longest does not necessarily get the object. And it is possible for a thread that got the object to loop around and get it again. However, this wouldn't be fair to the other threads, so the algorithm tries to prevent this. But there is no guarantee.

In reality, the algorithm Microsoft uses is simply the popular "first in, first out" scheme. The thread that has waited the longest for an object gets the object. However, actions can occur in the system that alter this behavior, making it less predictable. This is why Microsoft doesn't explicitly state how the algorithm works. One such action is a thread getting suspended. If a thread waits for an object and then the thread is suspended, the system forgets that the thread is waiting for the object. This is a feature because there is no reason to schedule a suspended thread. When the thread is later resumed, the system thinks that the thread just started waiting on the object.

While you debug a process, all threads within that process are suspended when breakpoints are hit. So debugging a process makes the "first in, first out" algorithm highly unpredictable because threads are frequently suspended and resumed.

Event Kernel Objects

Of all the kernel objects, events are by far the most primitive. They contain a usage count (as all kernel objects do), a Boolean value indicating whether the event is an auto-reset or manual-reset event, and another Boolean value indicating whether the event is signaled or nonsignaled.

Events signal that an operation has completed. There are two different types of event objects: manual-reset events and auto-reset events. When a manual-reset event is signaled, all threads waiting on the event become schedulable. When an auto-reset event is signaled, only one of the threads waiting on the event becomes schedulable.

Events are most commonly used when one thread performs initialization work and then signals another thread to perform the remaining work. The event is initialized as nonsignaled, and then after the thread completes its initial work, it sets the event to signaled. At this point, another thread, which has been waiting on the event, sees that the event is signaled and becomes schedulable. This second thread knows that the first thread has completed its work.

Here is the **CreateEvent** function, which creates an event kernel object:

```
HANDLE CreateEvent(
    PSECURITY_ATTRIBUTES psa,
    BOOL bManualReset,
    BOOL bInitialState,
    PCTSTR pszName);
```

In Chapter 3, "Kernel Objects," we discussed the mechanics of kernel objects—how to set their security, how usage counting is done, how their handles can be inheritable, and how objects can be shared by name. Because all of this should be familiar to you by now, I won't discuss the first and last parameters of this function.

The **bManualReset** parameter is a Boolean value that tells the system whether to create a manual-reset event (**TRUE**) or an auto reset event (**FALSE**). The **bInitialState** parameter indicates whether the event should be initialized to signaled (**TRUE**) or nonsignaled (**FALSE**). After the system creates the event object, **CreateEvent** returns the process-relative handle to the event object. Windows Vista provides the new **CreateEventEx** function to create an event:

```
HANDLE CreateEventEx(
    PSECURITY_ATTRIBUTES psa,
    PCTSTR pszName,
    DWORD dwFlags,
    DWORD dwDesiredAccess);
```

The **psa** and **pszName** parameters are the same as in **CreateEvent**. The **dwFlags** parameter accepts two bitmasks, as shown in Table 9-1.

Table 9-1   CreateEventEx Flags

Bitwise Constant from WinBase.h	Description
CREATE_EVENT_INITIAL_SET (0x00000002)	Equivalent to the **bInitialState** parameter passed to **CreateEvent**. If this bitwise value is set, the event should be initialized to signaled; otherwise, it should be set to nonsignaled.
CREATE_EVENT_MANUAL_RESET (0x00000001)	Equivalent to the **bManualReset** parameter passed to **CreateEvent**. If this bitwise value is set, the event is a manual-reset event; otherwise, it is an automatic-reset event.

The **dwDesiredAccess** parameter allows you to specify at creation time what access the returned handle has to the event. This is a way to create an event handle with reduced access, as the handle returned from **CreateEvent** is always granted full access. But what is more useful is that **CreateEventEx** allows you to open a potentially existing event requesting reduced access, whereas **CreateEvent** always requests full access. For example, **EVENT_MODIFY_STATE** (0x0002) is required to be allowed to call the **SetEvent**, **ResetEvent**, and **PulseEvent** functions that you will see in a moment. Read the dedicated page on MSDN (*http://msdn2.microsoft.com/en-us/library/ms686670.aspx*) for more details on these access rights.

Threads in other processes can gain access to the object by calling **CreateEvent** using the same value passed in the **pszName** parameter; by using inheritance; by using the **DuplicateHandle** function; or by calling **OpenEvent**, specifying a name in the **pszName** parameter that matches the name specified in the call to **CreateEvent**:

```
HANDLE OpenEvent(
   DWORD dwDesiredAccess,
   BOOL bInherit,
   PCTSTR pszName);
```

As always, you should call the **CloseHandle** function when you no longer require the event kernel object.

Once an event is created, you control its state directly. When you call **SetEvent**, you change the event to the signaled state:

```
BOOL SetEvent(HANDLE hEvent);
```

When you call **ResetEvent**, you change the event to the nonsignaled state:

```
BOOL ResetEvent(HANDLE hEvent);
```

It's that easy.

Microsoft has defined a successful wait side effect rule for an auto-reset event: an auto-reset event is automatically reset to the nonsignaled state when a thread successfully waits on the object. This is how auto-reset events got their name. It is usually unnecessary to call **ResetEvent** for an auto-reset event because the system automatically resets the event. In contrast, Microsoft has not defined a successful wait side effect for manual-reset events.

Let's run through a quick example of how you can use event kernel objects to synchronize threads. Here's the setup:

```
// Create a global handle to a manual-reset, nonsignaled event.
HANDLE g_hEvent;

int WINAPI _tWinMain(...) {

   // Create the manual-reset, nonsignaled event.
   g_hEvent = CreateEvent(NULL, TRUE, FALSE, NULL);

   // Spawn 3 new threads.
   HANDLE hThread[3];
   DWORD dwThreadID;
   hThread[0] = _beginthreadex(NULL, 0, WordCount, NULL, 0, &dwThreadID);
   hThread[1] = _beginthreadex(NULL, 0, SpellCheck, NULL, 0, &dwThreadID);
   hThread[2] = _beginthreadex(NULL, 0, GrammarCheck, NULL, 0, &dwThreadID);


   OpenFileAndReadContentsIntoMemory(...);

   // Allow all 3 threads to access the memory.
   SetEvent(g_hEvent);
   ...
}
```

```
DWORD WINAPI WordCount(PVOID pvParam) {

    // Wait until the file's data is in memory.
    WaitForSingleObject(g_hEvent, INFINITE);

    // Access the memory block.
    ...
    return(0);
}

DWORD WINAPI SpellCheck (PVOID pvParam) {

    // Wait until the file's data is in memory.
    WaitForSingleObject(g_hEvent, INFINITE);

    // Access the memory block.
    ...
    return(0);
}

DWORD WINAPI GrammarCheck (PVOID pvParam) {

    // Wait until the file's data is in memory.
    WaitForSingleObject(g_hEvent, INFINITE);

    // Access the memory block.
    ...
    return(0);
}
```

When this process starts, it creates a manual-reset, nonsignaled event and saves the handle in a global variable. This makes it easy for other threads in this process to access the same event object. Now three threads are spawned. These threads wait until a file's contents are read into memory, and then each thread accesses the data: one thread does a word count, another runs the spelling checker, and the third runs the grammar checker. The code for these three thread functions starts out identically: each thread calls **WaitForSingleObject**, which suspends the thread until the file's contents have been read into memory by the primary thread.

Once the primary thread has the data ready, it calls **SetEvent**, which signals the event. At this point, the system makes all three secondary threads schedulable—they all get CPU time and access the memory block. Notice that all three threads will access the memory in a read-only fashion. This is the only reason why all three threads can run simultaneously. Also note that if the machine has multiple CPUs on it, all of these threads can truly execute simultaneously, getting a lot of work done in a short amount of time.

If you use an auto-reset event instead of a manual-reset event, the application behaves quite differently. The system allows only one secondary thread to become schedulable after the primary thread calls **SetEvent**. Again, there is no guarantee as to which thread the system will make schedulable. The remaining two secondary threads will continue to wait.

The thread that becomes schedulable has exclusive access to the memory block. Let's rewrite the thread functions so that each function calls **SetEvent** (just like the **_tWinMain** function does) just before returning. The thread functions now look like this:

```
DWORD WINAPI WordCount(PVOID pvParam) {

   // Wait until the file's data is in memory.
   WaitForSingleObject(g_hEvent, INFINITE);

   // Access the memory block.
   ...
   SetEvent(g_hEvent);
   return(0);
}

DWORD WINAPI SpellCheck (PVOID pvParam) {

   // Wait until the file's data is in memory.
   WaitForSingleObject(g_hEvent, INFINITE);

   // Access the memory block.
   ...
   SetEvent(g_hEvent);
   return(0);
}

DWORD WINAPI GrammarCheck (PVOID pvParam) {

   // Wait until the file's data is in memory.
   WaitForSingleObject(g_hEvent, INFINITE);

   // Access the memory block.
   ...
   SetEvent(g_hEvent);
   return(0);
}
```

When a thread has finished its exclusive pass over the data, it calls **SetEvent**, which allows the system to make one of the two waiting threads schedulable. Again, we don't know which thread the system will choose, but this thread will have its own exclusive pass over the memory block. When this thread is done, it will call **SetEvent** as well, causing the third and last thread to get its exclusive pass over the memory block. Note that when you use an auto-reset event, there is no problem if each secondary thread accesses the memory block in a read/write fashion; the threads are no longer required to consider the data read-only. This example clearly demonstrates the difference between using a manual-reset event and an auto-reset event.

For the sake of completeness, I'll mention one more function that you can use with events:

```
BOOL PulseEvent(HANDLE hEvent);
```

PulseEvent makes an event signaled and then immediately nonsignaled; it's just like calling **SetEvent** immediately followed by **ResetEvent**. If you call **PulseEvent** on a manual-reset event, any and all threads waiting on the event when it is pulsed are schedulable. If you call **PulseEvent** on an auto-reset event, only one waiting thread becomes schedulable. If no threads are waiting on the event when it is pulsed, there is no effect.

PulseEvent is not very useful. In fact, I've never used it in any practical application because you have no idea what threads, if any, will see the pulse and become schedulable. Since you can't know the state of any threads when you call **PulseEvent**, the function is just not that useful. That said, I'm sure that in some scenarios **PulseEvent** might come in handy—but none spring to mind. See the discussion of the **SignalObjectAndWait** function later in this chapter for a little more information on **PulseEvent**.

The Handshake Sample Application

The Handshake (09-Handshake.exe) application demonstrates the use of auto-reset events. The source code files and resource files for the application are in the 09-Handshake directory on the companion content Web page. When you run Handshake, the following dialog box appears:

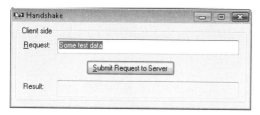

Handshake accepts a request string, reverses all the characters in the string, and places the result in the Result field. What makes Handshake exciting is the way it accomplishes this heroic task.

Handshake solves a common programming problem. You have a client and a server that want to talk to each other. Initially, the server has nothing to do, so it enters a wait state. When the client is ready to submit a request to the server, it places the request into a shared memory buffer and then signals an event so that the server thread knows to examine the data buffer and process the client's request. While the server thread is busy processing the request, the client's thread needs to enter a wait state until the server has the request's result ready. So the client enters a wait state until the server signals a different event that indicates that the result is ready to be processed by the client. When the client wakes up again, it knows that the result is in the shared data buffer and can present the result to the user.

When the application starts, it immediately creates two nonsignaled, auto-reset event objects. One event, **g_hevtRequestSubmitted**, indicates when a request is ready for the server. This event is waited on by the server thread and is signaled by the client thread. The second event, **g_hevt-ResultReturned**, indicates when the result is ready for the client. The client thread waits on this event, and the server thread is responsible for signaling it.

After the events are created, the server thread is spawned and executes the **ServerThread** function. This function immediately has the server wait for a client's request. Meanwhile, the primary thread, which is also the client thread, calls **DialogBox**, which displays the application's user interface. You can enter some text in the Request field, and then, when you click the Submit Request To Server button, the request string is placed in a buffer that is shared between the client and the server threads, and the **g_hevtRequestSubmitted** event is signaled. The client thread then waits for the server's result by waiting on the **g_hevtResultReturned** event.

The server wakes, reverses the string in the shared memory buffer, and then signals the **g_hevt-ResultReturned** event. The server's thread loops back around, waiting for another client request. Notice that this application never calls **ResetEvent** because it is unnecessary: auto-reset events are automatically reset to the nonsignaled state after a successful wait. Meanwhile, the client thread detects that the **g_hevtResultReturned** event has becomes signaled. It wakes and copies the string from the shared memory buffer into the Result field of the user interface.

Perhaps this application's only remaining notable feature is how it shuts down. To shut down the application, you simply close the dialog box. This causes the call to **DialogBox** in **_tWinMain** to return. At this point, the primary thread sets the global variable **g_hMainDlg** to **NULL** and copies a special string into the shared buffer and wakes the server's thread to process this special request. The primary thread waits for the server thread to acknowledge receipt of the request and for the server thread to terminate. When the server thread detects this special client request string and **g_hMainDlg** has a **NULL** value, it exits its loop and the thread just terminates. The secret request is never treated as a shutdown request as long as the main dialog is displayed thanks to the not-NULL check on the **g_hMainDlg** value.

I chose to have the primary thread wait for the server thread to die by calling **WaitForMultiple-Objects** so that you would see how this function is used. In reality, I could have just called **WaitForSingleObject**, passing in the server thread's handle, and everything would have worked exactly the same.

Once the primary thread knows that the server thread has stopped executing, I call **CloseHandle** three times to properly destroy all the kernel objects that the application was using. Of course, the system would do this for me automatically, but it just feels better to me when I do it myself. I like being in control of my code at all times.

```cpp
Handshake.cpp
/******************************************************************************
Module:  Handshake.cpp
Notices: Copyright (c) 2008 Jeffrey Richter & Christophe Nasarre
******************************************************************************/


#include "..\CommonFiles\CmnHdr.h"      /* See Appendix A. */
#include <windowsx.h>
#include <tchar.h>
#include "Resource.h"


///////////////////////////////////////////////////////////////////////////////


// This event is signaled when the client has a request for the server
HANDLE g_hevtRequestSubmitted;

// This event is signaled when the server has a result for the client
HANDLE g_hevtResultReturned;

// The buffer shared between the client and server threads
TCHAR  g_szSharedRequestAndResultBuffer[1024];
```

```
// The special value sent from the client that causes the
// server thread to terminate cleanly.
TCHAR  g_szServerShutdown[] = TEXT("Server Shutdown");

// The server thread will check that the main dialog is no longer alive
// when the shutdown message is received.
HWND   g_hMainDlg;


///////////////////////////////////////////////////////////////////////////


// This is the code executed by the server thread
DWORD WINAPI ServerThread(PVOID pvParam) {

   // Assume that the server thread is to run forever
   BOOL fShutdown = FALSE;

   while (!fShutdown) {

      // Wait for the client to submit a request
      WaitForSingleObject(g_hevtRequestSubmitted, INFINITE);

      // Check to see if the client wants the server to terminate
      fShutdown =
         (g_hMainDlg == NULL) &&
         (_tcscmp(g_szSharedRequestAndResultBuffer, g_szServerShutdown) == 0);

      if (!fShutdown) {
         // Process the client's request (reverse the string)
         _tcsrev(g_szSharedRequestAndResultBuffer);
      }

      // Let the client process the request's result
      SetEvent(g_hevtResultReturned);
   }

   // The client wants us to shut down, exit
   return(0);
}


///////////////////////////////////////////////////////////////////////////


BOOL Dlg_OnInitDialog(HWND hwnd, HWND hwndFocus, LPARAM lParam) {

   chSETDLGICONS(hwnd, IDI_HANDSHAKE);

   // Initialize the edit control with some test data request
   Edit_SetText(GetDlgItem(hwnd, IDC_REQUEST), TEXT("Some test data"));
```

```
        // Store the main dialog window handle
        g_hMainDlg = hwnd;

        return(TRUE);
}


////////////////////////////////////////////////////////////////////////////


void Dlg_OnCommand(HWND hwnd, int id, HWND hwndCtl, UINT codeNotify) {

    switch (id) {

        case IDCANCEL:
            EndDialog(hwnd, id);
            break;

        case IDC_SUBMIT:   // Submit a request to the server thread

            // Copy the request string into the shared data buffer
            Edit_GetText(GetDlgItem(hwnd, IDC_REQUEST),
                g_szSharedRequestAndResultBuffer,
                _countof(g_szSharedRequestAndResultBuffer));

            // Let the server thread know that a request is ready in the buffer
            SetEvent(g_hevtRequestSubmitted);

            // Wait for the server to process the request and give us the result
            WaitForSingleObject(g_hevtResultReturned, INFINITE);

            // Let the user know the result
            Edit_SetText(GetDlgItem(hwnd, IDC_RESULT),
                g_szSharedRequestAndResultBuffer);

            break;
    }
}


////////////////////////////////////////////////////////////////////////////


INT_PTR WINAPI Dlg_Proc(HWND hwnd, UINT uMsg, WPARAM wParam, LPARAM lParam) {

    switch (uMsg) {
        chHANDLE_DLGMSG(hwnd, WM_INITDIALOG, Dlg_OnInitDialog);
        chHANDLE_DLGMSG(hwnd, WM_COMMAND,    Dlg_OnCommand);
    }

    return(FALSE);
}


////////////////////////////////////////////////////////////////////////////
```

```
int WINAPI _tWinMain(HINSTANCE hInstanceExe, HINSTANCE, PTSTR, int) {

   // Create & initialize the 2 nonsignaled, auto-reset events
   g_hevtRequestSubmitted = CreateEvent(NULL, FALSE, FALSE, NULL);
   g_hevtResultReturned   = CreateEvent(NULL, FALSE, FALSE, NULL);

   // Spawn the server thread
   DWORD dwThreadID;
   HANDLE hThreadServer = chBEGINTHREADEX(NULL, 0, ServerThread, NULL,
      0, &dwThreadID);

   // Execute the client thread's user interface
   DialogBox(hInstanceExe, MAKEINTRESOURCE(IDD_HANDSHAKE), NULL, Dlg_Proc);
   g_hMainDlg = NULL;

   // The client's UI is closing, have the server thread shut down
   _tcscpy_s(g_szSharedRequestAndResultBuffer,
      _countof(g_szSharedRequestAndResultBuffer), g_szServerShutdown);
   SetEvent(g_hevtRequestSubmitted);

   // Wait for the server thread to acknowledge the shutdown AND
   // wait for the server thread to fully terminate
   HANDLE h[2];
   h[0] = g_hevtResultReturned;
   h[1] = hThreadServer;
   WaitForMultipleObjects(2, h, TRUE, INFINITE);

   // Properly clean up everything
   CloseHandle(hThreadServer);
   CloseHandle(g_hevtRequestSubmitted);
   CloseHandle(g_hevtResultReturned);

   // The client thread terminates with the whole process
   return(0);
}

/////////////////////////////// End of File ///////////////////////////////
```

Waitable Timer Kernel Objects

Waitable timers are kernel objects that signal themselves at a certain time or at regular intervals. They are most commonly used to have some operation performed at a certain time.

To create a waitable timer, you simply call **CreateWaitableTimer**:

```
HANDLE CreateWaitableTimer(
   PSECURITY_ATTRIBUTES psa,
   BOOL bManualReset,
   PCTSTR pszName);
```

The **psa** and **pszName** parameters are discussed in Chapter 3. Of course, a process can obtain its own process-relative handle to an existing waitable timer by calling **OpenWaitableTimer**:

```
HANDLE OpenWaitableTimer(
   DWORD dwDesiredAccess,
   BOOL bInheritHandle,
   PCTSTR pszName);
```

As with events, the **bManualReset** parameter indicates a manual-reset or auto-reset timer. When a manual-reset timer is signaled, all threads waiting on the timer become schedulable. When an auto-reset timer is signaled, only one waiting thread becomes schedulable.

Waitable timer objects are always created in the nonsignaled state. You must call the **SetWaitable-Timer** function to tell the timer when you want it to become signaled:

```
BOOL SetWaitableTimer(
   HANDLE hTimer,
   const LARGE_INTEGER *pDueTime,
   LONG lPeriod,
   PTIMERAPCROUTINE pfnCompletionRoutine,
   PVOID pvArgToCompletionRoutine,
   BOOL bResume);
```

This function takes several parameters and can be quite confusing to use. Obviously, the **hTimer** parameter indicates the timer that you want to set. The next two parameters, **pDueTime** and **lPeriod**, are used together. The **pDueTime** parameter indicates when the timer should go off for the first time, and the **lPeriod** parameter indicates how frequently the timer should go off after that. The following code sets a timer to go off for the first time on January 1, 2008, at 1:00 P.M., and then to go off every six hours after that:

```
// Declare our local variables.
HANDLE hTimer;
SYSTEMTIME st;
FILETIME ftLocal, ftUTC;
LARGE_INTEGER liUTC;

// Create an auto-reset timer.
hTimer = CreateWaitableTimer(NULL, FALSE, NULL);

// First signaling is at January 1, 2008, at 1:00 P.M. (local time).
st.wYear         = 2008; // Year
st.wMonth        = 1;    // January
st.wDayOfWeek    = 0;    // Ignored
st.wDay          = 1;    // The first of the month
st.wHour         = 13;   // 1PM
st.wMinute       = 0;    // 0 minutes into the hour
st.wSecond       = 0;    // 0 seconds into the minute
st.wMilliseconds = 0;    // 0 milliseconds into the second

SystemTimeToFileTime(&st, &ftLocal);

// Convert local time to UTC time.
LocalFileTimeToFileTime(&ftLocal, &ftUTC);
// Convert FILETIME to LARGE_INTEGER because of different alignment.
liUTC.LowPart  = ftUTC.dwLowDateTime;
liUTC.HighPart = ftUTC.dwHighDateTime;
```

```
// Set the timer.
SetWaitableTimer(hTimer, &liUTC, 6 * 60 * 60 * 1000,
    NULL, NULL, FALSE); ...
```

The preceding code first initializes a **SYSTEMTIME** structure that indicates when the timer should first go off (be signaled). I set this time in local time—the correct time for the machine's time zone. **SetWaitableTimer**'s second parameter is prototyped as a **const LARGE_INTEGER ***, and therefore it cannot accept a **SYSTEMTIME** structure directly. However, a **FILETIME** structure and a **LARGE_INTEGER** structure have identical binary formats: both structures contain two 32-bit values. So we can convert our **SYSTEMTIME** structure to a **FILETIME** structure. The next problem is that **SetWaitableTimer** expects the time always to be passed to it in Coordinated Universal Time (UTC) time. You can call **LocalFileTimeToFileTime** to easily make this conversion.

Because **FILETIME** and **LARGE_INTEGER** structures have identical binary formats, you might be tempted to pass the address of the **FILETIME** structure directly to **SetWaitableTimer**, as follows:

```
// Set the timer.
SetWaitableTimer(hTimer, (PLARGE_INTEGER) &ftUTC,
    6 * 60 * 60 * 1000, NULL, NULL, FALSE);
```

In fact, this is what I originally did. However, this is a big mistake! Though **FILETIME** and **LARGE_INTEGER** structures have identical binary formats, the alignment requirements of both structures are different. The address of all **FILETIME** structures must begin on a 32-bit boundary, but the address of all **LARGE_INTEGER** structures must begin on a 64-bit boundary. Whether calling **SetWaitableTimer** and passing it a **FILETIME** structure works correctly depends on whether the **FILETIME** structure happens to be on a 64-bit boundary. However, the compiler ensures that **LARGE_INTEGER** structures always begin on 64-bit boundaries, so the proper thing to do (the thing that is guaranteed to work all the time) is to copy the **FILETIME**'s members into a **LARGE_INTEGER**'s members and then pass the address of the **LARGE_INTEGER** to **SetWaitableTimer**.

> **Note**   The *x86* processors deal with unaligned data references silently. So passing the address of a **FILETIME** to **SetWaitableTimer** always works when your application is running on an *x86* CPU. However, other processors do not handle unaligned references as silently. In fact, most other processors raise an **EXCEPTION_DATATYPE_MISALIGNMENT** exception that causes your process to terminate. Alignment errors are the biggest cause of problems when you port code that works on *x86* computers to other processors. If you pay attention to alignment issues now, you can save months of porting effort later! For more information about alignment issues, see Chapter 13, "Windows Memory Architecture."

Now, to have the timer go off every six hours after January 1, 2008, at 1:00 P.M., we turn our attention to the **lPeriod** parameter. This parameter indicates, in milliseconds, how often the timer should go off after it initially goes off. For six hours, I pass 21,600,000 (6 hours * 60 minutes per hour * 60 seconds per minute * 1000 milliseconds per second). By the way, **SetWaitableTimer** does not fail if you pass it an absolute time in the past, such as January 1, 1975, at 1:00 P.M.

Instead of setting an absolute time that the timer should first go off, you can have the timer go off at a time relative to calling **SetWaitableTimer**. You simply pass a negative value in the **pDueTime** parameter. The value you pass must be in 100-nanosecond intervals. Because we don't normally think in intervals of 100 nanoseconds, you might find this useful: 1 second = 1,000 milliseconds = 1,000,000 microseconds = 10,000,000 100-nanoseconds.

The following code sets a timer to initially go off 5 seconds after the call to **SetWaitableTimer**:

```
// Declare our local variables.
HANDLE hTimer;
LARGE_INTEGER li;

// Create an auto-reset timer.
hTimer = CreateWaitableTimer(NULL, FALSE, NULL);

// Set the timer to go off 5 seconds after calling SetWaitableTimer.
// Timer unit is 100 nanoseconds.
const int nTimerUnitsPerSecond = 10000000;

// Negate the time so that SetWaitableTimer knows we
// want relative time instead of absolute time.
li.QuadPart = -(5 * nTimerUnitsPerSecond);

// Set the timer.
SetWaitableTimer(hTimer, &li, 6 * 60 * 60 * 1000,
   NULL, NULL, FALSE); ...
```

Usually, you want a one-shot timer that signals itself once and never signals itself again. To accomplish this, you simply pass **0** for the **lPeriod** parameter. You can then call **CloseHandle** to close the timer, or you can call **SetWaitableTimer** again to reset the time, giving it new criteria to follow.

SetWaitableTimer's last parameter, **bResume**, is useful for computers that support suspend and resume. Usually, you pass **FALSE** for this argument, as I've done in the preceding code fragments. However, if you're writing a meeting–planner type of application in which you want to set timers that remind the user of scheduled meetings, you should pass **TRUE**. When the timer goes off, it takes the machine out of suspend mode (if it's in suspend mode) and wakes up the threads that are waiting on the timer. The application then plays a sound and presents a message box telling the user of the upcoming meeting. If you pass **FALSE** for the **bResume** parameter, the timer object becomes signaled but any threads that it wakes up do not get CPU time until the machine is somehow resumed (usually by the user waking it up).

Our discussion of waitable timers would not be complete without talking about **Cancel-WaitableTimer**:

```
BOOL CancelWaitableTimer(HANDLE hTimer);
```

This simple function takes the handle of a timer and cancels it so that the timer never goes off unless there is a subsequent call to **SetWaitableTimer** to reset the timer. If you ever want to change the criteria for a timer, you don't have to call **CancelWaitableTimer** before calling **Set-WaitableTimer**. Each call to **SetWaitableTimer** cancels the criteria for the timer before setting the new criteria.

Having Waitable Timers Queue APC Entries

So far, you've learned how to create a timer and how to set the timer. You also know how to wait on the timer by passing its handle to the **WaitForSingleObject** or **WaitForMultipleObjects** functions. Microsoft also allows timers to queue an asynchronous procedure call (APC) to the thread that calls **SetWaitableTimer** when the timer is signaled.

Normally, when you call **SetWaitableTimer**, you pass **NULL** for both the **pfnCompletion-Routine** and **pvArgToCompletionRoutine** parameters. When **SetWaitableTimer** sees **NULL** for these parameters, it knows to signal the timer object when the time comes due. However, if you prefer to have the timer queue an APC when the time comes due, you must pass the address of a timer APC routine, which you must implement. The function should look like this:

```
VOID APIENTRY TimerAPCRoutine(PVOID pvArgToCompletionRoutine,
    DWORD dwTimerLowValue, DWORD dwTimerHighValue) {

    // Do whatever you want here.
}
```

I've named the function **TimerAPCRoutine**, but you can name it anything you like. This function is called using the same thread that called **SetWaitableTimer** when the timer goes off if and only if the calling thread is in an *alertable state*. In other words, the thread must be waiting in a call to **SleepEx**, **WaitForSingleObjectEx**, **WaitForMultipleObjectsEx**, **MsgWaitForMultiple-ObjectsEx**, or **SignalObjectAndWait**. If the thread is not waiting in one of these functions, the system does not queue the timer APC routine. This prevents the thread's APC queue from becoming overloaded with timer APC notifications, which can waste an enormous amount of memory inside the system. Chapter 10, "Synchronous and Asynchronous Device I/O," provides more details about the notion of alertable state.

If your thread is in an alertable wait when the timer goes off, the system makes your thread call the callback routine. The first parameter to the callback routine is the same value that you passed to **SetWaitableTimer**'s **pvArgToCompletionRoutine** parameter. You can pass some context information (usually a pointer to a structure that you define) to the **TimerAPCRoutine**. The remaining two parameters, **dwTimerLowValue** and **dwTimerHighValue**, indicate when the timer went off. The following code takes this information and shows it to the user:

```
VOID APIENTRY TimerAPCRoutine(PVOID pvArgToCompletionRoutine,
    DWORD dwTimerLowValue, DWORD dwTimerHighValue) {

    FILETIME ftUTC, ftLocal;
    SYSTEMTIME st;
    TCHAR szBuf[256];

    // Put the time in a FILETIME structure.
    ftUTC.dwLowDateTime = dwTimerLowValue;
    ftUTC.dwHighDateTime = dwTimerHighValue;

    // Convert the UTC time to the user's local time.
    FileTimeToLocalFileTime(&ftUTC, &ftLocal);

    // Convert the FILETIME to the SYSTEMTIME structure
    // required by GetDateFormat and GetTimeFormat.
    FileTimeToSystemTime(&ftLocal, &st);
```

```
   // Construct a string with the
   // date/time that the timer went off.
   GetDateFormat(LOCALE_USER_DEFAULT, DATE_LONGDATE,
      &st, NULL, szBuf, _countof(szBuf));
   _tcscat_s(szBuf, _countof(szBuf), TEXT(" "));
   GetTimeFormat(LOCALE_USER_DEFAULT, 0,
      &st, NULL, _tcschr(szBuf, TEXT('\0')),
      (int)(_countof(szBuf) - _tcslen(szBuf)));

   // Show the time to the user.
   MessageBox(NULL, szBuf, TEXT("Timer went off at..."), MB_OK);
}
```

Only after all APC entries have been processed does an alertable function return. Therefore, you must make sure that your **TimerAPCRoutine** function finishes executing before the timer becomes signaled again so that APC entries are not queued faster than they can be processed.

This code shows the proper way to use timers and APCs:

```
void SomeFunc() {
   // Create a timer. (It doesn't matter whether it's manual-reset
   // or auto-reset.)
   HANDLE hTimer = CreateWaitableTimer(NULL, TRUE, NULL);

   // Set timer to go off in 5 seconds.
   LARGE_INTEGER li = { 0 };
   SetWaitableTimer(hTimer, &li, 5000, TimerAPCRoutine, NULL, FALSE);

   // Wait in an alertable state for the timer to go off.
   SleepEx(INFINITE, TRUE);

   CloseHandle(hTimer);
}
```

One final word: a thread should not wait on a timer's handle while also waiting for the same timer alertably. Take a look at this code:

```
HANDLE hTimer = CreateWaitableTimer(NULL, FALSE, NULL);
SetWaitableTimer(hTimer, ..., TimerAPCRoutine,...);
WaitForSingleObjectEx(hTimer, INFINITE, TRUE);
```

You should not write code like this because the call to **WaitForSingleObjectEx** is actually waiting on the timer twice: alertably and with a kernel object handle. When the timer becomes signaled, the wait is successful and the thread wakes, which takes the thread out of the alertable state, and the APC routine is not called. As I said earlier, you won't often have a reason to use an APC routine with waitable timers because you can always wait for the timer to be signaled and then do what you want.

Timer Loose Ends

Timers are frequently used in communication protocols. For example, if a client makes a request of a server and the server doesn't respond in a certain amount of time, the client assumes that the server is not available. Today, client machines typically communicate with many servers simultaneously. If you were to create a timer kernel object for every single request, system performance would be hampered. You can imagine that it would be possible, for most applications, to create a single timer object and simply change the due time as necessary.

This managing of due times and resetting of the timer can be tedious; few applications go through the effort. However, among the new thread-pooling functions (covered in Chapter 11, "The Windows Thread Pool") is a function called **CreateThreadpoolTimer** that does all this work for you. If you find yourself creating and managing several timer objects, take a look at this function to reduce your application's overhead.

While it is nice that timers can queue APC entries, most applications written today do not use APCs; they use the I/O completion port mechanism. In the past, I have needed a thread in my own thread pool (managed with an I/O completion port) to wake up at specific timer intervals. Unfortunately, waitable timers do not offer this facility. To accomplish this, I have had to create a single thread whose sole job is to set and wait on a waitable timer. When the timer becomes signaled, the thread calls **PostQueuedCompletionStatus** to force an event to a thread in my thread pool.

One last note: any seasoned Windows developer will immediately compare waitable timers and User timers (set with the **SetTimer** function). The biggest difference is that User timers require a lot of additional user interface infrastructure in your application, which makes them more resource intensive. Also, waitable timers are kernel objects, which means that they can be shared by multiple threads and are securable.

User timers generate **WM_TIMER** messages that come back to the thread that called **SetTimer** (for callback timers) or the thread that created the window (for window-based timers). So only one thread is notified when a User timer goes off. Multiple threads, on the other hand, can wait on waitable timers, and several threads can be scheduled if the timer is a manual-reset timer.

If you are going to perform user-interface-related events in response to a timer, it is probably easier to structure your code using User timers because using a waitable timer requires that your threads wait for messages as well as kernel objects. (If you want to restructure your code, use the **MsgWait-ForMultipleObjects** function, which exists for exactly this purpose.) Finally, with waitable timers, you're more likely to be notified when the time actually expires. The **WM_TIMER** messages are always the lowest-priority messages and are retrieved when no other messages are in a thread's queue. Waitable timers are not treated any differently than other kernel objects; if the timer goes off and your thread is waiting, your thread will wake up.

Semaphore Kernel Objects

Semaphore kernel objects are used for resource counting. They contain a usage count, as all kernel objects do, but they also contain two additional signed 32-bit values: a maximum resource count and a current resource count. The maximum resource count identifies the maximum number of resources that the semaphore can control; the current resource count indicates the number of these resources that are currently available.

To put this in perspective, let's see how an application might use semaphores. Let's say that I'm developing a server process in which I have allocated a buffer that can hold client requests. I've hard-coded the size of the buffer so that it can hold a maximum of five client requests at a time. If a new client attempts to contact the server while five requests are outstanding, the new client is turned away with an error indicating that the server is busy and the client should try again later.

When my server process initializes, it creates a thread pool consisting of five threads, and each thread is ready to process individual client requests as they come in.

Initially, no clients have made any requests, so my server doesn't allow any of the threads in the pool to be schedulable. However, if three client requests come in simultaneously, three threads in the pool should be schedulable. You can handle this monitoring of resources and scheduling of threads very nicely using a semaphore: the maximum resource count is set to **5** because that is the size of my hard-coded buffer. The current resource count is initially set to **0** because no clients have made any requests. As client requests are accepted, the current resource count is incremented, and as client requests are handed off to server pool threads, the current resource count is decremented.

The rules for a semaphore are as follows:

- If the current resource count is greater than **0**, the semaphore is signaled.
- If the current resource count is **0**, the semaphore is nonsignaled.
- The system never allows the current resource count to be negative.
- The current resource count can never be greater than the maximum resource count.

When you use a semaphore, do not confuse the semaphore object's usage count with its current resource count.

This function creates a semaphore kernel object:

```
HANDLE CreateSemaphore(
   PSECURITY_ATTRIBUTE psa,
   LONG lInitialCount,
   LONG lMaximumCount,
   PCTSTR pszName);
```

The **psa** and **pszName** parameters are discussed in Chapter 3. You can also use the following function to directly provide access rights in the **dwDesiredAccess** parameter. Notice that the **dwFlags** is reserved and should be set to **0**.

```
HANDLE CreateSemaphoreEx(
   PSECURITY_ATTRIBUTES psa,
   LONG lInitialCount,
   LONG lMaximumCount,
   PCTSTR pszName,
   DWORD dwFlags,
   DWORD dwDesiredAccess);
```

Of course, another process can obtain its own process-relative handle to an existing semaphore by calling **OpenSemaphore**:

```
HANDLE OpenSemaphore(
   DWORD dwDesiredAccess,
   BOOL bInheritHandle,
   PCTSTR pszName);
```

The **lMaximumCount** parameter tells the system the maximum number of resources that your application can handle. Because this is a signed, 32-bit value, you can have as many as 2,147,483,647 resources. The **lInitialCount** parameter indicates how many of these resources are initially (currently) available. When my server process initializes, there are no client requests, so I call **CreateSemaphore** as follows:

```
HANDLE hSemaphore = CreateSemaphore(NULL, 0, 5, NULL);
```

This creates a semaphore with a maximum resource count of **5**, but initially **0** resources are available. (Incidentally, the kernel object's usage count is **1** because I just created this kernel object; don't get the counters confused.) Because the current resource count is initialized to **0**, the semaphore is nonsignaled. Any threads that wait on the semaphore are therefore placed in a wait state.

A thread gains access to a resource by calling a wait function, passing the handle of the semaphore guarding the resource. Internally, the wait function checks the semaphore's current resource count and if its value is greater than **0** (the semaphore is signaled), the counter is decremented by **1** and the calling thread remains schedulable. The nifty thing about semaphores is that they perform this test-and-set operation atomically; that is, when you request a resource from a semaphore, the operating system checks whether the resource is available and decrements the count of available resources without letting another thread interfere. Only after the resource count has been decremented does the system allow another thread to request access to a resource.

If the wait function determines that the semaphore's current resource count is **0** (the semaphore is nonsignaled), the system places the calling thread in a wait state. When another thread increments the semaphore's current resource count, the system remembers the waiting thread (or threads) and allows it to become schedulable (decrementing its current resource count appropriately).

A thread increments a semaphore's current resource count by calling **ReleaseSemaphore**:

```
BOOL ReleaseSemaphore(
    HANDLE hSemaphore,
    LONG lReleaseCount,
    PLONG plPreviousCount);
```

This function simply adds the value in **lReleaseCount** to the semaphore's current resource count. Usually, you pass **1** for the **lReleaseCount** parameter, but this is certainly not required; I often pass values of **2** or more. The function also returns the current resource count's original value in ***plPreviousCount**. Few applications actually care about this value, so fortunately you can pass **NULL** to ignore it.

Sometimes it is useful to know the current resource count of a semaphore without actually altering the count, but there is no function that queries a semaphore's current resource count value. At first, I thought that calling **ReleaseSemaphore** and passing **0** for the **lReleaseCount** parameter might work by returning the actual count in ***plPreviousCount**. But this doesn't work; **Release-Semaphore** fills the long variable with **0**. Next, I tried passing a really big number as the second parameter, hoping that it would not affect the current resource count because it would take it over the maximum. Again, **ReleaseSemaphore** filled ***plPreviousCount** with **0**. Unfortunately, there is just no way to get the current resource count of a semaphore without altering it.

Mutex Kernel Objects

Mutex kernel objects ensure that a thread has mutual exclusive access to a single resource. In fact, this is how the mutex got its name. A mutex object contains a usage count, thread ID, and recursion counter. Mutexes behave identically to critical sections. However, mutexes are kernel objects, while critical sections are user-mode synchronization objects (except if contention is high, as you saw in Chapter 8, "Thread Synchronization in User Mode"). This means that mutexes are slower than critical sections. But it also means that threads in different processes can access a single mutex, and it means that a thread can specify a timeout value while waiting to gain access to a resource.

The thread ID identifies which thread in the system currently owns the mutex, and the recursion counter indicates the number of times that this thread owns the mutex. Mutexes have many uses and are among the most frequently used kernel objects. Typically, they are used to guard a block of memory that is accessed by multiple threads. If multiple threads were to update the memory block simultaneously, the data in the block would be corrupted. Mutexes ensure that any thread accessing the memory block has exclusive access to the block so that the integrity of the data is maintained.

The rules for a mutex are as follows:

- If the thread ID is **0** (an invalid thread ID), the mutex is not owned by any thread and is signaled.
- If the thread ID is a nonzero value, a thread owns the mutex and the mutex is nonsignaled.
- Unlike all the other kernel objects, mutexes have special code in the operating system that allows them to violate the normal rules. (I'll explain this exception shortly.)

To use a mutex, one process must first create the mutex by calling **CreateMutex**:

```
HANDLE CreateMutex(
    PSECURITY_ATTRIBUTES psa,
    BOOL bInitialOwner,
    PCTSTR pszName);
```

The **psa** and **pszName** parameters are discussed in Chapter 3. You can also use the following function to directly provide access rights in the **dwDesiredAccess** parameter. The **dwFlags** parameter replaces the **bInitialOwned** parameter of **CreateMutex**: **0** means **FALSE**, and **CREATE_MUTEX_INITIAL_OWNER** is equivalent to **TRUE**.

```
HANDLE CreateMutexEx(
    PSECURITY_ATTRIBUTES psa,
    PCTSTR pszName,
    DWORD dwFlags,
    DWORD dwDesiredAccess);
```

Of course, another process can obtain its own process-relative handle to an existing mutex by calling **OpenMutex**:

```
HANDLE OpenMutex(
    DWORD dwDesiredAccess,
    BOOL bInheritHandle,
    PCTSTR pszName);
```

The **bInitialOwner** parameter controls the initial state of the mutex. If you pass **FALSE** (the usual case), both the mutex object's thread ID and recursion counter are set to **0**. This means that the mutex is unowned and is therefore signaled.

If you pass **TRUE** for **bInitialOwner**, the object's thread ID is set to the calling thread's ID and the recursion counter is set to **1**. Because the thread ID is a nonzero value, the mutex is initially nonsignaled.

A thread gains access to the shared resource by calling a wait function, passing the handle of the mutex guarding the resource. Internally, the wait function checks the thread ID to see if it is **0** (the mutex is signaled). If the thread ID is **0**, the thread ID is set to the calling thread's ID, the recursion counter is set to **1**, and the calling thread remains schedulable.

If the wait function detects that the thread ID is not **0** (the mutex is nonsignaled), the calling thread enters a wait state. The system remembers this and when the mutex's thread ID is set back to **0**, the system sets the thread ID to the waiting thread's ID, sets the recursion counter to **1**, and allows the waiting thread to be schedulable again. As always, these checks and changes to the mutex kernel object are performed atomically.

For mutexes, there is one special exception to the normal kernel object signaled/nonsignaled rules. Let's say that a thread attempts to wait on a nonsignaled mutex object. In this case, the thread is usually placed in a wait state. However, the system checks to see whether the thread attempting to acquire the mutex has the same thread ID as recorded inside the mutex object. If the thread IDs match, the system allows the thread to remain schedulable—even though the mutex was nonsignaled. We don't see this "exceptional" behavior applied to any other kernel object anywhere in the system. Every time a thread successfully waits on a mutex, the object's recursion counter is incremented. The only way the recursion counter can have a value greater than **1** is if the thread waits on the same mutex multiple times, taking advantage of this rule exception.

Once a thread has successfully waited on a mutex, the thread knows that it has exclusive access to the protected resource. Any other threads that attempt to gain access to the resource (by waiting on the same mutex) are placed in a wait state. When the thread that currently has access to the resource no longer needs its access, it must release the mutex by calling the **ReleaseMutex** function:

```
BOOL ReleaseMutex(HANDLE hMutex);
```

This function decrements the object's recursion counter by **1**. If a thread successfully waits on a mutex object multiple times, that thread has to call **ReleaseMutex** the same number of times before the object's recursion counter becomes **0**. When the recursion counter hits **0**, the thread ID is also set to **0** and the object becomes signaled.

When the object becomes signaled, the system checks to see whether any other threads are waiting on the mutex. If so, the system "fairly" selects one of the waiting threads and gives it ownership of the mutex. This means, of course, that the thread ID is set to the selected thread's ID and the recursion counter is set to **1**. If no other thread is waiting on the mutex, the mutex stays in the signaled state so that the next thread that waits on the mutex immediately gets it.

Abandonment Issues

Mutex objects are different from all other kernel objects because they have a notion of "thread ownership." None of the other kernel objects that we've discussed in this chapter remembers which thread successfully waited on it; only mutexes keep track of this. This thread ownership concept for mutexes is the reason why mutexes have the special rule exception that allows a thread to acquire the mutex even when it is nonsignaled.

This exception applies not only to a thread that is attempting to acquire a mutex, it also applies to threads attempting to release a mutex. When a thread calls **ReleaseMutex**, the function checks to see whether the calling thread's ID matches the thread ID in the mutex object. If the IDs match, the recursion counter is decremented as described earlier. If the thread IDs don't match, **ReleaseMutex** does nothing and returns **FALSE** (indicating failure) back to the caller. Making a call to **nGetLastError** at this time will return **ERROR_NOT_OWNER** (attempt to release mutex not owned by caller).

So if a thread owning a mutex terminates (using **ExitThread**, **TerminateThread**, **ExitProcess**, or **TerminateProcess**) before releasing the mutex, what happens to the mutex and the other threads that are waiting on it? The answer is that the system considers the mutex to be *abandoned*— the thread that owns it can never release it because the thread has died.

Because the system keeps track of all mutex and thread kernel objects, it knows exactly when mutexes become abandoned. When a mutex becomes abandoned, the system automatically resets the mutex object's thread ID to **0** and its recursion counter to **0**. Then the system checks to see whether any threads are currently waiting for the mutex. If so, the system "fairly" selects a waiting thread, sets the thread ID to the selected thread's ID, and sets the recursion counter to **1**; the selected thread becomes schedulable.

This is the same as before except that the wait function does not return the usual **WAIT_OBJECT_0** value to the thread. Instead, the wait function returns the special value of **WAIT_ABANDONED**. This special return value (which applies only to mutex objects) indicates that the mutex the thread was waiting on was owned by another thread that was terminated before it finished using the shared resource. This is not the best situation to be in. The newly scheduled thread has no idea what state the resource is currently in—the resource might be totally corrupt. You have to decide for yourself what your application should do in this case.

In real life, most applications never check explicitly for the **WAIT_ABANDONED** return value because a thread is rarely just terminated. (This whole discussion provides another great example of why you should never call the **TerminateThread** function.)

Mutexes vs. Critical Sections

Mutexes and critical sections have identical semantics with respect to scheduling waiting threads. However, they differ in some of their other attributes. Table 9-2 compares them.

Table 9-2   Comparison of Mutexes and Critical Sections

Characteristic	Mutex	Critical Section
Performance	Slow	Fast
Can be used across process boundaries	Yes	No
Declaration	`HANDLE hmtx;`	`CRITICAL_SECTION cs;`
Initialization	`hmtx = CreateMutex (NULL, FALSE, NULL);`	`InitializeCriticalSection(&cs);`
Cleanup	`CloseHandle(hmtx);`	`DeleteCriticalSection(&cs);`
Infinite wait	`WaitForSingleObject (hmtx, INFINITE);`	`EnterCriticalSection(&cs);`
0 wait	`WaitForSingleObject (hmtx, 0);`	`TryEnterCriticalSection(&cs);`
Arbitrary wait	`WaitForSingleObject (hmtx, dwMilliseconds);`	Not possible
Release	`ReleaseMutex(hmtx);`	`LeaveCriticalSection(&cs);`
Can be waited on with other kernel objects	Yes (use `WaitForMultiple-Objects` or similar function)	No

The Queue Sample Application

The Queue (09-Queue.exe) application uses a mutex and a semaphore to control a queue of simple data elements. You have already seen how **SRWLock** and condition variables could be used to manage this kind of queue in Chapter 8. Here, you will see how to make the queue thread-safe and easier to manipulate from the different threads. The source code and resource files for the application are in the 09-Queue directory on the companion content Web page. When you run Queue, the following dialog box appears.

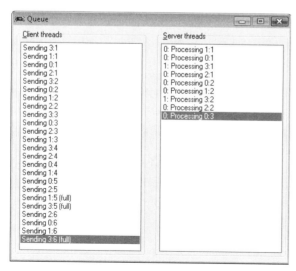

As in Chapter 8, when Queue initializes, it creates four client threads and two server threads. Each client thread sleeps for some period of time and then appends a request element to a queue. As each element is queued, the Client Threads list box is updated. Each entry indicates which client thread appended the entry and which entry it was. For example, the first entry in the list box indicates that client thread 3 appended its first request. Then client threads 1, 0, and 2 appended their first request, followed by client thread 3 appending its second request, and so on.

The server threads have nothing to do until at least one element appears in the queue. When an element appears, a single server thread wakes up to process the request. The Server Threads list box shows the status of the server threads. The first entry shows that server thread 0 is processing a request from client thread 1. The request being processed is the client thread's first request. The second entry shows server thread 0 processing client thread 0's first request, and so on.

In this example, the server threads cannot process the client's requests quickly enough and the queue fills to maximum capacity. I initialized the queue data structure so that it can hold no more than 10 elements at a single time; this causes the queue to fill quickly. Plus, there are four client threads and only two server threads. We see that the queue is full when client thread 3 attempts to append its fifth request to the queue.

OK, so that's what you see. What's more interesting is how it works. The queue is managed and controlled by a thread-safe C++ class, **CQueue**:

```
class CQueue {
public:
   struct ELEMENT {
      int m_nThreadNum, m_nRequestNum;
      // Other element data should go here.
   };
   typedef ELEMENT* PELEMENT;

private:
   PELEMENT m_pElements;        // Array of elements to be processed
   int      m_nMaxElements;     // # of elements in the array
   HANDLE   m_h[2];             // Mutex & semaphore handles
   HANDLE   &m_hmtxQ;           // Reference to m_h[0]
   HANDLE   &m_hsemNumElements; // Reference to m_h[1]

public:
   CQueue(int nMaxElements);
   ~CQueue();

   BOOL Append(PELEMENT pElement, DWORD dwMilliseconds);
   BOOL Remove(PELEMENT pElement, DWORD dwMilliseconds);
};
```

The public **ELEMENT** structure inside this class defines what a queue data element looks like. The actual content is not particularly important. For this sample application, clients place their client thread number and their request number in this element so that the servers can display this information in their list box when they process the retrieved element. A real-life application would generally not require this information.

For the private members, we have **m_pElements**, which points to a fixed-size array of **ELEMENT** structures. This is the data that needs protecting from the multiple client/server threads. The **m_nMaxElements** member indicates how large this array is when the **CQueue** object is constructed. The next member, **m_h**, is an array of two kernel object handles. To properly protect the queue's data elements, you need two kernel objects: a mutex and a semaphore. In the **CQueue** constructor, these two objects are created and their handles are placed in this array.

As you'll see shortly, the code sometimes calls **WaitForMultipleObjects**, passing the address to the handle array. You'll also see that sometimes the code needs to refer to just one of these kernel object handles. To make the code more readable and maintainable, I also declare two handle reference members, **m_hmtxQ** and **m_hsemNumElements**. When the **CQueue** constructor executes, it initializes these handle reference members to **m_h[0]** and **m_h[1]**, respectively.

You should now have no trouble understanding **CQueue**'s constructor and destructor methods, so let's turn our attention to the **Append** method. This method attempts to append an **ELEMENT** to the queue. But first, the thread must make sure that it has exclusive access to the queue. The **Append** method does this by calling **WaitForSingleObject**, passing the handle of the **m_hmtxQ** mutex. If **WAIT_OBJECT_0** is returned, the thread has exclusive access to the queue.

Next, the **Append** method must attempt to increment the number of elements in the queue by calling **ReleaseSemaphore** and passing a release count of **1**. If **ReleaseSemaphore** is successful, the queue is not full and the new element can be appended. Fortunately, **ReleaseSemaphore** also returns the previous count of queue elements in the **lPreviousCount** variable. This tells you exactly which array index the new element should be placed in. After copying the element into the queue's array, the function returns. Once the element is completely appended to the queue, **Append** calls **ReleaseMutex** so that other threads can access the queue. The remaining parts of the **Append** function have to do with failure cases and error handling.

Now let's look at how a server thread calls the **Remove** method to extract an element from the queue. First, the thread must make sure that it has exclusive access to the queue, and the queue must have at least one element in it. Certainly, a server thread has no reason to wake if no elements are in the queue. So the **Remove** method first calls **WaitForMultipleObjects**, passing both the mutex and the semaphore's handles. Only when both of these objects are signaled should a server thread wake up.

If **WAIT_OBJECT_0** is returned, the thread has exclusive access to the queue and at least one element must be in the queue. At this point, the code extracts the element at index 0 in the array and then shifts the remaining elements in the array down one. This is not the most efficient way to implement a queue because memory copies like this are expensive, but our purpose here is to demonstrate thread synchronization. Finally, **ReleaseMutex** is called so that other threads can safely access the queue.

Note that the semaphore object keeps track of how many elements are in the queue at any given time. You can see how this number is incremented: the **Append** method calls **ReleaseSemaphore** when a new element is appended to the queue. But you don't immediately see how this count is decremented when an element is removed from the queue. The decrementing is done by the **Remove** method's call to **WaitForMultipleObjects**. Remember that the side effect of successfully waiting on a semaphore is that its count is decremented by one. This is very convenient for us.

Now that you understand how the **CQueue** class works, the rest of the source code is easy to understand.

```
Queue.cpp
/******************************************************************************
Module:  Queue.cpp
Notices: Copyright (c) 2008 Jeffrey Richter & Christophe Nasarre
******************************************************************************/


#include "..\CommonFiles\CmnHdr.h"      /* See Appendix A. */
#include <windowsx.h>
#include <tchar.h>
#include <StrSafe.h>
#include "Resource.h"


///////////////////////////////////////////////////////////////////////////////


class CQueue {
public:
   struct ELEMENT {
      int m_nThreadNum, m_nRequestNum;
      // Other element data should go here
   };
   typedef ELEMENT* PELEMENT;

private:
   PELEMENT m_pElements;       // Array of elements to be processed
   int      m_nMaxElements;    // Maximum # of elements in the array
   HANDLE   m_h[2];            // Mutex & semaphore handles
   HANDLE   &m_hmtxQ;          // Reference to m_h[0]
   HANDLE   &m_hsemNumElements; // Reference to m_h[1]

public:
   CQueue(int nMaxElements);
   ~CQueue();

   BOOL Append(PELEMENT pElement, DWORD dwMilliseconds);
   BOOL Remove(PELEMENT pElement, DWORD dwMilliseconds);
};


///////////////////////////////////////////////////////////////////////////////


CQueue::CQueue(int nMaxElements)
   : m_hmtxQ(m_h[0]), m_hsemNumElements(m_h[1]) {

   m_pElements = (PELEMENT)
      HeapAlloc(GetProcessHeap(), 0, sizeof(ELEMENT) * nMaxElements);
   m_nMaxElements = nMaxElements;
   m_hmtxQ = CreateMutex(NULL, FALSE, NULL);
   m_hsemNumElements = CreateSemaphore(NULL, 0, nMaxElements, NULL);
}
```

```
/////////////////////////////////////////////////////////////////////////


CQueue::~CQueue() {

   CloseHandle(m_hsemNumElements);
   CloseHandle(m_hmtxQ);
   HeapFree(GetProcessHeap(), 0, m_pElements);
}


/////////////////////////////////////////////////////////////////////////


BOOL CQueue::Append(PELEMENT pElement, DWORD dwTimeout) {

   BOOL fOk = FALSE;
   DWORD dw = WaitForSingleObject(m_hmtxQ, dwTimeout);

   if (dw == WAIT_OBJECT_0) {
      // This thread has exclusive access to the queue

      // Increment the number of elements in the queue
      LONG lPrevCount;
      fOk = ReleaseSemaphore(m_hsemNumElements, 1, &lPrevCount);
      if (fOk) {
         // The queue is not full, append the new element
         m_pElements[lPrevCount] = *pElement;
      } else {

         // The queue is full, set the error code and return failure
         SetLastError(ERROR_DATABASE_FULL);
      }

      // Allow other threads to access the queue
      ReleaseMutex(m_hmtxQ);

   } else {
      // Timeout, set error code and return failure
      SetLastError(ERROR_TIMEOUT);
   }

   return(fOk);   // Call GetLastError for more info
}


/////////////////////////////////////////////////////////////////////////


BOOL CQueue::Remove(PELEMENT pElement, DWORD dwTimeout) {

   // Wait for exclusive access to queue and for queue to have element.
   BOOL fOk = (WaitForMultipleObjects(_countof(m_h), m_h, TRUE, dwTimeout)
      == WAIT_OBJECT_0);
```

```
    if (fOk) {
        // The queue has an element, pull it from the queue
        *pElement = m_pElements[0];

        // Shift the remaining elements down
        MoveMemory(&m_pElements[0], &m_pElements[1],
            sizeof(ELEMENT) * (m_nMaxElements - 1));

        // Allow other threads to access the queue
        ReleaseMutex(m_hmtxQ);

    } else {
        // Timeout, set error code and return failure
        SetLastError(ERROR_TIMEOUT);
    }

    return(fOk);   // Call GetLastError for more info
}


///////////////////////////////////////////////////////////////////////////


CQueue g_q(10);                       // The shared queue
volatile BOOL g_fShutdown = FALSE;    // Signals client/server threads to die
HWND g_hwnd;                          // How client/server threads give status


// Handles to all client/server threads & number of client/server threads
HANDLE g_hThreads[MAXIMUM_WAIT_OBJECTS];
int    g_nNumThreads = 0;


///////////////////////////////////////////////////////////////////////////


DWORD WINAPI ClientThread(PVOID pvParam) {

    int nThreadNum = PtrToUlong(pvParam);
    HWND hwndLB = GetDlgItem(g_hwnd, IDC_CLIENTS);

    int nRequestNum = 0;
    while ((PVOID)1 !=
        InterlockedCompareExchangePointer(
            (PVOID*) &g_fShutdown, (PVOID)0, (PVOID)0)) {

        // Keep track of the current processed element
        nRequestNum++;

        TCHAR sz[1024];
        CQueue::ELEMENT e = { nThreadNum, nRequestNum };

        // Try to put an element on the queue
        if (g_q.Append(&e, 200)) {

            // Indicate which thread sent it and which request
```

```
                StringCchPrintf(sz, _countof(sz), TEXT("Sending %d:%d"),
                    nThreadNum, nRequestNum);
            } else {

                // Couldn't put an element on the queue
                StringCchPrintf(sz, _countof(sz), TEXT("Sending %d:%d (%s)"),
                    nThreadNum, nRequestNum, (GetLastError() == ERROR_TIMEOUT)
                        ? TEXT("timeout") : TEXT("full"));
            }

            // Show result of appending element
            ListBox_SetCurSel(hwndLB, ListBox_AddString(hwndLB, sz));
            Sleep(2500);   // Wait before appending another element
        }

    return(0);
}


///////////////////////////////////////////////////////////////////////////


DWORD WINAPI ServerThread(PVOID pvParam) {

    int nThreadNum = PtrToUlong(pvParam);
    HWND hwndLB = GetDlgItem(g_hwnd, IDC_SERVERS);

    while ((PVOID)1 !=
        InterlockedCompareExchangePointer(
            (PVOID*) &g_fShutdown, (PVOID)0, (PVOID)0)) {

        TCHAR sz[1024];
        CQueue::ELEMENT e;

        // Try to get an element from the queue
        if (g_q.Remove(&e, 5000)) {

            // Indicate which thread is processing it, which thread
            // sent it and which request we're processing
            StringCchPrintf(sz, _countof(sz), TEXT("%d: Processing %d:%d"),
                nThreadNum, e.m_nThreadNum, e.m_nRequestNum);

            // The server takes some time to process the request
            Sleep(2000 * e.m_nThreadNum);

        } else {
            // Couldn't get an element from the queue
            StringCchPrintf(sz, _countof(sz), TEXT("%d: (timeout)"), nThreadNum);
        }

        // Show result of processing element
        ListBox_SetCurSel(hwndLB, ListBox_AddString(hwndLB, sz));
    }

    return(0);
}
```

```
///////////////////////////////////////////////////////////////////////


BOOL Dlg_OnInitDialog(HWND hwnd, HWND hwndFocus, LPARAM lParam) {

   chSETDLGICONS(hwnd, IDI_QUEUE);

   g_hwnd = hwnd; // Used by client/server threads to show status

   DWORD dwThreadID;

   // Create the client threads
   for (int x = 0; x < 4; x++)
      g_hThreads[g_nNumThreads++] =
         chBEGINTHREADEX(NULL, 0, ClientThread, (PVOID) (INT_PTR) x,
            0, &dwThreadID);

   // Create the server threads
   for (int x = 0; x < 2; x++)
      g_hThreads[g_nNumThreads++] =
         chBEGINTHREADEX(NULL, 0, ServerThread, (PVOID) (INT_PTR) x,
            0, &dwThreadID);

   return(TRUE);
}


///////////////////////////////////////////////////////////////////////


void Dlg_OnCommand(HWND hwnd, int id, HWND hwndCtl, UINT codeNotify) {

   switch (id) {
      case IDCANCEL:
         EndDialog(hwnd, id);
         break;
   }
}


///////////////////////////////////////////////////////////////////////


INT_PTR WINAPI Dlg_Proc(HWND hwnd, UINT uMsg, WPARAM wParam, LPARAM lParam) {

   switch (uMsg) {
      chHANDLE_DLGMSG(hwnd, WM_INITDIALOG, Dlg_OnInitDialog);
      chHANDLE_DLGMSG(hwnd, WM_COMMAND,    Dlg_OnCommand);
   }
   return(FALSE);
}


///////////////////////////////////////////////////////////////////////
```

```
int WINAPI _tWinMain(HINSTANCE hinstExe, HINSTANCE, PTSTR pszCmdLine, int) {

   DialogBox(hinstExe, MAKEINTRESOURCE(IDD_QUEUE), NULL, Dlg_Proc);
   InterlockedExchangePointer(&g_fShutdown, TRUE);

   // Wait for all the threads to terminate & then clean up
   WaitForMultipleObjects(g_nNumThreads, g_hThreads, TRUE, INFINITE);
   while (g_nNumThreads--)
      CloseHandle(g_hThreads[g_nNumThreads]);

   return(0);
}


/////////////////////////////// End of File ///////////////////////////////
```

A Handy Thread Synchronization Object Chart

Table 9-3 summarizes how the various kernel objects behave with respect to thread synchronization.

Table 9-3   Kernel Objects and Thread Synchronization

Object	When Nonsignaled	When Signaled	Successful Wait Side Effect
Process	While process is still active	When process terminates (**Exit-Process**, **TerminateProcess**)	None
Thread	While thread is still active	When thread terminates (**Exit-Thread**, **TerminateThread**)	None
Job	When job's time has not expired	When job time expires	None
File	When I/O request is pending	When I/O request completes	None
Console input	No input exists	When input is available	None
File change notifications	No files have changed	When file system detects changes	Resets notification
Auto-reset event	**ResetEvent**, **PulseEvent**, or successful wait	When **SetEvent/PulseEvent** is called	Resets event
Manual-reset event	**ResetEvent** or **PulseEvent**	When **SetEvent/PulseEvent** is called	None
Auto-reset waitable timer	**CancelWaitableTimer** or successful wait	When time comes due (**SetWaitableTimer**)	Resets timer
Manual-reset waitable timer	**CancelWaitableTimer**	When time comes due (**SetWaitableTimer**)	None

Table 9-3   Kernel Objects and Thread Synchronization

Object	When Nonsignaled	When Signaled	Successful Wait Side Effect
Semaphore	Successful wait	When count > 0 (**ReleaseSemaphore**)	Decrements count by 15
Mutex	Successful wait	When unowned by a thread (**ReleaseMutex**)	Gives ownership to a thread
Critical section (user-mode)	Successful wait ((**Try**)**Enter-Critical-Section**)	When unowned by a thread (**LeaveCriticalSection**)	Gives ownership to a thread
SRWLock (user-mode)	Successful wait (**Acquire-SRWLock(Exclusive)**)	When unowned by a thread (**ReleaseSRWLock(Exclusive)**)	Gives ownership to a thread
Condition variable (user-mode)	Successful wait (**SleepConditionVariable***)	When woken up (**Wake(All)ConditionVariable**)	None

Interlocked (user-mode) functions never cause a thread to be unschedulable; they alter a value and return immediately.

Other Thread Synchronization Functions

WaitForSingleObject and **WaitForMultipleObjects** are the most commonly used functions for performing thread synchronization. However, Windows offers a few more functions that have slight variations. If you understand **WaitForSingleObject** and **WaitForMultipleObjects**, you'll have no trouble understanding how these other functions work. In this section, I'll briefly introduce some of them.

Asynchronous Device I/O

As you will see in detail in Chapter 10, asynchronous device I/O allows a thread to start a read or write operation without having to wait for the read or write operation to complete. For example, if a thread needs to load a large file into memory, the thread can tell the system to load the file into memory. Then, as the system loads the file, the thread can be busy performing other tasks—creating windows, initializing internal data structures, and so on. When the initialization is complete, the thread can suspend itself, waiting for the system to notify it that the file has been read.

Device objects are synchronizable kernel objects, which means that you can call **WaitForSingle-Object**, passing the handle of a file, socket, communication port, and so on. While the system performs the asynchronous I/O, the device object is in the nonsignaled state. As soon as the operation is complete, the system changes the state of the object to signaled so that the thread knows that the operation has completed. At this point, the thread continues execution.

WaitForInputIdle

A thread can also suspend itself by calling **WaitForInputIdle**:

```
DWORD WaitForInputIdle(
   HANDLE hProcess,
   DWORD dwMilliseconds);
```

This function waits until the process identified by **hProcess** has no input pending in the thread that created the application's first window. This function is useful for a parent process. The parent process spawns a child process to do some work. When the parent process' thread calls **Create-Process**, the parent's thread continues to execute while the child process initializes. The parent's thread might need to get the handle of a window created by the child. The only way for the parent's thread to know when the child process has been fully initialized is to wait until the child is no longer processing any input. So after the call to **CreateProcess**, the parent's thread places a call to **WaitForInputIdle**.

You can also use **WaitForInputIdle** when you need to force keystrokes into an application. Let's say that you post the following messages to the main window of an application:

WM_KEYDOWN	with a virtual key of **VK_MENU**
WM_KEYDOWN	with a virtual key of **VK_F**
WM_KEYUP	with a virtual key of **VK_F**
WM_KEYUP	with a virtual key of **VK_MENU**
WM_KEYDOWN	with a virtual key of **VK_O**
WM_KEYUP	with a virtual key of **VK_O**

This sequence sends Alt+F, O to an application, which, for most English-language applications, chooses the Open command from the application's File menu. This command opens a dialog box, but before the dialog box can appear, Windows must load the dialog box template from the file and cycle through all the controls in the template, calling **CreateWindow** for each one. This can take some time. So the application that posted the **WM_KEY*** messages can call **WaitForInputIdle**, which causes the application to wait until the dialog box has been completely created and is ready for user input. The application can now force additional keys into the dialog box and its controls so that it can continue doing whatever it needs to do.

Developers who wrote for 16-bit Windows often faced this problem. Applications wanted to post messages to a window but didn't know exactly when the window was created and ready. The **WaitForInputIdle** function solves this problem.

MsgWaitForMultipleObjects(Ex)

A thread can call the **MsgWaitForMultipleObjects** or **MsgWaitForMultipleObjectsEx** function to cause the thread to wait for its own messages:

```
DWORD MsgWaitForMultipleObjects(
   DWORD dwCount,
   PHANDLE phObjects,
   BOOL bWaitAll,
   DWORD dwMilliseconds,
   DWORD dwWakeMask);
```

```
DWORD MsgWaitForMultipleObjectsEx(
   DWORD dwCount,
   PHANDLE phObjects,
   DWORD dwMilliseconds,
   DWORD dwWakeMask,
   DWORD dwFlags);
```

These functions are similar to the **WaitForMultipleObjects** function. The difference is that they allow a thread to be scheduled when a kernel object becomes signaled or when a window message needs dispatching to a window created by the calling thread.

A thread that creates windows and performs user-interface related tasks should use **MsgWaitFor-MultipleObjectsEx** instead of **WaitForMultipleObjects** because the latter prohibits the thread's user-interface from responding to the user.

WaitForDebugEvent

Windows has excellent debugging support built right into the operating system. When a debugger starts executing, it attaches itself to a debuggee. The debugger simply sits idle, waiting for the operating system to notify it of debug events related to the debuggee. A debugger waits for these events by calling the **WaitForDebugEvent** function:

```
BOOL WaitForDebugEvent(
   PDEBUG_EVENT pde,
   DWORD dwMilliseconds);
```

When a debugger calls this function, the debugger's thread is suspended. The system notifies the debugger that a debug event has occurred by allowing the call to **WaitForDebugEvent** to return. The structure pointed to by the **pde** parameter is filled by the system before it awakens the thread. This structure contains information about the debug event that has just occurred. Read the "Escape from DLL Hell with Custom Debugging and Instrumentation Tools and Utilities, Part 2" article on MSDN Magazine for a detailed explanation of writing your own debugger (*http://msdn.microsoft.com/msdnmag/issues/02/08/EscapefromDLLHell/*).

SignalObjectAndWait

The **SignalObjectAndWait** function signals a kernel object and waits on another kernel object in a single atomic operation:

```
DWORD SignalObjectAndWait(
   HANDLE hObjectToSignal,
   HANDLE hObjectToWaitOn,
   DWORD dwMilliseconds,
   BOOL bAlertable);
```

When you call this function, the **hObjectToSignal** parameter must identify a mutex, semaphore, or event. Any other type of object causes the function to return **WAIT_FAILED**, and **GetLastError** returns **ERROR_INVALID_HANDLE**. Internally, the function examines the type of object and performs the equivalent of **ReleaseMutex**, **ReleaseSemaphore** (with a count of **1**), or **SetEvent**, respectively.

The **hObjectToWaitOn** parameter can identify any of the following kernel objects: mutex, semaphore, event, timer, process, thread, job, console input, and change notification. As usual, the **dwMilliseconds** parameter indicates how long the function should wait for this object to become signaled, and the **bAlertable** flag indicates whether the thread should be able to process any queued asynchronous procedure calls while the thread is waiting.

The function returns one of the following values: **WAIT_OBJECT_0**, **WAIT_TIMEOUT**, **WAIT_FAILED**, **WAIT_ABANDONED** (discussed earlier in this chapter), or **WAIT_IO_COMPLETION**.

This function is a welcome addition to Windows for two reasons. First, because you often need to signal one object and wait on another, having a single function that does both operations saves processing time. Each time you call a function that causes your thread to jump from user-mode to kernel-mode code, approximately 200 CPU cycles need to execute (on *x*86 platforms) and even more are needed for thread rescheduling. For example, code such as this causes at least a lot of CPU cycles to execute:

```
ReleaseMutex(hMutex);
WaitForSingleObject(hEvent, INFINITE);
```

In high-performance server applications, **SignalObjectAndWait** saves a lot of processing time.

Second, without the **SignalObjectAndWait** function, one thread cannot know when another thread is in a wait state. This knowledge is useful for functions such as **PulseEvent**. As mentioned earlier in this chapter, **PulseEvent** signals an event and immediately resets it. If no threads are currently waiting on the event, no events catch the pulse. I've seen people write code like this:

```
// Perform some work. ... SetEvent(hEventWorkerThreadDone);
WaitForSingleObject(hEventMoreWorkToBeDone, INFINITE);
// Do more work. ...
```

A worker thread performs some code and then calls **SetEvent** to indicate that the work is done. Another thread executes code like this:

```
WaitForSingleObject(hEventWorkerThreadDone);
PulseEvent(hEventMoreWorkToBeDone);
```

The worker thread's code fragment is poorly designed because it does not work reliably. After the worker thread calls **SetEvent**, the other thread might wake up immediately and call **PulseEvent**. The worker thread is preempted and hasn't had a chance to return from its call to **SetEvent**, let alone call **WaitForSingleObject**. The result is that the signaling of the **hEventMoreWorkTo-BeDone** event is missed entirely by the worker thread.

If you rewrite the worker thread's code to call **SignalObjectAndWait** as shown here, the code will work reliably because the signaling and wait is performed atomically:

```
// Perform some work. ... SignalObjectAndWait(hEventWorkerThreadDone,
   hEventMoreWorkToBeDone, INFINITE, FALSE);
// Do more work. ...
```

When the nonworker thread wakes up, it can be 100-percent sure that the worker thread is waiting on the **hEventMoreWorkToBeDone** event and is therefore guaranteed to see the event pulsed.

Detecting Deadlocks with the Wait Chain Traversal API

Developing multithreaded applications is one of the most complicated tasks, but debugging them to find a bug related to locks is even more complicated, especially deadlocks or infinite waits. The Wait Chain Traversal (WCT) set of functions is an API new to Windows Vista that enables you to list locks and detect deadlocks within a process and even across processes. Windows keeps track of the synchronization mechanisms or reasons for locks shown in Table 9-4.

Table 9-4   Types of Synchronization Mechanisms Tracked by WCT

Possible Locks	Description
Critical sections	Windows keeps track of which thread owns which section structure.
Mutexes	Windows keeps track of which thread owns which mutex. Even abandoned mutexes are detected.
Processes and threads	Windows keeps track of which thread is waiting for a process or a thread to terminate.
SendMessage calls	As you've seen in "Deadlock Issues When Stopping Threads" on page 236, it is important to know which thread is waiting for a **SendMessage** call to return.
COM initialization and calls	The calls to **CoCreateInstance** and COM object methods are tracked.
Advanced Local Procedure Call (ALPC)	The ALPC has replaced Local Procedure Call in Windows Vista as the new undocumented kernel interprocess communication (IPC) mechanism.

Caution   The **SRWLock** synchronization mechanism presented in Chapter 8 is not tracked by WCT. Also note that many kernel objects—such as events, semaphores, and waitable timers—are not tracked, as any thread could signal any of these objects at any time, thereby waking a blocking thread.

The LockCop Sample Application

The LockCop application, 09-LockCop.exe, shows how to use the WCT functions to produce a very useful utility. The source code and resource files for the application are in the 09-LockCop directory on the companion content Web page. When you start the program and choose an application with deadlocks from the Processes combo box, the window shown in Figure 9-1 appears, making visible threads in a deadlock.

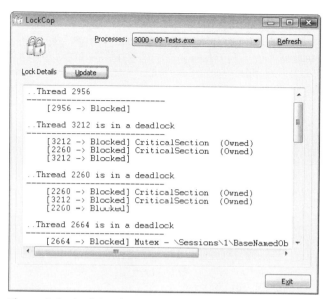

Figure 9-1   LockCop in action

LockCop first enumerates the set of processes currently running with ToolHelp32 presented in Chapter 4, "Processes," and places each process' ID and name in the Processes combo box. When you select a process, each of its threads is listed with its ID, if it is in a deadlock situation, and with its *wait chain*. MSDN online help defines a wait chain as follows:

> *"A wait chain is an alternating sequence of threads and synchronization objects; each thread waits for the object that follows it, which is owned by the subsequent thread in the chain."*

Let's look at an example to make it clear. In Figure 9-1, the thread 3212 is part of a deadlock and its wait chain explains the following situation:

- The thread 3212 is blocked on a critical section. (Let's call it CS1.)
- This critical section (CS1) is owned by another thread (2260) that is blocked on a critical section. (Let's call it CS2.)
- This critical section (CS2) is owned by the first thread, 3212.

To sum up: thread 3212 is waiting for thread 2260 to release a critical section, while thread 2260 is waiting for thread 3212 to release another critical section. This is a typical deadlock situation, as explained in "Accessing Multiple Logical Resources Simultaneously" on page 238.

Basically, all the information displayed by the LockCop application is produced by calling the various WCT functions. To make working with the WCT functions a little easier, I created a CWCT C++ class (contained in the WaitChainTraversal.h file). This class makes the traversal of the wait chain easy for you. You simply derive a class from CWCT that overrides the two virtual methods in bold in the following class definition and you call **ParseThreads** with the ID of the process you are interested in as a parameter at run time:

```
class CWCT
{
public:
   CWCT();
   ~CWCT();

   // Enumerate all the threads running in the given process,
   // and for each, dump the wait chain
   void ParseThreads(DWORD PID);


protected:
   // Implement this method to be called before each thread is analyzed
   // Note: if nodeCount is 0, it was not possible to analyze this thread
   virtual void OnThread(DWORD TID, BOOL bDeadlock, DWORD nodeCount);

   // Implement this method to be called for each wait node
   virtual void OnChainNodeInfo(DWORD rootTID, DWORD currentNode,
      WAITCHAIN_NODE_INFO nodeInfo);

   // Return the number of nodes in the current thread chain
   DWORD GetNodesInChain();

   // Return the PID of the parsed process
   DWORD GetPID();


private:
   void InitCOM();
   void ParseThread(DWORD TID);


private:
   // Handle of the WCT session
   HWCT _hWCTSession;

   // Handle of OLE32.DLL module
   HMODULE _hOLE32DLL;

   DWORD _PID;
   DWORD _dwNodeCount;
};
```

When a CWCT instance is constructed, **RegisterWaitChainCOMCallback** is called to register
the COM context with WCT (see the **InitCOM** method for implementation details) and a wait
chain session is opened by calling the following function:

```
HWCT OpenThreadWaitChainSession(
   DWORD dwFlags,
   PWAITCHAINCALLBACK callback);
```

The value of the **dwFlags** parameter is **0** if you want a synchronous session or **WCT_ASYNC_OPEN_ FLAG** if the session should be asynchronous. In the asynchronous case, you pass a pointer to your callback function as the second parameter. If your system is operating under heavy memory pressure, retrieving a long wait chain can take a long time. This is a case where it is more interesting to open an asynchronous session than a synchronous one, because you can cancel the wait chain traversal by calling **CloseThreadWaitChainSession**. However, the CWCT class traverses the wait chain in a synchronous way, so **0** is passed for **dwFlags** and the callback parameter is set to **NULL**. In the CWCT destructor, the WCT session is closed by passing the session handle returned by **OpenThreadWaitChainSession** to **CloseThreadWaitChainSession**.

The threads enumeration for a given process is encapsulated in the **ParseThreads** function, based on a ToolHelp snapshot as explained in Chapter 4:

```
void CWCT::ParseThreads(DWORD PID) {

    _PID = PID;

    // List all threads in the given process
    CToolhelp th(TH32CS_SNAPTHREAD, PID);
    THREADENTRY32 te = { sizeof(te) };
    BOOL fOk = th.ThreadFirst(&te);
    for (; fOk; fOk = th.ThreadNext(&te)) {
        // Only parse threads of the given process
        if (te.th32OwnerProcessID == PID) {
            ParseThread(te.th32ThreadID);
        }
    }
}
```

The **ParseThread** method is the heart of the wait chain traversal:

```
void CWCT::ParseThread(DWORD TID) {

    WAITCHAIN_NODE_INFO  chain[WCT_MAX_NODE_COUNT];
    DWORD                dwNodesInChain;
    BOOL                 bDeadlock;

    dwNodesInChain = WCT_MAX_NODE_COUNT;

    // Get the chain for the current thread
    if (!GetThreadWaitChain(_hWCTSession, NULL, WCTP_GETINFO_ALL_FLAGS,
            TID, &dwNodesInChain, chain, &bDeadlock)) {

        _dwNodeCount = 0;
        OnThread(TID, FALSE, 0);
        return;
    }

    // Start the chain processing for the current thread
    _dwNodeCount = min(dwNodesInChain, WCT_MAX_NODE_COUNT);
    OnThread(TID, bDeadlock, dwNodesInChain);
```

```
// For each node in the chain, call the virtual method with details
for (
    DWORD current = 0;
    current < min(dwNodesInChain, WCT_MAX_NODE_COUNT);
    current++
    ) {
    OnChainNodeInfo(TID, current, chain[current]);
}
}
```

The **GetThreadWaitChain** function fills up an array of **WAITCHAIN_NODE_INFO**, each element describing either a blocked thread or a synchronization mechanism upon which a thread blocks:

```
BOOL WINAPI GetThreadWaitChain(
    HWCT hWctSession,
    DWORD_PTR pContext,
    DWORD dwFlags,
    DWORD TID,
    PDWORD pNodeCount,
    PWAITCHAIN_NODE_INFO pNodeInfoArray,
    LPBOOL pbIsCycle
);
```

The handle returned by **OpenThreadWaitChainSession** is passed as the **hWctSession** parameter. In the case of an asynchronous session, you can pass any additional information in the **pContext** parameter. The **dwFlags** parameter allows you to refine out-of-process scenarios you are interested in with the bitwise flags shown in Table 9-5.

Table 9-5   GetThreadWaitChain Flags

dwFlags Value	Description
WCT_OUT_OF_PROC_FLAG (0x1)	If this flag is not set, the wait chain will not contain node information for threads in processes different from the process where the current thread runs. Set this flag if you are building multiprocess systems or systems that spawn processes and wait for them to end.
WCT_OUT_OF_PROC_CS_FLAG (0x4)	Gather critical section details within processes different from the process where the current thread runs. Set this flag if you are building multiprocess systems or systems that spawn processes and wait for them to end.
WCT_OUT_OF_PROC_COM_FLAG (0x2)	Important when working with MTA COM servers.
WCTP_GETINFO_ALL_FLAGS	All of the previous flags at the same time.

The **TID** parameter is the ID of the thread from which you are interested in starting the wait chain. The details of the chain are returned in the last three parameters:

- The **DWORD** pointed to by **pNodeCount** contains the number of nodes in the chain.
- The nodes of the chain are stored in the array passed in the **pNodeInfoArray** parameter.
- If a deadlock is detected, the Boolean variable pointed to by the **pbIsCycle** parameter is set to **TRUE**.

When **ParseThread** is executed for each thread of the given process, your override of **OnThread** is called once with the ID of the thread as the first parameter, **bDeadLock** set to **TRUE** if a deadlock is found, and **nodeCount** containing the number of nodes in the wait chain for this thread (with **0** meaning that a problem occurred, such as access denied). Your **OnChainNodeInfo** override gets called once per node of the wait chain with **rootTID** containing the ID of the thread passed to **OnThread**, the 0-based index of the current node passed in **currentNode**, and the description of the wait chain node stored in **nodeInfo** as a **WAITCHAIN_NODE_INFO** structure defined in the wct.h header file.

```
typedef struct _WAITCHAIN_NODE_INFO
{
    WCT_OBJECT_TYPE ObjectType;
    WCT_OBJECT_STATUS ObjectStatus;

    union {
        struct {
            WCHAR ObjectName[WCT_OBJNAME_LENGTH];
            LARGE_INTEGER Timeout;      // Not implemented in v1
            BOOL Alertable;             // Not implemented in v1
        } LockObject;

        struct {
            DWORD ProcessId;
            DWORD ThreadId;
            DWORD WaitTime;
            DWORD ContextSwitches;
        } ThreadObject;
    };

} WAITCHAIN_NODE_INFO, *PWAITCHAIN_NODE_INFO;
```

The type of node is defined by the **ObjectType** field, which takes the following values from the **WCT_OBJECT_TYPE** enumeration. Table 9-6 shows all possible node object types.

Table 9-6   Wait Chain Node Object Types

WCT_OBJECT_TYPE	Description of the Node in the Chain
WctThreadType	Thread in the chain that is blocked.
WctCriticalSectionType	The owned object is a critical section.
WctSendMessageType	Blocked on a **SendMessage** call.
WctMutexType	The owned object is a mutex.
WctAlpcType	Blocked on an ALPC call.
WctComType	Waiting for a COM call to return.
WctThreadWaitType	Waiting on a thread to end.
WctProcessWaitType	Waiting on a process to terminate.
WctComActivationType	Waiting on a **CoCreateInstance** call to return.
WctUnknownType	Placeholder for a future API extension.

The **ThreadObject** view of the union is meaningful only when **ObjectType** is set to **WctThread-Type**. In all other cases, the **LockObject** view should be taken into account instead. A thread wait chain always starts with a **WctThreadType** thread node corresponding to the **rootTID** parameter received by **OnChainNodeInfo**.

The **ObjectStatus** field details the status of the thread if the **ObjectType** field is **WctThread-Type**; otherwise, it details the status of the lock described by the node based on the **WCT_OBJECT_STATUS** enumeration shown next:

```
typedef enum _WCT_OBJECT_STATUS
{
    WctStatusNoAccess = 1,          // ACCESS_DENIED for this object
    WctStatusRunning,               // Thread status
    WctStatusBlocked,               // Thread status
    WctStatusPidOnly,               // Thread status
    WctStatusPidOnlyRpcss,          // Thread status
    WctStatusOwned,                 // Dispatcher object status
    WctStatusNotOwned,              // Dispatcher object status
    WctStatusAbandoned,             // Dispatcher object status
    WctStatusUnknown,               // All objects
    WctStatusError,                 // All objects
    WctStatusMax
} WCT_OBJECT_STATUS;
```

The LockCop application has a companion project called 09-BadLock that implements a large set of deadlocks and infinite locks. You should select it in LockCop to better understand how WCT fills up the **WAITCHAIN_NODE_INFO** structure depending on the kind of lock.

> **Note**   This LockCop tool will help you diagnose infinite locks and deadlocks in your application with one known limitation in Windows Vista: **WaitForMultipleObjects** is not supported. If your code is calling this function to wait for several objects at the same time, you will be able to find a cycle in the wait chains of the corresponding threads with LockCop, but no explicit deadlock will be detected when **GetThreadWaitChain** returns and your **OnThread** override gets called.

Chapter 10

Synchronous and Asynchronous Device I/O

I can't stress enough the importance of this chapter, which covers the Microsoft Windows technologies that enable you to design high-performance, scalable, responsive, and robust applications. A scalable application handles a large number of concurrent operations as efficiently as it handles a small number of concurrent operations. For a service application, typically these operations are processing client requests that arrive at unpredictable times and require an unpredictable amount of processing power. These requests usually arrive from I/O devices such as network adapters; processing the requests frequently requires additional I/O devices such as disk files.

In Microsoft Windows applications, threads are the best facility available to help you partition work. Each thread is assigned to a processor, which allows a multiprocessor machine to execute multiple operations simultaneously, increasing throughput. When a thread issues a synchronous device I/O request, the thread is temporarily suspended until the device completes the I/O request. This suspension hurts performance because the thread is unable to do useful work, such as initiate another client's request for processing. So, in short, you want to keep your threads doing useful work all the time and avoid having them block.

To help keep threads busy, you need to make your threads communicate with one another about the operations they will perform. Microsoft has spent years researching and testing in this area and has developed a finely tuned mechanism to create this communication. This mechanism, called the *I/O completion port*, can help you create high-performance, scalable applications. By using the I/O completion port, you can make your application's threads achieve phenomenal throughput by reading and writing to devices without waiting for the devices to respond.

The I/O completion port was originally designed to handle device I/O, but over the years, Microsoft has architected more and more operating system facilities that fit seamlessly into the I/O completion port model. One example is the job kernel object, which monitors its processes and sends event notifications to an I/O completion port. The Job Lab sample application detailed in Chapter 5, "Jobs," demonstrates how I/O completion ports and job objects work together.

Throughout my many years as a Windows developer, I have found more and more uses for the I/O completion port, and I feel that every Windows developer must fully understand how the I/O completion port works. Even though I present the I/O completion port in this chapter about device I/O, be aware that the I/O completion port doesn't have to be used with device I/O at all—simply put, it is an awesome interthread communication mechanism with an infinite number of uses.

From this fanfare, you can probably tell that I'm a huge fan of the I/O completion port. My hope is that by the end of this chapter, you will be too. But instead of jumping right into the details of the I/O completion port, I'm going to explain what Windows originally offered developers for device I/O. This will give you a much greater appreciation for the I/O completion port. In "I/O Completion Ports" on page 320 I'll discuss the I/O completion port.

Opening and Closing Devices

One of the strengths of Windows is the sheer number of devices that it supports. In the context of this discussion, I define a device to be anything that allows communication. Table 10-1 lists some devices and their most common uses.

Table 10-1   Various Devices and Their Common Uses

Device	Most Common Use
File	Persistent storage of arbitrary data
Directory	Attribute and file compression settings
Logical disk drive	Drive formatting
Physical disk drive	Partition table access
Serial port	Data transmission over a phone line
Parallel port	Data transmission to a printer
Mailslot	One-to-many transmission of data, usually over a network to a machine running Windows
Named pipe	One-to-one transmission of data, usually over a network to a machine running Windows
Anonymous pipe	One-to-one transmission of data on a single machine (never over the network)
Socket	Datagram or stream transmission of data, usually over a network to any machine supporting sockets (The machine need not be running Windows.)
Console	A text window screen buffer

This chapter discusses how an application's threads communicate with these devices without waiting for the devices to respond. Windows tries to hide device differences from the software developer as much as possible. That is, once you open a device, the Windows functions that allow you to read and write data to the device are the same no matter what device you are communicating with. Although only a few functions are available for reading and writing data regardless of the device, devices are certainly different from one another. For example, it makes sense to set a baud rate for a serial port, but a baud rate has no meaning when using a named pipe to communicate over a network (or over the local machine). Devices are subtly different from one another, and I will not attempt to address all their nuances. However, I will spend some time addressing files because files are so common. To perform any type of I/O, you must first open the desired device and get a handle to it. The way you get the handle to a device depends on the particular device. Table 10-2 lists various devices and the functions you should call to open them.

Table 10-2   Functions for Opening Various Devices

Device	Function Used to Open the Device
File	**CreateFile** (**pszName** is pathname or UNC pathname).
Directory	**CreateFile** (**pszName** is directory name or UNC directory name). Windows allows you to open a directory if you specify the **FILE_FLAG_BACKUP_SEMANTICS** flag in the call to **CreateFile**. Opening the directory allows you to change the directory's attributes (to normal, hidden, and so on) and its time stamp.
Logical disk drive	**CreateFile** (**pszName** is "\\.\x:"). Windows allows you to open a logical drive if you specify a string in the form of "\\.\x:" where x is a drive letter. For example, to open drive A, you specify "\\.\A:". Opening a drive allows you to format the drive or determine the media size of the drive.
Physical disk drive	**CreateFile** (**pszName** is "\\.\PHYSICALDRIVEx"). Windows allows you to open a physical drive if you specify a string in the form of "\\.\PHYSICALDRIVEx" where x is a physical drive number. For example, to read or write to physical sectors on the user's first physical hard disk, you specify "\\.\PHYSICALDRIVE0". Opening a physical drive allows you to access the hard drive's partition tables directly. Opening the physical drive is potentially dangerous; an incorrect write to the drive could make the disk's contents inaccessible by the operating system's file system.
Serial port	**CreateFile** (**pszName** is "COMx").
Parallel port	**CreateFile** (**pszName** is "LPTx").
Mailslot server	**CreateMailslot** (**pszName** is "\\.\mailslot\mailslotname").
Mailslot client	**CreateFile** (**pszName** is "\\servername\mailslot\mailslotname").
Named pipe server	**CreateNamedPipe** (**pszName** is "\\.\pipe\pipename").
Named pipe client	**CreateFile** (**pszName** is "\\servername\pipe\pipename").
Anonymous pipe	**CreatePipe** client and server.
Socket	**socket**, **accept**, or **AcceptEx**.
Console	**CreateConsoleScreenBuffer** or **GetStdHandle**.

Each function in Table 10-2 returns a handle that identifies the device. You can pass the handle to various functions to communicate with the device. For example, you call **SetCommConfig** to set the baud rate of a serial port:

```
BOOL SetCommConfig(
   HANDLE         hCommDev,
   LPCOMMCONFIG   pCC,
   DWORD          dwSize);
```

And you use **SetMailslotInfo** to set the time-out value when waiting to read data:

```
BOOL SetMailslotInfo(
   HANDLE hMailslot,
   DWORD  dwReadTimeout);
```

As you can see, these functions require a handle to a device for their first argument.

When you are finished manipulating a device, you must close it. For most devices, you do this by calling the very popular **CloseHandle** function:

```
BOOL CloseHandle(HANDLE hObject);
```

However, if the device is a socket, you must call **closesocket** instead:

```
int closesocket(SOCKET s);
```

Also, if you have a handle to a device, you can find out what type of device it is by calling **GetFileType**:

```
DWORD GetFileType(HANDLE hDevice);
```

All you do is pass to the **GetFileType** function the handle to a device, and the function returns one of the values listed in Table 10-3.

Table 10-3   Values Returned by the GetFileType Function

Value	Description
FILE_TYPE_UNKNOWN	The type of the specified file is unknown.
FILE_TYPE_DISK	The specified file is a disk file.
FILE_TYPE_CHAR	The specified file is a character file, typically an LPT device or a console.
FILE_TYPE_PIPE	The specified file is either a named pipe or an anonymous pipe.

A Detailed Look at *CreateFile*

The **CreateFile** function, of course, creates and opens disk files, but don't let the name fool you—it opens lots of other devices as well:

```
HANDLE CreateFile(
   PCTSTR pszName,
   DWORD  dwDesiredAccess,
   DWORD  dwShareMode,
   PSECURITY_ATTRIBUTES psa,
   DWORD  dwCreationDisposition,
   DWORD  dwFlagsAndAttributes,
   HANDLE hFileTemplate);
```

As you can see, **CreateFile** requires quite a few parameters, allowing for a great deal of flexibility when opening a device. At this point, I'll discuss all these parameters in detail.

When you call **CreateFile**, the **pszName** parameter identifies the device type as well as a specific instance of the device.

The **dwDesiredAccess** parameter specifies how you want to transmit data to and from the device. You can pass these four generic values, which are described in Table 10-4. Certain devices allow for additional access control flags. For example, when opening a file, you can specify access flags such as **FILE_READ_ATTRIBUTES**. See the Platform SDK documentation for more information about these flags.

Table 10-4   Generic Values That Can Be Passed for CreateFile's dwDesiredAccess Parameter

Value	Meaning
0	You do not intend to read or write data to the device. Pass **0** when you just want to change the device's configuration settings—for example, if you want to change only a file's time stamp.
GENERIC_READ	Allows read-only access from the device.
GENERIC_WRITE	Allows write-only access to the device. For example, this value can be used to send data to a printer and by backup software. Note that **GENERIC_WRITE** does not imply **GENERIC_READ**.
GENERIC_READ | GENERIC_WRITE	Allows both read and write access to the device. This value is the most common because it allows the free exchange of data.

The **dwShareMode** parameter specifies device-sharing privileges. It controls how the device can be opened by additional calls to **CreateFile** while you still have the device opened yourself (that is, you haven't closed the device yet by calling **CloseHandle**). Table 10-5 describes the possible values that can be passed for the **dwShareMode** parameter.

Table 10-5   Values Related to I/O That Can Be Passed for CreateFile's dwShareMode Parameter

Value	Meaning
0	You require exclusive access to the device. If the device is already opened, your call to **CreateFile** fails. If you successfully open the device, future calls to **CreateFile** fail.
FILE_SHARE_READ	You require that the data maintained by the device can't be changed by any other kernel object referring to this device. If the device is already opened for write or exclusive access, your call to **CreateFile** fails. If you successfully open the device, future calls to **CreateFile** fail if **GENERIC_WRITE** access is requested.
FILE_SHARE_WRITE	You require that the data maintained by the device can't be read by any other kernel object referring to this device. If the device is already opened for read or exclusive access, your call to **CreateFile** fails. If you successfully open the device, future calls to **CreateFile** fail if **GENERIC_READ** access is requested.
FILE_SHARE_READ | FILE_SHARE_WRITE	You don't care if the data maintained by the device is read or written to by any other kernel object referring to this device. If the device is already opened for exclusive access, your call to **CreateFile** fails. If you successfully open the device, future calls to **CreateFile** fail when exclusive read, exclusive write, or exclusive read/write access is requested.
FILE_SHARE_DELETE	You don't care if the file is logically deleted or moved while you are working with the file. Internally, Windows marks a file for deletion and deletes it when all open handles to the file are closed.

Note If you are opening a file, you can pass a pathname that is up to **MAX_PATH** (defined as 260 in WinDef.h) characters long. However, you can transcend this limit by calling **CreateFileW** (the Unicode version of **CreateFile**) and precede the pathname with "\\?\". Calling **CreateFileW** removes the prefix and allows you to pass a path that is almost 32,000 Unicode characters long. Remember, however, that you must use fully qualified paths when using this prefix; the system does not process relative directories such as "." and "..". Also, each individual component of the path is still limited to **MAX_PATH** characters. Don't be surprised to also see the **_MAX_PATH** constant in various source code because this is what C/C++ standard libraries define in stdlib.h as 260.

The **psa** parameter points to a **SECURITY_ATTRIBUTES** structure that allows you to specify security information and whether or not you'd like **CreateFile**'s returned handle to be inheritable. The security descriptor inside this structure is used only if you are creating a file on a secure file system such as NTFS; the security descriptor is ignored in all other cases. Usually, you just pass **NULL** for the **psa** parameter, indicating that the file is created with default security and that the returned handle is noninheritable.

The **dwCreationDisposition** parameter is most meaningful when **CreateFile** is being called to open a file as opposed to another type of device. Table 10-6 lists the possible values that you can pass for this parameter.

Table 10-6   Values That Can Be Passed for CreateFile's dwCreationDisposition Parameter

Value	Meaning
CREATE_NEW	Tells **CreateFile** to create a new file and to fail if a file with the same name already exists.
CREATE_ALWAYS	Tells **CreateFile** to create a new file regardless of whether a file with the same name already exists. If a file with the same name already exists, **CreateFile** overwrites the existing file.
OPEN_EXISTING	Tells **CreateFile** to open an existing file or device and to fail if the file or device doesn't exist.
OPEN_ALWAYS	Tells **CreateFile** to open the file if it exists and to create a new file if it doesn't exist.
TRUNCATE_EXISTING	Tells **CreateFile** to open an existing file, truncate its size to 0 bytes, and fail if the file doesn't already exist.

Note When you are calling **CreateFile** to open a device other than a file, you must pass **OPEN_EXISTING** for the **dwCreationDisposition** parameter.

CreateFile's **dwFlagsAndAttributes** parameter has two purposes: it allows you to set flags that fine-tune the communication with the device, and if the device is a file, you also get to set the file's attributes. Most of these communication flags are signals that tell the system how you intend to access the device. The system can then optimize its caching algorithms to help your application work more efficiently. I'll describe the communication flags first and then discuss the file attributes.

CreateFile Cache Flags

This section describes the various **CreateFile** cache flags, focusing on file system objects. For other kernel objects such as mailslots, you should refer to the MSDN documentation to get more specific details.

FILE_FLAG_NO_BUFFERING   This flag indicates not to use any data buffering when accessing a file. To improve performance, the system caches data to and from disk drives. Normally, you do not specify this flag, and the cache manager keeps recently accessed portions of the file system in memory. This way, if you read a couple of bytes from a file and then read a few more bytes, the file's data is most likely loaded in memory and the disk has to be accessed only once instead of twice, greatly improving performance. However, this process does mean that portions of the file's data are in memory twice: the cache manager has a buffer, and you called some function (such as **ReadFile**) that copied some of the data from the cache manager's buffer into your own buffer.

When the cache manager is buffering data, it might also read ahead so that the next bytes you're likely to read are already in memory. Again, speed is improved by reading more bytes than necessary from the file. Memory is potentially wasted if you never attempt to read further in the file. (See the **FILE_FLAG_SEQUENTIAL_SCAN** and **FILE_FLAG_RANDOM_ACCESS** flags, discussed next, for more about reading ahead.)

By specifying the **FILE_FLAG_NO_BUFFERING** flag, you tell the cache manager that you do not want it to buffer any data—you take on this responsibility yourself! Depending on what you're doing, this flag can improve your application's speed and memory usage. Because the file system's device driver is writing the file's data directly into the buffers that you supply, you must follow certain rules:

- You must always access the file by using offsets that are exact multiples of the disk volume's sector size. (Use the **GetDiskFreeSpace** function to determine the disk volume's sector size.)
- You must always read/write a number of bytes that is an exact multiple of the sector size.
- You must make sure that the buffer in your process' address space begins on an address that is integrally divisible by the sector size.

FILE_FLAG_SEQUENTIAL_SCAN and FILE_FLAG_RANDOM_ACCESS   These flags are useful only if you allow the system to buffer the file data for you. If you specify the **FILE_FLAG_NO_BUFFERING** flag, both of these flags are ignored.

If you specify the **FILE_FLAG_SEQUENTIAL_SCAN** flag, the system thinks you are accessing the file sequentially. When you read some data from the file, the system actually reads more of the file's data than the amount you requested. This process reduces the number of hits to the hard disk and improves the speed of your application. If you perform any direct seeks on the file, the system has spent a little extra time and memory caching data that you are not accessing. This is perfectly OK, but if you do it often, you'd be better off specifying the **FILE_FLAG_RANDOM_ACCESS** flag. This flag tells the system not to pre-read file data.

To manage a file, the cache manager must maintain some internal data structures for the file—the larger the file, the more data structures required. When working with extremely large files, the cache manager might not be able to allocate the internal data structures it requires and will fail to open the file. To access extremely large files, you must open the file using the **FILE_FLAG_NO_ BUFFERING** flag.

FILE_FLAG_WRITE_THROUGH   This is the last cache-related flag. It disables intermediate caching of file-write operations to reduce the potential for data loss. When you specify this flag, the system writes all file modifications directly to the disk. However, the system still maintains an internal cache of the file's data, and file-read operations use the cached data (if available) instead of reading data directly from the disk. When this flag is used to open a file on a network server, the Windows file-write functions do not return to the calling thread until the data is written to the server's disk drive.

That's it for the buffer-related communication flags. Now let's discuss the remaining communication flags.

Miscellaneous *CreateFile* Flags

This section describes the other flags that exist to customize **CreateFile** behaviors outside of caching.

FILE_FLAG_DELETE_ON_CLOSE   Use this flag to have the file system delete the file after all handles to it are closed. This flag is most frequently used with the **FILE_ATTRIBUTE_TEMPORARY** attribute. When these two flags are used together, your application can create a temporary file, write to it, read from it, and close it. When the file is closed, the system automatically deletes the file–what a convenience!

FILE_FLAG_BACKUP_SEMANTICS   Use this flag in backup and restore software. Before opening or creating any files, the system normally performs security checks to be sure that the process trying to open or create a file has the requisite access privileges. However, backup and restore software is special in that it can override certain file security checks. When you specify the **FILE_FLAG_ BACKUP_SEMANTICS** flag, the system checks the caller's access token to see whether the Backup/ Restore File and Directories privileges are enabled. If the appropriate privileges are enabled, the system allows the file to be opened. You can also use the **FILE_FLAG_BACKUP_SEMANTICS** flag to open a handle to a directory.

FILE_FLAG_POSIX_SEMANTICS   In Windows, filenames are case-preserved, whereas filename searches are case-insensitive. However, the POSIX subsystem requires that filename searches be case-sensitive. The **FILE_FLAG_POSIX_SEMANTICS** flag causes **CreateFile** to use a case-sensitive filename search when creating or opening a file. Use the **FILE_FLAG_POSIX_SEMANTICS** flag with extreme caution–if you use it when you create a file, that file might not be accessible to Windows applications.

FILE_FLAG_OPEN_REPARSE_POINT   In my opinion, this flag should have been called **FILE_FLAG_ IGNORE_REPARSE_POINT** because it tells the system to ignore the file's reparse attribute (if it exists). Reparse attributes allow a file system filter to modify the behavior of opening, reading, writing, and closing a file. Usually, the modified behavior is desired, so using the **FILE_FLAG_OPEN_ REPARSE_POINT** flag is not recommended.

FILE_FLAG_OPEN_NO_RECALL   This flag tells the system not to restore a file's contents from offline storage (such as tape) back to online storage (such as a hard disk). When files are not accessed for long periods of time, the system can transfer the file's contents to offline storage, freeing up hard disk space. When the system does this, the file on the hard disk is not destroyed; only the data in the file is destroyed. When the file is opened, the system automatically restores the data from offline storage. The **FILE_FLAG_OPEN_NO_RECALL** flag instructs the system not to restore the data and causes I/O operations to be performed against the offline storage medium.

FILE_FLAG_OVERLAPPED   This flag tells the system that you want to access a device asynchronously. You'll notice that the default way of opening a device is synchronous I/O (not specifying **FILE_FLAG_OVERLAPPED**). Synchronous I/O is what most developers are used to. When you read data from a file, your thread is suspended, waiting for the information to be read. Once the information has been read, the thread regains control and continues executing.

Because device I/O is slow when compared with most other operations, you might want to consider communicating with some devices asynchronously. Here's how it works: Basically, you call a function to tell the operating system to read or write data, but instead of waiting for the I/O to complete, your call returns immediately, and the operating system completes the I/O on your behalf using its own threads. When the operating system has finished performing your requested I/O, you can be notified. Asynchronous I/O is the key to creating high-performance, scalable, responsive, and robust applications. Windows offers several methods of asynchronous I/O, all of which are discussed in this chapter.

File Attribute Flags

Now it's time to examine the attribute flags for **CreateFile**'s **dwFlagsAndAttributes** parameter, described in Table 10-7. These flags are completely ignored by the system unless you are creating a brand new file and you pass **NULL** for **CreateFile**'s **hFileTemplate** parameter. Most of the attributes should already be familiar to you.

Table 10-7   File Attribute Flags That Can Be Passed for CreateFile's dwFlagsAndAttributes Parameter

Flag	Meaning
FILE_ATTRIBUTE_ARCHIVE	The file is an archive file. Applications use this flag to mark files for backup or removal. When **CreateFile** creates a new file, this flag is automatically set.
FILE_ATTRIBUTE_ENCRYPTED	The file is encrypted.
FILE_ATTRIBUTE_HIDDEN	The file is hidden. It won't be included in an ordinary directory listing.
FILE_ATTRIBUTE_NORMAL	The file has no other attributes set. This attribute is valid only when it's used alone.
FILE_ATTRIBUTE_NOT_CONTENT_INDEXED	The file will not be indexed by the content indexing service.
FILE_ATTRIBUTE_OFFLINE	The file exists, but its data has been moved to offline storage. This flag is useful for hierarchical storage systems.
FILE_ATTRIBUTE_READONLY	The file is read-only. Applications can read the file but can't write to it or delete it.
FILE_ATTRIBUTE_SYSTEM	The file is part of the operating system or is used exclusively by the operating system.
FILE_ATTRIBUTE_TEMPORARY	The file's data will be used only for a short time. The file system tries to keep the file's data in RAM rather than on disk to keep the access time to a minimum.

Use **FILE_ATTRIBUTE_TEMPORARY** if you are creating a temporary file. When **CreateFile** creates a file with the temporary attribute, **CreateFile** tries to keep the file's data in memory instead of on the disk. This makes accessing the file's contents much faster. If you keep writing to the file and the system can no longer keep the data in RAM, the operating system will be forced to start writing the data to the hard disk. You can improve the system's performance by combining the **FILE_ATTRIBUTE_TEMPORARY** flag with the **FILE_FLAG_DELETE_ON_CLOSE** flag (discussed earlier). Normally, the system flushes a file's cached data when the file is closed. However, if the system sees that the file is to be deleted when it is closed, the system doesn't need to flush the file's cached data.

In addition to all these communication and attribute flags, a number of flags allow you to control the security quality of service when opening a named-pipe device. Because these flags are specific to named pipes only, I will not discuss them here. To learn about them, please read about the **CreateFile** function in the Platform SDK documentation.

CreateFile's last parameter, **hFileTemplate**, identifies the handle of an open file or is **NULL**. If **hFileTemplate** identifies a file handle, **CreateFile** ignores the attribute flags in the **dwFlagsAndAttributes** parameter completely and uses the attributes associated with the file identified by **hFileTemplate**. The file identified by **hFileTemplate** must have been opened with the **GENERIC_READ** flag for this to work. If **CreateFile** is opening an existing file (as opposed to creating a new file), the **hFileTemplate** parameter is ignored.

If **CreateFile** succeeds in creating or opening a file or device, the handle of the file or device is returned. If **CreateFile** fails, **INVALID_HANDLE_VALUE** is returned.

> **Note**   Most Windows functions that return a handle return **NULL** when the function fails. However, **CreateFile** returns **INVALID_HANDLE_VALUE** (defined as −1) instead. I have often seen code like this, which is incorrect:
>
> ```
> HANDLE hFile = CreateFile(...);
> if (hFile == NULL) {
>    // We'll never get in here
> } else {
>    // File might or might not be created OK
> }
> ```
>
> Here's the correct way to check for an invalid file handle:
>
> ```
> HANDLE hFile = CreateFile(...);
> if (hFile == INVALID_HANDLE_VALUE) {
>    // File not created
> } else {
>    // File created OK
> }
> ```

Working with File Devices

Because working with files is so common, I want to spend some time addressing issues that apply specifically to file devices. This section shows how to position a file's pointer and change a file's size.

The first issue you must be aware of is that Windows was designed to work with extremely large files. Instead of representing a file's size using 32-bit values, the original Microsoft designers chose to use 64-bit values. This means that theoretically a file can reach a size of 16 EB (exabytes).

Dealing with 64-bit values in a 32-bit operating system makes working with files a little unpleasant because a lot of Windows functions require you to pass a 64-bit value as two separate 32-bit values. But as you'll see, working with the values is not too difficult and, in normal day-to-day operations, you probably won't need to work with a file greater than 4 GB. This means that the high 32 bits of the file's 64-bit size will frequently be 0 anyway.

Getting a File's Size

When working with files, quite often you will need to acquire the file's size. The easiest way to do this is by calling **GetFileSizeEx**:

```
BOOL GetFileSizeEx(
   HANDLE          hFile,
   PLARGE_INTEGER pliFileSize);
```

The first parameter, **hFile**, is the handle of an opened file, and the **pliFileSize** parameter is the address of a **LARGE_INTEGER** union. This union allows a 64-bit signed value to be referenced as two 32-bit values or as a single 64-bit value, and it can be quite convenient when working with file sizes and offsets. Here is (basically) what the union looks like:

```
typedef union _LARGE_INTEGER {
   struct {
      DWORD LowPart;     // Low  32-bit unsigned value
      LONG HighPart;     // High 32-bit signed value
   };
   LONGLONG QuadPart;    // Full 64-bit signed value
} LARGE_INTEGER, *PLARGE_INTEGER;
```

In addition to **LARGE_INTEGER**, there is a **ULARGE_INTEGER** structure representing an unsigned 64-bit value:

```
typedef union _ULARGE_INTEGER {
   struct {
      DWORD LowPart;     // Low  32-bit unsigned value
      DWORD HighPart;    // High 32-bit unsigned value
   };
   ULONGLONG QuadPart;   // Full 64-bit unsigned value
} ULARGE_INTEGER, *PULARGE_INTEGER;
```

Another very useful function for getting a file's size is **GetCompressedFileSize**:

```
DWORD GetCompressedFileSize(
    PCTSTR pszFileName,
    PDWORD pdwFileSizeHigh);
```

This function returns the file's physical size, whereas **GetFileSizeEx** returns the file's logical size. For example, consider a 100-KB file that has been compressed to occupy 85 KB. Calling **GetFile-SizeEx** returns the logical size of the file—100 KB—whereas **GetCompressedFileSize** returns the actual number of bytes on disk occupied by the file—85 KB.

Unlike **GetFileSizeEx**, **GetCompressedFileSize** takes a filename passed as a string instead of taking a handle for the first parameter. The **GetCompressedFileSize** function returns the 64-bit size of the file in an unusual way: the low 32 bits of the file's size are the function's return value. The high 32 bits of the file's size are placed in the **DWORD** pointed to by the **pdwFileSizeHigh** parameter. Here the use of the **ULARGE_INTEGER** structure comes in handy:

```
ULARGE_INTEGER ulFileSize;
ulFileSize.LowPart = GetCompressedFileSize(TEXT("SomeFile.dat"),
    &ulFileSize.HighPart);

// 64-bit file size is now in ulFileSize.QuadPart
```

Positioning a File Pointer

Calling **CreateFile** causes the system to create a file kernel object that manages operations on the file. Inside this kernel object is a file pointer. This file pointer indicates the 64-bit offset within the file where the next synchronous read or write should be performed. Initially, this file pointer is set to 0, so if you call **ReadFile** immediately after a call to **CreateFile**, you will start reading the file from offset 0. If you read 10 bytes of the file into memory, the system updates the pointer associated with the file handle so that the next call to **ReadFile** starts reading at the eleventh byte in the file at offset 10. For example, look at this code, in which the first 10 bytes from the file are read into the buffer, and then the next 10 bytes are read into the buffer:

```
BYTE pb[10];
DWORD dwNumBytes;
HANDLE hFile = CreateFile(TEXT("MyFile.dat"), ...); // Pointer set to 0
ReadFile(hFile, pb, 10, &dwNumBytes, NULL);   // Reads bytes  0 - 9
ReadFile(hFile, pb, 10, &dwNumBytes, NULL);   // Reads bytes 10 - 19
```

Because each file kernel object has its own file pointer, opening the same file twice gives slightly different results:

```
BYTE pb[10];
DWORD dwNumBytes;
HANDLE hFile1 = CreateFile(TEXT("MyFile.dat"), ...); // Pointer set to 0
HANDLE hFile2 = CreateFile(TEXT("MyFile.dat"), ...); // Pointer set to 0
ReadFile(hFile1, pb, 10, &dwNumBytes, NULL);   // Reads bytes 0 - 9
ReadFile(hFile2, pb, 10, &dwNumBytes, NULL);   // Reads bytes 0 - 9
```

In this example, two different kernel objects manage the same file. Because each kernel object has its own file pointer, manipulating the file with one file object has no effect on the file pointer maintained by the other object, and the first 10 bytes of the file are read twice.

I think one more example will help make all this clear:

```
BYTE pb[10];
DWORD dwNumBytes;
HANDLE hFile1 = CreateFile(TEXT("MyFile.dat"), ...); // Pointer set to 0
HANDLE hFile2;
DuplicateHandle(
   GetCurrentProcess(), hFile1,
   GetCurrentProcess(), &hFile2,
   0, FALSE, DUPLICATE_SAME_ACCESS);
ReadFile(hFile1, pb, 10, &dwNumBytes, NULL);    // Reads bytes  0 - 9
ReadFile(hFile2, pb, 10, &dwNumBytes, NULL);    // Reads bytes 10 - 19
```

In this example, one file kernel object is referenced by two file handles. Regardless of which handle is used to manipulate the file, the one file pointer is updated. As in the first example, different bytes are read each time.

If you need to access a file randomly, you will need to alter the file pointer associated with the file's kernel object. You do this by calling **SetFilePointerEx**:

```
BOOL SetFilePointerEx(
    HANDLE          hFile,
    LARGE_INTEGER   liDistanceToMove,
    PLARGE_INTEGER  pliNewFilePointer,
    DWORD           dwMoveMethod);
```

The **hFile** parameter identifies the file kernel object whose file pointer you want to change. The **liDistanceToMove** parameter tells the system by how many bytes you want to move the pointer. The number you specify is added to the current value of the file's pointer, so a negative number has the effect of stepping backward in the file. The last parameter of **SetFilePointerEx**, **dwMoveMethod**, tells **SetFilePointerEx** how to interpret the **liDistanceToMove** parameter. Table 10-8 describes the three possible values you can pass via **dwMoveMethod** to specify the starting point for the move.

Table 10-8   Values That Can Be Passed for SetFilePointerEx's dwMoveMethod Parameter

Value	Meaning
FILE_BEGIN	The file object's file pointer is set to the value specified by the **liDistanceToMove** parameter. Note that **liDistanceToMove** is interpreted as an unsigned 64-bit value.
FILE_CURRENT	The file object's file pointer has the value of **liDistanceToMove** added to it. Note that **liDistanceToMove** is interpreted as a signed 64-bit value, allowing you to seek backward in the file.
FILE_END	The file object's file pointer is set to the logical file size plus the **liDistanceToMove** parameter. Note that **liDistanceToMove** is interpreted as a signed 64-bit value, allowing you to seek backward in the file.

After **SetFilePointerEx** has updated the file object's file pointer, the new value of the file pointer is returned in the **LARGE_INTEGER** pointed to by the **pliNewFilePointer** parameter. You can pass **NULL** for **pliNewFilePointer** if you're not interested in the new pointer value.

Here are a few facts to note about **SetFilePointerEx**:

- Setting a file's pointer beyond the end of the file's current size is legal. Doing so does not actually increase the size of the file on disk unless you write to the file at this position or call **SetEndOfFile**.

- When using **SetFilePointerEx** with a file opened with **FILE_FLAG_NO_BUFFERING**, the file pointer can be positioned only on sector-aligned boundaries. The FileCopy sample application later in this chapter demonstrates how to do this properly.

- Windows does not offer a **GetFilePointerEx** function, but you can use **SetFile-PointerEx** to move the pointer by 0 bytes to get the desired effect, as shown in the following code snippet:

```
LARGE_INTEGER liCurrentPosition = { 0 };
SetFilePointerEx(hFile, liCurrentPosition, &liCurrentPosition, FILE_CURRENT);
```

Setting the End of a File

Usually, the system takes care of setting the end of a file when the file is closed. However, you might sometimes want to force a file to be smaller or larger. On those occasions, call

```
BOOL SetEndOfFile(HANDLE hFile);
```

This **SetEndOfFile** function truncates or extends a file's size to the size indicated by the file object's file pointer. For example, if you wanted to force a file to be 1024 bytes long, you'd use **SetEndOfFile** this way:

```
HANDLE hFile = CreateFile(...);
LARGE_INTEGER liDistanceToMove;
liDistanceToMove.QuadPart = 1024;
SetFilePointerEx(hFile, liDistanceToMove, NULL, FILE_BEGIN);
SetEndOfFile(hFile);
CloseHandle(hFile);
```

Using Windows Explorer to examine the properties of this file reveals that the file is exactly 1024 bytes long.

Performing Synchronous Device I/O

This section discusses the Windows functions that allow you to perform synchronous device I/O. Keep in mind that a device can be a file, mailslot, pipe, socket, and so on. No matter which device is used, the I/O is performed using the same functions.

Without a doubt, the easiest and most commonly used functions for reading from and writing to devices are **ReadFile** and **WriteFile**:

```
BOOL ReadFile(
    HANDLE        hFile,
    PVOID         pvBuffer,
    DWORD         nNumBytesToRead,
    PDWORD        pdwNumBytes,
    OVERLAPPED*   pOverlapped);

BOOL WriteFile(
    HANDLE        hFile,
    CONST VOID    *pvBuffer,
    DWORD         nNumBytesToWrite,
    PDWORD        pdwNumBytes,
    OVERLAPPED*   pOverlapped);
```

The **hFile** parameter identifies the handle of the device you want to access. When the device is opened, you must not specify the **FILE_FLAG_OVERLAPPED** flag, or the system will think that you want to perform asynchronous I/O with the device. The **pvBuffer** parameter points to the buffer to which the device's data should be read or to the buffer containing the data that should be written to the device. The **nNumBytesToRead** and **nNumBytesToWrite** parameters tell **ReadFile** and **WriteFile** how many bytes to read from the device and how many bytes to write to the device, respectively.

The **pdwNumBytes** parameters indicate the address of a **DWORD** that the functions fill with the number of bytes successfully transmitted to and from the device. The last parameter, **pOverlapped**, should be **NULL** when performing synchronous I/O. You'll examine this parameter in more detail shortly when asynchronous I/O is discussed.

Both **ReadFile** and **WriteFile** return **TRUE** if successful. By the way, **ReadFile** can be called only for devices that were opened with the **GENERIC_READ** flag. Likewise, **WriteFile** can be called only when the device is opened with the **GENERIC_WRITE** flag.

Flushing Data to the Device

Remember from our look at the **CreateFile** function that you can pass quite a few flags to alter the way in which the system caches file data. Some other devices, such as serial ports, mailslots, and pipes, also cache data. If you want to force the system to write cached data to the device, you can call **FlushFileBuffers**:

```
BOOL FlushFileBuffers(HANDLE hFile);
```

The **FlushFileBuffers** function forces all the buffered data associated with a device that is identified by the **hFile** parameter to be written. For this to work, the device has to be opened with the **GENERIC_WRITE** flag. If the function is successful, **TRUE** is returned.

Synchronous I/O Cancellation

Functions that do synchronous I/O are easy to use, but they block any other operations from occurring on the thread that issued the I/O until the request is completed. A great example of this is a **CreateFile** operation. When a user performs mouse and keyboard input, window messages are inserted into a queue that is associated with the thread that created the window that the input is destined for. If that thread is stuck inside a call to **CreateFile**, waiting for **CreateFile** to return, the window messages are not getting processed and all the windows created by the thread are frozen. The most common reason why applications hang is because their threads are stuck waiting for synchronous I/O operations to complete!

With Windows Vista, Microsoft has added some big features in an effort to alleviate this problem. For example, if a console (CUI) application hangs because of synchronous I/O, the user is now able to hit Ctrl+C to gain control back and continue using the console; the user no longer has to kill the console process. Also, the new Vista file open/save dialog box allows the user to press the Cancel button when opening a file is taking an excessively long time (typically, as a result of attempting to access a file on a network server).

To build a responsive application, you should try to perform asynchronous I/O operations as much as possible. This typically also allows you to use very few threads in your application, thereby saving resources (such as thread kernel objects and stacks). Also, it is usually easy to offer your users the ability to cancel an operation when you initiate it asynchronously. For example, Internet Explorer allows the user to cancel (via a red X button or the Esc key) a Web request if it is taking too long and the user is impatient.

Unfortunately, certain Windows APIs, such as **CreateFile**, offer no way to call the methods asynchronously. Although some of these methods do ultimately time out if they wait too long (such as when attempting to access a network server), it would be best if there was an application programming interface (API) that you could call to force the thread to abort waiting and to just cancel the synchronous I/O operation. In Windows Vista, the following function allows you to cancel a pending synchronous I/O request for a given thread:

```
BOOL CancelSynchronousIo(HANDLE hThread);
```

The **hThread** parameter is a handle of the thread that is suspended waiting for the synchronous I/O request to complete. This handle must have been created with the **THREAD_TERMINATE** access. If this is not the case, **CancelSynchronousIo** fails and **GetLastError** returns **ERROR_ACCESS_DENIED**. When you create the thread yourself by using **CreateThread** or **_beginthreadex**, the returned handle has **THREAD_ALL_ACCESS**, which includes **THREAD_TERMINATE** access. However, if you are taking advantage of the thread pool or your cancellation code is called by a timer callback, you usually have to call **OpenThread** to get a thread handle corresponding to the current thread ID; don't forget to pass **THREAD_TERMINATE** as the first parameter.

If the specified thread was suspended waiting for a synchronous I/O operation to complete, **CancelSynchronousIo** wakes the suspended thread and the operation it was trying to perform returns failure; calling **GetLastError** returns **ERROR_OPERATION_ABORTED**. Also, **CancelSynchronousIo** returns **TRUE** to its caller.

Note that the thread calling **CancelSynchronousIo** doesn't really know where the thread that called the synchronous operation is. The thread could have been pre-empted and it has yet to actually communicate with the device; it could be suspended, waiting for the device to respond; or the device could have just responded, and the thread is in the process of returning from its call. If **CancelSynchronousIo** is called when the specified thread is not actually suspended waiting for the device to respond, **CancelSynchronousIo** returns **FALSE** and **GetLastError** returns **ERROR_NOT_FOUND**.

For this reason, you might want to use some additional thread synchronization (as discussed in Chapter 8, "Thread Synchronization in User Mode," and Chapter 9, "Thread Synchronization with

Kernel Objects") to know for sure whether you are cancelling a synchronous operation or not. However, in practice, this is usually not necessary, as it is typical for a user to initiate the cancellation and this usually happens because the user sees the application is suspended. Also, a user could try to initiate cancellation twice (or more) if the first attempt to cancel doesn't seem to work. By the way, Windows calls **CancelSynchronousIo** internally to allow the user to regain control of a command console and the file open/save dialog box.

> **Caution**   Cancellation of I/O requests depends on the driver implementing the corresponding system layer. It might happen that such a driver does not support cancellation. In that case, **CancelSynchronousIo** would have returned **TRUE** anyway because this function has found a request to be marked as being cancelled. The real cancellation of the request is left as the responsibility of the driver. An example of a driver that was updated to support synchronous cancellation for Windows Vista is the network redirector.

Basics of Asynchronous Device I/O

Compared to most other operations carried out by a computer, device I/O is one of the slowest and most unpredictable. The CPU performs arithmetic operations and even paints the screen much faster than it reads data from or writes data to a file or across a network. However, using asynchronous device I/O enables you to better use resources and thus create more efficient applications.

Consider a thread that issues an asynchronous I/O request to a device. This I/O request is passed to a device driver, which assumes the responsibility of actually performing the I/O. While the device driver waits for the device to respond, the application's thread is not suspended as it waits for the I/O request to complete. Instead, this thread continues executing and performs other useful tasks.

At some point, the device driver finishes processing the queued I/O request and must notify the application that data has been sent, data has been received, or an error has occurred. You'll learn how the device driver notifies you of I/O completions in "Receiving Completed I/O Request Notifications" on page 310. For now, let's concentrate on how to queue asynchronous I/O requests. Queuing asynchronous I/O requests is the essence of designing a high-performance, scalable application, and it is what the remainder of this chapter is all about.

To access a device asynchronously, you must first open the device by calling **CreateFile**, specifying the **FILE_FLAG_OVERLAPPED** flag in the **dwFlagsAndAttributes** parameter. This flag notifies the system that you intend to access the device asynchronously.

To queue an I/O request for a device driver, you use the **ReadFile** and **WriteFile** functions that you already learned about in "Performing Synchronous Device I/O" on page 302. For convenience, I'll list the function prototypes again:

```
BOOL ReadFile(
    HANDLE       hFile,
    PVOID        pvBuffer,
    DWORD        nNumBytesToRead,
    PDWORD       pdwNumBytes,
    OVERLAPPED*  pOverlapped);
```

```
BOOL WriteFile(
   HANDLE      hFile,
   CONST VOID  *pvBuffer,
   DWORD       nNumBytesToWrite,
   PDWORD      pdwNumBytes,
   OVERLAPPED* pOverlapped);
```

When either of these functions is called, the function checks to see if the device, identified by the **hFile** parameter, was opened with the **FILE_FLAG_OVERLAPPED** flag. If this flag is specified, the function performs asynchronous device I/O. By the way, when calling either function for asynchronous I/O, you can (and usually do) pass **NULL** for the **pdwNumBytes** parameter. After all, you expect these functions to return before the I/O request has completed, so examining the number of bytes transferred is meaningless at this time.

The *OVERLAPPED* Structure

When performing asynchronous device I/O, you must pass the address to an initialized **OVERLAPPED** structure via the **pOverlapped** parameter. The word "overlapped" in this context means that the time spent performing the I/O request overlaps the time your thread spends performing other tasks. Here's what an **OVERLAPPED** structure looks like:

```
typedef struct _OVERLAPPED {
   DWORD  Internal;      // [out] Error code
   DWORD  InternalHigh;  // [out] Number of bytes transferred
   DWORD  Offset;        // [in]  Low  32-bit file offset
   DWORD  OffsetHigh;    // [in]  High 32-bit file offset
   HANDLE hEvent;        // [in]  Event handle or data
} OVERLAPPED, *LPOVERLAPPED;
```

This structure contains five members. Three of these members—**Offset**, **OffsetHigh**, and **hEvent**—must be initialized prior to calling **ReadFile** or **WriteFile**. The other two members, **Internal** and **InternalHigh**, are set by the device driver and can be examined when the I/O operation completes. Here is a more detailed explanation of these member variables:

Offset and OffsetHigh When a file is being accessed, these members indicate the 64-bit offset in the file where you want the I/O operation to begin. Recall that each file kernel object has a file pointer associated with it. When issuing a synchronous I/O request, the system knows to start accessing the file at the location identified by the file pointer. After the operation is complete, the system updates the file pointer automatically so that the next operation can pick up where the last operation left off.

When performing asynchronous I/O, this file pointer is ignored by the system. Imagine what would happen if your code placed two asynchronous calls to **ReadFile** (for the same file kernel object). In this scenario, the system wouldn't know where to start reading for the second call to **ReadFile**. You probably wouldn't want to start reading the file at the same location used by the first call to **ReadFile**. You might want to start the second read at the byte in the file that followed the last byte that was read by the first call to **ReadFile**. To avoid the confusion of multiple asynchronous calls to the same object, all asynchronous I/O requests must specify the starting file offset in the **OVERLAPPED** structure.

Note that the **Offset** and **OffsetHigh** members are not ignored for nonfile devices—you must initialize both members to **0** or the I/O request will fail and **GetLastError** will return **ERROR_INVALID_PARAMETER**.

hEvent   This member is used by one of the four methods available for receiving I/O completion notifications. When using the alertable I/O notification method, this member can be used for your own purposes. I know many developers who store the address of a C++ object in **hEvent**. (This member will be discussed more in "Signaling an Event Kernel Object" on page 312.)

Internal   This member holds the processed I/O's error code. As soon as you issue an asynchronous I/O request, the device driver sets **Internal** to **STATUS_PENDING**, indicating that no error has occurred because the operation has not started. In fact, the macro **HasOverlappedIoCompleted**, which is defined in WinBase.h, allows you to check whether an asynchronous I/O operation has completed. If the request is still pending, **FALSE** is returned; if the I/O request is completed, **TRUE** is returned. Here is the macro's definition:

```
#define HasOverlappedIoCompleted(pOverlapped) \
    ((pOverlapped)->Internal != STATUS_PENDING)
```

InternalHigh   When an asynchronous I/O request completes, this member holds the number of bytes transferred.

When first designing the **OVERLAPPED** structure, Microsoft decided not to document the **Internal** and **InternalHigh** members (which explains their names). As time went on, Microsoft realized that the information contained in these members would be useful to developers, so it documented them. However, Microsoft didn't change the names of the members because the operating system source code referenced them frequently, and Microsoft didn't want to modify the code.

> **Note**   When an asynchronous I/O request completes, you receive the address of the **OVERLAPPED** structure that was used when the request was initiated. Having more contextual information passed around with an **OVERLAPPED** structure is frequently useful—for example, if you wanted to store the handle of the device used to initiate the I/O request inside the **OVERLAPPED** structure. The **OVERLAPPED** structure doesn't offer a device handle member or other potentially useful members for storing context, but you can solve this problem quite easily.
>
> I frequently create a C++ class that is derived from an **OVERLAPPED** structure. This C++ class can have any additional information in it that I want. When my application receives the address of an **OVERLAPPED** structure, I simply cast the address to a pointer of my C++ class. Now I have access to the **OVERLAPPED** members and any additional context information my application needs. The FileCopy sample application at the end of this chapter demonstrates this technique. See my **CIOReq** C++ class in the FileCopy sample application for the details.

Asynchronous Device I/O Caveats

You should be aware of a couple of issues when performing asynchronous I/O. First, the device driver doesn't have to process queued I/O requests in a first-in first-out (FIFO) fashion. For example, if a thread executes the following code, the device driver will quite possibly write to the file and then read from the file:

```
OVERLAPPED o1 = { 0 };
OVERLAPPED o2 = { 0 };
BYTE bBuffer[100];
ReadFile (hFile, bBuffer, 100, NULL, &o1);
WriteFile(hFile, bBuffer, 100, NULL, &o2);
```

A device driver typically executes I/O requests out of order if doing so helps performance. For example, to reduce head movement and seek times, a file system driver might scan the queued I/O request list looking for requests that are near the same physical location on the hard drive.

The second issue you should be aware of is the proper way to perform error checking. Most Windows functions return **FALSE** to indicate failure or nonzero to indicate success. However, the **ReadFile** and **WriteFile** functions behave a little differently. An example might help to explain.

When attempting to queue an asynchronous I/O request, the device driver might choose to process the request synchronously. This can occur if you're reading from a file and the system checks whether the data you want is already in the system's cache. If the data is available, your I/O request is not queued to the device driver; instead, the system copies the data from the cache to your buffer, and the I/O operation is complete. The driver always performs certain operations synchronously, such as NTFS file compression, extending the length of a file or appending information to a file. For more information about operations that are always performed synchronously, please see *http://support.microsoft.com/default.aspx?scid=kb%3Ben-us%3B156932.*

ReadFile and **WriteFile** return a nonzero value if the requested I/O was performed synchronously. If the requested I/O is executing asynchronously, or if an error occurred while calling **ReadFile** or **WriteFile**, FALSE is returned. When **FALSE** is returned, you must call **GetLastError** to determine specifically what happened. If **GetLastError** returns **ERROR_IO_PENDING**, the I/O request was successfully queued and will complete later.

If **GetLastError** returns a value other than **ERROR_IO_PENDING**, the I/O request could not be queued to the device driver. Here are the most common error codes returned from **GetLastError** when an I/O request can't be queued to the device driver:

ERROR_INVALID_USER_BUFFER or ERROR_NOT_ENOUGH_MEMORY   Each device driver maintains a fixed-size list (in a nonpaged pool) of outstanding I/O requests. If this list is full, the system can't queue your request, **ReadFile** and **WriteFile** return FALSE, and **GetLastError** reports one of these two error codes (depending on the driver).

ERROR_NOT_ENOUGH_QUOTA   Certain devices require that your data buffer's storage be page locked so that the data cannot be swapped out of RAM while the I/O is pending. This page-locked storage requirement is certainly true of file I/O when using the **FILE_FLAG_NO_BUFFERING** flag. However, the system restricts the amount of storage that a single process can page lock. If **ReadFile** and **WriteFile** cannot page lock your buffer's storage, the functions return FALSE and **GetLastError** reports **ERROR_NOT_ENOUGH_QUOTA**. You can increase a process' quota by calling **SetProcessWorkingSetSize**.

How should you handle these errors? Basically, these errors occur because a number of outstanding I/O requests have not yet completed, so you need to allow some pending I/O requests to complete and then reissue the calls to **ReadFile** and **WriteFile**.

The third issue you should be aware of is that the data buffer and **OVERLAPPED** structure used to issue the asynchronous I/O request must not be moved or destroyed until the I/O request has completed. When queuing an I/O request to a device driver, the driver is passed the *address* of the data buffer and the *address* of the **OVERLAPPED** structure. Notice that just the address is passed, not the actual block. The reason for this should be quite obvious: memory copies are very expensive and waste a lot of CPU time.

When the device driver is ready to process your queued request, it transfers the data referenced by the **pvBuffer** address, and it accesses the file's offset member and other members contained within the **OVERLAPPED** structure pointed to by the **pOverlapped** parameter. Specifically, the device driver updates the **Internal** member with the I/O's error code and the **InternalHigh** member with the number of bytes transferred.

> **Note**   It is absolutely essential that these buffers not be moved or destroyed until the I/O request has completed; otherwise, memory will be corrupted. Also, you must allocate and initialize a unique **OVERLAPPED** structure for each I/O request.

The preceding note is very important and is one of the most common bugs developers introduce when implementing an asynchronous device I/O architecture. Here's an example of what *not* to do:

```
VOID ReadData(HANDLE hFile) {
   OVERLAPPED o = { 0 };
   BYTE b[100];
   ReadFile(hFile, b, 100, NULL, &o);
}
```

This code looks fairly harmless, and the call to **ReadFile** is perfect. The only problem is that the function returns after queuing the asynchronous I/O request. Returning from the function essentially frees the buffer and the **OVERLAPPED** structure from the thread's stack, but the device driver is not aware that **ReadData** returned. The device driver still has two memory addresses that point to the thread's stack. When the I/O completes, the device driver is going to modify memory on the thread's stack, corrupting whatever happens to be occupying that spot in memory at the time. This bug is particularly difficult to find because the memory modification occurs asynchronously. Sometimes the device driver might perform I/O synchronously, in which case you won't see the bug. Sometimes the I/O might complete right after the function returns, or it might complete over an hour later, and who knows what the stack is being used for then.

Canceling Queued Device I/O Requests

Sometimes you might want to cancel a queued device I/O request before the device driver has processed it. Windows offers a few ways to do this:

- You can call **CancelIo** to cancel all I/O requests queued by the calling thread for the specified handle (unless the handle has been associated with an I/O completion port):

```
BOOL CancelIo(HANDLE hFile);
```

- You can cancel all queued I/O requests, regardless of which thread queued the request, by closing the handle to a device itself.

- When a thread dies, the system automatically cancels all I/O requests issued by the thread, except for requests made to handles that have been associated with an I/O completion port.

- If you need to cancel a single, specific I/O request submitted on a given file handle, you can call **CancelIoEx**:

```
BOOL CancelIoEx(HANDLE hFile, LPOVERLAPPED pOverlapped);.
```

With **CancelIoEx**, you are able to cancel pending I/O requests emitted by a thread different from the calling thread. This function marks as canceled all I/O requests that are pending on **hFile** and associated with the given **pOverlapped** parameter. Because each outstanding I/O request should have its own **OVERLAPPED** structure, each call to **CancelIoEx** should cancel just one outstanding request. However, if the **pOverlapped** parameter is **NULL**, **CancelIoEx** cancels all outstanding I/O requests for the specified **hFile**.

> **Note**   Canceled I/O requests complete with an error code of **ERROR_OPERATION_ABORTED**.

Receiving Completed I/O Request Notifications

At this point, you know how to queue an asynchronous device I/O request, but I haven't discussed how the device driver notifies you after the I/O request has completed.

Windows offers four different methods (briefly described in Table 10-9) for receiving I/O completion notifications, and this chapter covers all of them. The methods are shown in order of complexity, from the easiest to understand and implement (signaling a device kernel object) to the hardest to understand and implement (I/O completion ports).

Table 10-9   Methods for Receiving I/O Completion Notifications

Technique	Summary
Signaling a device kernel object	Not useful for performing multiple simultaneous I/O requests against a single device. Allows one thread to issue an I/O request and another thread to process it.
Signaling an event kernel object	Allows multiple simultaneous I/O requests against a single device. Allows one thread to issue an I/O request and another thread to process it.
Using alertable I/O	Allows multiple simultaneous I/O requests against a single device. The thread that issued an I/O request must also process it.
Using I/O completion ports	Allows multiple simultaneous I/O requests against a single device. Allows one thread to issue an I/O request and another thread to process it. This technique is highly scalable and has the most flexibility.

As stated at the beginning of this chapter, the I/O completion port is the hands-down best method of the four for receiving I/O completion notifications. By studying all four, you'll learn why Microsoft added the I/O completion port to Windows and how the I/O completion port solves all the problems that exist for the other methods.

Signaling a Device Kernel Object

Once a thread issues an asynchronous I/O request, the thread continues executing, doing useful work. Eventually, the thread needs to synchronize with the completion of the I/O operation. In other words, you'll hit a point in your thread's code at which the thread can't continue to execute unless the data from the device is fully loaded into the buffer.

In Windows, a device kernel object can be used for thread synchronization, so the object can either be in a signaled or nonsignaled state. The **ReadFile** and **WriteFile** functions set the device kernel object to the nonsignaled state just before queuing the I/O request. When the device driver completes the request, the driver sets the device kernel object to the signaled state.

A thread can determine whether an asynchronous I/O request has completed by calling either **WaitForSingleObject** or **WaitForMultipleObjects**. Here is a simple example:

```
HANDLE hFile = CreateFile(..., FILE_FLAG_OVERLAPPED, ...);
BYTE bBuffer[100];
OVERLAPPED o = { 0 };
o.Offset = 345;

BOOL bReadDone = ReadFile(hFile, bBuffer, 100, NULL, &o);
DWORD dwError = GetLastError();

if (!bReadDone && (dwError == ERROR_IO_PENDING)) {
   // The I/O is being performed asynchronously; wait for it to complete
   WaitForSingleObject(hFile, INFINITE);
   bReadDone = TRUE;
}

if (bReadDone) {
   // o.Internal contains the I/O error
   // o.InternalHigh contains the number of bytes transferred
   // bBuffer contains the read data
} else {
   // An error occurred; see dwError
}
```

This code issues an asynchronous I/O request and then immediately waits for the request to finish, defeating the purpose of asynchronous I/O! Obviously, you would never actually write code similar to this, but the code does demonstrate important concepts, which I'll summarize here:

- The device must be opened for asynchronous I/O by using the **FILE_FLAG_OVERLAPPED** flag.
- The **OVERLAPPED** structure must have its **Offset**, **OffsetHigh**, and **hEvent** members initialized. In the code example, I set them all to **0** except for **Offset**, which I set to **345** so that **ReadFile** reads data from the file starting at byte 346.
- **ReadFile**'s return value is saved in **bReadDone**, which indicates whether the I/O request was performed synchronously.

- If the I/O request was not performed synchronously, I check to see whether an error occurred or whether the I/O is being performed asynchronously. Comparing the result of **GetLastError** with **ERROR_IO_PENDING** gives me this information.

- To wait for the data, I call **WaitForSingleObject**, passing the handle of the device kernel object. As you saw in Chapter 9, calling this function suspends the thread until the kernel object becomes signaled. The device driver signals the object when it completes the I/O. After **WaitForSingleObject** returns, the I/O is complete and I set **bReadDone** to **TRUE**.

- After the read completes, you can examine the data in **bBuffer**, the error code in the **OVERLAPPED** structure's **Internal** member, and the number of bytes transferred in the **OVERLAPPED** structure's **InternalHigh** member.

- If a true error occurred, **dwError** contains the error code giving more information.

Signaling an Event Kernel Object

The method for receiving I/O completion notifications just described is very simple and straightforward, but it turns out not to be all that useful because it does not handle multiple I/O requests well. For example, suppose you were trying to carry out multiple asynchronous operations on a single file at the same time. Say that you wanted to read 10 bytes from the file and write 10 bytes to the file simultaneously. The code might look like this:

```
HANDLE hFile = CreateFile(..., FILE_FLAG_OVERLAPPED, ...);

BYTE bReadBuffer[10];
OVERLAPPED oRead = { 0 };
oRead.Offset = 0;
ReadFile(hFile, bReadBuffer, 10, NULL, &oRead);

BYTE bWriteBuffer[10] = { 0, 1, 2, 3, 4, 5, 6, 7, 8, 9 };
OVERLAPPED oWrite = { 0 };
oWrite.Offset = 10;
WriteFile(hFile, bWriteBuffer, _countof(bWriteBuffer), NULL, &oWrite);
...
WaitForSingleObject(hFile, INFINITE);

// We don't know what completed: Read? Write? Both?
```

You can't synchronize your thread by waiting for the device to become signaled because the object becomes signaled as soon as either of the operations completes. If you call **WaitForSingleObject**, passing it the device handle, you will be unsure whether the function returned because the read operation completed, the write operation completed, or both operations completed. Clearly, there needs to be a better way to perform multiple, simultaneous asynchronous I/O requests so that you don't run into this predicament—fortunately, there is.

The last member of the **OVERLAPPED** structure, **hEvent**, identifies an event kernel object. You must create this event object by calling **CreateEvent**. When an asynchronous I/O request completes, the device driver checks to see whether the **hEvent** member of the **OVERLAPPED** structure is **NULL**. If **hEvent** is not **NULL**, the driver signals the event by calling **SetEvent**. The driver also sets the device object to the signaled state just as it did before. However, if you are using events to determine when a device operation has completed, you shouldn't wait for the device object to become signaled—wait for the event instead.

> **Note** To improve performance slightly, you can tell Windows not to signal the file object when the operation completes. You do so by calling the **SetFileCompletionNotifica-tionModes** function:
>
> ```
> BOOL SetFileCompletionNotificationModes(HANDLE hFile, UCHAR uFlags);
> ```
>
> The **hFile** parameter identifies a file handle, and the **uFlags** parameter indicates how Windows should modify its normal behavior with respect to completing an I/O operation. If you pass the **FILE_SKIP_SET_EVENT_ON_HANDLE** flag, Windows will not signal the file handle when operations on the file complete. Note that the **FILE_SKIP_SET_EVENT_ON_HANDLE** flag is very poorly named; a better name would have been something like **FILE_SKIP_SIGNAL**.

If you want to perform multiple asynchronous device I/O requests simultaneously, you must create a separate event object for each request, initialize the **hEvent** member in each request's **OVERLAPPED** structure, and then call **ReadFile** or **WriteFile**. When you reach the point in your code at which you need to synchronize with the completion of the I/O request, simply call **WaitForMultipleObjects**, passing in the event handles associated with each outstanding I/O request's **OVERLAPPED** structures. With this scheme, you can easily and reliably perform multiple asynchronous device I/O operations simultaneously and use the same device object. The following code demonstrates this approach:

```
HANDLE hFile = CreateFile(..., FILE_FLAG_OVERLAPPED, ...);

BYTE bReadBuffer[10];
OVERLAPPED oRead = { 0 };
oRead.Offset = 0;
oRead.hEvent = CreateEvent(...);
ReadFile(hFile, bReadBuffer, 10, NULL, &oRead);

BYTE bWriteBuffer[10] = { 0, 1, 2, 3, 4, 5, 6, 7, 8, 9 };
OVERLAPPED oWrite = { 0 };
oWrite.Offset = 10;
oWrite.hEvent = CreateEvent(...);
WriteFile(hFile, bWriteBuffer, _countof(bWriteBuffer), NULL, &oWrite);
...

HANDLE h[2];
h[0] = oRead.hEvent;
h[1] = oWrite.hEvent;
DWORD dw = WaitForMultipleObjects(2, h, FALSE, INFINITE);
switch (dw - WAIT_OBJECT_0) {
   case 0:   // Read completed
      break;

   case 1:   // Write completed
      break;
}
```

This code is somewhat contrived and is not *exactly* what you'd do in a real-life application, but it does illustrate my point. Typically, a real-life application has a loop that waits for I/O requests to complete. As each request completes, the thread performs the desired task, queues another asynchronous I/O request, and loops back around, waiting for more I/O requests to complete.

GetOverlappedResult

Recall that originally Microsoft was not going to document the **OVERLAPPED** structure's **Internal** and **InternalHigh** members, which meant it needed to provide another way for you to know how many bytes were transferred during the I/O processing and get the I/O's error code. To make this information available to you, Microsoft created the **GetOverlappedResult** function:

```
BOOL GetOverlappedResult(
    HANDLE      hFile,
    OVERLAPPED* pOverlapped,
    PDWORD      pdwNumBytes,
    BOOL        bWait);
```

Microsoft now documents the **Internal** and **InternalHigh** members, so the **GetOverlapped-Result** function is not very useful. However, when I was first learning asynchronous I/O, I decided to reverse engineer the function to help solidify concepts in my head. The following code shows how **GetOverlappedResult** is implemented internally:

```
BOOL GetOverlappedResult(
    HANDLE hFile,
    OVERLAPPED* po,
    PDWORD pdwNumBytes,
    BOOL bWait) {


    if (po->Internal == STATUS_PENDING) {
        DWORD dwWaitRet = WAIT_TIMEOUT;
        if (bWait) {
            // Wait for the I/O to complete
            dwWaitRet = WaitForSingleObject(
                (po->hEvent != NULL) ? po->hEvent : hFile, INFINITE);
        }

        if (dwWaitRet == WAIT_TIMEOUT) {
            // I/O not complete and we're not supposed to wait
            SetLastError(ERROR_IO_INCOMPLETE);
            return(FALSE);
        }

        if (dwWaitRet != WAIT_OBJECT_0) {
            // Error calling WaitForSingleObject
            return(FALSE);
        }
    }

    // I/O is complete; return number of bytes transferred
    *pdwNumBytes = po->InternalHigh;

    if (SUCCEEDED(po->Internal)) {
        return(TRUE);   // No I/O error
    }

    // Set last error to I/O error
    SetLastError(po->Internal);
    return(FALSE);
}
```

Alertable I/O

The third method available to you for receiving I/O completion notifications is called *alertable I/O*. At first, Microsoft touted alertable I/O as the absolute best mechanism for developers who wanted to create high-performance, scalable applications. But as developers started using alertable I/O, they soon realized that it was not going to live up to the promise.

I have worked with alertable I/O quite a bit, and I'll be the first to tell you that alertable I/O is horrible and should be avoided. However, to make alertable I/O work, Microsoft added some infrastructure into the operating system that I have found to be extremely useful and valuable. As you read this section, concentrate on the infrastructure that is in place and don't get bogged down in the I/O aspects.

Whenever a thread is created, the system also creates a queue that is associated with the thread. This queue is called the asynchronous procedure call (APC) queue. When issuing an I/O request, you can tell the device driver to append an entry to the calling thread's APC queue. To have completed I/O notifications queued to your thread's APC queue, you call the **ReadFileEx** and **WriteFileEx** functions:

```
BOOL ReadFileEx(
    HANDLE      hFile,
    PVOID       pvBuffer,
    DWORD       nNumBytesToRead,
    OVERLAPPED* pOverlapped,
    LPOVERLAPPED_COMPLETION_ROUTINE pfnCompletionRoutine);
```

```
BOOL WriteFileEx(
    HANDLE      hFile,
    CONST VOID  *pvBuffer,
    DWORD       nNumBytesToWrite,
    OVERLAPPED* pOverlapped,
    LPOVERLAPPED_COMPLETION_ROUTINE pfnCompletionRoutine);
```

Like **ReadFile** and **WriteFile**, **ReadFileEx** and **WriteFileEx** issue I/O requests to a device driver, and the functions return immediately. The **ReadFileEx** and **WriteFileEx** functions have the same parameters as the **ReadFile** and **WriteFile** functions, with two exceptions. First, the ***Ex** functions are not passed a pointer to a **DWORD** that gets filled with the number of bytes transferred; this information can be retrieved only by the callback function. Second, the ***Ex** functions require that you pass the address of a callback function, called a *completion routine*. This routine must have the following prototype:

```
VOID WINAPI CompletionRoutine(
    DWORD       dwError,
    DWORD       dwNumBytes,
    OVERLAPPED* po);
```

When you issue an asynchronous I/O request with **ReadFileEx** and **WriteFileEx**, the functions pass the address of this function to the device driver. When the device driver has completed the I/O request, it appends an entry in the issuing thread's APC queue. This entry contains the address of the completion routine function and the address of the **OVERLAPPED** structure used to initiate the I/O request.

> **Note** By the way, when an alertable I/O completes, the device driver does not attempt to signal an event object. In fact, the device does not reference the **OVERLAPPED** structure's **hEvent** member at all. Therefore, you can use the **hEvent** member for your own purposes if you like.

When the thread is in an alertable state (discussed shortly), the system examines its APC queue and, for every entry in the queue, the system calls the completion function, passing it the I/O error code, the number of bytes transferred, and the address of the **OVERLAPPED** structure. Note that the error code and number of bytes transferred can also be found in the **OVERLAPPED** structure's **Internal** and **InternalHigh** members. (As I mentioned earlier, Microsoft originally didn't want to document these, so it passed them as parameters to the function.)

I'll get back to this completion routine function shortly. First let's look at how the system handles the asynchronous I/O requests. The following code queues three different asynchronous operations:

```
hFile = CreateFile(..., FILE_FLAG_OVERLAPPED, ...);

ReadFileEx(hFile, ...);    // Perform first ReadFileEx
WriteFileEx(hFile, ...);   // Perform first WriteFileEx
ReadFileEx(hFile, ...);    // Perform second ReadFileEx

SomeFunc();
```

If the call to **SomeFunc** takes some time to execute, the system completes the three operations before **SomeFunc** returns. While the thread is executing the **SomeFunc** function, the device driver is appending completed I/O entries to the thread's APC queue. The APC queue might look something like this:

```
first WriteFileEx completed
second ReadFileEx completed
first ReadFileEx completed
```

The APC queue is maintained internally by the system. You'll also notice from the list that the system can execute your queued I/O requests in any order, and that the I/O requests that you issue last might be completed first and vice versa. Each entry in your thread's APC queue contains the address of a callback function and a value that is passed to the function.

As I/O requests complete, they are simply queued to your thread's APC queue—the callback routine is not immediately called because your thread might be busy doing something else and cannot be interrupted. To process entries in your thread's APC queue, the thread must put itself in an alertable state. This simply means that your thread has reached a position in its execution where it can handle being interrupted. Windows offers six functions that can place a thread in an alertable state:

```
DWORD SleepEx(
   DWORD dwMilliseconds,
   BOOL  bAlertable);

DWORD WaitForSingleObjectEx(
   HANDLE hObject,
   DWORD  dwMilliseconds,
   BOOL   bAlertable);

DWORD WaitForMultipleObjectsEx(
   DWORD    cObjects,
   CONST HANDLE* phObjects,
   BOOL     bWaitAll,
   DWORD    dwMilliseconds,
   BOOL     bAlertable);

BOOL SignalObjectAndWait(
   HANDLE hObjectToSignal,
   HANDLE hObjectToWaitOn,
   DWORD  dwMilliseconds,
   BOOL   bAlertable);

BOOL GetQueuedCompletionStatusEx(
   HANDLE hCompPort,
   LPOVERLAPPED_ENTRY pCompPortEntries,
   ULONG ulCount,
   PULONG pulNumEntriesRemoved,
   DWORD dwMilliseconds,
   BOOL bAlertable);

DWORD MsgWaitForMultipleObjectsEx(
   DWORD    nCount,
   CONST HANDLE* pHandles,
   DWORD    dwMilliseconds,
   DWORD    dwWakeMask,
   DWORD    dwFlags);
```

The last argument to the first five functions is a Boolean value indicating whether the calling thread should place itself in an alertable state. For **MsgWaitForMultipleObjectsEx**, you must use the **MWMO_ALERTABLE** flag to have the thread enter an alertable state. If you're familiar with the **Sleep**, **WaitForSingleObject**, and **WaitForMultipleObjects** functions, you shouldn't be surprised to learn that, internally, these non-**Ex** functions call their **Ex** counterparts, always passing **FALSE** for the **bAlertable** parameter.

When you call one of the six functions just mentioned and place your thread in an alertable state, the system first checks your thread's APC queue. If at least one entry is in the queue, the system does not put your thread to sleep. Instead, the system pulls the entry from the APC queue and your thread calls the callback routine, passing the routine the completed I/O request's error code, number of bytes transferred, and address of the **OVERLAPPED** structure. When the callback routine returns to the system, the system checks for more entries in the APC queue. If more entries exist, they are processed. However, if no more entries exist, your call to the alertable function returns. Something to keep in mind is that if any entries are in your thread's APC queue when you call any of these functions, your thread never sleeps!

The only time these functions suspend your thread is when no entries are in your thread's APC queue at the time you call the function. While your thread is suspended, the thread will wake up if the kernel object (or objects) that you're waiting on becomes signaled or if an APC entry appears in your thread's queue. Because your thread is in an alertable state, as soon as an APC entry appears, the system wakes your thread and empties the queue (by calling the callback routines). Then the functions immediately return to the caller—your thread does not go back to sleep waiting for kernel objects to become signaled.

The return value from these six functions indicates why they have returned. If they return **WAIT_IO_COMPLETION** (or if **GetLastError** returns **WAIT_IO_COMPLETION**), you know that the thread is continuing to execute because at least one entry was processed from the thread's APC queue. If the methods return for any other reason, the thread woke up because the sleep period expired, the specified kernel object or objects became signaled, or a mutex was abandoned.

The Bad and the Good of Alertable I/O

At this point, we've discussed the mechanics of performing alertable I/O. Now you need to know about the two issues that make alertable I/O a horrible method for doing device I/O:

Callback functions   Alertable I/O requires that you create callback functions, which makes implementing your code much more difficult. These callback functions typically don't have enough contextual information about a particular problem to guide you, so you end up placing a lot of information in global variables. Fortunately, these global variables don't need to be synchronized because the thread calling one of the six alterable functions is the same thread executing the callback functions. A single thread can't be in two places at one time, so the variables are safe.

Threading issues   The real big problem with alertable I/O is this: The thread issuing the I/O request must also handle the completion notification. If a thread issues several requests, that thread must respond to each request's completion notification, even if other threads are sitting completely idle. Because there is no load balancing, the application doesn't scale well.

Both of these problems are pretty severe, so I strongly discourage the use of alertable I/O for device I/O. I'm sure you guessed by now that the I/O completion port mechanism, discussed in the next section, solves both of the problems I just described. I promised to tell you some good stuff about the alertable I/O infrastructure, so before I move on to the I/O completion port, I'll do that.

Windows offers a function that allows you to manually queue an entry to a thread's APC queue:

```
DWORD QueueUserAPC(
    PAPCFUNC  pfnAPC,
    HANDLE    hThread,
    ULONG_PTR dwData);
```

The first parameter is a pointer to an APC function that must have the following prototype:

```
VOID WINAPI APCFunc(ULONG_PTR dwParam);
```

The second parameter is the handle of the thread for which you want to queue the entry. Note that this thread can be any thread in the system. If **hThread** identifies a thread in a different process' address space, **pfnAPC** must specify the memory address of a function that is in the address space of the target thread's process. The last parameter to **QueueUserAPC**, **dwData**, is a value that simply gets passed to the callback function.

Even though **QueueUserAPC** is prototyped as returning a **DWORD**, the function actually returns a **BOOL** indicating success or failure. You can use **QueueUserAPC** to perform extremely efficient inter-thread communication, even across process boundaries. Unfortunately, however, you can pass only a single value.

QueueUserAPC can also be used to force a thread out of a wait state. Suppose you have a thread calling **WaitForSingleObject**, waiting for a kernel object to become signaled. While the thread is waiting, the user wants to terminate the application. You know that threads should cleanly destroy themselves, but how do you force the thread waiting on the kernel object to wake up and kill itself? **QueueUserAPC** is the answer.

The following code demonstrates how to force a thread out of a wait state so that the thread can exit cleanly. The main function spawns a new thread, passing it the handle of some kernel object. While the secondary thread is running, the primary thread is also running. The secondary thread (executing the **ThreadFunc** function) calls **WaitForSingleObjectEx**, which suspends the thread, placing it in an alertable state. Now, say that the user tells the primary thread to terminate the application. Sure, the primary thread could just exit, and the system would kill the whole process. However, this approach is not very clean, and in many scenarios, you'll just want to kill an operation without terminating the whole process.

So the primary thread calls **QueueUserAPC**, which places an APC entry in the secondary thread's APC queue. Because the secondary thread is in an alertable state, it now wakes and empties its APC queue by calling the **APCFunc** function. This function does absolutely nothing and just returns. Because the APC queue is now empty, the thread returns from its call to **WaitForSingleObjectEx** with a return value of **WAIT_IO_COMPLETION**. The **ThreadFunc** function checks specifically for this return value, knowing that it received an APC entry indicating that the thread should exit.

```
// The APC callback function has nothing to do
VOID WINAPI APCFunc(ULONG_PTR dwParam) {
   // Nothing to do in here
}

UINT WINAPI ThreadFunc(PVOID pvParam) {
   HANDLE hEvent = (HANDLE) pvParam;   // Handle is passed to this thread

   // Wait in an alertable state so that we can be forced to exit cleanly
   DWORD dw = WaitForSingleObjectEx(hEvent, INFINITE, TRUE);
   if (dw == WAIT_OBJECT_0) {
      // Object became signaled
   }
   if (dw == WAIT_IO_COMPLETION) {
      // QueueUserAPC forced us out of a wait state
      return(0);   // Thread dies cleanly
   }
   ...
   return(0);
}
```

```
void main() {
   HANDLE hEvent = CreateEvent(...);
   HANDLE hThread = (HANDLE) _beginthreadex(NULL, 0,
      ThreadFunc, (PVOID) hEvent, 0, NULL);
   ...

   // Force the secondary thread to exit cleanly
   QueueUserAPC(APCFunc, hThread, NULL);
   WaitForSingleObject(hThread, INFINITE);
   CloseHandle(hThread);
   CloseHandle(hEvent);
}
```

I know that some of you are thinking that this problem could have been solved by replacing the call to **WaitForSingleObjectEx** with a call to **WaitForMultipleObjects** and by creating another event kernel object to signal the secondary thread to terminate. For my simple example, your solution would work. However, if my secondary thread called **WaitForMultipleObjects** to wait until all objects became signaled, **QueueUserAPC** would be the only way to force the thread out of a wait state.

I/O Completion Ports

Windows is designed to be a secure, robust operating system running applications that service literally thousands of users. Historically, you've been able to architect a service application by following one of two models:

Serial model   A single thread waits for a client to make a request (usually over the network). When the request comes in, the thread wakes and handles the client's request.

Concurrent model   A single thread waits for a client request and then creates a new thread to handle the request. While the new thread is handling the client's request, the original thread loops back around and waits for another client request. When the thread that is handling the client's request is completely processed, the thread dies.

The problem with the serial model is that it does not handle multiple, simultaneous requests well. If two clients make requests at the same time, only one can be processed at a time; the second request must wait for the first request to finish processing. A service that is designed using the serial approach cannot take advantage of multiprocessor machines. Obviously, the serial model is good only for the simplest of server applications, in which few client requests are made and requests can be handled very quickly. A Ping server is a good example of a serial server.

Because of the limitations in the serial model, the concurrent model is extremely popular. In the concurrent model, a thread is created to handle each client request. The advantage is that the thread waiting for incoming requests has very little work to do. Most of the time, this thread is sleeping. When a client request comes in, the thread wakes, creates a new thread to handle the request, and then waits for another client request. This means that incoming client requests are handled expediently. Also, because each client request gets its own thread, the server application scales well and can easily take advantage of multiprocessor machines. So if you are using the concurrent model and upgrade the hardware (add another CPU), the performance of the server application improves.

Service applications using the concurrent model were implemented using Windows. The Windows team noticed that application performance was not as high as desired. In particular, the team noticed that handling many simultaneous client requests meant that many threads were running in the system concurrently. Because all these threads were *runnable* (not suspended and waiting for something to happen), Microsoft realized that the Windows kernel spent too much time context switching between the running threads, and the threads were not getting as much CPU time to do their work. To make Windows an awesome server environment, Microsoft needed to address this problem. The result is the I/O completion port kernel object.

Creating an I/O Completion Port

The theory behind the I/O completion port is that the number of threads running concurrently must have an upper bound—that is, 500 simultaneous client requests cannot allow 500 runnable threads to exist. What, then, is the proper number of concurrent, runnable threads? Well, if you think about this question for a moment, you'll come to the realization that if a machine has two CPUs, having more than two runnable threads—one for each processor—really doesn't make sense. As soon as you have more runnable threads than CPUs available, the system has to spend time performing thread context switches, which wastes precious CPU cycles—a potential deficiency of the concurrent model.

Another deficiency of the concurrent model is that a new thread is created for each client request. Creating a thread is cheap when compared to creating a new process with its own virtual address space, but creating threads is far from free. The service application's performance can be improved if a pool of threads is created when the application initializes, and these threads hang around for the duration of the application. I/O completion ports were designed to work with a pool of threads.

An I/O completion port is probably the most complex kernel object. To create an I/O completion port, you call **CreateIoCompletionPort**:

```
HANDLE CreateIoCompletionPort(
    HANDLE      hFile,
    HANDLE      hExistingCompletionPort,
    ULONG_PTR   CompletionKey,
    DWORD       dwNumberOfConcurrentThreads);
```

This function performs two different tasks: it creates an I/O completion port, and it associates a device with an I/O completion port. This function is overly complex, and in my opinion, Microsoft should have split it into two separate functions. When I work with I/O completion ports, I separate these two capabilities by creating two tiny functions that abstract the call to **CreateIoCompletionPort**. The first function I write is called **CreateNewCompletionPort**, and I implement it as follows:

```
HANDLE CreateNewCompletionPort(DWORD dwNumberOfConcurrentThreads) {

    return(CreateIoCompletionPort(INVALID_HANDLE_VALUE, NULL, 0,
        dwNumberOfConcurrentThreads));
}
```

This function takes a single argument, **dwNumberOfConcurrentThreads**, and then calls the Windows **CreateIoCompletionPort** function, passing in hard-coded values for the first three parameters and **dwNumberOfConcurrentThreads** for the last parameter. You see, the first three parameters to **CreateIoCompletionPort** are used only when you are associating a device with a completion port. (I'll talk about this shortly.) To create just a completion port, I pass **INVALID_HANDLE_VALUE**, **NULL**, and **0**, respectively, to **CreateIoCompletionPort**'s first three parameters.

The **dwNumberOfConcurrentThreads** parameter tells the I/O completion port the maximum number of threads that should be runnable at the same time. If you pass **0** for the **dwNumberOf-ConcurrentThreads** parameter, the completion port defaults to allowing as many concurrent threads as there are CPUs on the host machine. This is usually exactly what you want so that extra context switching is avoided. You might want to increase this value if the processing of a client request requires a lengthy computation that rarely blocks, but increasing this value is strongly discouraged. You might experiment with the **dwNumberOfConcurrentThreads** parameter by trying different values and comparing your application's performance on your target hardware.

You'll notice that **CreateIoCompletionPort** is about the only Windows function that creates a kernel object but does not have a parameter that allows you to pass the address of a **SECURITY_ATTRIBUTES** structure. This is because completion ports are intended for use within a single process only. The reason will be clear to you when I explain how to use completion ports.

Associating a Device with an I/O Completion Port

When you create an I/O completion port, the kernel actually creates five different data structures, as shown in Figure 10-1. You should refer to this figure as you continue reading.

The first data structure is a device list indicating the device or devices associated with the port. You associate a device with the port by calling **CreateIoCompletionPort**. Again, I created my own function, **AssociateDeviceWithCompletionPort**, which abstracts the call to **CreateIoCompletionPort**:

```
BOOL AssociateDeviceWithCompletionPort(
   HANDLE hCompletionPort, HANDLE hDevice, DWORD dwCompletionKey) {

   HANDLE h = CreateIoCompletionPort(hDevice, hCompletionPort, dwCompletionKey, 0);
   return(h == hCompletionPort);
}
```

AssociateDeviceWithCompletionPort appends an entry to an existing completion port's device list. You pass to the function the handle of an existing completion port (returned by a previous call to **CreateNewCompletionPort**), the handle of the device (this can be a file, a socket, a mailslot, a pipe, and so on), and a completion key (a value that has meaning to you; the operating system doesn't care what you pass here). Each time you associate a device with the port, the system appends this information to the completion port's device list.

> **Note** The **CreateIoCompletionPort** function is complex, and I recommend that you mentally separate the two reasons for calling it. There is one advantage to having the function be so complex: you can create an I/O completion port and associate a device with it at the same time. For example, the following code opens a file and creates a new completion port, associating the file with it. All I/O requests to the file complete with a completion key of **CK_FILE**, and the port allows as many as two threads to execute concurrently.
>
> ```
> #define CK_FILE    1
> HANDLE hFile = CreateFile(...);
> HANDLE hCompletionPort = CreateIoCompletionPort(hFile, NULL, CK_FILE, 2);
> ```

Device List

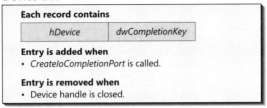

I/O Completion Queue (FIFO)

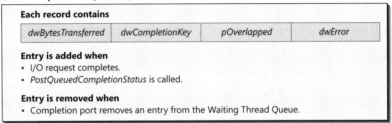

Waiting Thread Queue (LIFO)

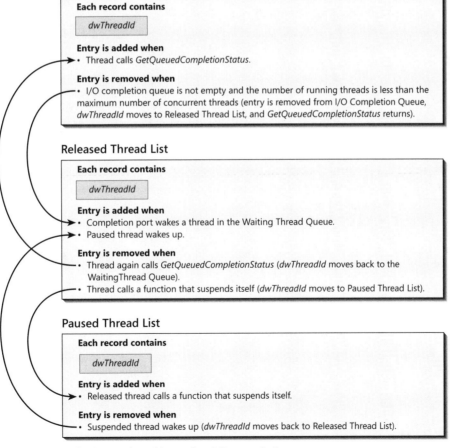

Released Thread List

Paused Thread List

Figure 10-1   The internal workings of an I/O completion port

The second data structure is an I/O completion queue. When an asynchronous I/O request for a device completes, the system checks to see whether the device is associated with a completion port and, if it is, the system appends the completed I/O request entry to the end of the completion port's I/O completion queue. Each entry in this queue indicates the number of bytes transferred, the completion key value that was set when the device was associated with the port, the pointer to the I/O request's **OVERLAPPED** structure, and an error code. I'll discuss how entries are removed from this queue shortly.

> **Note**   Issuing an I/O request to a device and not having an I/O completion entry queued to the I/O completion port is possible. This is not usually necessary, but it can come in handy occasionally—for example, when you send data over a socket and you don't care whether the data actually makes it or not.
>
> To issue an I/O request without having a completion entry queued, you must load the **OVERLAPPED** structure's **hEvent** member with a valid event handle and bitwise-**OR** this value with 1, like this:
>
> ```
> Overlapped.hEvent = CreateEvent(NULL, TRUE, FALSE, NULL);
> Overlapped.hEvent = (HANDLE) ((DWORD_PTR) Overlapped.hEvent | 1);
> ReadFile(..., &Overlapped);
> ```
>
> Now you can issue your I/O request, passing the address of this **OVERLAPPED** structure to the desired function (such as **ReadFile** above).
>
> It would be nice if you didn't have to create an event just to stop the queuing of the I/O completion. I would like to be able to do the following, but it doesn't work:
>
> ```
> Overlapped.hEvent = 1;
> ReadFile(..., &Overlapped);
> ```
>
> Also, don't forget to reset the low-order bit before closing this event handle:
>
> ```
> CloseHandle((HANDLE) ((DWORD_PTR) Overlapped.hEvent & ~1));
> ```

Architecting Around an I/O Completion Port

When your service application initializes, it should create the I/O completion port by calling a function such as **CreateNewCompletionPort**. The application should then create a pool of threads to handle client requests. The question you ask now is, "How many threads should be in the pool?" This is a tough question to answer, and I will address it in more detail later in "How Many Threads in the Pool?" on page 328. For now, a standard rule of thumb is to take the number of CPUs on the host machine and multiply it by 2. So on a dual-processor machine, you should create a pool of four threads.

All the threads in the pool should execute the same function. Typically, this thread function performs some sort of initialization and then enters a loop that should terminate when the service process is instructed to stop. Inside the loop, the thread puts itself to sleep waiting for device I/O requests to complete to the completion port. Calling **GetQueuedCompletionStatus** does this:

```
BOOL GetQueuedCompletionStatus(
    HANDLE        hCompletionPort,
    PDWORD        pdwNumberOfBytesTransferred,
    PULONG_PTR    pCompletionKey,
    OVERLAPPED**  ppOverlapped,
    DWORD         dwMilliseconds);
```

The first parameter, **hCompletionPort**, indicates which completion port the thread is interested in monitoring. Many service applications use a single I/O completion port and have all I/O request notifications complete to this one port. Basically, the job of **GetQueuedCompletionStatus** is to put the calling thread to sleep until an entry appears in the specified completion port's I/O completion queue or until the specified time-out occurs (as specified in the **dwMilliseconds** parameter).

The third data structure associated with an I/O completion port is the waiting thread queue. As each thread in the thread pool calls **GetQueuedCompletionStatus**, the ID of the calling thread is placed in this waiting thread queue, enabling the I/O completion port kernel object to always know which threads are currently waiting to handle completed I/O requests. When an entry appears in the port's I/O completion queue, the completion port wakes one of the threads in the waiting thread queue. This thread gets the pieces of information that make up a completed I/O entry: the number of bytes transferred, the completion key, and the address of the **OVERLAPPED** structure. This information is returned to the thread via the **pdwNumberOfBytesTransferred**, **pCompletionKey**, and **ppOverlapped** parameters passed to **GetQueuedCompletionStatus**.

Determining the reason that **GetQueuedCompletionStatus** returned is somewhat difficult. The following code demonstrates the proper way to do it:

```
DWORD dwNumBytes;
ULONG_PTR CompletionKey;
OVERLAPPED* pOverlapped;

// hIOCP is initialized somewhere else in the program
BOOL bOk = GetQueuedCompletionStatus(hIOCP,
   &dwNumBytes, &CompletionKey, &pOverlapped, 1000);
DWORD dwError = GetLastError();

if (bOk) {
   // Process a successfully completed I/O request
} else {
   if (pOverlapped != NULL) {
      // Process a failed completed I/O request
      // dwError contains the reason for failure
   } else {
      if (dwError == WAIT_TIMEOUT) {
         // Time-out while waiting for completed I/O entry
      } else {
         // Bad call to GetQueuedCompletionStatus
         // dwError contains the reason for the bad call
      }
   }
}
```

As you would expect, entries are removed from the I/O completion queue in a first-in first-out fashion. However, as you might not expect, threads that call **GetQueuedCompletionStatus** are awakened in a last-in first-out (LIFO) fashion. The reason for this is again to improve performance. For example, say that four threads are waiting in the waiting thread queue. If a single completed I/O entry appears, the last thread to call **GetQueuedCompletionStatus** wakes up to process the entry. When this last thread is finished processing the entry, the thread again calls **GetQueued-CompletionStatus** to enter the waiting thread queue. Now if another I/O completion entry appears, the same thread that processed the first entry is awakened to process the new entry.

As long as I/O requests complete so slowly that a single thread can handle them, the system just keeps waking the one thread, and the other three threads continue to sleep. By using this LIFO algorithm, threads that don't get scheduled can have their memory resources (such as stack space) swapped out to the disk and flushed from a processor's cache. This means having many threads waiting on a completion port isn't bad. If you do have several threads waiting but few I/O requests completing, the extra threads have most of their resources swapped out of the system anyway.

In Windows Vista, if you expect a large number of I/O requests to be constantly submitted, instead of multiplying the number of threads to wait on the completion port and incurring the increasing cost of the corresponding context switches, you can retrieve the result of several I/O requests at the same time by calling the following function:

```
BOOL GetQueuedCompletionStatusEx(
  HANDLE hCompletionPort,
  LPOVERLAPPED_ENTRY pCompletionPortEntries,
  ULONG ulCount,
  PULONG pulNumEntriesRemoved,
  DWORD dwMilliseconds,
  BOOL bAlertable);
```

The first parameter, **hCompletionPort**, indicates which completion port the thread is interested in monitoring. The entries present in the specified completion port's I/O completion queue when this function is called are retrieved, and their description is copied into the **pCompletionPort-Entries** array parameter. The **ulCount** parameter indicates how many entries can be copied in this array, and the long value pointed to by **pulNumEntriesRemoved** receives the exact number of I/O requests that were extracted from the completion queue.

Each element of the **pCompletionPortEntries** array is an **OVERLAPPED_ENTRY** that stores the pieces of information that make up a completed I/O entry: the completion key, the address of the **OVERLAPPED** structure, the result code (error) of the I/O request, and the number of bytes transferred.

```
typedef struct _OVERLAPPED_ENTRY {
    ULONG_PTR lpCompletionKey;
    LPOVERLAPPED lpOverlapped;
    ULONG_PTR Internal;
    DWORD dwNumberOfBytesTransferred;
} OVERLAPPED_ENTRY, *LPOVERLAPPED_ENTRY;
```

The **Internal** field is opaque and should not be used.

If the last **bAlertable** parameter is set to **FALSE**, the function waits for a completed I/O request to be queued on the completion port until the specified time-out occurs (as specified in the **dwMilliseconds** parameter). If the **bAlertable** parameter is set to **TRUE** and there is no completed I/O request in the queue, the thread enters an alertable state as explained earlier in this chapter.

> **Note**   When you issue an asynchronous I/O request to a device that is associated with a completion port, Windows queues the result to the completion port. Windows does this even if the asynchronous request is performed synchronously in order to give the programmer a consistent programming model. However, maintaining this consistent programming model hurts performance slightly because the completed request information must be placed in the port and a thread must extract it from the port.
>
> To improve performance slightly, you can tell Windows not to queue a synchronously performed asynchronous request to the completion port associated with the device by calling the **SetFileCompletionNotificationModes** function (described in "Signaling an Event Kernel Object" on page 312) passing it the **FILE_SKIP_COMPLETION_PORT_ON_SUCCESS** flag.
>
> The extremely performance-conscious programmer might also want to consider use of the **SetFileIoOverlappedRange** function. (See the Platform SDK documentation for more information.)

How the I/O Completion Port Manages the Thread Pool

Now it's time to discuss why I/O completion ports are so useful. First, when you create the I/O completion port, you specify the number of threads that can run concurrently. As I said, you usually set this value to the number of CPUs on the host machine. As completed I/O entries are queued, the I/O completion port wants to wake up waiting threads. However, the completion port wakes up only as many threads as you have specified. So if four I/O requests complete and four threads are waiting in a call to **GetQueuedCompletionStatus**, the I/O completion port will allow only two threads to wake up; the other two threads continue to sleep. As each thread processes a completed I/O entry, the thread again calls **GetQueuedCompletionStatus**. The system sees that more entries are queued and wakes the same threads to process the remaining entries.

If you're thinking about this carefully, you should notice that something just doesn't make a lot of sense: if the completion port only ever allows the specified number of threads to wake up concurrently, why have more threads waiting in the thread pool? For example, suppose I'm running on a machine with two CPUs and I create the I/O completion port, telling it to allow no more than two threads to process entries concurrently. But I create four threads (twice the number of CPUs) in the thread pool. It seems as though I am creating two additional threads that will never be awakened to process anything.

But I/O completion ports are very smart. When a completion port wakes a thread, the completion port places the thread's ID in the fourth data structure associated with the completion port, a released thread list. (See Figure 10-1.) This allows the completion port to remember which threads it awakened and to monitor the execution of these threads. If a released thread calls any function that places the thread in a wait state, the completion port detects this and updates its internal data structures by moving the thread's ID from the released thread list to the paused thread list (the fifth and final data structure that is part of an I/O completion port).

The goal of the completion port is to keep as many entries in the released thread list as are specified by the concurrent number of threads value used when creating the completion port. If a released thread enters a wait state for any reason, the released thread list shrinks and the completion port releases another waiting thread. If a paused thread wakes, it leaves the paused thread list and reenters the released thread list. This means that the released thread list can now have more entries in it than are allowed by the maximum concurrency value.

> **Note** Once a thread calls **GetQueuedCompletionStatus**, the thread is "assigned" to the specified completion port. The system assumes that all assigned threads are doing work on behalf of the completion port. The completion port wakes threads from the pool only if the number of running assigned threads is less than the completion port's maximum concurrency value.
>
> You can break the thread/completion port assignment in one of three ways:
>
> - Have the thread exit.
> - Have the thread call **GetQueuedCompletionStatus**, passing the handle of a different I/O completion port.
> - Destroy the I/O completion port that the thread is currently assigned to.

Let's tie all of this together now. Say that we are again running on a machine with two CPUs. We create a completion port that allows no more than two threads to wake concurrently, and we create four threads that are waiting for completed I/O requests. If three completed I/O requests get queued to the port, only two threads are awakened to process the requests, reducing the number of runnable threads and saving context-switching time. Now if one of the running threads calls **Sleep**, **WaitForSingleObject**, **WaitForMultipleObjects**, **SignalObjectAndWait**, a synchronous I/O call, or any function that would cause the thread not to be runnable, the I/O completion port would detect this and wake a third thread immediately. The goal of the completion port is to keep the CPUs saturated with work.

Eventually, the first thread will become runnable again. When this happens, the number of runnable threads will be higher than the number of CPUs in the system. However, the completion port again is aware of this and will not allow any additional threads to wake up until the number of threads drops below the number of CPUs. The I/O completion port architecture presumes that the number of runnable threads will stay above the maximum for only a short time and will die down quickly as the threads loop around and again call **GetQueuedCompletionStatus**. This explains why the thread pool should contain more threads than the concurrent thread count set in the completion port.

How Many Threads in the Pool?

Now is a good time to discuss how many threads should be in the thread pool. Consider two issues. First, when the service application initializes, you want to create a minimum set of threads so that you don't have to create and destroy threads on a regular basis. Remember that creating and destroying threads wastes CPU time, so you're better off minimizing this process as much as possible. Second, you want to set a maximum number of threads because creating too many threads wastes system resources. Even if most of these resources can be swapped out of RAM, minimizing the use of system resources and not wasting even paging file space is to your advantage, if you can manage it.

You will probably want to experiment with different numbers of threads. Most services (including Microsoft Internet Information Services) use heuristic algorithms to manage their thread pools. I recommend that you do the same. For example, you can create the following variables to manage the thread pool:

```
LONG g_nThreadsMin;    // Minimum number of threads in pool
LONG g_nThreadsMax;    // Maximum number of threads in pool
LONG g_nThreadsCrnt;   // Current number of threads in pool
LONG g_nThreadsBusy;   // Number of busy threads in pool
```

When your application initializes, you can create the **g_nThreadsMin** number of threads, all executing the same thread pool function. The following pseudocode shows how this thread function might look:

```
DWORD WINAPI ThreadPoolFunc(PVOID pv) {

   // Thread is entering pool
   InterlockedIncrement(&g_nThreadsCrnt);
   InterlockedIncrement(&g_nThreadsBusy);

   for (BOOL bStayInPool = TRUE; bStayInPool;) {

      // Thread stops executing and waits for something to do
      InterlockedDecrement(&m_nThreadsBusy);
      BOOL bOk = GetQueuedCompletionStatus(...);
      DWORD dwIOError = GetLastError();

      // Thread has something to do, so it's busy
      int nThreadsBusy = InterlockedIncrement(&m_nThreadsBusy);

      // Should we add another thread to the pool?
      if (nThreadsBusy == m_nThreadsCrnt) {    // All threads are busy
         if (nThreadsBusy < m_nThreadsMax) {   // The pool isn't full
            if (GetCPUUsage() < 75) {   // CPU usage is below 75%

               // Add thread to pool
               CloseHandle(chBEGINTHREADEX(...));
            }
         }
      }

      if (!bOk && (dwIOError == WAIT_TIMEOUT)) {   // Thread timed out
         // There isn't much for the server to do, and this thread
         // can die even if it still has outstanding I/O requests
         bStayInPool = FALSE;
      }

      if (bOk || (po != NULL)) {
         // Thread woke to process something; process it
         ...

         if (GetCPUUsage() > 90) {        // CPU usage is above 90%
            if (g_nThreadsCrnt > g_nThreadsMin) { // Pool above min
               bStayInPool = FALSE;    // Remove thread from pool
            }
         }
      }
   }
}
```

```
    // Thread is leaving pool
    InterlockedDecrement(&g_nThreadsBusy);
    InterlockedDecrement(&g_nThreadsCurrent);
    return(0);
}
```

This pseudocode shows how creative you can get when using an I/O completion port. The **Get-CPUUsage** function is not part of the Windows API. If you want its behavior, you'll have to implement the function yourself. In addition, you must make sure that the thread pool always contains at least one thread in it, or clients will never get tended to. Use my pseudocode as a guide, but your particular service might perform better if structured differently.

> **Note**   Earlier in this chapter, in "Canceling Queued Device I/O Requests" on page 309, I said that the system automatically cancels all pending I/O requests issued by a thread when that thread terminates. Before Windows Vista, when a thread issued an I/O request against a device associated with a completion port, it was mandatory that the thread remain alive until the request completed; otherwise, Windows canceled any outstanding requests made by the thread. With Windows Vista, this is no longer necessary: threads can now issue requests and terminate; the request will still be processed and the result will be queued to the completion port.

Many services offer a management tool that allows an administrator to have some control over the thread pool's behavior—for example, to set the minimum and maximum number of threads, the CPU time usage thresholds, and also the maximum concurrency value used when creating the I/O completion port.

Simulating Completed I/O Requests

I/O completion ports do not have to be used with device I/O at all. This chapter is also about interthread communication techniques, and the I/O completion port kernel object is an awesome mechanism to use to help with this. In "Alertable I/O" on page 315, I presented the **QueueUserAPC** function, which allows a thread to post an APC entry to another thread. I/O completion ports have an analogous function, **PostQueuedCompletionStatus**:

```
BOOL PostQueuedCompletionStatus(
    HANDLE      hCompletionPort,
    DWORD       dwNumBytes,
    ULONG_PTR   CompletionKey,
    OVERLAPPED* pOverlapped);
```

This function appends a completed I/O notification to an I/O completion port's queue. The first parameter, **hCompletionPort**, identifies the completion port that you want to queue the entry for. The remaining three parameters—**dwNumBytes**, **CompletionKey**, and **pOverlapped**—indicate the values that should be returned by a thread's call to **GetQueuedCompletionStatus**. When a thread pulls a simulated entry from the I/O completion queue, **GetQueuedCompletionStatus** returns **TRUE**, indicating a successfully executed I/O request.

The **PostQueuedCompletionStatus** function is incredibly useful—it gives you a way to communicate with all the threads in your pool. For example, when the user terminates a service application, you want all the threads to exit cleanly. But if the threads are waiting on the completion port and no I/O requests are coming in, the threads can't wake up. By calling **PostQueuedCompletion-Status** once for each thread in the pool, each thread can wake up, examine the values returned from **GetQueuedCompletionStatus**, see that the application is terminating, and clean up and exit appropriately.

You must be careful when using a thread termination technique like the one I just described. My example works because the threads in the pool are dying and not calling **GetQueuedCompletion-Status** again. However, if you want to notify each of the pool's threads of something and have them loop back around to call **GetQueuedCompletionStatus** again, you will have a problem because the threads wake up in a LIFO order. So you will have to employ some additional thread synchronization in your application to ensure that each pool thread gets the opportunity to see its simulated I/O entry. Without this additional thread synchronization, one thread might see the same notification several times.

> **Note**   In Windows Vista, when you call **CloseHandle** passing the handle of a completion port, all threads waiting in a call to **GetQueuedCompletionStatus** wake up and **FALSE** is returned to them. A call to **GetLastError** will return **ERROR_INVALID_HANDLE**; the threads can use this to know that it is time to die gracefully.

The FileCopy Sample Application

The FileCopy sample application (10-FileCopy.exe), shown at the end of this chapter, demonstrates the use of I/O completion ports. The source code and resource files for the application are in the 10-FileCopy directory on the companion content Web page. The program simply copies a file specified by the user to a new file called FileCopy.cpy. When the user executes FileCopy, the dialog box shown in Figure 10-2 appears.

Figure 10-2   The dialog box for the FileCopy sample application

The user clicks the Pathname button to select the file to be copied, and the Pathname and File Size fields are updated. When the user clicks the Copy button, the program calls the **FileCopy** function, which does all the hard work. Let's concentrate our discussion on the **FileCopy** function.

When preparing to copy, **FileCopy** opens the source file and retrieves its size, in bytes. I want the file copy to execute as blindingly fast as possible, so the file is opened using the **FILE_FLAG_NO_BUFFERING** flag. Opening the file with the **FILE_FLAG_NO_BUFFERING** flag allows me to access the file directly, bypassing the additional memory copy overhead incurred when allowing the system's cache to "help" access the file. Of course, accessing the file directly means slightly more work for me: I must always access the file using offsets that are multiples of the disk volume's sector size, and I must read and write data that is a multiple of the sector's size as well. I chose to transfer the file's data in **BUFFSIZE** (64 KB) chunks, which is guaranteed to be a multiple of the sector size. This is why I round up the source file's size to a multiple of **BUFFSIZE**. You'll also notice that the source file is opened with the **FILE_FLAG_OVERLAPPED** flag so that I/O requests against the file are performed asynchronously.

The destination file is opened similarly: both the **FILE_FLAG_NO_BUFFERING** and **FILE_FLAG_OVERLAPPED** flags are specified. I also pass the handle of the source file as **CreateFile**'s **hFileTemplate** parameter when creating the destination file, causing the destination file to have the same attributes as the source.

> **Note** Once both files are open, the destination file size is immediately set to its maximum size by calling **SetFilePointerEx** and **SetEndOfFile**. Adjusting the destination file's size now is extremely important because NTFS maintains a high-water marker that indicates the highest point at which the file was written. If you read past this marker, the system knows to return zeros. If you write past the marker, the file's data from the old high-water marker to the write offset is filled with zeros, your data is written to the file, and the file's high-water marker is updated. This behavior satisfies C2 security requirements pertaining to not presenting prior data. When you write to the end of a file on an NTFS partition, causing the high-water marker to move, NTFS must perform the I/O request synchronously even if asynchronous I/O was desired. If the **FileCopy** function didn't set the size of the destination file, none of the overlapped I/O requests would be performed asynchronously.

Now that the files are opened and ready to be processed, **FileCopy** creates an I/O completion port. To make working with I/O completion ports easier, I created a small C++ class, CIOCP, that is a very simple wrapper around the I/O completion port functions. This class can be found in the IOCP.h file discussed in Appendix A, "The Build Environment." **FileCopy** creates an I/O completion port by creating an instance (named **iocp**) of my CIOCP class.

The source file and destination file are associated with the completion port by calling the CIOCP's **AssociateDevice** member function. When associated with the completion port, each device is assigned a completion key. When an I/O request completes against the source file, the completion key is **CK_READ**, indicating that a read operation must have completed. Likewise, when an I/O request completes against the destination file, the completion key is **CK_WRITE**, indicating that a write operation must have completed.

Now we're ready to initialize a set of I/O requests (**OVERLAPPED** structures) and their memory buffers. The **FileCopy** function keeps four (**MAX_PENDING_IO_REQS**) I/O requests outstanding at any one time. For applications of your own, you might prefer to allow the number of I/O requests to dynamically grow or shrink as necessary. In the FileCopy program, the **CIOReq** class encapsulates a single I/O request. As you can see, this C++ class is derived from an **OVERLAPPED** structure but contains some additional context information. **FileCopy** allocates an array of **CIOReq** objects and calls the **AllocBuffer** method to associate a **BUFFSIZE**-sized data buffer with each I/O request object. The data buffer is allocated using the **VirtualAlloc** function. Using **VirtualAlloc** ensures that the block begins on an even allocation-granularity boundary, which satisfies the requirement of the **FILE_FLAG_NO_BUFFERING** flag: the buffer must begin on an address that is evenly divisible by the volume's sector size.

To issue the initial read requests against the source file, I perform a little trick: I post four **CK_WRITE** I/O completion notifications to the I/O completion port. When the main loop runs, the thread waits on the port and wakes immediately, thinking that a write operation has completed. This causes the thread to issue a read request against the source file, which really starts the file copy.

The main loop terminates when there are no outstanding I/O requests. As long as I/O requests are outstanding, the interior of the loop waits on the completion port by calling CIOCP's **GetStatus** method (which calls **GetQueuedCompletionStatus** internally). This call puts the thread to sleep until an I/O request completes to the completion port. When **GetQueuedCompletionStatus** returns, the returned completion key, **CompletionKey**, is checked. If **CompletionKey** is **CK_READ**, an I/O request against the source file is completed. I then call the **CIOReq**'s **Write** method to issue a write I/O request against the destination file. If **CompletionKey** is **CK_WRITE**, an I/O request against the destination file is completed. If I haven't read beyond the end of the source file, I call **CIOReq**'s **Read** method to continue reading the source file.

When there are no more outstanding I/O requests, the loop terminates and cleans up by closing the source and destination file handles. Before **FileCopy** returns, it must do one more task: it must fix the size of the destination file so that it is the same size as the source file. To do this, I reopen the destination file without specifying the **FILE_FLAG_NO_BUFFERING** flag. Because I am not using this flag, file operations do not have to be performed on sector boundaries. This allows me to shrink the size of the destination file to the same size as the source file.

```cpp
/******************************************************************************
Module:  FileCopy.cpp
Notices: Copyright (c) 2008 Jeffrey Richter & Christophe Nasarre
******************************************************************************/


#include "stdafx.h"
#include "Resource.h"


///////////////////////////////////////////////////////////////////////////////


// Each I/O request needs an OVERLAPPED structure and a data buffer
class CIOReq : public OVERLAPPED {
public:
   CIOReq() {
      Internal = InternalHigh = 0;
      Offset = OffsetHigh = 0;
      hEvent = NULL;
      m_nBuffSize = 0;
      m_pvData = NULL;
   }

   ~CIOReq() {
      if (m_pvData != NULL)
         VirtualFree(m_pvData, 0, MEM_RELEASE);
   }

   BOOL AllocBuffer(SIZE_T nBuffSize) {
      m_nBuffSize = nBuffSize;
      m_pvData = VirtualAlloc(NULL, m_nBuffSize, MEM_COMMIT, PAGE_READWRITE);
      return(m_pvData != NULL);
   }
```

```
    BOOL Read(HANDLE hDevice, PLARGE_INTEGER pliOffset = NULL) {
       if (pliOffset != NULL) {
          Offset     = pliOffset->LowPart;
          OffsetHigh = pliOffset->HighPart;
       }
       return(::ReadFile(hDevice, m_pvData, m_nBuffSize, NULL, this));
    }

    BOOL Write(HANDLE hDevice, PLARGE_INTEGER pliOffset = NULL) {
       if (pliOffset != NULL) {
          Offset     = pliOffset->LowPart;
          OffsetHigh = pliOffset->HighPart;
       }
       return(::WriteFile(hDevice, m_pvData, m_nBuffSize, NULL, this));
    }

private:
   SIZE_T m_nBuffSize;
   PVOID  m_pvData;
};


///////////////////////////////////////////////////////////////////////////


#define BUFFSIZE            (64 * 1024) // The size of an I/O buffer
#define MAX_PENDING_IO_REQS 4           // The maximum # of I/Os


// The completion key values indicate the type of completed I/O.
#define CK_READ  1
#define CK_WRITE 2


///////////////////////////////////////////////////////////////////////////


BOOL FileCopy(PCTSTR pszFileSrc, PCTSTR pszFileDst) {

   BOOL fOk = FALSE;    // Assume file copy fails
   LARGE_INTEGER liFileSizeSrc = { 0 }, liFileSizeDst;

   try {
      {
      // Open the source file without buffering & get its size
      CEnsureCloseFile hFileSrc = CreateFile(pszFileSrc, GENERIC_READ,
         FILE_SHARE_READ, NULL, OPEN_EXISTING,
         FILE_FLAG_NO_BUFFERING | FILE_FLAG_OVERLAPPED, NULL);
      if (hFileSrc.IsInvalid()) goto leave;

      // Get the file's size
      GetFileSizeEx(hFileSrc, &liFileSizeSrc);
```

```
// Nonbuffered I/O requires sector-sized transfers.
// I'll use buffer-size transfers since it's easier to calculate.
liFileSizeDst.QuadPart = chROUNDUP(liFileSizeSrc.QuadPart, BUFFSIZE);

// Open the destination file without buffering & set its size
CEnsureCloseFile hFileDst = CreateFile(pszFileDst, GENERIC_WRITE,
   0, NULL, CREATE_ALWAYS,
   FILE_FLAG_NO_BUFFERING | FILE_FLAG_OVERLAPPED, hFileSrc);
if (hFileDst.IsInvalid()) goto leave;

// File systems extend files synchronously. Extend the destination file
// now so that I/Os execute asynchronously improving performance.
SetFilePointerEx(hFileDst, liFileSizeDst, NULL, FILE_BEGIN);
SetEndOfFile(hFileDst);

// Create an I/O completion port and associate the files with it.
CIOCP iocp(0);
iocp.AssociateDevice(hFileSrc, CK_READ);  // Read from source file
iocp.AssociateDevice(hFileDst, CK_WRITE); // Write to destination file

// Initialize record-keeping variables
CIOReq ior[MAX_PENDING_IO_REQS];
LARGE_INTEGER liNextReadOffset = { 0 };
int nReadsInProgress  = 0;
int nWritesInProgress = 0;

// Prime the file copy engine by simulating that writes have completed.
// This causes read operations to be issued.
for (int nIOReq = 0; nIOReq < _countof(ior); nIOReq++) {

   // Each I/O request requires a data buffer for transfers
   chVERIFY(ior[nIOReq].AllocBuffer(BUFFSIZE));
   nWritesInProgress++;
   iocp.PostStatus(CK_WRITE, 0, &ior[nIOReq]);
}

// Loop while outstanding I/O requests still exist
while ((nReadsInProgress > 0) || (nWritesInProgress > 0)) {

   // Suspend the thread until an I/O completes
   ULONG_PTR CompletionKey;
   DWORD dwNumBytes;
   CIOReq* pior;
   iocp.GetStatus(&CompletionKey, &dwNumBytes, (OVERLAPPED**) &pior, INFINITE);

   switch (CompletionKey) {
   case CK_READ:  // Read completed, write to destination
      nReadsInProgress--;
      pior->Write(hFileDst);  // Write to same offset read from source
      nWritesInProgress++;
      break;
```

```
                case CK_WRITE: // Write completed, read from source
                    nWritesInProgress--;
                    if (liNextReadOffset.QuadPart < liFileSizeDst.QuadPart) {
                        // Not EOF, read the next block of data from the source file.
                        pior->Read(hFileSrc, &liNextReadOffset);
                        nReadsInProgress++;
                        liNextReadOffset.QuadPart += BUFFSIZE; // Advance source offset
                    }
                    break;
            }
        }
        fOk = TRUE;
        }
    leave:;
    }
    catch (...) {
    }

    if (fOk) {
        // The destination file size is a multiple of the page size. Open the
        // file WITH buffering to shrink its size to the source file's size.
        CEnsureCloseFile hFileDst = CreateFile(pszFileDst, GENERIC_WRITE,
            0, NULL, OPEN_EXISTING, 0, NULL);
        if (hFileDst.IsValid()) {

            SetFilePointerEx(hFileDst, liFileSizeSrc, NULL, FILE_BEGIN);
            SetEndOfFile(hFileDst);
        }
    }

    return(fOk);
}


///////////////////////////////////////////////////////////////////////////////


BOOL Dlg_OnInitDialog(HWND hWnd, HWND hWndFocus, LPARAM lParam) {

    chSETDLGICONS(hWnd, IDI_FILECOPY);

    // Disable Copy button since no file is selected yet.
    EnableWindow(GetDlgItem(hWnd, IDOK), FALSE);
    return(TRUE);
}


///////////////////////////////////////////////////////////////////////////////


void Dlg_OnCommand(HWND hWnd, int id, HWND hWndCtl, UINT codeNotify) {

    TCHAR szPathname[_MAX_PATH];
```

```
   switch (id) {
   case IDCANCEL:
      EndDialog(hWnd, id);
      break;

   case IDOK:
      // Copy the source file to the destination file.
      Static_GetText(GetDlgItem(hWnd, IDC_SRCFILE),
         szPathname, sizeof(szPathname));
      SetCursor(LoadCursor(NULL, IDC_WAIT));
      chMB(FileCopy(szPathname, TEXT("FileCopy.cpy"))
         ? "File Copy Successful" : "File Copy Failed");
      break;

   case IDC_PATHNAME:
      OPENFILENAME ofn = { OPENFILENAME_SIZE_VERSION_400 };
      ofn.hwndOwner = hWnd;
      ofn.lpstrFilter = TEXT("*.*\0");
      lstrcpy(szPathname, TEXT("*.*"));
      ofn.lpstrFile = szPathname;
      ofn.nMaxFile = _countof(szPathname);
      ofn.lpstrTitle = TEXT("Select file to copy");
      ofn.Flags = OFN_EXPLORER | OFN_FILEMUSTEXIST;
      BOOL fOk = GetOpenFileName(&ofn);
      if (fOk) {
         // Show user the source file's size
         Static_SetText(GetDlgItem(hWnd, IDC_SRCFILE), szPathname);
         CEnsureCloseFile hFile = CreateFile(szPathname, 0, 0, NULL,
            OPEN_EXISTING, 0, NULL);
         if (hFile.IsValid()) {
            LARGE_INTEGER liFileSize;
            GetFileSizeEx(hFile, &liFileSize);
            // NOTE: Only shows bottom 32 bits of size
            SetDlgItemInt(hWnd, IDC_SRCFILESIZE, liFileSize.LowPart, FALSE);
         }
      }
      EnableWindow(GetDlgItem(hWnd, IDOK), fOk);
      break;
   }
}


///////////////////////////////////////////////////////////////////////


INT_PTR WINAPI Dlg_Proc(HWND hWnd, UINT uMsg, WPARAM wParam, LPARAM lParam) {

   switch (uMsg) {
   chHANDLE_DLGMSG(hWnd, WM_INITDIALOG, Dlg_OnInitDialog);
   chHANDLE_DLGMSG(hWnd, WM_COMMAND,    Dlg_OnCommand);
   }
   return(FALSE);
}
```

```
//////////////////////////////////////////////////////////////////////////

int WINAPI _tWinMain(HINSTANCE hInstExe, HINSTANCE, PTSTR pszCmdLine, int) {

   DialogBox(hInstExe, MAKEINTRESOURCE(IDD_FILECOPY), NULL, Dlg_Proc);
   return(0);
}


/////////////////////////////// End of File //////////////////////////////
```

Chapter 11
The Windows Thread Pool

In Chapter 10, "Synchronous and Asynchronous Device I/O," we discussed how the Microsoft Windows I/O completion port kernel object provides a queue of I/O requests and how it dispatches threads to process these queued items in an intelligent way. However, the I/O completion port dispatches threads that are waiting on it; you still have to manage the creation and destruction of these threads yourself.

Everybody has opinions on how to manage the creation and destruction of threads. I've created several different implementations of thread pools myself over the years, each one fine-tuned for a particular scenario. To make things easier for developers, Windows provides a thread pool mechanism (built around the I/O completion port) to make thread creation, destruction, and general management easier. This new general-purpose thread pool might not be right for every situation, but it often fits the bill and can save you countless hours of development time.

The new thread pooling functions let you do the following:

- Call a function asynchronously
- Call a function at a timed interval
- Call a function when a single kernel object becomes signaled
- Call a function when asynchronous I/O requests complete

Note Microsoft introduced thread pool application programming interfaces (APIs) into Windows starting with Windows 2000. With Windows Vista, Microsoft has re-architected the thread pool and, in so doing, has also introduced a new set of thread pool APIs. Of course, Windows Vista still supports the older Windows 2000 APIs for backward compatibility, but it is recommended that you use the new APIs if your application doesn't need to run on versions of Windows prior to Vista. This chapter focuses on the new thread APIs introduced with Windows Vista; older editions of this book focused on the older APIs, which are not covered in this edition.

When a process initializes, it doesn't have any of the overhead associated with thread pool components. However, as soon as one of the new thread pooling functions is called, kernel resources are created for the process and some stay around until the process terminates. As you can see, the overhead of using the thread pool depends on the usage: threads, other kernel objects, and internal data structures become allocated on behalf of your process. So you must carefully consider what the thread pool will and won't do for you: don't just blindly use these functions.

OK, enough with the disclaimers. Let's see what this stuff does.

Scenario 1: Call a Function Asynchronously

To execute a function asynchronously using the thread pool, you simply define a function that matches the following prototype:

```
VOID NTAPI SimpleCallback(
    PTP_CALLBACK_INSTANCE pInstance, // See "Callback Termination Actions" section
    PVOID pvContext);
```

Then you submit a request to the thread pool to have one of its threads execute the function. To submit a request to the thread pool, you simply call the following function:

```
BOOL TrySubmitThreadpoolCallback(
    PTP_SIMPLE_CALLBACK pfnCallback,
    PVOID pvContext,
    PTP_CALLBACK_ENVIRON pcbe); // See "Customized Thread Pools" section
```

This function adds a *work item* to the thread pool's queue (by calling **PostQueuedCompletion-Status**) and returns **TRUE** if successful; it returns **FALSE** if unsuccessful. When calling **TrySubmitThreadpoolCallback**, the **pfnCallback** parameter identifies the function you wrote that matches the **SimpleCallback** prototype, the **pvContext** parameter identifies a value that should be passed to your function (in its **pvContext** parameter), and for the **PTP_CALLBACK_ENVIRON** parameter you can simply pass **NULL**. (I'll explain this parameter later in "Customized Thread Pools" on page 356.) I'll also explain **SimpleCallback**'s **pInstance** parameter later. (See "Callback Termination Actions" on page 355.)

Notice that you never need to call **CreateThread** yourself. A default thread pool is automatically created for your process, and a thread within the pool calls your callback function. Also, this thread is not immediately destroyed after it processes the client's request. It goes back into the thread pool so that it is ready to handle any other queued work item. The thread pool continuously reuses its threads rather than constantly creating and destroying threads. This results in a significant performance improvement for your application because it takes a lot of time to create and destroy a thread. Of course, if the thread pool determines that your application is best served by creating another thread pool thread it will do so, and if it determines that the thread pool has more threads than it needs, it will destroy some of its threads. Unless you really know what you're doing, it is best to trust the thread pool's internal algorithms here and let it fine-tune itself automatically to the workload of your application.

Explicitly Controlling a Work Item

In some circumstances, such as lack of memory or quota limitations, the call to **TrySubmit-ThreadpoolCallback** might fail. This is not acceptable when several actions are supposed to work in coordination, such as a timer counting on a work item to cancel another action. When the timer is set, you have to be sure that the cancellation work item will be submitted and processed by the thread pool. However, when the timer expires, the memory availability or quota conditions can be different than when the timer was created, and the call to **TrySubmitThreadpoolCallback** might fail. In that case, you create a work item object at the same time the timer is created and hold onto it until you explicitly need to submit the work item to the thread pool.

Each time you call **TrySubmitThreadpoolCallback**, internally a work item is allocated on your behalf. If you plan to submit a large bunch of work items, it would be better for performance and memory consumption to create the work item once and submit it several times. You create a work item by using the following function:

```
PTP_WORK CreateThreadpoolWork(
   PTP_WORK_CALLBACK pfnWorkHandler,
   PVOID pvContext,
   PTP_CALLBACK_ENVIRON pcbe);  // See "Customized Thread Pools" section
```

This function creates a user-mode structure in memory to store its three parameters and returns a pointer to it. The **pfnWorkHandler** parameter is a pointer to the function that will eventually be called by a thread pool thread to process the work item. The **pvContext** parameter can be any value; it is simply passed to the callback function. The function name you pass for the **pfn-WorkHandler** parameter must match the following prototype:

```
VOID CALLBACK WorkCallback(
   PTP_CALLBACK_INSTANCE Instance,
   PVOID Context,
   PTP_WORK Work);
```

When you want to submit a request to the thread pool, you call the **SubmitThreadpoolWork** function:

```
VOID SubmitThreadpoolWork(PTP_WORK pWork);
```

You can now assume that the queuing (and therefore the invoking of the callback function via a thread pool thread) will succeed. In fact, this is why **SubmitThreadpoolWork** has a **VOID** return type.

> **Caution** If you submit the same work item several times, your callback function will be called each time with the same **pvContext** value that was specified when the work item was created. Therefore, if you want to reuse the same work item to execute multiple actions, you need to be aware of this behavior. Most likely, you will want to execute the actions sequentially so that you can uniquely identify them.

If you have another thread that wants to either cancel the submitted work item or suspend itself waiting for the work item to complete its processing, you can call the following function:

```
VOID WaitForThreadpoolWorkCallbacks(
   PTP_WORK pWork,
   BOOL     bCancelPendingCallbacks);
```

The **pWork** parameter points to the work item created and submitted by your earlier calls to **CreateThreadpoolWork** and **SubmitThreadpoolWork**. If the work item has not been submitted yet, this function returns immediately without taking any action.

If you pass **TRUE** for the **bCancelPendingCallbacks** parameter, **WaitForThreadpoolWork-Callbacks** will try to cancel the previously submitted work item. If a thread pool thread is currently processing the work item, it will not be interrupted and **WaitForThreadpoolWork-Callbacks** will wait for the work item to complete before returning. If the work item has been submitted but no thread has processed it yet, it is marked as canceled and the function returns immediately. When the completion port extracts the item from its queue, the thread pool will know not to call the callback method, preventing the work item from even starting to execute.

If you pass **FALSE** for the **bCancelPendingCallbacks** parameter, **WaitForThreadpoolWork-Callbacks** will suspend the calling thread until the specified work item has completed its processing and the thread pool thread that was executing the work item has returned back to the thread pool to process another work item.

> **Note**   If you have submitted multiple work items using a single **PTP_WORK** object, **Wait-ForThreadpoolWorkCallbacks** will wait for all the submissions to be processed by the thread pool if you pass **FALSE** for the **bCancelPendingCallbacks** parameter. If you pass **TRUE** for the **bCancelPendingCallbacks** parameter, **WaitForThreadpoolWorkCall-backs** will wait only until the currently running items have completed.

When you don't need the work item any more, you should free it by calling **CloseThreadpool-Work** with the pointer to the work item as a single parameter:

```
VOID CloseThreadpoolWork(PTP_WORK pwk);
```

The Batch Sample Application

The Batch application (11-Batch.exe), listed next, shows how to use the thread pool's work item functions to implement batch processing of several actions, each notifying the user interface thread about its state, prefixed by the current thread ID. This application implements a simple solution for knowing when the whole batch is over, as shown in Figure 11-1.

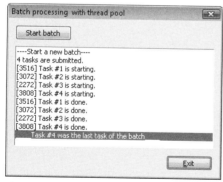

Figure 11-1   Output generated by the Batch application.

The source code and resource files for the application are in the 11-Batch directory on the book's companion content Web page.

```
/*****************************************************************************
Module:  Batch.cpp
Notices: Copyright (c) 2008 Jeffrey Richter & Christophe Nasarre
*****************************************************************************/


#include "stdafx.h"
#include "Batch.h"


///////////////////////////////////////////////////////////////////////////


// Global variables
HWND      g_hDlg = NULL;
PTP_WORK g_pWorkItem = NULL;
volatile LONG g_nCurrentTask = 0;


// Global definitions
#define WM_APP_COMPLETED (WM_APP+123)


///////////////////////////////////////////////////////////////////////////


void AddMessage(LPCTSTR szMsg) {

   HWND hListBox = GetDlgItem(g_hDlg, IDC_LB_STATUS);
   ListBox_SetCurSel(hListBox, ListBox_AddString(hListBox, szMsg));
}


///////////////////////////////////////////////////////////////////////////


void NTAPI TaskHandler(PTP_CALLBACK_INSTANCE Instance, PVOID Context, PTP_WORK Work) {

   LONG currentTask = InterlockedIncrement(&g_nCurrentTask);

   TCHAR szMsg[MAX_PATH];
   StringCchPrintf(
      szMsg, _countof(szMsg),
      TEXT("[%u] Task #%u is starting."), GetCurrentThreadId(), currentTask);
   AddMessage(szMsg);

   // Simulate a lot of work
   Sleep(currentTask * 1000);

   StringCchPrintf(
      szMsg, _countof(szMsg),
      TEXT("[%u] Task #%u is done."), GetCurrentThreadId(), currentTask);
   AddMessage(szMsg);
```

```c
      if (InterlockedDecrement(&g_nCurrentTask) == 0)
      {
         // Notify the UI thread for completion.
         PostMessage(g_hDlg, WM_APP_COMPLETED, 0, (LPARAM)currentTask);
      }
}


/////////////////////////////////////////////////////////////////////////////


void OnStartBatch() {

   // Disable Start button
   Button_Enable(GetDlgItem(g_hDlg, IDC_BTN_START_BATCH), FALSE);

   AddMessage(TEXT("----Start a new batch----"));

   // Submit 4 tasks by using the same work item
   SubmitThreadpoolWork(g_pWorkItem);
   SubmitThreadpoolWork(g_pWorkItem);
   SubmitThreadpoolWork(g_pWorkItem);
   SubmitThreadpoolWork(g_pWorkItem);

   AddMessage(TEXT("4 tasks are submitted."));
}


/////////////////////////////////////////////////////////////////////////////


void Dlg_OnCommand(HWND hWnd, int id, HWND hWndCtl, UINT codeNotify) {

   switch (id) {
      case IDOK:
      case IDCANCEL:
         EndDialog(hWnd, id);
         break;

      case IDC_BTN_START_BATCH:
         OnStartBatch();
         break;
   }
}


BOOL Dlg_OnInitDialog(HWND hWnd, HWND hWndFocus, LPARAM lParam) {

   // Keep track of main dialog window for error messages
   g_hDlg = hWnd;

   return(TRUE);
}
```

```
/////////////////////////////////////////////////////////////////////


INT_PTR WINAPI Dlg_Proc(HWND hWnd, UINT uMsg, WPARAM wParam, LPARAM lParam) {

   switch (uMsg) {
      chHANDLE_DLGMSG(hWnd, WM_INITDIALOG, Dlg_OnInitDialog);
      chHANDLE_DLGMSG(hWnd, WM_COMMAND,    Dlg_OnCommand);
      case WM_APP_COMPLETED: {
         TCHAR szMsg[MAX_PATH+1];
         StringCchPrintf(
            szMsg, _countof(szMsg),
            TEXT("____Task #%u was the last task of the batch____"), lParam);
         AddMessage(szMsg);

         // Don't forget to enable the button
         Button_Enable(GetDlgItem(hWnd, IDC_BTN_START_BATCH), TRUE);
      }
      break;
   }

   return(FALSE);
}



int APIENTRY _tWinMain(HINSTANCE hInstance, HINSTANCE, LPTSTR pCmdLine, int) {

   // Create the work item that will be used by all tasks
   g_pWorkItem = CreateThreadpoolWork(TaskHandler, NULL, NULL);
   if (g_pWorkItem == NULL) {
      MessageBox(NULL, TEXT("Impossible to create the work item for tasks."),
         TEXT(""), MB_ICONSTOP);
      return(-1);
   }

   DialogBoxParam(hInstance, MAKEINTRESOURCE(IDD_MAIN), NULL, Dlg_Proc,
      _ttoi(pCmdLine));

   // Don't forget to delete the work item
   // Note that it is not mandatory here since the process is exiting
   CloseThreadpoolWork(g_pWorkItem);

   return(0);
}


//////////////////////////// End of File /////////////////////////////
```

Before the main window is created, a single work item is created. If this operation fails, the application ends after a message box pops up to explain the problem. When you click on the Start batch button, the work item is submitted four times to the default thread pool through **SubmitThreadpoolWork**. The button is also disabled to avoid having another batch being submitted. The callback processed by a thread pool thread atomically increments the global task counter by using **InterlockedIncrement** (as explained in Chapter 8, "Thread Synchronization in User Mode") and adding one entry into the log when it starts and another one when it is done.

Just before the **TaskHandler** function returns, the global task count is atomically decremented by using **InterlockedDecrement**. If this was the last task to process, a dedicated message is posted to the main window that takes care of adding a final message to the log before enabling the Start button again. Another solution for detecting the end of the batch is to spawn a thread that simply calls **WaitForThreadpoolWorkCallbacks(g_pWorkItem, FALSE)**. When this function call returns, you are sure that the thread pool has processed all the submissions of this work item.

Scenario 2: Call a Function at a Timed Interval

Sometimes applications need to perform certain tasks at certain times. Windows offers a waitable timer kernel object (described in Chapter 9, "Thread Synchronization with Kernel Objects") that makes it easy to get a time-based notification. Many programmers create a waitable timer object for each time-based task that the application will perform, but this is unnecessary and wastes system resources. Instead, you can create a single waitable timer, set it to the next due time, and then reset the timer for the next time, and so on. However, the code to accomplish this is tricky to write. Fortunately, you can let the thread pool functions manage this for you.

To schedule a work item to be executed at a certain time, you first need to define a callback function with the following prototype:

```
VOID CALLBACK TimeoutCallback(
   PTP_CALLBACK_INSTANCE pInstance,   // See "Callback Termination Actions" section
   PVOID pvContext,
   PTP_TIMER pTimer);
```

Then inform the thread pool when to invoke your function by calling the following function:

```
PTP_TIMER CreateThreadpoolTimer(
   PTP_TIMER_CALLBACK pfnTimerCallback,
   PVOID pvContext,
   PTP_CALLBACK_ENVIRON pcbe);   // See "Customized Thread Pools" section
```

This function works similarly to the **CreateThreadpoolWork** function discussed in the previous section. The **pfnTimerCallback** parameter must refer to a function matching the **Timeout-Callback** prototype, and the value passed in the **pvContext** parameter will be passed to this function each time it is called. When called, your **TimerCallback** function's **pTimer** parameter will also receive a pointer to the object created and returned by the **CreateThreadpoolTimer** function.

When you want to register the timer with the thread pool, you call the **SetThreadpoolTimer** function:

```
VOID SetThreadpoolTimer(
   PTP_TIMER pTimer,
   PFILETIME pftDueTime,
   DWORD msPeriod,
   DWORD msWindowLength);
```

The **pTimer** parameter identifies the **TP_TIMER** object returned from **CreateThreadpoolTimer**. The **pftDueTime** parameter indicates when the callback will be called for the first time. To specify a due time relative to the time when you call this function, you pass a negative value (in milliseconds), with −1 being a special case to start immediately. To specify an absolute time, you specify a positive value measured in 100-nanosecond units since January 1, 1600.

If you want the timer to fire just once, pass **0** for the **msPeriod** parameter. However, if you want the thread pool to call your function periodically, specify a nonzero value for **msPeriod** (indicating how many milliseconds to wait before calling your **TimerCallback** function again). The **msWindowLength** parameter is used to introduce some randomness in the execution of the callback, which will occur anywhere from the current due time to the current due time plus **msWindowLength** milliseconds. This is particularly useful when you have several timers expiring with almost the same frequency but you don't want too many collisions—this avoids having to add a call to **Sleep** with a random value in your callbacks.

Another effect of the **msWindowLength** parameter is to group several timers together. If you have a large number of timers that end around the same time, you might prefer to group them in order to avoid too many context switches. For example, if timer A ends in 5 milliseconds and timer B ends in 6 milliseconds, the callback for timer A gets called when 5 milliseconds elapse, and then the thread goes back into the pool to sleep. Just after, it wakes up again to process the callback of timer B, and so on. To avoid the context switches and put threads into and take them out of the pool, you can set an **msWindowLength** of 2 for timer A and the same for timer B. The thread pool now knows that timer A expects its callback to be called between 5 and 7 milliseconds, while timer B expects to be triggered between 6 and 8 milliseconds from now. In this case, the thread pool knows that it is more efficient to batch the two timers at the same time, in 6 milliseconds. That way, only one thread will wake up, execute the callback of timer A, and then execute the callback of timer B before going back to sleep in the pool. This optimization is particularly important when your timers are very close in time and the cost of waking a thread up and putting it back to sleep becomes important compared to the frequency of timers.

I should point out that once the timers are set, you can modify an existing timer by calling **SetThreadpoolTimer**, passing a pointer to a previously set timer in the **pTimer** parameter. However, you can pass new values for the **pftDueTime**, **msPeriod**, and **msWindowLength** parameters. In fact, you can pass **NULL** for the **pftDueTime** parameter, which tells the thread pool to stop invoking your **TimerCallback** function. This is a good way to pause a timer without destroying the timer object, especially within the callback itself.

Also, you can determine if a timer has been set (that is, it has a **pftDueTime** value of non-**NULL**) by calling **IsThreadpoolTimerSet**:

```
BOOL IsThreadpoolTimerSet(PTP_TIMER pti);
```

Finally, you can have a thread wait for a timer to complete by calling **WaitForThreadpoolTimerCallbacks**, and you can free the timer's memory by calling the **CloseThreadpoolTimer** function. These two functions work similarly to the **WaitForThreadpoolWork** and **CloseThreadpoolWork** functions discussed earlier in this chapter.

The Timed Message Box Sample Application

The Timed Message Box application (11-TimedMsgBox.exe), listed next, shows how to use the thread pool's timer functions to implement a message box that automatically closes if the user doesn't respond within a certain amount of time. The source code and resource files for the application are in the 11-TimedMsgBox directory on the book's companion content Web page.

When you start the program, it sets a global variable, **g_nSecLeft**, to 10. This indicates the number of seconds that the user has to respond to the message box. The **CreateThreadpoolTimer** function is called to create a thread pool timer that is passed to **SetThreadpoolTimer**, instructing the thread pool to call the **MsgBoxTimeout** function every second, starting in one second. Once everything has been initialized, **MessageBox** is called and presents the following message box to the user:

While waiting for the user to respond, the **MsgBoxTimeout** function is called by a thread pool thread. This function finds the window handle for the message box, decrements the global **g_nSecLeft** variable, and updates the string in the message box. After **MsgBoxTimeout** has been called the first time, the message box looks like this:

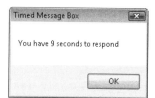

When **MsgBoxTimeout** is called for the ninth time, the **g_nSecLeft** variable becomes 1 and **MsgBoxTimeout** calls **EndDialog** to destroy the message box. The primary thread's call to **MessageBox** returns, **CloseThreadpoolTimer** is called to tell the thread pool that the timer is no longer needed and also to stop calling the **MsgBoxTimeout** function. Then another message box appears, telling the user that he or she didn't respond to the first message box within the allotted period:

If the user does respond before the time runs out, the following message box appears:

```
/**********************************************************************
Module:  TimedMsgBox.cpp
Notices: Copyright (c) 2008 Jeffrey Richter & Christophe Nasarre
**********************************************************************/


#include "..\CommonFiles\CmnHdr.h"     /* See Appendix A. */
#include <tchar.h>
#include <StrSafe.h>


///////////////////////////////////////////////////////////////////


// The caption of our message box
TCHAR g_szCaption[100];


// How many seconds we'll display the message box
int g_nSecLeft = 0;


// This is STATIC window control ID for a message box
#define ID_MSGBOX_STATIC_TEXT    0x0000ffff


///////////////////////////////////////////////////////////////////


VOID CALLBACK MsgBoxTimeoutCallback(
   PTP_CALLBACK_INSTANCE   pInstance,
   PVOID                   pvContext,
   PTP_TIMER               pTimer
   ) {
   // NOTE: Due to a thread race condition, it is possible (but very unlikely)
   // that the message box will not be created when we get here.
   HWND hwnd = FindWindow(NULL, g_szCaption);

   if (hwnd != NULL) {
      if (g_nSecLeft == 1) {
         // The time is up; force the message box to exit.
         EndDialog(hwnd, IDOK);
         return;
      }
   }
```

```
        // The window does exist; update the time remaining.
        TCHAR szMsg[100];
        StringCchPrintf(szMsg, _countof(szMsg),
            TEXT("You have %d seconds to respond"), --g_nSecLeft);
        SetDlgItemText(hwnd, ID_MSGBOX_STATIC_TEXT, szMsg);
    } else {

        // The window does not exist yet; do nothing this time.
        // We'll try again in another second.
    }
}

int WINAPI _tWinMain(HINSTANCE, HINSTANCE, PTSTR, int) {

    _tcscpy_s(g_szCaption, 100, TEXT("Timed Message Box"));

    // How many seconds we'll give the user to respond
    g_nSecLeft = 10;

    // Create the threadpool timer object
    PTP_TIMER lpTimer =
        CreateThreadpoolTimer(MsgBoxTimeoutCallback, NULL, NULL);

    if (lpTimer == NULL) {
        TCHAR szMsg[MAX_PATH];
        StringCchPrintf(szMsg, _countof(szMsg),
            TEXT("Impossible to create the timer: %u"), GetLastError());
        MessageBox(NULL, szMsg, TEXT("Error"), MB_OK | MB_ICONERROR);

        return(-1);
    }

    // Start the timer in one second to trigger every 1 second
    ULARGE_INTEGER ulRelativeStartTime;
    ulRelativeStartTime.QuadPart = (LONGLONG) -(10000000);  // start in 1 second
    FILETIME ftRelativeStartTime;
    ftRelativeStartTime.dwHighDateTime = ulRelativeStartTime.HighPart;
    ftRelativeStartTime.dwLowDateTime  = ulRelativeStartTime.LowPart;
    SetThreadpoolTimer(
        lpTimer,
        &ftRelativeStartTime,
        1000, // Triggers every 1000 milliseconds
        0);

    // Display the message box
    MessageBox(NULL, TEXT("You have 10 seconds to respond"),
        g_szCaption, MB_OK);

    // Clean up the timer
    CloseThreadpoolTimer(lpTimer);
```

```
    // Let us know if the user responded or if we timed out
    MessageBox(
        NULL, (g_nSecLeft == 1) ? TEXT("Timeout") : TEXT("User responded"),
        TEXT("Result"), MB_OK);

    return(0);
}


/////////////////////////////// End of File ///////////////////////////////
```

Before we move on to another scenario, let me point out a couple of additional items. Setting a periodic timer guarantees that your work item is queued at every interval. If you create a periodic timer that fires every 10 seconds, your callback function is called every 10 seconds. Be aware that this could happen using multiple threads within the thread pool; you might have to synchronize portions of your work item function. Also, notice that if the thread pool is overloaded, the timer work item might be delayed. For example, if you've set the maximum number of threads in your pool to a low number, the thread pool will have to delay invoking your callback function.

If you don't like this behavior and prefer that your lengthy work items be queued 10 seconds after each one executes, you have to follow another path and build a kind of smart one-shot timer:

1. You change nothing during the creation of the timer by using **CreateThreadpoolTimer**.

2. Call **SetThreadpoolTimer**, but passing **0** as the **msPeriod** parameter to indicate a one-shot timer.

3. When the work to be done is finished, you restart the timer with the same **msPeriod** parameter set to **0**.

4. Last but not least, when the time comes to definitively stop the timer, before executing **CloseThreadpoolTimer**, call **WaitForThreadpoolTimerCallbacks** with **TRUE** as the last parameter to tell the thread pool that no more work items should be processed for this timer. If you forget to do so, the callback gets called and an exception is triggered when **SetThreadpoolTimer** executes.

Notice that if you really need a one-shot timer, call **SetThreadpoolTimer** with **0** as the **msPeriod** parameter and in the callback, destroy the timer with **CloseThreadpoolTimer** before returning to be sure to clean up the thread pool resources.

Scenario 3: Call a Function When a Single Kernel Object Becomes Signaled

Microsoft discovered that many applications spawn threads simply to wait for a kernel object to become signaled. Once the object is signaled, the thread posts some sort of notification to another thread and then loops back, waiting for the object to signal again. This is exactly the scenario you saw earlier in the Batch example, where a dedicated work item was needed to monitor when the real actions were finished by waiting for kernel events signaled when each real action callback ended. Some developers even write code in which several threads wait on a single object. This is incredibly wasteful of system resources. Sure, there is a lot less overhead involved in creating threads than with creating processes, but threads are not free. Each thread has a stack, and a lot of CPU instructions are required to create and destroy threads. You should always try to minimize this.

If you want to register a work item to be executed when a kernel object is signaled, you follow a workflow quite similar to what we've already discussed in this chapter. First, you write a function that matches the following prototype:

```
VOID CALLBACK WaitCallback(
    PTP_CALLBACK_INSTANCE pInstance,  // See "Callback Termination Actions" section
    PVOID Context,
    PTP_WAIT Wait,
    TP_WAIT_RESULT WaitResult);
```

Then you create a thread pool wait object by calling **CreateThreadpoolWait**:

```
PTP_WAIT CreateThreadpoolWait(
    PTP_WAIT_CALLBACK    pfnWaitCallback,
    PVOID                pvContext,
    PTP_CALLBACK_ENVIRON pcbe);  // See "Customized Thread Pools" section
```

Then, when ready, you bind a kernel object to this thread pool wait object by calling the following function:

```
VOID SetThreadpoolWait(
    PTP_WAIT  pWaitItem,
    HANDLE    hObject,
    PFILETIME pftTimeout);
```

Obviously, the **pWaitItem** parameter identifies the object returned from **CreateThreadpool-Wait**. The **hObject** parameter identifies some kernel object that, when signaled, causes the thread pool to invoke your **WaitCallback** function. And, the **pftTimeout** parameter indicates how long the thread pool should wait for the kernel object to become signaled. Pass **0** to not wait at all, pass a negative value to indicate a relative time, pass a positive value to indicate an absolute time, and pass **NULL** to indicate an infinite amount of time.

Internally, the thread pool has one thread that calls the **WaitForMultipleObjects** function (discussed in Chapter 9), passing in to it the set of handles that have been registered via the **SetThreadpoolWait** function and **FALSE** for its **bWaitAll** parameter so that the thread pool thread wakes up whenever any of the handles becomes signaled. Because **WaitForMultiple-Objects** has a limit of 64 (MAXIMUM_WAIT_OBJECTS) handles that it can wait on at once (as discussed in Chapter 9), the thread pool really uses one thread per 64 kernel objects, which is pretty efficient.

Also, because **WaitForMultipleObjects** doesn't allow you to pass the same handle to it multiple times, you should make sure that you do not use **SetThreadpoolWait** to register the same handle multiple times. However, you can call **DuplicateHandle** and register the original handle and the duplicated handle individually.

When the kernel object is signaled or when the timeout expires, some thread pool thread will invoke your **WaitCallback** function (shown earlier). Most of the parameters are self-explanatory, with the exception of the last parameter: **WaitResult**. The **WaitResult** parameter, of type

TP_WAIT_RESULT (which is itself a **DWORD**), indicates the reason why your **WaitCallback** function is being called. The possible values are shown in Table 11-1.

Table 11-1   Possible WaitResult Values

WaitResult Value	Explanation
WAIT_OBJECT_0	Your callback function receives this value if the kernel object passed to **SetThreadpoolWait** has been signaled before the specified timeout has elapsed.
WAIT_TIMEOUT	Your callback function receives this value if the kernel object passed to **SetThreadpoolWait** has not been signaled before the specified time-out has elapsed.
WAIT_ABANDONED_0	Your callback function receives this value if the kernel object passed to **SetThreadpoolWait** refers to a mutex and the mutex was abandoned, as explained in "Abandonment Issues" on page 267.

Once a thread pool thread calls your callback function, the corresponding wait item is inactive. "Inactive" means that you need to register it again by making another call to **SetThreadpoolWait** if you want your callback function called again when the same kernel object gets signaled.

Let's say that you register a wait on a process kernel object. Once that process object becomes signaled, it stays signaled. In this case, you wouldn't want to register the wait item again with the same process handle. However, you can reuse the wait item by calling **SetThreadpoolWait**, passing a different kernel object handle or simply passing **NULL** to remove it from the pool.

Finally, you can have a thread wait for the wait item to complete by calling **WaitForThreadpool-WaitCallbacks** and you free the wait item's memory by calling the **CloseThreadpoolWait** function. These two functions work similarly to the **WaitForThreadpoolWork** and **Close-ThreadpoolWork** functions discussed earlier in this chapter.

> **Note**   Never have your callback method call **WaitForThreadpoolWork** passing a reference to its own work item, as that will cause a deadlock situation. This happens because the thread will block until it exits, which it can't do at this point. Also, you should make sure that the kernel object handle you pass to **SetThreadpoolWait** is not closed while the thread pool is still waiting on it. Finally, you probably do not want to signal a registered event by using **PulseEvent**, as there is no guarantee that the thread pool is actually waiting for the event at the moment **PulseEvent** is called.

Scenario 4: Call a Function When Asynchronous I/O Requests Complete

In Chapter 10, I talked about how to perform asynchronous I/O operations efficiently using the Windows I/O completion port. In that chapter, I explained how you could create a thread pool where the threads wait on the I/O completion port. Fortunately, the thread pool being discussed throughout this chapter manages the creation and destruction of threads for you, and these threads internally wait on an I/O completion port. However, when you open a file or device, you must associate the file/device with the thread pool's I/O completion port. Then you must tell the thread pool which function of yours to invoke when the asynchronous I/O operations you make of the file/device complete.

First, you must write a function that matches the following prototype:

```
VOID CALLBACK OverlappedCompletionRoutine(
    PTP_CALLBACK_INSTANCE pInstance,    // See "Callback Termination Actions" section
    PVOID                 pvContext,
    PVOID                 pOverlapped,
    ULONG                 IoResult,
    ULONG_PTR             NumberOfBytesTransferred,
    PTP_IO                pIo);
```

When an I/O operation completes, this method will be passed a pointer to the **OVERLAPPED** structure you used when calling **ReadFile** or **WriteFile** to initiate the I/O operation (via the **pOverlapped** parameter). The result of the operation is passed via the **IoResult** parameter; if the I/O was successful, this parameter will contain **NO_ERROR**. The number of bytes transferred is passed via the **NumberOfBytesTransferred** parameter, and a pointer to the thread pool's I/O item is passed via the **pIo** parameter. The **pInstance** parameter is described in "Callback Termination Actions" on the next page.

Then you create a thread pool I/O object by calling **CreateThreadpoolIo**, passing into it the handle of the file/device (opened by calling the **CreateFile** function with the **FILE_FLAG_OVER-LAPPED** flag) that you want to associate with the thread pool's internal I/O completion port:

```
PTP_IO CreateThreadpoolIo(
    HANDLE                hDevice,
    PTP_WIN32_IO_CALLBACK pfnIoCallback,
    PVOID                 pvContext,
    PTP_CALLBACK_ENVIRON  pcbe);  // See "Customized Thread Pools" section
```

Then, when ready, you associate the file/device embedded in the I/O item with the thread pool's internal I/O completion port by calling the following function:

```
VOID StartThreadpoolIo(PTP_IO pio);
```

Note that you must call **StartThreadpoolIo** before every call to **ReadFile** and **WriteFile**. If you fail to call **StartThreadpoolIo** before issuing each I/O request, your **Overlapped-CompletionRoutine** callback function will not be called.

If you want to stop your callback function from getting called after issuing an I/O request, you can call this function:

```
VOID CancelThreadpoolIo(PTP_IO pio);
```

You must also call **CancelThreadpoolIo** if **ReadFile** or **WriteFile** fail to issue the request—for example, if either returns **FALSE** and **GetLastError** returns a value other than **ERROR_IO_PENDING**.

When you are finished using a file/device, you call **CloseHandle** to close it and you disassociate it from the thread pool by calling this function:

```
VOID CloseThreadpoolIo(PTP_IO pio);
```

And you can have another thread wait for an outstanding I/O request to complete by calling this function:

```
VOID WaitForThreadpoolIoCallbacks(
   PTP_IO pio,
   BOOL bCancelPendingCallbacks);
```

If **TRUE** is passed for the **bCancelPendingCallbacks** parameter, the completion will not be called (if it hasn't yet started). This is similar to calling the **CancelThreadpoolIo** function.

Callback Termination Actions

The thread pool makes it convenient for a callback method to describe some operations that should be performed as your callback function returns. Your callback function uses the opaque **pInstance** parameter (of the **PTP_CALLBACK_INSTANCE** data type), which is passed to it to call one of the following functions:

```
VOID LeaveCriticalSectionWhenCallbackReturns(
   PTP_CALLBACK_INSTANCE pci, PCRITICAL_SECTION pcs);
VOID ReleaseMutexWhenCallbackReturns(PTP_CALLBACK_INSTANCE pci, HANDLE mut);
VOID ReleaseSemaphoreWhenCallbackReturns(PTP_CALLBACK_INSTANCE pci,
   HANDLE sem, DWORD crel);
VOID SetEventWhenCallbackReturns(PTP_CALLBACK_INSTANCE pci, HANDLE evt);
VOID FreeLibraryWhenCallbackReturns(PTP_CALLBACK_INSTANCE pci, HMODULE mod);
```

As its name implies, the **pInstance** parameter identifies the instance of the work, timer, wait, or I/O item that the thread pool thread is currently processing. For each function in the preceding list, Table 11-2 indicates the corresponding termination action taken by the thread pool.

Table 11-2   Callback Termination Functions and Their Actions

Function	Termination Action
LeaveCriticalSection-WhenCallbackReturns	When the callback returns, the thread pool automatically calls **LeaveCriticalSection**, passing the specified **CRITICAL_SECTION** structure.
ReleaseMutex-WhenCallbackReturns	When the callback returns, the thread pool automatically calls **ReleaseMutex**, passing the specified **HANDLE**.
ReleaseSemaphore-WhenCallbackReturns	When the callback returns, the thread pool automatically calls **ReleaseSemaphore**, passing the specified **HANDLE**.
SetEvent-WhenCallbackReturns	When the callback returns, the thread pool automatically calls **SetEvent**, passing the specified **HANDLE**.
FreeLibrary-WhenCallbackReturns	When the callback returns, the thread pool automatically calls **FreeLibrary**, passing the specified **HMODULE**.

The first four functions give you a way to notify another thread that the thread pool thread's work item has completed some task. The last function (**FreeLibraryWhenCallbackReturns**) gives you a way to unload a dynamic-link library (DLL) when the callback function returns. This is particularly useful in the case where the callback function is implemented inside a DLL and you want the DLL unloaded after the callback function completes its work. Of course, you can't have the callback function itself call **FreeLibrary** because its code would then no longer exist in the process, causing an access violation to occur as soon as **FreeLibrary** tried to return back to the callback method.

> **Important**   Only one termination effect is applied by the thread pool thread for a given callback instance. So you cannot ask for an event and a mutex to be both signaled when your item has been processed. The last function you call overwrites the previous one.

In addition to these termination functions, there are two additional functions that apply to a callback instance:

```
BOOL CallbackMayRunLong(PTP_CALLBACK_INSTANCE pci);
VOID DisassociateCurrentThreadFromCallback(PTP_CALLBACK_INSTANCE pci);
```

The **CallbackMayRunLong** function isn't really about termination action so much as it is about notifying the thread pool about this item's processing behavior. A callback function should call the **CallbackMayRunLong** function if it thinks that processing will take a long time. The thread pool resists creating new threads, so a long-running item has the potential to starve other items that are queued in the thread pool. If **CallbackMayRunLong** returns **TRUE**, the thread pool has other threads in the thread pool capable of processing queued items. However, if **CallbackMayRunLong** returns **FALSE**, the thread pool does not have other threads available to process items, and to maintain an efficiently-running thread pool, it would be best for this item to break up its work into smaller chunks (queuing each chunk separately to the thread pool). The first chunk of work can execute using the current thread.

A callback method calls the fairly advanced **DisassociateCurrentThreadFromCallback** function to inform the thread pool that it has logically finished its work, allowing any thread that might be blocked inside a call to **WaitForThreadpoolWorkCallbacks**, **WaitForThreadpoolTimer-Callbacks**, **WaitForThreadpoolWaitCallbacks**, or **WaitForThreadpoolIoCallbacks** to return early without waiting for the thread pool thread to actually return from its callback function.

Customized Thread Pools

Whenever you call **CreateThreadpoolWork**, **CreateThreadpoolTimer**, **CreateThreadpool-Wait**, or **CreateThreadpoolIo**, you have the opportunity to pass a **PTP_CALLBACK_ENVIRON** parameter. When you pass **NULL** for this parameter, you are queuing up your item to your process' default thread pool, which is configured in such a way as to work well with most applications.

However, at times you might want to use a thread pool that is configured specially for your application's needs. For example, you might want to modify the minimum or maximum number of running threads in the pool. Or perhaps your application would just benefit from having multiple thread pools within it that can be created and destroyed independently of each other.

You can create a new thread pool in your application by calling the following function:

```
PTP_POOL CreateThreadpool(PVOID reserved);
```

Currently, the **reserved** parameter is, well, reserved, and therefore you should pass **NULL**. This parameter might become meaningful in a future version of Windows. This function returns a

PTP_POOL value that refers to a new thread pool. You can now set the minimum and maximum number of threads in the thread pool by calling these functions:

```
BOOL SetThreadpoolThreadMinimum(PTP_POOL pThreadPool, DWORD cthrdMin);
BOOL SetThreadpoolThreadMaximum(PTP_POOL pThreadPool, DWORD cthrdMost);
```

The thread pool always keeps the specified minimum number of threads around in the pool and allows the number of threads in the pool to grow to the maximum number of threads specified. By the way, the default thread pool has the minimum number of threads set to 1 and its maximum number of threads set to 500.

In some rare scenarios, Windows cancels a request for information if the thread making the request terminates. Let's take the **RegNotifyChangeKeyValue** function as an example. When a thread calls this function, it passes a handle to an event that Windows will set when some registry value changes. However, if the thread that called the **RegNotifyChangeKeyValue** function terminates, Windows will no longer set the event.

Thread pools create and destroy their threads whenever they feel it's necessary to improve efficiency. So, if a thread pool thread were to call the **RegNotifyChangeKeyValue** function, it is possible (and even likely) that the thread pool would terminate this thread at some point and Windows would no longer notify the application that the registry has changed. Perhaps the best way to solve this particular problem is by calling **CreateThread** to create a dedicated thread whose purpose is to call the **RegNotifyChangeKeyValue** function and not terminate. However, another solution would be to create a thread pool specifying the same number for the minimum and maximum number of threads. This way, the thread pool creates a set of threads that are never destroyed. Now, you can have a thread pool thread call a function such as **RegNotifyChangeKey-Value** and be assured that Windows will always notify your application whenever the registry changes.

When your application no longer needs a customized thread pool that it has created, it should destroy the thread pool by calling **CloseThreadpool**:

```
VOID CloseThreadpool(PTP_POOL pThreadPool);
```

After calling this function, no more items can be queued to the thread pool. Any thread pool threads that are currently processing items complete their processing and then terminate. Also, any items still in the thread pool that have not started processing will be canceled.

Once you have created your own thread pool and specified the minimum and maximum number of threads it can have, you can initialize a *callback environment* that contains some additional settings or configuration that can apply to a work item.

The WinNT.h header file defines a thread pool callback environment data structure as follows:

```
typedef struct _TP_CALLBACK_ENVIRON {
    TP_VERSION                        Version;
    PTP_POOL                          Pool;
    PTP_CLEANUP_GROUP                 CleanupGroup;
    PTP_CLEANUP_GROUP_CANCEL_CALLBACK CleanupGroupCancelCallback;
    PVOID                             RaceDll;
    struct _ACTIVATION_CONTEXT       *ActivationContext;
    PTP_SIMPLE_CALLBACK               FinalizationCallback;
```

```
  union {
    DWORD                              Flags;
    struct {
      DWORD                                LongFunction :  1;
      DWORD                                Private      : 31;
    } s;
  } u;
} TP_CALLBACK_ENVIRON, *PTP_CALLBACK_ENVIRON;
```

Although you can examine this data structure and manipulate its fields manually, you should not. You should think of the data structure as being opaque, and you should manipulate its fields by calling various functions defined in the WinBase.h header file. To initialize the structure to a known good state, you first call the following function:

```
VOID InitializeThreadpoolEnvironment(PTP_CALLBACK_ENVIRON pcbe);
```

This inline function sets all the fields to **0**, except **Version**, which gets set to **1**. As always, when you no longer need to use a thread pool callback environment, you should clean it up nicely by calling **DestroyThreadpoolEnvironment**:

```
VOID DestroyThreadpoolEnvironment(PTP_CALLBACK_ENVIRON pcbe);
```

To submit a work item to a thread pool, the environment must indicate which thread pool should process the item. You can specify a particular thread pool by calling **SetThreadpoolCallback-Pool**, passing it a **PTP_POOL** value (returned by **CreateThreadpool**):

```
VOID SetThreadpoolCallbackPool(PTP_CALLBACK_ENVIRON pcbe, PTP_POOL pThreadPool);
```

If you do not call **SetThreadpoolCallbackPool**, the **TP_CALLBACK_ENVIRON**'s Pool field remains **NULL** and work items queued using this environment are queued to the process' default thread pool.

Call the **SetThreadpoolCallbackRunsLong** function to tell the environment that items typically take a long time to process. This causes the thread pool to create threads more quickly in an attempt to service items more fairly rather than most efficiently:

```
VOID SetThreadpoolCallbackRunsLong(PTP_CALLBACK_ENVIRON pcbe);
```

Call the **SetThreadpoolCallbackLibrary** function to ensure that a particular DLL remains loaded in the process' address space while outstanding items exist in the thread pool:

```
VOID SetThreadpoolCallbackLibrary(PTP_CALLBACK_ENVIRON pcbe, PVOID mod);
```

Basically, the **SetThreadpoolCallbackLibrary** function exists to remove the potential for a race condition that might result in a deadlock. This is a pretty advanced feature; see the Platform SDK documentation for more information about it.

Gracefully Destroying a Thread Pool: Cleanup Groups

Thread pools handle lots of items being queued into them from various sources. This can make it difficult to know exactly when a thread pool is finished with items so that it can be destroyed gracefully. To help coordinate graceful thread pool cleanup, the thread pool offers *cleanup groups*. Note that the discussion in this section doesn't apply to the default thread pool, as it cannot be destroyed. It lives as long as the lifetime of the process, and Windows destroys and cleans up everything when a process terminates.

In this section, we've already talked about how to initialize a **TP_CALLBACK_ENVIRON** structure, which can be used when queuing items to a private thread pool. To gracefully destroy a private thread pool, you'll first need to create a cleanup group by calling **CreateThreadpoolCleanup-Group**:

```
PTP_CLEANUP_GROUP CreateThreadpoolCleanupGroup();
```

Then associate this cleanup group with an already pool-bound **TP_CALLBACK_ENVIRON** structure by calling the following function:

```
VOID SetThreadpoolCallbackCleanupGroup(
  PTP_CALLBACK_ENVIRON pcbe,
  PTP_CLEANUP_GROUP ptpcg,
  PTP_CLEANUP_GROUP_CANCEL_CALLBACK pfng);
```

Internally, this function sets the **PTP_CALLBACK_ENVIRON** structure's **CleanupGroup** and **CleanupGroupCancelCallback** fields. When you call this function, the **pfng** parameter can identify the address of a callback function that will be called if the cleanup group is canceled. If you specify a non-**NULL** value for the **pfng** parameter, the function must have the following prototype:

```
VOID CALLBACK CleanupGroupCancelCallback(
  PVOID pvObjectContext,
  PVOID pvCleanupContext);
```

Each time you call **CreateThreadpoolWork**, **CreateThreadpoolTimer**, **CreateThreadpool-Wait**, or **CreateThreadpoolIo** while passing a non-**NULL** pointer to a **PTP_CALLBACK_ENVIRON** for the last parameter, the item created is added to the corresponding callback environment's cleanup group to indicate a potentially queued item that is being added to the pool. After each of these items completes, if you call **CloseThreadpoolWork**, **CloseThreadpoolTimer**, **Close-ThreadpoolWait**, and **CloseThreadpoolIo**, you are implicitly removing each item from the cleanup group.

Now, when your application wants to destroy the thread pool, it can call this function:

```
VOID CloseThreadpoolCleanupGroupMembers(
  PTP_CLEANUP_GROUP ptpcg,
  BOOL bCancelPendingCallbacks,
  PVOID pvCleanupContext);
```

This function is similar to the various **WaitForThreadpool*** functions (such as **WaitForThread-poolWork**) we've already discussed in this chapter. When a thread calls **CloseThreadpool-CleanupGroupMembers**, the function waits until all the items remaining in the thread pool's work group (that is, the items that have been created but have not yet been closed) are finished processing. Optionally, the caller can pass **TRUE** for the **bCancelPendingCallbacks** parameter, which will simply cancel all the submitted work items that have not been processed yet, and the function will return after all the currently-running items have completed. If **TRUE** is passed for the **bCancel-PendingCallbacks** parameter and if the address of a **CleanupGroupCancelCallback** function was passed to the **SetThreadpoolCallbackCleanupGroup**'s **pfng** parameter, your function will be called once for each item being canceled. In your **CleanupGroupCancelCallback** function, the **pvObjectContext** parameter will contain the context of each item being canceled. (The context is set via the **CreateThreadpool*** function's **pvContext** parameter). In your **CleanupGroup-CancelCallback** function, the **pvCleanupContext** parameter will contain the context that was passed via the **CloseThreadpoolCleanupGroupMembers** function's **pvCleanupContext** parameter.

If you call **CloseThreadpoolCleanupGroupMembers**, passing **FALSE** for the **bCancelPending-Callbacks** parameter, before returning, the thread pool will take the time to process all the remaining queued items. Notice that you can pass **NULL** for the **pvCleanupContext** parameter because your **CleanupGroupCancelCallback** function will never be called.

After all the work items are either canceled or processed, you then call **CloseThreadpool-CleanupGroup** to release the resources owned by the cleanup group:

```
VOID WINAPI CloseThreadpoolCleanupGroup(PTP_CLEANUP_GROUP ptpcg);
```

Finally, you can call **DestroyThreadpoolEnvironment** and **CloseThreadpool**; the thread pool is now gracefully shut down.

Chapter 12
Fibers

Microsoft added fibers to Windows to make it easy to port existing UNIX server applications to Windows. UNIX server applications are single-threaded (by the Windows definition) but can serve multiple clients. In other words, the developers of UNIX applications have created their own threading architecture library, which they use to simulate pure threads. This threading package creates multiple stacks, saves certain CPU registers, and switches among them to service the client requests.

Obviously, to get the best performance, these UNIX applications must be redesigned; the simulated threading library should be replaced with the pure threads offered by Windows. However, this redesign can take several months or longer to complete, so companies are first porting their existing UNIX code to Windows so that they can ship something to the Windows market.

Problems can arise when you port UNIX code to Windows. In particular, the way in which Windows manages a thread stack is much more complex than simply allocating memory. Windows stacks start out with relatively little physical storage and grow as necessary. This process is described in Chapter 16, "A Thread's Stack." Porting is also complicated by the structured exception-handling mechanism (described in Chapter 23, "Termination Handlers," Chapter 24, "Exception Handlers and Software Exceptions," and Chapter 25, "Unhandled Exceptions, Vectored Exception Handling, and C++ Exceptions").

To help companies port their code more quickly and correctly to Windows, Microsoft added fibers to the operating system. In this chapter, we'll examine the concept of a fiber, the functions that manipulate fibers, and how to take advantage of fibers. Keep in mind, of course, that you should avoid fibers in favor of more properly designed applications that use Windows native threads.

Working with Fibers

The first thing to note is that the Windows kernel implements threads. The operating system has intimate knowledge of threads, and it schedules them according to the algorithm defined by Microsoft. A fiber is implemented in user-mode code; the kernel does not have knowledge of fibers, and they are scheduled according to the algorithm you define. Because you define the fiber-scheduling algorithm, fibers are nonpreemptively scheduled as far as the kernel is concerned.

The next thing to be aware of is that a single thread can contain one or more fibers. As far as the kernel is concerned, a thread is preemptively scheduled and is executing code. However, the thread executes one fiber's code at a time—you decide which fiber. (These concepts will become clearer as we go on.)

The first step you must perform when you use fibers is to turn your existing thread into a fiber. You do this by calling **ConvertThreadToFiber**:

```
PVOID ConvertThreadToFiber(PVOID pvParam);
```

This function allocates memory (about 200 bytes) for the fiber's execution context. This execution context consists of the following elements:

- A user-defined value that is initialized to the value passed to **ConvertThreadToFiber**'s **pvParam** argument
- The head of a structured exception-handling chain
- The top and bottom memory addresses of the fiber's stack (When you convert a thread to a fiber, this is also the thread's stack.)
- Various CPU registers, including a stack pointer, an instruction pointer, and others

By default, on an x86 system, the CPU's floating-point state information is not part of the CPU registers that are maintained on a per-fiber basis, which can cause data corruption to occur if your fiber performs floating-point operations. To override the default, you should call the new **ConvertThreadToFiberEx** function, which allows you to pass **FIBER_FLAG_FLOAT_SWITCH** for the **dwFlags** parameter:

```
PVOID ConvertThreadToFiberEx(
    PVOID pvParam,
    DWORD dwFlags);
```

After you allocate and initialize the fiber execution context, you associate the address of the execution context with the thread. The thread has been converted to a fiber, and the fiber is running on this thread. **ConvertThreadToFiber** actually returns the memory address of the fiber's execution context. You need to use this address later, but you should never read from or write to the execution context data yourself—the fiber functions manipulate the contents of the structure for you when necessary. Now if your fiber (thread) returns or calls **ExitThread**, the fiber and thread both die.

There is no reason to convert a thread to a fiber unless you plan to create additional fibers to run on the same thread. To create another fiber, the thread (the currently running fiber) calls **CreateFiber**:

```
PVOID CreateFiber(
    DWORD dwStackSize,
    PFIBER_START_ROUTINE pfnStartAddress,
    PVOID pvParam);
```

CreateFiber first attempts to create a new stack whose size is indicated by the **dwStackSize** parameter. Usually 0 is passed, which, by default, creates a stack that can grow to 1 MB in size but initially has two pages of storage committed to it. If you specify a nonzero size, a stack is reserved and committed using the specified size. If you are using a lot of fibers, you might want to consume less memory for their respective stacks. In that case, instead of calling **CreateFiber**, you can use the following function:

```
PVOID CreateFiberEx(
    SIZE_T dwStackCommitSize,
    SIZE_T dwStackReserveSize,
    DWORD dwFlags,
    PFIBER_START_ROUTINE pStartAddress,
    PVOID pvParam);
```

The **dwStackCommitSize** parameter sets the part of the stack that is initially committed. The **dwStackReserveSize** parameter allows you to reserve an amount of virtual memory. The **dwFlags** parameter accepts the same **FIBER_FLAG_FLOAT_SWITCH** value as **ConvertThreadTo-FiberEx** does to add the floating-point state to the fiber context. The other parameters are the same as for **CreateFiber**.

Next, **CreateFiber(Ex)** allocates a new fiber execution context structure and initializes it. The user-defined value is set to the value passed to the **pvParam** parameter, the top and bottom memory addresses of the new stack are saved, and the memory address of the fiber function (passed as the **pfnStartAddress** argument) is saved.

The **pfnStartAddress** argument specifies the address of a fiber routine that you must implement and that must have the following prototype:

```
VOID WINAPI FiberFunc(PVOID pvParam);
```

When the fiber is scheduled for the first time, this function executes and is passed the **pvParam** value that was originally passed to **CreateFiber**. You can do whatever you like in this fiber function. However, the function is prototyped as returning **VOID**—not because the return value has no meaning, but because this function should never return at all! If a fiber function does return, the thread and all the fibers created on it are destroyed immediately.

Like **ConvertThreadToFiber(Ex)**, **CreateFiber(Ex)** returns the memory address of the fiber's execution context. However, unlike **ConvertThreadToFiber(Ex)**, this new fiber does not execute because the currently running fiber is still executing. Only one fiber at a time can execute on a single thread. To make the new fiber execute, you call **SwitchToFiber**:

```
VOID SwitchToFiber(PVOID pvFiberExecutionContext);
```

SwitchToFiber takes a single parameter, **pvFiberExecutionContext**, which is the memory address of a fiber's execution context as returned by a previous call to **ConvertThreadTo-Fiber(Ex)** or **CreateFiber(Ex)**. This memory address tells the function which fiber to schedule. Internally, **SwitchToFiber** performs the following steps:

1. It saves some of the current CPU registers, including the instruction pointer register and the stack pointer register, in the currently running fiber's execution context.

2. It loads the registers previously saved in the soon-to-be-running fiber's execution context into the CPU registers. These registers include the stack pointer register so that this fiber's stack is used when the thread continues execution.

3. It associates the fiber's execution context with the thread; the thread runs the specified fiber.

4. It sets the thread's instruction pointer to the saved instruction pointer. The thread (fiber) continues execution where this fiber last executed.

SwitchToFiber is the only way for a fiber to get any CPU time. Because your code must explicitly call **SwitchToFiber** at the appropriate times, you are in complete control of the fiber scheduling. Keep in mind that fiber scheduling has nothing to do with thread scheduling. The thread that the fibers run on can always be preempted by the operating system. When the thread is scheduled, the currently selected fiber runs—no other fiber runs unless **SwitchToFiber** is explicitly called.

To destroy a fiber, you call **DeleteFiber**:

```
VOID DeleteFiber(PVOID pvFiberExecutionContext);
```

This function deletes the fiber indicated by the **pvFiberExecutionContext** parameter, which is, of course, the address of a fiber's execution context. This function frees the memory used by the fiber's stack and then destroys the fiber's execution context. But if you pass the address of the fiber that is currently associated with the thread, the function calls **ExitThread** internally, which causes the thread and all the fibers created on the thread to die.

DeleteFiber is usually called by one fiber to delete another. The deleted fiber's stack is destroyed, and the fiber's execution context is freed. Notice the difference here between fibers and threads: threads usually kill themselves by calling **ExitThread**. In fact, it is considered bad form for one thread to terminate another thread using **TerminateThread**. If you do call **TerminateThread**, the system does not destroy the terminated thread's stack. We can take advantage of this ability of a fiber to cleanly delete another fiber—I'll discuss how when I explain the sample application later in this chapter. When all fibers are deleted, it is also possible to remove the fiber state from the original thread that called **ConvertThreadToFiber(Ex)** by using **ConvertFiberToThread**, releasing the last pieces of memory that made the thread a fiber.

If you need to store information on a per-fiber basis, you can use the *Fiber Local Storage*, or FLS, functions. These functions do for fibers what the TLS functions (discussed in Chapter 6, "Thread Basics") do for threads. You first call **FlsAlloc** to allocate an FLS slot that can be used by all fibers running in the current process. This function takes a single parameter: a callback function that is called either when a fiber gets destroyed or when the FLS slot is deleted by a call to **FlsFree**. You store per-fiber data in an FLS slot by calling **FlsSetValue**, and you retrieve it with **FlsGetValue**. If you need to know whether or not you are running in a fiber execution context, simply check the Boolean return value of **IsThreadAFiber**.

Several additional fiber functions are provided for your convenience. A thread can execute a single fiber at a time, and the operating system always knows which fiber is currently associated with the thread. If you want to get the address of the currently running fiber's execution context, you can call **GetCurrentFiber**:

```
PVOID GetCurrentFiber();
```

The other convenient function is **GetFiberData**:

```
PVOID GetFiberData();
```

As I've mentioned, each fiber's execution context contains a user-defined value. This value is initialized with the value that is passed as the **pvParam** argument to **ConvertThreadToFiber(Ex)** or **CreateFiber(Ex)**. This value is also passed as an argument to a fiber function. **GetFiberData** simply looks in the currently executing fiber's execution context and returns the saved value.

Both **GetCurrentFiber** and **GetFiberData** are fast and are usually implemented as intrinsic functions, which means that the compiler generates the code for these functions inline.

The Counter Sample Application

The Counter application (12-Counter.exe), which produces the dialog box shown in Figure 12-1, uses fibers to implement background processing. When you run the application, the dialog box appears. (I recommend that you run the application to really understand what's happening and to see the behavior as you read along.)

Figure 12-1   The Counter application's dialog box

You can think of this application as a superminiature spreadsheet consisting of two cells. The first cell is a writable cell implemented as an edit control (labeled Count To), and the second cell is a read-only cell implemented as a static control (labeled Answer). When you change the number in the edit control, the Answer cell automatically recalculates. For this simple application, the recalculation is a counter that starts at 0 and increments slowly until the value in the Answer cell becomes the same value as the entered number. For demonstration purposes, the static control at the bottom of the dialog box updates to indicate which fiber is currently executing. This fiber can be either the user interface fiber or the recalculation fiber.

To test the application, type **5** in the edit control. The Currently Running Fiber field changes to Recalculation, and the number in the Answer field slowly increments from 0 to 5. When the counting is finished, the Currently Running Fiber field changes back to User Interface and the thread goes to sleep. Now, in the edit control, type **0** after the 5 (making 50) and watch the counting start over from 0 and go to 50. But this time, while the Answer field increments, move the window on the screen. You'll notice that the recalculation fiber is preempted and that the user interface fiber is rescheduled so that the application's user interface stays responsive to the user. When you stop moving the window, the recalculation fiber is rescheduled and the Answer field continues counting from where it left off.

One last thing to test: while the recalculation fiber is counting, change the number in the edit control. Again, notice that the user interface is responsive to your input—but also notice that when you stop typing, the recalculation fiber starts counting from the beginning. This is exactly the kind of behavior that you want in a full-blown spreadsheet application.

Keep in mind that no critical sections or other thread synchronization objects are used in this application—everything is done using a single thread consisting of two fibers.

Let's discuss how this application is implemented. When the process' primary thread starts by executing **_tWinMain** (at the end of the listing), **ConvertThreadToFiber** is called to turn the thread into a fiber and to allow us to create another fiber later. Then a modeless dialog box is created, which is the application's main window. Next, a state variable is initialized to indicate the background processing state (BPS). This state variable is the **bps** member contained in the global **g_FiberInfo** variable. Three states are possible, as described in Table 12-1.

Table 12-1   Possible States for the Counter Application

State	Description
BPS_DONE	The recalculation ran to completion, and the user has not changed anything that would require a recalculation.
BPS_STARTOVER	The user has changed something that requires a recalculation to start from the beginning.
BPS_CONTINUE	The recalculation was started but has not finished. Also, the user has not changed anything that would require the recalculation to start over from the beginning.

The background processing state variable is examined in the thread's message loop, which is more complicated than a normal message loop. Here is what the message loop does:

- If a window message exists (the user interface is active), it processes the message. Keeping the user interface responsive is always a higher priority than recalculating values.

- If the user interface has nothing to do, it checks to see whether any recalculations need to be performed. (The background processing state is **BPS_STARTOVER** or **BPS_CONTINUE**.)

- If there are no recalculations to do (**BPS_DONE**), it suspends the thread by calling **WaitMessage**; only a user interface event can cause a recalculation to be required.

- If the dialog box is dismissed, it stops the calculation fiber with **DeleteFiber** and **ConvertFiberToThread** is called to clean up the user interface (UI) fiber and return in a non-fiber mode before **_WinMain** exits.

If the user-interface fiber has nothing to do and the user has just changed the value in the edit control, we need to start the recalculation over from the beginning (**BPS_STARTOVER**). The first thing to realize is that we might already have a recalculation fiber running. If this is the case, we must delete the fiber and create a new fiber that will start counting from the beginning. The user interface fiber calls **DeleteFiber** to destroy the existing recalculation fiber. This is where fibers (as opposed to threads) come in handy. Deleting the recalculation fiber is perfectly OK: the fiber's stack and execution context are completely and cleanly destroyed. If we were to use threads instead of fibers, the user interface thread would not destroy the recalculation thread cleanly—we'd have to use some form of interthread communication and wait for the recalculation thread to die on its own. Once we know that no recalculation fiber exists, we need to switch the UI thread into fiber mode if this is not already the case. Then we can create a new recalculation fiber and set the background processing state to **BPS_CONTINUE**.

When the user interface is idle and the recalculation fiber has something to do, we schedule it time by calling **SwitchToFiber**. **SwitchToFiber** does not return until the recalculation fiber calls **SwitchToFiber** again, passing the address of the user interface fiber's execution context.

The **FiberFunc** function contains the code executed by the recalculation fiber. This fiber function is passed the address of the global **g_FiberInfo** structure so that it knows the handle of the dialog box window, the address of the user-interface fiber's execution context, and the current background processing state. The address of this structure need not be passed because it is in a global variable, but I wanted to demonstrate how to pass arguments to fiber functions. Besides, passing the address places fewer dependencies on the code, which is always a good practice.

The fiber function first updates the status control in the dialog box to indicate that the recalculation fiber is executing. Then it gets the number in the edit control and enters a loop that starts counting from 0 to the number. Each time the number is about to be incremented, **GetQueue-Status** is called to see whether any messages have shown up in the thread's message queue. (All fibers running on a single thread share the thread's message queue.) When a message shows up, the user-interface fiber has something to do; because we want the user-interface fiber to take priority over the recalculations, **SwitchToFiber** is called immediately so that the user-interface fiber can process the message. After the message has been processed, the user-interface fiber reschedules the recalculation fiber (as described earlier) and the background processing continues.

When there are no messages to be processed, the recalculation fiber updates the Answer field in the dialog box and then sleeps for 200 milliseconds. In production code, you should remove the call to **Sleep**; I include it here to exaggerate the time required to perform the recalculation.

When the recalculation fiber finishes calculating the answer, the background processing state variable is set to **BPS_DONE** and a call to **SwitchToFiber** reschedules the user-interface fiber. At this point, the calculation fiber is deleted, and the UI fiber is converted back to a thread. Now the user interface fiber has nothing to do; it calls **WaitMessage**, suspending the thread so that no CPU time is wasted.

Notice that each fiber stores in an FLS slot an identifier string ("User interface" or "Computation") that is printed to log different events, such as when a fiber is deleted or when the FLS slot gets destroyed thanks to the FLS callback that is set when the slot is allocated. This callback takes advantage of the **IsThreadAFiber** function to detect whether or not the FLS slot value can be used.

Part III
Memory Management

Chapter 13
Windows Memory Architecture

The memory architecture used by an operating system is the most important key to understanding how the operating system does what it does. When you start working with a new operating system, many questions come to mind. "How do I share data between two applications?", "Where does the system store the information I'm looking for?", and "How can I make my program run more efficiently?" are just a few.

I have found that more often than not, a good understanding of how the system manages memory can help determine the answers to these questions quickly and accurately. This chapter explores the memory architecture used by Microsoft Windows.

A Process' Virtual Address Space

Every process is given its very own virtual address space. For 32-bit processes, this address space is 4 GB because a 32-bit pointer can have any value from 0x00000000 through 0xFFFFFFFF. This range allows a pointer to have one of 4,294,967,296 values, which covers a process' 4-GB range. For 64-bit processes, this address space is 16 EB (exabytes) because a 64-bit pointer can have any value from 0x00000000'00000000 through 0xFFFFFFFF'FFFFFFFF. This range allows a pointer to have one of 18,446,744,073,709,551,616 values, which covers a process' 16-EB range. This is quite a range!

Because every process receives its own private address space, when a thread in a process is running, that thread can access memory that belongs only to its process. The memory that belongs to all other processes is hidden and inaccessible to the running thread.

Note In Windows, the memory belonging to the operating system itself is also hidden from the running thread, which means that the thread cannot accidentally access the operating system's data.

As I said, every process has its own private address space. Process A can have a data structure stored in its address space at address 0x12345678, while Process B can have a totally different data structure stored in *its* address space—at address 0x12345678. When threads running in Process A access memory at address 0x12345678, these threads are accessing Process A's data structure. When threads running in Process B access memory at address 0x12345678, these threads are accessing Process B's data structure. Threads running in Process A cannot access the data structure in Process B's address space, and vice versa.

Before you get all excited about having so much address space for your application, keep in mind that this is *virtual* address space—not physical storage. This address space is simply a range of memory addresses. Physical storage needs to be assigned or mapped to portions of the address space before you can successfully access data without raising access violations. We will discuss how this is done later in this chapter.

How a Virtual Address Space Is Partitioned

Each process' virtual address space is split into partitions. The address space is partitioned based on the underlying implementation of the operating system. Partitions vary slightly among the different Microsoft Windows kernels. Table 13-1 shows how each platform partitions a process' address space.

As you can see, the 32-bit Windows kernel and 64-bit Windows kernel have nearly identical partitions; what differs are the partition sizes and locations. Let's examine how the system uses each of these partitions.

Table 13-1   How a Process' Address Space Is Partitioned

Partition	x86 32-Bit Windows	x86 32-Bit Windows with 3 GB User-Mode	x64 64-Bit Windows	IA-64 64-Bit Windows
NULL-Pointer Assignment	0x00000000 0x0000FFFF	0x00000000 0x0000FFFF	0x00000000'00000000 0x00000000'0000FFFF	0x00000000'00000000 0x00000000'0000FFFF
User-Mode	0x00010000 0x7FFEFFFF	0x00010000 0xBFFEFFFF	0x00000000'00010000 0x000007FF'FFFEFFFF	0x00000000'00010000 0x000006FB'FFFEFFFF
64-KB Off-Limits	0x7FFF0000 0x7FFFFFFF	0xBFFF0000 0xBFFFFFFF	0x000007FF'FFFF0000 0x000007FF'FFFFFFFF	0x000006FB'FFFF0000 0x000006FB'FFFFFFFF
Kernel-Mode	0x80000000 0xFFFFFFFF	0xC0000000 0xFFFFFFFF	0x00000800'00000000 0xFFFFFFFF'FFFFFFFF	0x000006FC'00000000

Null-Pointer Assignment Partition

The partition of the process' address space from 0x00000000 to 0x0000FFFF inclusive is set aside to help programmers catch NULL-pointer assignments. If a thread in your process attempts to read from or write to a memory address in this partition, an access violation is raised.

Error checking is often not performed religiously in C/C++ programs. For example, the following code performs no error checking:

```
int* pnSomeInteger = (int*) malloc(sizeof(int));
*pnSomeInteger = 5;
```

If **malloc** cannot find enough memory to satisfy the request, it returns **NULL**. However, this code doesn't check for that possibility—it assumes that the allocation was successful and proceeds to access memory at address 0x00000000. Because this partition of the address space is off-limits, a memory access violation occurs and the process is terminated. This feature helps developers find bugs in their applications. Notice that you can't even reserve virtual memory in this address range with functions of the Win32 application programming interface (API).

User-Mode Partition

This partition is where the process' address space resides. The usable address range and approximate size of the user-mode partition depends on the CPU architecture, as shown in Table 13-2.

Table 13-2 CPU Architectures, Their Usable User-Mode Address Range and the Range's Size

CPU Architecture	Usable User-Mode Partition Address Range	Usable User-Mode Partition Size
*x*86 (normal)	0x00010000 → 0x7FFEFFFF	~2 GB
*x*86 w/3 GB	0x00010000 → 0xBFFFFFFF	~3 GB
*x*64	0x00000000'00010000 → 0x000007FF'FFFEFFFF	~8192 GB
IA-64	0x00000000'00010000 → 0x000006FB'FFFEFFFF	~7152 GB

A process cannot use pointers to read from, write to, or in any way access another process' data residing in this partition. For all applications, this partition is where the bulk of the process' data is maintained. Because each process gets its own partition for data, applications are far less likely to be corrupted by other applications, making the whole system more robust.

> **Note** In Windows, all .exe and dynamic-link library (DLL) modules load in this area. Each process might load these DLLs at a different address within this partition (although this is very unlikely). The system also maps all memory-mapped files accessible to this process within this partition.

When I first looked at my 32-bit process' address space, I was surprised to see that the amount of usable address space was less than half of my process' overall address space. After all, does the kernel-mode partition really need the top half of the address space? Actually, the answer is yes. The system needs this space for the kernel code, device driver code, device I/O cache buffers, non-paged pool allocations, process page tables, and so on. In fact, Microsoft is squeezing the kernel into this 2-GB space. In 64-bit Windows, the kernel finally gets the room it truly needs.

Getting a Larger User-Mode Partition in *x*86 Windows

Some applications, such as Microsoft SQL Server, would benefit from a user-mode address space larger than 2 GB in order to improve performance and scalability by having more application data addressable. So the *x*86 version of Windows offers a mode to increase the user-mode partition up to a maximum of 3 GB. To have all processes use a larger-than-2-GB user-mode partition and a smaller-than-1-GB kernel-mode partition, you need to configure the boot configuration data (BCD) in Windows and then reboot the machine. (Read the white paper available at *http://www.microsoft.com/whdc/system/platform/firmware/bcd.mspx* for more details about the BCD.)

To configure the BCD, you need to execute BCDEdit.exe with the /**set** switch with the **Increase-UserVA** parameter. For example, **bcdedit /set IncreaseUserVa 3072** tells Windows to reserve, for all processes, a 3-GB user-mode address space region and a 1-GB kernel-mode address space region. The "x86 w/3 GB" row in Table 13-2 shows how the address space looks when the **IncreaseUserVa** value is set to **3072**. The minimum value accepted for **IncreaseUserVa** is **2048**, corresponding to the 2-GB default. If you want to explicitly reset this parameter, execute the following command: **bcdedit /deletevalue IncreaseUserVa**.

> **Tip**   When you need to figure out the current value of the parameters of the BCD, simply type **bcdedit /enum** on the command line. (Go to *http://msdn2.microsoft.com/en-us/library/ aa906211.aspx* for more information about BCDEdit parameters.)

In early versions of Windows, Microsoft didn't allow applications to access their address space above 2 GB. So some creative developers decided to leverage this and, in their code, they would use the high bit in a pointer as a flag that had meaning only to their applications. Then when the application accessed the memory address, code executed that cleared the high bit of the pointer before the memory address was used. Well, as you can imagine, when an application runs in a user-mode environment greater than 2 GB, the application fails in a blaze of fire.

Microsoft had to create a solution that allowed this application to work in a large user-mode address space environment. When the system is about to run an application, it checks to see if the application was linked with the /**LARGEADDRESSAWARE** linker switch. If so, the application is claiming that it does not do anything funny with memory addresses and is fully prepared to take advantage of a large user-mode address space. On the other hand, if the application was not linked with the /**LARGEADDRESSAWARE** switch, the operating system reserves any user-mode space between 2 GB and the start of kernel mode. This prevents any memory allocations from being created at a memory address whose high bit is set.

Note that all the code and data required by the kernel is squeezed tightly into a 2-GB partition. So reducing the kernel address space to less than 2 GB restricts the number of threads, stacks, and other resources that the system can create. In addition, the system can use a maximum of only 64 GB of RAM, unlike the 128-GB maximum available when the default of 2 GB is used.

> **Note**   An executable's **LARGEADDRESSAWARE** flag is checked when the operating system creates the process' address space. The system ignores this flag for DLLs. DLLs *must* be written to behave correctly in a large 2+ GB user-mode partition or their behavior is undefined.

Getting a 2-GB User-Mode Partition in 64-Bit Windows

Microsoft realizes that many developers will want to port their existing 32-bit applications to a 64-bit environment as quickly and easily as possible. However, there is a lot of source code in which pointers are assumed to be 32-bit values. Simply rebuilding the application will cause pointer truncation errors and improper memory accesses.

However, if the system could somehow guarantee that no memory allocations would ever be made above 0x00000000'7FFFFFFF, the application would work fine. Truncating a 64-bit address to a

32-bit address when the high 33 bits are 0 causes no problem whatsoever. The system can provide this guarantee by running the application in an *address space sandbox* that limits a process' usable address space to the bottom 2 GB.

By default, when you invoke a 64-bit application, the system reserves all the user-mode address space starting at 0x0000000'80000000. This ensures that all memory allocations are created in the bottom 2 GB of the 64-bit address space. This is the address space sandbox. For most applications, this is more than enough address space anyway. To allow a 64-bit application to access its full user-mode partition, the application must be built using the **/LARGEADDRESSAWARE** linker switch.

> **Note** An executable's **LARGEADDRESSAWARE** flag is checked when the operating system creates the process' 64-bit address space. The system ignores this flag for DLLs. DLLs *must* be written to behave correctly in a full 4-TB user-mode partition or their behavior is undefined.

Kernel-Mode Partition

This partition is where the operating system's code resides. The code for thread scheduling, memory management, file systems support, networking support, and all device drivers is loaded in this partition. Everything residing in this partition is shared among all processes. Although this partition is just above the user-mode partition in every process, all code and data in this partition is completely protected. If your application code attempts to read or write to a memory address in this partition, your thread raises an access violation. By default, the access violation causes the system to display a message box to the user, and then the system terminates your application. See Chapter 23, "Termination Handlers," Chapter 24, "Exception Handlers and Software Exceptions," and Chapter 25, "Unhandled Exceptions, Vectored Exception Handling, and C++ Exceptions," for more information about access violations and how to handle them.

> **Note** In 64-bit Windows, the 8-TB user-mode partition looks greatly out of proportion to the 16,777,208-TB kernel-mode partition. It's not that the kernel-mode partition requires all of this virtual address space. It's just that a 64-bit address space is enormous and most of that address space is unused. The system allows our applications to use 8 TB and allows the kernel to use what it needs; the majority of the kernel-mode partition is just not used. Fortunately, the system does not require any internal data structures to maintain the unused portions of the kernel-mode partition.

Regions in an Address Space

When a process is created and given its address space, the bulk of this usable address space is *free*, or unallocated. To use portions of this address space, you must allocate regions within it by calling **VirtualAlloc** (discussed in Chapter 15, "Using Virtual Memory in Your Own Applications"). The act of allocating a region is called *reserving*.

Whenever you reserve a region of address space, the system ensures that the region begins on an *allocation granularity* boundary. The allocation granularity can vary from one CPU platform to another. However, as of this writing, all the CPU platforms use the same allocation granularity of 64 KB—that is, allocation requests are rounded to a 64-KB boundary.

When you reserve a region of address space, the system ensures that the size of the region is a multiple of the system's *page* size. A page is a unit of memory that the system uses in managing memory. Like the allocation granularity, the page size can vary from one CPU to another. The *x86* and *x64* systems use a 4-KB page size, but the IA-64 uses an 8-KB page size.

> **Note**   Sometimes the system reserves regions of address space on behalf of your process. For example, the system allocates a region of address space to store a *process environment block* (PEB). A PEB is a small data structure created, manipulated, and destroyed entirely by the system. When a process is created, the system allocates a region of address space for the PEB.
>
> The system also needs to create *thread environment blocks* (TEBs) to help manage all the threads that currently exist in the process. The regions for these TEBs will be reserved and released as threads in the process are created and destroyed.
>
> Although the system demands that any of your requests to reserve address space regions begin on an allocation granularity boundary (64 KB on all platforms), the system itself is not subjected to the same limitation. It is extremely likely that the region reserved for your process' PEB and TEBs will not start on a 64-KB boundary. However, these reserved regions will still have to be a multiple of the CPU's page size.

If you attempt to reserve a 10-KB region of address space, the system will automatically round up your request and reserve a region whose size is a multiple of the page size. This means that on *x86* and *x64* systems, the system will reserve a region that is 12 KB; on an IA-64 system, the system will reserve a 16-KB region.

When your program's algorithms no longer need to access a reserved region of address space, the region should be freed. This process is called *releasing* the region of address space and is accomplished by calling the **VirtualFree** function.

Committing Physical Storage Within a Region

To use a reserved region of address space, you must allocate physical storage and then map this storage to the reserved region. This process is called *committing* physical storage. Physical storage is always committed in pages. To commit physical storage to a reserved region, you again call the **VirtualAlloc** function.

When you commit physical storage to regions, you do not have to commit physical storage to the entire region. For example, you can reserve a region that is 64 KB and then commit physical storage to the second and fourth pages within the region. Figure 13-1 shows what a process' address space might look like. Notice that the address space is different depending on which CPU platform you're running on. The address space on the left shows what happens on *x86/x64* machines (which have a 4-KB page), and the address space on the right shows what happens on an IA-64 machine (which has 8-KB pages).

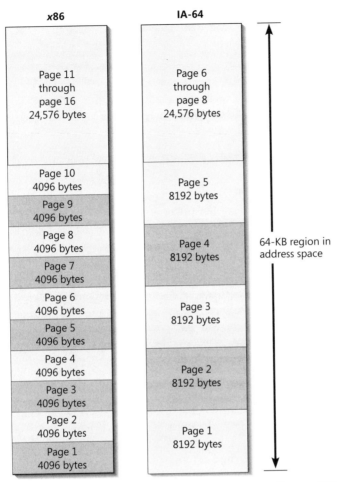

Figure 13-1 Example process address spaces for different CPUs

When your program's algorithms no longer need to access committed physical storage in the reserved region, the physical storage should be freed. This process is called *decommitting* the physical storage and is accomplished by calling the **VirtualFree** function.

Physical Storage and the Paging File

In older operating systems, physical storage was considered to be the amount of RAM that you had in your machine. In other words, if you had 16 MB of RAM in your machine, you could load and run applications that used up to 16 MB of RAM. Today's operating systems have the ability to make disk space look like memory. The file on the disk is typically called a *paging file*, and it contains the virtual memory that is available to all processes.

Of course, for virtual memory to work, a great deal of assistance is required from the CPU itself. When a thread attempts to access a byte of storage, the CPU must know whether that byte is in RAM or on the disk.

From an application's perspective, a paging file transparently increases the amount of RAM (or storage) that the application can use. If you have 1 GB of RAM in your machine and also have a 1-GB paging file on your hard disk, the applications you're running believe that your machine has a grand total of 2 GB of RAM.

Of course, you don't actually have 2 GB of RAM. Instead, the operating system, in coordination with the CPU, saves portions of RAM to the paging file and loads portions of the paging file back into RAM as the running applications need them. Because a paging file increases the apparent amount of RAM available for applications, the use of a paging file is optional. If you don't have a paging file, the system just thinks that there is less RAM available for applications to use. However, users are strongly encouraged to use paging files so that they can run more applications and those applications can work on larger data sets. It is best to think of physical storage as data stored in a paging file on a disk drive (usually a hard disk drive). So when an application commits physical storage to a region of address space by calling the **VirtualAlloc** function, space is actually allocated from a file on the hard disk. The size of the system's paging file is the most important factor in determining how much physical storage is available to applications; the amount of RAM you have has very little effect.

Now when a thread in your process attempts to access a block of data in the process' address space (outside of a memory-mapped file as shown in Chapter 17, "Memory-Mapped Files"), one of two things can happen, as shown in the simplified flowchart in Figure 13-2. (Read *Microsoft Windows Internals* by Mark Russinovich and David Solomon from Microsoft Press for more details.)

In the first possibility, the data that the thread is attempting to access is in RAM. In this case, the CPU maps the data's virtual memory address to the physical address in memory, and then the desired access is performed.

In the second possibility, the data that the thread is attempting to access is not in RAM but is contained somewhere in the paging file. In this case, the attempted access is called a *page fault*, and the CPU notifies the operating system of the attempted access. The operating system then locates a free page of memory in RAM; if a free page cannot be found, the system must free one. If a page has not been modified, the system can simply free the page. But if the system needs to free a page that was modified, it must first copy the page from RAM to the paging file. Next the system goes to the paging file, locates the block of data that needs to be accessed, and loads the data into the free page of memory. The operating system then updates its table indicating that the data's virtual memory address now maps to the appropriate physical memory address in RAM. The CPU now retries the instruction that generated the initial page fault, but this time the CPU is able to map the virtual memory address to a physical RAM address and access the block of data.

The more often the system needs to copy pages of memory to the paging file and vice versa, the more your hard disk thrashes and the slower the system runs. (*Thrashing* means that the operating system spends all its time swapping pages in and out of memory instead of running programs.) Thus by adding more RAM to your computer, you reduce the amount of thrashing necessary to run your applications, which will, of course, greatly improve the system's performance. So here is a general rule of thumb: to make your machine run faster, add more RAM. In fact, for most situations, you'll get a better performance boost from adding RAM than you will by getting a faster CPU.

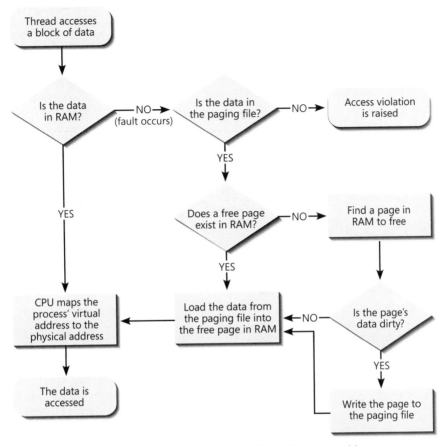

Figure 13-2 Translating a virtual address to a physical storage address

Physical Storage Not Maintained in the Paging File

After reading the previous section, you must be thinking that the paging file can get pretty large if many programs are all running at once—especially if you're thinking that every time you run a program the system must reserve regions of address space for the process' code and data, commit physical storage to these regions, and then copy the code and data from the program's file on the hard disk to the committed physical storage in the paging file.

The system does not do what I just described; if it did, it would take a very long time to load a program and start it running. Instead, when you invoke an application, the system opens the application's .exe file and determines the size of the application's code and data. Then the system reserves a region of address space and notes that the physical storage associated with this region is the .exe file itself. That's right—instead of allocating space from the paging file, the system uses the actual contents, or *image*, of the .exe file as the program's reserved region of address space. This, of course, makes loading an application very fast and allows the size of the paging file to remain small.

When a program's file image (that is, an .exe or a DLL file) on the hard disk is used as the physical storage for a region of address space, it is called a *memory-mapped file*. When an .exe or a DLL is loaded, the system automatically reserves a region of address space and maps the file's image to this region. However, the system also offers a set of functions that allow you to map data files to a region of address space. We will talk about memory-mapped files much more in Chapter 17.

Windows is capable of using multiple paging files. If multiple paging files exist on different physical hard drives, the system can perform much faster because it can write to the multiple drives simultaneously. From Control Panel, you can add and remove paging files by following the steps below:

1. Select the Performance Information And Tools applet.
2. Click the Advanced Tools link.
3. Click the Adjust The Appearance And Performance Of Windows link.
4. Choose the Advanced tab, and click the Change button of the Virtual Memory section.

The following figure shows what this dialog box looks like:

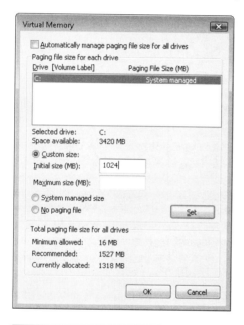

Note   When an .exe or a DLL file is loaded from a floppy disk, Windows copies the entire file from the floppy into the system's RAM. In addition, the system allocates enough storage from the paging file to hold the file's image. This storage is written to only if the system chooses to trim a page of RAM that currently contains a part of the file's image. If the load on the system's RAM is light, the file always runs directly from RAM.

Microsoft was forced to make image files executed from floppies work this way so that setup applications would work correctly. Often a setup program begins with one floppy, which the user removes from the drive in order to insert another floppy. If the system needs to go back to the first floppy to load some of the .exe's or the DLL's code, it is, of course, no longer in the floppy drive. However, because the system copied the file to RAM (and is backed by the paging file), it will have no trouble accessing the setup program.

The system does not copy to RAM image files on other removable media such as CD-ROMs or network drives unless the image is linked using the **/SWAPRUN:CD** or **/SWAPRUN:NET** switches.

Protection Attributes

Individual pages of physical storage allocated can be assigned different protection attributes. The protection attributes are shown in Table 13-3.

Table 13-3   Protection Attributes for Memory Pages

Protection Attribute	Description
PAGE_NOACCESS	Attempts to read from, write to, or execute code in this page raise an access violation.
PAGE_READONLY	Attempts to write to or execute code in this page raise an access violation.
PAGE_READWRITE	Attempts to execute code in this page raise an access violation.
PAGE_EXECUTE	Attempts to read or write memory in this page raise an access violation.
PAGE_EXECUTE_READ	Attempts to write to memory in this page raise an access violation.
PAGE_EXECUTE_READWRITE	There is nothing you can do to this page to raise an access violation.
PAGE_WRITECOPY	Attempts to execute code in this page raise an access violation. Attempts to write to memory in this page cause the system to give the process its own private copy of the page (backed by the paging file).
PAGE_EXECUTE_WRITECOPY	There is nothing you can do to this region to raise an access violation. Attempts to write to memory in this page cause the system to give the process its own private copy of the page (backed by the paging file).

Some malware applications write code into areas of memory intended for data (such as a thread's stack) and then the application executes the malicious code. Windows' *Data Execution Prevention (DEP)* feature provides protection against this type of malware attack. With DEP enabled, the operating system uses the **PAGE_EXECUTE_*** protections only on regions of memory that are intended to have code execute; other protections (typically **PAGE_READWRITE**) are used for regions of memory intended to have data in them (such as thread stacks and the application's heaps).

When the CPU attempts to execute code in a page that does not have the **PAGE_EXECUTE_*** protection, the CPU throws an access violation exception.

The structured exception handling mechanism supported by Windows—as detailed in Chapters 23, 24, and 25—is even more protected. When you build your code with the **/SAFESEH** linker switch, the exception handlers are registered in a special table in the image file. That way, when an exception handler is about to execute, the operating system checks whether or not this handler is registered in the table before allowing it to run.

For more details about DEP, read the Microsoft white paper, "03_CIF_Memory_Protection.DOC," which is downloadable at http://go.microsoft.com/fwlink/?LinkId=28022.

Copy-on-Write Access

The protection attributes listed in the preceding table should all be fairly self-explanatory except the last two: **PAGE_WRITECOPY** and **PAGE_EXECUTE_WRITECOPY**. These attributes exist to conserve RAM usage and paging file space. Windows supports a mechanism that allows two or more processes to share a single block of storage. So if 10 instances of Notepad are running, all instances share the application's code and data pages. Having all instances share the same storage pages greatly improves the performance of the system—but this does require that all instances consider the storage to be read-only or execute-only. If a thread in one instance wrote to the storage modifying it, the storage as seen by the other instances would also be modified, causing total chaos.

To prevent this chaos, *copy-on-write* protection is assigned to the shared block of storage by the operating system. When an .exe or a .dll module is mapped into an address space, the system calculates how many pages are writable. (Usually, the pages containing code are marked as **PAGE_EXECUTE_READ** while the pages containing data are marked **PAGE_READWRITE**.) Then the system allocates storage from the paging file to accommodate these writable pages. This paging file storage is not used unless the module's writable pages are actually written to.

When a thread in one process attempts to write to a shared block, the system intervenes and performs the following steps:

1. The system finds a free page of memory in RAM. Note that this free page will be backed by one of the pages allocated in the paging file when the module was first mapped into the process' address space. Because the system allocated all the potentially required paging file space when the module was first mapped, this step cannot possibly fail.

2. The system copies the contents of the page attempting to be modified to the free page found in step 1. This free page will be assigned either **PAGE_READWRITE** or **PAGE_EXECUTE_READWRITE** protection. The original page's protection and data does not change at all.

3. The system then updates the process' page tables so that the accessed virtual address now translates to the new page of RAM.

After the system has performed these steps, the process can access its own private instance of this page of storage. In Chapter 17, sharing storage and copy-on-write protection are covered in much more detail.

In addition, you should not pass either **PAGE_WRITECOPY** or **PAGE_EXECUTE_WRITECOPY** when you are reserving address space or committing physical storage using the **VirtualAlloc** function. Doing so will cause the call to **VirtualAlloc** to fail; calling **GetLastError** returns **ERROR_INVALID_PARAMETER**. These two attributes are used by the operating system when it maps .exe and DLL file images.

Special Access Protection Attribute Flags

In addition to the protection attributes already discussed, there are three protection attribute flags: **PAGE_NOCACHE**, **PAGE_WRITECOMBINE**, and **PAGE_GUARD**. You use these three flags by bitwise **OR**ing them with any of the protection attributes except **PAGE_NOACCESS**.

The first of these protection attribute flags, **PAGE_NOCACHE**, disables caching of the committed pages. This flag is not recommended for general use—it exists mostly for hardware device-driver developers who need to manipulate memory buffers.

The second protection attribute flag, **PAGE_WRITECOMBINE**, is also for device-driver developers. It allows multiple writes to a single device to be combined together in order to improve performance.

The last protection attribute flag, **PAGE_GUARD**, allows an application to receive a notification (via an exception) when a byte on a page has been written to. There are some clever uses for this flag. Windows uses this flag when it creates a thread's stack. See Chapter 16, "A Thread's Stack," for more information about this flag.

Bringing It All Home

In this section, we'll bring address spaces, partitions, regions, blocks, and pages all together. The best way to start is by examining a virtual memory map that shows all the regions of address space within a single process. The process happens to be the VMMap sample application presented in Chapter 14, "Exploring Virtual Memory." To fully understand the process' address space, we'll begin by discussing the address space as it appears when VMMap is running under Windows on a 32-bit *x86* machine. A sample address space map is shown in Table 13-4.

Table 13-4   A Sample Address Space Map Showing Regions Under Windows on a 32-Bit *x86* Machine

Base Address	Type	Size	Blocks	Protection Attr(s)	Description
00000000	Free	65536			
00010000	Mapped	65536	1	-RW-	
00020000	Private	4096	1	-RW-	
00021000	Free	61440			
00030000	Private	1048576	3	-RW-	Thread Stack
00130000	Mapped	16384	1	-R--	
00134000	Free	49152			
00140000	Mapped	12288	1	-R--	
00143000	Free	53248			
00150000	Mapped	819200	4	-R--	
00218000	Free	32768			
00220000	Mapped	1060864	1	-R--	
00323000	Free	53248			
00330000	Private	4096	1	-RW-	
00331000	Free	61440			
00340000	Mapped	20480	1	-RWC	\Device\HarddiskVolume1\Windows\System32\en-US\user32.dll.mui
00345000	Free	45056			
00350000	Mapped	8192	1	-R--	
00352000	Free	57344			
00360000	Mapped	4096	1	-RW-	
00361000	Free	61440			

Table 13-4   A Sample Address Space Map Showing Regions Under Windows on a 32-Bit *x86* Machine

Base Address	Type	Size	Blocks	Protection Attr(s)	Description
00370000	Mapped	8192	1	-R--	
00372000	Free	450560			
003E0000	Private	65536	2	-RW-	
003F0000	Free	65536			
00400000	Image	126976	7	ERWC	C:\Apps\14 VMMap.exe
0041F000	Free	4096			
00420000	Mapped	720896	1	-R--	
004D0000	Free	458752			
00540000	Private	65536	2	-RW-	
00550000	Free	196608			
00580000	Private	65536	2	-RW-	
00590000	Free	196608			
005C0000	Private	65536	2	-RW-	
005D0000	Free	262144			
00610000	Private	1048576	2	-RW-	
00710000	Mapped	3661824	1	-R--	\Device\HarddiskVolume1\Windows\System32\locale.nls
00A8E000	Free	8192			
00A90000	Mapped	3145728	2	-R--	
00D90000	Mapped	3661824	1	-R--	\Device\HarddiskVolume1\Windows\System32\locale.nls
0110E000	Free	8192			
01110000	Private	1048576	2	-RW-	
01210000	Private	524288	2	-RW-	
01290000	Free	65536			
012A0000	Private	262144	2	-RW-	
012E0000	Free	1179648			
01400000	Mapped	2097152	1	-R--	
01600000	Mapped	4194304	1	-R--	
01A00000	Free	1900544			
01BD0000	Private	65536	2	-RW-	
01BE0000	Mapped	4194304	1	-R--	
01FE0000	Free	235012096			
739B0000	Image	634880	9	ERWC	C:\Windows\WinSxS\x86_micro-soft.vc80.crt_1fc8b3b9a1e18e3b_8.0.50727.312_none_10b2ee7b9bffc2c7\MSVCR80.dll

Table 13-4   A Sample Address Space Map Showing Regions Under Windows on a 32-Bit *x*86 Machine

Base Address	Type	Size	Blocks	Protection Attr(s)	Description
73A4B000	Free	24072192			
75140000	Image	1654784	7	ERWC	C:\Windows\WinSxS\x86_micro-soft.windows.common-controls_6595b64144ccf1df_6.0.6000.16386_none_5d07289e07e1d100\comctl32.dll
752D4000	Free	1490944			
75440000	Image	258048	5	ERWC	C:\Windows\system32\uxtheme.dll
7547F000	Free	15208448			
76300000	Image	28672	4	ERWC	C:\Windows\system32\PSAPI.dll
76307000	Free	626688			
763A0000	Image	512000	7	ERWC	C:\Windows\system32\USP10.dll
7641D000	Free	12288			
76420000	Image	307200	5	ERWC	C:\Windows\system32\GDI32.dll
7646B000	Free	20480			
76470000	Image	36864	4	ERWC	C:\Windows\system32\LPK.dll
76479000	Free	552960			
76500000	Image	348160	4	ERWC	C:\Windows\system32\SHLWAPI.dll
76555000	Free	1880064			
76720000	Image	696320	7	ERWC	C:\Windows\system32\msvcrt.dll
767CA000	Free	24576			
767D0000	Image	122880	4	ERWC	C:\Windows\system32\IMM32.dll
767EE000	Free	8192			
767F0000	Image	647168	5	ERWC	C:\Windows\system32\USER32.dll
7688E000	Free	8192			
76890000	Image	815104	4	ERWC	C:\Windows\system32\MSCTF.dll
76957000	Free	36864			
76960000	Image	573440	4	ERWC	C:\Windows\system32\OLEAUT32.dll
769EC000	Free	868352			
76AC0000	Image	798720	4	ERWC	C:\Windows\system32\RPCRT4.dll
76B83000	Free	2215936			
76DA0000	Image	884736	5	ERWC	C:\Windows\system32\kernel32.dll
76E78000	Free	32768			
76E80000	Image	1327104	5	ERWC	C:\Windows\system32\ole32.dll
76FC4000	Free	11649024			
77AE0000	Image	1171456	9	ERWC	C:\Windows\system32\ntdll.dll
77BFE000	Free	8192			

Table 13-4   A Sample Address Space Map Showing Regions Under Windows on a 32-Bit *x86* Machine

Base Address	Type	Size	Blocks	Protection Attr(s)	Description
77C00000	Image	782336	7	ERWC	C:\Windows\system32\ADVAPI32.dll
77CBF000	Free	128126976			
7F6F0000	Mapped	1048576	2	-R--	
7F7F0000	Free	8126464			
7FFB0000	Mapped	143360	1	-R--	
7FFD3000	Free	4096			
7FFD4000	Private	4096	1	-RW-	
7FFD5000	Free	40960			
7FFDF000	Private	4096	1	-RW-	
7FFE0000	Private	65536	2	-R--	

The address space map in Table 13-4 shows the various regions in the process' address space. There is one region shown per line, and each line contains six columns.

The first, or leftmost, column shows the region's base address. You'll notice that we start walking the process' address space with the region at address 0x00000000 and end with the last region of usable address space, which begins at address 0x7FFE0000. All regions are contiguous. You'll also notice that almost all the base addresses for non-free regions start on a multiple of 64 KB. This is because of the allocation granularity of address space reservation imposed by the system. A region that does not start on an allocation granularity boundary represents a region that was allocated by operating system code on your process' behalf.

The second column shows the region's type, which is one of the four values—Free, Private, Image, or Mapped—described in the Table 13-5.

Table 13-5   Memory Region Types

Type	Description
Free	The region's virtual addresses are not backed by any storage. This address space is not reserved; the application can reserve a region either at the shown base address or anywhere within the free region.
Private	The region's virtual addresses are backed by the system's paging file.
Image	The region's virtual addresses were originally backed by a memory-mapped image file (such as an .exe or a DLL file). The virtual addresses might not be backed by the image file anymore. For example, when a global variable in a module's image is written to, the copy-on-write mechanism backs the specific page from the paging file instead of the original image file.
Mapped	The region's virtual addresses were originally backed by a memory-mapped data file. The virtual addresses might not be backed by the data file anymore. For example, a data file might be mapped using copy-on-write protection. Any writes to the file cause the specific pages to be backed by the paging file instead of the original data.

The way that my VMMap application calculates this column might lead to misleading results. When the region is not free, the VMMap sample application guesses which of the three remaining values applies—there is no function we can call to request this region's exact usage. I calculate this column's value by scanning all the blocks within the region and taking an educated guess. You should examine my code in Chapter 14 to better understand the way I calculate a column's value.

The third column shows the number of bytes that were reserved for the region. For example, the system mapped the image of User32.dll at memory address 0x767F0000. When the system reserved address space for this image, it needed to reserve 647,168 bytes. The number in the third column will always be a multiple of the CPU's page size (4096 bytes for an *x86* system). You might notice a difference between the file size on disk and the number of bytes required to map it into memory. The PE file produced by the linker is compacted as much as possible to preserve disk space. However, when Windows maps the PE file into the process' virtual address space, each section must begin on its own page boundary and be a multiple of the system's page size. This means that a PE file typically requires more virtual address space than its file size.

The fourth column shows the number of blocks within the reserved region. A *block* is a set of contiguous pages that all have the same protection attributes and that are all backed by the same type of physical storage—I'll talk more about this in the next section of this chapter. For free regions, this value will always be 0 because no storage can be committed within a free region. (Nothing is displayed in the fourth column for a free region.) For the non-free region, this value can be anywhere from 1 to a maximum number for region size or page size. For example, the region that begins at memory address 0x767F0000 has a region size of 647,168 bytes. Because this process is running on an *x86* CPU, for which the page size is 4096 bytes, the maximum number of different committed blocks is 158 (647,168/4096); the map shows that there are 5 blocks in the region.

The fifth column on the line shows the region's protection attributes. The individual letters represent the following: *E* = execute, *R* = read, *W* = write, and *C* = copy-on-write. If the region does not show any of these protection attributes, the region has no access protection. The free regions show no protection attributes because unreserved regions do not have protection attributes associated with them. Neither the guard protection attribute flag nor the no-cache protection attribute flag will ever appear here; these flags have meaning only when associated with physical storage, not reserved address space. Protection attributes are given to a region for the sake of efficiency only, and they are always overridden by protection attributes assigned to physical storage.

The sixth and last column shows a text description of what's in the region. For free regions, this column will always be blank; for private regions, it will usually be blank because VMMap has no way of knowing why the application reserved this private region of address space. However, VMMap can identify private regions that contain a thread's stack. VMMap can usually detect thread stacks because they will commonly have a block of physical storage within them with the guard protection attribute. However, when a thread's stack is full it will not have a block with the guard protection attribute, and VMMap will be unable to detect it.

For image regions, VMMap displays the full pathname of the file that is mapped into the region. VMMap obtains this information using the PSAPI functions (mentioned at the end of Chapter 4, "Processes"). VMMap can show regions backed by data files by calling the **GetMappedFileName** function, and it can show regions backed by executable image files by calling the ToolHelp functions, also mentioned in Chapter 4.

Inside the Regions

It is possible to break down the regions even further than shown in Table 13-4. Table 13-6 shows the same address space map as Table 13-4, but the blocks contained inside each region are also displayed.

Table 13-6   A Sample Address Space Map Showing Regions and Blocks Under Windows on a 32-Bit *x*86 Machine

Base Address	Type	Size	Blocks	Protection Attr(s)	Description
00000000	Free	65536			
00010000	Mapped	65536	1	-RW-	
00010000	Mapped	65536		-RW- ---	
00020000	Private	4096	1	-RW-	
00020000	Private	4096		-RW- ---	
00021000	Free	61440			
00030000	Private	1048576	3	-RW-	Thread Stack
00030000	Reserve	774144		-RW- ---	
. . .	. . .	. . .	. . .	. . .	. . .
00330000	Private	4096	1	-RW-	
00330000	Private	4096		-RW- ---	
00331000	Free	61440			
00340000	Mapped	20480	1	-RWC	\Device\HarddiskVolume1\Windows\System32\en-US\user32.dll.mui
00340000	Mapped	20480		-RWC ---	
. . .	. . .	. . .	. . .	. . .	. . .
003F0000	Free	65536			
00400000	Image	126976	7	ERWC	C:\Apps\14 VMMap.exe
00400000	Image	4096		-R-- ---	
00401000	Image	8192		ERW- ---	
00403000	Image	57344		ERWC ---	
00411000	Image	32768		ER-- ---	
00419000	Image	8192		-R-- ---	
0041B000	Image	8192		-RW- ---	
0041D000	Image	8192		-R-- ---	
0041F000	Free	4096			
. . .	. . .	. . .	. . .	. . .	. . .
739B0000	Image	634880	9	ERWC	C:\Windows\WinSxS\x86_microsoft.vc80.crt_1fc8b3b9a1e18e3b_8.0.50727.312_none_10b2ee7b9bffc2c7\MSVCR80.dll
739B0000	Image	4096		-R-- ---	

Table 13-6   A Sample Address Space Map Showing Regions and Blocks Under Windows on a 32-Bit *x86* Machine

Base Address	Type	Size	Blocks	Protection Attr(s)	Description
739B1000	Image	405504		ER-- ---	
73A14000	Image	176128		-R-- ---	
73A3F000	Image	4096		-RW- ---	
73A40000	Image	4096		-RWC ---	
73A41000	Image	4096		-RW- ---	
73A42000	Image	4096		-RWC ---	
73A43000	Image	12288		-RW- ---	
73A46000	Image	20480		-R-- ---	
73A4B000	Free	24072192			
75140000	Image	1654784	7	ERWC	C:\Windows\WinSxS\x86_micro-soft.windows.common-controls_6595b64144ccf1df_6.0.6000.16386_none_5d07289e07e1d100\comctl32.dll
75140000	Image	4096		-R-- ---	
75141000	Image	1273856		ER-- ---	
75278000	Image	4096		-RW- ---	
75279000	Image	4096		-RWC ---	
7527A000	Image	8192		-RW- ---	
7527C000	Image	40960		-RWC ---	
75286000	Image	319488		-R-- ---	
752D4000	Free	1490944			
. . .	. . .	. . .	. . .	. . .	. . .
767F0000	Image	647168	5	ERWC	C:\Windows\system32\USER32.dll
767F0000	Image	4096		-R-- ---	
767F1000	Image	430080		ER-- ---	
7685A000	Image	4096		-RW- ---	
7685B000	Image	4096		-RWC ---	
7685C000	Image	204800		-R-- ---	
7688E000	Free	8192			
. . .	. . .	. . .	. . .	. . .	. . .
76DA0000	Image	884736	5	ERWC	C:\Windows\system32\kernel32.dll
76DA0000	Image	4096		-R-- ---	
76DA1000	Image	823296		ER-- ---	
76E6A000	Image	8192		-RW- ---	
76E6C000	Image	4096		-RWC ---	
76E6D000	Image	45056		-R-- ---	

Table 13-6   A Sample Address Space Map Showing Regions and Blocks Under Windows on a 32-Bit *x*86 Machine

Base Address	Type	Size	Blocks	Protection Attr(s)	Description
76E78000	Free	32768			
. . .	. . .	. . .	. . .	. . .	. . .
7FFDF000	Private	4096	1	-RW-	
7FFDF000	Private	4096		-RW- ---	
7FFE0000	Private	65536	2	-R--	
7FFE0000	Private	4096		-R-- ---	
7FFE1000	Reserve	61440		-R-- ---	

Of course, free regions do not expand at all because they have no committed pages of storage within them. Each block line shows four columns, which I'll explain here.

The first column shows the address of a set of pages all having the same state and protection attributes. For example, a single page (4096 bytes) of memory with read-only protection is committed at address 0x767F0000. At address 0x767F1000, there is a block of 105 pages (430,080 bytes) of committed storage that has execute and read protection. If both of these blocks had the same protection attributes, the two would be combined and would appear as a single 106-page (434,176-byte) entry in the memory map.

The second column shows what type of physical storage is backing the block within the reserved region. One of five possible values can appear in this column: Free, Private, Mapped, Image, or Reserve. A value of Private, Mapped, or Image indicates that the block is backed by physical storage in the paging file, a data file, or a loaded .exe or DLL file, respectively. If the value is Free or Reserve, the block is not backed by any physical storage at all.

For the most part, the same type of physical storage backs all the committed blocks within a single region. However, it is possible for different committed blocks within a single region to be backed by different types of physical storage. For example, a memory-mapped file image will be backed by an .exe or a DLL file. If you were to write to a single page in this region that had **PAGE_WRITECOPY** or **PAGE_EXECUTE_WRITECOPY**, the system would make your process a private copy of the page backed by the paging file instead of the file image. This new page would have the same attributes as the original page without the copy-on-write protection attribute.

The third column shows the size of the block. All blocks are contiguous within a region—there will not be any gaps.

The fourth column shows the number of blocks within the reserved region.

The fifth column shows the protection attributes and protection attribute flags of the block. A block's protection attributes override the protection attributes of the region that contains the block. The possible protection attributes are identical to those that can be specified for a region; however, the protection attribute flags **PAGE_GUARD**, **PAGE_NOCACHE**, and **PAGE_WRITECOMBINE**— which are never associated with a region—can be associated with a block.

The Importance of Data Alignment

In this section, we leave the discussion of a process' virtual address space and discuss the important topic of data alignment. Data alignment is not so much a part of the operating system's memory architecture as it is a part of the CPU's architecture.

CPUs operate most efficiently when they access properly aligned data. Data is aligned when the memory address of the data modulo of the data's size is 0. For example, a **WORD** value should always start on an address that is evenly divided by 2, a **DWORD** value should always start on an address that is evenly divided by 4, and so on. When the CPU attempts to read a data value that is not properly aligned, the CPU will do one of two things. It will either raise an exception or the CPU will perform multiple, aligned memory accesses to read the full misaligned data value.

Here is some code that accesses misaligned data:

```
VOID SomeFunc(PVOID pvDataBuffer) {

   // The first byte in the buffer is some byte of information
   char c = * (PBYTE) pvDataBuffer;

   // Increment past the first byte in the buffer
   pvDataBuffer = (PVOID)((PBYTE) pvDataBuffer + 1);

   // Bytes 2-5 contain a double-word value
   DWORD dw = * (DWORD *) pvDataBuffer;

   // The line above raises a data misalignment exception on some CPUs
...
```

Obviously, if the CPU performs multiple memory accesses, the performance of your application is hampered. At best, it will take the system twice as long to access a misaligned value as it will to access an aligned value—but the access time could be even worse! To get the best performance for your application, you'll want to write your code so that the data is properly aligned.

Let's take a closer look at how the x86 CPU handles data alignment. The x86 CPU contains a special bit flag in its **EFLAGS** register called the AC (alignment check) flag. By default, this flag is set to zero when the CPU first receives power. When this flag is zero, the CPU automatically does whatever it has to in order to successfully access misaligned data values. However, if this flag is set to 1, the CPU issues an INT 17H interrupt whenever there is an attempt to access misaligned data. The x86 version of Windows never alters this CPU flag bit. Therefore, you will never see a data misalignment exception occur in an application when it is running on an x86 processor. The same behavior happens when running on an AMD x86-64 CPU, where, by default, the hardware takes care of misalignment fault fixup.

Now let's turn our attention to the IA-64 CPU. The IA-64 CPU cannot automatically fix up misaligned data accesses. Instead, when a misaligned data access occurs, the CPU notifies the operating system. Windows now decides if it should raise a data misalignment exception—or it can execute additional instructions that silently correct the problem and allow your code to continue executing. By default, when you install Windows on an IA-64 machine, the operating system automatically transforms a misalignment fault into an **EXCEPTION_DATATYPE_MISALIGNMENT** exception. However, you can alter this behavior. You can tell the system to silently correct misaligned data accesses for all threads in your process by having one of your process' threads call the **SetErrorMode** function:

```
UINT SetErrorMode(UINT fuErrorMode);
```

For our discussion, the flag in question is the **SEM_NOALIGNMENTFAULTEXCEPT** flag. When this flag is set, the system automatically corrects for misaligned data accesses. When this flag is reset, the system does not correct for misaligned data accesses but instead raises data misalignment exceptions. Once you change this flag, you can't update it again during the process' lifetime.

Note that changing this flag affects all threads contained within the process that owns the thread that makes the call. In other words, changing this flag will not affect any threads contained in any other processes. You should also note that a process' error mode flags are inherited by any child processes. Therefore, you might want to temporarily reset this flag before calling the **Create-Process** function (although you usually don't do this for the **SEM_NOALIGNMENTFAULTEXCEPT** flag because it can't be reset once set).

Of course, you can call **SetErrorMode**, passing the **SEM_NOALIGNMENTFAULTEXCEPT** flag, regardless of which CPU platform you are running on. However, the results are not always the same. For x86 and x64 systems, this flag is always on and cannot be turned off. You can use the Windows Reliability and Performance Monitor to see how many alignment fixups per second the system is performing. The following figure shows what the Add Counters dialog box looks like just before you add this counter to the chart:

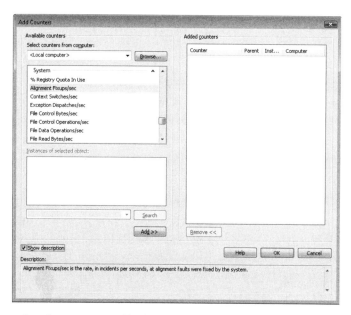

What this counter really shows is the number of times per second the CPU notifies the operating system of misaligned data accesses. If you monitor this counter on an x86 machine, you'll see that it always reports zero fixups per second. This is because the x86 CPU itself is performing the fixups and doesn't notify the operating system. Because the x86 CPU performs the fixup instead of the operating system, accessing misaligned data on an x86 machine is not nearly as bad a performance hit as that of CPUs that require software (the Windows operating system code) to do the fixup. As you can see, simply calling **SetErrorMode** is enough to make your application work correctly. But this solution is definitely not the most efficient.

Microsoft's C/C++ compiler for the IA-64 supports a special keyword called **__unaligned**. You use the **__unaligned** modifier just as you would use the **const** or **volatile** modifiers, except that the **__unaligned** modifier is meaningful only when applied to pointer variables. When you access data via an unaligned pointer, the compiler generates code that assumes that the data is not aligned properly and adds the additional CPU instructions necessary to access the data. The code shown here is a modified version of the code shown earlier. This new version takes advantage of the **__unaligned** keyword:

```
VOID SomeFunc(PVOID pvDataBuffer) {

   // The first byte in the buffer is some byte of information
   char c = * (PBYTE) pvDataBuffer;

   // Increment past the first byte in the buffer
   pvDataBuffer = (PVOID)((PBYTE) pvDataBuffer + 1);

   // Bytes 2-5 contain a double-word value
   DWORD dw = * (__unaligned DWORD *) pvDataBuffer;

   // The line above causes the compiler to generate additional
   // instructions so that several aligned data accesses are performed
   // to read the DWORD.
   // Note that a data misalignment exception is not raised.
...
```

The instructions added by the compiler are still much more efficient than letting the CPU trap the misaligned data access and having the operating system correct the problem. In fact, if you monitor the Alignment Fixups/sec counter, you'll see that accesses via unaligned pointers have no effect on the chart. Notice that the compiler will generate the additional instructions even in the case where the structure is aligned and, so, make the code less efficient in that case.

Finally, the **__unaligned** keyword is not supported by the *x86* version of the Microsoft Visual C/C++ compiler. I assume that Microsoft felt that this wasn't necessary because of the speed at which the CPU itself can perform the fixups. However, this also means that the *x86* compiler will generate errors when it encounters the **__unaligned** keyword. So if you are trying to create a single source code base for your application, you'll want to use the **UNALIGNED** and **UNALIGNED64** macros instead of the **__unaligned** keyword. The **UNALIGNED*** macros are defined in WinNT.h as follows:

```
#if defined(_M_MRX000) || defined(_M_ALPHA) || defined(_M_PPC) ||
    defined(_M_IA64) || defined(_M_AMD64)
   #define ALIGNMENT_MACHINE
   #define UNALIGNED __unaligned
   #if defined(_WIN64)
      #define UNALIGNED64 __unaligned
   #else
      #define UNALIGNED64
   #endif
```

```
#else
    #undef ALIGNMENT_MACHINE
    #define UNALIGNED
    #define UNALIGNED64
#endif
```

Chapter 14
Exploring Virtual Memory

In the last chapter, we discussed how the system manages virtual memory, how each process receives its own private address space, and what a process' address space looks like. In this chapter, we move away from the abstract and examine some of the Microsoft Windows functions that give us information about the system's memory management and about the virtual address space in a process.

System Information

Many operating system values are dependent on the host machine: page size, allocation granularity size, and so on. These values should never be hard-coded into your source code. Instead, you should always retrieve these values when your process initializes and use the retrieved values within your source code. The **GetSystemInfo** function retrieves the values relevant to the host machine:

```
VOID GetSystemInfo(LPSYSTEM_INFO psi);
```

You must pass the address of a **SYSTEM_INFO** structure to this function. The function will initialize all of the structure's members and return. Here is what the **SYSTEM_INFO** data structure looks like:

```
typedef struct _SYSTEM_INFO {
   union {
      struct {
         WORD wProcessorArchitecture;
         WORD wReserved;
      };
   };
   DWORD       dwPageSize;
   LPVOID      lpMinimumApplicationAddress;
   LPVOID      lpMaximumApplicationAddress;
   DWORD_PTR dwActiveProcessorMask;
   DWORD       dwNumberOfProcessors;
   DWORD       dwProcessorType;
   DWORD       dwAllocationGranularity;
   WORD        wProcessorLevel;
   WORD        wProcessorRevision;
} SYSTEM_INFO, *LPSYSTEM_INFO;
```

When the system boots, it determines what the values of these members should be. For any given system, the values will always be the same, so you will never need to call this function more than once for any given process. **GetSystemInfo** exists so that an application can query these values at run time. Of all the members in the structure, only four of them have anything to do with memory. These four members are explained in Table 14-1.

Table 14-1   Members of SYSTEM_INFO

Member Name	Description
dwPageSize	Shows the CPU's page size. On *x86* and *x64* machines, this value is 4096 bytes; and on IA-64 machines, this value is 8192 bytes.
lpMinimumApplicationAddress	Gives the minimum memory address of every process' usable address space. This value is 65,536, or 0x00010000, because the first 64 KB of every process' address space is always free.
lpMaximumApplicationAddress	Gives the highest memory address usable within each process' private address space.
dwAllocationGranularity	Shows the granularity of a reserved region of address space. As of this writing, this value is 65,536 on all Windows platforms.

The other members of this structure are not at all related to memory management; I explain them in Table 14-2 for completeness.

Table 14-2   Members of SYSTEM_INFO That Are Not Related to Memory

Member Name	Description
wReserved	Reserved for future use; do not reference.
dwNumberOfProcessors	Indicates the number of CPUs in the machine. Notice that this field will contain 2 on a machine with a dual-core processor.
dwActiveProcessorMask	A bitmask indicating which CPUs are active (allowed to run threads).
dwProcessorType	Obsolete; do not reference.
wProcessorArchitecture	Indicates the processor architecture, such as *x86*, *x64*, or IA-64.
wProcessorLevel	Breaks down the process architecture further, such as specifying Intel Pentium III or IV. You should avoid this field and call **IsProcessorFeaturePresent** instead to determine the capabilities of the CPU.
wProcessorRevision	Breaks down the processor level further.

> **Tip** If you need more details about the processors available on a machine, you should take
> advantage of the **GetLogicalProcessorInformation** function as shown in the following
> code snippet:

```
void ShowProcessors() {
   PSYSTEM_LOGICAL_PROCESSOR_INFORMATION pBuffer = NULL;
   DWORD dwSize = 0;
   DWORD procCoreCount;

   BOOL bResult = GetLogicalProcessorInformation(pBuffer, &dwSize);
   if (GetLastError() != ERROR_INSUFFICIENT_BUFFER) {
      _tprintf(TEXT("Impossible to get processor information\n"));
      return;
   }

   pBuffer = (PSYSTEM_LOGICAL_PROCESSOR_INFORMATION)malloc(dwSize);
   bResult = GetLogicalProcessorInformation(pBuffer, &dwSize);
   if (!bResult) {
       free(pBuffer);

      _tprintf(TEXT("Impossible to get processor information\n"));
      return;
   }

   procCoreCount = 0;
   DWORD lpiCount = dwSize / sizeof(SYSTEM_LOGICAL_PROCESSOR_INFORMATION);
   for(DWORD current = 0; current < lpiCount; current++) {
      if (pBuffer[current].Relationship == RelationProcessorCore) {
         if (pBuffer[current].ProcessorCore.Flags == 1) {
            _tprintf(TEXT("   + one CPU core (HyperThreading)\n"));
         } else {
            _tprintf(TEXT("   + one CPU socket\n"));
         }
         procCoreCount++;
      }
   }
    _tprintf(TEXT("   -> %d active CPU(s)\n"), procCoreCount);

   free(pBuffer);
}
```

To allow 32-bit applications to run on a 64-bit version of Windows, Microsoft provides an emulation layer called *Windows 32-bit On Windows 64-bit*, also known as WOW64. When a 32-bit application is running via WOW64, **GetSystemInfo** might not return the same values it would if the
application were running as a native 64-bit application. For example, the **dwPageSize** field of the
SYSTEM_INFO structure will contain 4 KB for the former and 8 KB for the latter if running on an
IA-64 machine. If you need to know whether or not a process is running on WOW64, you call the
following function:

```
BOOL IsWow64Process(
  HANDLE hProcess,
  PBOOL pbWow64Process);
```

The first parameter is the handle of the process you are interested in, such as what is returned by **GetCurrentProcess** for the running application. If **IsWow64Process** returns **FALSE**, it is usually because of invalid values given as parameters. If the function returns **TRUE**, the Boolean value pointed to by the **pbWow64Process** parameter is set to **FALSE** in the case of a 32-bit executable running on a 32-bit Windows version and also for a 64-bit application running on a 64-bit Windows version. So it will be set to **TRUE** only for a 32-bit application running on WOW64. In that case, you need to call **GetNativeSystemInfo** to retrieve the nonemulated values in a **SYSTEM_INFO** structure:

```
void GetNativeSystemInfo(
  LPSYSTEM_INFO pSystemInfo);
```

Instead of calling **IsWow64Process**, you could call the **IsOS** function defined in ShlWApi.h, passing **OS_WOW6432** as its parameter. If **IsOS** returns **TRUE**, the calling 32-bit application is running via WOW64. If **FALSE** is returned, the calling 32-bit application is running natively on a 32-bit Windows system.

 Note You should take a look at the "Best Practices for WOW64" white paper at *http://www.microsoft.com/whdc/system/platform/64bit/WoW64_bestprac.mspx* for more details about the 32-bit emulation provided by 64-bit Windows.

The System Information Sample Application

The SysInfo.cpp listing shows the source code of a simple program that calls **GetSystemInfo** and displays the information returned in the **SYSTEM_INFO** structure. The source code and resource files for the application are in the 14-SysInfo directory on the companion content Web page. Figure 14-1 shows the results of running the SysInfo application on several different platforms:

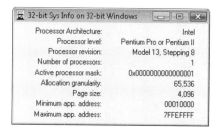

Figure 14-1 These dialog boxes show a 32-bit application running on 32-bit Windows (upper left); a 32-bit application running on 32-bit Windows with a dual-core processor (upper right); a 32-bit application running on 64-bit Windows (lower left); and a 64-bit application running on 64-bit Windows (lower right).

SysInfo.cpp

```
/*************************************************************************
Module:  SysInfo.cpp
Notices: Copyright (c) 2008 Jeffrey Richter & Christophe Nasarre
*************************************************************************/


#include "..\CmnHdr.h"      /* See Appendix A. */
#include <windowsx.h>
#include <tchar.h>
#include <stdio.h>
#include "Resource.h"
#include <StrSafe.h>


///////////////////////////////////////////////////////////////////////////



// This function accepts a number and converts it to a
// string, inserting commas where appropriate.
PTSTR BigNumToString(LONG lNum, PTSTR szBuf, DWORD chBufSize) {

   TCHAR szNum[100];
   StringCchPrintf(szNum, _countof(szNum), TEXT("%d"), lNum);
   NUMBERFMT nf;
   nf.NumDigits = 0;
   nf.LeadingZero = FALSE;
   nf.Grouping = 3;
   nf.lpDecimalSep = TEXT(".");
   nf.lpThousandSep = TEXT(",");
   nf.NegativeOrder = 0;
   GetNumberFormat(LOCALE_USER_DEFAULT, 0, szNum, &nf, szBuf, chBufSize);
   return(szBuf);
}


///////////////////////////////////////////////////////////////////////////



void ShowCPUInfo(HWND hWnd, WORD wProcessorArchitecture, WORD wProcessorLevel,
   WORD wProcessorRevision) {

   TCHAR szCPUArch[64]  = TEXT("(unknown)");
   TCHAR szCPULevel[64] = TEXT("(unknown)");
   TCHAR szCPURev[64]   = TEXT("(unknown)");

   switch (wProcessorArchitecture) {
      // Notice that AMD processors are seen as PROCESSOR_ARCHITECTURE_INTEL.
      // In the Registry, the content of the "VendorIdentifier" key under
      // HKEY_LOCAL_MACHINE\HARDWARE\DESCRIPTION\System\CentralProcessor\0
      // is either "GenuineIntel" or "AuthenticAMD"
      //
```

```
// Read http://download.intel.com/design/Xeon/applnots/24161831.pdf
// for Model numeric codes.
// http://www.amd.com/us-en/assets/content_type/white_papers_and_tech_docs/
// 20734.pdf should be used for AMD processors Model numeric codes.
//
case PROCESSOR_ARCHITECTURE_INTEL:
   _tcscpy_s(szCPUArch, _countof(szCPUArch), TEXT("Intel"));
  switch (wProcessorLevel) {
  case 3: case 4:
     StringCchPrintf(szCPULevel, _countof(szCPULevel), TEXT("80%c86"),
        wProcessorLevel + TEXT('0'));
     StringCchPrintf(szCPURev, _countof(szCPURev), TEXT("%c%d"),
        HIBYTE(wProcessorRevision) + TEXT('A'),
        LOBYTE(wProcessorRevision));
     break;

  case 5:
     _tcscpy_s(szCPULevel, _countof(szCPULevel), TEXT("Pentium"));
     StringCchPrintf(szCPURev, _countof(szCPURev),
        TEXT("Model %d, Stepping %d"),
        HIBYTE(wProcessorRevision), LOBYTE(wProcessorRevision));
     break;

  case 6:
     switch (HIBYTE(wProcessorRevision)) { // Model
        case 1:
           _tcscpy_s(szCPULevel, _countof(szCPULevel),
              TEXT("Pentium Pro"));
           break;

        case 3:
        case 5:
           _tcscpy_s(szCPULevel, _countof(szCPULevel),
              TEXT("Pentium II"));
           break;

        case 6:
           _tcscpy_s(szCPULevel, _countof(szCPULevel),
              TEXT("Celeron"));
           break;

        case 7:
        case 8:
        case 11:
           _tcscpy_s(szCPULevel, _countof(szCPULevel),
              TEXT("Pentium III"));
           break;

        case 9:
        case 13:
           _tcscpy_s(szCPULevel, _countof(szCPULevel),
              TEXT("Pentium M"));
           break;
```

```
                case 10:
                    _tcscpy_s(szCPULevel, _countof(szCPULevel),
                        TEXT("Pentium Xeon"));
                    break;

                case 15:
                    _tcscpy_s(szCPULevel, _countof(szCPULevel),
                        TEXT("Core 2 Duo"));
                    break;

                default:
                    _tcscpy_s(szCPULevel, _countof(szCPULevel),
                        TEXT("Unknown Pentium"));
                    break;
            }
            StringCchPrintf(szCPURev, _countof(szCPURev),
                TEXT("Model %d, Stepping %d"),
                HIBYTE(wProcessorRevision), LOBYTE(wProcessorRevision));
            break;

        case 15:
            _tcscpy_s(szCPULevel, _countof(szCPULevel), TEXT("Pentium 4"));
            StringCchPrintf(szCPURev, _countof(szCPURev),
                TEXT("Model %d, Stepping %d"),
                HIBYTE(wProcessorRevision), LOBYTE(wProcessorRevision));
            break;
        }
        break;

    case PROCESSOR_ARCHITECTURE_IA64:
        _tcscpy_s(szCPUArch, _countof(szCPUArch), TEXT("IA-64"));
        StringCchPrintf(szCPULevel, _countof(szCPULevel), TEXT("%d"),
            wProcessorLevel);
        StringCchPrintf(szCPURev, _countof(szCPURev), TEXT("Model %c, Pass %d"),
            HIBYTE(wProcessorRevision) + TEXT('A'),
            LOBYTE(wProcessorRevision));
        break;

    case PROCESSOR_ARCHITECTURE_AMD64:
        _tcscpy_s(szCPUArch, _countof(szCPUArch), TEXT("AMD64"));
        StringCchPrintf(szCPULevel, _countof(szCPULevel), TEXT("%d"),
            wProcessorLevel);
        StringCchPrintf(szCPURev, _countof(szCPURev), TEXT("Model %c, Pass %d"),
            HIBYTE(wProcessorRevision) + TEXT('A'),
            LOBYTE(wProcessorRevision));
        break;


    case PROCESSOR_ARCHITECTURE_UNKNOWN:
    default:
        _tcscpy_s(szCPUArch, _countof(szCPUArch), TEXT("Unknown"));
        break;
}
```

```
      SetDlgItemText(hWnd, IDC_PROCARCH,  szCPUArch);
      SetDlgItemText(hWnd, IDC_PROCLEVEL, szCPULevel);
      SetDlgItemText(hWnd, IDC_PROCREV,   szCPURev);
}


void ShowBitness(HWND hWnd) {
   TCHAR szFullTitle[100];
   TCHAR szTitle[32];
   GetWindowText(hWnd, szTitle, _countof(szTitle));

#if defined(_WIN32)
   BOOL bIsWow64 = FALSE;
   if (!IsWow64Process(GetCurrentProcess(), &bIsWow64)) {
      chFAIL("Failed to get WOW64 state.");
      return;
   }

   if (bIsWow64) {
      StringCchPrintf(szFullTitle, _countof(szFullTitle),
         TEXT("32-bit %s on WOW64"), szTitle);
   } else {
      StringCchPrintf(szFullTitle, _countof(szFullTitle),
         TEXT("32-bit %s on 32-bit Windows"), szTitle);
   }
#elif defined(_WIN64)
// 64-bit applications can only run on 64-bit Windows,
// so there is nothing special to check except the
// _WIN64 symbol set by the compiler.
   StringCchPrintf(szFullTitle, _countof(szFullTitle),
      TEXT("64-bit %s"), szTitle);
#endif

   SetWindowText(hWnd, szFullTitle);
}



///////////////////////////////////////////////////////////////////////////////


BOOL Dlg_OnInitDialog(HWND hWnd, HWND hWndFocus, LPARAM lParam) {

   chSETDLGICONS(hWnd, IDI_SYSINFO);

   SYSTEM_INFO sinf;
   GetSystemInfo(&sinf);

   ShowCPUInfo(hWnd, sinf.wProcessorArchitecture,
      sinf.wProcessorLevel, sinf.wProcessorRevision);

   TCHAR szBuf[50];
   SetDlgItemText(hWnd, IDC_PAGESIZE,
      BigNumToString(sinf.dwPageSize, szBuf, _countof(szBuf)));
```

```
    StringCchPrintf(szBuf, _countof(szBuf), TEXT("%p"),
       sinf.lpMinimumApplicationAddress);
    SetDlgItemText(hWnd, IDC_MINAPPADDR, szBuf);

    StringCchPrintf(szBuf, _countof(szBuf), TEXT("%p"),
       sinf.lpMaximumApplicationAddress);
    SetDlgItemText(hWnd, IDC_MAXAPPADDR, szBuf);

    StringCchPrintf(szBuf, _countof(szBuf), TEXT("0x%016I64X"),
       (__int64) sinf.dwActiveProcessorMask);
    SetDlgItemText(hWnd, IDC_ACTIVEPROCMASK, szBuf);

    SetDlgItemText(hWnd, IDC_NUMOFPROCS,
       BigNumToString(sinf.dwNumberOfProcessors, szBuf, _countof(szBuf)));

    SetDlgItemText(hWnd, IDC_ALLOCGRAN,
       BigNumToString(sinf.dwAllocationGranularity, szBuf, _countof(szBuf)));

    ShowBitness(hWnd);

    return(TRUE);
}


///////////////////////////////////////////////////////////////////////////


void Dlg_OnCommand(HWND hWnd, int id, HWND hWndCtl, UINT codeNotify) {

    switch (id) {
       case IDCANCEL:
          EndDialog(hWnd, id);
          break;
    }
}


///////////////////////////////////////////////////////////////////////////


INT_PTR WINAPI Dlg_Proc(HWND hDlg, UINT uMsg, WPARAM wParam, LPARAM lParam) {

    switch (uMsg) {
       chHANDLE_DLGMSG(hDlg, WM_INITDIALOG, Dlg_OnInitDialog);
       chHANDLE_DLGMSG(hDlg, WM_COMMAND,    Dlg_OnCommand);
    }
    return(FALSE);
}


///////////////////////////////////////////////////////////////////////////
```

```
int WINAPI _tWinMain(HINSTANCE hInstExe, HINSTANCE, PTSTR, int) {

   DialogBox(hInstExe, MAKEINTRESOURCE(IDD_SYSINFO), NULL, Dlg_Proc);
   return(0);
}



/////////////////////////////// End of File ///////////////////////////////
```

Virtual Memory Status

A Windows function called **GlobalMemoryStatus** retrieves dynamic information about the current state of memory:

```
VOID GlobalMemoryStatus(LPMEMORYSTATUS pmst);
```

I think that this function is poorly named—**GlobalMemoryStatus** implies that the function is somehow related to the global heaps in 16-bit Windows. I think that **GlobalMemoryStatus** should have been called something like **VirtualMemoryStatus** instead.

When you call **GlobalMemoryStatus**, you must pass the address of a **MEMORYSTATUS** structure. The **MEMORYSTATUS** data structure is shown here:

```
typedef struct _MEMORYSTATUS {
   DWORD dwLength;
   DWORD dwMemoryLoad;
   SIZE_T dwTotalPhys;
   SIZE_T dwAvailPhys;
   SIZE_T dwTotalPageFile;
   SIZE_T dwAvailPageFile;
   SIZE_T dwTotalVirtual;
   SIZE_T dwAvailVirtual;
} MEMORYSTATUS, *LPMEMORYSTATUS;
```

Before calling **GlobalMemoryStatus**, you must initialize the **dwLength** member to the size of the structure in bytes—that is, the size of a **MEMORYSTATUS** structure. This initialization allows Microsoft to add members to this structure in future versions of Windows without breaking existing applications. When you call **GlobalMemoryStatus**, it will initialize the remainder of the structure's members and return. The VMStat sample application in the next section describes the various members and their meanings.

If you anticipate that your application will run on machines with more than 4 GB of RAM or if the total swap file size might be larger than 4 GB, you might want to use the new **GlobalMemory-StatusEx** function:

```
BOOL GlobalMemoryStatusEx(LPMEMORYSTATUSEX pmst);
```

You must pass to this function the address of the new **MEMORYSTATUSEX** structure:

```
typedef struct _MEMORYSTATUSEX {
   DWORD dwLength;
   DWORD dwMemoryLoad;
   DWORDLONG ullTotalPhys;
   DWORDLONG ullAvailPhys;
   DWORDLONG ullTotalPageFile;
   DWORDLONG ullAvailPageFile;
   DWORDLONG ullTotalVirtual;
   DWORDLONG ullAvailVirtual;
   DWORDLONG ullAvailExtendedVirtual;
} MEMORYSTATUSEX, *LPMEMORYSTATUSEX;
```

This structure is identical to the original **MEMORYSTATUS** structure except that all the size members are 64 bits wide, allowing for values greater than 4 GB. The member at the end, **ullAvail-ExtendedVirtual**, indicates the size of unreserved memory in the very large memory (VLM) portion of the virtual address space of the calling process. This VLM portion applies only to certain CPU architectures in certain configurations.

Memory Management on NUMA Machines

As presented in Chapter 7, "Thread Scheduling, Priorities, and Affinities," CPUs on Non-Uniform Memory Access (NUMA) machines have access to memory on their own nodes as well as on other nodes. However, a CPU accessing memory on its own node is significantly faster than when a CPU accesses memory on a foreign node. By default, when a thread commits physical storage, the operating system tries to back the physical storage with RAM from the CPU's own node to improve access time performance. Only if insufficient RAM is available will Windows use RAM from a foreign node to back the storage.

When you are calling **GlobalMemoryStatusEx**, the value returned through the **ullAvailPhys** parameter is the sum of the available memory across all nodes. Call the following function to get the amount of memory on a specific NUMA node:

```
BOOL GetNumaAvailableMemoryNode(
   UCHAR uNode,
   PULONGLONG pulAvailableBytes);
```

The **LONGLONG** variable pointed to by the **pulAvailableBytes** parameter receives the amount of memory for the node identified by the **uNode** parameter. You can easily tell which NUMA node a CPU resides on by calling the **GetNumaProcessorNode** function:

```
BOOL WINAPI GetNumaProcessorNode(
  UCHAR Processor,
  PUCHAR NodeNumber);
```

The total number of nodes in the system is retrieved by calling the following function:

```
BOOL GetNumaHighestNodeNumber(PULONG pulHighestNodeNumber);
```

Given a node, from 0 to the value set to the variable pointed to by the **pulHighestNodeNumber** parameter, you can query the list of CPUs that reside on the node by calling the following function:

```
BOOL GetNumaNodeProcessorMask(
    UCHAR uNode,
    PULONGLONG pulProcessorMask);
```

The **uNode** parameter is the numeric identifier of the node, and the **LONGLONG** variable pointed to by the **pulProcessorMask** parameter will receive a bitmask: for a position in the mask, if the bit is set, the corresponding processor is part of the node.

As already described, Windows automatically tries to keep a thread and its RAM on the same node to improve performance. However, Windows also offers functions that you can call to control the thread and memory affinity manually. (See Chapter 15, "Using Virtual Memory in Your Own Applications," for more information.)

For more details about NUMA in Windows, you should read "Application Software Considerations for NUMA-Based Systems" at http://www.microsoft.com/whdc/system/platform/server/datacenter/numa_isv.mspx *and "NUMA Support"* (http://msdn2.microsoft.com/en-us/library/aa363804.aspx) *on MSDN.*

The Virtual Memory Status Sample Application

The VMStat application (14-VMStat.exe) displays a simple dialog box that lists the results of a call to **GlobalMemoryStatus**. The information inside the dialog box is updated once every second, so you might want to keep the application running while you work with other processes on your system. The source code and resource files for the application can be found in the 14-VMStat directory on the companion content Web page. The following figure shows the result of running this program on Windows Vista with a 1-GB machine:

The **dwMemoryLoad** member (shown as Memory Load) gives a rough estimate of how busy the memory management system is. This number can be anywhere from 0 through 100. The exact algorithm used to calculate this value varies in each version of Windows. In practice, the value reported by this member variable is useless.

The **dwTotalPhys** member (shown as TotalPhys) indicates the total number of bytes of physical memory (RAM) that exist. On this 1-GB machine, this value is 1,072,627,712, which is just 1,114,112 bytes under 1 GB. The reason that **GlobalMemoryStatus** does not report the full 1 GB is that the system reserves some storage as a nonpaged pool during the boot process. This memory is not even considered available to the kernel. The **dwAvailPhys** member (shown as AvailPhys) indicates the total number of bytes of physical memory available for allocation.

The **dwTotalPageFile** member (shown as TotalPageFile) indicates the maximum number of bytes that can be contained in the paging file(s) on your hard disk(s). Although VMStat reported that the paging file is currently 2,414,112,768 bytes, the system can expand and shrink the paging file as it sees fit. The **dwAvailPageFile** member (shown as AvailPageFile) indicates that 1,741,586,432 bytes in the paging file(s) are not committed to any process and are currently available should a process decide to commit any private storage.

The **dwTotalVirtual** member (shown as TotalVirtual) indicates the total number of bytes that are private in each process' address space. The value 2,147,352,576 is 128 KB short of being exactly 2 GB. The two partitions from 0x00000000 through 0x0000FFFF and from 0x7FFF0000 through 0x7FFFFFFF of inaccessible address space account for the 128-KB difference.

The last member, **dwAvailVirtual** (shown as AvailVirtual), is the only member of the structure specific to the process calling **GlobalMemoryStatus**—all the other members apply to the system and would be the same regardless of which process was calling **GlobalMemoryStatus**. To calculate this value, **GlobalMemoryStatus** adds up all the free regions in the calling process' address space. The **dwAvailVirtual** value 2,106,437,632 indicates the amount of free address space that is available for VMStat to do with what it wants. If you subtract the **dwAvailVirtual** member from the **dwTotalVirtual** member, you'll see that VMStat has 40,914,944 bytes reserved in its virtual address space.

There is no member that indicates the amount of physical storage currently in use by the process. For a process, the pages of its address space kept in RAM are called its *working set*. For a given process, the following function defined in psapi.h allows you to retrieve the process' current and maximum working set sizes:

```
BOOL GetProcessMemoryInfo(
    HANDLE hProcess,
    PPROCESS_MEMORY_COUNTERS ppmc,
    DWORD cbSize);
```

The **hProcess** is the handle of the process you are interested in; this handle must have **PROCESS_QUERY_INFORMATION** and **PROCESS_VM_READ** access rights. For the current executing process, **GetCurrentProcess** returns a pseudohandle that fits this requirement. The **ppmc** parameter points to a **PROCESS_MEMORY_COUNTERS_EX** structure whose size is given through the **cbSize** parameter. If **GetProcessMemoryInfo** returns **TRUE**, the following structure contains details about the specified process:

```
typedef struct _PROCESS_MEMORY_COUNTERS_EX {
    DWORD cb;
    DWORD PageFaultCount;
    SIZE_T PeakWorkingSetSize;
    SIZE_T WorkingSetSize;
    SIZE_T QuotaPeakPagedPoolUsage;
    SIZE_T QuotaPagedPoolUsage;
    SIZE_T QuotaPeakNonPagedPoolUsage;
    SIZE_T QuotaNonPagedPoolUsage;
    SIZE_T PagefileUsage;
    SIZE_T PeakPagefileUsage;
    SIZE_T PrivateUsage;
} PROCESS_MEMORY_COUNTERS_EX,
  *PPROCESS_MEMORY_COUNTERS_EX;
```

The **WorkingSetSize** field contains the number of bytes in RAM used by the process identified by **hProcess** at the time the function is called (shown as WorkingSet). The **PeakWorkingSetSize** field contains the maximum number of bytes the process had in RAM at any one moment in time since the process started running.

Knowing a process' working set is extremely valuable because it tells you how much RAM your program requires to run once it reaches a steady state. Minimizing your application's working set will improve your application's performance. As you probably know, if Windows applications are running slowly, the best thing you can do (as an end user) to improve their performance is to increase the amount of RAM you have in the machine. Although Windows does have the ability to swap RAM to and from disk, this ability comes with a huge performance hit. Adding RAM means that Windows can reduce swapping, which improves performance. If you are a developer, you have control over how much memory your application needs residing in RAM at any given time; reducing your application's requirement will result in improved performance.

When tuning an application, in addition to minimizing its working set, you'll also want to know how much memory your application is explicitly allocating through functions such as **new**, **malloc**, or **VirtualAlloc**. This is exactly what the **PrivateUsage** field returns (shown as PrivateBytes). The rest of the chapter explains the functions you can use to get a clear view of a process' address space.

> **Note** For more details about the existing application programming interface (API) to monitor the operating system and process' memory, go to the "Memory Performance Information" page at *http://msdn2.microsoft.com/en-us/library/aa965225.aspx*.

Determining the State of an Address Space

Windows offers a function that lets you query certain information (for example, size, storage type, and protection attributes) about a memory address in your address space. In fact, the VMMap sample application shown later in this chapter uses this function to produce the virtual memory map dumps that appeared in Chapter 13, "Windows Memory Architecture." This function is called **VirtualQuery**:

```
DWORD VirtualQuery(
   LPCVOID pvAddress,
   PMEMORY_BASIC_INFORMATION pmbi,
   DWORD dwLength);
```

Windows also offers a function that allows one process to query memory information about another process:

```
DWORD VirtualQueryEx(
   HANDLE hProcess,
   LPCVOID pvAddress,
   PMEMORY_BASIC_INFORMATION pmbi,
   DWORD dwLength);
```

The two functions are identical except that **VirtualQueryEx** allows you to pass the handle of a process whose address space you want to query. Debuggers and other utilities most often use this function—nearly all applications will need only to call **VirtualQuery**. When you call **Virtual-Query(Ex)**, the **pvAddress** parameter must contain the virtual memory address that you want information about. The **pmbi** parameter is the address to a **MEMORY_BASIC_INFORMATION** structure that you must allocate. This structure is defined in WinNT.h as follows:

```
typedef struct _MEMORY_BASIC_INFORMATION {
    PVOID BaseAddress;
    PVOID AllocationBase;
    DWORD AllocationProtect;
    SIZE_T RegionSize;
    DWORD State;
    DWORD Protect;
    DWORD Type;
} MEMORY_BASIC_INFORMATION, *PMEMORY_BASIC_INFORMATION;
```

The last parameter, **dwLength**, specifies the size of the **MEMORY_BASIC_INFORMATION** structure. **VirtualQuery(Ex)** returns the number of bytes copied into the buffer.

Based on the address that you pass in the **pvAddress** parameter, **VirtualQuery(Ex)** fills the **MEMORY_BASIC_INFORMATION** structure with information about the range of adjoining pages that share the same state, protection attributes, and type. Table 14-3 offers a description of the structure's members.

Table 14-3 Members of MEMORY_BASIC_INFORMATION

Member Name	Description
BaseAddress	The same value as the **pvAddress** parameter rounded down to a page boundary.
AllocationBase	Identifies the base address of the region containing the address specified in the **pvAddress** parameter.
AllocationProtect	Identifies the protection attribute assigned to the region when it was initially reserved.
RegionSize	Identifies the size, in bytes, for all pages starting at **BaseAddress** that have the same protection attributes, state, and type as the page containing the address specified in the **pvAddress** parameter.
State	Identifies the state (**MEM_FREE**, **MEM_RESERVE**, or **MEM_COMMIT**) for all adjoining pages that have the same protection attributes, state, and type as the page containing the address specified in the **pvAddress** parameter. If the state is free, the **AllocationBase**, **Allocation-Protect**, **Protect**, and **Type** members are undefined. If the state is **MEM_RESERVE**, the **Protect** member is undefined.
Protect	Identifies the protection attribute (**PAGE_***) for all adjoining pages that have the same protection attributes, state, and type as the page containing the address specified in the **pvAddress** parameter.
Type	Identifies the type of physical storage (**MEM_IMAGE**, **MEM_MAPPED**, or **MEM_PRIVATE**) that is backing all adjoining pages that have the same protection attributes, state, and type as the page containing the address specified in the **pvAddress** parameter.

The *VMQuery* Function

When I was first learning about Windows memory architecture, I used **VirtualQuery** as my guide. In fact, if you examine the first edition of this book, you'll see that the VMMap sample application was much simpler than the version I present in the next section. In the old version, I had a simple loop that repeatedly called **VirtualQuery**, and for each call I simply constructed a single line containing the members of the **MEMORY_BASIC_INFORMATION** structure. I studied this dump and tried to piece the memory management architecture together while referring to the SDK documentation (which was rather poor at the time). Well, I've learned a lot since then. Although **VirtualQuery** and the **MEMORY_BASIC_INFORMATION** structure give you a lot of insight into what's going on, I now know that they don't give you enough information to really understand it all.

The problem is that the **MEMORY_BASIC_INFORMATION** structure does not return all the information that the system has stored internally. If you have a memory address and want to obtain some simple information about it, **VirtualQuery** is great. If you just want to know whether there is committed physical storage to an address or whether a memory address can be read from or written to, **VirtualQuery** works fine. But if you want to know the total size of a reserved region or the number of blocks in a region or whether a region contains a thread's stack, a single call to **VirtualQuery** is just not going to give you the information you're looking for.

To obtain much more complete memory information, I have created my own function, **VMQuery**:

```
BOOL VMQuery(
   HANDLE hProcess,
   LPCVOID pvAddress,
   PVMQUERY pVMQ);
```

This function is similar to **VirtualQueryEx** in that it takes a process handle (in **hProcess**), a memory address (in **pvAddress**), and a pointer to a structure that is to be filled (specified by **pVMQ**). This structure is a **VMQUERY** structure that I have also defined:

```
typedef struct {
   // Region information
   PVOID pvRgnBaseAddress;
   DWORD dwRgnProtection;  // PAGE_*
   SIZE_T RgnSize;
   DWORD dwRgnStorage;     // MEM_*: Free, Image, Mapped, Private
   DWORD dwRgnBlocks;
   DWORD dwRgnGuardBlks;   // If > 0, region contains thread stack
   BOOL bRgnIsAStack;      // TRUE if region contains thread stack

   // Block information
   PVOID pvBlkBaseAddress;
   DWORD dwBlkProtection;  // PAGE_*
   SIZE_T BlkSize;
   DWORD dwBlkStorage;     // MEM_*: Free, Reserve, Image, Mapped, Private
} VMQUERY, *PVMQUERY;
```

As you can see from just a quick glance, my **VMQUERY** structure contains much more information than the Windows **MEMORY_BASIC_INFORMATION** structure. My structure is divided into two distinct parts: region information and block information. The region portion describes information about the region, and the block portion includes information about the block containing the address specified by the **pvAddress** parameter. Table 14-4 describes all the members.

Table 14-4   Members of VMQUERY

Member Name	Description
pvRgnBaseAddress	Identifies the base address of the virtual address space region containing the address specified in the **pvAddress** parameter.
dwRgnProtection	Identifies the protection attribute (**PAGE_***) that was assigned to the region of address space when it was initially reserved.
RgnSize	Identifies the size, in bytes, of the region that was reserved.
dwRgnStorage	Identifies the type of physical storage that is used for the bulk of the blocks in the region. The value is one of the following: **MEM_FREE, MEM_IMAGE, MEM_MAPPED,** or **MEM_PRIVATE.**
dwRgnBlocks	Identifies the number of blocks contained within the region.
dwRgnGuardBlks	Identifies the number of blocks that have the **PAGE_GUARD** protection attribute flag turned on. This value will usually be either 0 or 1. If it's 1, that's a good indicator that the region was reserved to contain a thread's stack.
bRgnIsAStack	Identifies whether the region contains a thread's stack. This value is determined by taking a "best guess" because it is impossible to be 100-percent sure whether a region contains a stack.
pvBlkBaseAddress	Identifies the base address of the block that contains the address specified in the **pvAddress** parameter.
dwBlkProtection	Identifies the protection attribute for the block that contains the address specified in the **pvAddress** parameter.
BlkSize	Identifies the size, in bytes, of the block that contains the address specified in the **pvAddress** parameter.
dwBlkStorage	Identifies the content of the block that contains the address specified in the **pvAddress** parameter. The value is one of the following: **MEM_FREE, MEM_RESERVE, MEM_IMAGE, MEM_MAPPED,** or **MEM_PRIVATE.**

No doubt **VMQuery** must do a significant amount of processing, including many calls to **VirtualQueryEx**, to obtain all this information—which means it executes much more slowly than **VirtualQueryEx**. For this reason, you should think carefully when deciding which of these two functions to call. If you do not need the extra information obtained by **VMQuery**, call **VirtualQuery** or **VirtualQueryEx**.

The VMQuery.cpp file, listed next, shows how I obtain and massage all the information needed to set the members of the **VMQUERY** structure. The VMQuery.cpp and VMQuery.h files are in the 14-VMMap directory on the companion content Web page. Rather than go into detail in the text about how I process this data, I'll let my comments (sprinkled liberally throughout the code) speak for themselves.

VMQuery.cpp

```
/**************************************************************************
Module:  VMQuery.cpp
Notices: Copyright (c) 2008 Jeffrey Richter & Christophe Nasarre
**************************************************************************/


#include "..\CommonFiles\CmnHdr.h"      /* See Appendix A. */
#include <windowsx.h>
#include "VMQuery.h"


///////////////////////////////////////////////////////////////////////////


// Helper structure
typedef struct {
   SIZE_T RgnSize;
   DWORD  dwRgnStorage;      // MEM_*: Free, Image, Mapped, Private
   DWORD  dwRgnBlocks;
   DWORD  dwRgnGuardBlks;    // If > 0, region contains thread stack
   BOOL   bRgnIsAStack;      // TRUE if region contains thread stack
} VMQUERY_HELP;


// This global, static variable holds the allocation granularity value for
// this CPU platform. Initialized the first time VMQuery is called.
static DWORD gs_dwAllocGran = 0;


///////////////////////////////////////////////////////////////////////////


// Iterates through a region's blocks and returns findings in VMQUERY_HELP
static BOOL VMQueryHelp(HANDLE hProcess, LPCVOID pvAddress,
   VMQUERY_HELP *pVMQHelp) {

   ZeroMemory(pVMQHelp, sizeof(*pVMQHelp));

   // Get address of region containing passed memory address.
   MEMORY_BASIC_INFORMATION mbi;
   BOOL bOk = (VirtualQueryEx(hProcess, pvAddress, &mbi, sizeof(mbi))
      == sizeof(mbi));

   if (!bOk)
      return(bOk);   // Bad memory address, return failure

   // Walk starting at the region's base address (which never changes)
   PVOID pvRgnBaseAddress = mbi.AllocationBase;

   // Walk starting at the first block in the region (changes in the loop)
   PVOID pvAddressBlk = pvRgnBaseAddress;
```

```
      // Save the memory type of the physical storage block.
      pVMQHelp->dwRgnStorage = mbi.Type;


      for (;;) {
         // Get info about the current block.
         bOk = (VirtualQueryEx(hProcess, pvAddressBlk, &mbi, sizeof(mbi))
            == sizeof(mbi));
         if (!bOk)
            break;   // Couldn't get the information; end loop.


         // Is this block in the same region?
         if (mbi.AllocationBase != pvRgnBaseAddress)
            break;   // Found a block in the next region; end loop.


         // We have a block contained in the region.

         pVMQHelp->dwRgnBlocks++;                 // Add another block to the region
         pVMQHelp->RgnSize += mbi.RegionSize;  // Add block's size to region size


         // If block has PAGE_GUARD attribute, add 1 to this counter
         if ((mbi.Protect & PAGE_GUARD) == PAGE_GUARD)
            pVMQHelp->dwRgnGuardBlks++;


         // Take a best guess as to the type of physical storage committed to the
         // block. This is a guess because some blocks can convert from MEM_IMAGE
         // to MEM_PRIVATE or from MEM_MAPPED to MEM_PRIVATE; MEM_PRIVATE can
         // always be overridden by MEM_IMAGE or MEM_MAPPED.
         if (pVMQHelp->dwRgnStorage == MEM_PRIVATE)
            pVMQHelp->dwRgnStorage = mbi.Type;


         // Get the address of the next block.
         pvAddressBlk = (PVOID) ((PBYTE) pvAddressBlk + mbi.RegionSize);
      }


      // After examining the region, check to see whether it is a thread stack
      // Windows Vista: Assume stack if region has at least 1 PAGE_GUARD block
      pVMQHelp->bRgnIsAStack = (pVMQHelp->dwRgnGuardBlks > 0);


      return(TRUE);
}



///////////////////////////////////////////////////////////////////////////////


BOOL VMQuery(HANDLE hProcess, LPCVOID pvAddress, PVMQUERY pVMQ) {

   if (gs_dwAllocGran == 0) {
      // Set allocation granularity if this is the first call
      SYSTEM_INFO sinf;
      GetSystemInfo(&sinf);
      gs_dwAllocGran = sinf.dwAllocationGranularity;
   }


   ZeroMemory(pVMQ, sizeof(*pVMQ));
```

```
    // Get the MEMORY_BASIC_INFORMATION for the passed address.
    MEMORY_BASIC_INFORMATION mbi;
    BOOL bOk = (VirtualQueryEx(hProcess, pvAddress, &mbi, sizeof(mbi))
       == sizeof(mbi));

    if (!bOk)
       return(bOk);    // Bad memory address; return failure

    // The MEMORY_BASIC_INFORMATION structure contains valid information.
    // Time to start setting the members of our own VMQUERY structure.

    // First, fill in the block members. We'll fill the region members later.
    switch (mbi.State) {
       case MEM_FREE:       // Free block (not reserved)
          pVMQ->pvBlkBaseAddress = NULL;
          pVMQ->BlkSize = 0;
          pVMQ->dwBlkProtection = 0;
          pVMQ->dwBlkStorage = MEM_FREE;
          break;

       case MEM_RESERVE:    // Reserved block without committed storage in it.
          pVMQ->pvBlkBaseAddress = mbi.BaseAddress;
          pVMQ->BlkSize = mbi.RegionSize;

          // For an uncommitted block, mbi.Protect is invalid. So we will
          // show that the reserved block inherits the protection attribute
          // of the region in which it is contained.
          pVMQ->dwBlkProtection = mbi.AllocationProtect;
          pVMQ->dwBlkStorage = MEM_RESERVE;
          break;

       case MEM_COMMIT:     // Reserved block with committed storage in it.
          pVMQ->pvBlkBaseAddress = mbi.BaseAddress;
          pVMQ->BlkSize = mbi.RegionSize;
          pVMQ->dwBlkProtection = mbi.Protect;
          pVMQ->dwBlkStorage = mbi.Type;
          break;

       default:
          DebugBreak();
          break;
    }

    // Now fill in the region data members.
    VMQUERY_HELP VMQHelp;
    switch (mbi.State) {
       case MEM_FREE:       // Free block (not reserved)
          pVMQ->pvRgnBaseAddress = mbi.BaseAddress;
          pVMQ->dwRgnProtection  = mbi.AllocationProtect;
          pVMQ->RgnSize          = mbi.RegionSize;
          pVMQ->dwRgnStorage     = MEM_FREE;
          pVMQ->dwRgnBlocks      = 0;
          pVMQ->dwRgnGuardBlks   = 0;
          pVMQ->bRgnIsAStack     = FALSE;
          break;
```

```
    case MEM_RESERVE:    // Reserved block without committed storage in it.
        pVMQ->pvRgnBaseAddress = mbi.AllocationBase;
        pVMQ->dwRgnProtection  = mbi.AllocationProtect;

        // Iterate through all blocks to get complete region information.
        VMQueryHelp(hProcess, pvAddress, &VMQHelp);

        pVMQ->RgnSize          = VMQHelp.RgnSize;
        pVMQ->dwRgnStorage     = VMQHelp.dwRgnStorage;
        pVMQ->dwRgnBlocks      = VMQHelp.dwRgnBlocks;
        pVMQ->dwRgnGuardBlks   = VMQHelp.dwRgnGuardBlks;
        pVMQ->bRgnIsAStack     = VMQHelp.bRgnIsAStack;
        break;

    case MEM_COMMIT:     // Reserved block with committed storage in it.
        pVMQ->pvRgnBaseAddress = mbi.AllocationBase;
        pVMQ->dwRgnProtection  = mbi.AllocationProtect;

        // Iterate through all blocks to get complete region information.
        VMQueryHelp(hProcess, pvAddress, &VMQHelp);

        pVMQ->RgnSize          = VMQHelp.RgnSize;
        pVMQ->dwRgnStorage     = VMQHelp.dwRgnStorage;
        pVMQ->dwRgnBlocks      = VMQHelp.dwRgnBlocks;
        pVMQ->dwRgnGuardBlks   = VMQHelp.dwRgnGuardBlks;
        pVMQ->bRgnIsAStack     = VMQHelp.bRgnIsAStack;
        break;

    default:
        DebugBreak();
        break;
    }

    return(bOk);
}


/////////////////////////////// End of File ///////////////////////////////
```

The Virtual Memory Map Sample Application

The VMMap application (14-VMMap.exe) walks a process' address space and shows the regions and the blocks within regions. The source code and resource files for the application are in the 14-VMMap directory on the companion content Web page. When you start the program, the window shown on the next page appears.

I used the contents of this application's list box to produce the virtual memory map dumps presented in Table 13-2 on page 373 and Table 13-3 on page 381.

Each entry in the list box shows the result of information obtained by calling my **VMQuery** function. The main loop, in the **Refresh** function, looks like this:

```
BOOL bOk = TRUE;
PVOID pvAddress = NULL;
...

while (bOk) {

    VMQUERY vmq;
    bOk = VMQuery(hProcess, pvAddress, &vmq);

    if (bOk) {
        // Construct the line to be displayed, and add it to the list box.
        TCHAR szLine[1024];
        ConstructRgnInfoLine(hProcess, &vmq, szLine, sizeof(szLine));
        ListBox_AddString(hWndLB, szLine);

        if (bExpandRegions) {
            for (DWORD dwBlock = 0; bOk && (dwBlock < vmq.dwRgnBlocks);
                dwBlock++) {

                ConstructBlkInfoLine(&vmq, szLine, sizeof(szLine));
                ListBox_AddString(hWndLB, szLine);

                // Get the address of the next region to test.
                pvAddress = ((PBYTE) pvAddress + vmq.BlkSize);
                if (dwBlock < vmq.dwRgnBlocks - 1) {
                    // Don't query the memory info after the last block.
                    bOk = VMQuery(hProcess, pvAddress, &vmq);
                }
            }
        }
    }
}
```

```
        // Get the address of the next region to test.
        pvAddress = ((PBYTE) vmq.pvRgnBaseAddress + vmq.RgnSize);
    }
}
```

This loop starts walking from virtual address **NULL** and ends when **VMQuery** returns **FALSE**, indicating that it can no longer walk the process' address space. With each iteration of the loop, there is a call to **ConstructRgnInfoLine**; this function fills a character buffer with information about the region. Then this information is appended to the list box.

Within this main loop is a nested loop that iterates through each block in the region. Each iteration of this loop calls **ConstructBlkInfoLine** to fill a character buffer with information about the region's blocks. Then the information is appended to the list box. It's easy to walk the process' address space using the **VMQuery** function.

If you run the VMMap application on Windows Vista after a reboot (or compare the output from two different computers running Vista), you might notice that various dynamic-link libraries (DLLs) load at different addresses each time. This is because of a new feature called *Address Space Layout Randomization (ASLR)*, which allows Windows to select a different base address when loading a DLL for the first time. The goal of this base address randomization is to make the location of code in known DLLs more difficult for hackers to find, and therefore, reduce exploitation of this code by malware.

For example, a buffer or stack overflow is often used by hackers to force the course of execution to jump to a well-known address in a system DLL code function. With ASLR, there is one chance in 256 (or more) that the well-known address will be correct, which significantly reduces the chance that a hacker can easily or consistently exploit the overflow.

When the DLL is loaded, the ASLR rebase fixups are applied by the kernel and these modified pages are shared by all processes using the DLL. That is, memory is used efficiently because the fixups are not applied on a per-process basis.

> **Note**   Starting with Microsoft Visual Studio 2005 SP1, your own DLLs (and EXE files) can partake of the ASLR feature by using the **/dynamicbase** linker switch when you build your file. In fact, if you expect your DLL (or EXE) file to load at an address other than its base address, I recommend you use this switch because it allows your file's fixed-up pages to be shared across multiple processes, using memory efficiently.

Chapter 15

Using Virtual Memory in Your Own Applications

Microsoft Windows offers three mechanisms for manipulating memory:

- Virtual memory, which is best for managing large arrays of objects or structures
- Memory-mapped files, which are best for managing large streams of data (usually from files) and for sharing data between multiple processes running on a single machine
- Heaps, which are best for managing large numbers of small objects

In this chapter, we discuss the first method, virtual memory. Memory-mapped files and heaps are discussed in Chapter 17, "Memory-Mapped Files," and Chapter 18, "Heaps," respectively.

The functions for manipulating virtual memory allow you to directly reserve a region of address space, commit physical storage (from the paging file) to the region, and set your own protection attributes.

Reserving a Region in an Address Space

You reserve a region in your process' address space by calling **VirtualAlloc**:

```
PVOID VirtualAlloc(
   PVOID pvAddress,
   SIZE_T dwSize,
   DWORD fdwAllocationType,
   DWORD fdwProtect);
```

The first parameter, **pvAddress**, contains a memory address specifying where you would like the system to reserve the address space. Most of the time, you'll pass **NULL** for this parameter. This tells **VirtualAlloc** that the system, which keeps a record of free address ranges, should reserve the region wherever it sees fit. The system can reserve a region from anywhere in your process' address space—there are no guarantees that the system will allocate regions from the bottom of your address space up or vice versa. However, you can have some say over this allocation by using the **MEM_TOP_DOWN** flag, discussed later in this chapter.

For most programmers, the ability to choose a specific memory address where a region will be reserved is an unusual concept. When you allocated memory in the past, the operating system simply found a block of memory large enough to satisfy the request, allocated the block, and returned its address. But because each process has its own address space, you can specify the base memory address where you would like the operating system to reserve the region.

For example, say that you want to allocate a region starting 50 MB into your process' address space. In this case, you pass 52,428,800 (50 × 1024 × 1024) as the **pvAddress** parameter. If this memory address has a free region large enough to satisfy your request, the system will reserve the desired region and return. If a free region does not exist at the specified address or if the free region is not large enough, the system cannot satisfy your request and **VirtualAlloc** returns **NULL**. Note that any address you pass for the **pvAddress** parameter must always reside in your process' user-mode partition or the call to **VirtualAlloc** will fail, causing it to return **NULL**.

As I mentioned in Chapter 13, "Windows Memory Architecture," regions are always reserved on an allocation granularity boundary (64 KB for all implementations of Windows to date). So if you attempt to reserve a region starting at address 19,668,992 (300 × 65,536 + 8192) in your process' address space, the system rounds that address down to a multiple of 64 KB and reserves the region starting at address 19,660,800 (300 × 65,536).

If **VirtualAlloc** can satisfy your request, it returns a value indicating the base address of the reserved region. If you passed a specific address as **VirtualAlloc**'s **pvAddress** parameter, this return value is the same value that you passed to **VirtualAlloc** rounded down (if necessary) to a 64-KB boundary.

VirtualAlloc's second parameter, **dwSize**, specifies the size of the region you want to reserve in bytes. Because the system must always reserve regions in multiples of the CPU's page size, an attempt to reserve a region that spans 62 KB will result in reserving a region that spans 64 KB on machines that use 4-KB, 8-KB, or 16-KB pages.

VirtualAlloc's third parameter, **fdwAllocationType**, tells the system whether you want to reserve a region or commit physical storage. (This distinction is necessary because **VirtualAlloc** is also used to commit physical storage.) To reserve a region of address space, you must pass the **MEM_RESERVE** identifier as the value for the **fdwAllocationType** parameter.

If you're going to reserve a region that you don't expect to release for a long time, you might want to reserve the region at the highest memory address possible. That way, the region does not get reserved from the middle of your process' address space, where it can potentially cause fragmentation. If you want the system to reserve a region at the highest possible memory address, you must pass **NULL** for the **pvAddress** parameter and, for the **fdwAllocationType** parameter, you must also bitwise **OR** the **MEM_TOP_DOWN** flag with the **MEM_RESERVE** flag.

The last parameter, **fdwProtect**, indicates the protection attribute that should be assigned to the region. The protection attribute associated with the region has no effect on the committed storage mapped to the region. Regardless of the protection attribute assigned to a region, if no physical storage is committed, any attempt to access a memory address in the range will cause the thread to raise an access violation.

When reserving a region, assign the protection attribute that will be used most often with the storage committed to the region. For example, if you intend to commit physical storage with a protection attribute of **PAGE_READWRITE** (by far the most common protection attribute), you should reserve the region with **PAGE_READWRITE**. The system's internal record keeping behaves more efficiently when the region's protection attribute matches the committed storage's protection attribute.

You can use any of the following protection attributes: **PAGE_NOACCESS**, **PAGE_READWRITE**, **PAGE_READONLY**, **PAGE_EXECUTE**, **PAGE_EXECUTE_READ**, or **PAGE_EXECUTE_READWRITE**. However, you cannot specify either the **PAGE_WRITECOPY** attribute or the **PAGE_EXECUTE_WRITECOPY** attribute. If you do so, **VirtualAlloc** will not reserve the region and will return **NULL**. Also, you cannot use the protection attribute flags **PAGE_GUARD**, **PAGE_NOCACHE**, or **PAGE_WRITECOMBINE** when reserving regions—they can be used only with committed storage.

> **Note**   If your application is running on a Non-Uniform Memory Access (NUMA) machine, you can improve performance by forcing some of a process' virtual memory to be on a particular node's RAM by calling the following function:
>
> ```
> PVOID VirtualAllocExNuma(
>    HANDLE hProcess,
>    PVOID pvAddress,
>    SIZE_T dwSize,
>    DWORD  fdwAllocationType,
>    DWORD  fdwProtect,
>    DWORD  dwPreferredNumaNode);
> ```
>
> This function is identical to **VirtualAlloc** except that **VirtualAllocExNuma** has two additional parameters: **hProcess** and **dwPreferredNumaNode**. The **hProcess** parameter identifies the process whose virtual address space you want to reserve/commit. (Call the **GetCurrentProcess** function to manipulate your own process' virtual memory.) The **dwPreferredNumaNode** parameter indicates which node's RAM should be used to back the virtual memory pages.
>
> The Windows functions that allow you to figure out relations between nodes and processors on NUMA machines are covered in "Memory Management on NUMA Machines" on page 405.

Committing Storage in a Reserved Region

After you have reserved a region, you need to commit physical storage to the region before you can access the memory addresses contained within it. The system allocates physical storage committed to a region from the system's paging file. Physical storage is always committed on page boundaries and in page-size chunks.

To commit physical storage, you must call **VirtualAlloc** again. This time, however, you'll pass the **MEM_COMMIT** identifier instead of the **MEM_RESERVE** identifier for the **fdwAllocationType** parameter. You usually pass the same page protection attribute (most often **PAGE_READWRITE**) that was used when **VirtualAlloc** was called to reserve the region, although you can specify a different protection attribute.

From within the reserved region, you *must* tell **VirtualAlloc** where you want to commit physical storage and how much physical storage to commit. You do this by specifying the desired memory address in the **pvAddress** parameter and the amount of physical storage, in bytes, in the **dwSize** parameter. Note that you don't have to commit physical storage to the entire region at once.

Let's look at an example of how to commit storage. Say your application is running on an *x*86 CPU and the application reserves a 512-KB region starting at address 5,242,880. You would like your application to commit storage to the 6-KB portion of the reserved region starting 2 KB into the reserved region's address space. To do this, call **VirtualAlloc** using the **MEM_COMMIT** flag as follows:

```
VirtualAlloc((PVOID) (5242880 + (2 * 1024)), 6 * 1024,
    MEM_COMMIT, PAGE_READWRITE);
```

In this case, the system must commit 8 KB of physical storage, spanning the address range 5,242,880 through 5,251,071 (5,242,880 + 8 KB – 1 byte). Both of these committed pages have a protection attribute of **PAGE_READWRITE**. Protection attributes are assigned on a whole-page basis only. It is not possible to use different protection attributes for portions of the same page of storage. However, it is possible for one page in a region to have one protection attribute (such as **PAGE_READWRITE**) and for another page in the same region to have a different protection attribute (such as **PAGE_READONLY**).

Reserving a Region and Committing Storage Simultaneously

At times, you'll want to reserve a region and commit storage to it simultaneously. You can do this by placing a single call to **VirtualAlloc** as follows:

```
PVOID pvMem = VirtualAlloc(NULL, 99 * 1024,
    MEM_RESERVE | MEM_COMMIT, PAGE_READWRITE);
```

This call is a request to reserve a 99-KB region and commit 99 KB of physical storage to the region. When the system processes this call, it first searches your process' address space to find a contiguous area of unreserved address space large enough to hold 100 KB in 25 pages (on a 4-KB page machine) or 104 KB in 13 pages (on an 8-KB page machine).

The system searches the address space because I specified **NULL** as the **pvAddress** parameter. If I had specified a memory address for **pvAddress**, the system would see whether there was enough unreserved address space at that memory address. If the system could not find enough unreserved address space, **VirtualAlloc** would return **NULL**.

If a suitable region can be reserved, the system commits physical storage to the entire region. Both the region and the committed storage will be assigned **PAGE_READWRITE** protection.

Windows offers large-page support, which can improve the performance of manipulating large chunks of memory. Instead of allocating memory with page granularity as returned by the **Get-SystemInfo** function in the **dwPageSize** field of the **SYSTEM_INFO** structure, a large-page granularity is used, whose size is returned by the following function:

```
SIZE_T GetLargePageMinimum();
```

Notice that **GetLargePageMinimum** might return 0 if the CPU does not support large-page allocations. If you are allocating a block of memory that is at least as large as the value returned from **GetLargePageMinimum**, you can use Windows large-page support. To allocate the memory, you simply call **VirtualAlloc** with the **MEM_LARGE_PAGE** flag **OR**ed with the **fdwAllocationType** parameter. In addition, there are three other conditions that you must meet:

- You must allocate a block of memory that is a multiple of the value returned by **GetLarge-PageMinimum** in the **dwSize** parameter.

- When **VirtualAlloc** is called, **MEM_RESERVE | MEM_COMMIT** must be **OR**ed with the **fdwAllocationType** parameter. In other words, you must reserve and commit all the memory at once; you cannot reserve and sparsely commit.

- You must allocate all the memory specifying **PAGE_READWRITE** for **VirtualAlloc**'s **fdwProtect** parameter.

Windows considers memory allocated with the **MEM_LARGE_PAGE** flag to be unpageable; it must reside in RAM. This is one reason why memory allocated this way offers high performance. However, because RAM is scarce, calling **VirtualAlloc** with the **MEM_LARGE_PAGE** flag requires the caller to have the Lock Pages In Memory user right granted and enabled or the function fails. By default, this right isn't assigned to any user or group. If you want to run an interactive application that takes advantage of large pages, an administrator must grant you this right before you log on and run the application.

To turn on this right, perform the following steps:

1. Open the Local Security Policy entry in the Administrative Tools from the Start menu.

2. In the left-hand pane of the console, double-click to expand each of the following items: Security Settings and Local Policies. Select the User Rights Assignment item.

3. In the right-hand pane, select the Lock Pages In Memory attribute.

4. Select Properties from the Action menu to display the Lock Pages In Memory Properties dialog box. Click the Add User Or Group button. Use the Select Users Or Groups dialog box to add the users and/or groups that you want to assign the Lock Pages In Memory user right. Exit each of the dialog boxes by clicking the OK button.

User rights are granted when a user logs on. If you just granted the Lock Pages In Memory right to yourself, you must log off and log back on before it takes effect. Notice that, in addition to enabling the corresponding privilege at run time, the application must also run elevated as explained in "When Administrator Runs as a Standard User" on page 110.

Finally, **VirtualAlloc** returns the virtual address of the reserved and committed region, which is then saved in the **pvMem** variable. If the system couldn't find a large enough address space or commit the physical storage, **VirtualAlloc** returns **NULL**.

It is certainly possible when reserving a region and committing physical storage this way to pass a specific address as the **pvAddress** parameter to **VirtualAlloc**. Or you might need to have the system select a suitable region toward the top of your process' address space by **OR**ing the **MEM_TOP_DOWN** flag to the **fdwAllocationType** parameter and passing **NULL** for the **pvAddress** parameter.

When to Commit Physical Storage

Let's pretend you're implementing a spreadsheet application that supports 200 rows by 256 columns. For each cell, you need a **CELLDATA** structure that describes the contents of the cell. The easiest way for you to manipulate the two-dimensional matrix of cells would be to declare the following variable in your application:

```
CELLDATA CellData[200][256];
```

If the size of a **CELLDATA** structure were 128 bytes, the two-dimensional matrix would require 6,553,600 (200 × 256 × 128) bytes of physical storage. That's a lot of physical storage to allocate from the paging file right up front for a spreadsheet, especially when you consider that most users put information into only a few spreadsheet cells, leaving the majority unused. The memory usage would be very inefficient.

So, historically, spreadsheets have been implemented using other data structure techniques, such as linked lists. With the linked-list approach, **CELLDATA** structures have to be created only for the cells in the spreadsheet that actually contain data. Because most cells in a spreadsheet go unused, this method saves a tremendous amount of storage. However, this technique makes it much more difficult to obtain the contents of a cell. If you want to know the contents of the cell in row 5, column 10, you must walk through linked lists to find the desired cell, which makes the linked-list method slower than the declared-matrix method.

Virtual memory offers us a compromise between declaring the two-dimensional matrix up front and implementing linked lists. With virtual memory, you get the fast, easy access offered by the declared-matrix technique combined with the superior storage savings offered by the linked-list technique.

For you to obtain the advantages of the virtual memory technique, your program needs to follow these steps:

1. Reserve a region large enough to contain the entire matrix of **CELLDATA** structures. Reserving a region uses no physical storage at all.

2. When the user enters data into a cell, locate the memory address in the reserved region where the **CELLDATA** structure should go. Of course, no physical storage is mapped to this address yet, so any attempts to access memory at this address will raise an access violation.

3. Commit only enough physical storage to the memory address located in step 2 for a **CELLDATA** structure. (You can tell the system to commit physical storage to specific parts of the reserved region—a region can contain both parts that are mapped to physical storage and parts that are not.)

4. Set the members of the new **CELLDATA** structure.

Now that physical storage is mapped to the proper location, your program can access the storage without raising an access violation. This virtual memory technique is excellent because physical storage is committed only as the user enters data into the spreadsheet's cells. Because most of the cells in a spreadsheet are empty, most of the reserved region will not have physical storage committed to it.

The one problem with the virtual memory technique is that you must determine when physical storage needs to be committed. If the user enters data into a cell and then simply edits or changes that data, there is no need to commit physical storage—the storage for the cell's **CELLDATA** structure was committed the first time data was entered.

Also, the system always commits physical storage with page granularity. So when you attempt to commit physical storage for a single **CELLDATA** structure (as in step 2 of the procedure just shown), the system is actually committing a full page of storage. This is not as wasteful as it sounds: committing storage for a single **CELLDATA** structure has the effect of committing storage for other nearby **CELLDATA** structures. If the user then enters data into a neighboring cell—which is frequently the case—you might not need to commit additional physical storage.

There are four methods for determining whether to commit physical storage to a portion of a region:

- Always attempt to commit physical storage. Instead of checking to see whether physical storage is mapped to a portion of the region, have your program try to commit storage every time it calls **VirtualAlloc**. The system first checks to see whether storage has already been committed and, if so, does not commit additional physical storage. This approach is the easiest but has the disadvantage of making an additional function call every time a **CELLDATA** structure is altered, which makes your program perform more slowly.

- Determine (using the **VirtualQuery** function) whether physical storage has already been committed to the address space containing the **CELLDATA** structure. If it has been, do nothing else; if it hasn't been, call **VirtualAlloc** to commit the memory. This method is actually worse than the first one: it both increases the size of your code and slows down your program because of the additional call to **VirtualQuery**.

- Keep a record of which pages have been committed and which haven't. Doing so makes your application run faster: you avoid the call to **VirtualAlloc**, and your code can determine more quickly than the system can whether storage has already been committed. The disadvantage is that you must keep track of the page commit information somehow, which could be either very simple or very difficult depending on your specific situation.

- Use structured exception handling (SEH)—the best method. SEH is an operating system feature that causes the system to notify your application when certain situations occur. Essentially, you set up your application with an exception handler, and then, whenever an attempt is made to access uncommitted memory, the system notifies your application of the problem. Your application then commits the memory and tells the system to retry the instruction that caused the exception. This time the memory access succeeds, and the program continues running as though there had never been a problem. This method is the most advantageous because it requires the least amount of work from you (meaning less code) and because your program will run at full speed. A complete discussion of the SEH mechanism is saved for Chapter 23, "Termination Handlers," Chapter 24, "Exception Handlers and Software Exceptions," and Chapter 25, "Unhandled Exceptions, Vectored Exception Handling, and C++ Exceptions." The Spreadsheet sample application in Chapter 25 illustrates exactly how to use virtual memory as I've just described.

Decommitting Physical Storage and Releasing a Region

To decommit physical storage mapped to a region or release an entire region of address space, call the **VirtualFree** function:

```
BOOL VirtualFree(
    LPVOID pvAddress,
    SIZE_T dwSize,
    DWORD fdwFreeType);
```

Let's first examine the simple case of calling **VirtualFree** to release a reserved region. When your process will no longer be accessing the physical storage within a region, you can release the entire reserved region, and all the physical storage committed to the region, by making a single call to **VirtualFree**.

For this call, the **pvAddress** parameter must be the base address of the region. This address is the same address that **VirtualAlloc** returned when the region was reserved. The system knows the size of the region at the specified memory address, so you can pass **0** for the **dwSize** parameter. In fact, you must pass **0** for the **dwSize** parameter or the call to **VirtualFree** will fail. For the third parameter, **fdwFreeType**, you must pass **MEM_RELEASE** to tell the system to decommit all physical storage mapped to the region and to release the region. When releasing a region, you must release all the address space that was reserved by the region. For example, you cannot reserve a 128-KB region and then decide to release only 64 KB of it. You must release all 128 KB.

When you want to decommit some physical storage from the region without releasing the region, you also call **VirtualFree**. To decommit some physical storage, you must pass the memory address that identifies the first page to be decommitted in **VirtualFree**'s **pvAddress** parameter. You must also specify the number of bytes to free in the **dwSize** parameter and the **MEM_DECOMMIT** identifier in the **fdwFreeType** parameter.

Like committing, decommitting is done with page granularity. That is, specifying a memory address in the middle of a page decommits the entire page. And, of course, if **pvAddress + dwSize** falls in the middle of a page, the whole page that contains this address is decommitted as well. So all pages that fall within the range of **pvAddress** to **pvAddress + dwSize** are decommitted.

If **dwSize** is **0** and **pvAddress** is the base address for the allocated region, **VirtualFree** will decommit the complete range of allocated pages. After the pages of physical storage have been decommitted, the freed physical storage is available to any other process in the system; any attempt to access the decommitted memory results in an access violation.

When to Decommit Physical Storage

In practice, knowing when it's OK to decommit memory is very tricky. Consider the spreadsheet example again. If your application is running on an *x86* machine, each page of storage is 4 KB and can hold 32 (4096/128) **CELLDATA** structures. If the user deletes the contents of **Cell-Data[0][1]**, you might be able to decommit the page of storage as long as cells **CellData[0][0]** through **CellData[0][31]** are also not in use. But how do you know? You can tackle this problem in different ways:

- Without a doubt, the easiest solution is to design a **CELLDATA** structure that is exactly one page in size. Then, because there is always one structure per page, you can simply decommit the page of physical storage when you no longer need the data in the structure. Even if your data structures were, say, multiples of a page 8 KB or 12 KB for *x*86 CPUs (these would be unusually large structures), decommitting memory would still be pretty easy. Of course, to use this method you must define your data structures to meet the page size of the CPU you're targeting—not how we usually write our programs.

- A more practical solution is to keep a record of which structures are in use. To save memory, you might use a bitmap. So if you have an array of 100 structures, you also maintain an array of 100 bits. Initially, all the bits are set to **0**, indicating that no structures are in use. As you use the structures, you set the corresponding bits to **1**. Then, whenever you don't need a structure and you change its bit back to **0**, you check the bits of the adjacent structures that fall into the same page of memory. If none of the adjacent structures is in use, you can decommit the page.

- The last solution implements a garbage collection function. This scheme relies on the fact that the system sets all the bytes in a page to **0** when physical storage is first committed. To use this scheme, you must first set aside a **BOOL** (perhaps called **bInUse**) in your structure. Then, every time you put a structure in committed memory, you need to ensure that **bInUse** is set to **TRUE**.

As your application runs, you'll want to call the garbage collection function periodically. This function should traverse all the potential data structures. For each structure, the function first determines whether storage is committed for the structure; if so, the function checks the **bInUse** member to see whether it is **0**. A value of **0** means that the structure is not in use, whereas a value of **TRUE** means that it is in use. After the garbage collection function has checked all the structures that fall within a given page, it calls **VirtualFree** to decommit the storage if all the structures are not in use.

You can call the garbage collection function immediately after a structure is no longer considered to be in use, but doing so might take more time than you want to spend because the function cycles through all the possible structures. An excellent way to implement this function is to have it run as part of a lower-priority thread. In this way, you don't take time away from the thread executing the main application. Whenever the main application is idle or the main application's thread is performing file I/O, the system can schedule time to the garbage collection function.

Of all the methods I've listed, the first two are my personal favorites. However, if your structures are small (less than a page), I recommend using the last method.

The Virtual Memory Allocation Sample Application

The VMAlloc.cpp listing demonstrates how to use virtual memory techniques for manipulating an array of structures. The source code and resource files for the application are in the 15-VMAlloc directory on the companion content Web page. When you start the program, the following window appears:

Initially, no region of address space has been reserved for the array, and all the address space that would be reserved for it is free, as shown in the Memory Map area. When you click the Reserve Region (50, 2 KB Structures) button, VMAlloc calls **VirtualAlloc** to reserve the region, and the memory map is updated to reflect this. After **VirtualAlloc** reserves the region, the remaining buttons become active.

You can now type an index into the edit control to select an index, and then click the Use button. This has the effect of committing physical storage to the memory address where the array element is to be placed. When a page of storage is committed, the memory map is redrawn to reflect the state of the reserved region for the entire array. So if after reserving the region, you click the Use button to mark array elements 7 and 46 as *in use*, the window will look like the following window (when you are running the program on a 4-KB page machine):

Clicking the Clear button clears any element that is marked as in use. But doing so does not decommit the physical storage mapped to the array element because each page contains room for multiple structures—just because one is clear doesn't mean the others are too. If the memory were decommitted, the data in the other structures would be lost. Because clicking Clear doesn't affect the region's physical storage, the memory map is not updated when an array element is cleared.

However, when a structure is cleared, its **bInUse** member is set to **FALSE**. This setting is necessary so that the garbage collection routine can make its pass over all the structures and decommit storage that's no longer in use. If you haven't guessed it by now, the Garbage Collect button tells VMAlloc to execute its garbage collection routine. To keep things simple, I have not implemented the garbage collection routine on a separate thread.

To demonstrate the garbage collection function, clear the array element at index 46. Notice that the memory map does not change. Now click the Garbage Collect button. The program decommits the page of storage containing element 46, and the memory map is updated to reflect this, as shown in the following window. Note that the **GarbageCollect** function can easily be used in your own applications. I implemented it to work with arrays of any size data structures; the structures do not have to fit exactly in a page. The only requirement is that the first member of your structure must be a **BOOL** value, which indicates whether the structure is in use.

Finally, even though there is no visual display to inform you, all the committed memory is decommitted and the reserved region is freed when the window is destroyed.

This program contains another element that I haven't described yet. The program needs to determine the state of memory in the region's address space in three places:

- After changing the index, the program needs to enable the Use button and disable the Clear button or vice versa.

- In the garbage collection function, the program needs to see whether storage is committed before actually testing to see whether the **bInUse** flag is set.

- When updating the memory map, the program needs to know which pages are free, which are reserved, and which are committed.

VMAlloc performs all these tests by calling the **VirtualQuery** function, discussed in the previous chapter.

```
VMAlloc.cpp
/*********************************************************************
Module:  VMAlloc.cpp
Notices: Copyright (c) 2008 Jeffrey Richter & Christophe Nasarre
*********************************************************************/


#include "..\CmnHdr.h"     /* See Appendix A. */
#include <WindowsX.h>
#include <tchar.h>
#include "Resource.h"
#include <StrSafe.h>



///////////////////////////////////////////////////////////////////


// The number of bytes in a page on this host machine.
UINT g_uPageSize = 0;
```

```
// A dummy data structure used for the array.
typedef struct {
  BOOL bInUse;
  BYTE bOtherData[2048 - sizeof(BOOL)];
} SOMEDATA, *PSOMEDATA;


// The number of structures in the array
#define MAX_SOMEDATA    (50)

// Pointer to an array of data structures
PSOMEDATA g_pSomeData = NULL;

// The rectangular area in the window occupied by the memory map
RECT g_rcMemMap;


///////////////////////////////////////////////////////////////////////////


BOOL Dlg_OnInitDialog(HWND hWnd, HWND hWndFocus, LPARAM lParam) {

   chSETDLGICONS(hWnd, IDI_VMALLOC);

   // Initialize the dialog box by disabling all the nonsetup controls.
   EnableWindow(GetDlgItem(hWnd, IDC_INDEXTEXT),       FALSE);
   EnableWindow(GetDlgItem(hWnd, IDC_INDEX),           FALSE);
   EnableWindow(GetDlgItem(hWnd, IDC_USE),             FALSE);
   EnableWindow(GetDlgItem(hWnd, IDC_CLEAR),           FALSE);
   EnableWindow(GetDlgItem(hWnd, IDC_GARBAGECOLLECT), FALSE);

   // Get the coordinates of the memory map display.
   GetWindowRect(GetDlgItem(hWnd, IDC_MEMMAP), &g_rcMemMap);
   MapWindowPoints(NULL, hWnd, (LPPOINT) &g_rcMemMap, 2);

   // Destroy the window that identifies the location of the memory map
   DestroyWindow(GetDlgItem(hWnd, IDC_MEMMAP));

   // Put the page size in the dialog box just for the user's information.
   TCHAR szBuf[10];
   StringCchPrintf(szBuf, _countof(szBuf), TEXT("%d KB"), g_uPageSize / 1024);
   SetDlgItemText(hWnd, IDC_PAGESIZE, szBuf);

   // Initialize the edit control.
   SetDlgItemInt(hWnd, IDC_INDEX, 0, FALSE);

   return(TRUE);
}


///////////////////////////////////////////////////////////////////////////
```

```
void Dlg_OnDestroy(HWND hWnd) {

   if (g_pSomeData != NULL)
      VirtualFree(g_pSomeData, 0, MEM_RELEASE);
}


///////////////////////////////////////////////////////////////////////////


VOID GarbageCollect(PVOID pvBase, DWORD dwNum, DWORD dwStructSize) {

   UINT uMaxPages = dwNum * dwStructSize / g_uPageSize;
   for (UINT uPage = 0; uPage < uMaxPages; uPage++) {
      BOOL bAnyAllocsInThisPage = FALSE;
      UINT uIndex     = uPage * g_uPageSize / dwStructSize;
      UINT uIndexLast = uIndex + g_uPageSize / dwStructSize;

      for (; uIndex < uIndexLast; uIndex++) {
         MEMORY_BASIC_INFORMATION mbi;
         VirtualQuery(&g_pSomeData[uIndex], &mbi, sizeof(mbi));
         bAnyAllocsInThisPage = ((mbi.State == MEM_COMMIT) &&
            * (PBOOL) ((PBYTE) pvBase + dwStructSize * uIndex));

         // Stop checking this page, we know we can't decommit it.
         if (bAnyAllocsInThisPage) break;
      }

      if (!bAnyAllocsInThisPage) {
         // No allocated structures in this page; decommit it.
         VirtualFree(&g_pSomeData[uIndexLast - 1], dwStructSize, MEM_DECOMMIT);
      }
   }
}


///////////////////////////////////////////////////////////////////////////


void Dlg_OnCommand(HWND hWnd, int id, HWND hWndCtl, UINT codeNotify) {

   UINT uIndex = 0;

   switch (id) {
      case IDCANCEL:
         EndDialog(hWnd, id);
         break;

      case IDC_RESERVE:
         // Reserve enough address space to hold the array of structures.
         g_pSomeData = (PSOMEDATA) VirtualAlloc(NULL,
            MAX_SOMEDATA * sizeof(SOMEDATA), MEM_RESERVE, PAGE_READWRITE);
```

```
       // Disable the Reserve button and enable all the other controls.
       EnableWindow(GetDlgItem(hWnd, IDC_RESERVE),        FALSE);
       EnableWindow(GetDlgItem(hWnd, IDC_INDEXTEXT),      TRUE);
       EnableWindow(GetDlgItem(hWnd, IDC_INDEX),          TRUE);
       EnableWindow(GetDlgItem(hWnd, IDC_USE),            TRUE);
       EnableWindow(GetDlgItem(hWnd, IDC_GARBAGECOLLECT), TRUE);

       // Force the index edit control to have the focus.
       SetFocus(GetDlgItem(hWnd, IDC_INDEX));

       // Force the memory map to update
       InvalidateRect(hWnd, &g_rcMemMap, FALSE);
       break;

   case IDC_INDEX:
      if (codeNotify != EN_CHANGE)
         break;

      uIndex = GetDlgItemInt(hWnd, id, NULL, FALSE);
      if ((g_pSomeData != NULL) && chINRANGE(0, uIndex, MAX_SOMEDATA - 1)) {
         MEMORY_BASIC_INFORMATION mbi;
         VirtualQuery(&g_pSomeData[uIndex], &mbi, sizeof(mbi));
         BOOL bOk = (mbi.State == MEM_COMMIT);
         if (bOk)
            bOk = g_pSomeData[uIndex].bInUse;

         EnableWindow(GetDlgItem(hWnd, IDC_USE),   !bOk);
         EnableWindow(GetDlgItem(hWnd, IDC_CLEAR), bOk);

      } else {
         EnableWindow(GetDlgItem(hWnd, IDC_USE),    FALSE);
         EnableWindow(GetDlgItem(hWnd, IDC_CLEAR), FALSE);
      }
      break;


   case IDC_USE:
      uIndex = GetDlgItemInt(hWnd, IDC_INDEX, NULL, FALSE);
      // NOTE: New pages are always zeroed by the system
      VirtualAlloc(&g_pSomeData[uIndex], sizeof(SOMEDATA),
         MEM_COMMIT, PAGE_READWRITE);

      g_pSomeData[uIndex].bInUse = TRUE;

      EnableWindow(GetDlgItem(hWnd, IDC_USE),    FALSE);
      EnableWindow(GetDlgItem(hWnd, IDC_CLEAR), TRUE);

      // Force the Clear button control to have the focus.
      SetFocus(GetDlgItem(hWnd, IDC_CLEAR));

      // Force the memory map to update
      InvalidateRect(hWnd, &g_rcMemMap, FALSE);
      break;
```

```
        case IDC_CLEAR:
            uIndex = GetDlgItemInt(hWnd, IDC_INDEX, NULL, FALSE);
            g_pSomeData[uIndex].bInUse = FALSE;
            EnableWindow(GetDlgItem(hWnd, IDC_USE),    TRUE);
            EnableWindow(GetDlgItem(hWnd, IDC_CLEAR), FALSE);

            // Force the Use button control to have the focus.
            SetFocus(GetDlgItem(hWnd, IDC_USE));
            break;

        case IDC_GARBAGECOLLECT:
            GarbageCollect(g_pSomeData, MAX_SOMEDATA, sizeof(SOMEDATA));

            // Force the memory map to update
            InvalidateRect(hWnd, &g_rcMemMap, FALSE);
            break;
    }
}


///////////////////////////////////////////////////////////////////////////


void Dlg_OnPaint(HWND hWnd) {     // Update the memory map

    PAINTSTRUCT ps;
    BeginPaint(hWnd, &ps);

    UINT uMaxPages = MAX_SOMEDATA * sizeof(SOMEDATA) / g_uPageSize;
    UINT uMemMapWidth = g_rcMemMap.right - g_rcMemMap.left;

    if (g_pSomeData == NULL) {

        // The memory has yet to be reserved.
        Rectangle(ps.hdc, g_rcMemMap.left, g_rcMemMap.top,
            g_rcMemMap.right - uMemMapWidth % uMaxPages, g_rcMemMap.bottom);

    } else {

        // Walk the virtual address space, painting the memory map
        for (UINT uPage = 0; uPage < uMaxPages; uPage++) {

            UINT uIndex = uPage * g_uPageSize / sizeof(SOMEDATA);
            UINT uIndexLast = uIndex + g_uPageSize / sizeof(SOMEDATA);
            for (; uIndex < uIndexLast; uIndex++) {

                MEMORY_BASIC_INFORMATION mbi;
                VirtualQuery(&g_pSomeData[uIndex], &mbi, sizeof(mbi));

                int nBrush = 0;
                switch (mbi.State) {
                    case MEM_FREE:    nBrush = WHITE_BRUSH; break;
                    case MEM_RESERVE: nBrush = GRAY_BRUSH;  break;
                    case MEM_COMMIT:  nBrush = BLACK_BRUSH; break;
                }
```

```
                SelectObject(ps.hdc, GetStockObject(nBrush));
                Rectangle(ps.hdc,
                    g_rcMemMap.left + uMemMapWidth / uMaxPages * uPage,
                    g_rcMemMap.top,
                    g_rcMemMap.left + uMemMapWidth / uMaxPages * (uPage + 1),
                    g_rcMemMap.bottom);
            }
        }
    }

    EndPaint(hWnd, &ps);
}


///////////////////////////////////////////////////////////////////////////


INT_PTR WINAPI Dlg_Proc(HWND hWnd, UINT uMsg, WPARAM wParam, LPARAM lParam) {

    switch (uMsg) {
        chHANDLE_DLGMSG(hWnd, WM_INITDIALOG, Dlg_OnInitDialog);
        chHANDLE_DLGMSG(hWnd, WM_COMMAND,    Dlg_OnCommand);
        chHANDLE_DLGMSG(hWnd, WM_PAINT,      Dlg_OnPaint);
        chHANDLE_DLGMSG(hWnd, WM_DESTROY,    Dlg_OnDestroy);
    }
    return(FALSE);
}


///////////////////////////////////////////////////////////////////////////


int WINAPI _tWinMain(HINSTANCE hInstExe, HINSTANCE, PTSTR, int) {

    // Get the page size used on this CPU.
    SYSTEM_INFO si;
    GetSystemInfo(&si);
    g_uPageSize = si.dwPageSize;

    DialogBox(hInstExe, MAKEINTRESOURCE(IDD_VMALLOC), NULL, Dlg_Proc);
    return(0);
}

/////////////////////////////// End of File ///////////////////////////////
```

Changing Protection Attributes

Although the practice is rare, it is possible to change the protection attributes associated with a page or pages of committed physical storage. For example, say you've developed code to manage a linked list, the nodes of which you are keeping in a reserved region. You could design the functions that process the linked list so that they change the protection attributes of the committed storage to **PAGE_READWRITE** at the start of each function and then back to **PAGE_NOACCESS** just before each function terminates.

By doing this, you protect your linked-list data from other bugs hiding in your program. If any other code in your process has a stray pointer that attempts to access your linked-list data, an access violation is raised. Taking advantage of protection attributes can be incredibly useful when you're trying to locate hard-to-find bugs in your application.

You can alter the protection rights of a page of memory by calling **VirtualProtect**:

```
BOOL VirtualProtect(
    PVOID pvAddress,
    SIZE_T dwSize,
    DWORD flNewProtect,
    PDWORD pflOldProtect);
```

Here, **pvAddress** points to the base address of the memory (which must be in your process' user-mode partition), **dwSize** indicates the number of bytes for which you want to change the protection attribute, and **flNewProtect** can represent any one of the **PAGE_*** protection attribute identifiers except for **PAGE_WRITECOPY** and **PAGE_EXECUTE_WRITECOPY**.

The last parameter, **pflOldProtect**, is the address of a **DWORD** that **VirtualProtect** will fill in with the protection attribute originally associated with the byte at **pvAddress**. Even though many applications don't need this information, you must pass a valid address for this parameter, or the function fails.

Of course, protection attributes are associated with entire pages of storage and cannot be assigned to individual bytes. So if you were to call **VirtualProtect** on a 4-KB page machine using the following code, you would end up assigning **PAGE_NOACCESS** protection to two pages of storage:

```
VirtualProtect(pvRgnBase + (3 * 1024), 2 * 1024,
    PAGE_NOACCESS, &flOldProtect);
```

VirtualProtect cannot be used to change the protection of pages that span different reserved regions. If you have adjoining reserved regions and you want to alter the page protection on the pages within these regions, you must make multiple calls to **VirtualProtect**.

Resetting the Contents of Physical Storage

When you modify the contents of various pages of physical storage, the system tries to keep the changes in RAM as long as possible. However, while applications are running, a demand might be placed on your system's RAM as pages are being loaded from .exe files, DLL files, and/or the paging file. As the system looks for pages of RAM to satisfy recent load requests, the system will have to swap modified pages of RAM to the system's paging file.

Windows offers a feature that allows an application to improve its performance—the resetting of physical storage. Resetting storage means that you are telling the system that the data on one or more pages of storage is not modified. If the system is searching for a page of RAM and chooses a modified page, the system must write the page of RAM to the paging file. This operation is slow and hurts performance. For most applications, you want the system to preserve your modified pages in the system's paging file.

However, certain applications use storage for short periods of time and then no longer require that the contents of that storage be preserved. To help performance, an application can tell the system not to preserve desired pages of storage in the system's paging file. This is basically a way for an application to tell the system that a data page has not been modified. So if the system chooses to use a page of RAM for another purpose, the page's contents don't have to be preserved in the paging file, thus increasing performance. An application resets storage by calling **VirtualAlloc**, passing the **MEM_RESET** flag in the third parameter.

If the pages referenced in the call to **VirtualAlloc** are in the paging file, the system discards them. The next time the application accesses the storage, new RAM pages that are first initialized to zeros are used. If you reset pages that are currently in RAM, they are marked as not modified so that they will never be written to the paging file. Note that although the content of the RAM page is *not* zeroed, you should not continue to read from this page of storage. If the system doesn't need the page of RAM, it will contain the original contents. However, if the system needs the page of RAM, the system can take it. Then when you attempt to access the page's contents, the system will give you a new page that has been zeroed. Because you have no control over this behavior, you must assume that the contents of the page are garbage after you reset the page.

Keep in mind a couple of additional things when you reset storage. First, when you call **Virtual-Alloc**, the base address is usually rounded down to a page boundary and the number of bytes is rounded up to an integral number of pages. Rounding the base address and number of bytes this way would be very dangerous to do when resetting storage; therefore, **VirtualAlloc** rounds these values in the opposite direction when you pass **MEM_RESET**. For example, let's say that you had the following code:

```
PINT pnData = (PINT) VirtualAlloc(NULL, 1024,
   MEM_RESERVE | MEM_COMMIT, PAGE_READWRITE);
pnData[0] = 100;
pnData[1] = 200;
VirtualAlloc((PVOID) pnData, sizeof(int), MEM_RESET, PAGE_READWRITE);
```

This code commits one page of storage and then says that the first 4 bytes (**sizeof(int)**) are no longer necessary and can be reset. However, as with all storage operations, everything must be done on page boundaries and in page increments. As it turns out, the call to reset the storage above fails: **VirtualAlloc** returns **NULL**, and **GetLastError** gives **ERROR_INVALID_ADDRESS** (defined as 487 in WinError.h) as the reason. Why? Because when you pass **MEM_RESET** to **VirtualAlloc**, the base address that you pass to the function is rounded up to a page boundary. This is done to ensure that important data in the same page but before the given address is not thrown away by mistake. In the preceding example, rounding the number of bytes down makes it 0, and it is illegal to reset 0 bytes. The number of bytes is also rounded down to an integral number of pages for the same reason: if the garbage data does not fill up an entire page, you don't want to reset the whole page because it might contain valid data at the end. Doing so, the operating system ensures that only entire garbage pages are reset.

The second thing to remember about resetting storage is that the **MEM_RESET** flag must always be used by itself and cannot be **OR**ed with any other flags. The following call always fails and returns **NULL**:

```
PVOID pvMem = VirtualAlloc(NULL, 1024,
   MEM_RESERVE | MEM_COMMIT | MEM_RESET, PAGE_READWRITE);
```

It really doesn't make any sense to combine the **MEM_RESET** flag with any other flag, anyway.

Finally, note that calling **VirtualAlloc** with **MEM_RESET** requires that you pass a valid page protection value even though this value will not be used by the function.

The MemReset Sample Application

The MemReset.cpp listing demonstrates how the **MEM_RESET** flag works. The source code and resource files for the application are in the 15-MemReset directory on the companion content Web page.

The first thing that the MemReset.cpp code does is reserve and commit a region of physical storage. Because the size passed to **VirtualAlloc** is 1024, the system automatically rounds this value up to the system's page size. Now a string is copied into this buffer using **_tcscpy_s**, causing the contents of the page to be modified. If the system later decides it needs the page of RAM occupied by our data page, the system first writes the data that is in our page to the system's paging file. When our application later attempts to access this data, the system automatically reloads the page from the paging file into another page of RAM so that we can successfully access the data.

After writing the string to the page of storage, the code presents the user with a message box asking whether the data needs to be accessed at a later time. If the user responds by clicking the No button, the code forces the operating system to believe that the data in the page is not modified by calling **VirtualAlloc** and passing the **MEM_RESET** flag.

To demonstrate that the storage has been reset, we need to force a heavy demand on the system's RAM. We can do this with the following three-step process:

1. Call **GlobalMemoryStatus** to get the total amount of RAM in the machine.
2. Call **VirtualAlloc** to commit this amount of storage. This operation is very fast because the system doesn't actually allocate RAM for the storage until the process attempts to touch the pages. Don't be surprised if **VirtualAlloc** returns **NULL** when you run this code on the latest computer: you might have more RAM than the size of the available process address space!
3. Call **ZeroMemory** so that the newly committed pages are touched. This will place a heavy burden on the system's RAM, causing some pages that are currently in RAM to be written to the paging file.

If the user indicated that that data will be accessed later, the data is not reset and will be swapped back into RAM later when it is accessed. However, if the user indicated that the data will not be accessed later, the data is reset and the system will not write it out to the paging file, thereby improving our application's performance.

After **ZeroMemory** returns, the code compares the contents of the data page with the string originally written to it. If the data wasn't reset, the contents are guaranteed to be the same. If the data page was reset, the contents might or might not be the same. In the MemReset program, the contents will never be the same because all pages in RAM are forced to be written to the paging file. However, if the dummy region were smaller than the total amount of RAM in the machine, the original contents could possibly still be in RAM. As I pointed out earlier, be careful about this!

MemReset.cpp

```
/**************************************************************************
Module:  MemReset.cpp
Notices: Copyright (c) 2008 Jeffrey Richter & Christophe Nasarre
**************************************************************************/


#include "..\CmnHdr.h"      /* See Appendix A. */
#include <tchar.h>



///////////////////////////////////////////////////////////////////////////


int WINAPI _tWinMain(HINSTANCE, HINSTANCE, PTSTR, int) {

   TCHAR szAppName[]  = TEXT("MEM_RESET tester");
   TCHAR szTestData[] = TEXT("Some text data");

   // Commit a page of storage and modify its contents.
   PTSTR pszData = (PTSTR) VirtualAlloc(NULL, 1024,
      MEM_RESERVE | MEM_COMMIT, PAGE_READWRITE);
   _tcscpy_s(pszData, 1024, szTestData);

   if (MessageBox(NULL, TEXT("Do you want to access this data later?"),
      szAppName, MB_YESNO) == IDNO) {

      // We want this page of storage to remain in our process, but the
      // contents aren't important to us anymore.
      // Tell the system that the data is not modified.

      // Note: Because MEM_RESET destroys data, VirtualAlloc rounds
      // the base address and size parameters to their safest range.
      // Here is an example:
      //    VirtualAlloc(pvData, 5000, MEM_RESET, PAGE_READWRITE)
      // resets 0 pages on CPUs where the page size is greater than 4 KB
      // and resets 1 page on CPUs with a 4 KB page. So that our call to
      // VirtualAlloc to reset memory below always succeeds, VirtualQuery
      // is called first to get the exact region size.
      MEMORY_BASIC_INFORMATION mbi;
      VirtualQuery(pszData, &mbi, sizeof(mbi));
      VirtualAlloc(pszData, mbi.RegionSize, MEM_RESET, PAGE_READWRITE);
   }

   // Commit as much storage as there is physical RAM.
   MEMORYSTATUS mst;
   GlobalMemoryStatus(&mst);
   PVOID pvDummy = VirtualAlloc(NULL, mst.dwTotalPhys,
      MEM_RESERVE | MEM_COMMIT, PAGE_READWRITE);

   // Touch all the pages in the dummy region so that any
   // modified pages in RAM are written to the paging file.
   if (pvDummy != NULL)
      ZeroMemory(pvDummy, mst.dwTotalPhys);
```

```
   // Compare our data page with what we originally wrote there.
   if (_tcscmp(pszData, szTestData) == 0) {

      // The data in the page matches what we originally put there.
      // ZeroMemory forced our page to be written to the paging file.
      MessageBox(NULL, TEXT("Modified data page was saved."),
         szAppName, MB_OK);
   } else {

      // The data in the page does NOT match what we originally put there
      // ZeroMemory didn't cause our page to be written to the paging file
      MessageBox(NULL, TEXT("Modified data page was NOT saved."),
         szAppName, MB_OK);
   }

   // Don't forget to release these parts of the address space.
   // Note that it is not mandatory here since the application is exiting.
   if (pvDummy != NULL)
      VirtualFree(pvDummy, 0, MEM_RELEASE);
   VirtualFree(pszData, 0, MEM_RELEASE);

   return(0);
}


///////////////////////////// End of File //////////////////////////////////
```

Address Windowing Extensions

As days go by, applications require more and more memory. This is especially true of server applications: As an increasing number of clients make requests of the server, the server's performance diminishes. To improve performance, the server application needs to keep more of its data in RAM and reduce disk paging. Other classes of applications—such as database, engineering, and scientific—also require the ability to manipulate large blocks of storage. For all these applications, a 32-bit address space is just not enough room.

To help these applications, Windows offers a feature called Address Windowing Extensions (AWE). Microsoft had two goals when creating AWE:

- Allow applications to allocate RAM that is never swapped by the operating system to or from disk.
- Allow an application to access more RAM than fits within the process' address space.

Basically, AWE provides a way for an application to allocate one or more blocks of RAM. When allocated, these blocks are not visible in the process' address space. Then the application reserves a region of address space (using **VirtualAlloc**), which becomes the address window. The application then calls a function that assigns one RAM block at a time to the address window. Assigning a RAM block to the address window is extremely fast (usually on the order of a few milliseconds).

Obviously, only one RAM block at a time can be accessed via a single address window. This makes your code more difficult to implement because you must explicitly call functions within your code to assign different RAM blocks to the address window as you need them.

The following code shows how to use AWE:

```
// First, reserve a 1MB region for the address window
ULONG_PTR ulRAMBytes = 1024 * 1024;
PVOID pvWindow = VirtualAlloc(NULL, ulRAMBytes,
   MEM_RESERVE | MEM_PHYSICAL, PAGE_READWRITE);

// Get the number of bytes in a page for this CPU platform
SYSTEM_INFO sinf;
GetSystemInfo(&sinf);

// Calculate the required number of RAM pages for the
// desired number of bytes
ULONG_PTR ulRAMPages = (ulRAMBytes + sinf.dwPageSize - 1) / sinf.dwPageSize;

// Allocate array for RAM page's page frame numbers
ULONG_PTR* aRAMPages = (ULONG_PTR*) new ULONG_PTR[ulRAMPages];

// Allocate the pages of RAM (requires Lock Pages in Memory user right)
AllocateUserPhysicalPages(
   GetCurrentProcess(), // Allocate the storage for our process
   &ulRAMPages,         // Input: # of RAM pages, Output: # pages allocated
   aRAMPages);          // Output: Opaque array indicating pages allocated

// Assign the RAM pages to our window
MapUserPhysicalPages(pvWindow,  // The address of the address window
   ulRAMPages,                  // Number of entries in array
   aRAMPages);                  // Array of RAM pages

// Access the RAM pages via the pvWindow virtual address
. . .
// Free the block of RAM pages
FreeUserPhysicalPages(
   GetCurrentProcess(), // Free the RAM allocated for our process
   &ulRAMPages,         // Input: # of RAM pages, Output: # pages freed
   aRAMPages);          // Input: Array indicating the RAM pages to free

// Destroy the address window
VirtualFree(pvWindow, 0, MEM_RELEASE);
delete[] aRAMPages;
```

As you can see, using AWE is simple. Now, let me point out a few interesting things about this code.

The call to **VirtualAlloc** reserves a 1-MB address window. Usually, the address window is much bigger. You must select a size that is appropriate for the size of the RAM blocks your application requires. Of course, the largest contiguous free block available in your address space determines the largest window you can create. The **MEM_RESERVE** flag indicates that I am just reserving a region of addresses. The **MEM_PHYSICAL** flag indicates that this region will eventually be backed by physical RAM storage. One limitation of AWE is that all storage mapped to the address window must be readable and writable; hence, **PAGE_READWRITE** is the only valid protection that can be passed to **VirtualAlloc**. In addition, you cannot use the **VirtualProtect** function to alter this protection.

Allocating physical RAM is simply a matter of calling **AllocateUserPhysicalPages**:

```
BOOL AllocateUserPhysicalPages(
    HANDLE hProcess,
    PULONG_PTR pulRAMPages,
    PULONG_PTR aRAMPages);
```

This function allocates the number of RAM pages specified in the value pointed to by the **pulRAM-Pages** parameter and assigns these pages to the process identified by the **hProcess** parameter.

Each page of RAM is assigned a *page frame number* by the operating system. As the system selects pages of RAM for the allocation, it populates the array—pointed to by the **aRAMPages** parameter— with each RAM page's page frame number. The page frame numbers themselves are not useful in any way to your application; you should not examine the contents of this array, and you most definitely should not alter any of the values in this array. Note that you neither know which pages of RAM were allocated to this block nor should you care. When the address window shows the pages in the RAM block, they appear as a contiguous block of memory. This makes the RAM easy to use and frees you from having to understand exactly what the system is doing internally.

When the function returns, the value in **pulRAMPages** indicates the number of pages that the function successfully allocated. This will usually be the same value that you passed to the function, but it can also be a smaller value.

Only the owning process can use the allocated RAM pages; AWE does not allow the RAM pages to be mapped into another process' address space. Therefore, you cannot share RAM blocks between processes.

> **Note** Of course, physical RAM is a very precious resource and an application can allocate only whatever RAM has not already been dedicated. You should use AWE sparingly or your process and other processes will excessively page storage to and from disk, severely hurting overall performance. In addition, less available RAM adversely affects the system's ability to create new processes, threads, and other resources. An application can use the **Global-MemoryStatusEx** function to monitor physical memory use.
>
> To help protect the allocation of RAM, the **AllocateUserPhysicalPages** function requires the caller to have the Lock Pages In Memory user right granted and enabled, or the function fails. Look at "Reserving a Region and Committing Storage Simultaneously" on page 422 to see how you turn on this user right in Windows Vista.

Now that I've created the address window and allocated a RAM block, I assign the block to the window by calling **MapUserPhysicalPages**:

```
BOOL MapUserPhysicalPages(
    PVOID pvAddressWindow,
    ULONG_PTR ulRAMPages,
    PULONG_PTR aRAMPages);
```

The first parameter, **pvAddressWindow**, indicates the virtual address of the address window, and the second two parameters, **ulRAMPages** and **aRAMPages**, indicate how many and which pages of RAM to make visible in this address window. If the window is smaller than the number of pages you're attempting to map, the function fails. Microsoft's main goal for this function was to make it execute extremely fast. Typically, **MapUserPhysicalPages** is able to map the RAM block in just a few microseconds.

> **Note**   You can also call **MapUserPhysicalPages** to unassign the current RAM block by passing **NULL** for the **aRAMPages** parameter. Here is an example:
>
> ```
> // Un-assign the RAM block from the address window
> MapUserPhysicalPages(pvWindow, ulRAMPages, NULL);
> ```

Once the RAM block has been assigned to the address window, you can easily access the RAM storage simply by referencing virtual addresses relative to the address window's base address (**pvWindow** in my sample code).

When you no longer need the RAM block, you should free it by calling **FreeUserPhysicalPages**:

```
BOOL FreeUserPhysicalPages(
   HANDLE hProcess,
   PULONG_PTR pulRAMPages,
   PULONG_PTR aRAMPages);
```

The first parameter, **hProcess**, indicates which process owns the RAM pages you're attempting to free. The second two parameters indicate how many pages and the page frame numbers of those pages that are to be freed. If this RAM block is currently mapped to the address window, it is unmapped and then freed.

Finally, to completely clean up, I free the address window merely by calling **VirtualFree** and passing the base virtual address of the window, **0** for the region's size, and **MEM_RELEASE**.

My simple code example creates a single address window and a single RAM block. This allows my application access to RAM that will not be swapped to or from disk. However, an application can create several address windows and can allocate several RAM blocks. These RAM blocks can be assigned to any of the address windows, but the system does not allow a single RAM block to appear in two address windows simultaneously.

64-bit Windows fully supports AWE; porting a 32-bit application that uses AWE is easy and straightforward. However, AWE is less useful for a 64-bit application because a process' address space is so large. AWE is still useful because it allows the application to allocate physical RAM that is not swapped to or from disk.

The AWE Sample Application

The AWE application (15-AWE.exe), listed next, demonstrates how to create multiple address windows and how to assign different storage blocks to these windows. The source code and resource files for the application are in the 15-AWE directory on the companion content Web page. When you start the program, it internally creates two address window regions and allocates two RAM blocks.

Initially, the first RAM block is populated with the string "Text in Storage 0" and the second RAM block is populated with the string "Text in Storage 1." Then the first RAM block is assigned to the first address window and the second RAM block is assigned to the second address window. The application's window reflects this.

Using this window, you can perform some experiments. First, you assign RAM blocks to address windows using each address window's combo box. The combo box also offers a No Storage option that unmaps any storage from the address window. Second, editing the text updates the RAM block currently selected in the address window.

If you attempt to assign the same RAM block to the two address windows simultaneously, the following message box appears because AWE doesn't support this.

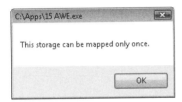

The source code for this sample application is clear-cut. To make working with AWE easier, I created three C++ classes contained in the AddrWindows.h file. The first class, **CSystemInfo**, is a very simple wrapper around the **GetSystemInfo** function. The other two classes each create an instance of the **CSystemInfo** class.

The second C++ class, **CAddrWindow**, encapsulates an address window. Basically, the **Create** method reserves an address window, the **Destroy** method destroys the address window, the **UnmapStorage** method unmaps any RAM block currently assigned to the address window, and the **PVOID** cast operator method simply returns the virtual address of the address window.

The third C++ class, **CAddrWindowStorage**, encapsulates a RAM block that may be assigned to a **CAddrWindow** object. The **Allocate** method enables the Lock Pages In Memory user right, attempts to allocate the RAM block, and then disables the user right. The **Free** method frees the RAM block. The **HowManyPagesAllocated** method returns the number of pages successfully allocated. The **MapStorage** and **UnmapStorage** methods map and unmap the RAM block to or from a **CAddrWindow** object.

Using these C++ classes made implementing the sample application much easier. The sample application creates two **CAddrWindow** objects and two **CAddrWindowStorage** objects. The rest of the code is just a matter of calling the correct method for the proper object at the right time.

Notice that a manifest has been added to the application so that Windows will always pop up the privilege elevation request to the user as explained in "Elevating a Process Automatically" on page 113.

AWE.cpp

```
/******************************************************************************
Module:  AWE.cpp
Notices: Copyright (c) 2008 Jeffrey Richter & Christophe Nasarre
******************************************************************************/


#include "..\CmnHdr.h"      /* See Appendix A. */
#include <Windowsx.h>
#include <tchar.h>
#include "AddrWindow.h"
#include "Resource.h"
#include <StrSafe.h>


///////////////////////////////////////////////////////////////////////////////


CAddrWindow g_aw[2];                 // 2 memory address windows
CAddrWindowStorage g_aws[2];         // 2 storage blocks
const ULONG_PTR g_nChars = 1024;     // 1024 character buffers
const DWORD g_cbBufferSize = g_nChars * sizeof(TCHAR);


///////////////////////////////////////////////////////////////////////////////


BOOL Dlg_OnInitDialog(HWND hWnd, HWND hWndFocus, LPARAM lParam) {

   chSETDLGICONS(hWnd, IDI_AWE);

   // Create the 2 memory address windows
   chVERIFY(g_aw[0].Create(g_cbBufferSize));
   chVERIFY(g_aw[1].Create(g_cbBufferSize));

   // Create the 2 storage blocks
   if (!g_aws[0].Allocate(g_cbBufferSize)) {
      chFAIL("Failed to allocate RAM.\nMost likely reason: "
         "you are not granted the Lock Pages in Memory user right.");
   }
   chVERIFY(g_aws[1].Allocate(g_nChars * sizeof(TCHAR)));

   // Put some default text in the 1st storage block
   g_aws[0].MapStorage(g_aw[0]);
   _tcscpy_s((PTSTR) (PVOID) g_aw[0], g_cbBufferSize, TEXT("Text in Storage 0"));

   // Put some default text in the 2nd storage block
   g_aws[1].MapStorage(g_aw[0]);
   _tcscpy_s((PTSTR) (PVOID) g_aw[0], g_cbBufferSize, TEXT("Text in Storage 1"));
```

```
   // Populate the dialog box controls
   for (int n = 0; n <= 1; n++) {
      // Set the combo box for each address window
      int id = ((n == 0) ? IDC_WINDOW0STORAGE : IDC_WINDOW1STORAGE);
      HWND hWndCB = GetDlgItem(hWnd, id);
      ComboBox_AddString(hWndCB, TEXT("No storage"));
      ComboBox_AddString(hWndCB, TEXT("Storage 0"));
      ComboBox_AddString(hWndCB, TEXT("Storage 1"));

      // Window 0 shows Storage 0, Window 1 shows Storage 1
      ComboBox_SetCurSel(hWndCB, n + 1);
      FORWARD_WM_COMMAND(hWnd, id, hWndCB, CBN_SELCHANGE, SendMessage);
      Edit_LimitText(GetDlgItem(hWnd,
         (n == 0) ? IDC_WINDOW0TEXT : IDC_WINDOW1TEXT), g_nChars);
   }

   return(TRUE);
}


///////////////////////////////////////////////////////////////////////////


void Dlg_OnCommand(HWND hWnd, int id, HWND hWndCtl, UINT codeNotify) {

   switch (id) {

   case IDCANCEL:
      EndDialog(hWnd, id);
      break;

   case IDC_WINDOW0STORAGE:
   case IDC_WINDOW1STORAGE:
      if (codeNotify == CBN_SELCHANGE) {

         // Show different storage in address window
         int nWindow  = ((id == IDC_WINDOW0STORAGE) ? 0 : 1);
         int nStorage = ComboBox_GetCurSel(hWndCtl) - 1;

         if (nStorage == -1) {   // Show no storage in this window
            chVERIFY(g_aw[nWindow].UnmapStorage());
         } else {
            if (!g_aws[nStorage].MapStorage(g_aw[nWindow])) {
               // Couldn't map storage in window
               chVERIFY(g_aw[nWindow].UnmapStorage());
               ComboBox_SetCurSel(hWndCtl, 0);  // Force "No storage"
               chMB("This storage can be mapped only once.");
            }
         }
```

```
            // Update the address window's text display
            HWND hwndText = GetDlgItem(hWnd,
                ((nWindow == 0) ? IDC_WINDOW0TEXT : IDC_WINDOW1TEXT));
            MEMORY_BASIC_INFORMATION mbi;
            VirtualQuery(g_aw[nWindow], &mbi, sizeof(mbi));
            // Note: mbi.State == MEM_RESERVE if no storage is in address window
            EnableWindow(hwndText, (mbi.State == MEM_COMMIT));
            Edit_SetText(hwndText, IsWindowEnabled(hwndText)
                ? (PCTSTR) (PVOID) g_aw[nWindow] : TEXT("(No storage)"));
        }
        break;

    case IDC_WINDOW0TEXT:
    case IDC_WINDOW1TEXT:
        if (codeNotify == EN_CHANGE) {
            // Update the storage in the address window
            int nWindow = ((id == IDC_WINDOW0TEXT) ? 0 : 1);
            Edit_GetText(hWndCtl, (PTSTR) (PVOID) g_aw[nWindow], g_nChars);
        }
        break;
    }
}


///////////////////////////////////////////////////////////////////////////////


INT_PTR WINAPI Dlg_Proc(HWND hWnd, UINT uMsg, WPARAM wParam, LPARAM lParam) {

    switch (uMsg) {
        chHANDLE_DLGMSG(hWnd, WM_INITDIALOG, Dlg_OnInitDialog);
        chHANDLE_DLGMSG(hWnd, WM_COMMAND,    Dlg_OnCommand);
    }

    return(FALSE);
}


///////////////////////////////////////////////////////////////////////////////


int WINAPI _tWinMain(HINSTANCE hInstExe, HINSTANCE, PTSTR, int) {

    DialogBox(hInstExe, MAKEINTRESOURCE(IDD_AWE), NULL, Dlg_Proc);
    return(0);
}


/////////////////////////////// End of File ///////////////////////////////////
```

AddrWindow.h

```
/******************************************************************************
Module:  AddrWindow.h
Notices: Copyright (c) 2008 Jeffrey Richter & Christophe Nasarre
******************************************************************************/


#pragma once


///////////////////////////////////////////////////////////////////////////


#include "..\CmnHdr.h"      /* See Appendix A. */
#include <tchar.h>


///////////////////////////////////////////////////////////////////////////


class CSystemInfo : public SYSTEM_INFO {
public:
   CSystemInfo() { GetSystemInfo(this); }
};


///////////////////////////////////////////////////////////////////////////


class CAddrWindow {
public:
   CAddrWindow()  { m_pvWindow = NULL; }
   ~CAddrWindow() { Destroy(); }

   BOOL Create(SIZE_T dwBytes, PVOID pvPreferredWindowBase = NULL) {
      // Reserve address window region to view physical storage
      m_pvWindow = VirtualAlloc(pvPreferredWindowBase, dwBytes,
         MEM_RESERVE | MEM_PHYSICAL, PAGE_READWRITE);
      return(m_pvWindow != NULL);
   }

   BOOL Destroy() {
      BOOL bOk = TRUE;
      if (m_pvWindow != NULL) {
         // Destroy address window region
         bOk = VirtualFree(m_pvWindow, 0, MEM_RELEASE);
         m_pvWindow = NULL;
      }
      return(bOk);
   }
```

```
    BOOL UnmapStorage() {
        // Unmap all storage from address window region
        MEMORY_BASIC_INFORMATION mbi;
        VirtualQuery(m_pvWindow, &mbi, sizeof(mbi));
        return(MapUserPhysicalPages(m_pvWindow,
            mbi.RegionSize / sm_sinf.dwPageSize, NULL));
    }

    // Returns virtual address of address window
    operator PVOID() { return(m_pvWindow); }

private:
    PVOID m_pvWindow;     // Virtual address of address window region
    static CSystemInfo sm_sinf;
};


///////////////////////////////////////////////////////////////////////////


CSystemInfo CAddrWindow::sm_sinf;


///////////////////////////////////////////////////////////////////////////


class CAddrWindowStorage {
public:
    CAddrWindowStorage()  { m_ulPages = 0; m_pulUserPfnArray = NULL; }
    ~CAddrWindowStorage() { Free(); }

    BOOL Allocate(ULONG_PTR ulBytes) {
        // Allocate storage intended for an address window

        Free();  // Clean up this object's existing address window

        // Calculate number of pages from number of bytes
        m_ulPages = (ulBytes + sm_sinf.dwPageSize - 1) / sm_sinf.dwPageSize;

        // Allocate array of page frame numbers
        m_pulUserPfnArray = (PULONG_PTR)
            HeapAlloc(GetProcessHeap(), 0, m_ulPages * sizeof(ULONG_PTR));

        BOOL bOk = (m_pulUserPfnArray != NULL);
        if (bOk) {
            // The "Lock Pages in Memory" privilege must be enabled
            EnablePrivilege(SE_LOCK_MEMORY_NAME, TRUE);
            bOk = AllocateUserPhysicalPages(GetCurrentProcess(),
                &m_ulPages, m_pulUserPfnArray);
            EnablePrivilege(SE_LOCK_MEMORY_NAME, FALSE);
        }
        return(bOk);
    }
```

```
   BOOL Free() {
      BOOL bOk = TRUE;
      if (m_pulUserPfnArray != NULL) {
         bOk = FreeUserPhysicalPages(GetCurrentProcess(),
            &m_ulPages, m_pulUserPfnArray);
         if (bOk) {
            // Free the array of page frame numbers
            HeapFree(GetProcessHeap(), 0, m_pulUserPfnArray);
            m_ulPages = 0;
            m_pulUserPfnArray = NULL;
         }
      }
      return(bOk);
   }

   ULONG_PTR HowManyPagesAllocated() { return(m_ulPages); }

   BOOL MapStorage(CAddrWindow& aw) {
      return(MapUserPhysicalPages(aw,
         HowManyPagesAllocated(), m_pulUserPfnArray));
   }

   BOOL UnmapStorage(CAddrWindow& aw) {
      return(MapUserPhysicalPages(aw,
         HowManyPagesAllocated(), NULL));
   }

private:
   static BOOL EnablePrivilege(PCTSTR pszPrivName, BOOL bEnable = TRUE) {

      BOOL bOk = FALSE;     // Assume function fails
      HANDLE hToken;

      // Try to open this process' access token
      if (OpenProcessToken(GetCurrentProcess(),
         TOKEN_ADJUST_PRIVILEGES, &hToken)) {

         // Attempt to modify the "Lock Pages in Memory" privilege
         TOKEN_PRIVILEGES tp = { 1 };
         LookupPrivilegeValue(NULL, pszPrivName, &tp.Privileges[0].Luid);
         tp.Privileges[0].Attributes = bEnable ? SE_PRIVILEGE_ENABLED : 0;
         AdjustTokenPrivileges(hToken, FALSE, &tp, sizeof(tp), NULL, NULL);
         bOk = (GetLastError() == ERROR_SUCCESS);
         CloseHandle(hToken);
      }
      return(bOk);
   }
```

```
private:
   ULONG_PTR  m_ulPages;          // Number of storage pages
   PULONG_PTR m_pulUserPfnArray; // Page frame number array

private:
   static CSystemInfo sm_sinf;
};


/////////////////////////////////////////////////////////////////////////////


CSystemInfo CAddrWindowStorage::sm_sinf;

/////////////////////////////// End of File ///////////////////////////////
```

Chapter 16
A Thread's Stack

Sometimes the system reserves regions in your own process' address space. I mentioned in Chapter 13, "Windows Memory Architecture," that this happens for process and thread environment blocks. Another time that the system reserves regions in your own process' address space is for a thread's stack.

Whenever a thread is created, the system reserves a region of address space for the thread's stack (each thread gets its very own stack) and also commits some physical storage to this reserved region. By default, the system reserves 1 MB of address space and commits two pages of storage. However, these defaults can be changed by specifying either the **/F** option to the Microsoft C++ compiler or the **/STACK** option to Microsoft's C++ linker when you build your application:

```
/Freserve
/STACK:reserve[,commit]
```

When you build your application, the linker embeds the desired stack size into your .exe or .dll file's PE header. When a thread's stack is created, the system reserves a region of address space matching the size indicated in the file's PE header. However, you can override the amount of storage that is initially committed when you call the **CreateThread** or **_beginthreadex** function. Both functions have a parameter that allows you to override the storage that is initially committed to the stack's address space region. If you specify **0** for this parameter, the system uses the commit size indicated by the PE header. For the remainder of this discussion, I'll assume we're using the default stack sizes: 1 MB of reserved region, with storage committed one page at a time.

Figure 16-1 shows what a stack region (reserved starting at address 0x08000000) might look like on a machine whose page size is 4 KB. The stack's region and all the physical storage committed to it have a page protection of **PAGE_READWRITE**.

After reserving this region, the system commits physical storage to the top two pages of the region. Just before allowing the thread to begin execution, the system sets the thread's stack pointer register to point to the end of the top page of the stack region (an address very close to 0x08100000). This page is where the thread will begin using its stack. The second page from the top is called the *guard page*. As the thread increases its call tree by calling more functions, the thread needs more stack space.

Memory Address	State of Page
0x080FF000	Top of stack: committed page
0x080FE000	Committed page with guard protection attribute flag
0x080FD000	Reserved page
0x08003000	Reserved page
0x08002000	Reserved page
0x08001000	Reserved page
0x08000000	Bottom of stack: reserved page

Figure 16-1   What a thread's stack region looks like when it is first created

Whenever the thread attempts to access storage in the guard page, the system is notified. In response, the system commits another page of storage just below the guard page. Then the system removes the guard page protection flag from the current guard page and assigns it to the newly committed page of storage. This technique allows the stack storage to increase only as the thread requires it. Eventually, if the thread's call tree continues to expand, the stack region will look like Figure 16-2.

Referring to Figure 16-2, assume that the thread's call tree is very deep and that the stack pointer CPU register points to the stack memory address 0x08003004. Now, when the thread calls another function, the system has to commit more physical storage. However, when the system commits physical storage to the page at address 0x08001000, the system does not do exactly what it did when committing physical storage to the rest of the stack's memory region. Figure 16-3 shows what the stack's reserved memory region looks like.

Memory Address	State of Page
0x080FF000	Top of stack: committed page
0x080FE000	Committed page
0x080FD000	Committed page
0x08003000	Committed page
0x08002000	Committed page with guard protection attribute flag
0x08001000	Reserved page
0x08000000	Bottom of stack: reserved page

Figure 16-2   A nearly full thread's stack region

Memory Address	State of Page
0x080FF000	Top of stack: committed page
0x080FE000	Committed page
0x080FD000	Committed page
0x08003000	Committed page
0x08002000	Committed page
0x08001000	Committed page
0x08000000	Bottom of stack: reserved page

Figure 16-3   A full thread stack region

As you'd expect, the page starting at address 0x08002000 has the guard attribute removed, and physical storage is committed to the page starting at 0x08001000. The difference is that the system does not apply the guard attribute to the new page of physical storage (0x08001000). This means that the stack's reserved address space region contains all the physical storage that it can ever contain. The bottommost page is always reserved and never gets committed. I will explain the reason for this shortly.

The system performs one more action when it commits physical storage to the page at address 0x08001000–it raises an **EXCEPTION_STACK_OVERFLOW** exception, which has a value of 0xC00000FD. By using structured exception handling (SEH), your program will be notified of this condition and can recover gracefully. For more information on SEH, see Chapter 23, "Termination Handlers," Chapter 24, "Exception Handlers and Software Exceptions," and Chapter 25, "Unhandled Exceptions, Vectored Exception Handling, and C++ Exceptions." The Summation sample at the end of this chapter demonstrates how to recover gracefully from stack overflows.

If the thread continues to use the stack after the stack overflow exception is raised, all the memory in the page at 0x08001000 will be used and the thread will attempt to access memory in the page starting at 0x08000000. When the thread attempts to access this reserved (uncommitted) memory, the system raises an access violation exception. If this access violation exception is raised while the thread is attempting to access the stack, the thread is in deep trouble. The system takes control at this point and shifts control to the Windows Error Reporting service, which pops up the following dialog box before terminating the process–not just the thread, but the whole process.

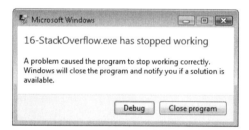

An application can have the system raise the **EXCEPTION_STACK_OVERFLOW** exception earlier by calling the **SetThreadStackGuarantee** function. This function ensures that the specified number of bytes exist above the reserved (uncommitted) memory page, which allows the application to use more than one page of stack space before Windows Error Reporting takes over to terminate the process.

> **Important** The system raises an **EXCEPTION_STACK_OVERFLOW** exception when a thread's last guard page is touched. If this exception is caught and the thread's execution continues, the system will not raise the exception for this thread again because there are no more guard pages. To receive future **EXCEPTION_STACK_OVERFLOW** exceptions for this thread, your application must reset the guard page. This is easily accomplished by calling the C run-time library's **_resetstkoflw** function (defined in malloc.h).

Now I will explain why the bottommost page of a stack's region is always reserved. Doing so protects against accidental overwriting of other data being used by the process. You see, it's possible that at address 0x07FFF000 (one page below 0x08000000) another region of address space has committed physical storage. If the page at 0x08000000 contained physical storage, the system would not catch attempts by the thread to access the reserved stack region. If the stack were to dip below the reserved stack region, the code in your thread would overwrite other data in your process' address space—a very, very difficult bug to catch.

Another difficult bug to catch is *stack underflow*. To see what a stack underflow is, examine the following code:

```
int WINAPI WinMain (HINSTANCE hInstExe, HINSTANCE,
   PTSTR pszCmdLine, int nCmdShow) {

   BYTE aBytes[100];
   aBytes[10000] = 0; // Stack underflow

   return(0);
}
```

When this function's assignment statement is executed, an attempt is made to access memory beyond the end of the thread's stack. Of course, the compiler and the linker will not catch the bug in the code just shown, and an access violation will not necessarily be raised when the statement executes because it is possible to have another region immediately after your thread's stack. If this happens and you attempt to access memory beyond your stack, you might corrupt memory related to another part of your process—and the system will *not* detect this corruption. Here is a code snippet that shows a case where the stack underflow will always trigger a corruption because a memory block is allocated just after the stack of a thread:

```
DWORD WINAPI ThreadFunc(PVOID pvParam) {

   BYTE aBytes[0x10];

   // Figure out where the stack is in the virtual address space
   // See Chapter 14 for more details about VirtualQuery
   MEMORY_BASIC_INFORMATION mbi;
   SIZE_T size = VirtualQuery(aBytes, &mbi, sizeof(mbi));

   // Allocate a block of memory just after the 1 MB stack
   SIZE_T s = (SIZE_T)mbi.AllocationBase + 1024*1024;
   PBYTE pAddress = (PBYTE)s;
   BYTE* pBytes = (BYTE*)VirtualAlloc(pAddress, 0x10000,
      MEM_COMMIT | MEM_RESERVE, PAGE_READWRITE);

   // Trigger an unnoticeable stack underflow
   aBytes[0x10000] = 1; // Write in the allocated block, past the stack

   ...

   return(0);
}
```

The C/C++ Run-Time Library's Stack-Checking Function

The C/C++ run-time library contains a stack-checking function. As your source code is compiled, the compiler generates calls to this function automatically when necessary. The purpose of the stack-checking function is to make sure that pages are appropriately committed to your thread's stack. Let's look at an example. Here's a small function that requires a lot of memory for its local variables:

```
void SomeFunction () {
   int nValues[4000];

   // Do some processing with the array.
   nValues[0] = 0;  // Some assignment
}
```

This function will require at least 16,000 bytes (4000 × **sizeof(int)**; each integer is 4 bytes) of stack space to accommodate the array of integers. Usually, the code a compiler generates to allocate this stack space simply decrements the CPU's stack pointer by 16,000 bytes. However, the system does not commit physical storage to this lower area of the stack's region until an attempt is made to access the memory address.

On a system with a 4-KB or 8-KB page size, this limitation could cause a problem. If the first access to the stack is at an address that is below the guard page (as shown on the assignment line in the preceding code), the thread will be accessing reserved memory and the system will raise an access violation. To ensure that you can successfully write functions like the one just shown, the compiler inserts calls to the C run-time library's stack-checking function.

When compiling your program, the compiler knows the page size for the CPU system you are targeting. The x86/x64 compiler knows that pages are 4 KB, and the IA-64 compiler knows that pages are 8 KB. As the compiler encounters each function in your program, it determines the amount of stack space required for the function; if the function requires more stack space than the target system's page size, the compiler automatically inserts a call to the stack-checking function.

The following pseudocode shows what the stack-checking function does. I say *pseudocode* because this function is usually implemented in assembly language by the compiler vendors.

```
// The C run-time library knows the page size for the target system.
#ifdef _M_IA64
#define PAGESIZE    (8 * 1024)    // 8-KB page
#else
#define PAGESIZE    (4 * 1024)    // 4-KB page
#endif

void StackCheck(int nBytesNeededFromStack) {
   // Get the stack pointer position.
   // At this point, the stack pointer has NOT been decremented
   // to account for the function's local variables.
   PBYTE pbStackPtr = (CPU's stack pointer);

   while (nBytesNeededFromStack >= PAGESIZE) {
      // Move down a page on the stack--should be a guard page.
      pbStackPtr -= PAGESIZE;
```

```
      // Access a byte on the guard page--forces new page to be
      // committed and guard page to move down a page.
      pbStackPtr[0] = 0;

      // Reduce the number of bytes needed from the stack.
      nBytesNeededFromStack -= PAGESIZE;
   }

   // Before returning, the StackCheck function sets the CPU's
   // stack pointer to the address below the function's
   // local variables.
}
```

Microsoft Visual C++ does offer the **/GS** compiler switch, which allows you to control the page-size threshold that the compiler uses to determine when to add the automatic call to **StackCheck**. (Read *http://msdn2.microsoft.com/en-us/library/9598wk25(VS.80).aspx* for more details about this compiler switch.) You should use this compiler switch only if you know exactly what you are doing and have a special need for it. For 99.99999 percent of all applications and DLLs written, this switch should not be used.

> **Note**   The Microsoft C/C++ compiler provides switches that help you to detect stack corruptions at run time. When you create a C++ project, the **/RTCsu** compiler switch (*http://msdn2.microsoft.com/en-us/library/8wtf2dfz(VS.80).aspx*) is set by default for your DEBUG build. If a local variable array overrun occurs at run time, the injected code detects it and you are notified when the erring function returns. The **/RTC** switches are available only for DEBUG build.
>
> However, for your RELEASE build, you should set the **/GS** compiler switch. This switch tells the compiler to add code that stores the state of the stack as a *cookie* before a function is called, and it checks the integrity of the stack after the function returns. With these checks in place, malware attempting to trigger a buffer overrun to redirect the flow of execution to its code, by overwriting the return address on the stack, cannot happen because the check against the cookie detects it and terminates the application. For a very detailed analysis of the **/GS** compiler option, refer to *http://www.symantec.com/avcenter/reference/GS_Protections_in_Vista.pdf* and "Compiler Security Checks In Depth" (*http://msdn2.microsoft.com/en-us/library/aa290051(VS.71).aspx*).

The Summation Sample Application

The Summation (16-Summation.exe) sample application shown later in this chapter demonstrates how to use exception filters and exception handlers to recover gracefully from a stack overflow. The source code and resource files for the application are in the 16-Summation directory on the companion content Web page. You might want to review the chapters on SEH to fully understand how this application works.

The Summation application sums all the numbers from 0 through **x**, where **x** is a number entered by the user. Of course, the simplest way to do this is to create a function called **Sum** that simply performs the following calculation:

```
Sum = (x * (x + 1)) / 2;
```

However, for this sample, I have written the **Sum** function to be recursive so that it uses a lot of stack space if you enter large numbers.

When the program starts, it displays the dialog box shown here:

In this dialog box, you can enter a number in the edit control and then click the Calculate button. This causes the program to create a new thread whose sole responsibility is to total all the numbers between 0 and **x**. While the new thread is running, the program's primary thread waits for the result by calling **WaitForSingleObject**, passing the new thread's handle. When the new thread terminates, the system wakes the primary thread. The primary thread retrieves the sum by getting the new thread's exit code through a call to **GetExitCodeThread**. Finally—and this is extremely important—the primary thread closes its handle to the new thread so that the system can completely destroy the thread object and so that our application does not have a resource leak.

Now the primary thread examines the summation thread's exit code. The exit code **UINT_MAX** indicates that an error occurred—the summation thread overflowed the stack while totaling the numbers—and the primary thread will display a message box to this effect. If the exit code is not **UINT_MAX**, the summation thread completed successfully and the exit code is the summation. In this case, the primary thread will simply put the summation answer in the dialog box.

Now let's turn to the summation thread. The thread function for this thread is called **SumThreadFunc**. When the primary thread creates this thread, it is passed the number of integers that it should total as its only parameter, **pvParam**. The function then initializes the **uSum** variable to **UINT_MAX**, which means that the function is assuming that it will not complete successfully. Next **SumThreadFunc** sets up SEH so that it can catch any exception that might be raised while the thread executes. The recursive **Sum** function is then called to calculate the sum.

If the sum is calculated successfully, **SumThreadFunc** simply returns the value of the **uSum** variable; this is the thread's exit code. However, if an exception is raised while the **Sum** function is executing, the system will immediately evaluate the SEH filter expression. In other words, the system will call the **FilterFunc** function and pass it the code that identifies the raised exception. For a stack overflow exception, this code is **EXCEPTION_STACK_OVERFLOW**. If you want to see the program gracefully handle a stack overflow exception, tell the program to sum the first 44,000 numbers.

My **FilterFunc** function is simple. It checks to see if a stack overflow exception was raised, and if not, it returns **EXCEPTION_CONTINUE_SEARCH**. Otherwise, the filter returns **EXCEPTION_EXECUTE_HANDLER**. This indicates to the system that the filter was expecting this exception and that the code contained in the **except** block should execute. For this sample application, the exception handler has nothing special to do, but it allows the thread to exit gracefully with a return code of **UINT_MAX** (the value in **uSumNum**). The parent thread will see this special return value and display a warning message to the user.

The final thing that I want to discuss is why I execute the **Sum** function in its own thread instead of just setting up an SEH block in the primary thread and calling the **Sum** function from within the **try** block. I created this additional thread for four reasons.

First, each time a thread is created, it gets its very own 1-MB stack region. If I called the **Sum** function from within the primary thread, some of the stack space would already be in use and the **Sum** function would not be able to use its full 1 MB of stack space. Granted, my sample is a simple program and is probably not using all that much stack, but other programs will probably be more complicated. I can easily imagine a situation in which **Sum** might successfully total the integers from 0 through 1000. Then when **Sum** is called again later, the stack might be deeper, causing a stack overflow to occur when **Sum** is trying only to total the integers from 0 through 750. So to make the **Sum** function behave more consistently, I ensure that it has a full stack that has not been used by any other code.

The second reason for using a separate thread is that a thread is notified only once of a stack overflow exception. If I called the **Sum** function in the primary thread and a stack overflow occurred, the exception could be trapped and handled gracefully. However, at this point all of the stack's reserved address space is committed with physical storage, and there are no more pages with the guard protection flag turned on. If the user performs another sum, the **Sum** function could overflow the stack and a stack overflow exception would not be raised. Instead, an access violation exception would be raised, and it would be too late to handle this situation gracefully. Of course, I could fix this problem by calling the C run-time library's **_resetstkoflw** function.

The third reason for using a separate thread is so that the physical storage for its stack can be freed. Take this scenario as an example: The user asks the **Sum** function to calculate the sum of the integers from 0 through 30,000. This will require quite a bit of physical storage to be committed to the stack region. Then the user might do several summations in which the highest number is only 5000. In this case, a large amount of storage is committed to the stack region but is no longer being used. This physical storage is allocated from the paging file. Rather than leave this storage committed, it's better to free the storage, giving it back to the system and other processes. By having the **SumThreadFunc** thread terminate, the system automatically reclaims the physical storage that was committed to the stack's region.

The final reason for using a separate thread is that reusing one thread to do all the summation work would require thread synchronization in order to coordinate when the thread should start executing and how it should return its results. The simplest approach (for this simple application) is just to spawn a new thread each time, passing it the value I want it to sum up to, and then just wait for the thread to exit to get the result.

```
Summation.cpp
/******************************************************************************
Module:  Summation.cpp
Notices: Copyright (c) 2008 Jeffrey Richter & Christophe Nasarre
******************************************************************************/


#include "..\CommonFiles\CmnHdr.h"     /* See Appendix A. */
#include <windowsx.h>
#include <limits.h>
#include <tchar.h>
#include "Resource.h"


//////////////////////////////////////////////////////////////////////////////
```

```
// An example of calling Sum for uNum = 0 through 9
// uNum: 0 1 2 3  4  5  6  7  8  9 ...
// Sum:  0 1 3 6 10 15 21 28 36 45 ...
UINT Sum(UINT uNum) {

   // Call Sum recursively.
   return((uNum == 0) ? 0 : (uNum + Sum(uNum - 1)));
}


///////////////////////////////////////////////////////////////////////////


LONG WINAPI FilterFunc(DWORD dwExceptionCode) {

   return((dwExceptionCode == STATUS_STACK_OVERFLOW)
      ? EXCEPTION_EXECUTE_HANDLER : EXCEPTION_CONTINUE_SEARCH);
}


///////////////////////////////////////////////////////////////////////////


// The separate thread that is responsible for calculating the sum.
// I use a separate thread for the following reasons:
//    1. A separate thread gets its own 1 MB of stack space.
//    2. A thread can be notified of a stack overflow only once.
//    3. The stack's storage is freed when the thread exits.
DWORD WINAPI SumThreadFunc(PVOID pvParam) {

   // The parameter pvParam contains the number of integers to sum.
   UINT uSumNum = PtrToUlong(pvParam);

   // uSum contains the summation of the numbers from 0 through uSumNum.
   // If the sum cannot be calculated, a sum of UINT_MAX is returned.
   UINT uSum = UINT_MAX;

   __try {
      // To catch the stack overflow exception, we must
      // execute the Sum function while inside an SEH block.
      uSum = Sum(uSumNum);
   }
   __except (FilterFunc(GetExceptionCode())) {
      // If we get in here, it's because we have trapped a stack overflow.
      // We can now do whatever is necessary to gracefully continue execution.
      // This sample application has nothing to do, so no code is placed
      // in this exception handler block.
   }

   // The thread's exit code is the sum of the first uSumNum
   // numbers, or UINT_MAX if a stack overflow occurred.
   return(uSum);
}


///////////////////////////////////////////////////////////////////////////
```

```
BOOL Dlg_OnInitDialog(HWND hWnd, HWND hWndFocus, LPARAM lParam) {

   chSETDLGICONS(hWnd, IDI_SUMMATION);

   // Don't accept integers more than 9 digits long
   Edit_LimitText(GetDlgItem(hWnd, IDC_SUMNUM), 9);

   return(TRUE);
}


///////////////////////////////////////////////////////////////////////////////


void Dlg_OnCommand(HWND hWnd, int id, HWND hWndCtl, UINT codeNotify) {

   switch (id) {
      case IDCANCEL:
         EndDialog(hWnd, id);
         break;

      case IDC_CALC:
         // Get the number of integers the user wants to sum.
         BOOL bSuccess = TRUE;
         UINT uSum = GetDlgItemInt(hWnd, IDC_SUMNUM, &bSuccess, FALSE);
         if (!bSuccess) {
            MessageBox(hWnd, TEXT("Please enter a valid numeric value!"),
               TEXT("Invalid input..."), MB_ICONINFORMATION | MB_OK);
            SetFocus(GetDlgItem(hWnd, IDC_CALC));
            break;
         }

         // Create a thread (with its own stack) that is
         // responsible for performing the summation.
         DWORD dwThreadId;
         HANDLE hThread = chBEGINTHREADEX(NULL, 0,
            SumThreadFunc, (PVOID) (UINT_PTR) uSum, 0, &dwThreadId);

         // Wait for the thread to terminate.
         WaitForSingleObject(hThread, INFINITE);

         // The thread's exit code is the resulting summation.
         GetExitCodeThread(hThread, (PDWORD) &uSum);

         // Allow the system to destroy the thread kernel object
         CloseHandle(hThread);

         // Update the dialog box to show the result.
         if (uSum == UINT_MAX) {
            // If result is UINT_MAX, a stack overflow occurred.
            SetDlgItemText(hWnd, IDC_ANSWER, TEXT("Error"));
            chMB("The number is too big, please enter a smaller number");
```

```
          } else {
            // The sum was calculated successfully;
            SetDlgItemInt(hWnd, IDC_ANSWER, uSum, FALSE);
          }
          break;
      }
}


////////////////////////////////////////////////////////////////////////////


INT_PTR WINAPI Dlg_Proc(HWND hWnd, UINT uMsg, WPARAM wParam, LPARAM lParam) {

   switch (uMsg) {
      chHANDLE_DLGMSG(hWnd, WM_INITDIALOG, Dlg_OnInitDialog);
      chHANDLE_DLGMSG(hWnd, WM_COMMAND,    Dlg_OnCommand);
   }
   return(FALSE);
}


////////////////////////////////////////////////////////////////////////////


int WINAPI _tWinMain(HINSTANCE hInstExe, HINSTANCE, PTSTR, int) {

   DialogBox(hInstExe, MAKEINTRESOURCE(IDD_SUMMATION), NULL, Dlg_Proc);
   return(0);
}

////////////////////////////// End of File.//////////////////////////////////
```

Chapter 17
Memory-Mapped Files

Working with files is something almost every application must do, and it's always a hassle. Should your application open the file, read it, and close the file, or should it open the file and use a buffering algorithm to read from and write to different portions of the file? Microsoft Windows offers the best of both worlds: memory-mapped files.

Like virtual memory, memory-mapped files allow you to reserve a region of address space and commit physical storage to the region. The difference is that the physical storage comes from a file that is already on the disk instead of the system's paging file. Once the file has been mapped, you can access it as if the whole file were loaded in memory.

Memory-mapped files are used for three different purposes:

■ The system uses memory-mapped files to load and execute .exe and dynamic-link library (DLL) files. This greatly conserves both paging file space and the time required for an application to begin executing.

■ You can use memory-mapped files to access a data file on disk. This shelters you from performing file I/O operations on the file and from buffering the file's contents.

■ You can use memory-mapped files to allow multiple processes running on the same machine to share data with each other. Windows does offer other methods for communicating data among processes—but these other methods are implemented using memory-mapped files, making memory-mapped files the most efficient way for multiple processes on a single machine to communicate with one another.

In this chapter, we will examine each of these uses for memory-mapped files.

7

Memory-Mapped Executables and DLLs

When a thread calls **CreateProcess**, the system performs the following steps:

1. The system locates the .exe file specified in the call to **CreateProcess**. If the .exe file cannot be found, the process is not created and **CreateProcess** returns **FALSE**.

2. The system creates a new process kernel object.

3. The system creates a private address space for this new process.

4. The system reserves a region of address space large enough to contain the .exe file. The desired location of this region is specified inside the .exe file itself. By default, an .exe file's base address is 0x00400000. (This address might be different for a 64-bit application running on 64-bit Windows.) However, you can override this when you create your application's .exe file by using the linker's /**BASE** option when you link your application.

5. The system notes that the physical storage backing the reserved region is in the .exe file on disk instead of the system's paging file.

After the .exe file has been mapped into the process' address space, the system accesses a section of the .exe file that lists the DLLs containing functions that the code in the .exe calls. The system then calls **LoadLibrary** for each of these DLLs, and if any of the DLLs require additional DLLs, the system calls **LoadLibrary** to load those DLLs as well. Every time **LoadLibrary** is called to load a DLL, the system performs steps similar to steps 4 and 5 just listed:

1. The system reserves a region of address space large enough to contain the DLL file. The desired location of this region is specified inside the DLL file itself. By default, Microsoft's linker sets the DLL's base address to 0x10000000 for an x86 DLL and 0x00400000 for an x64 DLL. However, you can override this when you build your DLL by using the linker's /**BASE** option. All the standard system DLLs that ship with Windows have different base addresses so that they don't overlap if loaded into a single address space.

2. If the system is unable to reserve a region at the DLL's preferred base address, either because the region is occupied by another DLL or .exe or because the region just isn't big enough, the system will then try to find another region of address space to reserve for the DLL. It is unfortunate when a DLL cannot load at its preferred base address for two reasons. First, the system might not be able to load the DLL if it does not have relocation information. (You can remove relocation information from a DLL when it is created by using the linker's /**FIXED** switch. This makes the DLL file smaller, but it also means that the DLL *must* load at its preferred address or it can't load at all.) Second, the system must perform some relocations within the DLL. These relocations require additional storage from the system's paging file; they also increase the amount of time needed to load the DLL.

3. The system notes that the physical storage backing the reserved region is in the DLL file on disk instead of in the system's paging file. If Windows has to perform relocations because the DLL could not load at its preferred base address, the system also notes that some of the physical storage for the DLL is mapped to the paging file.

If for some reason the system is unable to map the .exe and all the required DLLs, the system displays a message box to the user and frees the process' address space and the process object. **CreateProcess** will return **FALSE** to its caller; the caller can call **GetLastError** to get a better idea of why the process could not be created.

After all the .exe and DLL files have been mapped into the process' address space, the system can begin executing the .exe file's startup code. After the .exe file has been mapped, the system takes care of all the paging, buffering, and caching. For example, if code in the .exe causes it to jump to the address of an instruction that isn't loaded into memory, a fault will occur. The system detects the fault and automatically loads the page of code from the file's image into a page of RAM. Then the system maps the page of RAM to the proper location in the process' address space and allows the thread to continue executing as though the page of code were loaded all along. Of course, all this is invisible to the application. This process is repeated each time any thread in the process attempts to access code or data that is not loaded into RAM.

Static Data Is Not Shared by Multiple Instances of an Executable or a DLL

When you create a new process for an application that is already running, the system simply opens another memory-mapped view of the file-mapping object that identifies the executable file's image and creates a new process object and a new thread object (for the primary thread). The system also assigns new process and thread IDs to these objects. By using memory-mapped files, multiple running instances of the same application can share the same code and data in RAM.

Note one small problem here. Processes use a flat address space. When you compile and link your program, all the code and data are thrown together as one large entity. The data is separated from the code but only to the extent that it follows the code in the .exe file. (See the following note for more detail.) The following illustration shows a simplified view of how the code and data for an application are loaded into virtual memory and then mapped into an application's address space.

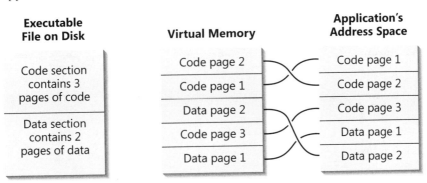

As an example, let's say that a second instance of an application is run. The system simply maps the pages of virtual memory containing the file's code and data into the second application's address space, as shown next.

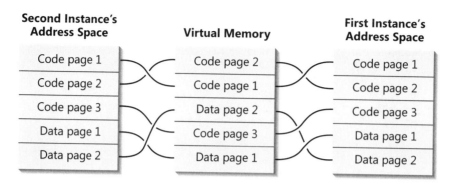

Note Actually, the contents of a file are broken down into sections. The code is in one section, and the global variables are in another. Sections are aligned on page boundaries. An application can determine the page size being used by calling **GetSystemInfo**. In the .exe or DLL file, the code section usually precedes the data section.

If one instance of the application alters some global variables residing in a data page, the memory contents for all instances of the application change. This type of change could cause disastrous effects and must not be allowed.

The system prohibits this by using the copy-on-write feature of the memory management system. Any time an application attempts to write to its memory-mapped file, the system catches the attempt, allocates a new block of memory for the page containing the memory the application is trying to write to, copies the contents of the page, and allows the application to write to this newly allocated memory block. As a result, no other instances of the same application are affected. The following illustration shows what happens when the first instance of an application attempts to change a global variable in data page 2:

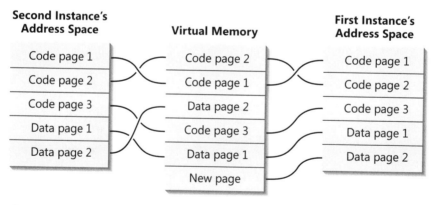

The system allocated a new page of virtual memory (labeled as "New page" in the image above) and copied the contents of data page 2 into it. The first instance's address space is changed so that the new data page is mapped into the address space at the same location as the original address page. Now the system can let the process alter the global variable without fear of altering the data for another instance of the same application.

A similar sequence of events occurs when an application is being debugged. Let's say that you're running multiple instances of an application and want to debug only one instance. You access your debugger and set a breakpoint in a line of source code. The debugger modifies your code by changing one of your assembly language instructions to an instruction that causes the debugger to activate itself. So you have the same problem again. When the debugger modifies the code, it causes all instances of the application to activate the debugger when the changed assembly instruction is executed. To fix this situation, the system again uses copy-on-write memory. When the system senses that the debugger is attempting to change the code, it allocates a new block of memory, copies the page containing the instruction into the new page, and allows the debugger to modify the code in the page copy.

> **Note**   When a process is loaded, the system examines all the file image's pages. The system commits storage in the paging file immediately for pages that would normally be protected with the copy-on-write attribute. These pages are simply committed; they are not touched in any way. When a page in the file image is accessed, the system loads the appropriate page. If that page is never modified, it can be discarded from memory and reloaded when necessary. If the file's page is modified, however, the system swaps the modified page to one of the previously committed pages in the paging file.

Sharing Static Data Across Multiple Instances of an Executable or a DLL

The fact that global and static data is not shared by multiple mappings of the same .exe or DLL is a safe default. However, on some occasions it is useful and convenient for multiple mappings of an .exe to share a single instance of a variable. For example, Windows offers no easy way to determine whether the user is running multiple instances of an application. But if you could get all the instances to share a single global variable, this global variable could reflect the number of instances running. When the user invoked an instance of the application, the new instance's thread could simply check the value of the global variable (which had been updated by another instance), and if the count were greater than 1, the second instance could notify the user that only one instance of the application is allowed to run and the second instance would terminate.

This section discusses a technique that allows you to share variables among all instances of an .exe or a DLL. But before we dive too deeply into the details, you'll need a little background information....

Every .exe or DLL file image is composed of a collection of sections. By convention, each standard section name begins with a period. For example, when you compile your program, the compiler places all the code in a section called *.text*. The compiler also places all the uninitialized data in a *.bss* section and all the initialized data in a *.data* section.

Each section has a combination of the following attributes associated with it, as shown in Table 17-1.

Table 17-1   Section Attributes

Attribute	Meaning
READ	The bytes in the section can be read from.
WRITE	The bytes in the section can be written to.
EXECUTE	The bytes in the section can be executed.
SHARED	The bytes in the section are shared across multiple instances. (This attribute effectively turns off the copy-on-write mechanism.)

Using the Microsoft Visual Studio DumpBin utility (with the **/Headers** switch), you can see the list of sections in an .exe or DLL image file. The following excerpt was generated by running DumpBin on an executable file:

```
SECTION HEADER #1
   .text name
  11A70 virtual size
   1000 virtual address
  12000 size of raw data
   1000 file pointer to raw data
      0 file pointer to relocation table
      0 file pointer to line numbers
      0 number of relocations
      0 number of line numbers
60000020 flags
        Code
        Execute Read

SECTION HEADER #2
  .rdata name
    1F6 virtual size
  13000 virtual address
   1000 size of raw data
  13000 file pointer to raw data
      0 file pointer to relocation table
      0 file pointer to line numbers
      0 number of relocations
      0 number of line numbers
40000040 flags
        Initialized Data
        Read Only

SECTION HEADER #3
   .data name
    560 virtual size
  14000 virtual address
   1000 size of raw data
  14000 file pointer to raw data
      0 file pointer to relocation table
      0 file pointer to line numbers
      0 number of relocations
      0 number of line numbers
C0000040 flags
        Initialized Data
        Read Write
```

```
SECTION HEADER #4
  .idata name
     58D virtual size
   15000 virtual address
    1000 size of raw data
   15000 file pointer to raw data
       0 file pointer to relocation table
       0 file pointer to line numbers
       0 number of relocations
       0 number of line numbers
C0000040 flags
         Initialized Data
         Read Write

SECTION HEADER #5
  .didat name
     7A2 virtual size
   16000 virtual address
    1000 size of raw data
   16000 file pointer to raw data
       0 file pointer to relocation table
       0 file pointer to line numbers
       0 number of relocations
       0 number of line numbers
C0000040 flags
         Initialized Data
         Read Write

SECTION HEADER #6
  .reloc name
     26D virtual size
   17000 virtual address
    1000 size of raw data
   17000 file pointer to raw data
       0 file pointer to relocation table
       0 file pointer to line numbers
       0 number of relocations
       0 number of line numbers
42000040 flags
         Initialized Data
         Discardable
         Read Only

    Summary
        1000 .data
        1000 .didat
        1000 .idata
        1000 .rdata
        1000 .reloc
       12000 .text
```

Table 17-2 shows some of the more common section names and explains each section's purpose.

Table 17-2   Executable Common Sections

Section Name	Purpose
`.bss`	Uninitialized data
`.CRT`	Read-only C run-time data
`.data`	Initialized data
`.debug`	Debugging information
`.didata`	Delay imported names table
`.edata`	Exported names table
`.idata`	Imported names table
`.rdata`	Read-only run-time data
`.reloc`	Relocation table information
`.rsrc`	Resources
`.text`	.exe's or DLL's code
`.textbss`	Generated by the C++ compiler when the Incremental Linking option is enabled
`.tls`	Thread-local storage
`.xdata`	Exception-handling table

In addition to using the standard sections created by the compiler and the linker, you can create your own sections when you compile using the following directive:

```
#pragma data_seg("sectionname")
```

So, for example, I can create a section called "Shared" that contains a single **LONG** value, as follows:

```
#pragma data_seg("Shared")
LONG g_lInstanceCount = 0;
#pragma data_seg()
```

When the compiler compiles this code, it creates a new section called Shared and places all the *initialized* data variables that it sees after the pragma in this new section. In the preceding example, the variable is placed in the Shared section. Following the variable, the *#pragma data_seg()* line tells the compiler to stop putting initialized variables in the Shared section and to start putting them back in the default data section. It is extremely important to remember that the compiler will store only initialized variables in the new section. For example, if I had removed the initialization from the previous code fragment (as shown in the following code), the compiler would have put this variable in a section other than the Shared section:

```
#pragma data_seg("Shared")
LONG g_lInstanceCount;
#pragma data_seg()
```

The Microsoft Visual C++ compiler offers an *allocate* declaration specifier, however, that does allow you to place uninitialized data in any section you desire. Take a look at the following code:

```
// Create Shared section & have compiler place initialized data in it.
#pragma data_seg("Shared")

// Initialized, in Shared section
int a = 0;

// Uninitialized, not in Shared section
int b;

// Have compiler stop placing initialized data in Shared section.
#pragma data_seg()

// Initialized, in Shared section
__declspec(allocate("Shared")) int c = 0;

// Uninitialized, in Shared section
__declspec(allocate("Shared")) int d;

// Initialized, not in Shared section
int e = 0;

// Uninitialized, not in Shared section
int f;
```

The comments shown make it clear which section the specified variable will be placed in. For the *allocate* declaration specification to work properly, the section must first be created. Therefore, the code just shown would not compile if the first *#pragma data_seg* line in the preceding code were removed.

Probably the most common reason to put variables in their own section is to share them among multiple mappings of an .exe or a DLL. By default, each mapping of an .exe or a DLL gets its very own set of variables. However, you can group into their own section any variables that you want to share among all mappings of that module. When you group variables, the system doesn't create new instances of the variables for every mapping of the .exe or the DLL.

Simply telling the compiler to place certain variables in their own section is not enough to share those variables. You must also tell the linker that the variables in a particular section are to be shared. You can do this by using the **/SECTION** switch on the linker's command line:

```
/SECTION:name,attributes
```

Following the colon, type the name of the section for which you want to alter attributes. In our example, we want to change the attributes of the Shared section. So we'd construct our linker switch as follows:

```
/SECTION:Shared,RWS
```

After the comma, we specify the desired attributes: use *R* for READ, *W* for WRITE, *E* for EXECUTE, and *S* for SHARED. The switch shown indicates that the data in the Shared section is readable, writable, and shared. If you want to change the attributes of more than one section, you must specify the **/SECTION** switch multiple times—once for each section for which you want to change attributes.

You can also embed linker switches right inside your source code using this syntax:

```
#pragma comment(linker, "/SECTION:Shared,RWS")
```

This line tells the compiler to embed the preceding string inside a special section of the generated .obj file named ".drectve". When the linker combines all the .obj modules together, the linker examines each .obj module's ".drectve" section and pretends that all the strings were passed to the linker as command-line arguments. I use this technique all the time because it is so convenient—if you move a source code file into a new project, you don't have to remember to set linker switches in the Visual C++ Project Properties dialog box.

Although you can create shared sections, Microsoft discourages the use of shared sections for two reasons. First, sharing memory in this way can potentially violate security. Second, sharing variables means that an error in one application can affect the operation of another application because there is no way to protect a block of data from being randomly written to by an application.

Imagine that you have written two applications, each requiring the user to enter a password. However, you decide to add a feature to your applications that makes things a little easier on the user: If the user is already running one of the applications when the second is started, the second application examines the contents of shared memory to get the password. This way, the user doesn't need to reenter the password if one of the programs is already being used.

This sounds innocent enough. After all, no other applications but your own load the DLL and know where to find the password contained within the shared section. However, hackers lurk about, and if they want to get your password, all they need to do is write a small program of their own to load your company's DLL and monitor the shared memory blocks. When the user enters a password, the hacker's program can learn the user's password.

An industrious program such as the hacker's might also try to guess repeatedly at passwords and write them to the shared memory. Once the program guesses the correct password, it can send all kinds of commands to one of the two applications. Perhaps this problem could be solved if there were a way to grant access to only certain applications for loading a particular DLL. But currently this is not the case—any program can call **LoadLibrary** to explicitly load a DLL.

The Application Instances Sample Application

The Application Instances sample application (17-AppInst.exe), presented next, shows how an application can know how many instances of itself are running at any one time. The source code and resource files for the application are in the 17-AppInst directory on this book's companion content Web page. When you run the AppInst program, its dialog box appears, indicating that one instance of the application is running:

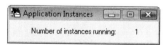

If you run a second instance of the application, both instances' dialog boxes change to reflect that two instances are now running:

You can run and kill as many instances as you like—the number will always be accurately reflected in whichever instances remain.

Near the top of AppInst.cpp, you'll see the following lines:

```
// Tell the compiler to put this initialized variable in its own Shared
// section so it is shared by all instances of this application.
#pragma data_seg("Shared")
volatile LONG g_lApplicationInstances = 0;
#pragma data_seg()


// Tell the linker to make the Shared section
// readable, writable, and shared.
#pragma comment(linker, "/Section:Shared,RWS")
```

These lines create a section called Shared that will have read, write, and shared protection. Within this section is one variable: **g_lApplicationInstances**. All instances of this application share this variable. Note that the variable is volatile so that the optimizer doesn't get too smart for our own good.

When each instance's **_tWinMain** function executes, the **g_lApplicationInstances** variable is incremented by 1; and before **_tWinMain** exits, this variable is decremented by 1. I use **Inter-lockedExchangeAdd** to alter this variable because multiple threads will access this shared resource.

When each instance's dialog box appears, the **Dlg_OnInitDialog** function is called. This function broadcasts to all top-level windows a registered window message (whose message ID is contained in the **g_uMsgAppInstCountUpdate** variable):

```
PostMessage(HWND_BROADCAST, g_uMsgAppInstCountUpdate, 0, 0);
```

All the windows in the system will ignore this registered window message except for Application Instances windows. When one of our windows receives this message, the code in **Dlg_Proc** simply updates the number in the dialog box to reflect the current number of instances (maintained in the shared **g_lApplicationInstances** variable).

AppInst.cpp

```
/**************************************************************************
Module:   AppInst.cpp
Notices:  Copyright (c) 2008 Jeffrey Richter & Christophe Nasarre
**************************************************************************/


#include "..\CmnHdr.h"      /* See Appendix A. */
#include <windowsx.h>
#include <tchar.h>
#include "Resource.h"


///////////////////////////////////////////////////////////////////////////


// The system-wide window message, unique to the application
UINT g_uMsgAppInstCountUpdate = WM_APP+123;


///////////////////////////////////////////////////////////////////////////


// Tell the compiler to put this initialized variable in its own Shared
// section so it is shared by all instances of this application.
#pragma data_seg("Shared")
volatile LONG g_lApplicationInstances = 0;
#pragma data_seg()

// Tell the linker to make the Shared section readable, writable, and shared.
#pragma comment(linker, "/Section:Shared,RWS")


///////////////////////////////////////////////////////////////////////////


BOOL Dlg_OnInitDialog(HWND hWnd, HWND hWndFocus, LPARAM lParam) {

   chSETDLGICONS(hWnd, IDI_APPINST);

   // Force the static control to be initialized correctly.
   PostMessage(HWND_BROADCAST, g_uMsgAppInstCountUpdate, 0, 0);
   return(TRUE);
}


///////////////////////////////////////////////////////////////////////////
```

```
void Dlg_OnCommand(HWND hWnd, int id, HWND hWndCtl, UINT codeNotify) {

   switch (id) {
      case IDCANCEL:
         EndDialog(hWnd, id);
         break;
   }
}


/////////////////////////////////////////////////////////////////////////////


INT_PTR WINAPI Dlg_Proc(HWND hWnd, UINT uMsg, WPARAM wParam, LPARAM lParam) {

   if (uMsg == g_uMsgAppInstCountUpdate) {
      SetDlgItemInt(hWnd, IDC_COUNT, g_lApplicationInstances, FALSE);
   }

   switch (uMsg) {
      chHANDLE_DLGMSG(hWnd, WM_INITDIALOG, Dlg_OnInitDialog);
      chHANDLE_DLGMSG(hWnd, WM_COMMAND,    Dlg_OnCommand);
   }
   return(FALSE);
}


/////////////////////////////////////////////////////////////////////////////


int WINAPI _tWinMain(HINSTANCE hInstExe, HINSTANCE, PTSTR, int) {

   // Get the numeric value of the systemwide window message used to notify
   // all top-level windows when the module's usage count has changed.
   g_uMsgAppInstCountUpdate =
      RegisterWindowMessage(TEXT("MsgAppInstCountUpdate"));

   // There is another instance of this application running
   InterlockedExchangeAdd((PLONG) &g_lApplicationInstances, 1);

   DialogBox(hInstExe, MAKEINTRESOURCE(IDD_APPINST), NULL, Dlg_Proc);

   // This instance of the application is terminating
   InterlockedExchangeAdd((PLONG) &g_lApplicationInstances, -1);

   // Have all other instances update their display
   PostMessage(HWND_BROADCAST, g_uMsgAppInstCountUpdate, 0, 0);

   return(0);
}

/////////////////////////////// End of File //////////////////////////////////
```

Memory-Mapped Data Files

The operating system makes it possible to memory map a data file into your process' address space. Thus it is very convenient to manipulate large streams of data.

To understand the power of using memory-mapped files this way, let's look at four possible methods of implementing a program to reverse the order of all the bytes in a file.

Method 1: One File, One Buffer

The first and theoretically simplest method involves allocating a block of memory large enough to hold the entire file. The file is opened, its contents are read into the memory block, and the file is closed. With the contents in memory, we can now reverse all the bytes by swapping the first byte with the last, the second byte with the second-to-last, and so on. This swapping continues until you reach the middle of the file. After all the bytes have been swapped, you reopen the file and over-write its contents with the contents of the memory block.

This method is pretty easy to implement but has two major drawbacks. First, a memory block the size of the file must be allocated. This might not be so bad if the file is small, but what if the file is huge—say, 2 GB? A 32-bit system will not allow the application to commit a block of physical storage that large. Large files require a different method.

Second, if the process is interrupted in the middle—while the reversed bytes are being written back out to the file—the contents of the file will be corrupted. The simplest way to guard against this is to make a copy of the original file before reversing its contents. If the whole process succeeds, you can delete the copy of the file. Unfortunately, this safeguard requires additional disk space.

Method 2: Two Files, One Buffer

In the second method, you open the existing file and create a new file of 0 length on the disk. Then you allocate a small internal buffer—say, 8 KB. You seek to the end of the original file minus 8 KB, read the last 8 KB into the buffer, reverse the bytes, and write the buffer's contents to the newly created file. The process of seeking, reading, reversing, and writing repeats until you reach the beginning of the original file. Some special—but not extensive—handling is required if the file's length is not an exact multiple of 8 KB. After the original file is fully processed, both files are closed and the original file is deleted.

This method is a bit more complicated to implement than the first one. It uses memory much more efficiently because only an 8-KB chunk is ever allocated, but it has two big problems. First, the processing is slower than in the first method because on each iteration you must perform a seek on the original file before performing a read. Second, this method can potentially use a large amount of hard disk space. If the original file is 1 GB, the new file will grow to be 1 GB as the process continues. Just before the original file is deleted, the two files will occupy 2 GB of disk space. This is 1 GB more than should be required—a disadvantage that leads us to the next method.

Method 3: One File, Two Buffers

For this method, let's say the program initializes by allocating two separate 8-KB buffers. The program reads the first 8 KB of the file into one buffer and the last 8 KB of the file into the other buffer. The process then reverses the contents of both buffers and writes the contents of the first buffer back to the end of the file and the contents of the second buffer back to the beginning of the same file. Each iteration continues by moving blocks from the front and back of the file in 8-KB chunks. Some special handling is required if the file's length is not an exact multiple of 16 KB and the two 8-KB chunks overlap. This special handling is more complex than the special handling in the previous method, but it's nothing that should scare off a seasoned programmer.

Compared with the previous two methods, this method is better at conserving hard disk space. Because everything is read from and written to the same file, no additional disk space is required. As for memory use, this method is also not too bad, using only 16 KB. Of course, this method is probably the most difficult to implement. Like the first method, this method can result in corruption of the data file if the process is somehow interrupted.

Now let's take a look at how this process might be accomplished using memory-mapped files.

Method 4: One File, Zero Buffers

When using memory-mapped files to reverse the contents of a file, you open the file and then tell the system to reserve a region of virtual address space. You tell the system to map the first byte of the file to the first byte of this reserved region. You can then access the region of virtual memory as though it actually contained the file. In fact, if there were a single 0 byte at the end of a text file, you could simply call the C run-time function **_tcsrev** to reverse the data in the file because it is usable simply as an in-memory text string.

This method's great advantage is that the system manages all the file caching for you. You don't have to allocate any memory, load file data into memory, write data back to the file, or free any memory blocks. Unfortunately, the possibility that an interruption such as a power failure could corrupt data still exists with memory-mapped files.

Using Memory-Mapped Files

To use a memory-mapped file, you must perform three steps:

1. Create or open a file kernel object that identifies the file on disk that you want to use as a memory-mapped file.

2. Create a file-mapping kernel object that tells the system the size of the file and how you intend to access the file.

3. Tell the system to map all or part of the file-mapping object into your process' address space.

When you are finished using the memory-mapped file, you must perform three steps to clean up:

1. Tell the system to unmap the file-mapping kernel object from your process' address space.

2. Close the file-mapping kernel object.

3. Close the file kernel object.

The next five sections discuss all these steps in more detail.

Step 1: Creating or Opening a File Kernel Object

To create or open a file kernel object, always call the **CreateFile** function:

```
HANDLE CreateFile(
    PCSTR pszFileName,
    DWORD dwDesiredAccess,
    DWORD dwShareMode,
    PSECURITY_ATTRIBUTES psa,
    DWORD dwCreationDisposition,
    DWORD dwFlagsAndAttributes,
    HANDLE hTemplateFile);
```

The **CreateFile** function takes quite a few parameters that have been described in "A Detailed Look at *CreateFile*" on page 292. For this discussion, I'll concentrate only on the first three: **pszFileName**, **dwDesiredAccess**, and **dwShareMode**.

As you might guess, the first parameter, **pszFileName**, identifies the name (including an optional path) of the file that you want to create or open. The second parameter, **dwDesiredAccess**, specifies how you intend to access the contents of the file. You can specify one of the four values shown in Table 17-3.

Table 17-3   File Desired Access Rights

Value	Meaning
0	You cannot read from or write to the file's contents. Specify **0** when you just want to get a file's attributes.
GENERIC_READ	You can read from the file.
GENERIC_WRITE	You can write to the file.
GENERIC_READ | GENERIC_WRITE	You can read from the file and write to the file.

When creating or opening a file for use as a memory-mapped file, select the access flag or flags that make the most sense for how you intend to access the file's data. For memory-mapped files, you must open the file for read-only access or read-write access, so you'll want to specify either **GENERIC_READ** or **GENERIC_READ | GENERIC_WRITE**, respectively.

The third parameter, **dwShareMode**, tells the system how you want to share this file. You can specify one of the four values shown in Table 17-4 for **dwShareMode**.

Table 17-4   File Sharing Modes

Value	Meaning
0	Any other attempts to open the file fail.
FILE_SHARE_READ	Other attempts to open the file using **GENERIC_WRITE** fail.
FILE_SHARE_WRITE	Other attempts to open the file using **GENERIC_READ** fail.
FILE_SHARE_READ | FILE_SHARE_WRITE	Other attempts to open the file succeed.

If **CreateFile** successfully creates or opens the specified file, a handle to a file kernel object is returned; otherwise, **INVALID_HANDLE_VALUE** is returned.

> **Note**   Most Windows functions that return a handle return **NULL** when they are unsuccessful. **CreateFile**, however, returns **INVALID_HANDLE_VALUE**, which is defined as **((HANDLE) -1)**.

Step 2: Creating a File-Mapping Kernel Object

Calling **CreateFile** tells the operating system the location of the file mapping's physical storage. The pathname that you pass indicates the exact location on the disk (or on the network or the CD-ROM, for example) of the physical storage that is backing the file mapping. Now you must tell the system how much physical storage the file-mapping object requires. You do this by calling **CreateFileMapping**:

```
HANDLE CreateFileMapping(
   HANDLE hFile,
   PSECURITY_ATTRIBUTES psa,
   DWORD fdwProtect,
   DWORD dwMaximumSizeHigh,
   DWORD dwMaximumSizeLow,
   PCTSTR pszName);
```

The first parameter, **hFile**, identifies the handle of the file you want mapped into the process' address space. This handle is returned by the previous call to **CreateFile**. The **psa** parameter is a pointer to a **SECURITY_ATTRIBUTES** structure for the file-mapping kernel object; usually **NULL** is passed (which provides default security and the returned handle is noninheritable).

As I pointed out at the beginning of this chapter, creating a memory-mapped file is just like reserving a region of address space and then committing physical storage to the region. It's just that the physical storage for a memory-mapped file comes from a file on a disk rather than from space allocated from the system's paging file. When you create a file-mapping object, the system does not reserve a region of address space and map the file's storage to the region. (I'll describe how to do this in the next section.) However, when the system does map the storage to the process' address space, the system must know what protection attribute to assign to the pages of physical storage. **CreateFileMapping**'s **fdwProtect** parameter allows you to specify the protection attributes. Most of the time, you will specify one of the three protection attributes listed in Table 17-5.

In addition to the aforementioned page protections, there are five section attributes that you can bitwise **OR** in the **CreateFileMapping** function's **fdwProtect** parameter. A "section" is just another word for a *memory mapping*, and this kernel object type is shown by Process Explorer from Sysinternals (*http://www.microsoft.com/technet/sysinternals/Security/ProcessExplorer.mspx*).

The first of these attributes, **SEC_NOCACHE**, tells the system that none of the file's memory-mapped pages are to be cached. So as you write data to the file, the system will update the file's data on the disk more often than it normally would. This flag, like the **PAGE_NOCACHE** protection attribute, exists for the device driver developer and is not usually used by applications.

Table 17-5   Page Protection Attributes

Protection Attribute	Meaning
PAGE_READONLY	When the file-mapping object is mapped, you can read the file's data. You must have passed **GENERIC_READ** to **CreateFile**.
PAGE_READWRITE	When the file-mapping object is mapped, you can read and write to the file's data. You must have passed **GENERIC_READ | GENERIC_WRITE** to **CreateFile**.
PAGE_WRITECOPY	When the file-mapping object is mapped, you can read and write to the file's data. Writing causes a private copy of the page to be created. You must have passed either **GENERIC_READ** or **GENERIC_READ | GENERIC_WRITE** to **CreateFile**.
PAGE_EXECUTE_READ	When the file-mapping object is mapped, you can read the file's data, which can also be executed. You must have passed **GENERIC_READ** and **GENERIC_EXECUTE** to **CreateFile**.
PAGE_EXECUTE_READWRITE	When the file-mapping object is mapped, you can read and write to the file's data, which can also be executed. You must have passed **GENERIC_READ**, **GENERIC_WRITE**, and **GENERIC_EXECUTE** to **CreateFile**.

The second section attribute, **SEC_IMAGE**, tells the system that the file you are mapping is a portable executable (PE) file image. When the system maps this file into your process' address space, the system examines the file's contents to determine which protection attributes to assign to the various pages of the mapped image. For example, a PE file's code section (**.text**) is usually mapped with **PAGE_EXECUTE_READ** attributes, whereas the PE file's data section (**.data**) is usually mapped with **PAGE_READWRITE** attributes. Specifying the **SEC_IMAGE** attribute tells the system to map the file's image and to set the appropriate page protections.

The next two attributes, **SEC_RESERVE** and **SEC_COMMIT**, are mutually exclusive and do not apply when you are using a memory-mapped data file. These two flags will be discussed in "Sparsely Committed Memory-Mapped Files" on page 504. When creating a memory-mapped data file, you should not specify either of these flags. **CreateFileMapping** will ignore them.

The last attribute, **SEC_LARGE_PAGES**, tells Windows to use large pages of RAM for a memory-mapped image. This attribute is valid only for PE image files or memory-only mapped files; it is not possible to use it for mapping your own data files in memory. As explained in "Reserving a Region and Committing Storage Simultaneously" on page 422 for **VirtualAlloc**, the following conditions must be met:

■   You need to commit the memory by **OR**ing the **SEC_COMMIT** attribute when you call **Create-FileMapping**.

■   The size of the mapping must be greater than the value returned by the **GetLargePage-Minimum** function. (See the explanation for the **dwMaximumSizeHigh** and **dwMaximum-SizeLow** parameters that follows.)

- The mapping must be defined with the **PAGE_READWRITE** protection attribute.
- The Lock Pages In Memory user right must be granted and enabled or the call to the **Create-FileMapping** function will fail.

CreateFileMapping's next two parameters, **dwMaximumSizeHigh** and **dwMaximumSizeLow**, are the most important parameters. The main purpose of the **CreateFileMapping** function is to ensure that enough physical storage is available for the file-mapping object. These two parameters tell the system the maximum size of the file in bytes. Two 32-bit values are required because Windows supports file sizes that can be expressed using a 64-bit value; the **dwMaximumSizeHigh** parameter specifies the high 32 bits, and the **dwMaximumSizeLow** parameter specifies the low 32 bits. For files that are less than 4 GB, **dwMaximumSizeHigh** will always be **0**.

Using a 64-bit value means that Windows can process files as large as 16 EB (exabytes). If you want to create the file-mapping object so that it reflects the current size of the file, you can pass **0** for both parameters. If you intend only to read from the file or to access the file without changing its size, pass **0** for both parameters. If you intend to append data to the file, you will want to choose a maximum file size that leaves you some breathing room. If the file on disk currently contains 0 bytes, you can't pass two zeros to **CreateFileMapping**'s **dwMaximumSizeHigh** and **dwMaximumSizeLow** parameters. Doing so tells the system that you want a file-mapping object with 0 bytes of storage in it. This is an error and **CreateFileMapping** will return **NULL**.

If you've paid attention so far, you must be thinking that something is terribly wrong here. It's nice that Windows supports files and file-mapping objects that can be anywhere up to 16 EB, but how are you ever going to map a file that big into a 32-bit process' address space, which has a maximum limit of 4 GB (little of which is even usable)? I'll explain how you can accomplish this in the next section. Of course, a 64-bit process has a 16-EB address space so that you can work with much larger file mappings, but a similar limitation still exists if the file is super-big.

To really understand how **CreateFile** and **CreateFileMapping** work, you should try the following experiment. Take the following code, build it, and then run it in a debugger. As you single-step through each statement, jump to a command shell and execute a **dir** command on the C:\ directory. Notice the changes that are appearing in the directory as you execute each statement in the debugger.

```
int WINAPI _tWinMain(HINSTANCE, HINSTANCE, PTSTR, int) {

   // Before executing the line below, C:\ does not have
   // a file called "MMFTest.Dat"
   HANDLE hFile = CreateFile(TEXT("C:\\MMFTest.Dat"),
      GENERIC_READ | GENERIC_WRITE,
      FILE_SHARE_READ | FILE_SHARE_WRITE, NULL, CREATE_ALWAYS,
      FILE_ATTRIBUTE_NORMAL, NULL);

   // Before executing the line below, the MMFTest.Dat
   // file does exist but has a file size of 0 bytes.
   HANDLE hFileMap = CreateFileMapping(hFile, NULL, PAGE_READWRITE,
      0, 100, NULL);

   // After executing the line above, the MMFTest.Dat
   // file has a size of 100 bytes.
```

```
    // Cleanup
    CloseHandle(hFileMap);
    CloseHandle(hFile);

    // When the process terminates, MMFTest.Dat remains
    // on the disk with a size of 100 bytes.
    return(0);
}
```

If you call **CreateFileMapping**, passing the **PAGE_READWRITE** flag, the system checks to make sure that the associated data file on the disk is at least the same size as the size specified in the **dwMaximumSizeHigh** and **dwMaximumSizeLow** parameters. If the file is smaller than the specified size, **CreateFileMapping** makes the file on the disk larger by extending its size. This enlargement is required so that the physical storage will already exist when the file is used later as a memory-mapped file. If the file-mapping object is being created with the **PAGE_READONLY** or the **PAGE_WRITECOPY** flag, the size specified to **CreateFileMapping** must be no larger than the physical size of the disk file. This is because you won't be able to append any data to the file.

The last parameter of **CreateFileMapping**, **pszName**, is a zero-terminated string that assigns a name to this file-mapping object. The name is used to share the object with another process. (An example of this is shown later in this chapter. Chapter 3, "Kernel Objects," also discusses kernel object sharing in greater detail.) A memory-mapped data file usually doesn't need to be shared; therefore, this parameter is usually **NULL**.

The system creates the file-mapping object and returns a handle identifying the object back to the calling thread. If the system cannot create the file-mapping object, a **NULL** handle value is returned. Again, please remember that **CreateFile** returns **INVALID_HANDLE_VALUE** (defined as −1) when it fails and **CreateFileMapping** returns **NULL** when it fails. Don't get these error values confused.

Step 3: Mapping the File's Data into the Process' Address Space

After you have created a file-mapping object, you still need to have the system reserve a region of address space for the file's data and commit the file's data as the physical storage that is mapped to the region. You do this by calling **MapViewOfFile**:

```
PVOID MapViewOfFile(
    HANDLE hFileMappingObject,
    DWORD dwDesiredAccess,
    DWORD dwFileOffsetHigh,
    DWORD dwFileOffsetLow,
    SIZE_T dwNumberOfBytesToMap);
```

The **hFileMappingObject** parameter identifies the handle of the file-mapping object, which was returned by the previous call to either **CreateFileMapping** or **OpenFileMapping** (discussed later in this chapter). The **dwDesiredAccess** parameter identifies how the data can be accessed. That's right, we must again specify how we intend to access the file's data. You can specify one of the five possible values shown in Table 17-6.

Table 17-6   Memory-Mapped File Desired Access Rights

Value	Meaning
FILE_MAP_WRITE	You can read and write to file data. **CreateFileMapping** had to be called by passing **PAGE_READWRITE**.
FILE_MAP_READ	You can read file data. **CreateFileMapping** could be called with either of the protection attributes: **PAGE_READONLY** or **PAGE_READWRITE**.
FILE_MAP_ALL_ACCESS	Same as **FILE_MAP_WRITE	FILE_MAP_READ	FILE_MAP_COPY**.
FILE_MAP_COPY	You can read and write to file data. Writing causes a private copy of the page to be created. **CreateFileMapping** must be called only with the **PAGE_WRITECOPY** protection attribute.
FILE_MAP_EXECUTE	The data can be executed as code. **CreateFileMapping** could be called with **PAGE_EXECUTE_READWRITE** or **PAGE_EXECUTE_READ** protection attributes.

It certainly seems strange and annoying that Windows requires all these protection attributes to be set over and over again. I assume this was done to give an application as much control as possible over data protection.

The remaining three parameters have to do with reserving the region of address space and mapping the physical storage to the region. When you map a file into your process' address space, you don't have to map the entire file at once. Instead, you can map only a small portion of the file into the address space. A portion of a file that is mapped into your process' address space is called a *view*, which explains how **MapViewOfFile** got its name.

When you map a view of a file into your process' address space, you must specify two things. First, you must tell the system which byte in the data file should be mapped as the first byte in the view. You do this using the **dwFileOffsetHigh** and **dwFileOffsetLow** parameters. Because Windows supports files that can be up to 16 EB in size, you must specify this byte-offset using a 64-bit value, of which the high 32 bits are passed in the **dwFileOffsetHigh** parameter and the low 32 bits are passed in the **dwFileOffsetLow** parameter. Note that the offset in the file must be a multiple of the system's allocation granularity. (To date, all implementations of Windows have an allocation granularity of 64 KB.) "System Information" on page 395 shows how to obtain the allocation granularity value for a given system.

Second, you must tell the system how much of the data file to map into the address space. This is the same thing as specifying how large a region of address space to reserve. You specify this size using the **dwNumberOfBytesToMap** parameter. If you specify a size of **0**, the system will attempt to map a view starting with the specified offset within the file to the end of the entire file. Notice that **MapViewOfFile** needs only to find a region large enough for the view requested, regardless of the size of the entire file-mapping object.

If you specify the **FILE_MAP_COPY** flag when calling **MapViewOfFile**, the system commits physical storage from the system's paging file. The amount of space committed is determined by the **dwNumberOfBytesToMap** parameter. As long as you do nothing more than read from the file's mapped view, the system never uses these committed pages in the paging file. However, the first time any thread in your process writes to any memory address within the file's mapped view, the system will grab one of the committed pages from the paging file, copy the page of original data to this paging-file page, and then map this copied page into your process' address space. From this point on, the threads in your process are accessing a local copy of the data and cannot read or modify the original data.

When the system makes the copy of the original page, the system changes the protection of the page from **PAGE_WRITECOPY** to **PAGE_READWRITE**. The following code fragment explains it all:

```
// Open the file that we want to map.
HANDLE hFile = CreateFile(pszFileName, GENERIC_READ | GENERIC_WRITE, 0, NULL,
   OPEN_ALWAYS, FILE_ATTRIBUTE_NORMAL, NULL);

// Create a file-mapping object for the file.
HANDLE hFileMapping = CreateFileMapping(hFile, NULL, PAGE_WRITECOPY,
   0, 0, NULL);

// Map a copy-on-write view of the file; the system will commit
// enough physical storage from the paging file to accommodate
// the entire file. All pages in the view will initially have
// PAGE_WRITECOPY access.
PBYTE pbFile = (PBYTE) MapViewOfFile(hFileMapping, FILE_MAP_COPY,
   0, 0, 0);

// Read a byte from the mapped view.
BYTE bSomeByte = pbFile[0];
// When reading, the system does not touch the committed pages in
// the paging file. The page keeps its PAGE_WRITECOPY attribute.

// Write a byte to the mapped view.
pbFile[0] = 0;
// When writing for the first time, the system grabs a committed
// page from the paging file, copies the original contents of the
// page at the accessed memory address, and maps the new page
// (the copy) into the process' address space. The new page has
// an attribute of PAGE_READWRITE.

// Write another byte to the mapped view.
pbFile[1] = 0;
// Because this byte is now in a PAGE_READWRITE page, the system
// simply writes the byte to the page (backed by the paging file).

// When finished using the file's mapped view, unmap it.
// UnmapViewOfFile is discussed in the next section.
UnmapViewOfFile(pbFile);
// The system decommits the physical storage from the paging file.
// Any writes to the pages are lost.

// Clean up after ourselves.
CloseHandle(hFileMapping);
CloseHandle(hFile);
```

> **Note** If your application runs on a Non-Uniform Memory Access (NUMA) machine, improved performance is obtained by having the RAM used to back the data on the same node as the CPU running the thread that will access the data. By default, when a thread maps a view of a memory-mapped file, Windows automatically tries to use RAM on the same node as the thread's ideal CPU. However, if you know that a thread might migrate to a CPU on another node, you can override the default by calling **CreateFileMappingNuma** and explicitly indicating which NUMA node the RAM should be allocated from in the last parameter (**dwPreferredNumaNode**):
>
> ```
> HANDLE CreateFileMappingNuma(
>    HANDLE hFile,
>    PSECURITY_ATTRIBUTES psa,
>    DWORD fdwProtect,
>    DWORD dwMaximumSizeHigh,
>    DWORD dwMaximumSizeLow,
>    PCTSTR pszName,
>    DWORD dwPreferredNumaNode
> );
> ```
>
> Now, when **MapViewOfFile** is called, it will know to use the node specified when **CreateFileMappingNuma** was called. In addition, Windows offers a **MapViewOfFileExNuma** function, which can be used to override the NUMA node that was specified in the call to **CreateFileMappingNuma**. Here is the **MapViewOfFileExNuma** function's **dwPreferredNumaNode** parameter:
>
> ```
> PVOID MapViewOfFileExNuma(
>    HANDLE hFileMappingObject,
>    DWORD dwDesiredAccess,
>    DWORD dwFileOffsetHigh,
>    DWORD dwFileOffsetLow,
>    SIZE_T dwNumberOfBytesToMap,
>    LPVOID lpBaseAddress,
>    DWORD dwPreferredNumaNode
> );
> ```
>
> The Windows functions that allow you to determine the relationship between NUMA nodes and CPUs are covered in "Memory Management on NUMA Machines" on page 405. You can also find out how NUMA support affects memory allocation at the end of the "Reserving a Region in an Address Space" section that starts on page 419.

Step 4: Unmapping the File's Data from the Process' Address Space

When you no longer need to keep a file's data mapped to a region of your process' address space, you can release the region by calling

```
BOOL UnmapViewOfFile(PVOID pvBaseAddress);
```

The only parameter, **pvBaseAddress**, specifies the base address of the returned region. This value must be the same value returned from a call to **MapViewOfFile**. You must remember to call **UnmapViewOfFile**. If you do not call this function, the reserved region won't be released until your process terminates. Whenever you call **MapViewOfFile**, the system always reserves a new region within your process' address space—any previously reserved regions are *not* released.

In the interest of speed, the system buffers the pages of the file's data and doesn't update the disk image of the file immediately while working with the file's mapped view. If you need to ensure that your updates have been written to disk, you can force the system to write a portion or all of the modified data back to the disk image by calling **FlushViewOfFile**:

```
BOOL FlushViewOfFile(
   PVOID pvAddress,
   SIZE_T dwNumberOfBytesToFlush);
```

The first parameter is the address of a byte contained within a view of a memory-mapped file. The function rounds down the address you pass here to a page boundary. The second parameter indicates the number of bytes that you want flushed. The system will round this number up so that the total number of bytes is an integral number of pages. If you call **FlushViewOfFile** and none of the data has been changed, the function simply returns without writing anything to the disk.

For a memory-mapped file whose storage is over a network, **FlushViewOfFile** guarantees that the file's data has been written from the workstation. However, **FlushViewOfFile** cannot guarantee that the server machine that is sharing the file has written the data to the remote disk drive because the server might be caching the file's data. To ensure that the server writes the file's data, you should pass the **FILE_FLAG_WRITE_THROUGH** flag to the **CreateFile** function whenever you create a file-mapping object for the file and then map the view of the file-mapping object. If you use this flag to open the file, **FlushViewOfFile** will return only when all of the file's data has been stored on the server's disk drive.

Keep in mind one special characteristic of the **UnmapViewOfFile** function. If the view was originally mapped using the **FILE_MAP_COPY** flag, any changes you made to the file's data were actually made to a copy of the file's data stored in the system's paging file. In this case, if you call **Unmap-ViewOfFile**, the function has nothing to update on the disk file and simply causes the pages in the paging file to be freed—the data is lost.

If you want to preserve the changed data, you must take additional measures yourself. For example, you might want to create another file-mapping object (using **PAGE_READWRITE**) from the same file and map this new file-mapping object into your process' address space using the **FILE_MAP_WRITE** flag. Then you could scan the first view looking for pages with the **PAGE_READWRITE** protection attribute. Whenever you found a page with this attribute, you could examine its contents and decide whether to write the changed data to the file. If you do not want to update the file with the new data, keep scanning the remaining pages in the view until you reach the end. If you do want to save the changed page of data, however, just call **MoveMemory** to copy the page of data from the first view to the second view. Because the second view is mapped with **PAGE_READWRITE** protection, the **MoveMemory** function will be updating the actual contents of the file on the disk. You can use this method to determine changes and preserve your file's data.

Steps 5 and 6: Closing the File-Mapping Object and the File Object

It goes without saying that you should always close any kernel objects you open. Forgetting to do so will cause resource leaks while your process continues to run. Of course, when your process terminates, the system automatically closes any objects your process opened but forgot to close. But if your process does not terminate for a while, you will accumulate resource handles. You should always write clean, "proper" code that closes any objects you have opened. To close the file-mapping object and the file object, you simply need to call the **CloseHandle** function twice—once for each handle.

Let's look at this process a little more closely. The following pseudocode shows an example of memory-mapping a file:

```
HANDLE hFile = CreateFile(...);
HANDLE hFileMapping = CreateFileMapping(hFile, ...);
PVOID pvFile = MapViewOfFile(hFileMapping, ...);

// Use the memory-mapped file.

UnmapViewOfFile(pvFile);
CloseHandle(hFileMapping);
CloseHandle(hFile);
```

The preceding code shows the "expected" method for manipulating memory-mapped files. However, what it does not show is that the system increments the usage counts of the file object and the file-mapping object when you call **MapViewOfFile**. This side effect is significant because it means that we could rewrite the preceding code fragment as follows:

```
HANDLE hFile = CreateFile(...);
HANDLE hFileMapping = CreateFileMapping(hFile, ...);
CloseHandle(hFile);
PVOID pvFile = MapViewOfFile(hFileMapping, ...);
CloseHandle(hFileMapping);

// Use the memory-mapped file.

UnmapViewOfFile(pvFile);
```

When you work with memory-mapped files, you will commonly open the file, create the file-mapping object, and then use the file-mapping object to map a view of the file's data into the process' address space. Because the system increments the internal usage counts of the file object and the file-mapping object, you can close these objects at the beginning of your code and eliminate potential resource leaks.

If you will be creating additional file-mapping objects from the same file or mapping multiple views of the same file-mapping object, you cannot call **CloseHandle** *early*—you'll need the handles later to make the additional calls to **CreateFileMapping** and **MapViewOfFile**, respectively.

The File Reverse Sample Application

The File Reverse application (17-FileRev.exe) listed on page 490 demonstrates how to use memory-mapped files to reverse the contents of an ANSI or Unicode text file. The source code and resource files for the application are in the 17-FileRev directory on the companion content Web page. When you start the program, the window shown on the next page appears.

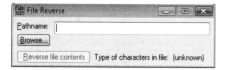

FileRev first allows you to first select a file. When you click the Reverse File Contents button, the function reverses all the characters contained within the file. The program will work correctly only on text files; it will not work correctly on binary files. FileRev determines whether the text file is ANSI or Unicode by calling the **IsTextUnicode** function (discussed in Chapter 2, "Working with Characters and Strings").

When you click the Reverse File Contents button, FileRev makes a copy of the specified file called FileRev.dat. It does this so that the original file won't become unusable because its contents have been reversed. Next, FileRev calls the **FileReverse** function, which is responsible for reversing the file; **FileReverse** calls the **CreateFile** function, opening FileRev.dat for reading and writing.

As I said earlier, the easiest way to reverse the contents of the file is to call the C run-time function **_strrev**. As with all C strings, the last character of the string must be a zero terminator. Because text files do not end with a zero character, FileRev must append one to the file. It does so by first calling **GetFileSize**:

```
dwFileSize = GetFileSize(hFile, NULL);
```

Now that you're armed with the length of the file, you can create the file-mapping object by calling **CreateFileMapping**. The file-mapping object is created with a length of **dwFileSize** plus the size of a wide character (for the zero character). After the file-mapping object is created, a view of the object is mapped into FileRev's address space. The **pvFile** variable contains the return value from **MapViewOfFile** and points to the first byte of the text file.

The next step is to write a zero character at the end of the file and to reverse the string:

```
PSTR pchANSI = (PSTR) pvFile;
pchANSI[dwFileSize / sizeof(CHAR)] = 0;
```

In a text file, every line is terminated by a return character (**'\r'**) followed by a newline character (**'\n'**). Unfortunately, when we call **_strrev** to reverse the file, these characters also get reversed. For the reversed text file to be loaded into a text editor, every occurrence of the **"\n\r"** pair needs to be converted back to its original **"\r\n"** order. This conversion is the job of the following loop:

```
while (pchANSI != NULL) {
   // We have found an occurrence....
   *pchANSI++ = '\r';   // Change '\n' to '\r'.
   *pchANSI++ = '\n';   // Change '\r' to '\n'.
   pchANSI = strstr(pchANSI, "\n\r"); // Find the next occurrence.
}
```

When you examine simple code like this, you can easily forget that you are actually manipulating the contents of a file on a disk drive (which shows you how powerful memory-mapped files are).

After the file has been reversed, FileRev must clean up by unmapping the view of the file-mapping object and closing all the kernel object handles. In addition, FileRev must remove the zero character added to the end of the file (remember that **_strrev** doesn't reverse the position of the terminating zero character). If you don't remove the zero character, the reversed file would be 1 character larger, and calling FileRev again would not reverse the file back to its original form. To remove the trailing zero character, you need to drop back a level and use the file-management functions instead of manipulating the file through memory mapping.

Forcing the reversed file to end at a specific location requires positioning the file pointer at the desired location (the end of the original file) and calling the **SetEndOfFile** function:

```
SetFilePointer(hFile, dwFileSize, NULL, FILE_BEGIN);
SetEndOfFile(hFile);
```

> **Note** **SetEndOfFile** must be called after the view is unmapped and the file-mapping object is closed; otherwise, the function returns **FALSE** and **GetLastError** returns **ERROR_USER_MAPPED_FILE**. This error indicates that the end-of-file operation cannot be performed on a file that is associated with a file-mapping object.

The last thing FileRev does is spawn an instance of Notepad so that you can look at the reversed file. The window in the following illustration shows the result of running FileRev on its own FileRev.cpp file.

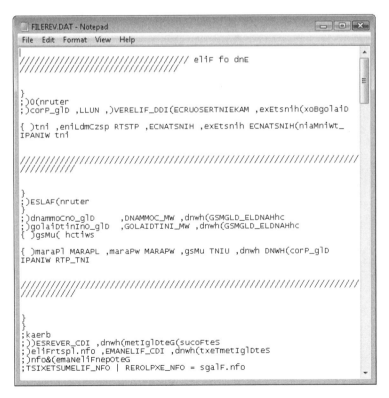

FileRev.cpp

```
/*****************************************************************************
Module:  FileRev.cpp
Notices: Copyright (c) 2008 Jeffrey Richter & Christophe Nasarre
*****************************************************************************/


#include "..\CmnHdr.h"      /* See Appendix A. */
#include <windowsx.h>
#include <tchar.h>
#include <commdlg.h>
#include <string.h>          // For _strrev
#include "Resource.h"


///////////////////////////////////////////////////////////////////////////


#define FILENAME  TEXT("FileRev.dat")


///////////////////////////////////////////////////////////////////////////


BOOL FileReverse(PCTSTR pszPathname, PBOOL pbIsTextUnicode) {

   *pbIsTextUnicode = FALSE;  // Assume text is Unicode

   // Open the file for reading and writing.
   HANDLE hFile = CreateFile(pszPathname, GENERIC_WRITE | GENERIC_READ, 0,
      NULL, OPEN_EXISTING, FILE_ATTRIBUTE_NORMAL, NULL);

   if (hFile == INVALID_HANDLE_VALUE) {
      chMB("File could not be opened.");
      return(FALSE);
   }

   // Get the size of the file (I assume the whole file can be mapped).
   DWORD dwFileSize = GetFileSize(hFile, NULL);

   // Create the file-mapping object. The file-mapping object is 1 character
   // bigger than the file size so that a zero character can be placed at the
   // end of the file to terminate the string (file). Because I don't yet know
   // if the file contains ANSI or Unicode characters, I assume worst case
   // and add the size of a WCHAR instead of CHAR.
   HANDLE hFileMap = CreateFileMapping(hFile, NULL, PAGE_READWRITE,
      0, dwFileSize + sizeof(WCHAR), NULL);

   if (hFileMap == NULL) {
      chMB("File map could not be opened.");
      CloseHandle(hFile);
      return(FALSE);
   }
```

```
// Get the address where the first byte of the file is mapped into memory.
PVOID pvFile = MapViewOfFile(hFileMap, FILE_MAP_WRITE, 0, 0, 0);

if (pvFile == NULL) {
   chMB("Could not map view of file.");
   CloseHandle(hFileMap);
   CloseHandle(hFile);
   return(FALSE);
}

// Does the buffer contain ANSI or Unicode?
int iUnicodeTestFlags = -1;    // Try all tests
*pbIsTextUnicode = IsTextUnicode(pvFile, dwFileSize, &iUnicodeTestFlags);

if (!*pbIsTextUnicode) {
   // For all the file manipulations below, we explicitly use ANSI
   // functions because we are processing an ANSI file.

   // Put a zero character at the very end of the file.
   PSTR pchANSI = (PSTR) pvFile;
   pchANSI[dwFileSize / sizeof(CHAR)] = 0;

   // Reverse the contents of the file.
   _strrev(pchANSI);

   // Convert all "\n\r" combinations back to "\r\n" to
   // preserve the normal end-of-line sequence.
   pchANSI = strstr(pchANSI, "\n\r"); // Find first '\n\r'.

   while (pchANSI != NULL) {
      // We have found an occurrence....
      *pchANSI++ = '\r';    // Change '\n' to '\r'.
      *pchANSI++ = '\n';    // Change '\r' to '\n'.
      pchANSI = strstr(pchANSI, "\n\r"); // Find the next occurrence.
   }

} else {
   // For all the file manipulations below, we explicitly use Unicode
   // functions because we are processing a Unicode file.

   // Put a zero character at the very end of the file.
   PWSTR pchUnicode = (PWSTR) pvFile;
   pchUnicode[dwFileSize / sizeof(WCHAR)] = 0;

   if ((iUnicodeTestFlags & IS_TEXT_UNICODE_SIGNATURE) != 0) {
      // If the first character is the Unicode BOM (byte-order-mark),
      // 0xFEFF, keep this character at the beginning of the file.
      pchUnicode++;
   }

   // Reverse the contents of the file.
   _wcsrev(pchUnicode);
```

```
         // Convert all "\n\r" combinations back to "\r\n" to
         // preserve the normal end-of-line sequence.
         pchUnicode = wcsstr(pchUnicode, L"\n\r"); // Find first '\n\r'.

         while (pchUnicode != NULL) {
            // We have found an occurrence....
            *pchUnicode++ = L'\r';   // Change '\n' to '\r'.
            *pchUnicode++ = L'\n';   // Change '\r' to '\n'.
            pchUnicode = wcsstr(pchUnicode, L"\n\r"); // Find the next occurrence.
         }
      }

      // Clean up everything before exiting.
      UnmapViewOfFile(pvFile);
      CloseHandle(hFileMap);

      // Remove trailing zero character added earlier.
      SetFilePointer(hFile, dwFileSize, NULL, FILE_BEGIN);
      SetEndOfFile(hFile);
      CloseHandle(hFile);

      return(TRUE);
}


///////////////////////////////////////////////////////////////////////////


BOOL Dlg_OnInitDialog(HWND hWnd, HWND hWndFocus, LPARAM lParam) {

   chSETDLGICONS(hWnd, IDI_FILEREV);

   // Initialize the dialog box by disabling the Reverse button
   EnableWindow(GetDlgItem(hWnd, IDC_REVERSE), FALSE);
   return(TRUE);
}


///////////////////////////////////////////////////////////////////////////


void Dlg_OnCommand(HWND hWnd, int id, HWND hWndCtl, UINT codeNotify) {

   TCHAR szPathname[MAX_PATH];

   switch (id) {
      case IDCANCEL:
         EndDialog(hWnd, id);
         break;

      case IDC_FILENAME:
         EnableWindow(GetDlgItem(hWnd, IDC_REVERSE),
            Edit_GetTextLength(hWndCtl) > 0);
         break;
```

```
      case IDC_REVERSE:
         GetDlgItemText(hWnd, IDC_FILENAME, szPathname, _countof(szPathname));

         // Make copy of input file so that we don't destroy it
         if (!CopyFile(szPathname, FILENAME, FALSE)) {
            chMB("New file could not be created.");
            break;
         }

         BOOL bIsTextUnicode;
         if (FileReverse(FILENAME, &bIsTextUnicode)) {
            SetDlgItemText(hwnd, IDC_TEXTTYPE,
               bIsTextUnicode ? TEXT("Unicode") : TEXT("ANSI"));

            // Spawn Notepad to see the fruits of our labors.
            STARTUPINFO si = { sizeof(si) };
            PROCESS_INFORMATION pi;
            TCHAR sz[] = TEXT("Notepad ") FILENAME;
            if (CreateProcess(NULL, sz,
               NULL, NULL, FALSE, 0, NULL, NULL, &si, &pi)) {

               CloseHandle(pi.hThread);
               CloseHandle(pi.hProcess);
            }
         }
         break;

      case IDC_FILESELECT:
         OPENFILENAME ofn = { OPENFILENAME_SIZE_VERSION_400 };
         ofn.hwndOwner = hWnd;
         ofn.lpstrFile = szPathname;
         ofn.lpstrFile[0] = 0;
         ofn.nMaxFile = _countof(szPathname);
         ofn.lpstrTitle = TEXT("Select file for reversing");
         ofn.Flags = OFN_EXPLORER | OFN_FILEMUSTEXIST;
         GetOpenFileName(&ofn);
         SetDlgItemText(hWnd, IDC_FILENAME, ofn.lpstrFile);
         SetFocus(GetDlgItem(hWnd, IDC_REVERSE));
         break;
   }
}


///////////////////////////////////////////////////////////////////////////////


INT_PTR WINAPI Dlg_Proc(HWND hWnd, UINT uMsg, WPARAM wParam, LPARAM lParam) {

   switch (uMsg) {
      chHANDLE_DLGMSG(hWnd, WM_INITDIALOG,  Dlg_OnInitDialog);
      chHANDLE_DLGMSG(hWnd, WM_COMMAND,     Dlg_OnCommand);
   }
   return(FALSE);
}
```

```
///////////////////////////////////////////////////////////////////////////


int WINAPI _tWinMain(HINSTANCE hInstExe, HINSTANCE, PTSTR, int) {

   DialogBox(hInstExe, MAKEINTRESOURCE(IDD_FILEREV), NULL, Dlg_Proc);
   return(0);
}


/////////////////////////// End of File ///////////////////////////////
```

Processing a Big File Using Memory-Mapped Files

In an earlier section, I said I would tell you how to map a 16-EB file into a small address space. Well, you can't. Instead, you must map a view of the file that contains only a small portion of the file's data. You should start by mapping a view of the very beginning of the file. When you've finished accessing the first view of the file, you can unmap it and then map a new view starting at an offset deeper within the file. You'll need to repeat this process until you access the complete file. This certainly makes dealing with large memory-mapped files less convenient, but fortunately most files are small enough that this problem doesn't usually come up.

Let's look at an example using an 8-GB file and a 32-bit address space. Here is a routine that counts all the 0 bytes in a binary data file in several steps:

```
__int64 CountOs(void) {

   // Views must always start on a multiple
   // of the allocation granularity
   SYSTEM_INFO sinf;
   GetSystemInfo(&sinf);

   // Open the data file.
   HANDLE hFile = CreateFile(TEXT("C:\\HugeFile.Big"), GENERIC_READ,
      FILE_SHARE_READ, NULL, OPEN_EXISTING, FILE_FLAG_SEQUENTIAL_SCAN, NULL);

   // Create the file-mapping object.
   HANDLE hFileMapping = CreateFileMapping(hFile, NULL,
      PAGE_READONLY, 0, 0, NULL);

   DWORD dwFileSizeHigh;
   __int64 qwFileSize = GetFileSize(hFile, &dwFileSizeHigh);
   qwFileSize += (((__int64) dwFileSizeHigh) << 32);

   // We no longer need access to the file object's handle.
   CloseHandle(hFile);

   __int64 qwFileOffset = 0, qwNumOfOs = 0;

   while (qwFileSize > 0) {
```

```
    // Determine the number of bytes to be mapped in this view
    DWORD dwBytesInBlock = sinf.dwAllocationGranularity;
    if (qwFileSize < sinf.dwAllocationGranularity)
        dwBytesInBlock = (DWORD) qwFileSize;

    PBYTE pbFile = (PBYTE) MapViewOfFile(hFileMapping, FILE_MAP_READ,
        (DWORD) (qwFileOffset >> 32),          // Starting byte
        (DWORD) (qwFileOffset & 0xFFFFFFFF),   // in file
        dwBytesInBlock);                       // # of bytes to map

    // Count the number of 0s in this block.
    for (DWORD dwByte = 0; dwByte < dwBytesInBlock; dwByte++) {
        if (pbFile[dwByte] == 0)
        qwNumOf0s++;
    }

    // Unmap the view; we don't want multiple views
    // in our address space.
    UnmapViewOfFile(pbFile);

    // Skip to the next set of bytes in the file.
    qwFileOffset += dwBytesInBlock;
    qwFileSize -= dwBytesInBlock;
    }

    CloseHandle(hFileMapping);
    return(qwNumOf0s);
}
```

This algorithm maps views of 64 KB (the allocation granularity size) or less. Also, remember that **MapViewOfFile** requires that the file offset parameters be a multiple of the allocation granularity size. As each view is mapped into the address space, the scanning for zeros continues. After each 64-KB chunk of the file has been mapped and scanned, it's time to tidy up by closing the file-mapping object.

Memory-Mapped Files and Coherence

The system allows you to map multiple views of the same data of a file. For example, you can map the first 10 KB of a file into a view and then map the first 4 KB of that same file into a separate view. As long as you are mapping the same file-mapping object, the system ensures that the viewed data is *coherent*. For example, if your application alters the contents of the file in one view, all other views are updated to reflect the changes. This is because even though the page is mapped into the process' virtual address space more than once, the system really has the data in only a single page of RAM. If multiple processes are mapping views of a single data file, the data is still coherent because there is still only one instance of each page of RAM within the data file—it's just that the pages of RAM are mapped into multiple process address spaces.

Note Windows allows you to create several file-mapping objects that are backed by a single data file. Windows does *not* guarantee that views of these different file-mapping objects will be coherent. It guarantees only that multiple views of a single file-mapping object will be coherent.

When we're working with files, however, there is no reason why another application can't call **CreateFile** to open the same file that another process has mapped. This new process can then read from and write to the file using the **ReadFile** and **WriteFile** functions. Of course, whenever a process makes these calls, it must be either reading file data from or writing file data to a memory buffer. This memory buffer must be one the process itself created, not the memory that is being used by the mapped files. Problems can arise when two applications have opened the same file: one process can call **ReadFile** to read a portion of the file, modify the data, and write it back out using **WriteFile** without the file-mapping object of the second process being aware of the first process' actions. For this reason, it is recommended that when you call **CreateFile** for files that will be memory mapped, you specify **0** as the value of the **dwShareMode** parameter. Doing so tells the system that you want exclusive access to the file and that no other process can open it.

Read-only files do not have coherence problems, making them good candidates for memory-mapped files. Memory-mapped files should never be used to share writable files over a network because the system cannot guarantee coherent views of the data. If someone's computer updates the contents of the file, someone else's computer with the original data in memory will not know that the information has changed.

Specifying the Base Address of a Memory-Mapped File

Just as you can use the **VirtualAlloc** function to suggest an initial address to reserve address space, you can also use the **MapViewOfFileEx** function instead of the **MapViewOfFile** function to suggest that a file be mapped into a particular address:

```
PVOID MapViewOfFileEx(
    HANDLE hFileMappingObject,
    DWORD dwDesiredAccess,
    DWORD dwFileOffsetHigh,
    DWORD dwFileOffsetLow,
    SIZE_T dwNumberOfBytesToMap,
    PVOID pvBaseAddress);
```

All the parameters and the return value for this function are identical to those of the **MapViewOf-File** function with the single exception of the last parameter, **pvBaseAddress**. In this parameter, you specify a target address for the file you're mapping. As with **VirtualAlloc**, the target address you specify should be on an allocation granularity boundary (64 KB); otherwise, **MapViewOf-FileEx** returns **NULL**, indicating an error, and **GetLastError** will return 1132 (**ERROR_MAPPED_ALIGNMENT**).

If the system can't map the file at this location (usually because the file is too large and would overlap another reserved address space), the function fails and returns **NULL**. **MapViewOfFileEx** does not attempt to locate another address space that can accommodate the file. Of course, you can specify **NULL** as the **pvBaseAddress** parameter—in which case, **MapViewOfFileEx** behaves exactly the same as **MapViewOfFile**.

MapViewOfFileEx is useful when you're using memory-mapped files to share data with other processes. As an example, you might need a memory-mapped file at a particular address when two or more applications are sharing a group of data structures containing pointers to other data structures. A linked list is a perfect example. In a linked list, each node, or element, of the list contains the memory address of another element in the list. To walk the list, you must know the address of the first element and then reference the member of the element that contains the address of the next element. This can be a problem when you're using memory-mapped files.

If one process prepares the linked list in a memory-mapped file and then shares this file with another process, it is possible that the other process will map the file into a completely different location in its address space. When the second process attempts to walk the linked list, it looks at the first element of the list, retrieves the memory address of the next element, and then tries to reference this next element. However, the address of the next element in the first node will be incorrect for this second process.

You can solve this problem in two ways. First, the second process can simply call **MapViewOf-FileEx** instead of **MapViewOfFile** when it maps the memory-mapped file containing the linked list into its own address space. Of course, this method requires that the second process know where the first process originally mapped the file when constructing the linked list. When the two applications have been designed to interact with each other—which is most likely the case—this isn't a problem: the address can be hard-coded into both, or one process can notify the other process using another form of interprocess communication, such as sending a message to a window.

The second method for solving the problem is for the process that creates the linked list to store in each node the offset from within the address space where the next node is located. This requires that the application add the offset to the base address of the memory-mapped file in order to access each node. This method is not great: it can be slow, it makes the program bigger (because of the additional code the compiler generates to perform all the calculations), and it can be quite error prone. However, it is certainly a viable method, and the Microsoft compiler offers assistance for based pointers using the **__based** keyword.

 Note   When calling **MapViewOfFileEx**, you must specify an address that is in your process' user-mode partition, or **MapViewOfFileEx** will return **NULL**.

Implementation Details of Memory-Mapped Files

Windows *requires* a process to call **MapViewOfFile** before the file's data is accessible in the process' address space. If one process calls **MapViewOfFile**, the system reserves a region of address space for the view in the calling process' address space—no other process can see the view. If another process wants to access the data in the same file-mapping object, a thread in the second process must call **MapViewOfFile**, and the system will reserve a region for the view in the second process' address space.

It is important to note that the memory address returned by the first process' call to **MapViewOf-File** will most likely *not* be the same memory address returned by the second process' call to **MapViewOfFile**. This is true even though both processes are mapping a view of the same file-mapping object.

Let's look at another implementation detail. Here is a small program that maps two views of a single file-mapping object:

```
int WINAPI _tWinMain (HINSTANCE, HINSTANCE, PTSTR, int) {

   // Open an existing file--it must be bigger than 64 KB.
   HANDLE hFile = CreateFile(pszCmdLine, GENERIC_READ | GENERIC_WRITE,
      0, NULL, OPEN_EXISTING, FILE_ATTRIBUTE_NORMAL, NULL);

   // Create a file-mapping object backed by the data file.
   HANDLE hFileMapping = CreateFileMapping(hFile, NULL,
      PAGE_READWRITE, 0, 0, NULL);

   // Map a view of the whole file into our address space.
   PBYTE pbFile = (PBYTE) MapViewOfFile(hFileMapping,
      FILE_MAP_WRITE, 0, 0, 0);

   // Map a view of the file (starting 64 KB in) into our address space
   PBYTE pbFile2 = (PBYTE) MapViewOfFile(hFileMapping,
      FILE_MAP_WRITE, 0, 65536, 0);

   // Show that the two views are not 64 KB away from each other
   // in the address space, meaning that there is no overlap.
   int iDifference = int(pbFile2 - pbFile);
   TCHAR szMsg[100];
   StringCchPrintf(szMsg, _countof(szMsg),
      TEXT("Pointers difference = %d KB"), iDifference / 1024);
   MessageBox(NULL, szMsg, NULL, MB_OK);

   UnmapViewOfFile(pbFile2);
   UnmapViewOfFile(pbFile);
   CloseHandle(hFileMapping);
   CloseHandle(hFile);

   return(0);
}
```

The two calls to **MapViewOfFile** in the preceding code segment cause Windows to reserve two different address space regions. The size of the first region is the size of the file-mapping object, and the size of the second region is the size of the file-mapping object minus 64 KB. Even though there are two different and nonoverlapping regions, the data is guaranteed to be coherent because both views are made from the same file-mapping object.

Using Memory-Mapped Files to Share Data Among Processes

Windows has always excelled at offering mechanisms that allow applications to share data and information quickly and easily. These mechanisms include RPC, COM, OLE, DDE, window messages (especially **WM_COPYDATA**), the Clipboard, mailslots, pipes, sockets, and so on. In Windows, the lowest-level mechanism for sharing data on a single machine is the memory-mapped file. That's right, all of the mechanisms I mention ultimately use memory-mapped files to do their dirty work if all the processes communicating are on the same machine. If you require high-performance with low overhead, the memory-mapped file is the hands-down best mechanism to use.

This data sharing is accomplished by having two or more processes map views of the same file-mapping object, which means they are sharing the same pages of physical storage. As a result, when one process writes to data in a view of a shared file-mapping object, the other processes see the change instantly in their views. Note that for multiple processes to share a single file-mapping object, all processes must use exactly the same name for the file-mapping object.

Let's look at an example: starting an application. When an application starts, the system calls **CreateFile** to open the .exe file on the disk. The system then calls **CreateFileMapping** to create a file-mapping object. Finally the system calls **MapViewOfFileEx** (with the **SEC_IMAGE** flag) on behalf of the newly created process so that the .exe file is mapped into the process' address space. **MapViewOfFileEx** is called instead of **MapViewOfFile** so that the file's image is mapped to the base address stored in the .exe file's image. The system creates the process' primary thread, puts the address of the first byte of executable code of this mapped view in the thread's instruction pointer, and then lets the CPU start executing the code.

If the user runs a second instance of the same application, the system sees that a file-mapping object already exists for the desired .exe file and doesn't create a new file object or file-mapping object. Instead, the system maps a view of the file a second time, this time in the context of the newly created process' address space. What the system has done is map the identical file into two address spaces simultaneously. Obviously, this is a more efficient use of memory because both processes are sharing the same pages of physical storage containing portions of the code that are executing.

As with all kernel objects, you can use three techniques to share the objects with multiple processes: handle inheritance, naming, and handle duplication. See Chapter 3 for a detailed explanation of all three techniques.

Memory-Mapped Files Backed by the Paging File

So far, I've discussed techniques that allow you to map a view of a file that resides on a disk drive. Many applications create some data while they run and need to transfer the data or share it with another process. It would be terribly inconvenient if the applications had to create a data file on a disk drive and store the data there in order to share it.

Microsoft realized this and added the ability to create memory-mapped files that are backed by the system's paging file rather than a dedicated hard disk file. This method is almost identical to the method for creating a memory-mapped disk file except that it's even easier. For one thing, there is no need to call **CreateFile** because you will not be creating or opening a dedicated file. Instead, you simply call **CreateFileMapping**, as you would normally and pass **INVALID_HANDLE_VALUE** as the **hFile** parameter. This tells the system that you are not creating a file-mapping object whose physical storage resides in a file on the disk; instead, you want the system to commit physical storage from the system's paging file. The amount of storage allocated is determined by **Create-FileMapping**'s **dwMaximumSizeHigh** and **dwMaximumSizeLow** parameters.

After you have created this file-mapping object and mapped a view of it into your process' address space, you can use it as you would any region of memory. If you want to share this data with other processes, call **CreateFileMapping** and pass a zero-terminated string as the **pszName** parameter. Then other processes that want to access the storage can call **CreateFileMapping** or **Open-FileMapping** and pass the same name.

When a process no longer needs access to the file-mapping object, that process should call **Close-Handle**. When all the handles are closed, the system will reclaim the committed storage from the system's paging file.

> **Note**   Here is an interesting problem that has caught unsuspecting programmers by surprise. Can you guess what is wrong with the following code fragment?
>
> ```
> HANDLE hFile = CreateFile(...);
> HANDLE hMap = CreateFileMapping(hFile, ...);
> if (hMap == NULL)
>     return(GetLastError());
> ...
> ```
>
> If the call shown to **CreateFile** fails, it returns **INVALID_HANDLE_VALUE**. However, the unsuspecting programmer who wrote this code didn't test to check whether the file was created successfully. When **CreateFileMapping** is called, **INVALID_HANDLE_VALUE** is passed in the **hFile** parameter, which causes the system to create a file mapping using storage from the paging file instead of the intended disk file. Any additional code that uses the memory-mapped file will work correctly. However, when the file-mapping object is destroyed, all the data that was written to the file-mapping storage (the paging file) will be destroyed by the system. At this point, the developer sits and scratches his or her head, wondering what went wrong! You must always check **CreateFile**'s return value to see if an error occurred because **CreateFile** can fail for so many reasons!

The Memory-Mapped File Sharing Sample Application

The Memory-Mapped File Sharing application (17-MMFShare.exe) listed next demonstrates how to use memory-mapped files to transfer data among two or more separate processes. The source code and resource files for the application are in the 17-MMFShare directory on the companion content Web page.

You're going to need to execute at least two instances of MMFShare. Each instance creates its own dialog box, shown here:

To transfer data from one instance of MMFShare to another, type the data to be transferred into the Data edit box. Then click the Create Mapping Of Data button. When you do, MMFShare calls **CreateFileMapping** to create a 4-KB memory-mapped file object backed by the system's paging file and names the object **MMFSharedData**. If MMFShare sees that a file-mapping object with this name already exists, it displays a message box notifying you that it could not create the object. If, on the other hand, MMFShare succeeds in creating the object, it proceeds to map a view of the file into the process' address space and copies the data from the edit control into the memory-mapped file.

After the data has been copied, MMFShare unmaps the view of the file, disables the Create Mapping Of Data button, and enables the Close Mapping Of Data button. At this point, a memory-mapped file named **MMFSharedData** is just sitting somewhere in the system. No processes have mapped a view to the data contained in the file.

If you now go to another instance of MMFShare and click on this instance's Open Mapping And Get Data button, MMFShare attempts to locate a file-mapping object called **MMFSharedData** by calling **OpenFileMapping**. If an object of this name cannot be found, MMFShare notifies you by displaying another message box. If MMFShare finds the object, it maps a view of the object into its process' address space, copies the data from the memory-mapped file into the edit control of the dialog box, and unmaps and closes the file-mapping object. Voilà! You have transferred data from one process to another.

The Close Mapping Of Data button in the dialog box is used to close the file-mapping object, which frees up the storage in the paging file. If no file-mapping object exists, no other instance of MMF-Share will be able to open one and get data from it. Also, if one instance has created a memory-mapped file, no other instance is allowed to create one and overwrite the data contained within the file.

```cpp
MMFShare.cpp
/******************************************************************************
Module:  MMFShare.cpp
Notices: Copyright (c) 2008 Jeffrey Richter & Christophe Nasarre
******************************************************************************/


#include "..\CmnHdr.h"     /* See Appendix A. */
#include <windowsx.h>
#include <tchar.h>
#include "Resource.h"


///////////////////////////////////////////////////////////////////////////////


BOOL Dlg_OnInitDialog(HWND hWnd, HWND hWndFocus, LPARAM lParam) {

   chSETDLGICONS(hWnd, IDI_MMFSHARE);

   // Initialize the edit control with some test data.
   Edit_SetText(GetDlgItem(hWnd, IDC_DATA), TEXT("Some test data"));

   // Disable the Close button because the file can't
   // be closed if it was never created or opened.
   Button_Enable(GetDlgItem(hWnd, IDC_CLOSEFILE), FALSE);
   return(TRUE);
}


///////////////////////////////////////////////////////////////////////////////


void Dlg_OnCommand(HWND hWnd, int id, HWND hWndCtl, UINT codeNotify) {

   // Handle of the open memory-mapped file
   static HANDLE s_hFileMap = NULL;
```

```
switch (id) {
  case IDCANCEL:
    EndDialog(hWnd, id);
    break;

  case IDC_CREATEFILE:
    if (codeNotify != BN_CLICKED)
      break;

    // Create a paging file-backed MMF to contain the edit control text.
    // The MMF is 4 KB at most and is named MMFSharedData.
    s_hFileMap = CreateFileMapping(INVALID_HANDLE_VALUE, NULL,
      PAGE_READWRITE, 0, 4 * 1024, TEXT("MMFSharedData"));

    if (s_hFileMap != NULL) {

      if (GetLastError() == ERROR_ALREADY_EXISTS) {
        chMB("Mapping already exists - not created.");
        CloseHandle(s_hFileMap);

      } else {

        // File mapping created successfully.

        // Map a view of the file into the address space.
        PVOID pView = MapViewOfFile(s_hFileMap,
          FILE_MAP_READ | FILE_MAP_WRITE, 0, 0, 0);

        if (pView != NULL) {
          // Put edit text into the MMF.
          Edit_GetText(GetDlgItem(hWnd, IDC_DATA),
            (PTSTR) pView, 4 * 1024);

          // Protect the MMF storage by unmapping it.
          UnmapViewOfFile(pView);

          // The user can't create another file right now.
          Button_Enable(hWndCtl, FALSE);

          // The user closed the file.
          Button_Enable(GetDlgItem(hWnd, IDC_CLOSEFILE), TRUE);

        } else {
          chMB("Can't map view of file.");
        }
      }

    } else {
      chMB("Can't create file mapping.");
    }
    break;
```

```
      case IDC_CLOSEFILE:
         if (codeNotify != BN_CLICKED)
            break;

         if (CloseHandle(s_hFileMap)) {
            // User closed the file, fix up the buttons.
            Button_Enable(GetDlgItem(hWnd, IDC_CREATEFILE), TRUE);
            Button_Enable(hWndCtl, FALSE);
         }
         break;

      case IDC_OPENFILE:
         if (codeNotify != BN_CLICKED)
            break;

         // See if a memory-mapped file named MMFSharedData already exists.
         HANDLE hFileMapT = OpenFileMapping(FILE_MAP_READ | FILE_MAP_WRITE,
            FALSE, TEXT("MMFSharedData"));

         if (hFileMapT != NULL) {
            // The MMF does exist, map it into the process' address space.
            PVOID pView = MapViewOfFile(hFileMapT,
               FILE_MAP_READ | FILE_MAP_WRITE, 0, 0, 0);

            if (pView != NULL) {

               // Put the contents of the MMF into the edit control.
               Edit_SetText(GetDlgItem(hWnd, IDC_DATA), (PTSTR) pView);
               UnmapViewOfFile(pView);
            } else {
               chMB("Can't map view.");
            }

            CloseHandle(hFileMapT);

         } else {
            chMB("Can't open mapping.");
         }
         break;
   }
}


//////////////////////////////////////////////////////////////////////////////


INT_PTR WINAPI Dlg_Proc(HWND hWnd, UINT uMsg, WPARAM wParam, LPARAM lParam) {

   switch (uMsg) {
      chHANDLE_DLGMSG(hWnd, WM_INITDIALOG, Dlg_OnInitDialog);
      chHANDLE_DLGMSG(hWnd, WM_COMMAND,    Dlg_OnCommand);
   }
   return(FALSE);
}
```

```
//////////////////////////////////////////////////////////////////////////

int WINAPI _tWinMain(HINSTANCE hInstExe, HINSTANCE, PTSTR, int) {

   DialogBox(hInstExe, MAKEINTRESOURCE(IDD_MMFSHARE), NULL, Dlg_Proc);
   return(0);
}


///////////////////////////// End of File //////////////////////////////////
```

Sparsely Committed Memory-Mapped Files

In all the discussion of memory-mapped files so far, we see that the system requires that all storage for the memory-mapped file be committed either in the data file on disk or in the paging file. This means that we can't use storage as efficiently as we might like. Let's return to the discussion of the spreadsheet from "When to Decommit Physical Storage" on page 426. Let's say that you want to share the entire spreadsheet with another process. If we were to use memory-mapped files, we would need to commit the physical storage for the entire spreadsheet:

```
CELLDATA CellData[200][256];
```

If a **CELLDATA** structure is 128 bytes, this array requires 6,553,600 (200 × 256 × 128) bytes of physical storage. As I said in an earlier chapter, "That's a lot of physical storage to allocate from the paging file right up front for a spreadsheet, especially when you consider that most users put information into only a few spreadsheet cells, leaving the majority unused."

It should be obvious that we would prefer to share the spreadsheet as a file-mapping object without having to commit all the physical storage up front. **CreateFileMapping** offers a way to do this by specifying either the **SEC_RESERVE** or **SEC_COMMIT** flag in the **fdwProtect** parameter.

These flags are meaningful only if you're creating a file-mapping object that is backed by the system's paging file. The **SEC_COMMIT** flag causes **CreateFileMapping** to commit storage from the system's paging file. This is also the result if you specify neither flag.

When you call **CreateFileMapping** and pass the **SEC_RESERVE** flag, the system does not commit physical storage from the system's paging file; it just returns a handle to the file-mapping object. You can now call **MapViewOfFile** or **MapViewOfFileEx** to create a view of this file-mapping object. **MapViewOfFile** and **MapViewOfFileEx** will reserve a region of address space and will not commit any physical storage to back the region. Any attempts to access a memory address in the reserved region will cause the thread to raise an access violation.

What we have here is a region of reserved address space and a handle to a file-mapping object that identifies the region. Other processes can use the same file-mapping object to map a view of the same region of address space. Physical storage is still not committed to the region, and if threads in other processes attempt to access a memory address of the view in their regions, these threads will raise access violations.

Now here is where things get exciting. To commit physical storage to the shared region, all a thread has to do is call **VirtualAlloc**:

```
PVOID VirtualAlloc(
    PVOID pvAddress,
    SIZE_T dwSize,
    DWORD fdwAllocationType,
    DWORD fdwProtect);
```

We already discussed this function in great detail in Chapter 15. Calling **VirtualAlloc** to commit physical storage to the memory-mapped view region is just like calling **VirtualAlloc** to commit storage to a region initially reserved by a simple call to **VirtualAlloc** using the **MEM_RESERVE** flag. And just as you can commit storage sparsely in a region reserved with **VirtualAlloc**, you can also commit storage sparsely within a region reserved by **MapViewOfFile** or **MapViewOfFileEx**. However, when you commit storage to a region reserved by **MapViewOfFile** or **MapViewOfFileEx**, all the processes that have mapped a view of the same file-mapping object can now successfully access the committed pages.

Using the **SEC_RESERVE** flag and **VirtualAlloc**, we can successfully share the spreadsheet application's **CellData** matrix with other processes—and use physical storage quite efficiently.

> **Note**   You cannot use the **VirtualFree** function to decommit storage from a memory-mapped file that was reserved with the **SEC_RESERVE** flag.

The NT File System (NTFS) offers support for sparse files. This is a terrific feature. Using this sparse file feature, you can easily create and work with sparse memory-mapped files in which the storage is contained in a normal disk file rather than in the system's paging file.

Here is an example of how you could use this: Let's say that you want to create an MMF to store recorded audio data. As the user speaks, you want to write the digital audio data into a memory buffer and have that buffer be backed by a file on the disk. A sparse MMF would certainly be the easiest and most efficient way to implement this in your code. The problem is that you don't know how long the user will speak before clicking on the Stop button. You might need a file large enough for five minutes of data or five hours—a pretty big difference! When using a sparse MMF, however, size really doesn't matter.

The Sparse Memory-Mapped File Sample Application

The MMF Sparse application (17-MMFSparse.exe), listed next, demonstrates how to create a memory-mapped file backed by an NTFS sparse file. The source code and resource files for the application are in the 17-MMFSparse directory on the companion content Web page. When you start the program, the window on the next page appears.

When you click the Create A 1MB (1024 KB) Sparse MMF button, the program attempts to create a sparse file called MMFSparse in the current directory. If the corresponding drive is not an NTFS volume, this will fail and the process will terminate. If your NTFS volume is on another drive letter, you'll have to modify the source code and rebuild it to see how the application works.

Once the sparse file is created, it is mapped into the process' address space. The Allocated Ranges edit control at the bottom shows which parts of the file are actually backed by disk storage. Initially, the file will have no storage in it and the edit control will contain the text "No allocated ranges in the file."

To read a byte, simply enter a number into the Offset edit box and click the Read Byte button. The number you enter is multiplied by 1024 (1 KB), and the byte at that location is read and placed in the Byte edit box. If you read from any portion that has no backing storage, you will always read a zero byte. If you read from a portion of the file that does have backing storage, you will read whatever byte is there.

To write a byte, simply enter a number into the Offset edit box and also enter a byte value (0–255) into the Byte edit box. Then, when you click the Write Byte button, the offset number is multiplied by 1024 and the byte at that location is changed to reflect the specified byte value. This write can cause the file system to commit backing storage for a portion of the file. After any read or write operation, the Allocated Ranges edit control is always updated to show you which portions of the file are actually backed by storage. The window presented next shows what the dialog box looks like after writing just a single byte at offset 1,024,000 (1000 × 1024).

In this figure, notice that there is just one allocated range starting at logical offset 983,040 bytes into the file and that 65,536 bytes of backing storage have been allocated. You can also use Windows Explorer to locate the MMFSparse file and display its property page, as shown here:

Notice that the property page indicates that the file's size is 1 MB (this is the virtual size of the file), but the file actually occupies only 64 KB of disk space.

The last button, Free All Allocated Regions, causes the program to free all the storage for the file; this feature frees up disk space and makes all the bytes in the file appear as zeros.

Let's talk about how the program works. To make things easier, I created a **CSparseStream** C++ class (implemented in the SparseStream.h file). This class encapsulates the tasks that you can perform with a sparse file or stream. Then, in the MMFSparse.cpp file, I created another C++ class, **CMMFSparse**, that is derived from the **CSparseStream** class. So a **CMMFSparse** object will have all the features of a **CSparseStream** plus a few more that are specific to using a sparse stream as a memory-mapped file. The process has a single, global instance of a **CMMFSparse** object called **g_mmf**. The application references this global variable throughout its code to manipulate the sparse memory-mapped file.

In the **WM_INITDIALOG** message handler, if the volume does not support sparse files (checked by calling the **CSparseStream::DoesFileSystemSupportSparseStreams** static helper function), an error message pops up and the application ends. When the user clicks the Create A 1MB (1024 KB) Sparse MMF button, **CreateFile** is called to create a new file on the NTFS disk partition. This is a normal, ordinary file. But then I use my global **g_mmf** object and call its **Initialize** method, passing the handle of this file and the maximum size of the file (1 MB). Internally, the **Initialize** method calls **CreateFileMapping** to create the file-mapping kernel object using the specified size and then calls **MapViewOfFile** to make the sparse file visible in the process' address space.

When the **Initialize** method returns, the **Dlg_ShowAllocatedRanges** function is called. This function internally calls Windows functions that enumerate the logical ranges of the sparse files that have storage actually allocated to them. The starting offset and length of each allocated range is shown in the edit control at the bottom of the dialog box. When the **g_mmf** object is first initialized, the file on the disk actually has 0 bytes of physical storage allocated for it; the edit control will reflect this.

At this point, the user can attempt to read from or write to bytes within the sparse memory-mapped file. For an attempted write, the user's offset and byte values are obtained from their respective edit controls, and the memory address within the **g_mmf** object is written to. Writing to **g_mmf** can cause the file system to allocate storage to this logical portion of the file, but the allocation is transparent to the application.

If the user attempts to read a byte from the **g_mmf** object, the read might attempt to read a logical byte within the file where storage has been allocated or the byte might identify a byte where storage has not been allocated. If the byte does not have storage allocated, reading the byte returns 0. Again, this is transparent to the application. If storage does exist for the byte being read, the actual value is of course returned.

The last thing that the application demonstrates is how to reset the file so that all of its allocated ranges are freed and the file doesn't actually require any disk storage. The user frees all the allocated ranges by clicking the Free All Allocated Regions button. Windows cannot free all the allocated ranges for a file that is memory-mapped, so the first thing that the application does is call the **g_mmf** object's **ForceClose** method. Internally, the **ForceClose** method calls **UnmapViewOfFile** and then calls **CloseHandle**, passing the handle of the file-mapping kernel object.

Next the **DecommitPortionOfStream** method is called, freeing all storage allocated for logical bytes 0 through 1 MB in the file. You must close the file handle to let the operating system flush the sparse state. Finally the file is reopened and the **Initialize** method is called again on the **g_mmf** object, which reinitializes the memory-mapped file into the process' address space. To prove that the file has had all its allocated storage freed, the **Dlg_ShowAllocatedRanges** function is called, which will display the "No allocated ranges in the file" string in the edit control.

One last thing: If you are using a sparse memory-mapped file in a real-life application, you might want to truncate the logical size of the file when you close it. Trimming the end of a sparse file that contains zero bytes doesn't actually affect the disk space, but it's still a nice thing to do—Windows Explorer and the command shell's **DIR** command can report a more accurate file size to the user. To set the end of file marker for a file, you can call the **SetFilePointer** and **SetEndOfFile** functions after calling the **ForceClose** method.

 Note   My Q&A article in April 1999 Microsoft System Journal (*http://www.microsoft.com/msj/ 0499/win32/win320499.aspx*) details how you can implement a growable memory-mapped file.

MMFSparse.cpp

```
/*****************************************************************************
Module:  MMFSparse.cpp
Notices: Copyright (c) 2008 Jeffrey Richter & Christophe Nasarre
*****************************************************************************/


#include "..\CmnHdr.h"     /* See Appendix A. */
#include <tchar.h>
#include <WindowsX.h>
#include <WinIoCtl.h>
#include "SparseStream.h"
#include <StrSafe.h>
#include "Resource.h"


///////////////////////////////////////////////////////////////////////////


// This class makes it easy to work with memory-mapped sparse files
class CMMFSparse : public CSparseStream {
private:
   HANDLE m_hFileMap;       // File-mapping object
   PVOID  m_pvFile;         // Address to start of mapped file

public:
   // Creates a Sparse MMF and maps it in the process' address space.
   CMMFSparse(HANDLE hStream = NULL, DWORD dwStreamSizeMaxLow = 0,
      DWORD dwStreamSizeMaxHigh = 0);

   // Closes a Sparse MMF
   virtual ~CMMFSparse() { ForceClose(); }
```

```cpp
  // Creates a sparse MMF and maps it in the process' address space.
  BOOL Initialize(HANDLE hStream, DWORD dwStreamSizeMaxLow,
    DWORD dwStreamSizeMaxHigh = 0);

  // MMF to BYTE cast operator returns address of first byte
  // in the memory-mapped sparse file.
  operator PBYTE() const { return((PBYTE) m_pvFile); }

  // Allows you to explicitly close the MMF without having
  // to wait for the destructor to be called.
  VOID ForceClose();
};


///////////////////////////////////////////////////////////////////////


CMMFSparse::CMMFSparse(HANDLE hStream, DWORD dwStreamSizeMaxLow,
  DWORD dwStreamSizeMaxHigh) {

  Initialize(hStream, dwStreamSizeMaxLow, dwStreamSizeMaxHigh);
}


///////////////////////////////////////////////////////////////////////


BOOL CMMFSparse::Initialize(HANDLE hStream, DWORD dwStreamSizeMaxLow,
  DWORD dwStreamSizeMaxHigh) {

  if (m_hFileMap != NULL)
    ForceClose();

  // Initialize to NULL in case something goes wrong
  m_hFileMap = m_pvFile = NULL;

  BOOL bOk = TRUE;   // Assume success

  if (hStream != NULL) {
    if ((dwStreamSizeMaxLow == 0) && (dwStreamSizeMaxHigh == 0)) {
      DebugBreak();  // Illegal stream size
    }

    CSparseStream::Initialize(hStream);
    bOk = MakeSparse();  // Make the stream sparse
    if (bOk) {
      // Create a file-mapping object
      m_hFileMap = ::CreateFileMapping(hStream, NULL, PAGE_READWRITE,
        dwStreamSizeMaxHigh, dwStreamSizeMaxLow, NULL);

      if (m_hFileMap != NULL) {
        // Map the stream into the process' address space
        m_pvFile = ::MapViewOfFile(m_hFileMap,
          FILE_MAP_WRITE | FILE_MAP_READ, 0, 0, 0);
```

```
            } else {
                // Failed to map the file, cleanup
                CSparseStream::Initialize(NULL);
                ForceClose();
                bOk = FALSE;
            }
        }
    }
    return(bOk);
}


///////////////////////////////////////////////////////////////////////////


VOID CMMFSparse::ForceClose() {

    // Clean up everything that was done successfully
    if (m_pvFile != NULL) {
        ::UnmapViewOfFile(m_pvFile);
        m_pvFile = NULL;
    }
    if (m_hFileMap != NULL) {
        ::CloseHandle(m_hFileMap);
        m_hFileMap = NULL;
    }
}


///////////////////////////////////////////////////////////////////////////


#define STREAMSIZE      (1 * 1024 * 1024)    // 1 MB (1024 KB)
HANDLE g_hStream = INVALID_HANDLE_VALUE;
CMMFSparse g_mmf;
TCHAR g_szPathname[MAX_PATH] = TEXT("\0");


///////////////////////////////////////////////////////////////////////////


BOOL Dlg_OnInitDialog(HWND hWnd, HWND hWndFocus, LPARAM lParam) {

    chSETDLGICONS(hWnd, IDI_MMFSPARSE);

    // Initialize the dialog box controls.
    EnableWindow(GetDlgItem(hWnd, IDC_OFFSET), FALSE);
    Edit_LimitText(GetDlgItem(hWnd, IDC_OFFSET), 4);
    SetDlgItemInt(hWnd, IDC_OFFSET, 1000, FALSE);

    EnableWindow(GetDlgItem(hWnd, IDC_BYTE), FALSE);
    Edit_LimitText(GetDlgItem(hWnd, IDC_BYTE), 3);
    SetDlgItemInt(hWnd, IDC_BYTE, 5, FALSE);
```

```
      EnableWindow(GetDlgItem(hWnd, IDC_WRITEBYTE), FALSE);
      EnableWindow(GetDlgItem(hWnd, IDC_READBYTE),  FALSE);
      EnableWindow(GetDlgItem(hWnd, IDC_FREEALLOCATEDREGIONS), FALSE);

      // Store the file in a writable folder
      GetCurrentDirectory(_countof(g_szPathname), g_szPathname);
      _tcscat_s(g_szPathname, _countof(g_szPathname), TEXT("\\MMFSparse"));

      // Check to see if the volume supports sparse files
      TCHAR szVolume[16];
      PTSTR pEndOfVolume = _tcschr(g_szPathname, _T('\\'));
      if (pEndOfVolume == NULL) {
         chFAIL("Impossible to find the Volume for the default document folder.");
         DestroyWindow(hWnd);
         return(TRUE);
      }
      _tcsncpy_s(szVolume, _countof(szVolume),
         g_szPathname, pEndOfVolume - g_szPathname + 1);
      if (!CSparseStream::DoesFileSystemSupportSparseStreams(szVolume)) {
         chFAIL("Volume of default document folder does not support sparse MMF.");
         DestroyWindow(hWnd);
         return(TRUE);
      }

      return(TRUE);
}


///////////////////////////////////////////////////////////////////////////////


void Dlg_ShowAllocatedRanges(HWND hWnd) {

      // Fill in the Allocated Ranges edit control
      DWORD dwNumEntries;
      FILE_ALLOCATED_RANGE_BUFFER* pfarb =
         g_mmf.QueryAllocatedRanges(&dwNumEntries);

      if (dwNumEntries == 0) {
         SetDlgItemText(hWnd, IDC_FILESTATUS,
            TEXT("No allocated ranges in the file"));
      } else {
         TCHAR sz[4096] = { 0 };
         for (DWORD dwEntry = 0; dwEntry < dwNumEntries; dwEntry++) {
            StringCchPrintf(_tcschr(sz, _T('\0')), _countof(sz) - _tcslen(sz),
               TEXT("Offset: %7.7u, Length: %7.7u\r\n"),
               pfarb[dwEntry].FileOffset.LowPart, pfarb[dwEntry].Length.LowPart);
         }
         SetDlgItemText(hWnd, IDC_FILESTATUS, sz);
      }
      g_mmf.FreeAllocatedRanges(pfarb);
}


///////////////////////////////////////////////////////////////////////////////
```

```
void Dlg_OnCommand(HWND hWnd, int id, HWND hWndCtl, UINT codeNotify) {

   switch (id) {
      case IDCANCEL:
         if (g_hStream != INVALID_HANDLE_VALUE)
            CloseHandle(g_hStream);
         EndDialog(hWnd, id);
         break;

      case IDC_CREATEMMF:
         {
         g_hStream = CreateFile(g_szPathname, GENERIC_READ | GENERIC_WRITE,
            0, NULL, CREATE_ALWAYS, FILE_ATTRIBUTE_NORMAL, NULL);
         if (g_hStream == INVALID_HANDLE_VALUE) {
            chFAIL("Failed to create file.");
            return;
         }

         // Create a 1MB (1024 KB) MMF using the file
         if (!g_mmf.Initialize(g_hStream, STREAMSIZE)) {
            chFAIL("Failed to initialize Sparse MMF.");
            CloseHandle(g_hStream);
            g_hStream = NULL;
            return;
         }
         Dlg_ShowAllocatedRanges(hWnd);

         // Enable/disable the other controls.
         EnableWindow(GetDlgItem(hWnd, IDC_CREATEMMF), FALSE);
         EnableWindow(GetDlgItem(hWnd, IDC_OFFSET),    TRUE);
         EnableWindow(GetDlgItem(hWnd, IDC_BYTE),      TRUE);
         EnableWindow(GetDlgItem(hWnd, IDC_WRITEBYTE), TRUE);
         EnableWindow(GetDlgItem(hWnd, IDC_READBYTE),  TRUE);
         EnableWindow(GetDlgItem(hWnd, IDC_FREEALLOCATEDREGIONS), TRUE);

         // Force the Offset edit control to have the focus.
         SetFocus(GetDlgItem(hWnd, IDC_OFFSET));
         }
         break;

      case IDC_WRITEBYTE:
         {
         BOOL bTranslated;
         DWORD dwOffset = GetDlgItemInt(hWnd, IDC_OFFSET, &bTranslated, FALSE);
         if (bTranslated) {
            g_mmf[dwOffset * 1024] = (BYTE)
               GetDlgItemInt(hWnd, IDC_BYTE, NULL, FALSE);
            Dlg_ShowAllocatedRanges(hWnd);
         }
         }
         break;
```

```
      case IDC_READBYTE:
         {
         BOOL bTranslated;
         DWORD dwOffset = GetDlgItemInt(hWnd, IDC_OFFSET, &bTranslated, FALSE);
         if (bTranslated) {
            SetDlgItemInt(hWnd, IDC_BYTE, g_mmf[dwOffset * 1024], FALSE);
            Dlg_ShowAllocatedRanges(hWnd);
         }
         }
         break;

      case IDC_FREEALLOCATEDREGIONS:
         // Normally the destructor causes the file-mapping to close.
         // But, in this case, we want to force it so that we can reset
         // a portion of the file back to all zeros.
         g_mmf.ForceClose();

         // We call ForceClose above because attempting to zero a portion of
         // the file while it is mapped causes DeviceIoControl to fail with
         // error ERROR_USER_MAPPED_FILE ("The requested operation cannot
         // be performed on a file with a user-mapped section open.")
         g_mmf.DecommitPortionOfStream(0, STREAMSIZE);

         // We need to close the file handle and reopen it in order to
         // flush the sparse state.
         CloseHandle(g_hStream);
         g_hStream = CreateFile(g_szPathname, GENERIC_READ | GENERIC_WRITE,
            0, NULL, CREATE_ALWAYS, FILE_ATTRIBUTE_NORMAL, NULL);
         if (g_hStream == INVALID_HANDLE_VALUE) {
            chFAIL("Failed to create file.");
            return;
         }

         // Reset the MMF wrapper for the new file handle.
         g_mmf.Initialize(g_hStream, STREAMSIZE);

         // Update the UI.
         Dlg_ShowAllocatedRanges(hWnd);
         break;
   }
}


///////////////////////////////////////////////////////////////////////////////


INT_PTR WINAPI Dlg_Proc(HWND hWnd, UINT uMsg, WPARAM wParam, LPARAM lParam) {

   switch (uMsg) {
      chHANDLE_DLGMSG(hWnd, WM_INITDIALOG, Dlg_OnInitDialog);
      chHANDLE_DLGMSG(hWnd, WM_COMMAND,    Dlg_OnCommand);
   }
   return(FALSE);
}
```

```
///////////////////////////////////////////////////////////////////////


int WINAPI _tWinMain(HINSTANCE hInstExe, HINSTANCE, PTSTR, int) {

   DialogBox(hInstExe, MAKEINTRESOURCE(IDD_MMFSPARSE), NULL, Dlg_Proc);
   return(0);
}


///////////////////////////// End of File //////////////////////////////
```

SparseStream.h

```
/******************************************************************************
Module:  SparseStream.h
Notices: Copyright (c) 2008 Jeffrey Richter & Christophe Nasarre
******************************************************************************/


#include "..\CommonFiles\CmnHdr.h"      /* See Appendix A. */
#include <WinIoCtl.h>


///////////////////////////////////////////////////////////////////////


#pragma once


///////////////////////////////////////////////////////////////////////


class CSparseStream {
public:
   static BOOL DoesFileSystemSupportSparseStreams(PCTSTR pszVolume);
   static BOOL DoesFileContainAnySparseStreams(PCTSTR pszPathname);

public:
   CSparseStream(HANDLE hStream = INVALID_HANDLE_VALUE) {
      Initialize(hStream);
   }

   virtual ~CSparseStream() { }

   void Initialize(HANDLE hStream = INVALID_HANDLE_VALUE) {
      m_hStream = hStream;
   }

public:
   operator HANDLE() const { return(m_hStream); }
```

```
public:
   BOOL IsStreamSparse() const;
   BOOL MakeSparse();
   BOOL DecommitPortionOfStream(
      __int64 qwFileOffsetStart, __int64 qwFileOffsetEnd);

   FILE_ALLOCATED_RANGE_BUFFER* QueryAllocatedRanges(PDWORD pdwNumEntries);
   BOOL FreeAllocatedRanges(FILE_ALLOCATED_RANGE_BUFFER* pfarb);

private:
   HANDLE m_hStream;

private:
   static BOOL AreFlagsSet(DWORD fdwFlagBits, DWORD fFlagsToCheck) {
      return((fdwFlagBits & fFlagsToCheck) == fFlagsToCheck);
   }
};


///////////////////////////////////////////////////////////////////////////


inline BOOL CSparseStream::DoesFileSystemSupportSparseStreams(
   PCTSTR pszVolume) {

   DWORD dwFileSystemFlags = 0;
   BOOL bOk = GetVolumeInformation(pszVolume, NULL, 0, NULL, NULL,
      &dwFileSystemFlags, NULL, 0);
   bOk = bOk && AreFlagsSet(dwFileSystemFlags, FILE_SUPPORTS_SPARSE_FILES);
   return(bOk);
}


///////////////////////////////////////////////////////////////////////////


inline BOOL CSparseStream::IsStreamSparse() const {

   BY_HANDLE_FILE_INFORMATION bhfi;
   GetFileInformationByHandle(m_hStream, &bhfi);
   return(AreFlagsSet(bhfi.dwFileAttributes, FILE_ATTRIBUTE_SPARSE_FILE));
}


///////////////////////////////////////////////////////////////////////////


inline BOOL CSparseStream::MakeSparse() {

   DWORD dw;
   return(DeviceIoControl(m_hStream, FSCTL_SET_SPARSE,
      NULL, 0, NULL, 0, &dw, NULL));
}
```

```
/////////////////////////////////////////////////////////////////////////

inline BOOL CSparseStream::DecommitPortionOfStream(
   __int64 qwOffsetStart, __int64 qwOffsetEnd) {

   // NOTE: This function does not work if this file is memory-mapped.
   DWORD dw;
   FILE_ZERO_DATA_INFORMATION fzdi;
   fzdi.FileOffset.QuadPart = qwOffsetStart;
   fzdi.BeyondFinalZero.QuadPart = qwOffsetEnd + 1;
   return(DeviceIoControl(m_hStream, FSCTL_SET_ZERO_DATA, (PVOID) &fzdi,
      sizeof(fzdi), NULL, 0, &dw, NULL));
}


/////////////////////////////////////////////////////////////////////////


inline BOOL CSparseStream::DoesFileContainAnySparseStreams(
   PCTSTR pszPathname) {

   DWORD dw = GetFileAttributes(pszPathname);
   return((dw == 0xffffffff)
      ? FALSE : AreFlagsSet(dw, FILE_ATTRIBUTE_SPARSE_FILE));
}


/////////////////////////////////////////////////////////////////////////


inline FILE_ALLOCATED_RANGE_BUFFER* CSparseStream::QueryAllocatedRanges(
   PDWORD pdwNumEntries) {

   FILE_ALLOCATED_RANGE_BUFFER farb;
   farb.FileOffset.QuadPart = 0;
   farb.Length.LowPart =
      GetFileSize(m_hStream, (PDWORD) &farb.Length.HighPart);

   // There is no way to determine the correct memory block size prior to
   // attempting to collect this data, so I just picked 100 * sizeof(*pfarb)
   DWORD cb = 100 * sizeof(farb);
   FILE_ALLOCATED_RANGE_BUFFER* pfarb = (FILE_ALLOCATED_RANGE_BUFFER*)
      HeapAlloc(GetProcessHeap(), HEAP_ZERO_MEMORY, cb);

   DeviceIoControl(m_hStream, FSCTL_QUERY_ALLOCATED_RANGES,
      &farb, sizeof(farb), pfarb, cb, &cb, NULL);
   *pdwNumEntries = cb / sizeof(*pfarb);
   return(pfarb);
}


/////////////////////////////////////////////////////////////////////////
```

```
inline BOOL CSparseStream::FreeAllocatedRanges(
   FILE_ALLOCATED_RANGE_BUFFER* pfarb) {

   // Free the queue entry's allocated memory
   return(HeapFree(GetProcessHeap(), 0, pfarb));
}

///////////////////////////// End Of File ///////////////////////////////
```

Chapter 18

Heaps

The third and last mechanism for manipulating memory is the use of heaps. Heaps are great for allocating lots of small blocks of data. For example, linked lists and trees are best managed using heaps rather than the virtual memory techniques discussed in Chapter 15, "Using Virtual Memory in Your Own Applications," or the memory-mapped file techniques discussed in Chapter 17, "Memory-Mapped Files." The advantage of heaps is that they allow you to ignore all the allocation granularity and page boundary stuff and concentrate on the task at hand. The disadvantage of heaps is that allocating and freeing memory blocks is slower than the other mechanisms and you lose the direct control over the committing and decommitting of physical storage.

Internally, a heap is a region of reserved address space. Initially, most of the pages within the reserved region are not committed with physical storage. As you make more allocations from the heap, the heap manager commits more physical storage to the heap. This physical storage is always allocated from the system's paging file. As you free blocks within a heap, the heap manager decommits the physical storage.

Microsoft does not document the exact rules that the heap follows for committing and decommitting storage. Microsoft is constantly performing stress tests and running different scenarios to determine the rules that work best most of the time with the best security. As applications and the hardware that runs them change, these rules will change. If this knowledge is critical to your application, don't use heaps. Instead, use the virtual memory functions (that is, **VirtualAlloc** and **VirtualFree**) so that you can control these rules yourself.

A Process' Default Heap

When a process initializes, the system creates a heap in the process' address space. This heap is called the process' *default heap*. By default, this heap's region of address space is 1 MB in size. However, the system can grow a process' default heap so that it becomes larger than this. You can change the default region size of 1 MB using the **/HEAP** linker switch when you create an application. Because a dynamic-link library (DLL) does not have a heap associated with it, you should not use the **/HEAP** switch when you are linking a DLL. The **/HEAP** switch has the following syntax:

```
/HEAP:reserve[,commit]
```

Many Windows functions require the process' default heap. For example, the core functions in Windows perform all of their operations using Unicode characters and strings. If you call an ANSI version of a Windows function, this ANSI version must convert the ANSI strings to Unicode strings and then call the Unicode version of the same function. To convert the strings, the ANSI function needs to allocate a block of memory to hold the Unicode version of the string. This block of memory is allocated from your process' default heap. Many other Windows functions require the use of temporary memory blocks; these blocks are allocated from the process' default heap. Also, the old 16-bit Windows functions **LocalAlloc** and **GlobalAlloc** make their memory allocations from the process' default heap.

Because the process' default heap is used by many of the Windows functions, and because your application has many threads simultaneously calling the various Windows functions, access to the default heap is serialized. In other words, the system guarantees that only one thread at a time can allocate or free blocks of memory in the default heap at any given time. If two threads attempt to simultaneously allocate a block of memory in the default heap, only one thread will be able to allocate a block; the other thread will be forced to wait until the first thread's block is allocated. Once the first thread's block is allocated, the heap functions will allow the second thread to allocate a block. This serialized access causes a small performance hit. If your application has only one thread and you want to have the fastest possible access to a heap, you should create your own separate heap and not use the process' default heap. Unfortunately, you cannot tell the Windows functions not to use the default heap, so their accesses to the heap are always serialized.

A single process can have several heaps at once. These heaps can be created and destroyed during the lifetime of the process. The default heap, however, is created before the process begins execution and is destroyed automatically when the process terminates. You cannot destroy the process' default heap. Each heap is identified with its own heap handle, and all the heap functions that allocate and free blocks within a heap require this heap handle as a parameter.

You can obtain the handle to your process' default heap by calling **GetProcessHeap**:

```
HANDLE GetProcessHeap();
```

Reasons to Create Additional Heaps

In addition to the process' default heap, you can create additional heaps in your process' address space. You would want to create additional heaps in your own applications for the following reasons:

- Component protection
- More efficient memory management
- Local access
- Avoiding thread synchronization overhead
- Quick free

Let's examine each reason in detail.

Component Protection

Imagine that your application needs to process two components: a linked list of **NODE** structures and a binary tree of **BRANCH** structures. You have two source code files: LinkList.cpp, which contains the functions that process the linked list of **NODE**s, and BinTree.cpp, which contains the functions that process the binary tree of **BRANCH**es.

If the **NODE**s and the **BRANCH**es are stored together in a single heap, the combined heap might look like Figure 18-1.

Now let's say that a bug in the linked-list code causes the 8 bytes after **NODE** 1 to be accidentally overwritten, which in turn causes the data in **BRANCH** 3 to be corrupted. When the code in Bin-Tree.cpp later attempts to traverse the binary tree, it will probably fail because of this memory corruption. Of course, this will lead you to believe that there is a bug in your binary-tree code when in fact the bug exists in the linked-list code. Because the different types of objects are mixed together in a single heap, tracking down and isolating bugs becomes significantly more difficult.

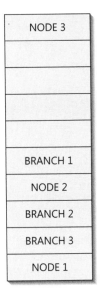

Figure 18-1   A single heap that stores NODEs and BRANCHes together

By creating two separate heaps—one for **NODE**s and the other for **BRANCH**es—you localize your problems. A small bug in your linked-list code does not compromise the integrity of your binary tree, and vice versa. It is still possible to have a bug in your code that causes a wild memory write to another heap, but this is a far less likely scenario.

More Efficient Memory Management

Heaps can be managed more efficiently by allocating objects of the same size within them. For example, let's say that every **NODE** structure requires 24 bytes and every **BRANCH** structure requires 32 bytes. All of these objects are allocated from a single heap. Figure 18-2 shows a fully occupied single heap with several **NODE** and **BRANCH** objects allocated within it. If **NODE** 2 and **NODE** 4 are freed, memory in the heap becomes fragmented. If you then attempt to allocate a **BRANCH** structure, the allocation will fail even though 48 bytes are available and a **BRANCH** needs only 32 bytes.

If each heap consisted only of objects that were the same size, freeing an object would guarantee that another object would fit perfectly into the freed object's space.

| NODE 3 |
| NODE 5 |
| NODE 4 |
| NODE 6 |
| BRANCH 5 |
| BRANCH 1 |
| NODE 2 |
| BRANCH 2 |
| BRANCH 3 |
| NODE 1 |

Figure 18-2   A single fragmented heap that contains several NODE and BRANCH objects

Local Access

There is a huge performance penalty whenever the system must swap a page of RAM to and from the system's paging file. If you keep accesses to memory localized to a small range of addresses, it is less likely that the system will need to swap pages between RAM and disk.

So, in designing an application, it's a good idea to allocate things close to each other if they will be accessed together. Returning to our linked list and binary tree example, traversing the linked list is not related in any way to traversing the binary tree. By keeping all the **NODE**s close together (in one heap), you can keep the **NODE**s in adjoining pages; in fact, it's likely that several **NODE**s will fit within a single page of physical memory. Traversing the linked list will not require that the CPU refer to several different pages of memory for each **NODE** access.

If you were to allocate both **NODE**s and **BRANCH**es in a single heap, the **NODE**s would not necessarily be close together. In a worst-case situation, you might be able to have only one **NODE** per page of memory, with the remainder of each page occupied by **BRANCH**es. In this case, traversing the linked list could cause page faults for each **NODE**, which would make the processing extremely slow.

Avoiding Thread Synchronization Overhead

As I'll explain shortly, heaps are serialized by default so that there is no chance of data corruption if multiple threads attempt to access the heap at the same time. However, the heap functions must execute additional code to keep the heap thread-safe. If you are performing lots of heap allocations, executing this additional code can really add up, taking a toll on your application's performance. When you create a new heap, you can tell the system that only one thread will access the heap and therefore the additional code will not execute. However, be careful—you are now taking on the responsibility of keeping the heap thread-safe. The system will not be looking out for you.

Quick Free

Finally, using a dedicated heap for some data structures allows you to free the entire heap without having to free each memory block explicitly within the heap. For example, when Windows Explorer walks the directory hierarchy of your hard drive, it must build a tree in memory. If you tell Windows Explorer to refresh its display, it could simply destroy the heap containing the tree and start over (assuming, of course, that it has used a dedicated heap only for the directory tree information). For many applications, this can be extremely convenient—and they'll run faster too.

How to Create an Additional Heap

You can create additional heaps in your process by having a thread call **HeapCreate**:

```
HANDLE HeapCreate(
   DWORD fdwOptions,
   SIZE_T dwInitialSize,
   SIZE_T dwMaximumSize);
```

The first parameter, **fdwOptions**, modifies how operations are performed on the heap. You can specify **0**, **HEAP_NO_SERIALIZE**, **HEAP_GENERATE_EXCEPTIONS**, **HEAP_CREATE_ENABLE_EXE-CUTE**, or a combination of these flags.

By default, a heap will serialize access to itself so that multiple threads can allocate and free blocks from the heap without the danger of corrupting the heap. When an attempt is made to allocate a block of memory from the heap, the **HeapAlloc** function (discussed later) must do the following:

1. Traverse the linked list of allocated and freed memory blocks
2. Find the address of a big enough free block
3. Allocate the new block by marking the free block as allocated
4. Add a new entry to the linked list of memory blocks

Here's an example that illustrates why you should avoid using the **HEAP_NO_SERIALIZE** flag. Let's say that two threads attempt to allocate blocks of memory from the same heap at the same time. Thread 1 executes steps 1 and 2 just listed and gets the address of a free memory block. However, before Thread 1 can execute step 3, it is preempted and Thread 2 gets a chance to execute steps 1 and 2. Because Thread 1 has not yet executed step 3, Thread 2 finds the address to the same free memory block.

With both threads having found what they believe to be a free memory block in the heap, Thread 1 updates the linked list, marking the new block as allocated. Thread 2 then also updates the linked list, marking the *same* block as allocated. Neither thread has detected a problem so far, but both threads receive an address to the exact same block of memory.

This type of bug can be very difficult to track down because it usually doesn't manifest itself immediately. Instead, the bug waits in the background until the most inopportune moment. Potential problems include the following:

- The linked list of memory blocks has been corrupted. This problem will not be discovered until an attempt to allocate or free a block is made.

- Both threads are sharing the same memory block. Thread 1 and Thread 2 might both write information to the same block. When Thread 1 examines the contents of the block, it will not recognize the data introduced by Thread 2.

- One thread might proceed to use the block and free it, causing the other thread to overwrite unallocated memory. This will corrupt the heap.

The solution to these problems is to allow a single thread exclusive access to the heap and its linked list until the thread has performed all necessary operations on the heap. The absence of the **HEAP_NO_SERIALIZE** flag does exactly this. It is safe to use the **HEAP_NO_SERIALIZE** flag only if one or more of the following conditions are true for your process:

1. Your process uses only a single thread.

2. Your process uses multiple threads, but only a single thread accesses the heap.

3. Your process uses multiple threads, but manages access to the heap itself by using other forms of mutual exclusion, such as critical sections, mutexes, and semaphores (as discussed in Chapter 8, "Thread Synchronization in User Mode," and Chapter 9, "Thread Synchronization with Kernel Objects").

If you're not sure whether to use the **HEAP_NO_SERIALIZE** flag, don't use it. Not using it will cause your threads to take a slight performance hit whenever a heap function is called, but you won't risk corrupting your heap and its data.

The **HEAP_GENERATE_EXCEPTIONS** flag causes the system to raise an exception whenever an attempt to allocate or reallocate a block of memory in the heap fails. An exception is just another way for the system to notify your application that an error has occurred. Sometimes it's easier to design your application to look for exceptions rather than to check for return values. Exceptions are discussed in Chapter 23, "Termination Handlers," Chapter 24, "Exception Handlers and Software Exceptions," and Chapter 25, "Unhandled Exceptions, Vectored Exception Handling, and C++ Exceptions."

> **Note**   By default, when you call a **Heap*** function, if the operating system detects that the heap is corrupted (such as when you have written past a block you have allocated), nothing special happens except an assertion if you are running under a debugger. However, exploits of internal heap structure corruption in the past have pushed Microsoft to add more controls and validations to detect this type of corruption as early as possible when it takes place.
>
> You can now ask the heap manager to raise an exception from any of the **Heap*** functions as soon as a corruption is detected. Here is the code that you need to execute:
>
> ```
> HeapSetInformation(NULL, HeapEnableTerminationOnCorruption, NULL, 0);
> ```
>
> The first parameter of **HeapSetInformation** is ignored when **HeapEnableTerminationOnCorruption** is passed for the second parameter: this strict policy is applied to all the heaps in the process. Also, once this feature is enabled for your process' heaps, it cannot be disabled.

If you expect to store executable code in the heap, you must use the last flag, **HEAP_CREATE_ENABLE_EXECUTE**. This is especially important with the Data Execution Prevention feature presented in Chapter 13, "Windows Memory Architecture." If you don't set this flag, Windows will raise an **EXCEPTION_ACCESS_VIOLATION** exception when you try to execute code from a memory block allocated on the heap.

The second parameter of **HeapCreate**, **dwInitialSize**, indicates the number of bytes initially committed to the heap. If necessary, **HeapCreate** rounds this value up to a multiple of the CPU's page size. The final parameter, **dwMaximumSize**, indicates the maximum size to which the heap can expand (the maximum amount of address space the system can reserve for the heap). If **dwMaximumSize** is greater than 0, you are creating a heap that has a maximum size. If you attempt to allocate a block that would cause the heap to go over its maximum, the attempt to allocate the block fails.

If **dwMaximumSize** is 0, you are creating a growable heap, which has no inherent limit. Allocating blocks from the heap simply makes the heap grow until physical storage is exhausted. If the heap is created successfully, **HeapCreate** returns a handle identifying the new heap. This handle is used by the other heap functions.

Allocating a Block of Memory from a Heap

Allocating a block of memory from a heap is simply a matter of calling **HeapAlloc**:

```
PVOID HeapAlloc(
   HANDLE hHeap,
   DWORD fdwFlags,
   SIZE_T dwBytes);
```

The first parameter, **hHeap**, identifies the handle of the heap from which an allocation should be made. The **dwBytes** parameter specifies the number of bytes that are to be allocated from the heap. The middle parameter, **fdwFlags**, allows you to specify flags that affect the allocation. Currently, only three flags are supported: **HEAP_ZERO_MEMORY**, **HEAP_GENERATE_EXCEPTIONS**, and **HEAP_NO_SERIALIZE**.

The purpose of the **HEAP_ZERO_MEMORY** flag should be fairly obvious. This flag causes the contents of the block to be filled with zeros before **HeapAlloc** returns. The second flag, **HEAP_GENERATE_EXCEPTIONS**, causes the **HeapAlloc** function to raise a software exception if insufficient memory is available in the heap to satisfy the request. When creating a heap with **HeapCreate**, you can specify the **HEAP_GENERATE_EXCEPTIONS** flag, which tells the heap that an exception should be raised when a block cannot be allocated. If you specify this flag when calling **HeapCreate**, you don't need to specify it when calling **HeapAlloc**. On the other hand, you might want to create the heap without using this flag. In this case, specifying this flag to **HeapAlloc** affects only the single call to **HeapAlloc**, not every call to this function.

If **HeapAlloc** fails and then raises an exception, the exception raised will be one of the two shown in Table 18-1.

Table 18-1   Exceptions Raised by HeapAlloc

Identifier	Meaning
STATUS_NO_MEMORY	The allocation attempt failed because of insufficient memory.
STATUS_ACCESS_VIOLATION	The allocation attempt failed because of heap corruption or improper function parameters.

If the block has been successfully allocated, **HeapAlloc** returns the address of the block. If the memory could not be allocated and **HEAP_GENERATE_EXCEPTIONS** was not specified, **HeapAlloc** returns **NULL**.

The last flag, **HEAP_NO_SERIALIZE**, allows you to force this individual call to **HeapAlloc** to not be serialized with other threads that are accessing the same heap. You should use this flag with extreme caution because the heap could become corrupted if other threads are manipulating the heap at the same time. Never use this flag when making an allocation from your process' default heap, as data could become corrupted: Other threads in your process could access the default heap at the same time.

> **Note**   It is recommended that you use **VirtualAlloc** when allocating large blocks (around 1 MB or more). Avoid using the heap functions for such large allocations.

If you are allocating a lot of blocks with different sizes, the default algorithm used by the heap manager to handle the internal allocations could lead to address space fragmentation: it is not possible to find a free block of a given size because all the available blocks don't have the right size. Since Windows XP and Windows Server 2003, you can force the operating system to use a *low-fragmentation heap* algorithm for the memory allocation. In the case of multiprocessor machines, the performance of the low-fragmentation heap is greatly enhanced. Here is the code you need to write to switch to a low-fragmentation heap:

```
ULONG HeapInformationValue = 2;
if (HeapSetInformation(
   hHeap, HeapCompatibilityInformation,
   &HeapInformationValue, sizeof(HeapInformationValue)) {
   // hHeap is turned into a low fragmentation heap
} else {
   // hHeap can't be turned into a low fragmentation heap.
   // Maybe because it has been created with the HEAP_NO_SERIALIZE flag
}
```

If you pass the handle returned by **GetProcessHeap** to **HeapSetInformation**, the default process heap is turned into a low-fragmentation heap. The call to **HeapSetInformation** fails if you pass a handle of a heap that has been created with the **HEAP_NO_SERIALIZE** flag. Notice that if your code is running under a debugger, certain heap debugging options are set that prevent the heap from becoming a low-fragmentation heap; you can turn off these debugging options by setting the **_NO_DEBUG_HEAP** environment variable to **1**. Note also that the heap manager itself monitors your allocations and can perform some internal optimizations. For example, a heap might automatically switch to a low-fragmentation heap if the heap manager detects that your application would benefit from it.

Changing the Size of a Block

Often it's necessary to alter the size of a memory block. Some applications initially allocate a larger than necessary block and then, after all the data has been placed into the block, reduce the size of the block. Some applications begin by allocating a small block of memory and then attempting to enlarge the block when more data needs to be copied into it. Resizing a memory block is accomplished by calling the **HeapReAlloc** function:

```
PVOID HeapReAlloc(
   HANDLE hHeap,
   DWORD fdwFlags,
   PVOID pvMem,
   SIZE_T dwBytes);
```

As always, the **hHeap** parameter indicates the heap containing the block you want to resize. The **fdwFlags** parameter specifies the flags that **HeapReAlloc** should use when attempting to resize the block. Only the following four flags are available: **HEAP_GENERATE_EXCEPTIONS**, **HEAP_NO_SERIALIZE**, **HEAP_ZERO_MEMORY**, and **HEAP_REALLOC_IN_PLACE_ONLY**.

The first two flags have the same meaning as when they are used with **HeapAlloc**. The **HEAP_ZERO_MEMORY** flag is useful only when you are resizing a block to make it larger. In this case, the additional bytes in the block will be zeroed. This flag has no effect if the block is being reduced.

The **HEAP_REALLOC_IN_PLACE_ONLY** flag tells **HeapReAlloc** that it is not allowed to move the memory block within the heap, which **HeapReAlloc** might attempt to do if the memory block were growing. If **HeapReAlloc** is able to enlarge the memory block without moving it, it will do so and return the original address of the memory block. On the other hand, if **HeapReAlloc** must move the contents of the block, the address of the new, larger block is returned. If the block is made smaller, **HeapReAlloc** returns the original address of the memory block. You specify the **HEAP_REALLOC_IN_PLACE_ONLY** flag if the block is part of a linked list or tree. In this case, other nodes in the list or tree might have pointers to this node, and relocating the node in the heap would corrupt the integrity of the linked list.

The remaining two parameters, **pvMem** and **dwBytes**, specify the current address of the block that you want to resize and the new size—in bytes—of the block. **HeapReAlloc** returns either the address of the new, resized block or **NULL** if the block cannot be resized.

Obtaining the Size of a Block

After a memory block has been allocated, the **HeapSize** function can be called to retrieve the actual size of the block:

```
SIZE_T HeapSize(
   HANDLE hHeap,
   DWORD fdwFlags,
   LPCVOID pvMem);
```

The **hHeap** parameter identifies the heap, and the **pvMem** parameter indicates the address of the block. The **fdwFlags** parameter can be either **0** or **HEAP_NO_SERIALIZE**.

Freeing a Block

When you no longer need the memory block, you can free it by calling **HeapFree**:

```
BOOL HeapFree(
   HANDLE hHeap,
   DWORD fdwFlags,
   PVOID pvMem);
```

HeapFree frees the memory block and returns **TRUE** if successful. The **fdwFlags** parameter can be either **0** or **HEAP_NO_SERIALIZE**. Calling this function might cause the heap manager to decommit some physical storage, but there are no guarantees.

Destroying a Heap

If your application no longer needs a heap that it created, you can destroy the heap by calling **HeapDestroy**:

```
BOOL HeapDestroy(HANDLE hHeap);
```

Calling **HeapDestroy** causes all the memory blocks contained within the heap to be freed, and it also causes the physical storage and reserved address space region occupied by the heap to be released back to the system. If the function is successful, **HeapDestroy** returns **TRUE**. If you don't explicitly destroy the heap before your process terminates, the system will destroy it for you. However, a heap is destroyed only when a process terminates. If a thread creates a heap, the heap won't be destroyed when the thread terminates.

The system will not allow the process' default heap to be destroyed until the process completely terminates. If you pass the handle to the process' default heap to **HeapDestroy**, the system simply ignores the call and returns **FALSE**.

Using Heaps with C++

One of the best ways to take advantage of heaps is to incorporate them into existing C++ programs. In C++, calling the **new** operator–instead of the normal C run-time routine **malloc**–performs class-object allocation. Then, when we no longer need the class object, the **delete** operator is called instead of the normal C run-time routine **free**. For example, let's say we have a class called **CSomeClass** and we want to allocate an instance of this class. To do this, we would use syntax similar to the following:

```
CSomeClass* pSomeClass = new CSomeClass;
```

When the C++ compiler examines this line, it first checks whether the **CSomeClass** class contains a member function for the **new** operator; if it does, the compiler generates code to call this function. If the compiler doesn't find a function overloading the **new** operator, the compiler generates code to call the standard C++ new operator function.

After you're done using the allocated object, you can destroy it by calling the **delete** operator:

```
delete pSomeClass;
```

By overloading the **new** and **delete** operators for our C++ class, we can easily take advantage of the heap functions. To do this, let's define our **CSomeClass** class in a header file like this:

```
class CSomeClass {
private:

    static HANDLE s_hHeap;
    static UINT s_uNumAllocsInHeap;

    // Other private data and member functions
    ...
```

```
public:
   void* operator new (size_t size);
   void operator delete (void* p);
   // Other public data and member functions
   ...
};
```

In this code fragment, I've declared two member variables, **s_hHeap** and **s_uNumAllocsInHeap**, as static variables. Because they are static, C++ will make all instances of **CSomeClass** share the same variables; that is, C++ will *not* allocate separate **s_hHeap** and **s_uNumAllocsInHeap** variables for each instance of the class that is created. This fact is important to us because we want all of our instances of **CSomeClass** to be allocated within the same heap.

The **s_hHeap** variable will contain the handle to the heap within which **CSomeClass** objects should be allocated. The **s_uNumAllocsInHeap** variable is simply a counter of how many **CSomeClass** objects are allocated within the heap. Every time a new **CSomeClass** object is allocated in the heap, **s_uNumAllocsInHeap** is incremented, and every time a **CSomeClass** object is destroyed, **s_uNumAllocsInHeap** is decremented. When **s_uNumAllocsInHeap** reaches **0**, the heap is no longer necessary and is freed. The code to manipulate the heap should be included in a .cpp file that looks like this:

```
HANDLE CSomeClass::s_hHeap = NULL;
UINT CSomeClass::s_uNumAllocsInHeap = 0;

void* CSomeClass::operator new (size_t size) {
   if (s_hHeap == NULL) {
      // Heap does not exist; create it.
      s_hHeap = HeapCreate(HEAP_NO_SERIALIZE, 0, 0);

      if (s_hHeap == NULL)
         return(NULL);
   }
   // The heap exists for CSomeClass objects.
   void* p = HeapAlloc(s_hHeap, 0, size);

   if (p != NULL) {
      // Memory was allocated successfully; increment
      // the count of CSomeClass objects in the heap.
      s_uNumAllocsInHeap++;
   }

   // Return the address of the allocated CSomeClass object.
   return(p);
}
```

Notice that I first defined the two static member variables, **s_hHeap** and **s_uNumAllocsInHeap**, at the top and initialized them as **NULL** and **0**, respectively.

The C++ **new** operator receives one parameter—**size**. This parameter indicates the number of bytes required to hold a **CSomeClass** object. The first task for our **new** operator function is to create a heap if one hasn't been created already. This is simply a matter of checking the **s_hHeap** variable to see whether it is **NULL**. If it is, a new heap is created by calling **HeapCreate**, and the handle that

HeapCreate returns is saved in **s_hHeap** so that the next call to the **new** operator will not create another heap but rather will use the heap we have just created.

When I called the **HeapCreate** function in the preceding code sample, I used the **HEAP_NO_SERIALIZE** flag because the remainder of the sample code is not multithread-safe. The other two parameters in the call to **HeapCreate** indicate the initial size and the maximum size of the heap, respectively. I chose **0** and **0** here. The first **0** means that the heap has no initial size; the second **0** means that the heap expands as needed. Depending on your needs, you might want to change either or both of these values.

You might think it would be worthwhile to pass the **size** parameter to the **new** operator function as the second parameter to **HeapCreate**. In this way, you could initialize the heap so that it is large enough to contain one instance of the class. Then the first time that **HeapAlloc** is called, it would execute faster because the heap wouldn't have to resize itself to hold the class instance. Unfortunately, things don't always work the way you want them to. Because each allocated memory block within the heap has an associated overhead, the call to **HeapAlloc** will still have to resize the heap so that it is large enough to contain the one class instance and its associated overhead.

Once the heap has been created, new **CSomeClass** objects can be allocated from it using **Heap-Alloc**. The first parameter is the handle to the heap, and the second parameter is the size of the **CSomeClass** object. **HeapAlloc** returns the address to the allocated block.

When the allocation is performed successfully, I increment the **s_uNumAllocsInHeap** variable so that I know there is one more allocation in the heap. The last thing the new operator does is return the address of the newly allocated **CSomeClass** object.

Well, that's it for creating a new **CSomeClass** object. Let's turn our attention to destroying a **CSomeClass** object when our application no longer needs it. This is the responsibility of the **delete** operator function, coded as follows:

```
void CSomeClass::operator delete (void* p) {
   if (HeapFree(s_hHeap, 0, p)) {
      // Object was deleted successfully.
      s_uNumAllocsInHeap--;
   }

   if (s_uNumAllocsInHeap == 0) {
      // If there are no more objects in the heap,
      // destroy the heap.
      if (HeapDestroy(s_hHeap)) {
         // Set the heap handle to NULL so that the new operator
         // will know to create a new heap if a new CSomeClass
         // object is created.
         s_hHeap = NULL;
      }
   }
}
```

The **delete** operator function receives only one parameter: the address of the object being deleted. The first thing the function does is call **HeapFree**, passing it the handle of the heap and the address of the object to be freed. If the object is freed successfully, **s_uNumAllocsInHeap** is decremented, indicating that one fewer **CSomeClass** object is in the heap. Next the function checks whether **s_uNumAllocsInHeap** is **0**. If it is, the function calls **HeapDestroy**, passing it the heap handle. If the heap is destroyed successfully, **s_hHeap** is set to **NULL**. This is extremely important because our program might attempt to allocate another **CSomeClass** object sometime in the future. When it does, the new operator will be called and will examine the **s_hHeap** variable to determine whether it should use an existing heap or create a new one.

This example demonstrates a convenient scheme for using multiple heaps. The example is easy to set up and can be incorporated into several of your classes. You will probably want to give some thought to inheritance, however. If you derive a new class using **CSomeClass** as a base class, the new class will inherit **CSomeClass**'s **new** and **delete** operators. The new class will also inherit **CSomeClass**'s heap, which means that when the **new** operator is applied to the derived class, the memory for the derived class object will be allocated from the same heap that **CSomeClass** is using. Depending on your situation, this might or might not be what you want. If the objects are very different in size, you might be setting yourself up for a situation in which the heap could fragment badly. You might also be making it harder to track down bugs in your code, as mentioned in "Component Protection" and "More Efficient Memory Management" on page 521.

If you want to use a separate heap for derived classes, simply duplicate what I did in the **CSomeClass** class. More specifically, include another set of **s_hHeap** and **s_uNumAllocsInHeap** variables, and copy the code over for the **new** and **delete** operators. When you compile it, the compiler will see that you have overloaded the **new** and **delete** operators for the derived class and will make calls to those functions instead of to the ones in the base class.

The only advantage to not creating a heap for each class is that you won't need to devote overhead and memory to each heap. However, the amount of overhead and memory the heaps tie up is not great and is probably worth the potential gains. The compromise might be to have each class use its own heap and to let derived classes share the base class's heap when your application has been well tested and is close to shipping. But be aware that fragmentation might still be a problem.

Miscellaneous Heap Functions

In addition to the heap functions I've already mentioned, Windows offers several more. In this section, I'll just briefly mention them.

The ToolHelp functions (mentioned at the end of Chapter 4, "Processes") allow you to enumerate a process' heaps as well as the allocations within those heaps. For more information, look up the following functions in the Platform SDK documentation: **Heap32First**, **Heap32Next**, **Heap32ListFirst**, and **Heap32ListNext**.

Because a process can have multiple heaps within its address space, the **GetProcessHeaps** function allows you to get the handles of the existing heaps:

```
DWORD GetProcessHeaps(
   DWORD dwNumHeaps,
   PHANDLE phHeaps);
```

To call **GetProcessHeaps**, you must first allocate an array of **HANDLE**s and then call the function as follows:

```
HANDLE hHeaps[25];
DWORD dwHeaps = GetProcessHeaps(25, hHeaps);
if (dwHeaps > 25) {
   // More heaps are in this process than we expected.
} else {
   // hHeaps[0] through hHeap[dwHeaps - 1]
   // identify the existing heaps.
}
```

Note that the handle of your process' default heap is also included in the array of heap handles when this function returns. The **HeapValidate** function validates the integrity of a heap:

```
BOOL HeapValidate(
   HANDLE hHeap,
   DWORD fdwFlags,
   LPCVOID pvMem);
```

You will usually call this function by passing a heap handle, a flag of **0** (the only other legal flag is **HEAP_NO_SERIALIZE**), and **NULL** for **pvMem**. This function will then walk the blocks within the heap, making sure that no blocks are corrupt. To make the function execute faster, you might want to pass the address of a specific block for the **pvMem** parameter. Doing so causes the function to check the validity of only the single block.

To coalesce free blocks within a heap and also decommit any pages of storage that do not contain allocated heap blocks, you can call

```
UINT HeapCompact(
   HANDLE hHeap,
   DWORD fdwFlags);
```

Normally, you'll pass **0** for the **fdwFlags** parameter, but you can also pass **HEAP_NO_SERIALIZE**.

The next two functions, **HeapLock** and **HeapUnlock**, are used together:

```
BOOL HeapLock(HANDLE hHeap);
BOOL HeapUnlock(HANDLE hHeap);
```

These functions are for thread synchronization purposes. When you call **HeapLock**, the calling thread becomes the owner of the specified heap. If any other thread calls a heap function (specifying the same heap handle), the system will suspend the calling thread and not allow it to wake until the heap is unlocked by calling **HeapUnlock**.

Functions such as **HeapAlloc**, **HeapSize**, **HeapFree**, and so on call **HeapLock** and **HeapUnlock** internally to make sure that access to the heap is serialized. It would be unusual for you ever to have to call **HeapLock** or **HeapUnlock** yourself.

The final heap function is **HeapWalk**:

```
BOOL HeapWalk(
   HANDLE hHeap,
   PPROCESS_HEAP_ENTRY pHeapEntry);
```

This function is useful for debugging purposes only. It allows you to walk the contents of a heap. You will call this function multiple times. Each time, you'll pass in the address of a **PROCESS_HEAP_ENTRY** structure that you must allocate and initialize:

```
typedef struct _PROCESS_HEAP_ENTRY {
    PVOID lpData;
    DWORD cbData;
    BYTE cbOverhead;
    BYTE iRegionIndex;
    WORD wFlags;
    union {
        struct {
            HANDLE hMem;
            DWORD dwReserved[ 3 ];
        } Block;
        struct {
            DWORD dwCommittedSize;
            DWORD dwUnCommittedSize;
            LPVOID lpFirstBlock;
            LPVOID lpLastBlock;
        } Region;
    };
} PROCESS_HEAP_ENTRY, *LPPROCESS_HEAP_ENTRY, *PPROCESS_HEAP_ENTRY;
```

When you start enumerating the blocks in the heap, you'll have to set the **lpData** member to **NULL**. This tells **HeapWalk** to initialize the members inside the structure. You can examine the members of the structure after each successful call to **HeapWalk**. To get to the next block in the heap, you just call **HeapWalk** again, passing the same heap handle and the address of the **PROCESS_HEAP_ENTRY** structure you passed on the previous call. When **HeapWalk** returns **FALSE**, there are no more blocks in the heap. See the Platform SDK documentation for a description of the members in the structure.

You will probably want to use the **HeapLock** and **HeapUnlock** functions around your **HeapWalk** loop so that other threads cannot allocate and free blocks of memory inside the heap while you're walking it.

Part IV
Dynamic-Link Libraries

Chapter 19

DLL Basics

Dynamic-link libraries (DLLs) have been the cornerstone of Microsoft Windows since the first version of the operating system. All the functions in the Windows application programming interface (API) are contained in DLLs. The three most important DLLs are Kernel32.dll, which contains functions for managing memory, processes, and threads; User32.dll, which contains functions for performing user-interface tasks such as window creation and message sending; and GDI32.dll, which contains functions for drawing graphical images and displaying text.

Windows also comes with several other DLLs that offer functions for performing more specialized tasks. For example, AdvAPI32.dll contains functions for object security, registry manipulation, and event logging; ComDlg32.dll contains the common dialog boxes (such as File Open and File Save); and ComCtl32.DLL supports all the common window controls.

In this chapter, you'll learn how to create DLLs for your own applications. Here are some reasons for using DLLs:

They extend the features of an application. Because DLLs can be dynamically loaded into a process' address space, an application can determine at run time what actions to perform and then load the code to execute those actions on demand. For example, a DLL is useful when one company creates a product and wants to allow other companies to extend or enhance the product.

They simplify project management. If different groups work on different modules during the development process, the project is easier to manage. However, an application should ship with as few files as possible. I know of one company that shipped a product with one hundred DLLs—up to five DLLs per programmer. The application's initialization time was horribly slow because the system had to open one hundred disk files before the program could do anything.

They help conserve memory. If two or more applications use the same DLL, the DLL has its pages in RAM once and the pages are shared by all of the applications. The C/C++ run-time library is a perfect example. Many applications use this library. If all these applications link to the static library, the code for functions such as **_tcscpy**, **malloc**, and so on exist in memory multiple times. However, if all these applications link to the DLL C/C++ run-time library, the code for these functions is in memory only once, which means that memory is used more efficiently.

They facilitate resource sharing. DLLs can contain resources such as dialog box templates, strings, icons, and bitmaps. Multiple applications can use DLLs to share these resources.

They facilitate localization. Applications frequently use DLLs to localize themselves. For example, an application that contains only code and no user interface components can load the DLL containing localized user interface components.

They help resolve platform differences.   The various versions of Windows offer different functions. Frequently, developers want to call new functions if they exist on the host version. However, if your source code contains a call to a new function and your application is about to run on a version of Windows that doesn't offer that function, the operating system loader will refuse to run your process. This is true even if you never actually call the function. If you keep these new functions in a DLL, however, applications can load on an older version of Windows. Of course, you still cannot successfully call the function.

They can serve special purposes.   Windows makes certain features available only to DLLs. For example, you can install certain hooks (set using **SetWindowsHookEx** and **SetWinEvent-Hook**) only if the hook notification function is contained in a DLL. You can extend Windows Explorer's shell by creating COM objects that must live inside a DLL. The same is true for ActiveX controls that can be loaded by a Web browser to create rich Web pages.

DLLs and a Process' Address Space

It is often easier to create a DLL than to create an application because a DLL usually consists of a set of autonomous functions that any application can use. There is usually no support code for processing message loops or creating windows within DLLs. A DLL is simply a set of source code modules, with each module containing a set of functions that an application (executable file) or another DLL will call. After all the source code files have been compiled, they are linked by the linker just as an application's executable file would be. However, for a DLL you must specify the **/DLL** switch to the linker. This switch causes the linker to emit slightly different information into the resulting DLL file image so that the operating system loader recognizes the file image as a DLL rather than an application.

Before an application (or another DLL) can call functions in a DLL, the DLL's file image must be mapped into the calling process' address space. You can do this using one of two methods: implicit load-time linking or explicit run-time linking. Implicit linking is discussed later in this chapter; explicit linking is discussed in Chapter 20, "DLL Advanced Techniques."

Once a DLL's file image is mapped into the calling process' address space, the DLL's functions are available to all the threads running within the process. In fact, the DLL loses almost all of its identity as a DLL: To the threads in the process, the DLL's code and data simply look like additional code and data that happen to be in the process' address space. When a thread calls a DLL function, the DLL function looks at the thread's stack to retrieve its passed parameters and uses the thread's stack for any local variables that it needs. In addition, any objects created by code in the DLL's functions are owned by the calling thread or process—a DLL never owns anything.

For example, if **VirtualAlloc** is called by a function in a DLL, the region of address space is reserved from the address space of the calling thread's process. If the DLL is later unmapped from the process' address space, the address space region remains reserved because the system does not keep track of the fact that a function in the DLL reserved the region. The reserved region is owned by the process and is freed only if a thread somehow calls the **VirtualFree** function or if the process terminates.

As you know, the global and static variables of an executable file are not shared between multiple running instances of the same executable. Windows ensures this by using the copy-on-write mechanism discussed in Chapter 13, "Windows Memory Architecture." Global and static variables in a DLL are handled in exactly the same way. When one process maps a DLL image file into its address space, the system creates instances of the global and static data variables as well.

Note   It is important to realize that a single address space consists of one executable module and several DLL modules. Some of these modules can link to a static version of the C/C++ run-time library, some of these modules might link to a DLL version of the C/C++ run-time library, and some of these modules (if not written in C/C++) might not require the C/C++ run-time library at all. Many developers make a common mistake because they forget that several C/C++ run-time libraries can be present in a single address space. Examine the following code:

```
VOID EXEFunc() {
   PVOID pv = DLLFunc();
   // Access the storage pointed to by pv...
   // Assumes that pv is in EXE's C/C++ run-time heap
   free(pv);
}

PVOID DLLFunc() {
   // Allocate block from DLL's C/C++ run-time heap
   return(malloc(100));
}
```

So, what do you think? Does the preceding code work correctly? Is the block allocated by the DLL's function freed by the EXE's function? The answer is: maybe. The code shown does not give you enough information. If both the EXE and the DLL link to the DLL C/C++ run-time library, the code works just fine. However, if one or both of the modules link to the static C/C++ run-time library, the call to **free** fails. I have seen developers write code similar to this too many times, and it has burned them all.

There is an easy fix for this problem. When a module offers a function that allocates memory, the module must also offer a function that frees memory. Let me rewrite the code just shown:

```
VOID EXEFunc() {
   PVOID pv = DLLFunc();
   // Access the storage pointed to by pv...
   // Makes no assumptions about C/C++ run-time heap
   DLLFreeFunc(pv);
}

PVOID DLLFunc() {
   // Allocate block from DLL's C/C++ run-time heap
   PVOID pv = malloc(100);
   return(pv);
}

BOOL DLLFreeFunc(PVOID pv) {
   // Free block from DLL's C/C++ run-time heap
   return(free(pv));
}
```

This code is correct and will always work. When you write a module, don't forget that functions in other modules might not even be written in C/C++ and therefore might not use **malloc** and **free** for memory allocations. Be careful not to make these assumptions in your code. By the way, this same argument holds true for the C++ **new** and **delete** operators while calling **malloc** and **free** internally.

The Overall Picture

To fully understand how DLLs work and how you and the system use DLLs, let's start out by examining the whole picture. Figure 19-1 summarizes how the components fit together.

For now, we'll concentrate on how executable and DLL modules implicitly link to one another. Implicit linking is by far the most common type of linking. Windows also supports explicit linking (which we'll discuss in Chapter 20).

BUILDING THE DLL

1) Header with exported prototypes/structures/symbols.
2) C/C++ source files implementing exported functions/variables.
3) Compiler produces .obj file for each C/C++ source file.
4) Linker combines .obj module producing DLL.
5) Linker also produces .lib file if at least one function/variable is exported.

BUILDING THE EXE

6) Header with imported prototypes/structures/symbols.
7) C/C++ source files referencing imported functions/variables.
8) Compiler produces .obj file for each C/C++ source file.
9) Linker combines .obj modules resolving references to imported functions/variables using .lib file producing .exe (containing import table-list of required DLLs and imported symbols).

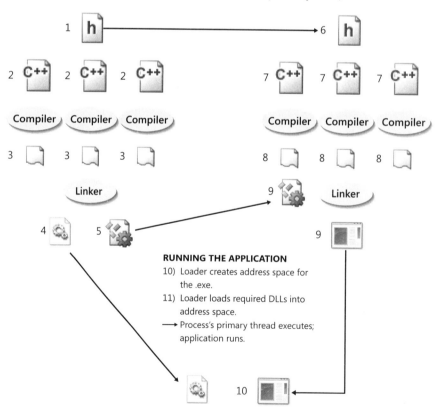

RUNNING THE APPLICATION

10) Loader creates address space for the .exe.
11) Loader loads required DLLs into address space.
→ Process's primary thread executes; application runs.

Figure 19-1   How a DLL is created and implicitly linked by an application

As you can see in Figure 19-1, several files and components come into play when a module (such as an executable file) makes use of functions and variables in a DLL. To simplify the discussion, I'll refer to "executable modules" as importing functions and variables from a DLL and "DLL modules" as exporting functions and variables for an executable module. However, be aware that DLL modules can (and often do) import functions and variables that are contained in other DLL modules.

To build an executable module that imports functions and variables from a DLL module, you must first build the DLL module. Then you can build the executable module.

Building a DLL requires the following steps:

1. You must first create a header file, which contains the function prototypes, structures, and symbols that you want to export from the DLL. This header file is included by all of your DLL's source code modules to help build the DLL. As you'll see later, this same header file is required when you build an executable module (or modules) that uses the functions and variables contained in your DLL.

2. You create the C/C++ source code module (or modules) that implements the functions and variables that you want in the DLL module. Because these source code modules are not required to build an executable module, the DLL company's source code can remain a company secret.

3. Building the DLL module causes the compiler to process each source code module, producing an .obj module (one .obj module per source code module).

4. After all the .obj modules are created, the linker combines the contents of all the .obj modules and produces a single DLL image file. This image file (or module) contains all the binary code and global/static data variables for the DLL. This file is required in order to execute the executable module.

5. If the linker detects that the DLL's source code module exports at least one function or variable, the linker also produces a single .lib file. This .lib file is small because it contains no functions or variables. It simply lists all the exported function and variable symbol names. This file is required in order to build the executable module.

    Once you build the DLL module, you can build the executable module by following these steps:

6. In all the source modules that reference functions, variables, data structures, or symbols, you must include the header file created by the DLL developer.

7. You create the C/C++ source code module (or modules) that implements the functions and variables that you want in the executable module. The code can, of course, reference functions and variables defined in the DLL's header file.

8. Building the executable module causes the compiler to process each source code module, producing an .obj module (one .obj module per source code module).

9. After all the .obj modules are created, the linker combines the contents of all the .obj modules and produces a single executable image file. This image file (or module) contains all the binary code and global/static data variables for the executable. The executable module also

contains an import section that lists all the DLL module names required by this executable. (See Chapter 17, "Memory-Mapped Files," for more on sections.) In addition, for each DLL name listed, the section indicates which function and variable symbols are referenced by the executable's binary code. The operating system loader parses the import section, as you'll see in a moment.

Once the DLL and the executable modules are built, a process can execute. When you attempt to run the executable module, the operating system's loader performs the following step.

10. The loader creates a virtual address space for the new process. The executable module is mapped into the new process' address space. The loader parses the executable module's import section. For every DLL name listed in the section, the loader locates the DLL module on the user's system and maps that DLL into the process' address space. Note that because a DLL module can import functions and variables from another DLL module, a DLL module might have its own import section. To fully initialize a process, the loader parses every module's import section and maps all required DLL modules into the process' address space. As you can see, initializing a process can be time consuming.

Once the executable module and all the DLL modules have been mapped into the process' address space, the process' primary thread can start executing and the application can run. The next few sections go into the process in further detail.

Building the DLL Module

When you create a DLL, you create a set of functions that an executable module (or other DLLs) can call. A DLL can export variables, functions, or C++ classes to other modules. In real life, you should avoid exporting variables because this removes a level of abstraction in your code and makes it more difficult to maintain your DLL's code. In addition, C++ classes can be exported only if the modules importing the C++ class are compiled using a compiler from the same vendor. For this reason, you should also avoid exporting C++ classes unless you know that the executable module developers use the same tools as the DLL module developers.

When you create a DLL, you should first establish a header file that contains the variables (type and name) and functions (prototype and name) that you want to export. This header file must also define any symbols and data structures that are used with the exported functions and variables. All of your DLL's source code modules should include this header file. Also, you must distribute this header file so that it can be included in any source code that might import these functions or variables. Having a single header file used by the DLL builder and the executable builder makes maintenance much easier.

Here is how you should code the single header file to include in both the executable and the DLL's source code files:

```
/**********************************************************************
Module:  MyLib.h
**********************************************************************/


#ifdef MYLIBAPI

// MYLIBAPI should be defined in all of the DLL's source
// code modules before this header file is included.

// All functions/variables are being exported.

#else

// This header file is included by an EXE source code module.
// Indicate that all functions/variables are being imported.
#define MYLIBAPI extern "C" __declspec(dllimport)

#endif

////////////////////////////////////////////////////////////////////

// Define any data structures and symbols here.

////////////////////////////////////////////////////////////////////

// Define exported variables here. (NOTE: Avoid exporting variables.)
MYLIBAPI int g_nResult;

////////////////////////////////////////////////////////////////////

// Define exported function prototypes here.
MYLIBAPI int Add(int nLeft, int nRight);

/////////////////////////// End of File ///////////////////////////
```

In each of your DLL's source code files, you should include the header file as follows:

```
/**********************************************************************
Module:  MyLibFile1.cpp
**********************************************************************/


// Include the standard Windows and C-Runtime header files here.
#include <windows.h>


// This DLL source code file exports functions and variables.
#define MYLIBAPI extern "C" __declspec(dllexport)

// Include the exported data structures, symbols, functions, and variables.
#include "MyLib.h"
```

```
////////////////////////////////////////////////////////////////////////

// Place the code for this DLL source code file here.
int g_nResult;


int Add(int nLeft, int nRight) {
   g_nResult = nLeft + nRight;
   return(g_nResult);
}

/////////////////////////// End of File ///////////////////////////////
```

When the DLL source code file just shown is compiled, **MYLIBAPI** is defined using **__declspec(dllexport)** before the MyLib.h header file. When the compiler sees **__declspec(dllexport)** modifying a variable, function, or C++ class, it knows that this variable, function, or C++ class is to be exported from the resulting DLL module. Notice that the **MYLIBAPI** identifier is placed in the header file before the definition of the variable to export and before the function to export.

Also notice that inside the source code file (MyLibFile1.cpp), the **MYLIBAPI** identifier does not appear before the exported variable and function. The **MYLIBAPI** identifier is not necessary here because the compiler remembers which variables or functions to export when it parses the header file.

You'll notice that the **MYLIBAPI** symbol includes the **extern "C"** modifier. You should use this modifier only if you are writing C++ code, not straight C code. Normally, C++ compilers mangle function and variable names, which can lead to severe linker problems. For example, imagine writing a DLL in C++ and an executable in straight C. When you build the DLL, the function name is mangled, but when you build the executable, the function name is not mangled. When the linker attempts to link the executable, it will complain that the executable refers to a symbol that does not exist. Using **extern "C"** tells the compiler not to mangle the variable or function names and thereby make the variable or function accessible to executable modules written in C, C++, or any other programming language.

So now you see how the DLL's source code files use this header file. But what about the executable's source code files? Well, executable source code files should not define **MYLIBAPI** before this header file. Because **MYLIBAPI** is not defined, the header file defines **MYLIBAPI** as **__declspec(dllimport)**. The compiler sees that the executable's source code imports variables and functions from the DLL module.

If you examine Microsoft's standard Windows header files, such as WinBase.h, you'll see that Microsoft uses basically the same technique that I've just described.

What Exporting Really Means

The only truly interesting thing I introduced in the previous section was the **__declspec(dllexport)** modifier. When Microsoft's C/C++ compiler sees this modifier before a variable, function prototype, or C++ class, it embeds some additional information in the resulting .obj file. The linker parses this information when all the .obj files for the DLL are linked.

When the DLL is linked, the linker detects this embedded information about the exported variable, function, or class and automatically produces a .lib file. This .lib file contains the list of symbols exported by the DLL. This .lib file is, of course, required to link any executable module that references this DLL's exported symbols. In addition to creating the .lib file, the linker embeds a table of exported symbols in the resulting DLL file. This *export section* contains the list (in alphabetical order) of exported variables, functions, and class symbols. The linker also places the relative virtual address (RVA), indicating where each symbol can be found in the DLL module.

Using the Microsoft Visual Studio DumpBin.exe utility (with the **-exports** switch), you can see what a DLL's export section looks like. The following is a fragment of Kernel32.dll's export section. (I've removed some of DUMPBIN's output so that it won't occupy too many pages in this book.)

```
C:\Windows\System32>DUMPBIN -exports Kernel32.DLL

Microsoft (R) COFF/PE Dumper Version 8.00.50727.42
Copyright (C) Microsoft Corporation. All rights reserved.


Dump of file Kernel32.DLL

File Type: DLL

  Section contains the following exports for KERNEL32.dll

    00000000 characteristics
    4549AD66 time date stamp Thu Nov 02 09:33:42 2006
        0.00 version
           1 ordinal base
        1207 number of functions
        1207 number of names

    ordinal hint RVA       name

          3    0           AcquireSRWLockExclusive (forwarded to
                           NTDLL.RtlAcquireSRWLockExclusive)
          4    1           AcquireSRWLockShared (forwarded to
                           NTDLL.RtlAcquireSRWLockShared)
          5    2 0002734D  ActivateActCtx = _ActivateActCtx@8
          6    3 000088E9  AddAtomA = _AddAtomA@4
          7    4 0001FD7D  AddAtomW = _AddAtomW@4
          8    5 000A30AF  AddConsoleAliasA = _AddConsoleAliasA@12
          9    6 000A306E  AddConsoleAliasW = _AddConsoleAliasW@12
         10    7 00087935  AddLocalAlternateComputerNameA =
                           _AddLocalAlternateComputerNameA@8
         11    8 0008784E  AddLocalAlternateComputerNameW =
                           _AddLocalAlternateComputerNameW@8
         12    9 00026159  AddRefActCtx = _AddRefActCtx@4
         13    A 00094456  AddSIDToBoundaryDescriptor =
                           _AddSIDToBoundaryDescriptor@8
        ...
       1205  4B4 0004328A  lstrlen = _lstrlenA@4
       1206  4B5 0004328A  lstrlenA = _lstrlenA@4
       1207  4B6 00049D35  lstrlenW = _lstrlenW@4
```

```
Summary

    3000  .data
    A000  .reloc
    1000  .rsrc
    C9000 .text
```

As you can see, the symbols are in alphabetical order and the numbers under the RVA column identify the offset in the DLL file image where the exported symbol can be found. The ordinal column is for backward compatibility with 16-bit Windows source code and should not be used in modern-day applications. The hint column is used by the system to improve performance and is not important for our discussion.

> **Note**   Many developers are used to exporting DLL functions by assigning functions an ordinal value. This is especially true of those who come from a 16-bit Windows background. However, Microsoft does not publish ordinal values for the system DLLs. When your executable or DLL links to any Windows function, Microsoft wants you to link using the symbol's name. If you link by ordinal, you run the risk that your application will not run on other or future Windows platforms.
>
> I asked Microsoft why it is getting away from ordinals and got this response: "We feel that the Portable Executable file format provides the benefit of ordinals (fast lookup) with the flexibility of import by name. We can add functions at any time. Ordinals are very hard to manage in a large project with multiple implementations."
>
> You can use ordinals for any DLLs that you create and have your executable files link to these DLLs by ordinal. Microsoft guarantees that this method will work even in future versions of the operating system. However, I am avoiding the use of ordinals in my own work and will link by name only from now on.

Creating DLLs for Use with Non–Visual C++ Tools

If you are using Microsoft Visual C++ to build both a DLL and an executable that will link to the DLL, you can safely skip this entire section. However, if you are building a DLL with Visual C++ that is to be linked with an executable file built using any vendor's tools, you must perform some additional work.

I already mentioned the issue of using the **extern "C"** modifier when you mix C and C++ programming. I also mentioned the issue of C++ classes and how because of name mangling you must use the same compiler vendor's tools. Another issue comes up even when you use straight C programming with multiple tool vendors. The problem is that Microsoft's C compiler mangles C functions even if you're not using C++ at all. This happens only if your function uses the **__stdcall** (WINAPI) calling convention. Unfortunately, this calling convention is the most popular type. When C functions are exported using **__stdcall**, Microsoft's compiler mangles the function names by prepending a leading underscore and adding a suffix of an @ sign followed by a number that indicates the count of bytes that are passed to the function as parameters. For example, this function is exported as **_MyFunc@8** in the DLL's export section.

```
__declspec(dllexport) LONG __stdcall MyFunc(int a, int b);
```

If you build an executable using another vendor's tools, it will attempt to link to a function named **MyFunc**—a function that does not exist in the Microsoft compiler–built DLL—and the link will fail.

To build a DLL with Microsoft's tools that is to be linked with other compiler vendors' tools, you must tell Microsoft's compiler to export the function names without mangling. You can do this in two ways. The first way is to create a .def file for your project and include in the .def file an **EXPORTS** section like this:

```
EXPORTS
   MyFunc
```

When Microsoft's linker parses this .def file, it sees that both **_MyFunc@8** and **MyFunc** are being exported. Because these two function names match (except for the mangling), the linker exports the function using the .def file name of **MyFunc** and does not export a function with the name of **_MyFunc@8** at all.

Now, you might think that if you build an executable with Microsoft's tools and attempt to link to the DLL containing the unmangled name, the linker will fail because it will try to link to a function called **_MyFunc@8**. Well, you'll be pleased to know that Microsoft's linker does the right thing and links the executable to the function named **MyFunc**.

If you want to avoid using a .def file, you can use the second way of exporting an unmangled version of the function. Inside one of the DLL's source code modules, you add a line like this:

```
#pragma comment(linker, "/export:MyFunc=_MyFunc@8")
```

This line causes the compiler to emit a linker directive telling the linker that a function called **MyFunc** is to be exported with the same entry point as a function called **_MyFunc@8**. This second technique is a bit less convenient than the first because you must mangle the function name yourself to construct the line. Also, when you use this second technique, the DLL actually exports two symbols identifying a single function—**MyFunc** and **_MyFunc@8**—whereas the first technique exports only the **MyFunc** symbol. The second technique doesn't buy you much—it just lets you avoid using a .def file.

Building the Executable Module

The following code fragment shows an executable source code file that imports the DLL's exported symbols and references those symbols in the code:

```
/*****************************************************************************
Module:  MyExeFile1.cpp
*****************************************************************************/

// Include the standard Windows and C-Runtime header files here.
#include <windows.h>
#include <strsafe.h>
#include <stdlib.h>

// Include the exported data structures, symbols, functions, and variables.
#include "MyLib\MyLib.h"

///////////////////////////////////////////////////////////////////////////////
```

```
int WINAPI _tWinMain(HINSTANCE, HINSTANCE, LPSTR, int) {

   int nLeft = 10, nRight = 25;

   TCHAR sz[100];
   StringCchPrintf(sz, _countof(sz), TEXT("%d + %d = %d"),
      nLeft, nRight, Add(nLeft, nRight));
   MessageBox(NULL, sz, TEXT("Calculation"), MB_OK);

   StringCchPrintf(sz, _countof(sz),
      TEXT("The result from the last Add is: %d"), g_nResult);
   MessageBox(NULL, sz, TEXT("Last Result"), MB_OK);
   return(0);
}

/////////////////////////// End of File ///////////////////////////
```

When you develop executable source code files, you must include the DLL's header file. Without it, the imported symbols will not be defined and the compiler will issue a lot of warnings and errors.

The executable source code file should not define **MYLIBAPI** before the DLL's header file. When the preceding executable source code file is compiled, **MYLIBAPI** is defined using **__declspec(dllimport)** by the MyLib.h header file. When the compiler sees **__declspec(dllimport)** modifying a variable, function, or C++ class, it knows that this symbol is to be imported from some DLL module. It doesn't know which DLL module, and it doesn't care. The compiler just wants to be sure that you access these imported symbols in the right way. Now, in the source code, you can simply refer to the imported symbols and everything will work.

Next, the linker must combine all the .obj modules to create the resulting executable module. The linker must determine which DLLs contain all the imported symbols that the code references. So you have to pass the DLL's .lib file to the linker. As mentioned before, the .lib file simply contains the list of symbols that a DLL module exports. The linker simply wants to know that a referenced symbol exists and which DLL module contains that symbol. If the linker resolves all the external symbol references, an executable module is born.

What Importing Really Means

The previous section introduced the **__declspec(dllimport)** modifier. When you import a symbol, you do not have to use the **__declspec(dllimport)** keyword—you can simply use the standard C **extern** keyword. However, the compiler can produce slightly more efficient code if it knows ahead of time that the symbol you are referencing will be imported from a DLL's .lib file. So I highly recommend that you use the **__declspec(dllimport)** keyword for imported function and data symbols. Microsoft does this for you when you call any of the standard Windows functions.

When the linker resolves the imported symbols, it embeds a special section called the *import section* in the resulting executable module. The import section lists the DLL modules required by this module and the symbols referenced from each DLL module.

Using Visual Studio's DumpBin.exe utility (with the **-imports** switch), you can see what a module's import section looks like. The following is a fragment of Calc.exe's import section. (Again, I've removed some of DUMPBIN's output so that it would not occupy too many pages in this book.)

```
C:\Windows\System32>DUMPBIN -imports Calc.exe

Microsoft (R) COFF/PE Dumper Version 8.00.50727.42
Copyright (C) Microsoft Corporation.  All rights reserved.


Dump of file calc.exe

File Type: EXECUTABLE IMAGE

  Section contains the following imports:

    SHELL32.dll
                10010CC Import Address Table
                1013208 Import Name Table
                FFFFFFFF time date stamp
                FFFFFFFF Index of first forwarder reference

      766EA0A5     110 ShellAboutW

    ADVAPI32.dll
                1001000 Import Address Table
                101313C Import Name Table
                FFFFFFFF time date stamp
                FFFFFFFF Index of first forwarder reference

      77CA8229     236 RegCreateKeyW
      77CC802D     278 RegSetValueExW
      77CD632E     268 RegQueryValueExW
      77CD64CC     22A RegCloseKey
  ...
    ntdll.dll
                1001250 Import Address Table
                101338C Import Name Table
                FFFFFFFF time date stamp
                FFFFFFFF Index of first forwarder reference

      77F0850D     548 WinSqmAddToStream

    KERNEL32.dll
                1001030 Import Address Table
                101316C Import Name Table
                FFFFFFFF time date stamp
                FFFFFFFF Index of first forwarder reference

      77E01890     24F GetSystemTimeAsFileTime
      77E47B0D     1AA GetCurrentProcessId
      77E2AA46     170 GetCommandLineW
      77E0918D     230 GetProfileIntW
  ...
```

```
Header contains the following bound import information:
   Bound to SHELL32.dll [4549BDB4] Thu Nov 02 10:43:16 2006
   Bound to ADVAPI32.dll [4549BCD2] Thu Nov 02 10:39:30 2006
   Bound to OLEAUT32.dll [4549BD95] Thu Nov 02 10:42:45 2006
   Bound to ole32.dll [4549BD92] Thu Nov 02 10:42:42 2006
   Bound to ntdll.dll [4549BDC9] Thu Nov 02 10:43:37 2006
   Bound to KERNEL32.dll [4549BD80] Thu Nov 02 10:42:24 2006
   Bound to GDI32.dll [4549BCD3] Thu Nov 02 10:39:31 2006
   Bound to USER32.dll [4549BDE0] Thu Nov 02 10:44:00 2006
   Bound to msvcrt.dll [4549BD61] Thu Nov 02 10:41:53 2006

Summary

      2000 .data
      2000 .reloc
     16000 .rsrc
     13000 .text
```

As you can see, the section has an entry for each DLL that Calc.exe requires: Shell32.dll, AdvAPI32.dll, OleAut32.dll, Ole32.dll, Ntdll.dll, Kernel32.dll, GDI32.dll, User32.dll, and MSVCRT.dll. Under each DLL's module name is the list of symbols that Calc.exe is importing from that particular module. For example, Calc calls the following functions contained in Kernel32.dll: **GetSystemTimeAsFileTime**, **GetCurrentProcessId**, **GetCommandLineW**, **GetProfileIntW**, and so on.

The number immediately to the left of the symbol name indicates the *hint* value of the symbol and is not pertinent to our discussion. The number on the far left of each symbol's line indicates the memory address where the symbol is located in the process' address space. This memory address appears only if the executable module is bound. You can see some additional binding information toward the end of DumpBin's output. (Binding is discussed in Chapter 20.)

Running the Executable Module

When an executable file is invoked, the operating system loader creates the virtual address space for the process. Then the loader maps the executable module into the process' address space. The loader examines the executable's import section and attempts to locate and map any required DLLs into the process' address space.

Because the import section contains just a DLL name without its pathname, the loader must search the user's disk drives for the DLL. Here is the loader's search order:

1. The directory containing the executable image file
2. The Windows system directory returned by **GetWindowsDirectory**
3. The 16-bit system directory—that is, the *System* subfolder under the Windows directory
4. The Windows directory returned by **GetSystemDirectory**
5. The process' current directory
6. The directories listed in the PATH environment variable

Notice that the application current directory is searched after the Windows directories. This change occurred in Windows XP SP2 to avoid having fake system DLLs be found and loaded from the application current directory instead of from their official location in the Windows directories. The MSDN online help mentions how a **DWORD** value under HKEY_LOCAL_MACHINE\SYSTEM\CurrentControlSet\Control\Session Manager could change this search order, but you should never set it if you don't want to allow malware to compromise your machine. Be aware that other things can affect how the loader searches for a DLL. (See Chapter 20 for more information.)

As the DLL modules are mapped into the process' address space, the loader checks each DLL's import section as well. If an import section exists (and usually it does), the loader continues to map the additional required DLL modules into the process' address space. The loader keeps track of the DLL modules that it is loading and maps a module only once even if multiple modules require that module.

If the loader cannot locate a required DLL module, the user sees the following message box:

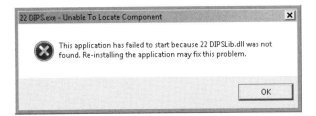

After all the DLL modules have been located and mapped into the process' address space, the loader fixes up all references to imported symbols. To do this, it again looks in each module's import section. For each symbol listed, the loader examines the designated DLL's export section to see if the symbol exists. If the symbol does not exist (which is very rare), the loader displays a message box similar to the following:

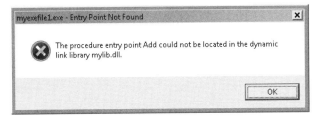

If the symbol does exist, the loader retrieves the RVA of the symbol and adds the virtual address of where the DLL module is loaded (the location of the symbol in the process' address space). It then saves this virtual address in the executable module's import section. Now, when the code references an imported symbol, it looks in the calling module's import section and grabs the address of the imported symbol, and it can thus successfully access the imported variable, function, or C++ class member function. Voilà—the dynamic link is complete, the process' primary thread begins executing, and the application is finally running!

Naturally, it takes the loader quite a bit of time to load all these DLL modules and fix up every module's import section with the proper addresses of all the imported symbols. Because all this work is done when the process initializes, there is no run-time performance hit for the application. For many applications, however, a slow initialization is unacceptable. To help improve your application's load time, you should rebase and bind your executable and DLL modules. Few developers know how to do this, which is unfortunate because these techniques are extremely important. The system would run much better if every company performed these techniques. In fact, I believe that operating systems should ship with a utility that automatically performs these operations. I'll discuss rebasing and binding in the next chapter.

Chapter 20

DLL Advanced Techniques

In the previous chapter, we discussed the basics of DLL linking and concentrated specifically on implicit linking, which is by far the most common form of DLL linking. The information in that chapter is all you'll ever need for most applications. However, you can do a lot more with dynamic-link libraries (DLLs). In this chapter, we'll discuss a hodgepodge of techniques that relate to DLLs. Most applications will not require these techniques, but they can be extremely useful, so you should know about them. I encourage you to at least read the "Rebasing Modules" and "Binding Modules" sections in this chapter because the techniques they describe can significantly improve the performance of your entire system.

Explicit DLL Module Loading and Symbol Linking

For a thread to call a function in a DLL module, the DLL's file image must be mapped into the address space of the calling thread's process. You can accomplish this in two ways. The first way is to have your application's source code simply reference symbols contained in the DLL. This causes the loader to implicitly load (and link) the required DLL when the application is invoked.

The second way is for the application to explicitly load the required DLL and explicitly link to the desired exported symbol while the application is running. In other words, while the application is running, a thread within it can decide that it wants to call a function within a DLL. That thread can explicitly load the DLL into the process' address space, get the virtual memory address of a function contained within the DLL, and then call the function using this memory address. The beauty of this technique is that everything is done while the application is running.

Figure 20-1 shows how an application explicitly loads a DLL and links to a symbol within it.

BUILDING THE DLL

1) Header with *exported* prototypes/structures/symbols.
2) C/C++ source files implementing exported functions/variables.
3) Compiler produces .obj file for each C/C++ source file.
4) Linker combines .obj module producing DLL.
5) Linker also produces .lib file if at least one function/variable is exported.
   NOTE: This .lib file is not used for explicit linking.

BUILDING THE EXE

6) Header with *imported* prototypes/structures/symbols (optional).
7) C/C++ source files that DO NOT reference imported functions/variables.
8) Compiler produces .obj file for each C/C++ source file.
9) Linker combines .obj modules producing .exe modules.
   NOTE: DLL's .lib file is not needed since there are no direct references to exported symbols. The .exe file does not contain an import table.

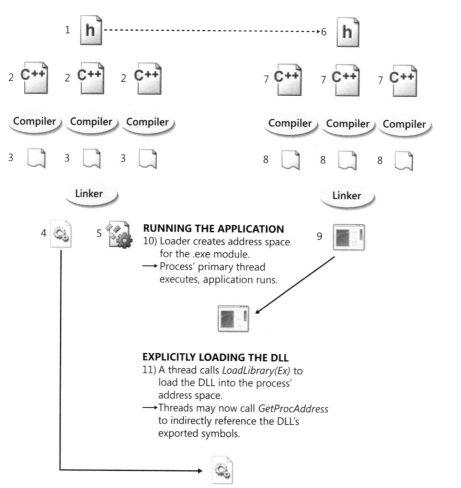

RUNNING THE APPLICATION

10) Loader creates address space for the .exe module.
   → Process' primary thread executes, application runs.

EXPLICITLY LOADING THE DLL

11) A thread calls *LoadLibrary(Ex)* to load the DLL into the process' address space.
   →Threads may now call *GetProcAddress* to indirectly reference the DLL's exported symbols.

Figure 20-1   How a DLL is created and explicitly linked by an application

Explicitly Loading the DLL Module

At any time, a thread in the process can decide to map a DLL into the process' address space by calling one of these two functions:

```
HMODULE LoadLibrary(PCTSTR pszDLLPathName);

HMODULE LoadLibraryEx(
   PCTSTR pszDLLPathName,
   HANDLE hFile,
   DWORD dwFlags);
```

Both of these functions locate a file image on the user's system (using the search algorithm discussed in the previous chapter) and attempt to map the DLL's file image into the calling process' address space. The **HMODULE** value returned from both functions identifies the virtual memory address where the file image is mapped. Notice that the two functions return an **HMODULE** value. This **HMODULE** type is equivalent to **HINSTANCE**, and both are interchangeable. The **HINSTANCE** parameter received by the **DllMain** entry point (discussed later in this chapter) is also the virtual memory address where the file image is mapped. If the DLL cannot be mapped into the process' address space, **NULL** is returned. To get more information about the error, you can call **GetLastError**.

You'll notice that the **LoadLibraryEx** function has two additional parameters: **hFile** and **dwFlags**. The **hFile** parameter is reserved for future use and must be **NULL** for now. For the **dwFlags** parameter, you must specify **0** or a combination of the **DONT_RESOLVE_DLL_REFER-ENCES**, **LOAD_LIBRARY_AS_DATAFILE**, **LOAD_LIBRARY_AS_DATAFILE_EXCLUSIVE**, **LOAD_LIBRARY_AS_IMAGE_RESOURCE**, **LOAD_WITH_ALTERED_SEARCH_PATH**, and **LOAD_IGNORE_CODE_AUTHZ_LEVEL** flags, which are discussed briefly next.

DONT_RESOLVE_DLL_REFERENCES

The **DONT_RESOLVE_DLL_REFERENCES** flag tells the system to map the DLL into the calling process' address space. Normally, when a DLL is mapped into a process' address space, the system calls a special function in the DLL, usually **DllMain** (discussed later in this chapter), which is used to initialize the DLL. The **DONT_RESOLVE_DLL_REFERENCES** flag causes the system to simply map the file image without calling **DllMain**.

In addition, a DLL might import functions contained in another DLL. When the system maps a DLL into a process' address space, it also checks to see whether the DLL requires any additional DLLs and automatically loads these as well. When the **DONT_RESOLVE_DLL_REFERENCES** flag is specified, the system does not automatically load any of these additional DLLs into the process' address space.

So you won't be able to call any exported function from this DLL without the risk of ending up with code that relies on either an internal structure that was not initialized or a referenced DLL that was not loaded. These reasons are good enough for you to avoid using this flag. If you want more details, you should read the "LoadLibraryEx(DONT_RESOLVE_DLL_REFERENCES) is fundamentally flawed" entry in Raymond Chen's blog at *http://blogs.msdn.com/oldnewthing/archive/2005/02/14/372266.aspx*.

LOAD_LIBRARY_AS_DATAFILE

The **LOAD_LIBRARY_AS_DATAFILE** flag is similar to the **DONT_RESOLVE_DLL_REFERENCES** flag in that the system simply maps the DLL into the process' address space as if it were a data file. The system spends no additional time preparing to execute any code in the file. For example, when a DLL is mapped into a process' address space, the system examines some information in the DLL to determine which page-protection attributes should be assigned to different sections of the file. If you don't specify the **LOAD_LIBRARY_AS_DATAFILE** flag, the system sets the page-protection attributes in the same way that it would if it were expecting to execute code in the file. For example, if you call **GetProcAddress** on a DLL loaded with this flag, **NULL** is returned and **GetLastError** returns **ERROR_MOD_NOT_FOUND**.

This flag is useful for several reasons. First, if you have a DLL that contains only resources and no functions, you can specify this flag so that the DLL's file image is mapped into the process' address space. You can then use the **HMODULE** value returned from **LoadLibraryEx** in calls to functions that load resources. Also, you can use the **LOAD_LIBRARY_AS_DATAFILE** flag if you want to use resources that are contained in an .exe file. Normally, loading an .exe file starts a new process, but you can also use the **LoadLibraryEx** function to map an .exe file's image into a process' address space. With the mapped .exe file's **HMODULE/HINSTANCE** value, you can access resources within it. Because an .exe file doesn't have the **DllMain** function, you must specify the **LOAD_LIBRARY_AS_DATAFILE** flag when you call **LoadLibraryEx** to load an .exe file.

LOAD_LIBRARY_AS_DATAFILE_EXCLUSIVE

This flag is similar to **LOAD_LIBRARY_AS_DATAFILE** except that the binary file is opened for exclusive access, forbidding any other application from modifying the file while your application uses it. This flag offers your application more security over the **LOAD_LIBRARY_AS_DATAFILE** flag, and therefore, it is recommended that your application use the **LOAD_LIBRARY_AS_DATAFILE_EXCLU-SIVE** flag unless you specifically require that other applications be able to modify the file's contents.

LOAD_LIBRARY_AS_IMAGE_RESOURCE

The **LOAD_LIBRARY_AS_IMAGE_RESOURCE** flag is similar to **LOAD_LIBRARY_AS_DATAFILE** but with one little difference: the *relative virtual addresses* (RVA) detailed in Chapter 19, "DLL Basics," are patched by the operating system when the DLL is loaded. So the RVAs can be used directly instead of having to translate them based on the address where the DLL has been loaded in memory. This is particularly handy when you need to parse a DLL for exploring its portable executable (PE) sections.

LOAD_WITH_ALTERED_SEARCH_PATH

The **LOAD_WITH_ALTERED_SEARCH_PATH** flag changes the search algorithm that **LoadLibraryEx** uses to locate the specified DLL file. Normally, **LoadLibraryEx** searches for files in the order shown on page 550. However, if the **LOAD_WITH_ALTERED_SEARCH_PATH** flag is specified, **Load-LibraryEx** searches for the file using the following three different algorithms based on what is passed to the **pszDLLPathName** parameter:

1. If **pszDLLPathName** does not contain the \ character, the standard search path shown in Chapter 19 is applied to find the DLL.

2. If **pszDLLPathName** contains the \ character, **LoadLibraryEx** behaves differently whether this parameter is a full pathname or a relative pathname:

    ❏ When a full pathname or a network share is passed as a parameter (such as C:\Apps\Libraries\MyLibrary.dll or \\server\share\MyLibrary.dll), **LoadLibraryEx** tries to directly load this particular DLL file. If the corresponding file does not exist, **NULL** is returned and **GetLastError** returns **ERROR_MOD_NOT_FOUND** without searching somewhere else.

    ❏ Otherwise, the **pszDLLPathName** is concatenated to the following folders before trying to load the corresponding file as a DLL:

        a. The process' current directory

        b. The Windows system directory

        c. The 16-bit system directory— that is, the System subfolder under the Windows directory

        d. The Windows directory

        e. The directories listed in the **PATH** environment variable

    Notice that if the "." or ".." characters are present in the **pszDLLPathName** parameter, they are taken into account to build a relative path at each step of the search. For example, passing **TEXT("..\\MyLibrary.dll")** as a parameter asks **LoadLibraryEx** to search MyLibrary.dll in the following locations:

        a. The folder containing the current directory

        b. The folder containing the Windows system directory (that is, the Windows directory)

        c. The folder containing the Windows 16-bit system directory

        d. The folder containing the Windows directory (usually a volume root)

        e. Each parent folder of the directories listed in the **PATH** environment variable

    The search stops as soon as a valid DLL is loaded from one of these folders.

3. When you build an application that is supposed to dynamically load libraries from a well-known folder, instead of using **LoadLibraryEx** with the **LOAD_WITH_ALTERED_SEARCH_PATH** flag or changing the application current directory, you should instead call **SetDll-Directory** with the library folder as a parameter. This function tells **LoadLibrary** and **LoadLibraryEx** to search with the following algorithm:

    a. The folder containing the application

    b. The folder set through **SetDllDirectory**

    c. The folder containing the Windows system directory (that is, the Windows directory)

    d. The folder containing the Windows 16-bit system directory

    e. The folder containing the Windows directory (usually a volume root)

    f. Each parent folder of the directories listed in the **PATH** environment variable

This search algorithm allows you to store your application and your shared DLLs into well-defined directories without any risk of loading other unexpected DLLs with the same name from the application's current directory, such as those set through a shortcut. Notice that if you call **SetDllDirectory** with an empty string—**TEXT("")**—as a parameter, the current directory is simply removed from the search steps. If you pass **NULL** instead, the default search algorithm is restored. Last but not least, **GetDllDirectory** returns the current value of this particular directory.

LOAD_IGNORE_CODE_AUTHZ_LEVEL

The **LOAD_IGNORE_CODE_AUTHZ_LEVEL** flag turns off the validation provided by WinSafer (also known as *Software Restriction Policies* or *Safer*), which was introduced in Windows XP and was designed to control the privileges that code would have during execution. This feature (which you can learn more about at *http://technet.microsoft.com/en-us/windowsvista/aa940985.aspx*) has been usurped in Windows Vista by way of the User Account Control (UAC) feature presented in Chapter 4, "Processes."

Explicitly Unloading the DLL Module

When the threads in the process no longer want to reference symbols in a DLL, you can explicitly unload the DLL from the process' address space by calling this function:

```
BOOL FreeLibrary(HMODULE hInstDll);
```

You must pass the **HMODULE** value that identifies the DLL you want to unload. This value was returned by an earlier call to **LoadLibrary(Ex)**.

You can also unload a DLL module from a process' address space by calling this function:

```
VOID FreeLibraryAndExitThread(
   HMODULE hInstDll,
   DWORD dwExitCode);
```

This function is implemented in Kernel32.dll as follows:

```
VOID FreeLibraryAndExitThread(HMODULE hInstDll, DWORD dwExitCode) {
   FreeLibrary(hInstDll);
   ExitThread(dwExitCode);
}
```

At first glance, this doesn't look like a big deal, and you might wonder why Microsoft went to the trouble of creating the **FreeLibraryAndExitThread** function. The reason has to do with the following scenario: Suppose you are writing a DLL that, when it is first mapped into a process' address space, creates a thread. When the thread finishes its work, it can unmap the DLL from the process' address space and terminate by calling **FreeLibrary** and then immediately calling **ExitThread**.

But if the thread calls **FreeLibrary** and **ExitThread** individually, a serious problem occurs. The problem, of course, is that the call to **FreeLibrary** unmaps the DLL from the process' address space immediately. By the time the call to **FreeLibrary** returns, the code that contains the call to **ExitThread** is no longer available and the thread will attempt to execute nothing. This causes an access violation, and the entire process is terminated!

However, if the thread calls **FreeLibraryAndExitThread**, this function calls **FreeLibrary**, causing the DLL to be immediately unmapped. The next instruction executed is in Kernel32.dll, not in the DLL that has just been unmapped. This means that the thread can continue executing and can call **ExitThread**. **ExitThread** causes the thread to terminate and does not return.

In reality, the **LoadLibrary** and **LoadLibraryEx** functions increment a per-process usage count associated with the specified library, and the **FreeLibrary** and **FreeLibraryAndExitThread** functions decrement the library's per-process usage count. For example, the first time you call **LoadLibrary** to load a DLL, the system maps the DLL's file image into the calling process' address space and sets the DLL's usage count to 1. If a thread in the same process later calls **LoadLibrary** to load the same DLL file image, the system does not map the DLL file image into the process' address space a second time. Instead, it simply increments the usage count associated with the DLL for that process.

For the DLL file image to be unmapped from the process' address space, threads in the process must call **FreeLibrary** twice—the first call simply decrements the DLL's usage count to 1, and the second call decrements the DLL's usage count to 0. When the system sees that a DLL's usage count has reached 0, it unmaps the DLL's file image from this process' address space. Any thread that attempts to call a function in the DLL raises an access violation because the code at the specified address is no longer mapped into the process' address space.

The system maintains a DLL's usage count on a per-process basis; that is, if a thread in Process A makes the following call and then a thread in Process B makes the same call, MyLib.dll is mapped into both processes' address spaces—the DLL's usage count for Process A and for Process B are both 1.

```
HMODULE hInstDll = LoadLibrary(TEXT("MyLib.dll"));
```

If a thread in Process B later calls the following function, the DLL's usage count for Process B becomes 0, and the DLL is unmapped from Process B's address space. However, the mapping of the DLL in Process A's address space is unaffected, and the DLL's usage count for Process A remains 1.

```
FreeLibrary(hInstDll);
```

A thread can determine whether a DLL is already mapped into its process' address space by calling the **GetModuleHandle** function:

```
HMODULE GetModuleHandle(PCTSTR pszModuleName);
```

For example, the following code loads MyLib.dll only if it is not already mapped into the process' address space:

```
HMODULE hInstDll = GetModuleHandle(TEXT("MyLib")); // DLL extension assumed
if (hInstDll == NULL) {
   hInstDll = LoadLibrary(TEXT("MyLib")); // DLL extension assumed
}
```

If you pass **NULL** to **GetModuleHandle**, the handle of the application executable is returned.

You can also determine the full pathname of a DLL (or an .exe) if you have only the DLL's **HINSTANCE/HMODULE** value by using the **GetModuleFileName** function:

```
DWORD GetModuleFileName(
    HMODULE hInstModule,
    PTSTR pszPathName,
    DWORD cchPath);
```

The first parameter is the DLL's (or .exe's) **HMODULE**. The second parameter, **pszPathName**, is the address of the buffer where the function puts the file image's full pathname. The third parameter, **cchPath**, specifies the size of the buffer in characters. If you pass **NULL** to the **hInstModule** parameter, **GetModuleFileName** returns the filename of the running application executable in **pszPathName**. "A Process Instance Handle" on page 73 provides additional details about these methods, the **__ImageBase** pseudo-variable, and **GetModuleHandleEx**.

Mixing **LoadLibrary** and **LoadLibraryEx** could result in situations where the same DLL is mapped in different locations in the same address space. For example, let's take the following code:

```
HMODULE hDll1 = LoadLibrary(TEXT("MyLibrary.dll"));
HMODULE hDll2 = LoadLibraryEx(TEXT("MyLibrary.dll"), NULL,
    LOAD_LIBRARY_AS_IMAGE_RESOURCE);
HMODULE hDll3 = LoadLibraryEx(TEXT("MyLibrary.dll"), NULL,
    LOAD_LIBRARY_AS_DATAFILE);
```

What value do you expect for **hDll1**, **hDll2**, and **hDll3**? Obviously, the same value if the same MyLibrary.dll file is loaded. Well... This is not so obvious when you change the order of calls like in the following code snippet:

```
HMODULE hDll1 = LoadLibraryEx(TEXT("MyLibrary.dll"), NULL,
    LOAD_LIBRARY_AS_DATAFILE);
HMODULE hDll2 = LoadLibraryEx(TEXT("MyLibrary.dll"), NULL,
    LOAD_LIBRARY_AS_IMAGE_RESOURCE);
HMODULE hDll3 = LoadLibrary(TEXT("MyLibrary.dll"));
```

In this case, **hDll1**, **hDll2**, and **hDll3** each contain a different value! When you call **Load-LibraryEx** with the **LOAD_LIBRARY_AS_DATAFILE**, **LOAD_LIBRARY_AS_DATAFILE_EXCLUSIVE**, or **LOAD_LIBRARY_AS_IMAGE_RESOURCE** flags, the operating system first checks whether the DLL was already loaded by a call to **LoadLibrary** or **LoadLibraryEx** but without these flags. If this is the case, the address where this DLL has been previously mapped into the address space is returned. However, if the DLL is not already loaded, Windows maps the DLL at an available location into the address space but does not consider it to be a fully loaded DLL. At this stage, **Get-ModuleFileName** returns **0** when called with this module handle as a parameter. This is a good way to recognize that a module handle corresponds to a DLL that is not usable for a dynamic function call through **GetProcAddress**, as you will discover in the next section.

Always remember that the mapping address returned by **LoadLibrary** and **LoadLibraryEx** should not be used interchangeably even if the same DLL on disk is supposed to be loaded.

Explicitly Linking to an Exported Symbol

Once a DLL module has been explicitly loaded, the thread must get the address of the symbol that it wants to reference by calling this function:

```
FARPROC GetProcAddress(
   HMODULE hInstDll,
   PCSTR pszSymbolName);
```

The **hInstDll** parameter, returned from a call to **LoadLibrary(Ex)** or **GetModuleHandle**, specifies the handle of the DLL containing the symbol. The **pszSymbolName** parameter can take one of two forms. The first form is the address of a zero-terminated string containing the name of the symbol whose address you want:

```
FARPROC pfn = GetProcAddress(hInstDll, "SomeFuncInDll");
```

Notice that the **pszSymbolName** parameter is prototyped as a **PCSTR**, as opposed to a **PCTSTR**. This means that the **GetProcAddress** function accepts only ANSI strings—you never pass Unicode strings to this function because the compiler/linker always stores symbol names as ANSI strings in the DLL's export section.

The second form of the **pszSymbolName** parameter indicates the ordinal number of the symbol whose address you want:

```
FARPROC pfn = GetProcAddress(hInstDll, MAKEINTRESOURCE(2));
```

This usage assumes that you know that the desired symbol name was assigned the ordinal value of 2 by the creator of the DLL. Again, let me reiterate that Microsoft strongly discourages the use of ordinals, so you won't often see this second usage of **GetProcAddress**.

Either method provides the address to the desired symbol contained in the DLL. If the requested symbol does not exist in the DLL module's export section, **GetProcAddress** returns **NULL** to indicate failure.

You should be aware that the first method of calling **GetProcAddress** is slower than the second because the system must perform string comparisons and searches on the symbol name string that was passed. With the second method, if you pass an ordinal number that hasn't been assigned to any of the exported functions, **GetProcAddress** might return a non-**NULL** value. This return value will trick your application into thinking that you have a valid address when you don't. Attempting to call this address will almost certainly cause the thread to raise an access violation. Early in my Windows programming career, I didn't fully understand this behavior and was burned by it several times—so watch out. (This behavior is yet another reason to avoid ordinals in favor of symbol names.)

Before being able to call the function pointer returned by **GetProcAddress**, you need to cast it into the right type that maps its signature. For example, **typedef void (CALLBACK *PFN_DUMPMOD-ULE)(HMODULE hModule);** is the signature of the type of the callback corresponding to the function **void DynamicDumpModule(HMODULE hModule)**. The following code shows how to dynamically call this function from a DLL that exports it:

```
PFN_DUMPMODULE pfnDumpModule =
   (PFN_DUMPMODULE)GetProcAddress(hDll, "DumpModule");
if (pfnDumpModule != NULL) {
   pfnDumpModule(hDll);
}
```

The DLL's Entry-Point Function

A DLL can have a single entry-point function. The system calls this entry-point function at various times, which I'll discuss shortly. These calls are informational and are usually used by a DLL to perform any per-process or per-thread initialization and cleanup. If your DLL doesn't require these notifications, you do not have to implement this function in your DLL source code. For example, if you create a DLL that contains only resources, you do not need to implement this function. If you do want to receive notifications in your DLL, you can implement an entry-point function that looks like the following.

```
BOOL WINAPI DllMain(HINSTANCE hInstDll, DWORD fdwReason, PVOID fImpLoad) {

   switch (fdwReason) {
      case DLL_PROCESS_ATTACH:
         // The DLL is being mapped into the process' address space.
         break;

      case DLL_THREAD_ATTACH:
         // A thread is being created.
         break;

      case DLL_THREAD_DETACH:
         // A thread is exiting cleanly.
         break;

      case DLL_PROCESS_DETACH:
         // The DLL is being unmapped from the process' address space.
         break;
   }
   return(TRUE);  // Used only for DLL_PROCESS_ATTACH
}
```

 Note The function name **DllMain** is case-sensitive. Many developers accidentally call the function **DLLMain** instead. This is an easy mistake to make because the term *DLL* is frequently represented in all capital letters. If you call the entry-point function anything but **DllMain**, your code will compile and link; however, your entry-point function will never be called and your DLL will never initialize.

The **hInstDll** parameter contains the instance handle of the DLL. Like the **hInstExe** parameter to **_tWinMain**, this value identifies the virtual memory address of where the DLL's file image was mapped in the process' address space. You usually save this parameter in a global variable so that you can use it in calls that load resources, such as **DialogBox** and **LoadString**. The last parameter, **fImpLoad**, is nonzero if the DLL is implicitly loaded and zero if the DLL is explicitly loaded.

The **fdwReason** parameter indicates why the system is calling the function. This parameter can have one of four values: **DLL_PROCESS_ATTACH**, **DLL_PROCESS_DETACH**, **DLL_THREAD_ATTACH**, or **DLL_THREAD_DETACH**. These are discussed in the following sections.

> **Note**   You must remember that DLLs use **DllMain** functions to initialize themselves. When your **DllMain** function executes, other DLLs in the same address space probably haven't executed their **DllMain** functions yet. This means that they have not initialized, so you should avoid calling functions imported from other DLLs. In addition, you should avoid calls to **LoadLibrary(Ex)** and **FreeLibrary** from inside **DllMain** because these functions can create dependency loops.
>
> The Platform SDK documentation states that your **DllMain** function should perform only simple initialization, such as setting up thread-local storage (discussed in Chapter 21, "Thread-Local Storage"), creating kernel objects, and opening files. You must also avoid calls to User, Shell, ODBC, COM, RPC, and socket functions (or functions that call these functions) because their DLLs might not have initialized yet or the functions might call **LoadLibrary(Ex)** internally, again creating a dependency loop.
>
> Also be aware that the same problems exist if you create global or static C++ objects because the constructor or destructor for these objects is called at the same time as your **DllMain** function.
>
> Read the "Best Practices for Creating DLLs" document available at *http://www.microsoft.com/whdc/driver/kernel/DLL_bestprac.mspx* for more constraints related to the process-wide lock acquired when a **DllMain** entry point executes.

The *DLL_PROCESS_ATTACH* Notification

When a DLL is first mapped into a process' address space, the system calls the DLL's **DllMain** function, passing it a value of **DLL_PROCESS_ATTACH** for the **fdwReason** parameter. This happens only when the DLL's file image is first mapped. If a thread later calls **LoadLibrary(Ex)** for a DLL that is already mapped into the process' address space, the operating system simply increments the DLL's usage count; it does not call the DLL's **DllMain** function again with a value of **DLL_PROCESS_ATTACH**.

When processing **DLL_PROCESS_ATTACH**, a DLL should perform any process-relative initialization required by functions contained within the DLL. For example, the DLL might contain functions that need to use their own heap (created in the process' address space). The DLL's **DllMain** function can create this heap by calling **HeapCreate** during its processing of the **DLL_PROCESS_ATTACH** notification. The handle to the created heap can be saved in a global variable that the DLL functions have access to.

When **DllMain** processes a **DLL_PROCESS_ATTACH** notification, **DllMain**'s return value indicates whether the DLL's initialization was successful. If, for example, the call to **HeapCreate** was successful, **DllMain** should return **TRUE**. If the heap could not be created, it should return **FALSE**. For any of the other **fdwReason** values—**DLL_PROCESS_DETACH**, **DLL_THREAD_ATTACH**, and **DLL_THREAD_DETACH**—the system ignores the return value from **DllMain**.

Of course, some thread in the system must be responsible for executing the code in the **DllMain** function. When a new process is created, the system allocates the process' address space and then maps the .exe file image and all the required DLL file images into the process' address space. Then it creates the process' primary thread and uses this thread to call each of the DLL's **DllMain** functions with a value of **DLL_PROCESS_ATTACH**. After all the mapped DLLs have responded to this notification, the system causes the process' primary thread to begin executing the executable module's C/C++ run-time startup code, followed by the executable module's entry-point function (**_tmain**, or **_tWinMain**). If any of the DLL's **DllMain** functions return **FALSE**, indicating unsuccessful initialization, the system terminates the entire process, removing all the file images from its address space and displaying a message box to the user stating that the process could not be started. Here is the message box that Windows Vista displays:

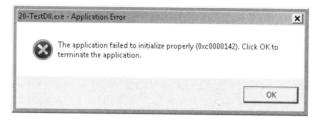

Now let's look at what happens when a DLL is loaded explicitly. When a thread in a process calls **LoadLibrary(Ex)**, the system locates the specified DLL and maps the DLL into the process' address space. Then the system calls the DLL's **DllMain** function with a value of **DLL_PROCESS_ATTACH**, using the thread that placed the call to **LoadLibrary(Ex)**. After the DLL's **DllMain** function has processed the notification, the system allows the call to **LoadLibrary(Ex)** to return, and the thread continues processing as normal. If the **DllMain** function returns **FALSE**, indicating that the initialization was unsuccessful, the system automatically unmaps the DLL's file image from the process' address space and the call to **LoadLibrary(Ex)** returns **NULL**.

The *DLL_PROCESS_DETACH* Notification

When a DLL is unmapped from a process' address space, the system calls the DLL's **DllMain** function, passing it an **fdwReason** value of **DLL_PROCESS_DETACH**. A DLL should perform any process-relative cleanup when it processes this value. For example, a DLL might call **HeapDestroy** to destroy a heap that it created during the **DLL_PROCESS_ATTACH** notification. Note that if a **DllMain** function returns **FALSE** when it receives a **DLL_PROCESS_ATTACH** notification, the **DllMain** function is not called with a **DLL_PROCESS_DETACH** notification. If the DLL is being unmapped because the process is terminating, the thread that calls the **ExitProcess** function is responsible for executing the **DllMain** function's code. Under normal circumstances, this is the application's primary thread. When your entry-point function returns to the C/C++ run-time library's startup code, the startup code explicitly calls the **ExitProcess** function to terminate the process.

If the DLL is being unmapped because a thread in the process called **FreeLibrary** or **FreeLibraryAndExitThread**, the thread that made the call executes the **DllMain** function code. If **FreeLibrary** is used, the thread does not return from this call until after the **DllMain** function has finished executing the **DLL_PROCESS_DETACH** notification.

Note that a DLL can prevent the process from dying. For example, **DllMain** might enter an infinite loop when it receives the **DLL_PROCESS_DETACH** notification. The operating system actually kills the process only after every DLL has completed processing the **DLL_PROCESS_DETACH** notification.

> **Note**   If a process terminates because some thread in the system calls **TerminateProcess**, the system does not call the DLL's **DllMain** function with a value of **DLL_PROCESS_DETACH**. This means that any DLLs mapped into the process' address space do not have a chance to perform any cleanup before the process terminates. This can result in the loss of data. You should use the **TerminateProcess** function only as a last resort!

Figure 20-2 shows the steps that are performed when a thread calls **LoadLibrary**. Figure 20-3 shows the steps that are performed when a thread calls **FreeLibrary**.

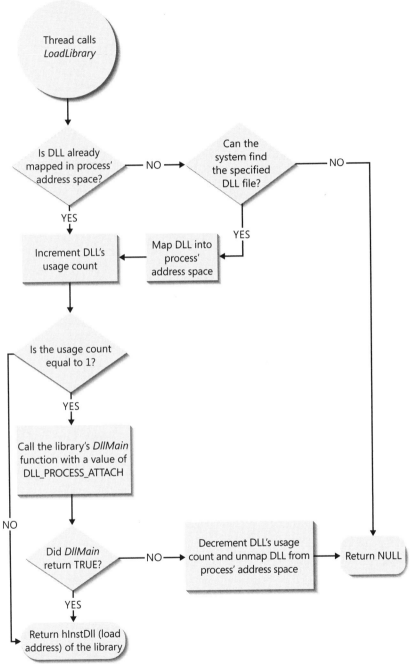

Figure 20-2   The steps performed by the system when a thread calls **LoadLibrary**

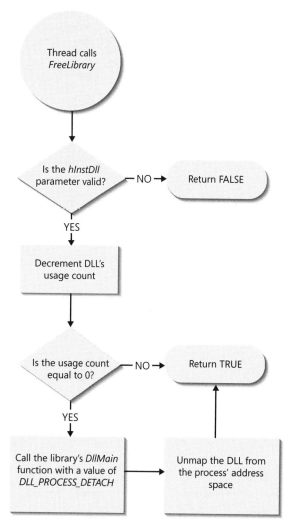

Figure 20-3   The steps performed by the system when a thread calls **FreeLibrary**

The *DLL_THREAD_ATTACH* Notification

When a thread is created in a process, the system examines all the DLL file images currently mapped into the process' address space and calls each one's **DllMain** function with a value of **DLL_THREAD_ATTACH**. This tells all the DLLs to perform any per-thread initialization. The newly created thread is responsible for executing the code in all the DLLs' **DllMain** functions. Only after all the DLLs have had a chance to process this notification does the system allow the new thread to begin executing its thread function.

If a process already has several threads running in it when a new DLL is mapped into its address space, the system does not call the DLL's **DllMain** function with a value of **DLL_THREAD_ATTACH** for any of the existing threads. It calls the DLL's **DllMain** function with a value of **DLL_THREAD_ATTACH** only if the DLL is mapped into the process' address space when a new thread is created.

Also note that the system does not call any **DllMain** functions with a value of **DLL_THREAD_ATTACH** for the process' primary thread. Any DLLs that are mapped into the process' address space when the process is first invoked receive the **DLL_PROCESS_ATTACH** notification but not the **DLL_THREAD_ATTACH** notification.

The *DLL_THREAD_DETACH* Notification

The preferred way for a thread to terminate is to have its thread function return. This causes the system to call **ExitThread** to kill the thread. **ExitThread** tells the system that the thread wants to die, but the system does not kill the thread right away. Instead, it takes the soon-to-be-dead thread and has it call all the mapped DLL's **DllMain** functions with a reason of **DLL_THREAD_DETACH**. This notification tells all the DLLs to perform any per-thread cleanup. For example, the DLL version of the C/C++ run-time library frees the data block that it uses to manage multithreaded applications.

Note that a DLL can prevent the thread from dying. For example, the **DllMain** function can enter an infinite loop when it receives the **DLL_THREAD_DETACH** notification. The operating system actually kills the thread only after every DLL has completed processing the **DLL_THREAD_DETACH** notification.

> **Note** If a thread terminates because a thread in the system calls **TerminateThread**, the system does not call all the DLLs' **DllMain** functions with a value of **DLL_THREAD_DETACH**. This means that any DLLs mapped into the process' address space do not have a chance to perform any cleanup before the thread terminates. This can result in the loss of data. As with **TerminateProcess**, use the **TerminateThread** function only as a last resort!

If any threads are still running when the DLL is detached, **DllMain** is not called with **DLL_THREAD_DETACH** for any of the threads. You might want to check for this in your **DLL_PROCESS_DETACH** processing so that you can perform any necessary cleanup.

Because of the aforementioned rules, the following situation might occur: A thread in a process calls **LoadLibrary** to load a DLL, causing the system to call the DLL's **DllMain** function with a value of **DLL_PROCESS_ATTACH**. (Note that the **DLL_THREAD_ATTACH** notification is not sent for this thread.) Next, the thread that loaded the DLL exits, causing the DLL's **DllMain** function to be called again—this time with a value of **DLL_THREAD_DETACH**. Notice that the DLL is notified that the thread is detaching even though it never received a **DLL_THREAD_ATTACH** notifying the library that the thread had attached. For this reason, you must be extremely careful when you perform any thread-specific cleanup. Fortunately, most programs are written so that the thread that calls **LoadLibrary** is the same thread that calls **FreeLibrary**.

Serialized Calls to *DllMain*

The system serializes calls to a DLL's **DllMain** function. To understand what this means, consider the following scenario. A process has two threads: Thread A and Thread B. The process also has a DLL, named SomeDLL.dll, mapped into its address space. Both threads are about to call the **CreateThread** function to create two more threads: Thread C and Thread D.

When Thread A calls **CreateThread** to create Thread C, the system calls SomeDLL.dll's **DllMain** function with a value of **DLL_THREAD_ATTACH**. While Thread C executes the code in the **DllMain** function, Thread B calls **CreateThread** to create Thread D. The system must call **DllMain** again with a value of **DLL_THREAD_ATTACH**, this time having Thread D execute the code. However, calls to **DllMain** are serialized by the system, and the system suspends Thread D until Thread C has completely processed the code in **DllMain** and returned.

After Thread C finishes processing **DllMain**, it can begin executing its thread function. Now the system wakes up Thread D and allows it to process the code in **DllMain**. When it returns, Thread D begins processing its thread function.

Normally, you don't even think about this **DllMain** serialization. The reason I'm making a big deal out of it is that I worked with someone who had a bug in his code caused by **DllMain** serialization. His code looked something like the following code:

```
BOOL WINAPI DllMain(HINSTANCE hInstDll, DWORD fdwReason, PVOID fImpLoad) {

   HANDLE hThread;
   DWORD dwThreadId;

   switch (fdwReason) {
   case DLL_PROCESS_ATTACH:
      // The DLL is being mapped into the process' address space.

      // Create a thread to do some stuff.
      hThread = CreateThread(NULL, 0, SomeFunction, NULL,
         0, &dwThreadId);

      // Suspend our thread until the new thread terminates.
      WaitForSingleObject(hThread, INFINITE);

      // We no longer need access to the new thread.
      CloseHandle(hThread);
      break;

   case DLL_THREAD_ATTACH:
      // A thread is being created.
      break;

   case DLL_THREAD_DETACH:
      // A thread is exiting cleanly.
      break;

   case DLL_PROCESS_DETACH:
      // The DLL is being unmapped from the process' address space.
      break;
   }
   return(TRUE);
}
```

It took us several hours to discover the problem with this code. Can you see it? When **DllMain** receives a **DLL_PROCESS_ATTACH** notification, a new thread is created. The system must call **DllMain** again with a value of **DLL_THREAD_ATTACH**. However, the new thread is suspended because the thread that caused the **DLL_PROCESS_ATTACH** notification to be sent to **DllMain** has not finished processing. The problem is the call to **WaitForSingleObject**. This function suspends the currently executing thread until the new thread terminates. However, the new thread never gets a chance to run, let alone terminate, because it is suspended—waiting for the current thread to exit the **DllMain** function. What we have here is a deadlock situation. Both threads are suspended forever!

When I first started thinking about how to solve this problem, I discovered the **DisableThread-LibraryCalls** function:

```
BOOL DisableThreadLibraryCalls(HMODULE hInstDll);
```

DisableThreadLibraryCalls tells the system that you do not want **DLL_THREAD_ATTACH** and **DLL_THREAD_DETACH** notifications sent to the specified DLL's **DllMain** function. It seemed reasonable to me that, if we told the system not to send DLL notifications to the DLL, the deadlock situation would not occur. However, when I tested my solution, which follows, I soon discovered that it didn't solve the problem.

```
BOOL WINAPI DllMain(HINSTANCE hInstDll, DWORD fdwReason, PVOID fImpLoad) {

    HANDLE hThread;
    DWORD dwThreadId;

    switch (fdwReason) {
    case DLL_PROCESS_ATTACH:
        // The DLL is being mapped into the process' address space.
        // Prevent the system from calling DllMain
        // when threads are created or destroyed.
        DisableThreadLibraryCalls(hInstDll);

        // Create a thread to do some stuff.
        hThread = CreateThread(NULL, 0, SomeFunction, NULL,
            0, &dwThreadId);

        // Suspend our thread until the new thread terminates.
        WaitForSingleObject(hThread, INFINITE);

        // We no longer need access to the new thread.
        CloseHandle(hThread);
        break;

    case DLL_THREAD_ATTACH:
        // A thread is being created.
        break;

    case DLL_THREAD_DETACH:
        // A thread is exiting cleanly.
        break;

    case DLL_PROCESS_DETACH:
        // The DLL is being unmapped from the process' address space.
        break;
    }
    return(TRUE);
}
```

Here is where the problem comes from: when a process is created, the system also creates a *lock* (a critical section in Windows Vista). Each process has its own lock—multiple processes do not share the same lock. This lock synchronizes all of a process' threads when the threads call the **DllMain** functions of the DLLs mapped into the process' address space. Note that this lock might disappear in a future Windows release.

When the **CreateThread** function is called, the system first creates the thread kernel object and the thread's stack. Then it internally calls the **WaitForSingleObject** function, passing the handle of the process' mutex object. Once the new thread has ownership of the mutex, the system makes the new thread call each DLL's **DllMain** function with a value of **DLL_THREAD_ATTACH**. Only then does the system call **ReleaseMutex** to relinquish ownership of the process' mutex object. Because the system works this way, adding the call to **DisableThreadLibraryCalls** does not prevent the threads from deadlocking. The only way I could think of to prevent the threads from being suspended was to redesign this part of the source code so that **WaitForSingleObject** is not called inside any DLL's **DllMain** function.

DllMain and the C/C++ Run-Time Library

In the preceding discussion of the **DllMain** function, I have assumed that you are using the Microsoft Visual C++ compiler to build your DLL. When you write a DLL, you'll probably need some startup assistance from the C/C++ run-time library. For example, say that you are building a DLL that contains a global variable and that this global variable is an instance of a C++ class. Before you can safely use the global variable inside your **DllMain** function, the variable must have its constructor called. This is a job for the C/C++ run-time library's DLL startup code.

When you link your DLL, the linker embeds the address of the DLL's entry-point function in the resulting DLL file image. You specify the address of this function using the linker's **/ENTRY** switch. By default, when you use Microsoft's linker and specify the **/DLL** switch, the linker assumes that the entry function is called **_DllMainCRTStartup**. This function is contained inside the C/C++ run time's library file and is statically linked in your DLL file's image when you link your DLL. (The function is statically linked even if you use the DLL version of the C/C++ run-time library.)

When your DLL file image is mapped into a process' address space, the system actually calls this **_DllMainCRTStartup** function instead of your **DllMain** function. Before forwarding all notifications to the **_DllMainCRTStartup** function, the **_DllMainCRTStartup** function handles the **DLL_PROCESS_ATTACH** notification to support the security features provided by the **/GS** switch. The **_DllMainCRTStartup** function initializes the C/C++ run-time library, and it ensures that any global or static C++ objects are constructed when **_DllMainCRTStartup** receives the **DLL_PROCESS_ATTACH** notification. After any C/C++ run-time initialization has been performed, the **_DllMainCRTStartup** function calls your **DllMain** function.

When the DLL receives a **DLL_PROCESS_DETACH** notification, the system again calls the **_DllMainCRTStartup** function. This time, the function calls your **DllMain** function, and when **DllMain** returns, **_DllMainCRTStartup** calls any destructors for any global or static C++ objects in the DLL. The **_DllMainCRTStartup** function doesn't do any special processing when it receives a **DLL_THREAD_ATTACH** or a **DLL_THREAD_DETACH** notification.

I mentioned earlier that you do not have to implement a **DllMain** function in your DLL's source code. If you don't have your own **DllMain** function, you can use the C/C++ run-time library's implementation of a **DllMain** function, which looks like this (if you're statically linking to the C/C++ run-time library):

```
BOOL WINAPI DllMain(HINSTANCE hInstDll, DWORD fdwReason, PVOID fImpLoad) {

   if (fdwReason == DLL_PROCESS_ATTACH)
      DisableThreadLibraryCalls(hInstDll);
   return(TRUE);
}
```

When the linker links your DLL, it links the C/C++ run-time library's implementation of the **DllMain** function if the linker cannot find a **DllMain** function in your DLL's .obj files. If you don't supply your own **DllMain** function, the C/C++ run-time library rightfully assumes that you don't care about **DLL_THREAD_ATTACH** and **DLL_THREAD_DETACH** notifications. To improve the performance of creating and destroying threads, **DisableThreadLibraryCalls** is called.

Delay-Loading a DLL

Microsoft Visual C++ offers a fantastic feature to make working with DLLs easier: delay-load DLLs. A delay-load DLL is a DLL that is implicitly linked but not actually loaded until your code attempts to reference a symbol contained within the DLL. Delay-load DLLs are helpful in these situations:

- If your application uses several DLLs, its initialization time might be slow because the loader maps all the required DLLs into the process' address space. One way to alleviate this problem is to spread out the loading of the DLLs as the process executes. Delay-load DLLs let you accomplish this easily.

- If you call a new function in your code and then try to run your application on an older version of the system in which the function does not exist, the loader reports an error and does not allow the application to run. You need a way to allow your application to run and then, if you detect (at run time) that the application is running on an older system, you don't call the missing function. For example, let's say that an application wants to use the new Thread Pool functions when running on Windows Vista and the old functions when running on older versions of Windows. When the application initializes, it calls **GetVersionEx** to determine the host operating system and properly calls the appropriate functions. Attempting to run this application on versions of Windows older than Windows Vista causes the loader to display an error message because the new Thread Pool functions don't exist on these operating systems. Again, delay-load DLLs let you solve this problem easily.

I've spent quite a bit of time playing with the delay-load DLL feature of Visual C++, and I must say that Microsoft has done an excellent job in implementing it. It offers many features and works equally well on all versions of Windows.

However, a couple of limitations are worth mentioning:

- It is not possible to delay-load a DLL that exports fields.

- The Kernel32.dll module cannot be delay-loaded because it must be loaded for **Load-Library** and **GetProcAddress** to be called.

- You should not call a delay-load function in a **DllMain** entry point because the process might crash.

Read "Constraints of Delay Loading DLLs" at *http://msdn2.microsoft.com/en-us/library/ yx1x886y(VS.80).aspx* for more details about the limitations that apply to delay-load usage.

Let's start with the easy stuff: getting delay-load DLLs to work. First, you create a DLL just as you normally would. You also create an executable as you normally would, but you do have to change a couple of linker switches and relink the executable. Here are the two linker switches you need to add:

- `/Lib:DelayImp.lib`
- `/DelayLoad:MyDll.dll`

> **Warning**   The **/DELAYLOAD** and **/DELAY** linker switches cannot be set within your source code through **#pragma comment(linker, "")**. You need to set these two linker switches through the project properties.

The Delay Loaded DLLs option is set through the Configuration Properties/Linker/Input page as shown here:

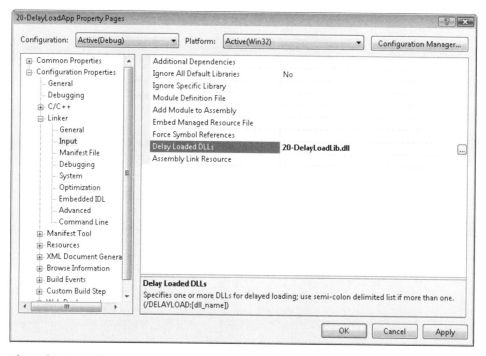

The Delay Loaded DLL option is set through the Configuration Properties/Linker/Advanced page as shown next:

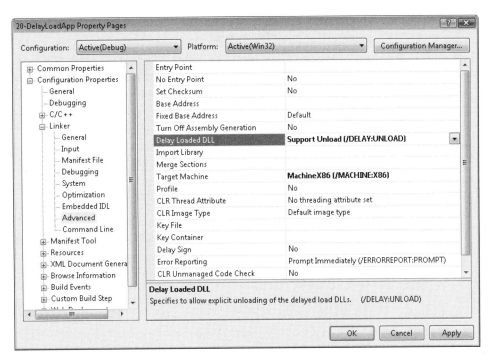

The **/Lib** switch tells the linker to embed a special function, **__delayLoadHelper2**, into your executable. The second switch tells the linker the following things:

- Remove MyDll.dll from the executable module's import section so that the operating system loader does not implicitly load the DLL when the process initializes.

- Embed a new Delay Import section (called .didata) in the executable that indicates which functions are being imported from MyDll.dll.

- Resolve calls to the delay-loaded functions by having calls jump to the **__delayLoad-Helper2** function.

When the application runs, a call to a delay-loaded function actually calls the **__delayLoad-Helper2** function instead. This function references the special Delay Import section and knows to call **LoadLibrary** followed by **GetProcAddress**. Once the address of the delay-loaded function is obtained, **__delayLoadHelper2** fixes up calls to that function so that future calls go directly to the delay-loaded function. Note that other functions in the same DLL still have to be fixed up the first time you call them. Also note that you can specify the **/DelayLoad** linker switch multiple times—once for every DLL that you want to delay-load.

OK, that's it. It's that simple! It is, really. But you should also consider a couple of other issues. Normally, when the operating system loader loads your executable, it tries to load the required DLLs. If a DLL can't be loaded, the loader displays an error message. But for delay-loaded DLLs, the existence of the DLL is not checked at initialization time. If the DLL can't be found when a delay-loaded function is called, the **__delayLoadHelper2** function raises a software exception. You can trap this exception using structured exception handling (SEH) and keep your application running. If you don't trap the exception, your process is terminated. (SEH is discussed in Chapter 23,

"Termination Handlers," Chapter 24, "Exception Handlers and Software Exceptions," and Chapter 25, "Unhandled Exceptions, Vectored Exception Handling, and C++ Exceptions.")

Another problem can occur when **__delayLoadHelper2** does find your DLL but the function you're trying to call isn't in the DLL. This can happen if the loader finds an old version of the DLL, for example. In this case, **__delayLoadHelper2** also raises a software exception and the same rules apply. The sample application presented in the next section shows how to properly write the SEH code to handle these errors.

You'll notice a lot of other stuff in the code that has nothing to do with SEH and error handling. It has to do with additional features that are available when you use delay-load DLLs. I'll describe these features shortly. If you don't use the more advanced features, you can delete this additional code.

As you can see, the Visual C++ team has defined two software exception codes: **VcppException(ERROR_SEVERITY_ERROR, ERROR_MOD_NOT_FOUND)** and **VcppException(ERROR_SEVERITY_ERROR, ERROR_PROC_NOT_FOUND)**. These indicate that the DLL module was not found and that the function was not found, respectively. My exception filter function, **DelayLoadDllExceptionFilter**, checks for these two exception codes. If neither code is thrown, the filter returns **EXCEPTION_CONTINUE_SEARCH**, as any good filter should. (Never swallow exceptions that you don't know how to handle.) However, if one of these codes is thrown, the **__delayLoadHelper2** function provides a pointer to a **DelayLoadInfo** structure containing some additional information. The **DelayLoadInfo** structure is defined in the Visual C++ DelayImp.h file as follows:

```
typedef struct DelayLoadInfo {
   DWORD           cb;         // Size of structure
   PCImgDelayDescr pidd;       // Raw data (everything is there)
   FARPROC *       ppfn;       // Points to address of function to load
   LPCSTR          szDll;      // Name of dll
   DelayLoadProc   dlp;        // Name or ordinal of procedure
   HMODULE         hmodCur;    // hInstance of loaded library
   FARPROC         pfnCur;     // Actual function that will be called
   DWORD           dwLastError;// Error received
} DelayLoadInfo, * PDelayLoadInfo;
```

This data structure is allocated and initialized by the **__delayLoadHelper2** function. As the function progresses through its work of dynamically loading the DLL and getting the address of the called function, it populates the members of this structure. Inside your SEH filter, the **szDll** member points to the name of the DLL you're attempting to load and the function you're attempting to look up is in the **dlp** member. Because you can look up functions by ordinal or by name, the **dlp** member looks like this:

```
typedef struct DelayLoadProc {
   BOOL fImportByName;
   union {
      LPCSTR szProcName;
      DWORD  dwOrdinal;
   };
} DelayLoadProc;
```

If the DLL successfully loads but does not contain the desired function, you might also look at the **hmodCur** member to see the memory address where the DLL is loaded. You can also check the

dwLastError member to see what error caused the exception to be raised, but this probably isn't necessary for an exception filter because the exception code tells you what happened. The **pfnCur** member contains the address of the desired function. This is always set to **NULL** in the exception filter because **__delayLoadHelper2** couldn't find the address of the function.

Of the remaining members, **cb** is for versioning, **pidd** points to the section embedded in the module that contains the list of delay-load DLLs and functions, and **ppfn** is the address where the function's address will go if the function is found. These last two members are used by the **__delayLoadHelper2** function internally. They are for super-advanced use; it is extremely unlikely that you will ever have to examine or understand them.

So far, I've explained the basics of using delay-load DLLs and properly recovering from error conditions. However, Microsoft's implementation of delay-load DLLs goes beyond what I have discussed so far. Your application can unload a delay-loaded DLL, for example. Let's say that your application requires a special DLL to print the user's document. This DLL is a perfect candidate to be a delay-load DLL because most of the time it probably won't be used. However, if the user chooses the Print command, you can call a function in the DLL and it will automatically load. This is great, but after the document is printed, the user probably won't print another document immediately, so you can unload the DLL and free system resources. If the user decides to print another document, the DLL will again be loaded on demand.

To unload a delay-loaded DLL, you must do two things. First, you must specify an additional linker switch (**/Delay:unload**) when you build your executable file. Second, you must modify your source code and place a call to the **__FUnloadDelayLoadedDLL2** function at the point where you want the DLL to be unloaded:

```
BOOL __FUnloadDelayLoadedDLL2(PCSTR szDll);
```

The **/Delay:unload** linker switch tells the linker to place another section inside the file. This section contains the information necessary to reset the functions you have already called so that they again call the **__delayLoadHelper2** function. When you call **__FUnloadDelayLoadedDLL2**, you pass it the name of the delay-load DLL that you want to unload. The function then goes to the unload section in the file and resets all of the DLL's function addresses. Then **__FUnloadDelay- LoadedDLL2** calls **FreeLibrary** to unload the DLL.

Let me point out a few important items. First, make sure that you don't call **FreeLibrary** yourself to unload the DLL or the function's address will not be reset; this will cause an access violation the next time you attempt to call a function in the DLL. Second, when you call **__FUnloadDelay- LoadedDLL2**, the DLL name you pass should not include a path and the letters in the name must be the same case that was used when you passed the DLL name to the **/DelayLoad** linker switch; otherwise, **__FUnloadDelayLoadedDLL2** will fail. Third, if you never intend to unload a delay-loaded DLL, do not specify the **/Delay:unload** linker switch and your executable file will be smaller in size. Finally, if you call **__FUnloadDelayLoadedDLL2** from a module that was not built with the **/Delay:unload** switch, nothing bad happens: **__FUnloadDelayLoadedDLL2** simply does nothing and returns **FALSE**.

Another feature of the delay-load DLLs is that by default, the functions that you call are bindable to memory addresses where the system thinks the function will be in a process' address. (I'll discuss binding later in this chapter.) Because creating bindable delay-load DLL sections makes your executable file bigger, the linker also supports a **/Delay:nobind** switch. Because binding is generally preferred, most applications should not use this linker switch.

The last feature of delay-load DLLs is for advanced users and really shows Microsoft's attention to detail. As the **__delayLoadHelper2** function executes, it can call hook functions that you provide. These functions receive notifications of **__delayLoadHelper2**'s progress and notifications of errors. In addition, these functions can override how the DLL is loaded and how the function's virtual memory address is obtained.

To get the notification or override behavior, you must do two things to your source code. First, you must write a hook function that looks like the **DliHook** function in DelayLoadApp.cpp. The **DliHook** skeleton function does not affect **__delayLoadHelper2**'s operation. To alter the behavior, start with the **DliHook** function and then modify it as necessary. Then tell **__delayLoadHelper2** the address of the function.

Inside the DelayImp.lib static-link library, two global variables are defined: **__pfnDliNotifyHook2** and **__pfnDliFailureHook2**. Both of these variables are of type **PfnDliHook**:

```
typedef FARPROC (WINAPI *PfnDliHook)(
    unsigned dliNotify,
    PDelayLoadInfo pdli);
```

As you can see, this is a function data type and matches the prototype of my **DliHook** function. Inside DelayImp.lib, the two variables are initialized to **NULL**, which tells **__delayLoadHelper2** not to call any hook functions. To have your hook function called, you must set one of these variables to your hook function's address. In my code, I simply add these two lines of code at global scope:

```
PfnDliHook __pfnDliNotifyHook2  = DliHook;
PfnDliHook __pfnDliFailureHook2 = DliHook;
```

As you can see, **__delayLoadHelper2** actually works with two callback functions. It calls one to report notifications and the other to report failures. Because the prototypes are identical for both functions, and the first parameter, **dliNotify**, tells why the function is being called, I always make life simpler by creating a single function and setting both variables to point to my one function.

> **Tip** The DependencyWalker utility from *www.DependencyWalker.com* allows you to list the link-time dependencies—both static and delay-load—but it also keeps track of the **LoadLibrary/GetProcAddress** calls at run time thanks to its profiling feature.

The DelayLoadApp Sample Application

The DelayLoadApp application (20-DelayLoadApp.exe), listed a bit later in this section, shows everything you need to do to take full advantage of delay-load DLLs. For demonstration purposes, a simple DLL is required; the code for that is in the 20-DelayLoadLib directory.

Because the application loads the 20-DelayLoadLib module, the loader does not map this module into the process' address space when you run the application. Inside the application, I periodically call the **IsModuleLoaded** function. This function simply displays a message box notifying you whether a module is loaded into the process' address space. When the application first starts, the 20-DelayLoadLib module is not loaded, causing the message box in Figure 20-4 to appear.

Figure 20-4   DelayLoadApp indicating that the 20-DelayLoadLib module is not loaded

The application then calls a function imported from the DLL, which causes the **__delayLoad-Helper2** function to automatically load the DLL. When the function returns, the message box in Figure 20-5 is displayed.

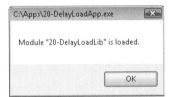

Figure 20-5   DelayLoadApp indicating that the 20-DelayLoadLib module is loaded

When this message box is dismissed, another function in the DLL is called. Because this function is in the same DLL, the DLL does not get loaded in the address space again, but the address of this new function is resolved and called.

At this point, **__FUnloadDelayLoadedDLL2** is called; it unloads the 20-DelayLoadLib module. Again, the call to **IsModuleLoaded** shows the message box in Figure 20-4. Finally, an imported function is again called, which reloads the 20-DelayLoadLib module, causing the last call to **IsModuleLoaded** to show the message box in Figure 20-5.

If all is OK, the application will work as I've described. However, if you delete the 20-DelayLoadLib module before running the application or if the module doesn't contain one of the imported functions, exceptions will be raised. The sample code shows how to recover "gracefully" (so to speak) from this situation.

Finally, the application shows how to properly set a delay-load hook function. My skeleton **DliHook** function doesn't do anything of interest. However, it does trap various notifications and shows what you can do when you receive these notifications.

DelayLoadApp.cpp

```
/*****************************************************************************
Module:  DelayLoadApp.cpp
Notices: Copyright (c) 2008 Jeffrey Richter & Christophe Nasarre
*****************************************************************************/


#include "..\CommonFiles\CmnHdr.h"      /* See Appendix A. */
#include <Windowsx.h>
#include <tchar.h>
#include <StrSafe.h>


///////////////////////////////////////////////////////////////////////////


#include <Delayimp.h>   // For error handling & advanced features
#include "..\20-DelayLoadLib\DelayLoadLib.h"     // My DLL function prototypes


///////////////////////////////////////////////////////////////////////////


// Statically link __delayLoadHelper2/__FUnloadDelayLoadedDLL2
#pragma comment(lib, "Delayimp.lib")

// Note: it is not possible to use #pragma comment(linker, "")
//        for /DELAYLOAD and /DELAY


// The name of the Delay-Load module (only used by this sample app)
TCHAR g_szDelayLoadModuleName[] = TEXT("20-DelayLoadLib");


///////////////////////////////////////////////////////////////////////////


// Forward function prototype
LONG WINAPI DelayLoadDllExceptionFilter(PEXCEPTION_POINTERS pep);


///////////////////////////////////////////////////////////////////////////


void IsModuleLoaded(PCTSTR pszModuleName) {

   HMODULE hmod = GetModuleHandle(pszModuleName);
   char sz[100];
#ifdef UNICODE
   StringCchPrintfA(sz, _countof(sz), "Module \"%S\" is %Sloaded.",
      pszModuleName, (hmod == NULL) ? L"not " : L"");
```

```
#else
   StringCchPrintfA(sz, _countof(sz), "Module \"%s\" is %sloaded.",
      pszModuleName, (hmod == NULL) ? "not " : "");
#endif
   chMB(sz);
}


/////////////////////////////////////////////////////////////////////////////


int WINAPI _tWinMain(HINSTANCE hInstExe, HINSTANCE, PTSTR pszCmdLine, int) {

   // Wrap all calls to delay-load DLL functions inside SEH
   __try {
      int x = 0;

      // If you're in the debugger, try the new Debug.Modules menu item to
      // see that the DLL is not loaded prior to executing the line below
      IsModuleLoaded(g_szDelayLoadModuleName);

      x = fnLib();  // Attempt to call delay-load function

      // Use Debug.Modules to see that the DLL is now loaded
      IsModuleLoaded(g_szDelayLoadModuleName);

      x = fnLib2(); // Attempt to call delay-load function

      // Unload the delay-loaded DLL
      // NOTE: Name must exactly match /DelayLoad:(DllName)
      __FUnloadDelayLoadedDLL2("20-DelayLoadLib.dll");

      // Use Debug.Modules to see that the DLL is now unloaded
      IsModuleLoaded(g_szDelayLoadModuleName);

      x = fnLib();  // Attempt to call delay-load function

      // Use Debug.Modules to see that the DLL is loaded again
      IsModuleLoaded(g_szDelayLoadModuleName);
   }
   __except (DelayLoadDllExceptionFilter(GetExceptionInformation())) {
      // Nothing to do in here, thread continues to run normally
   }

   // More code can go here...

   return(0);
}


/////////////////////////////////////////////////////////////////////////////
```

```
LONG WINAPI DelayLoadDllExceptionFilter(PEXCEPTION_POINTERS pep) {

   // Assume we recognize this exception
   LONG lDisposition = EXCEPTION_EXECUTE_HANDLER;

   // If this is a Delay-load problem, ExceptionInformation[0] points
   // to a DelayLoadInfo structure that has detailed error info
   PDelayLoadInfo pdli =
      PDelayLoadInfo(pep->ExceptionRecord->ExceptionInformation[0]);

   // Create a buffer where we construct error messages
   char sz[500] = { 0 };

   switch (pep->ExceptionRecord->ExceptionCode) {
   case VcppException(ERROR_SEVERITY_ERROR, ERROR_MOD_NOT_FOUND):
      // The DLL module was not found at runtime
      StringCchPrintfA(sz, _countof(sz), "Dll not found: %s", pdli->szDll);
      break;

   case VcppException(ERROR_SEVERITY_ERROR, ERROR_PROC_NOT_FOUND):
      // The DLL module was found, but it doesn't contain the function
      if (pdli->dlp.fImportByName) {
         StringCchPrintfA(sz, _countof(sz), "Function %s was not found in %s",
            pdli->dlp.szProcName, pdli->szDll);
      } else {
         StringCchPrintfA(sz, _countof(sz), "Function ordinal %d was not found in %s",
            pdli->dlp.dwOrdinal, pdli->szDll);
      }
      break;

   default:
      // We don't recognize this exception
      lDisposition = EXCEPTION_CONTINUE_SEARCH;
      break;
   }

   if (lDisposition == EXCEPTION_EXECUTE_HANDLER) {
      // We recognized this error and constructed a message, show it
      chMB(sz);
   }

   return(lDisposition);
}


///////////////////////////////////////////////////////////////////////////////


// Skeleton DliHook function that does nothing interesting
FARPROC WINAPI DliHook(unsigned dliNotify, PDelayLoadInfo pdli) {

   FARPROC fp = NULL;   // Default return value

   // NOTE: The members of the DelayLoadInfo structure pointed
   // to by pdli show the results of progress made so far.
```

```
  switch (dliNotify) {
  case dliStartProcessing:
      // Called when __delayLoadHelper2 attempts to find a DLL/function
      // Return 0 to have normal behavior or nonzero to override
      // everything (you will still get dliNoteEndProcessing)
      break;

  case dliNotePreLoadLibrary:
      // Called just before LoadLibrary
      // Return NULL to have __delayLoadHelper2 call LoadLibary
      // or you can call LoadLibrary yourself and return the HMODULE
      fp = (FARPROC) (HMODULE) NULL;
      break;

  case dliFailLoadLib:
      // Called if LoadLibrary fails
      // Again, you can call LoadLibary yourself here and return an HMODULE
      // If you return NULL, __delayLoadHelper2 raises the
      // ERROR_MOD_NOT_FOUND exception
      fp = (FARPROC) (HMODULE) NULL;
      break;

  case dliNotePreGetProcAddress:
      // Called just before GetProcAddress
      // Return NULL to have __delayLoadHelper2 call GetProcAddress,
      // or you can call GetProcAddress yourself and return the address
      fp = (FARPROC) NULL;
      break;

  case dliFailGetProc:
      // Called if GetProcAddress fails
      // You can call GetProcAddress yourself here and return an address
      // If you return NULL, __delayLoadHelper2 raises the
      // ERROR_PROC_NOT_FOUND exception
      fp = (FARPROC) NULL;
      break;

  case dliNoteEndProcessing:
      // A simple notification that __delayLoadHelper2 is done
      // You can examine the members of the DelayLoadInfo structure
      // pointed to by pdli and raise an exception if you desire
      break;
  }

  return(fp);
}


///////////////////////////////////////////////////////////////////////////


// Tell __delayLoadHelper2 to call my hook function
PfnDliHook __pfnDliNotifyHook2  = DliHook;
PfnDliHook __pfnDliFailureHook2 = DliHook;

//////////////////////////// End of File //////////////////////////////////
```

DelayLoadLib.cpp

```
/******************************************************************************
Module:  DelayLoadLib.cpp
Notices: Copyright (c) 2008 Jeffrey Richter & Christophe Nasarre
******************************************************************************/


#include "..\CommonFiles\CmnHdr.h"        /* See Appendix A. */
#include <Windowsx.h>
#include <tchar.h>


///////////////////////////////////////////////////////////////////////////////


#define DELAYLOADLIBAPI extern "C" __declspec(dllexport)
#include "DelayLoadLib.h"


///////////////////////////////////////////////////////////////////////////////


int fnLib() {

   return(321);
}


///////////////////////////////////////////////////////////////////////////////


int fnLib2() {

   return(123);
}


//////////////////////////////// End of File //////////////////////////////////
```

DelayLoadLib.h

```
/******************************************************************************
Module:  DelayLoadLib.h
Notices: Copyright (c) 2008 Jeffrey Richter & Christophe Nasarre
******************************************************************************/


#ifndef DELAYLOADLIBAPI
#define DELAYLOADLIBAPI extern "C" __declspec(dllimport)
#endif


///////////////////////////////////////////////////////////////////////////////
```

```
DELAYLOADLIBAPI int fnLib();
DELAYLOADLIBAPI int fnLib2();


///////////////////////////////// End of File /////////////////////////////////
```

Function Forwarders

A function forwarder is an entry in a DLL's export section that redirects a function call to another function in another DLL. For example, if you run the Visual C++ DumpBin utility on the Windows Vista Kernel32.dll, you'll see a part of the output that looks like this:

```
C:\Windows\System32>DumpBin -Exports Kernel32.dll       (some output omitted)
75    49    CloseThreadpoolIo (forwarded to NTDLL.TpReleaseIoCompletion)
76    4A    CloseThreadpoolTimer (forwarded to NTDLL.TpReleaseTimer)
77    4B    CloseThreadpoolWait (forwarded to NTDLL.TpReleaseWait)
78    4C    CloseThreadpoolWork (forwarded to NTDLL.TpReleaseWork)
      (remainder of output omitted)
```

This output shows four forwarded functions. Whenever your application calls **CloseThreadpoolIo**, **CloseThreadpoolTimer**, **CloseThreadpoolWait**, or **CloseThreadpoolWork**, your executable is dynamically linked with Kernel32.dll. When you invoke your executable, the loader loads Kernel32.dll and sees that forwarded functions are actually contained inside NTDLL.dll. It then loads the NTDLL.dll module as well. When your executable calls **CloseThreadpoolIo**, it is actually calling the **TpReleaseIoCompletion** function inside NTDLL.dll. A **CloseThreadpoolIo** function doesn't exist anywhere in the system!

If you call the following function, **GetProcAddress** looks in Kernel32's export section, sees that **CloseThreadpoolIo** is a forwarded function, and then calls **GetProcAddress** recursively, looking for **TpReleaseIoCompletion** inside NTDLL.dll's export section.

You can take advantage of function forwarders in your DLL module as well. The easiest way to do this is by using a **pragma** directive, as shown here:

```
// Function forwarders to functions in DllWork
#pragma comment(linker, "/export:SomeFunc=DllWork.SomeOtherFunc")
```

This **pragma** tells the linker that the DLL being compiled should export a function called **Some-Func**. But the actual implementation of **SomeFunc** is in another function called **SomeOtherFunc**, which is contained in a module called DllWork.dll. You must create separate **pragma** lines for each function you want to forward.

Known DLLs

Certain operating system–supplied DLLs get special treatment. These are called *known DLLs*. They are just like any other DLL except that the operating system always looks for them in the same directory in order to load them. Inside the registry is the following key:

```
HKEY_LOCAL_MACHINE\SYSTEM\CurrentControlSet\Control\
    Session Manager\KnownDLLs
```

Here's what this subkey looks like on my machine using the RegEdit.exe utility.

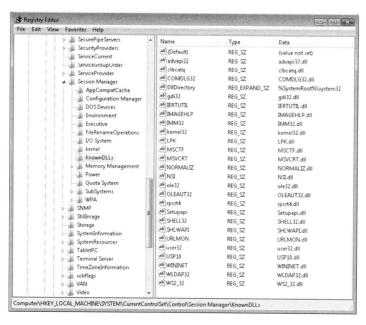

As you can see, this key contains a set of value names that are the names of certain DLLs. Each of these value names has value data that happens to be identical to the value name with a .dll file extension. (This does not have to be the case, however, as I'll show you in an upcoming example.) When **LoadLibrary** or **LoadLibraryEx** is called, the functions first check to see whether you are passing a DLL name that includes the .dll extension. If you are not, they search for the DLL using the normal search rules.

If you do specify a .dll extension, these functions remove the extension and then search the **KnownDLLs** registry key to see whether it contains a value name that matches. If no matching name is found, the normal search rules are used. But if a matching value name is found, the system looks up the associated value data and attempts to load a DLL using the value data instead. The system also begins searching for the DLL in the directory indicated by the **DllDirectory** value's data in the registry. By default, the **DllDirectory** value's data is %SystemRoot%\System32 on Windows Vista.

To illustrate, suppose we add the following value to the **KnownDLLs** registry key:

```
Value name: SomeLib
Value data: SomeOtherLib.dll
```

When we call the following function, the system uses the normal search rules to locate the file:

```
LoadLibrary(TEXT("SomeLib"));
```

However, if we call the following function, the system sees that there is a matching value name. (Remember that the system removes the .dll extension when it checks the registry value names.)

```
LoadLibrary(TEXT("SomeLib.dll"));
```

The system therefore attempts to load a library called SomeOtherLib.dll instead of SomeLib.dll. And it first looks for SomeOtherLib.dll in the %SystemRoot%\System32 directory. If it finds the file in this directory, it loads it. If the file is not in this directory, **LoadLibrary(Ex)** fails and returns **NULL**, and a call to **GetLastError** returns **2** (**ERROR_FILE_NOT_FOUND**).

DLL Redirection

When Windows was first developed, RAM and disk space were at a premium. So Windows was designed to share as many resources as possible to conserve these precious resources. To this end, Microsoft recommended that any modules shared by multiple applications, such as the C/C++ run-time library and the Microsoft Foundation Classes (MFC) DLLs, be placed in the Windows system directory. This allowed the system to locate the shared files easily.

As time went on, this became a serious problem because setup programs would overwrite files in this directory with older files or newer files that were not completely backward compatible. This prevented the user's other applications from running properly. Today, hard disks are big and cheap and RAM is also quite plentiful and relatively cheap. So Microsoft is now reversing itself and strongly recommending that you place all of your application's files in their own directory and never touch anything in the Windows system directory. This will prevent your application from harming other applications and will keep your application from being harmed by other applications.

To help you, Microsoft has added a DLL redirection feature since Windows 2000. This feature forces the operating system loader to load modules from your application's directory first. Only if the loader cannot find the file there will it search other directories.

To force the loader to always check the application's directory first, all you do is place a file in the application's directory. The contents of the file are ignored but the file must be called App-Name.local. For example, if you have an executable file called SuperApp.exe, the redirection file must be called SuperApp.exe.local.

Internally, **LoadLibrary(Ex)** has been modified to check for the existence of this file. If the file exists in the application's directory, the module in this directory is loaded. If the module doesn't exist in the application's directory, **LoadLibrary(Ex)** works as usual. Notice that, instead of creating a .local file, it is possible to create a folder with the same name instead. In that case, you can store all your DLLs in this folder for Windows to find them easily.

This feature is extremely useful for registered COM objects. It allows an application to place its COM object DLLs in its own directory so that other applications registering the same COM objects cannot interfere with your operation.

Notice that for security sake—because fake system DLLs could be loaded from the application folder instead of from the Windows system folders—this feature is disabled by default in Windows Vista. To enable it, you have to create in the registry the **DWORD DevOverrideEnable** entry under the HKLM\Software\Microsoft\WindowsNT\CurrentVersion\Image File Execution Options key and give it a value of **1**.

> **Note**   Since Windows XP and the rise of Microsoft .NET applications, you can take advantage of isolated applications and side-by-side assemblies even with unmanaged code, as detailed in "Isolated Applications and Side-by-side Assemblies" at *http://msdn2.microsoft.com/en-us/library/aa375193.aspx*.

Rebasing Modules

Every executable and DLL module has a *preferred base address*, which identifies the ideal memory address where the module should get mapped into a process' address space. When you build an executable module, the linker sets the module's preferred base address to 0x00400000. For a DLL module, the linker sets a preferred base address of 0x10000000. Using the Microsoft Visual Studio DumpBin utility (with the **/headers** switch), you can see an image's preferred base address. Here is an example of using DumpBin to dump its own header information:

```
C:\>DUMPBIN /headers dumpbin.exe

Microsoft (R) COFF/PE Dumper Version 8.00.50727.42
Copyright (C) Microsoft Corporation.  All rights reserved.

Dump of file dumpbin.exe

PE signature found

File Type: EXECUTABLE IMAGE

FILE HEADER VALUES
            14C machine (i386)
              3 number of sections
       4333ABD8 time date stamp Fri Sep 23 09:16:40 2005
              0 file pointer to symbol table
              0 number of symbols
             E0 size of optional header
            123 characteristics
                  Relocations stripped
                  Executable
                  Application can handle large (>2GB) addresses
                  32 bit word machine

OPTIONAL HEADER VALUES
            10B magic # (PE32)
           8.00 linker version
           1200 size of code
            800 size of initialized data
              0 size of uninitialized data
           170C entry point (0040170C)
```

```
  1000 base of code
  3000 base of data
400000 image base (00400000 to 00404FFF) <- Module's preferred base address
  1000 section alignment
   200 file alignment
  5.00 operating system version
  8.00 image version
  4.00 subsystem version
     0 Win32 version
  5000 size of image
   400 size of headers
 1306D checksum
     3 subsystem (Windows CUI)
  8000 DLL characteristics
          Terminal Server Aware
100000 size of stack reserve
  2000 size of stack commit
100000 size of heap reserve
  1000 size of heap commit
     0 loader flags
    10 number of directories
```

...

When this executable module is invoked, the operating system loader creates a virtual address for the new process. Then the loader maps the executable module at memory address 0x00400000 and the DLL module at 0x10000000. Why is this preferred base address so important? Let's look at this code:

```
int g_x;

void Func() {
   g_x = 5; // This is the important line.
}
```

When the compiler processes the **Func** function, the compiler and linker produce machine code that looks something like this:

```
MOV   [0x00414540], 5
```

In other words, the compiler and linker have created machine code that is actually hard-coded in the address of the **g_x** variable: 0x00414540. This address is in the machine code and absolutely identifies the location of the **g_x** variable in the process' address space. But, of course, this memory address is correct if and only if the executable module loads at its preferred base address: 0x00400000.

What if we had the exact same code in a DLL module? In that case, the compiler and linker would generate machine code that looks something like this:

```
MOV   [0x10014540], 5
```

Again, notice that the virtual memory address for the DLL's **g_x** variable is hard-coded in the DLL file's image on the disk drive. And again, this memory address is absolutely correct as long as the DLL does in fact load at its preferred base address.

OK, now let's say that you're designing an application that requires two DLLs. By default, the linker sets the .exe module's preferred base address to 0x00400000 and the linker sets the preferred base address for both DLLs to 0x10000000. If you attempt to run the .exe, the loader creates the virtual address space and maps the .exe module at the 0x00400000 memory address. Then the loader maps the first DLL to the 0x10000000 memory address. But now, when the loader attempts to map the second DLL into the process' address space, it can't possibly map it at the module's preferred base address. It must relocate the DLL module, placing it somewhere else.

Relocating an executable (or DLL) module is an absolutely horrible process, and you should take measures to avoid it. Let's see why. Suppose that the loader relocates the second DLL to address 0x20000000. In that case, the code that changes the **g_x** variable to **5** should be

```
MOV   [0x20014540], 5
```

But the code in the file's image looks like this:

```
MOV   [0x10014540], 5
```

If the code from the file's image is allowed to execute, some 4-byte value in the first DLL module will be overwritten with the value **5**. This can't possibly be allowed. The loader must somehow fix this code. When the linker builds your module, it embeds a relocation section in the resulting file. This section contains a list of byte offsets. Each byte offset identifies a memory address used by a machine code instruction. If the loader can map a module at its preferred base address, the module's relocation section is never accessed by the system. This is certainly what we want—you never want the relocation section to be used.

If, on the other hand, the module cannot be mapped at its preferred base address, the loader opens the module's relocation section and iterates though all the entries. For each entry found, the loader goes to the page of storage that contains the machine code instruction to be modified. It then grabs the memory address that the machine instruction is currently using and adds to the address the difference between the module's preferred base address and the address where the module actually got mapped.

So, in the preceding example, the second DLL was mapped at 0x20000000 but its preferred base address is 0x10000000. This yields a difference of 0x10000000, which is then added to the address in the machine code instruction, giving us this:

```
MOV   [0x20014540], 5
```

Now this code in the second DLL will reference its **g_x** variable correctly.

There are two major drawbacks when a module cannot load at its preferred base address:

- The loader has to iterate through the relocation section and modify a lot of the module's code. This produces a major performance hit and can really hurt an application's initialization time.
- As the loader writes to the module's code pages, the system's copy-on-write mechanism forces these pages to be backed by the system's paging file.

The second point is truly bad. It means that the module's code pages can no longer be discarded and reloaded from the module's file image on disk. Instead, the pages are swapped to and from the system's paging file as necessary. This hurts performance too. But wait, it gets worse. Because the paging file backs all the module's code pages, the system has less storage available for all processes running in the system. This restricts the size of users' spreadsheets, word-processing documents, CAD drawings, bitmaps, and so on.

By the way, you can create an executable or DLL module that doesn't have a relocation section in it. You do this by passing the **/FIXED** switch to the linker when you build the module. Using this switch makes the module smaller in bytes, but it means that the module cannot be relocated. If the module cannot load at its preferred base address, it cannot load at all. If the loader must relocate a module but no relocation section exists for the module, the loader kills the entire process and displays an "Abnormal Process Termination" message to the user.

For resource-only DLLs, this is a problem. A resource-only DLL contains no code, so linking the DLL using the **/FIXED** switch makes a lot of sense. However, if the resource-only DLL can't load at its preferred base address, the module can't load at all. This is ridiculous. To solve this problem, the linker allows you to create a module with information embedded in the header indicating that the module contains no relocation information because none is needed. The Windows loader works with this header information and allows a resource-only DLL to load without incurring any performance or paging file space penalties.

To create an image without any relocations, link the image using the **/SUBSYSTEM:WINDOWS, 5.0** switch or **/SUBSYSTEM:CONSOLE, 5.0** switch and do not specify the **/FIXED** switch. If the linker determines that nothing in the module is subject to relocation fixups, it omits the relocation section from the module and turns off a special **IMAGE_FILE_RELOCS_STRIPPED** flag in the header. When Windows loads the module, it sees that the module can be relocated (because the **IMAGE_FILE_RELOCS_STRIPPED** flag is off) but that the module has no relocations (because the relocation section doesn't exist). Note that this was a new feature of the Windows 2000 loader, which explains why the **/SUBSYSTEM** switch requires the **5.0** at the end.

You now understand the importance of the preferred base address. So if you have multiple modules that you're loading into a single address space, you must set different preferred base addresses for each module. The Visual Studio Project Properties dialog box makes this easy. All you do is select the Configuration Properties\Linker\Advanced section. In the Base Address field, which is blank by default, you enter a number. In the following figure, I've set my DLL module's base address to **0x20000000**.

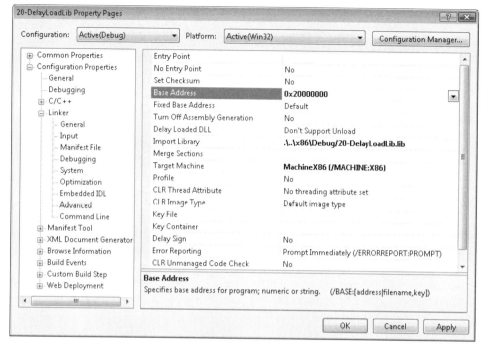

By the way, you should always load DLLs from high-memory addresses, working your way down to low-memory addresses to reduce fragmentation of the address space.

Note Preferred base addresses must always start on an allocation-granularity boundary. On all platforms to date, the system's allocation granularity is 64 KB. This could change in the future. Chapter 13, "Windows Memory Architecture," discusses allocation granularity in more detail.

OK, so that's all fine and good. But what if you're loading a lot of modules into a single address space? It would be nice if there were some easy way to set good preferred base addresses for all of them. Fortunately, there is.

Visual Studio ships with a utility called Rebase.exe. If you run Rebase without any command-line arguments, you get the following usage information:

```
usage: REBASE [switches]
              [-R image-root [-G filename] [-O filename] [-N filename]]
              image-names...

              One of -b and -i switches are mandatory.

              [-a] Does nothing
              [-b InitialBase] specify initial base address
              [-c coffbase_filename] generate coffbase.txt
                  -C includes filename extensions, -c does not
              [-d] top down rebase
              [-e SizeAdjustment] specify extra size to allow for image growth
```

```
[-f] Strip relocs after rebasing the image
[-i coffbase_filename] get base addresses from coffbase_filename
[-l logFilePath] write image bases to log file.
[-p] Does nothing
[-q] minimal output
[-s] just sum image range
[-u symbol_dir] Update debug info in .DBG along this path
[-v] verbose output
[-x symbol_dir] Same as -u
[-z] allow system file rebasing
[-?] display this message


[-R image_root] set image root for use by -G, -O, -N
[-G filename] group images together in address space
[-O filename] overlay images in address space
[-N filename] leave images at their original address
    -G, -O, -N, may occur multiple times.  File "filename"
    contains a list of files (relative to "image-root")


'image-names' can be either a file (foo.dll) or files (*.dll)
              or a file that lists other files (@files.txt).
              If you want to rebase to a fixed address (ala QFE)
              use the @@files.txt format where files.txt contains
              address/size combos in addition to the filename
```

The Rebase utility is described in the Platform SDK documentation, so I won't go into detail here. However, you can implement your own rebasing by simply calling the **ReBaseImage** function from the ImageHlp API:

```
BOOL ReBaseImage(
   PCSTR CurrentImageName,    // Pathname of file to be rebased
   PCSTR SymbolPath,          // Symbol file path so debug info
                              // is accurate
   BOOL bRebase,              // TRUE to actually do the work; FALSE
                              // to pretend
   BOOL bRebaseSysFileOk,     // FALSE to not rebase system images
   BOOL bGoingDown,           // TRUE to rebase the image below
                              // an address
   ULONG CheckImageSize,      // Maximum size that image can grow to (zero if don't care)
   ULONG* pOldImageSize,      // Receives original image size
   ULONG* pOldImageBase,      // Receives original image base address
   ULONG* pNewImageSize,      // Receives new image size
   ULONG* pNewImageBase,      // Receives new image base address
   ULONG TimeStamp);          // New timestamp for image if non zero
```

When you execute Rebase, passing it a set of image filenames, it does the following:

1. It simulates creating a process' address space.

2. It opens all the modules that would normally be loaded into this address space. It thus gets the preferred base address and size of each module.

3. It simulates relocating the modules in the simulated address space so that none of the modules overlap.

4. For the relocated modules, it parses that module's relocation section and modifies the code in the module file on disk.

5. It updates the header of each relocated module to reflect the new preferred base address.

Rebase is an excellent tool, and I strongly encourage you to use it. You should run it toward the end of your build cycle, after all your application's modules are built. Also, if you use Rebase, you can ignore setting the base address in the Project Properties dialog box. The linker will give the DLL a base of 0x10000000, but Rebase will override that.

By the way, you should never, ever rebase any of the modules that ship with the operating system. Microsoft runs Rebase on all the operating system–supplied files before shipping Windows so that none of the operating system modules overlap if you map them all into a single address space.

I added a special feature to the ProcessInfo.exe application presented in Chapter 4. The tool shows you the list of all modules that are in the process' address space. Under the BaseAddr column, you see the virtual memory address where the module is loaded. Right next to the BaseAddr column is the ImagAddr column. Usually this column is blank, which indicates that the module loaded at its preferred base address. You hope to see this for all modules. However, if another address appears in parentheses, the module did not load at its preferred base address and the number indicates the module's preferred base address as read from header information in the module's disk file.

Here is the ProcessInfo.exe tool looking at the devenv.exe process. Notice that one of the modules did not load at its preferred base address. You'll also notice that this module had a preferred base address of 0x00400000, indicating that it is the default address for an .exe and that the creator of this module did not worry about rebasing issues—shame on them.

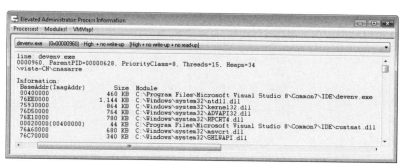

Binding Modules

Rebasing is very important and greatly improves the performance of the entire system. However, you can do even more to improve performance. Let's say that you have properly rebased all your application's modules. Recall from Chapter 19 our discussion about how the loader looks up the address of all the imported symbols. The loader writes the symbol's virtual address into the executable module's import section. This allows references to the imported symbols to actually get to the correct memory location.

Let's think about this for a second. If the loader is writing the virtual addresses of the imported symbols into the .exe module's import section, the pages that back the import section are written to. Because these pages are copy-on-write, the pages are backed by the paging file. So we have a problem that is similar to the rebasing problem: portions of the image file are swapped to and from the system's paging file instead of being discarded and reread from the file's disk image when necessary. Also, the loader has to resolve the addresses of all the imported symbols (for all modules), which can be time-consuming.

You can use the technique of binding a module so that your application can initialize faster and use less storage. Binding a module prepares that module's import section with the virtual addresses of all the imported symbols. To improve initialization time and to use less storage, you must do this before loading the module, of course.

Visual Studio ships with another utility called Bind.exe, which outputs the following information when you run it with no command-line arguments:

```
usage: BIND [switches] image-names...
            [-?] display this message
            [-c] no caching of import dlls
            [-o] disable new import descriptors
            [-p dll search path]
            [-s Symbol directory] update any associated .DBG file
            [-u] update the image
            [-v] verbose output
            [-x image name] exclude this image from binding
            [-y] allow binding on images located above 2G
```

The Bind utility is described in the Platform SDK documentation, so I won't go into detail here. However, like for Rebase, you can implement the same features by calling the **BindImageEx** function from the ImageHlp API:

```
BOOL BindImageEx(
    DWORD dwFlags,          // Flags giving fine control over the function
    PCSTR pszImageName,     // Pathname of file to be bound
    PCSTR pszDllPath,       // Search path used for locating image files
    PCSTR pszSymbolPath,    // Search path used to keep debug info accurate
    PIMAGEHLP_STATUS_ROUTINE pfnStatusRoutine);  // Callback function
```

The last parameter, **pfnStatusRoutine**, is the address of a callback function that is called periodically by **BindImageEx** so that you can monitor the bind process. Here is the prototype of the function:

```
BOOL WINAPI StatusRoutine(
    IMAGEHLP_STATUS_REASON Reason, // Module/procedure not found, etc.
    PCSTR pszImageName,     // Pathname of file being bound
    PCSTR pszDllName,       // Pathname of DLL
    ULONG_PTR VA,           // Computed virtual address
    ULONG_PTR Parameter);   // Additional info depending on Reason
```

When you execute Bind, passing it an image name, it does the following:

1. It opens the specified image file's import section.

2. For every DLL listed in the import section, it opens the DLL file and looks in its header to determine its preferred base address.

3. It looks up each imported symbol in the DLL's export section.

4. It takes the RVA of the symbol and adds to it the module's preferred base address. It writes the resulting expected virtual address of the imported symbol to the image file's import section.

5. It adds some additional information to the image file's import section. This information includes the name of all DLL modules that the image is bound to and the time stamp of those modules.

In Chapter 19, we used the DumpBin utility to examine Calc.exe's import section. The bottom of this output showed the bound import information added in step 5. Here is the relevant portion of the output again:

```
Header contains the following bound import information:
   Bound to SHELL32.dll [4549BDB4] Thu Nov 02 10:43:16 2006
   Bound to ADVAPI32.dll [4549BCD2] Thu Nov 02 10:39:30 2006
   Bound to OLEAUT32.dll [4549BD95] Thu Nov 02 10:42:45 2006
   Bound to ole32.dll [4549BD92] Thu Nov 02 10:42:42 2006
   Bound to ntdll.dll [4549BDC9] Thu Nov 02 10:43:37 2006
   Bound to KERNEL32.dll [4549BD80] Thu Nov 02 10:42:24 2006
   Bound to GDI32.dll [4549BCD3] Thu Nov 02 10:39:31 2006
   Bound to USER32.dll [4549BDE0] Thu Nov 02 10:44:00 2006
   Bound to msvcrt.dll [4549BD61] Thu Nov 02 10:41:53 2006
```

You can see which modules Calc.exe was bound to, and the number in square brackets indicates when Microsoft built each DLL module. This 32-bit time stamp value is expanded and shown as a human-readable string after the square brackets.

During this whole process, Bind makes two important assumptions:

- When the process initializes, the required DLLs actually load at their preferred base address. You can ensure this by using the Rebase utility described earlier.

- The location of the symbol referenced in the DLL's export section has not changed since binding was performed. The loader verifies this by checking each DLL's time stamp with the time stamp saved in step 5 above.

Of course, if the loader determines that either of these assumptions is false, Bind has not done anything useful and the loader must manually fix up the executable module's import section, just as it normally would. But if the loader sees that the module is bound, the required DLLs did load at their preferred base address, and the time stamps match, it actually has nothing to do. It doesn't have to relocate any modules, and it doesn't have to look up the virtual address of any imported functions. The application can simply start executing!

In addition, no storage is required from the system's paging file. This is fantastic—we have the best of all worlds here. It's amazing how many commercial applications ship today without proper rebasing and binding.

OK, so now you know that you should bind all the modules that you ship with your application. But when should you perform the bind? If you bind your modules at your company, you would bind them to the system DLLs that you've installed, which are unlikely to be what the user has installed. Because you don't know if your user is running Windows XP, Windows 2003, or Windows Vista, or whether these have service packs installed, you should perform binding as part of your application's setup.

Of course, if the user dual-boots Windows XP and Windows Vista, the bound modules will be incorrect for one of the operating systems. Also, if the user installs your application under Windows Vista and then upgrades to a service pack, the bind is also incorrect. There isn't much you or the user can do in these situations. Microsoft should ship a utility with the operating system that automatically rebinds every module after an operating system upgrade. But alas, no such utility exists.

Chapter 21
Thread-Local Storage

Sometimes it's helpful to associate data with an instance of an object. For example, window extra bytes associate data with a specific window by using the **SetWindowWord** and **SetWindowLong** functions. You can use Thread Local Storage (TLS) to associate data with a specific thread of execution. For example, you can associate the creation time of a thread with a thread. Then, when the thread terminates, you can determine the thread's lifetime.

The C/C++ run-time library uses TLS. Because the library was designed years before multithreaded applications, most functions in the library are intended for use with single-threaded applications. The **_tcstok_s** function is an excellent example. The first time an application calls **_tcstok_s**, the function passes the address to a string and saves the address of the string in its own static variable. When you make future calls to **_tcstok_s**, passing **NULL**, the function refers to the saved string address.

In a multithreaded environment, one thread might call **_tcstok_s** and then, before it can make another call, another thread might also call **_tcstok_s**. In this case, the second thread causes **_tcstok_s** to overwrite its static variable with a new address without the first thread's knowledge. The first thread's future calls to **_tcstok_s** use the second thread's string, which can lead to all kinds of bugs that are difficult to find and to fix.

To address this problem, the C/C++ run-time library uses TLS. Each thread is assigned its own string pointer that is reserved for use by the **_tcstok_s** function. Other C/C++ run-time functions that require the same treatment include **asctime** and **gmtime**.

TLS can be a lifesaver if your application relies heavily on global or static variables. Fortunately, developers tend to minimize the use of such variables and rely much more on automatic (stack-based) variables and data passing via function parameters. This is good because stack-based variables are always associated with a particular thread.

The standard C/C++ run-time library has been implemented and reimplemented by various compiler vendors; a C/C++ compiler wouldn't be worth buying if it didn't include the standard C/C++ library. Programmers have used it for years and will continue to do so, which means that the prototype and behavior of functions such as **_tcstok_s** must remain exactly as the standard C/C++ library describes them. If the C/C++ run-time library were to be redesigned today, it would be designed for environments that support multithreaded applications, and extreme measures would be taken to avoid the use of global and static variables.

In my own software projects, I avoid global variables as much as possible. If your application uses global and static variables, I strongly suggest that you examine each variable and investigate the possibilities for changing it to a stack-based variable. This effort can save you an enormous amount of time if you decide to add threads to your application, and even single-threaded applications can benefit.

You can use the two TLS techniques discussed in this chapter—dynamic TLS and static TLS—in both applications and dynamic-link libraries (DLLs). However, they're generally more useful when you create DLLs because DLLs often don't know the structure of the application to which they are linked. When you write an application, however, you typically know how many threads will be created and how those threads will be used. You can then create makeshift methods or, better yet, use stack-based methods (local variables) for associating data with each created thread. Nevertheless, application developers can also benefit from the information in this chapter.

Dynamic TLS

An application takes advantage of dynamic TLS by calling a set of four functions. These functions are actually most often used by DLLs. Figure 21-1 shows the internal data structures that Microsoft Windows uses for managing TLS.

The figure shows a single set of in-use flags for each process running in the system. Each flag is set to either **FREE** or **INUSE**, indicating whether the TLS slot is in use. Microsoft guarantees that at least **TLS_MINIMUM_AVAILABLE** bit flags are available. By the way, **TLS_MINIMUM_AVAILABLE** is defined as 64 in WinNT.h, and additional slots are allocated on demand to allow more than 1000 TLS slots! This should be more than enough slots for any application.

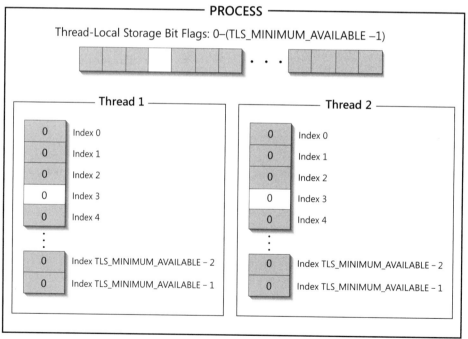

Figure 21-1   Internal data structures that manage TLS

To use dynamic TLS, you must first call **TlsAlloc**:

```
DWORD TlsAlloc();
```

This function instructs the system to scan the bit flags in the process and locate a **FREE** flag. The system then changes the flag from **FREE** to **INUSE**, and **TlsAlloc** returns the index of the flag in the bit array. A DLL (or an application) usually saves the index in a global variable. This is one of those times when a global variable is actually the better choice because the value is used on a per-process basis rather than a per-thread basis.

If **TlsAlloc** cannot find a **FREE** flag in the list, it returns **TLS_OUT_OF_INDEXES** (defined as 0xFFFFFFFF in WinBase.h). The first time **TlsAlloc** is called, the system recognizes that the first flag is **FREE** and changes the flag to **INUSE** and **TlsAlloc** returns **0**. That's 99 percent of what **TlsAlloc** does. I'll get to the other 1 percent later.

When a thread is created, an array of **TLS_MINIMUM_AVAILABLE PVOID** values is allocated, initialized to **0**, and associated with the thread by the system. As Figure 21-1 shows, each thread gets its own array and each **PVOID** in the array can store any value.

Before you can store information in a thread's **PVOID** array, you must know which index in the array is available for use—this is what the earlier call to **TlsAlloc** is for. Conceptually, **TlsAlloc** reserves an index for you. If **TlsAlloc** returns index 3, it is effectively saying that index 3 is reserved for you in every thread currently executing in the process as well as in any threads that might be created in the future.

To place a value in a thread's array, you call the **TlsSetValue** function:

```
BOOL TlsSetValue(
    DWORD dwTlsIndex,
    PVOID pvTlsValue);
```

This function puts a **PVOID** value, identified by the **pvTlsValue** parameter, into the thread's array at the index identified by the **dwTlsIndex** parameter. The value of **pvTlsValue** is associated with the thread making the call to **TlsSetValue**. If the call is successful, **TRUE** is returned.

A thread changes its own array when it calls **TlsSetValue**. But it cannot set a TLS value for another thread. I wish that there were another **Tls** function that allowed one thread to store data in another thread's array, but no such function exists. Currently, the only simple way to pass data from one thread to another is to pass a single value to **CreateThread** or **_beginthreadex**, which then passes the value to the thread function as its only parameter. Otherwise, you have to use the kind of synchronization mechanisms described in Chapter 8, "Thread Synchronization in User Mode," and Chapter 9, "Thread Synchronization with Kernel Objects," to ensure consistency of the exchanged data.

When you call **TlsSetValue**, you should always pass an index returned from an earlier call to **TlsAlloc**. Microsoft designed these functions to be as fast as possible and, in so doing, gave up error checking. If you pass an index that was never allocated by a call to **TlsAlloc**, the system stores the value in the thread's array anyway—no error check is performed.

To retrieve a value from a thread's array, you call **TlsGetValue**:

```
PVOID TlsGetValue(DWORD dwTlsIndex);
```

This function returns the value that was associated with the TLS slot at index **dwTlsIndex**. Like **TlsSetValue**, **TlsGetValue** looks only at the array that belongs to the calling thread. And again like **TlsSetValue**, **TlsGetValue** does check that the passed index is in the allocated range, but it is your responsibility to ensure that the content of the slot is valid before using it.

When you come to a point in your process where you no longer need to reserve a TLS slot among all threads, you should call **TlsFree**:

```
BOOL TlsFree(DWORD dwTlsIndex);
```

This function simply tells the system that this slot no longer needs to be reserved. The **INUSE** flag managed by the process' bit flags array is set to **FREE** again, and it might be allocated in the future if a thread later calls **TlsAlloc**. In addition, the content of the slot is set to **0** in all threads. **TlsFree** returns **TRUE** if the function is successful. Attempting to free a slot that was not allocated results in an error.

Using Dynamic TLS

Usually, if a DLL uses TLS, it calls **TlsAlloc** when its **DllMain** function is called with **DLL_PROCESS_ATTACH**, and it calls **TlsFree** when **DllMain** is called with **DLL_PROCESS_DETACH**. The calls to **TlsSetValue** and **TlsGetValue** are most likely made during calls to functions contained within the DLL.

One method for adding TLS to an application is to add it when you need it. For example, you might have a function in a DLL that works similarly to **_tcstok_s**. The first time your function is called, the thread passes a pointer to a 40-byte structure. You must save this structure so that future calls can reference it. You might code your function like this:

```
DWORD g_dwTlsIndex; // Assume that this is initialized
                    // with the result of a call to TlsAlloc.
...
void MyFunction(PSOMESTRUCT pSomeStruct) {
   if (pSomeStruct != NULL) {
      // The caller is priming this function.

      // See if we already allocated space to save the data.
      if (TlsGetValue(g_dwTlsIndex) == NULL) {
         // Space was never allocated. This is the first
         // time this function has ever been called by this thread.
         TlsSetValue(g_dwTlsIndex,
            HeapAlloc(GetProcessHeap(), 0, sizeof(*pSomeStruct)));
      }

      // Memory already exists for the data;
      // save the newly passed values.
      memcpy(TlsGetValue(g_dwTlsIndex), pSomeStruct,
         sizeof(*pSomeStruct));

   } else {

      // The caller already primed the function. Now it
      // wants to do something with the saved data.
```

```
      // Get the address of the saved data.
      pSomeStruct = (PSOMESTRUCT) TlsGetValue(g_dwTlsIndex);

      // The saved data is pointed to by pSomeStruct; use it.
      ...
}
```

If the application's thread never calls **MyFunction**, a memory block is never allocated for the thread.

It might seem that 64 TLS locations are more than you'll ever need. However, keep in mind that an application can dynamically link to several DLLs. One DLL can allocate 10 TLS indexes, a second DLL can allocate 5 indexes, and so on. So it is always best to reduce the number of TLS indexes you need. The best way to do this is to use the same method that **MyFunction** uses on the previous page. Sure, I can save all 40 bytes in multiple TLS indexes, but doing so is not only wasteful, it makes working with the data difficult. Instead, you should allocate a memory block for the data and simply save the pointer in a single TLS index just as **MyFunction** does. As I mentioned earlier, Windows dynamically allocates more TLS slots beyond the initial 64 slots. Microsoft increased this limit because many developers took a cavalier attitude toward using the slots, which denied slots to other DLLs and caused them to fail.

When I discussed the **TlsAlloc** function earlier, I described only 99 percent of what it did. To help you understand the remaining 1 percent, look at this code fragment:

```
DWORD dwTlsIndex;
PVOID pvSomeValue;
      ...
dwTlsIndex = TlsAlloc();
TlsSetValue(dwTlsIndex, (PVOID) 12345);
TlsFree(dwTlsIndex);

// Assume that the dwTlsIndex value returned from
// this call to TlsAlloc is identical to the index
// returned by the earlier call to TlsAlloc.
dwTlsIndex = TlsAlloc();

pvSomeValue = TlsGetValue(dwTlsIndex);
```

What do you think **pvSomeValue** contains after this code executes? 12345? The answer is **0**. **TlsAlloc**, before returning, cycles through every thread in the process and places **0** in each thread's array at the newly allocated index.

This is fortunate because an application might call **LoadLibrary** to load a DLL, and the DLL might call **TlsAlloc** to allocate an index. Then the thread might call **FreeLibrary** to remove the DLL. The DLL should free its index with a call to **TlsFree**, but who knows which values the DLL code placed in any of the thread's arrays? Next, a thread calls **LoadLibrary** to load a different DLL into memory. This DLL also calls **TlsAlloc** when it starts and gets the same index used by the previous DLL. If **TlsAlloc** didn't set the returned index for all threads in the process, a thread might see an old value and the code might not execute correctly.

For example, this new DLL might want to check whether memory for a thread has ever been allocated by calling **TlsGetValue**, as in the code fragment on the preceding page. If **TlsAlloc** doesn't clear out the array entry for every thread, the old data from the first DLL is still available. If a thread calls **MyFunction**, **MyFunction** thinks that a memory block has already been allocated and calls **memcpy** to copy the new data into what it thinks is a memory block. This could have disastrous results, but fortunately **TlsAlloc** initializes the array elements so that such a disaster can never happen.

Static TLS

Like dynamic TLS, static TLS associates data with a thread. However, static TLS is much easier to use in your code because you don't have to call any functions to take advantage of it.

Let's say that you want to associate a start time with every thread created by your application. All you do is declare the start-time variable as follows:

```
__declspec(thread) DWORD gt_dwStartTime = 0;
```

The **__declspec(thread)** prefix is a modifier that Microsoft added to the Visual C++ compiler. It tells the compiler that the corresponding variable should be placed in its own section in the executable or DLL file. The variable following **__declspec(thread)** must be declared as either a global variable or a static variable inside (or outside) a function. You can't declare a local variable to be of type **__declspec(thread)**. This shouldn't be a problem because local variables are always associated with a specific thread anyway. I use the **gt_** prefix for global TLS variables and **st_** for static TLS variables.

When the compiler compiles your program, it puts all the TLS variables into their own section, which is named, unsurprisingly enough, .tls. The linker combines all the .tls sections from all the object modules to produce one big .tls section in the resulting executable or DLL file.

For static TLS to work, the operating system must get involved. When your application is loaded into memory, the system looks for the .tls section in your executable file and dynamically allocates a block of memory large enough to hold all the static TLS variables. Every time the code in your application refers to one of these variables, the reference resolves to a memory location contained in the allocated block of memory. As a result, the compiler must generate additional code to reference the static TLS variables, which makes your application both larger in size and slower to execute. On an *x86* CPU, three additional machine instructions are generated for every reference to a static TLS variable.

If another thread is created in your process, the system traps it and automatically allocates another block of memory to contain the new thread's static TLS variables. The new thread has access only to its own static TLS variables and cannot access the TLS variables belonging to any other thread.

That's basically how static TLS works. Now let's add DLLs to the story. It's likely that your application will use static TLS variables and that you'll link to a DLL that also wants to use static TLS variables. When the system loads your application, it first determines the size of your application's .tls section and adds the value to the size of any .tls sections in any DLLs to which your application links. When threads are created in your process, the system automatically allocates a block of memory large enough to hold all the TLS variables required by your application and all the implicitly linked DLLs. This is pretty cool.

But let's look at what happens when your application calls **LoadLibrary** to link to a DLL that also contains static TLS variables. The system must look at all the threads that already exist in the process and enlarge their TLS memory blocks to accommodate the additional memory requirements of the new DLL. Also, if **FreeLibrary** is called to free a DLL containing static TLS variables, the memory block associated with each thread in the process should be compacted. The good news is that it is fully supported in Windows Vista.

Chapter 22
DLL Injection and API Hooking

In Microsoft Windows, each process gets its own private address space. When you use pointers to reference memory, the value of the pointer refers to a memory address in your own process' address space. Your process cannot create a pointer that references memory belonging to another process. So if your process has a bug that overwrites memory at a random address, the bug can't affect the memory used by another process.

Separate address spaces are a great advantage for both developers and users. For developers, the system is more likely to catch wild memory reads and writes. For users, the operating system is more robust because one application cannot bring down another process or the operating system. Of course, this robustness comes at a price: it is much harder to write applications that can communicate with or manipulate other processes.

Situations that require breaking through process boundary walls to access another process' address space include the following:

- When you want to subclass a window created by another process
- When you need debugging aids—for example, when you need to determine which dynamic-link libraries (DLLs) another process is using
- When you want to hook other processes

In this chapter, I'll show you several mechanisms you can use to inject a DLL into another process' address space. Once your DLL code is in another address space, you can wreak unlimited havoc on the other process. This should scare you—always think twice about whether this is something you really need to do.

DLL Injection: An Example

Let's say that you want to subclass an instance of a window created by another process. You might recall that subclassing allows you to alter the behavior of a window. To do this, you simply call

SetWindowLongPtr to change the window procedure address in the window's memory block to point to a new (your own) **WndProc**. The Platform SDK documentation states that an application cannot subclass a window created by another process. This is not exactly true. The problem with subclassing another process' window really has to do with process address space boundaries.

When you call **SetWindowLongPtr** to subclass a window, as shown below, you tell the system that all messages sent or posted to the window specified by **hWnd** should be directed to **MySubclassProc** instead of the window's normal window procedure:

```
SetWindowLongPtr(hWnd, GWLP_WNDPROC, MySubclassProc);
```

In other words, when the system needs to dispatch a message to the specified window's **WndProc**, it looks up the address and then makes a direct call to **WndProc**. In this example, the system sees that the address of the **MySubclassProc** function is associated with the window and makes a direct call to **MySubclassProc** instead.

The problem with subclassing a window created by another process is that the subclass procedure is in another address space. Figure 22-1 shows a simplified view of how a window procedure receives messages. Process A is running and has created a window. The User32.dll file is mapped into the address space of Process A. This mapping of User32.dll is responsible for receiving and dispatching all sent and posted messages destined for any window created by any thread running in Process A. When this mapping of User32.dll detects a message, it first determines the address of the window's **WndProc** and then calls it, passing the window handle, the message, and the **wParam** and **lParam** values. After **WndProc** processes the message, User32.dll loops back around and waits for another window message to be processed.

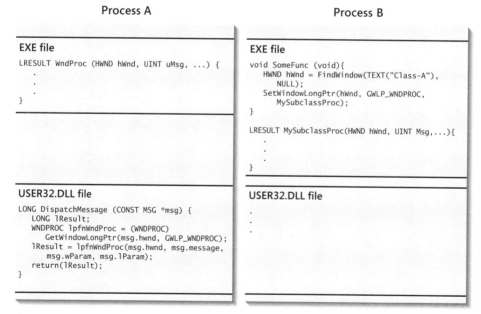

Figure 22-1   A thread in Process B attempting to subclass a window created by a thread in Process A

Now suppose that your process is Process B and you want to subclass a window created by a thread in Process A. Your code in Process B must first determine the handle to the window you want to subclass. This can happen in a variety of ways. The example shown in Figure 22-1 simply calls **FindWindow** to obtain the desired window. Next, the thread in Process B calls **SetWindowLongPtr** in an attempt to change the address of the window's **WndProc**. Notice that I said "attempt." This call does nothing and simply returns **NULL**. The code in **SetWindowLongPtr** checks to see whether one process is attempting to change the **WndProc** address for a window created by another process and simply ignores the call.

What if the **SetWindowLongPtr** function could change the window's **WndProc**? The system would associate the address of **MySubclassProc** with the specified window. Then, when this window was sent a message, the User32 code in Process A would retrieve the message, get the address of **MySubclassProc**, and attempt to call this address. But then you'd have a big problem. **MySubclassProc** would be in Process B's address space, but Process A would be the active process. Obviously, if User32 were to call this address, it would be calling an address in Process A's address space, and this would probably result in a memory access violation.

To avoid this problem, you want the system to know that **MySubclassProc** is in Process B's address space and then have the system perform a context switch before calling the subclass procedure. Microsoft did not implement this additional functionality for several reasons:

- Applications rarely need to subclass windows created by threads in other processes. Most applications subclass windows that they create, and the memory architecture of Windows does not hinder this.

- Switching active processes is very expensive in terms of CPU time.

- A thread in Process B would have to execute the code in **MySubclassProc**. Which thread should the system try to use? An existing thread or a new thread?

- How would User32.dll be able to tell whether the address associated with the window was for a procedure in another process or in the same process?

Because there are no great solutions to these problems, Microsoft decided not to allow **SetWindowLongPtr** to change the window procedure of a window created by another process.

However, you can subclass a window created by another process—you simply go about it in a different way. The question isn't really about subclassing—it's about process address space boundaries. If you could somehow get the code for your subclass procedure into Process A's address space, you could easily call **SetWindowLongPtr** and pass Process A's address to **MySubclassProc**. I call this technique "injecting" a DLL into a process' address space. I know several ways to do this. We'll discuss each of these in turn.

> **Note**   If you plan to subclass windows within the same process, you should take advantage of the **SetWindowSubclass**, **GetWindowSubclass**, **RemoveWindowSubclass**, and **Def-SubclassProc** functions as shown in "Subclassing Controls" at *http://msdn2.microsoft.com/en-us/library/ms649784.aspx*.

Injecting a DLL Using the Registry

If you've been using Windows for any length of time, you should be familiar with the registry. The configuration for the entire system is maintained in the registry, and you can alter the behavior of the system by tweaking its settings. The entries I'll discuss are under the following key:

```
HKEY_LOCAL_MACHINE\Software\Microsoft
   \Windows NT\CurrentVersion\Windows\
```

The following window shows what the entries in this key look like when viewed with Registry Editor:

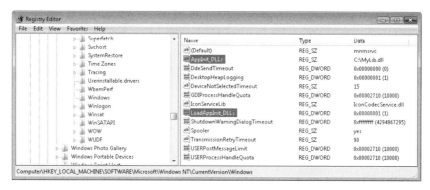

The value for the AppInit_Dlls key might contain a single DLL filename or a set of DLL filenames (separated by spaces or commas). Because spaces delimit filenames, you must avoid filenames that contain spaces. The first DLL filename listed might include a path, but any other DLLs that contain a path are ignored. For this reason, it is usually best to place your DLL in the Windows system directory so that paths need not be specified. In the window, I have set the value to a single DLL pathname, C:\MyLib.dll. For this key to be taken into account, you also need to create a **DWORD** key named LoadAppInit_Dlls with **1** as the value.

Then, when the User32.dll library is mapped into a new process, it receives a **DLL_PROCESS_ATTACH** notification. When this notification is processed, User32.dll retrieves the saved value of this key and calls **LoadLibrary** for each DLL specified in the string. As each library is loaded, the library's associated **DllMain** is called with an **fdwReason** value of **DLL_PROCESS_ATTACH** so that each library can initialize itself. Because the injected DLL is loaded so early in the process' lifetime, you must exercise caution when calling functions. There should be no problem calling functions in Kernel32.dll, but calling functions in some other DLL might cause problems, even a blue screen. User32.dll does not check whether each library has been successfully loaded or initialized.

Of all the methods for injecting a DLL, this is by far the easiest. All you do is add two values to an already existing registry key. But this technique also has some disadvantages:

- Your DLL is mapped only into processes that use User32.dll. All GUI-based applications use User32.dll, but most CUI-based applications do not. So if you need to inject your DLL into a compiler or linker, this method won't work.

- Your DLL is mapped into every GUI-based application, but you probably need to inject your library into only one or a few processes. The more processes your DLL is mapped into, the greater the chance of crashing the "container" processes. After all, threads running in these processes are executing your code. If your code enters an infinite loop or accesses memory incorrectly, you affect the behavior and robustness of the processes in which your code runs. Therefore, it is best to inject your library into as few processes as possible.

■ Your DLL is mapped into every GUI-based application for its entire lifetime. This is similar to the previous problem. Ideally, your DLL should be mapped into just the processes you need, and it should be mapped into those processes for the minimum amount of time. Suppose that when the user invokes your application, you want to subclass WordPad's main window. Your DLL doesn't have to be mapped into WordPad's address space until the user invokes your application. If the user later decides to terminate your application, you'll want to unsubclass WordPad's main window. In this case, your DLL no longer needs to be injected into WordPad's address space. It's best to keep your DLL injected only when necessary.

Injecting a DLL Using Windows Hooks

You can inject a DLL into a process' address space using hooks. To get hooks to work as they do in 16-bit Windows, Microsoft was forced to devise a mechanism that allows a DLL to be injected into the address space of another process.

Let's look at an example. Process A (a utility similar to Microsoft Spy++) installs a **WH_GETMESSAGE** hook to see messages processed by windows in the system. The hook is installed by calling **SetWindowsHookEx** as follows:

```
HHOOK hHook = SetWindowsHookEx(WH_GETMESSAGE, GetMsgProc,
   hInstDll, 0);
```

The first parameter, **WH_GETMESSAGE**, indicates the type of hook to install. The second parameter, **GetMsgProc**, identifies the address (in your address space) of the function that the system should call when a window is about to process a message. The third parameter, **hInstDll**, identifies the DLL that contains the **GetMsgProc** function. In Windows, a DLL's **hInstDll** value identifies the virtual memory address where the DLL is mapped into the process' address space. The last parameter, **0**, identifies the thread to hook. It is possible for one thread to call **SetWindowsHookEx** and to pass the ID of another thread in the system. By passing **0** for this parameter, we tell the system that we want to hook all GUI threads in the system.

Now let's take a look at what happens:

1. A thread in Process B prepares to dispatch a message to a window.

2. The system checks to see whether a **WH_GETMESSAGE** hook is installed on this thread.

3. The system checks to see whether the DLL containing the **GetMsgProc** function is mapped into Process B's address space.

4. If the DLL has not been mapped, the system forces the DLL to be mapped into Process B's address space and increments a lock count on the DLL's mapping in Process B.

5. The system looks at the DLL's **hInstDll** as it applies to Process B and checks to see whether the DLL's **hInstDll** is at the same location as it is when it applies to Process A.

   If the **hInstDlls** are the same, the memory address of the **GetMsgProc** function is also the same in the two process address spaces. In this case, the system can simply call the **GetMsgProc** function in Process A's address space.

If the **hInstDll**s are different, the system must determine the virtual memory address of the **GetMsgProc** function in Process B's address space. This address is determined using the following formula:

```
GetMsgProc B = hInstDll B + (GetMsgProc A - hInstDll A)
```

By subtracting **hInstDll A** from **GetMsgProc A**, you get the offset in bytes for the **GetMsgProc** function. Adding this offset to **hInstDll B** gives the location of the **GetMsgProc** function as it applies to the DLL's mapping in Process B's address space.

6. The system increments a lock count on the DLL's mapping in Process B.

7. The system calls the **GetMsgProc** function in Process B's address space.

8. When **GetMsgProc** returns, the system decrements a lock count on the DLL's mapping in Process B.

Note that when the system injects or maps the DLL containing the hook filter function, the whole DLL is mapped, not just the hook filter function. This means that any and all functions contained in the DLL now exist and can be called from threads running in Process B's context.

So, to subclass a window created by a thread in another process, you can first set a **WH_GETMESSAGE** hook on the thread that created the window, and then, when the **GetMsgProc** function is called, call **SetWindowLongPtr** to subclass the window. Of course, the subclass procedure must be in the same DLL as the **GetMsgProc** function.

Unlike the registry method of injecting a DLL, this method allows you to unmap the DLL when it is no longer needed in the other process' address space by simply calling the following:

```
BOOL UnhookWindowsHookEx(HHOOK hHook);
```

When a thread calls the **UnhookWindowsHookEx** function, the system cycles through its internal list of processes into which it had to inject the DLL and decrements the DLL's lock count. When the lock count reaches 0, the DLL is automatically unmapped from the process' address space. You'll recall that just before the system calls the **GetMsgProc** function, it increments the DLL's lock count. (See step 6 above.) This prevents a memory access violation. If this lock count is not incremented, another thread running in the system can call **UnhookWindowsHookEx** while Process B's thread attempts to execute the code in the **GetMsgProc** function.

All of this means that you can't subclass the window and immediately unhook the hook. The hook must stay in effect for the lifetime of the subclass.

The Desktop Item Position Saver (DIPS) Utility

The DIPS.exe application uses windows hooks to inject a DLL into Explorer.exe's address space. The source code and resource files for the application and DLL are in the 22-DIPS and 22-DIPSLib directories on the companion content Web page.

I generally use my laptop for business-related tasks, and I find that a screen resolution of 1400 by 1050 works best for me. However, I occasionally have to play a presentation through a video projector, and most are designed to support lower resolutions. So when I prepare my laptop for a presentation, I go to Control Panel's Display applet and change the resolution to whatever is required by the projector. When I'm done presenting, I go back to the Display applet and change the resolution back to 1400 by 1050.

This ability to change the display resolution on the fly is awesome and a welcome feature of Windows. However, I do despise one thing about changing the display resolution: the desktop icons don't remember where they were. I have several icons on my desktop to access applications immediately and to get to files that I use frequently. I have these icons positioned on my desktop just so. When I change the display resolution, the desktop window changes size and my icons are rearranged in a way that makes it impossible for me to find anything. Then, when I change the display resolution back, all my icons are rearranged again, in some new order. To fix this, I have to manually reposition all the desktop icons back to the way I like them—how annoying!

I hated manually rearranging these icons so much that I created the Desktop Item Position Saver utility, DIPS. DIPS consists of a small executable and a small DLL. When you run the executable, the following message box appears:

This message box shows how to use the utility. When you pass S as the command-line argument to DIPS, it creates the following registry subkey and adds a value for each item on your desktop window:

```
HKEY_CURRENT_USER\Software\Wintellect\Desktop Item Position Saver
```

Each item has a position value saved with it. You run DIPS S just before you change the screen resolution to play a game. When you're done playing the game, you change the screen resolution back to normal and run DIPS R. This causes DIPS to open the registry subkey, and for each item on your desktop that matches an item saved in the registry, the item's position is set back to where it was when you ran DIPS S.

At first, you might think that DIPS would be fairly easy to implement. After all, you simply get the window handle of the desktop's **ListView** control, send it messages to enumerate the items, get their positions, and then save this information in the registry. However, if you try this, you'll see that it is not quite this simple. The problem is that most common control window messages, such as **LVM_GETITEM** and **LVM_GETITEMPOSITION**, do not work across process boundaries.

Here's why: the **LVM_GETITEM** message requires that you pass the address of an **LV_ITEM** data structure for the message's **LPARAM** parameter. Because this memory address is meaningful only to the process that is sending the message, the process receiving the message cannot safely use it. So to make DIPS work as advertised, you must inject code into Explorer.exe that sends **LVM_GETITEM** and **LVM_GETITEMPOSITION** messages successfully to the desktop's **ListView** control.

> **Note**   You can send window messages across process boundaries to interact with built-in controls (such as button, edit, static, combo box, list box, and so on), but you can't do so with the new common controls. For example, you can send a list box control created by a thread in another process an **LB_GETTEXT** message where the **LPARAM** parameter points to a string buffer in the sending process. This works because Microsoft checks specifically to see whether an **LB_GETTEXT** message is being sent, and if so, the operating system internally creates memory-mapped files and copies the string data across process boundaries.
>
> Why did Microsoft decide to do this for the built-in controls and not for the new common controls? The answer is portability. In 16-bit Windows, in which all applications run in a single address space, one application could send an **LB_GETTEXT** message to a window created by another application. To port these 16-bit applications to Win32 easily, Microsoft went to the extra effort of making sure that this still works. However, when new common controls were created that do not exist in 16-bit Windows, there was no porting issue involved, so Microsoft chose not to do the additional work for the common controls.

When you run DIPS.exe, it first gets the window handle of the desktop's **ListView** control:

```
// The Desktop ListView window is the
// grandchild of the ProgMan window.
hWndLV = GetFirstChild(
   GetFirstChild(FindWindow(TEXT("ProgMan"), NULL)));
```

This code first looks for a window whose class is **ProgMan**. Even though no Program Manager application is running, the Windows Shell creates a window of this class for backward compatibility with applications that were designed for older versions of Windows. This **ProgMan** window has a single child window whose class is **SHELLDLL_DefView**. This child window also has a single child window whose class is **SysListView32**. This **SysListView32** window is the desktop's **ListView** control window. (By the way, I obtained all this information using Spy++.)

Once I have the **ListView**'s window handle, I can determine the ID of the thread that created the window by calling **GetWindowThreadProcessId**. I pass this ID to the **SetDIPSHook** function (implemented inside DIPSLib.cpp). **SetDIPSHook** installs a **WH_GETMESSAGE** hook on this thread and calls the following function to force Windows Explorer's thread to wake up:

```
PostThreadMessage(dwThreadId, WM_NULL, 0, 0);
```

Because I have installed a **WH_GETMESSAGE** hook on this thread, the operating system automatically injects my DIPSLib.dll file into Windows Explorer's address space and calls my **GetMsgProc** function. This function first checks to see whether it is being called for the first time; if so, it creates a hidden window with a caption of "Wintellect DIPS." Keep in mind that Windows Explorer's thread is creating this hidden window. While it does this, the DIPS.exe thread returns from **SetDIPSHook** and then calls this function:

```
GetMessage(&msg, NULL, 0, 0);
```

This call puts the thread to sleep until a message shows up in the queue. Even though DIPS.exe does not create any windows of its own, it still has a message queue, and messages can be placed in this queue only by calling **PostThreadMessage**. If you look at the code in DIPSLib.cpp's **GetMsgProc** function, you'll see that immediately after the call to **CreateDialog** is a call to **PostThreadMessage** that causes the DIPS.exe thread to wake up again. The thread ID was saved in a shared variable inside the **SetDIPSHook** function.

Notice that I use the thread's message queue for thread synchronization. There is absolutely nothing wrong with doing this, and sometimes it's much easier to synchronize threads in this way rather than using the various kernel objects (mutexes, semaphores, events, and so on). Windows has a rich API; take advantage of it.

When the thread in the DIPS executable wakes up, it knows that the server dialog box has been created and calls **FindWindow** to get the window handle. We now can use window messages to communicate between the client (the DIPS applications) and the server (the hidden dialog box). Because a thread running inside the context of Windows Explorer's process created the dialog box, we do face a few limitations on what we can do to Windows Explorer.

To tell our dialog box to save or restore the desktop icon positions, we simply send a message:

```
// Tell the DIPS window which ListView window to manipulate
// and whether the items should be saved or restored.
SendMessage(hWndDIPS, WM_APP, (WPARAM) hWndLV, bSave);
```

I have coded the dialog box's dialog box procedure to look for the **WM_APP** message. When it receives this message, the **WPARAM** parameter indicates the handle of the **ListView** control that is to be manipulated, and the **LPARAM** parameter is a Boolean value indicating whether the current item positions should be saved to the registry or whether the items should be repositioned based on the saved information read from the registry.

Because I use **SendMessage** instead of **PostMessage**, the function does not return until the operation is complete. If you want, you can add messages to the dialog box's dialog box procedure to give the program more control over the Windows Explorer process. When I finish communicating with the dialog box and want to terminate the server (so to speak), I send a **WM_CLOSE** message that tells the dialog box to destroy itself.

Finally, just before the DIPS application terminates, it calls **SetDIPSHook** again but passes **0** as the thread ID. The **0** is a sentinel value that tells the function to unhook the **WH_GETMESSAGE** hook. When the hook is uninstalled, the operating system automatically unloads the DIPSLib.dll file from Windows Explorer's address space, which means that the dialog box's dialog box procedure is no longer inside Windows Explorer's address space. It is important that the dialog box be destroyed first, before the hook is uninstalled; otherwise, the next message received by the dialog box causes Windows Explorer's thread to raise an access violation. If this happens, Windows Explorer is terminated by the operating system. You must be very careful when using DLL injection!

Dips.cpp

```
/**************************************************************************
Notices: Copyright (c) 2008 Jeffrey Richter & Christophe Nasarre
**************************************************************************/


#include "..\CommonFiles\CmnHdr.h"    /* See Appendix A. */
#include <WindowsX.h>
#include <tchar.h>
#include "Resource.h"
#include "..\22-DIPSLib\DIPSLib.h"


///////////////////////////////////////////////////////////////////////////


BOOL Dlg_OnInitDialog(HWND hWnd, HWND hWndFocus, LPARAM lParam) {

   chSETDLGICONS(hWnd, IDI_DIPS);
   return(TRUE);
}


///////////////////////////////////////////////////////////////////////////


void Dlg_OnCommand(HWND hWnd, int id, HWND hWndCtl, UINT codeNotify) {

   switch (id) {
      case IDC_SAVE:
      case IDC_RESTORE:
      case IDCANCEL:
         EndDialog(hWnd, id);
         break;
   }
}


///////////////////////////////////////////////////////////////////////////


BOOL WINAPI Dlg_Proc(HWND hWnd, UINT uMsg, WPARAM wParam, LPARAM lParam) {

   switch (uMsg) {
      chHANDLE_DLGMSG(hWnd, WM_INITDIALOG, Dlg_OnInitDialog);
      chHANDLE_DLGMSG(hWnd, WM_COMMAND,    Dlg_OnCommand);
   }

   return(FALSE);
}


///////////////////////////////////////////////////////////////////////////
```

```
int WINAPI _tWinMain(HINSTANCE hInstExe, HINSTANCE, PTSTR pszCmdLine, int) {

   // Convert command-line character to uppercase.
   CharUpperBuff(pszCmdLine, 1);
   TCHAR cWhatToDo = pszCmdLine[0];

   if ((cWhatToDo != TEXT('S')) && (cWhatToDo != TEXT('R'))) {

      // An invalid command-line argument; prompt the user.
      cWhatToDo = 0;
   }

   if (cWhatToDo == 0) {
      // No command-line argument was used to tell us what to
      // do; show usage dialog box and prompt the user.
      switch (DialogBox(hInstExe, MAKEINTRESOURCE(IDD_DIPS), NULL, Dlg_Proc)) {
         case IDC_SAVE:
            cWhatToDo = TEXT('S');
            break;

         case IDC_RESTORE:
            cWhatToDo = TEXT('R');
            break;
      }
   }

   if (cWhatToDo == 0) {
      // The user doesn't want to do anything.
      return(0);
   }

   // The Desktop ListView window is the grandchild of the ProgMan window.
   HWND hWndLV = GetFirstChild(GetFirstChild(
      FindWindow(TEXT("ProgMan"), NULL)));
   chASSERT(IsWindow(hWndLV));

   // Set hook that injects our DLL into the Explorer's address space. After
   // setting the hook, the DIPS hidden modeless dialog box is created. We
   // send messages to this window to tell it what we want it to do.
   chVERIFY(SetDIPSHook(GetWindowThreadProcessId(hWndLV, NULL)));

   // Wait for the DIPS server window to be created.
   MSG msg;
   GetMessage(&msg, NULL, 0, 0);

   // Find the handle of the hidden dialog box window.
   HWND hWndDIPS = FindWindow(NULL, TEXT("Wintellect DIPS"));

   // Make sure that the window was created.
   chASSERT(IsWindow(hWndDIPS));

   // Tell the DIPS window which ListView window to manipulate
   // and whether the items should be saved or restored.
   BOOL bSave = (cWhatToDo == TEXT('S'));
   SendMessage(hWndDIPS, WM_APP, (WPARAM) hWndLV, bSave);
```

```
      // Tell the DIPS window to destroy itself. Use SendMessage
      // instead of PostMessage so that we know the window is
      // destroyed before the hook is removed.
      SendMessage(hWndDIPS, WM_CLOSE, 0, 0);

      // Make sure that the window was destroyed.
      chASSERT(!IsWindow(hWndDIPS));

      // Unhook the DLL, removing the DIPS dialog box procedure
      // from the Explorer's address space.
      SetDIPSHook(0);

      return(0);
   }


   /////////////////////////////// End of File ////////////////////////////////
```

DIPSLib.cpp

```
/******************************************************************************
Module:  DIPSLib.cpp
Notices: Copyright (c) 2008 Jeffrey Richter & Christophe Nasarre
******************************************************************************/


#include "..\CommonFiles\CmnHdr.h"      /* See Appendix A. */
#include <WindowsX.h>
#include <CommCtrl.h>

#define DIPSLIBAPI __declspec(dllexport)
#include "DIPSLib.h"
#include "Resource.h"


///////////////////////////////////////////////////////////////////////////////


#ifdef _DEBUG
// This function forces the debugger to be invoked
void ForceDebugBreak() {
   __try { DebugBreak(); }
   __except(UnhandledExceptionFilter(GetExceptionInformation())) { }
}
#else
#define ForceDebugBreak()
#endif


///////////////////////////////////////////////////////////////////////////////
```

```c
// Forward references
LRESULT WINAPI GetMsgProc(int nCode, WPARAM wParam, LPARAM lParam);

INT_PTR WINAPI Dlg_Proc(HWND hWnd, UINT uMsg, WPARAM wParam, LPARAM lParam);


///////////////////////////////////////////////////////////////////////////


// Instruct the compiler to put the g_hHook data variable in
// its own data section called Shared. We then instruct the
// linker that we want to share the data in this section
// with all instances of this application.
#pragma data_seg("Shared")
HHOOK g_hHook = NULL;
DWORD g_dwThreadIdDIPS = 0;
#pragma data_seg()

// Instruct the linker to make the Shared section
// readable, writable, and shared.
#pragma comment(linker, "/section:Shared,rws")


///////////////////////////////////////////////////////////////////////////


// Nonshared variables
HINSTANCE g_hInstDll = NULL;


///////////////////////////////////////////////////////////////////////////


BOOL WINAPI DllMain(HINSTANCE hInstDll, DWORD fdwReason, PVOID fImpLoad) {

   switch (fdwReason) {

      case DLL_PROCESS_ATTACH:
         // DLL is attaching to the address space of the current process.
         g_hInstDll = hInstDll;
         break;

      case DLL_THREAD_ATTACH:
         // A new thread is being created in the current process.
         break;

      case DLL_THREAD_DETACH:
         // A thread is exiting cleanly.
         break;

      case DLL_PROCESS_DETACH:
         // The calling process is detaching the DLL from its address space.
         break;
   }
   return(TRUE);
}
```

```
///////////////////////////////////////////////////////////////////////


BOOL WINAPI SetDIPSHook(DWORD dwThreadId) {

   BOOL bOk = FALSE;

   if (dwThreadId != 0) {
      // Make sure that the hook is not already installed.
      chASSERT(g_hHook == NULL);

      // Save our thread ID in a shared variable so that our GetMsgProc
      // function can post a message back to the thread when the server
      // window has been created.
      g_dwThreadIdDIPS = GetCurrentThreadId();

      // Install the hook on the specified thread
      g_hHook = SetWindowsHookEx(WH_GETMESSAGE, GetMsgProc, g_hInstDll,
         dwThreadId);

      bOk = (g_hHook != NULL);
      if (bOk) {
         // The hook was installed successfully; force a benign message to
         // the thread's queue so that the hook function gets called.
         bOk = PostThreadMessage(dwThreadId, WM_NULL, 0, 0);
      }
   } else {

      // Make sure that a hook has been installed.
      chASSERT(g_hHook != NULL);
      bOk = UnhookWindowsHookEx(g_hHook);
      g_hHook = NULL;
   }

   return(bOk);
}


///////////////////////////////////////////////////////////////////////


LRESULT WINAPI GetMsgProc(int nCode, WPARAM wParam, LPARAM lParam) {

   static BOOL bFirstTime = TRUE;

   if (bFirstTime) {
      // The DLL just got injected.
      bFirstTime = FALSE;

      // Uncomment the line below to invoke the debugger
      // on the process that just got the injected DLL.
      // ForceDebugBreak();

      // Create the DIPS Server window to handle the client request.
      CreateDialog(g_hInstDll, MAKEINTRESOURCE(IDD_DIPS), NULL, Dlg_Proc);
```

```
            // Tell the DIPS application that the server is up
            // and ready to handle requests.
            PostThreadMessage(g_dwThreadIdDIPS, WM_NULL, 0, 0);
    }

    return(CallNextHookEx(g_hHook, nCode, wParam, lParam));
}


///////////////////////////////////////////////////////////////////////////////


void Dlg_OnClose(HWND hWnd) {

    DestroyWindow(hWnd);
}


///////////////////////////////////////////////////////////////////////////////


static const TCHAR g_szRegSubKey[] =
    TEXT("Software\\Wintellect\\Desktop Item Position Saver");


///////////////////////////////////////////////////////////////////////////////


void SaveListViewItemPositions(HWND hWndLV) {

    int nMaxItems = ListView_GetItemCount(hWndLV);

    // When saving new positions, delete the old position
    // information that is currently in the registry.
    LONG l = RegDeleteKey(HKEY_CURRENT_USER, g_szRegSubKey);

    // Create the registry key to hold the info
    HKEY hkey;
    l = RegCreateKeyEx(HKEY_CURRENT_USER, g_szRegSubKey, 0, NULL,
        REG_OPTION_NON_VOLATILE, KEY_SET_VALUE, NULL, &hkey, NULL);
    chASSERT(l == ERROR_SUCCESS);

    for (int nItem = 0; nItem < nMaxItems; nItem++) {

        // Get the name and position of a ListView item.
        TCHAR szName[MAX_PATH];
        ListView_GetItemText(hWndLV, nItem, 0, szName, _countof(szName));

        POINT pt;
        ListView_GetItemPosition(hWndLV, nItem, &pt);

        // Save the name and position in the registry.
        l = RegSetValueEx(hkey, szName, 0, REG_BINARY, (PBYTE) &pt, sizeof(pt));
        chASSERT(l == ERROR_SUCCESS);
    }
    RegCloseKey(hkey);
}
```

```
///////////////////////////////////////////////////////////////////////////

void RestoreListViewItemPositions(HWND hWndLV) {

   HKEY hkey;
   LONG l = RegOpenKeyEx(HKEY_CURRENT_USER, g_szRegSubKey,
      0, KEY_QUERY_VALUE, &hkey);
   if (l == ERROR_SUCCESS) {

      // If the ListView has AutoArrange on, temporarily turn it off.
      DWORD dwStyle = GetWindowStyle(hWndLV);
      if (dwStyle & LVS_AUTOARRANGE)
         SetWindowLong(hWndLV, GWL_STYLE, dwStyle & ~LVS_AUTOARRANGE);

      l = NO_ERROR;
      for (int nIndex = 0; l != ERROR_NO_MORE_ITEMS; nIndex++) {
         TCHAR szName[MAX_PATH];
         DWORD cbValueName = _countof(szName);

         POINT pt;
         DWORD cbData = sizeof(pt), nItem;

         // Read a value name and position from the registry.
         DWORD dwType;
         l = RegEnumValue(hkey, nIndex, szName, &cbValueName,
            NULL, &dwType, (PBYTE) &pt, &cbData);

         if (l == ERROR_NO_MORE_ITEMS)
            continue;

         if ((dwType == REG_BINARY) && (cbData == sizeof(pt))) {
            // The value is something that we recognize; try to find
            // an item in the ListView control that matches the name.
            LV_FINDINFO lvfi;
            lvfi.flags = LVFI_STRING;
            lvfi.psz = szName;
            nItem = ListView_FindItem(hWndLV, -1, &lvfi);
            if (nItem != -1) {
               // We found a match; change the item's position.
               ListView_SetItemPosition(hWndLV, nItem, pt.x, pt.y);
            }
         }
      }
      // Turn AutoArrange back on if it was originally on.
      SetWindowLong(hWndLV, GWL_STYLE, dwStyle);
      RegCloseKey(hkey);
   }
}

///////////////////////////////////////////////////////////////////////////
```

```
INT_PTR WINAPI Dlg_Proc(HWND hWnd, UINT uMsg, WPARAM wParam, LPARAM lParam) {

   switch (uMsg) {
      chHANDLE_DLGMSG(hWnd, WM_CLOSE, Dlg_OnClose);

      case WM_APP:
         // Uncomment the line below to invoke the debugger
         // on the process that just got the injected DLL.
         // ForceDebugBreak();

         if (lParam)
            SaveListViewItemPositions((HWND) wParam);
         else
            RestoreListViewItemPositions((HWND) wParam);
         break;
   }

   return(FALSE);
}

//////////////////////////// End of File ////////////////////////////
```

Injecting a DLL Using Remote Threads

The third method of injecting a DLL, using remote threads, offers the greatest flexibility. It requires that you understand several Windows features: processes, threads, thread synchronization, virtual memory management, DLLs, and Unicode. (If you're unclear about any of these features, please refer to their respective chapters in this book.) Most Windows functions allow a process to manipulate only itself. This restriction is good because it prevents one process from corrupting another process. However, a handful of functions do allow one process to manipulate another. Most of these functions were originally designed for debuggers and other tools. However, any application can call these functions.

Basically, this DLL injection technique requires that a thread in the target process call **Load-Library** to load the desired DLL. Because we can't easily control the threads in a process other than our own, this solution requires that we create a new thread in the target process. Because we create this thread ourselves, we can control what code it executes. Fortunately, Windows offers a function called **CreateRemoteThread** that makes it easy to create a thread in another process:

```
HANDLE CreateRemoteThread(
   HANDLE hProcess,
   PSECURITY_ATTRIBUTES psa,
   DWORD dwStackSize,
   PTHREAD_START_ROUTINE pfnStartAddr,
   PVOID pvParam,
   DWORD fdwCreate,
   PDWORD pdwThreadId);
```

CreateRemoteThread is identical to **CreateThread** except that it has one additional parameter, **hProcess**. This parameter identifies the process that will own the newly created thread. The

pfnStartAddr parameter identifies the memory address of the thread function. This memory address is, of course, relative to the remote process—the thread function's code cannot be in your own process' address space.

OK, so now you know how to create a thread in another process, but how do we get that thread to load our DLL? The answer is simple: we need the thread to call the **LoadLibrary** function:

```
HMODULE LoadLibrary(PCTSTR pszLibFile);
```

If you look up **LoadLibrary** in the WinBase.h header file, you'll find the following:

```
HMODULE WINAPI LoadLibraryA(LPCSTR  lpLibFileName);
HMODULE WINAPI LoadLibraryW(LPCWSTR lpLibFileName);
#ifdef UNICODE
#define LoadLibrary  LoadLibraryW
#else
#define LoadLibrary  LoadLibraryA
#endif // !UNICODE
```

There are actually two LoadLibrary functions: **LoadLibraryA** and **LoadLibraryW**. The only difference between them is the type of parameter that you pass to the function. If you have the library's filename stored as an ANSI string, you must call **LoadLibraryA**. (The *A* stands for *ANSI*.) If the filename is stored as a Unicode string, you must call **LoadLibraryW**. (The *W* stands for *wide characters*.) No single **LoadLibrary** function exists—only **LoadLibraryA** and **LoadLibraryW**. For most applications today, the **LoadLibrary** macro expands to **LoadLibraryW**.

Fortunately, the prototype for the **LoadLibrary** functions and the prototype for a thread function are identical. Here is a thread function's prototype:

```
DWORD WINAPI ThreadFunc(PVOID pvParam);
```

OK, the function prototypes are not exactly identical, but they are close enough. Both functions accept a single parameter and both return a value. Also, both use the same calling convention, WINAPI. This is extremely fortunate because all we have to do is create a new thread and have the thread function address be the address of the **LoadLibraryA** or **LoadLibraryW** function. Basically, all we need to do is execute a line of code that looks like this:

```
HANDLE hThread = CreateRemoteThread(hProcessRemote, NULL, 0,
   LoadLibraryW, L"C:\\MyLib.dll", 0, NULL);
```

Or, if you prefer ANSI, the line looks like this:

```
HANDLE hThread = CreateRemoteThread(hProcessRemote, NULL, 0,
   LoadLibraryA, "C:\\MyLib.dll", 0, NULL);
```

When the new thread is created in the remote process, the thread immediately calls the **Load-LibraryW** (or **LoadLibraryA**) function, passing to it the address of the DLL's pathname. This is easy. But there are two other problems.

The first problem is that you can't simply pass **LoadLibraryW** or **LoadLibraryA** as the fourth parameter to **CreateRemoteThread**, as I've shown in the preceding code. The reason is quite subtle. When you compile and link a program, the resulting binary contains an import section (described in Chapter 19, "DLL Basics"). This section consists of a series of thunks to imported functions. So when your code calls a function such as **LoadLibraryW**, the linker generates a call to a thunk in your module's import section. The thunk in turn jumps to the actual function.

If you use a direct reference to **LoadLibraryW** in the call to **CreateRemoteThread**, this resolves to the address of the **LoadLibraryW** thunk in your module's import section. Passing the address of the thunk as the starting address of the remote thread causes the remote thread to begin executing who-knows-what. The result is most likely an access violation. To force a direct call to the **Load-LibraryW** function, bypassing the thunk, you must get the exact memory location of **Load-LibraryW** by calling **GetProcAddress**.

The call to **CreateRemoteThread** assumes that Kernel32.dll is mapped to the same memory location in both the local and remote processes' address spaces. Every application requires Kernel32.dll, and in my experience the system maps Kernel32.dll to the same address in every process, even if this address might change between two reboots as you have seen with Address Space Layout Randomization (ASLR) in Chapter 14, "Exploring Virtual Memory." So we have to call **CreateRemoteThread** like this:

```
// Get the real address of LoadLibraryW in Kernel32.dll.
PTHREAD_START_ROUTINE pfnThreadRtn = (PTHREAD_START_ROUTINE)
   GetProcAddress(GetModuleHandle(TEXT("Kernel32")), "LoadLibraryW");

HANDLE hThread = CreateRemoteThread(hProcessRemote, NULL, 0,
   pfnThreadRtn, L"C:\\MyLib.dll", 0, NULL);
```

Or, again, if you prefer ANSI, do this:

```
// Get the real address of LoadLibraryA in Kernel32.dll.
PTHREAD_START_ROUTINE pfnThreadRtn = (PTHREAD_START_ROUTINE)
   GetProcAddress(GetModuleHandle(TEXT("Kernel32")), "LoadLibraryA");

HANDLE hThread = CreateRemoteThread(hProcessRemote, NULL, 0,
   pfnThreadRtn, "C:\\MyLib.dll", 0, NULL);
```

All right, this fixes one problem. But I said that there were two problems. The second problem has to do with the DLL pathname string. The string, **"C:\\MyLib.dll"**, is in the calling process' address space. The address of this string is given to the newly created remote thread, which passes it to **LoadLibraryW**. But when **LoadLibraryW** dereferences the memory address, the DLL pathname string is not there and the remote process' thread will probably raise an access violation; the unhandled exception message box is presented to the user, and the remote process is terminated. That's right, the remote process is terminated—not your process. You will have successfully crashed another process while your process continues to execute just fine!

To fix this, we need to get the DLL's pathname string into the remote process' address space. Then, when **CreateRemoteThread** is called, we need to pass it the address (relative to the remote process) of where we placed the string. Again, Windows offers a function, **VirtualAllocEx**, that allows one process to allocate memory in another process' address space:

```
PVOID VirtualAllocEx(
   HANDLE hProcess,
   PVOID pvAddress,
   SIZE_T dwSize,
   DWORD flAllocationType,
   DWORD flProtect);
```

Another function allows us to free this memory:

```
BOOL VirtualFreeEx(
    HANDLE hProcess,
    PVOID pvAddress,
    SIZE_T dwSize,
    DWORD dwFreeType);
```

Both of these functions are similar to their non-**Ex** versions (which are discussed in Chapter 15, "Using Virtual Memory in Your Own Applications"). The only difference is that these two functions require a handle to a process as their first argument. This handle indicates the process where the operation is to be performed.

Once we allocate memory for the string, we also need a way to copy the string from our process' address space over to the remote process' address space. Windows offers functions that allow one process to read from and write to another process' address space:

```
BOOL ReadProcessMemory(
    HANDLE hProcess,
    LPCVOID pvAddressRemote,
    PVOID pvBufferLocal,
    SIZE_T dwSize,
    SIZE_T* pdwNumBytesRead);

BOOL WriteProcessMemory(
    HANDLE hProcess,
    PVOID pvAddressRemote,
    LPCVOID pvBufferLocal,
    SIZE_T dwSize,
    SIZE_T* pdwNumBytesWritten);
```

The remote process is identified by the **hProcess** parameter. The **pvAddressRemote** parameters indicate the address in the remote process, **pvBufferLocal** is the address of memory in the local process, **dwSize** is the requested number of bytes to transfer, and **pdwNumBytesRead** and **pdwNumBytesWritten** indicate the number of bytes actually transferred; these values can be examined after the function returns.

Now that you understand all that I'm trying to do, let me summarize the steps you must take:

1. Use the **VirtualAllocEx** function to allocate memory in the remote process' address space.

2. Use the **WriteProcessMemory** function to copy the DLL's pathname to the memory allocated in step 1.

3. Use the **GetProcAddress** function to get the real address (inside Kernel32.dll) of the **LoadLibraryW** or **LoadLibraryA** function.

4. Use the **CreateRemoteThread** function to create a thread in the remote process that calls the proper **LoadLibrary** function, passing it the address of the memory allocated in step 1.

   At this point, the DLL has been injected into the remote process' address space, and the DLL's **DllMain** function receives a **DLL_PROCESS_ATTACH** notification and can execute the desired code. When **DllMain** returns, the remote thread returns from its call to **LoadLibraryW/A** back to the **BaseThreadStart** function (discussed in Chapter 6, "Thread Basics"). **BaseThreadStart** then calls **ExitThread**, causing the remote thread to die.

Now the remote process has the block of storage allocated in step 1 and the DLL still stuck in its address space. To clean this stuff up, we need to execute the following steps after the remote thread exists:

5. Use the **VirtualFreeEx** function to free the memory allocated in step 1.

6. Use the **GetProcAddress** function to get the real address (inside Kernel32.dll) of the **FreeLibrary** function.

7. Use the **CreateRemoteThread** function to create a thread in the remote process that calls the **FreeLibrary** function, passing the remote DLL's **HMODULE**.

That's basically it.

The Inject Library Sample Application

The 22-InjLib.exe application injects a DLL using the **CreateRemoteThread** function. The source code and resource files for the application and DLL are in the 22-InjLib and 22-ImgWalk directories on the companion content Web page. The program uses the following dialog box to accept the process ID of a running process:

You can obtain a process' ID by using the Task Manager that ships with Windows. Using the ID, the program attempts to open a handle to this running process by calling **OpenProcess**, requesting the appropriate access rights:

```
hProcess = OpenProcess(
   PROCESS_CREATE_THREAD |   // For CreateRemoteThread
   PROCESS_VM_OPERATION  |   // For VirtualAllocEx/VirtualFreeEx
   PROCESS_VM_WRITE,         // For WriteProcessMemory
   FALSE, dwProcessId);
```

If **OpenProcess** returns **NULL**, the application is not running under a security context that allows it to open a handle to the target process. Some processes—such as WinLogon, SvcHost, and Csrss—run under the local system account, which the logged-on user cannot alter. You might be able to open a handle to these processes if you are granted and enable the debug security privilege. The ProcessInfo sample in Chapter 4, "Processes," demonstrates how to do this.

If **OpenProcess** is successful, a buffer is initialized with the full pathname of the DLL that is to be injected. Then **InjectLib** is called, passing it the handle of the desired remote process and the pathname of the DLL to inject into it. Finally, when **InjectLib** returns, the program displays a message box indicating whether the DLL successfully loaded in the remote process; it then closes the handle to the process. That's all there is to it.

You might notice in the code that I make a special check to see whether the process ID passed is **0**. If so, I set the process ID to InjLib.exe's own process ID by calling **GetCurrentProcessId**. This way, when **InjectLib** is called, the DLL is injected into the process' own address space. This makes debugging easier. As you can imagine, when bugs popped up, it was sometimes difficult to determine whether the bugs were in the local process or in the remote process. Originally, I started debugging my code with two debuggers, one watching **InjLib** and the other watching the remote process. This turned out to be terribly inconvenient. It then dawned on me that **InjLib** can also inject a DLL into itself—that is, into the same address space as the caller. This made it much easier to debug my code.

As you can see at the top of the source code module, **InjectLib** is really a symbol that expands to either **InjectLibA** or **InjectLibW**, depending on how you're compiling the source code. The **InjectLibW** function is where all the magic happens. The comments speak for themselves, and I can't add much here. However, you'll notice that the **InjectLibA** function is short. It simply converts the ANSI DLL pathname to its Unicode equivalent and then calls the **InjectLibW** function to actually do the work. This approach is exactly what I recommended in Chapter 2, "Working with Characters and Strings." It also means that I only had to get the injection code running once—a nice timesaver.

InjLib.cpp

```
/**********************************************************************************
Module:  InjLib.cpp
Notices: Copyright (c) 2008 Jeffrey Richter & Christophe Nasarre
**********************************************************************************/


#include "..\CommonFiles\CmnHdr.h"      /* See Appendix A. */
#include <windowsx.h>
#include <stdio.h>
#include <tchar.h>
#include <malloc.h>          // For alloca
#include <TlHelp32.h>
#include "Resource.h"
#include <StrSafe.h>



///////////////////////////////////////////////////////////////////////////////


#ifdef UNICODE
   #define InjectLib InjectLibW
   #define EjectLib  EjectLibW
#else
   #define InjectLib InjectLibA
   #define EjectLib  EjectLibA
#endif   // !UNICODE



///////////////////////////////////////////////////////////////////////////////


BOOL WINAPI InjectLibW(DWORD dwProcessId, PCWSTR pszLibFile) {

   BOOL bOk = FALSE; // Assume that the function fails
   HANDLE hProcess = NULL, hThread = NULL;
   PWSTR pszLibFileRemote = NULL;
```

```
__try {
   // Get a handle for the target process.
   hProcess = OpenProcess(
      PROCESS_QUERY_INFORMATION |    // Required by Alpha
      PROCESS_CREATE_THREAD      |    // For CreateRemoteThread
      PROCESS_VM_OPERATION       |    // For VirtualAllocEx/VirtualFreeEx
      PROCESS_VM_WRITE,               // For WriteProcessMemory
      FALSE, dwProcessId);
   if (hProcess == NULL) __leave;

   // Calculate the number of bytes needed for the DLL's pathname
   int cch = 1 + lstrlenW(pszLibFile);
   int cb  = cch * sizeof(wchar_t);

   // Allocate space in the remote process for the pathname
   pszLibFileRemote = (PWSTR)
      VirtualAllocEx(hProcess, NULL, cb, MEM_COMMIT, PAGE_READWRITE);
   if (pszLibFileRemote == NULL) __leave;

   // Copy the DLL's pathname to the remote process' address space
   if (!WriteProcessMemory(hProcess, pszLibFileRemote,
      (PVOID) pszLibFile, cb, NULL)) __leave;

   // Get the real address of LoadLibraryW in Kernel32.dll
   PTHREAD_START_ROUTINE pfnThreadRtn = (PTHREAD_START_ROUTINE)
      GetProcAddress(GetModuleHandle(TEXT("Kernel32")), "LoadLibraryW");
   if (pfnThreadRtn == NULL) __leave;

   // Create a remote thread that calls LoadLibraryW(DLLPathname)
   hThread = CreateRemoteThread(hProcess, NULL, 0,
      pfnThreadRtn, pszLibFileRemote, 0, NULL);
   if (hThread == NULL) __leave;

   // Wait for the remote thread to terminate
   WaitForSingleObject(hThread, INFINITE);

   bOk = TRUE; // Everything executed successfully
}
__finally { // Now, we can clean everything up

   // Free the remote memory that contained the DLL's pathname
   if (pszLibFileRemote != NULL)
      VirtualFreeEx(hProcess, pszLibFileRemote, 0, MEM_RELEASE);

   if (hThread   != NULL)
      CloseHandle(hThread);

   if (hProcess != NULL)
      CloseHandle(hProcess);
}

return(bOk);
}
```

```
/////////////////////////////////////////////////////////////////////////

BOOL WINAPI InjectLibA(DWORD dwProcessId, PCSTR pszLibFile) {

   // Allocate a (stack) buffer for the Unicode version of the pathname
   SIZE_T cchSize = lstrlenA(pszLibFile) + 1;
   PWSTR pszLibFileW = (PWSTR)
      _alloca(cchSize * sizeof(wchar_t));

   // Convert the ANSI pathname to its Unicode equivalent
   StringCchPrintfW(pszLibFileW, cchSize, L"%S", pszLibFile);

   // Call the Unicode version of the function to actually do the work.
   return(InjectLibW(dwProcessId, pszLibFileW));
}


/////////////////////////////////////////////////////////////////////////


BOOL WINAPI EjectLibW(DWORD dwProcessId, PCWSTR pszLibFile) {

   BOOL bOk = FALSE; // Assume that the function fails
   HANDLE hthSnapshot = NULL;
   HANDLE hProcess = NULL, hThread = NULL;

   __try {
      // Grab a new snapshot of the process
      hthSnapshot = CreateToolhelp32Snapshot(TH32CS_SNAPMODULE, dwProcessId);
      if (hthSnapshot == INVALID_HANDLE_VALUE) __leave;

      // Get the HMODULE of the desired library
      MODULEENTRY32W me = { sizeof(me) };
      BOOL bFound = FALSE;
      BOOL bMoreMods = Module32FirstW(hthSnapshot, &me);
      for (; bMoreMods; bMoreMods = Module32NextW(hthSnapshot, &me)) {
         bFound = (_wcsicmp(me.szModule,  pszLibFile) == 0) ||
                  (_wcsicmp(me.szExePath, pszLibFile) == 0);
         if (bFound) break;
      }
      if (!bFound) __leave;

      // Get a handle for the target process.
      hProcess = OpenProcess(
         PROCESS_QUERY_INFORMATION |
         PROCESS_CREATE_THREAD     |
         PROCESS_VM_OPERATION,  // For CreateRemoteThread
         FALSE, dwProcessId);
      if (hProcess == NULL) __leave;

      // Get the real address of FreeLibrary in Kernel32.dll
      PTHREAD_START_ROUTINE pfnThreadRtn = (PTHREAD_START_ROUTINE)
         GetProcAddress(GetModuleHandle(TEXT("Kernel32")), "FreeLibrary");
```

```
      if (pfnThreadRtn == NULL) __leave;

      // Create a remote thread that calls FreeLibrary()
      hThread = CreateRemoteThread(hProcess, NULL, 0,
         pfnThreadRtn, me.modBaseAddr, 0, NULL);
      if (hThread == NULL) __leave;

      // Wait for the remote thread to terminate
      WaitForSingleObject(hThread, INFINITE);

      bOk = TRUE; // Everything executed successfully
   }
   __finally { // Now we can clean everything up

      if (hthSnapshot != NULL)
         CloseHandle(hthSnapshot);

      if (hThread    != NULL)
         CloseHandle(hThread);

      if (hProcess   != NULL)
         CloseHandle(hProcess);
   }

   return(bOk);
}


/////////////////////////////////////////////////////////////////////////////


BOOL WINAPI EjectLibA(DWORD dwProcessId, PCSTR pszLibFile) {

   // Allocate a (stack) buffer for the Unicode version of the pathname
   SIZE_T cchSize = lstrlenA(pszLibFile) + 1;
   PWSTR pszLibFileW = (PWSTR)
      _alloca(cchSize * sizeof(wchar_t));

   // Convert the ANSI pathname to its Unicode equivalent
      StringCchPrintfW(pszLibFileW, cchSize, L"%S", pszLibFile);

   // Call the Unicode version of the function to actually do the work.
   return(EjectLibW(dwProcessId, pszLibFileW));
}


/////////////////////////////////////////////////////////////////////////////


BOOL Dlg_OnInitDialog(HWND hWnd, HWND hWndFocus, LPARAM lParam) {

   chSETDLGICONS(hWnd, IDI_INJLIB);
   return(TRUE);
}
```

```
//////////////////////////////////////////////////////////////////////////

void Dlg_OnCommand(HWND hWnd, int id, HWND hWndCtl, UINT codeNotify) {

   switch (id) {
      case IDCANCEL:
         EndDialog(hWnd, id);
         break;

      case IDC_INJECT:
         DWORD dwProcessId = GetDlgItemInt(hWnd, IDC_PROCESSID, NULL, FALSE);
         if (dwProcessId == 0) {
            // A process ID of 0 causes everything to take place in the
            // local process; this makes things easier for debugging.
            dwProcessId = GetCurrentProcessId();
         }

         TCHAR szLibFile[MAX_PATH];
         GetModuleFileName(NULL, szLibFile, _countof(szLibFile));
         PTSTR pFilename = _tcsrchr(szLibFile, TEXT('\\')) + 1;
         _tcscpy_s(pFilename, _countof(szLibFile) - (szLibFile - szLibFile),
            TEXT("22-ImgWalk.DLL"));
         if (InjectLib(dwProcessId, szLibFile)) {
            chVERIFY(EjectLib(dwProcessId, szLibFile));
            chMB("DLL Injection/Ejection successful.");
         } else {
            chMB("DLL Injection/Ejection failed.");
         }
         break;
   }
}


//////////////////////////////////////////////////////////////////////////


INT_PTR WINAPI Dlg_Proc(HWND hWnd, UINT uMsg, WPARAM wParam, LPARAM lParam) {

   switch (uMsg) {
      chHANDLE_DLGMSG(hWnd, WM_INITDIALOG, Dlg_OnInitDialog);
      chHANDLE_DLGMSG(hWnd, WM_COMMAND,    Dlg_OnCommand);
   }
   return(FALSE);
}


//////////////////////////////////////////////////////////////////////////


int WINAPI _tWinMain(HINSTANCE hInstExe, HINSTANCE, PTSTR pszCmdLine, int) {

   DialogBox(hInstExe, MAKEINTRESOURCE(IDD_INJLIB), NULL, Dlg_Proc);
   return(0);
}

//////////////////////////// End of File ////////////////////////////////
```

The Image Walk DLL

22-ImgWalk.dll is a DLL that, once injected into a process' address space, can report on all the DLLs that the process is using. (The source code and resource files for the DLL are in the 22-ImgWalk directory on the companion content Web page.) For example, if I first run Notepad and then run 22-InjLib, passing it Notepad's process ID, InjLib injects 22-ImgWalk.dll into Notepad's address space. Once there, 22-ImgWalk determines which file images (executables and DLLs) are being used by Notepad and displays the following message box, which shows the results:

22-ImgWalk walks through a process' address space looking for mapped file images by repeatedly calling **VirtualQuery** to fill a **MEMORY_BASIC_INFORMATION** structure. With each iteration of the loop, 22-ImgWalk checks for a file pathname to concatenate with a string. This string appears in the message box. Here is the code of the **DllMain** entry point:

```
ImgWalk.cpp
/*********************************************************************************
Module:  ImgWalk.cpp
Notices: Copyright (c) 2008 Jeffrey Richter & Christophe Nasarre
*********************************************************************************/


#include "..\CommonFiles\CmnHdr.h"      /* See Appendix A. */
#include <tchar.h>


///////////////////////////////////////////////////////////////////////////////
```

```
BOOL WINAPI DllMain(HINSTANCE hInstDll, DWORD fdwReason, PVOID fImpLoad) {

   if (fdwReason == DLL_PROCESS_ATTACH) {
      char szBuf[MAX_PATH * 100] = { 0 };

      PBYTE pb = NULL;
      MEMORY_BASIC_INFORMATION mbi;
      while (VirtualQuery(pb, &mbi, sizeof(mbi)) == sizeof(mbi)) {

         int nLen;
         char szModName[MAX_PATH];

         if (mbi.State == MEM_FREE)
            mbi.AllocationBase = mbi.BaseAddress;

         if ((mbi.AllocationBase == hInstDll) ||
            (mbi.AllocationBase != mbi.BaseAddress) ||
            (mbi.AllocationBase == NULL)) {
            // Do not add the module name to the list
            // if any of the following is true:
            // 1. If this region contains this DLL
            // 2. If this block is NOT the beginning of a region
            // 3. If the address is NULL
            nLen = 0;
         } else {
            nLen = GetModuleFileNameA((HINSTANCE) mbi.AllocationBase,
               szModName, _countof(szModName));
         }

         if (nLen > 0) {
            wsprintfA(strchr(szBuf, 0), "\n%p-%s",
               mbi.AllocationBase, szModName);
         }

         pb += mbi.RegionSize;
      }

      // NOTE: Normally, you should not display a message box in DllMain
      // due to the loader lock described in Chapter 20. However, to keep
      // this sample application simple, I am violating this rule.
      chMB(&szBuf[1]);
   }

   return(TRUE);
}
```

/////////////////////////// End of File ///////////////////////////////

First, I check to see whether the region's base address matches the base address of the injected DLL. If it matches, I set **nLen** to **0** so that the injected library does not appear in the message box. If it doesn't match, I attempt to get the filename for the module loaded at the region's base address. If the **nLen** variable is greater than 0, the system recognizes that the address identifies a loaded module and the system fills the **szModName** buffer with the full pathname of the module. I then concatenate the module's **HINSTANCE** (base address) and its pathname with the **szBuf** string that will eventually be displayed in the message box. When the loop is finished, the DLL presents a message box with the final string as its contents.

Injecting a DLL with a Trojan DLL

Another way to inject a DLL is to replace a DLL that you know a process will load. For example, if you know that a process will load Xyz.dll, you can create your own DLL and give it the same file-name. Of course, you must rename the original Xyz.dll to something else.

Inside your Xyz.dll, you must export all the same symbols that the original Xyz.dll exported. You can do this easily using function forwarders (described in Chapter 20, "DLL Advanced Techniques"), which make it trivially simple to hook certain functions, but you should avoid using this technique because it is not version-resilient. If you replace a system DLL, for example, and Microsoft adds new functions in the future, your DLL will not have function forwarders for them. Applications that reference these new functions will be unable to load and execute.

If you have just a single application in which you want to use this technique, you can give your DLL a unique name and change the import section of the application's .exe module. More specifically, the import section contains the names of the DLLs required by a module. You can rummage through this import section in the file and alter it so that the loader loads your own DLL. This technique is not too bad, but you have to be pretty familiar with the .exe and DLL file formats.

Injecting a DLL as a Debugger

A debugger can perform special actions on a debuggee process. When a debuggee loads, the system automatically notifies the debugger when the debuggee's address space is ready but before the debuggee's primary thread executes any code. At this point, the debugger can force some code into the debuggee's address space (using **WriteProcessMemory**, for example) and then cause the debuggee's primary thread to execute that code.

This technique requires that you manipulate the debuggee thread's **CONTEXT** structure, which means that you must write CPU-specific code. You have to modify your source code to work correctly on different CPU platforms. In addition, you probably have to hand-code the machine language instructions that you want the debuggee to execute. Also, the relationship between a debugger and its debuggee is solid. By default, if the debugger terminates, Windows automatically kills the debuggee. However, a debugger can change this default behavior by calling **DebugSet-ProcessKillOnExit** with **FALSE** as a parameter. It is also possible to stop debugging a process without killing it, thanks to the **DebugActiveProcessStop** function.

Injecting Code with *CreateProcess*

If your process is spawning the process into which you want to inject code, things get a little easier. For one, your process (the parent process) can create the new process suspended. This approach allows you to alter the child process' state without affecting its execution, because it hasn't started executing anything yet. But the parent process also gets a handle to the child process' primary thread. Using this handle, you can alter what code the thread executes. You can solve the problem mentioned in the previous section because you can set the thread's instruction pointer to execute the code in the memory-mapped file.

Here is one way for your process to control what code the child process' primary thread executes:

1. Have your process spawn the child process suspended.
2. Retrieve the primary thread's starting memory address from the .exe module's file header.
3. Save the machine instructions at this memory address.
4. Force some hand-coded machine instructions at this address. The instructions should call **LoadLibrary** to load a DLL.
5. Resume the child process' primary thread so that this code executes.
6. Restore the original instructions back into the starting address.
7. Let the process continue execution from the starting address as if nothing had happened.

Steps 6 and 7 are tricky to get right because you have to change the code that you are currently executing. It is possible, however—I've seen it done.

This technique offers a lot of benefits. First, it gets the address space before the application executes. Second, because you're not a debugger, you can easily debug the application with the injected DLL. And finally, this technique works on both console and GUI applications.

Of course, this technique also has some disadvantages. You can inject the DLL only if your code is the parent process. And, of course, this technique is not CPU-independent; you must make modifications for different CPU platforms.

API Hooking: An Example

Injecting a DLL into a process' address space is a wonderful way to determine what's going on within a process. However, simply injecting a DLL doesn't give you enough information. You'll often want to know exactly how threads in a particular process are calling various functions, and you might want to modify what a Windows function does.

For example, I know of a company that produced a DLL that was loaded by a database product. The DLL's job was to enhance and extend the capabilities of the database product. When the database product was terminated, the DLL received a **DLL_PROCESS_DETACH** notification and only then executed all of its cleanup code. The DLL would call functions in other DLLs to close socket connections, files, and other resources, but by the time it received the **DLL_PROCESS_DETACH** notification, other DLLs in the process' address space had already gotten their **DLL_PROCESS_DETACH** notifications. So when the company's DLL tried to clean up, many of the functions it called would fail because the other DLLs had already uninitialized.

The company hired me to help them solve this problem, and I suggested that we hook the **ExitProcess** function. As you know, calling **ExitProcess** causes the system to notify the DLLs with **DLL_PROCESS_DETACH** notifications. By hooking the **ExitProcess** function, we ensured that the company's DLL was notified when **ExitProcess** was called. This notification would come in before any DLLs got a **DLL_PROCESS_DETACH** notification; therefore, all the DLLs in the process were still initialized and functioning properly. At this point, the company's DLL would know that the process was about to terminate and could perform all of its cleanup successfully. Then the operating system's **ExitProcess** function would be called, causing all the DLLs to receive their **DLL_PROCESS_DETACH** notifications and clean up. The company's DLL would have no special cleanup to perform when it received this notification because it had already done what it needed to do.

In this example, injecting the DLL came for free: the database application was already designed to allow this, and it loaded the company's DLL. When the company's DLL was loaded, it had to scan all the loaded executable and DLL modules for calls to **ExitProcess**. When it found calls to **ExitProcess**, the DLL had to modify the modules so that they would call a function in the company's DLL instead of the operating system's **ExitProcess** function. (This process is a lot simpler than it sounds.) Once the company's **ExitProcess** replacement function (or *hook function*, as it's more commonly called) executed its cleanup code, the operating system's **ExitProcess** function (in Kernel32.dll) was called.

This example shows a typical use for API hooking. It solved a very real problem with very little code.

API Hooking by Overwriting Code

API hooking isn't new—developers have been using API hooking methods for years. When it comes to solving the problem I just described, the first "solution" that everyone comes to is to hook by overwriting code. Here's how this works:

1. You locate the address of the function you want to hook in memory (say, **ExitProcess** in Kernel32.dll).

2. You save the first few bytes of this function in some memory of your own.

3. You overwrite the first few bytes of this function with a **JUMP CPU** instruction that jumps to the memory address of your replacement function. Of course, your replacement function must have exactly the same signature as the function you're hooking: all the parameters must be the same, the return value must be the same, and the calling convention must be the same.

4. Now, when a thread calls the hooked function, the **JUMP** instruction will actually jump to your replacement function. At this point, you can execute whatever code you'd like.

5. You unhook the function by taking the saved bytes (from step 2) and placing them back at the beginning of the hooked function.

6. You call the hooked function (which is no longer hooked), and the function performs its normal processing.

7. When the original function returns, you execute steps 2 and 3 again so that your replacement function will be called in the future.

This method was heavily used by 16-bit Windows programmers and worked just fine in that environment. Today, this method has several serious shortcomings, and I strongly discourage its use. First, it is CPU-dependent: **JUMP** instructions on *x*86, *x*64, IA-64, and other CPUs are different, and you must use hand-coded machine instructions to get this technique to work. Second, this method doesn't work at all in a preemptive, multithreaded environment. It takes time for a thread to overwrite the code at the beginning of a function. While the code is being overwritten, another thread might attempt to call the same function. The results are disastrous! So this method works only if you know that no more than one thread will attempt to call a particular function at any given time.

API Hooking by Manipulating a Module's Import Section

As it turns out, another API hooking technique solves both of the problems I've mentioned. This technique is easy to implement and is quite robust. But to understand it, you must understand how dynamic linking works. In particular, you must understand what's contained in a module's import section. Although I haven't gone into the nitty-gritty details of data structures and the like, I did spend a good bit of Chapter 19 explaining how this section is generated and what's in it. You can refer back to that chapter as you read the information that follows.

As you know, a module's import section contains the set of DLLs that the module requires in order to run. In addition, it contains the list of symbols that the module imports from each of the DLLs. When the module places a call to an imported function, the thread actually grabs the address of the desired imported function from the module's import section and then jumps to that address.

So, to hook a particular function, all you do is change the address in the module's import section. That's it. No CPU-dependent stuff. And because you're not modifying the function's code in any way, you don't need to worry about any thread synchronization issues.

The following function performs the magic. It looks in one module's import section for a reference to a symbol at a specific address. If such a reference exists, it changes the address of the symbol.

```
void CAPIHook::ReplaceIATEntryInOneMod(PCSTR pszCalleeModName,
  PROC pfnCurrent, PROC pfnNew, HMODULE hmodCaller) {

  // Get the address of the module's import section
  ULONG ulSize;

  // An exception was triggered by Explorer (when browsing the content of
  // a folder) into imagehlp.dll. It looks like one module was unloaded...
  // Maybe some threading problem: the list of modules from Toolhelp might
  // not be accurate if FreeLibrary is called during the enumeration.
  PIMAGE_IMPORT_DESCRIPTOR pImportDesc = NULL;
  __try {
    pImportDesc = (PIMAGE_IMPORT_DESCRIPTOR) ImageDirectoryEntryToData(
      hmodCaller, TRUE, IMAGE_DIRECTORY_ENTRY_IMPORT, &ulSize);
  }
  __except (InvalidReadExceptionFilter(GetExceptionInformation())) {
    // Nothing to do in here, thread continues to run normally
    // with NULL for pImportDesc
  }

  if (pImportDesc == NULL)
    return;  // This module has no import section or is no longer loaded


  // Find the import descriptor containing references to callee's functions
  for (; pImportDesc->Name; pImportDesc++) {
    PSTR pszModName = (PSTR) ((PBYTE) hmodCaller + pImportDesc->Name);
    if (lstrcmpiA(pszModName, pszCalleeModName) == 0) {

      // Get caller's import address table (IAT) for the callee's functions
      PIMAGE_THUNK_DATA pThunk = (PIMAGE_THUNK_DATA)
        ((PBYTE) hmodCaller + pImportDesc->FirstThunk);
```

```
          // Replace current function address with new function address
          for (; pThunk->u1.Function; pThunk++) {

              // Get the address of the function address
              PROC* ppfn = (PROC*) &pThunk->u1.Function;

              // Is this the function we're looking for?
              BOOL bFound = (*ppfn == pfnCurrent);
              if (bFound) {
                  if (!WriteProcessMemory(GetCurrentProcess(), ppfn, &pfnNew,
                        sizeof(pfnNew), NULL) && (ERROR_NOACCESS == GetLastError())) {
                      DWORD dwOldProtect;
                      if (VirtualProtect(ppfn, sizeof(pfnNew), PAGE_WRITECOPY,
                        &dwOldProtect)) {

                          WriteProcessMemory(GetCurrentProcess(), ppfn, &pfnNew,
                                sizeof(pfnNew), NULL);
                          VirtualProtect(ppfn, sizeof(pfnNew), dwOldProtect,
                                &dwOldProtect);
                      }
                  }
                  return;  // We did it, get out
              }
          }
      } // Each import section is parsed until the right entry is found and patched
  }
}
```

To help you see how you call this function, let me first start by explaining a potential environment. Let's say that we have a module called Database.exe. The code in this module calls the **Exit-Process** function contained in Kernel32.dll, but we want it to call the **MyExitProcess** function contained in my DbExtend.dll module. To accomplish this, we call **ReplaceIATEntryInOneMod** as follows:

```
PROC pfnOrig = GetProcAddress(GetModuleHandle("Kernel32"),
   "ExitProcess");
HMODULE hmodCaller = GetModuleHandle("Database.exe");


ReplaceIATEntryInOneMod(
   "Kernel32.dll", // Module containing the function (ANSI)
   pfnOrig,        // Address of function in callee
   MyExitProcess,  // Address of new function to be called
   hmodCaller);    // Handle of module that should call the new function
```

The first thing that **ReplaceIATEntryInOneMod** does is locate the **hmodCaller** module's import section by calling **ImageDirectoryEntryToData**, passing it **IMAGE_DIRECTORY_ENTRY_IMPORT**. If this function returns **NULL**, the DataBase.exe module has no import section and there is nothing to do. The call to **ImageDirectoryEntryToData** is protected by a **__try/__except** construct (detailed in Chapter 24, "Exception Handlers and Software Exceptions") to catch any unexpected exceptions from this function provided by ImageHlp.dll. This protection is required because it might happen that **ReplaceIATEntryInOneMod** gets called with an invalid module handle as the last parameter, which triggers a 0xC0000005 exception. This happens, for example, in the context of Windows Explorer, which dynamically loads and unloads DLLs very fast in a thread different from the thread where **ReplaceIATEntryInOneMod** is executed.

If the Database.exe module has an import section, **ImageDirectoryEntryToData** returns the address of the import section, which is a pointer of type **PIMAGE_IMPORT_DESCRIPTOR**. We must now look in the module's import section for the DLL that contains the imported function that we want to change. In this example, we're looking for the symbols that are being imported from "Kernel32.dll" (the first parameter passed to the **ReplaceIATEntryInOneMod** function). The **for** loop scans for the DLL module's name. Notice that all strings in a module's import section are written in ANSI (never Unicode). This is why I explicitly call the **lstrcmpiA** function instead of using the **lstrcmpi** macro.

If the loop terminates without locating any references to symbols inside "Kernel32.dll", the function returns and again does nothing. If the module's import section does reference symbols in "Kernel32.dll", we get the address to an array of **IMAGE_THUNK_DATA** structures that contains information about the imported symbols. Note that some compilers, such as Borland Delphi, generate more than one import section for the same module, and this is why we don't stop at the first match. Then, for each matching import section, we iterate through all the import symbols from "Kernel32.dll", looking for an address that matches the current address of the symbol. In our example, we're looking for an address that matches the address of the **ExitProcess** function.

If no address matches what we're looking for, this module must not import the desired symbol, and **ReplaceIATEntryInOneMod** simply returns. If the address is found, **WriteProcessMemory** is called to change the address of the replacement function. If an error occurs, the page protection is changed by using **VirtualProtect** and restored after the function pointer is patched.

From now on, when any thread executes code inside Database.exe's module that calls **Exit-Process**, the thread calls our replacement function. From this function, we can easily get the address of the real **ExitProcess** function inside Kernel32.dll and call it when we want the normal **ExitProcess** processing.

Note that the **ReplaceIATEntryInOneMod** function alters calls to functions made from code within a single module. But another DLL might be in the address space, and that DLL might have calls to **ExitProcess** as well. If a module other than Database.exe attempts to call **ExitProcess**, its call will succeed at calling the **ExitProcess** function in Kernel32.dll.

If you want to trap all calls to **ExitProcess** from all modules, you must call **ReplaceIATEntry-InOneMod** once for each module loaded in the process' address space. To this end, I've written another function called **ReplaceIATEntryInAllMods**. This function simply uses the ToolHelp functions to enumerate all the modules loaded in the process' address space and then calls **ReplaceIATEntryInOneMod** for each module, passing it the appropriate module handle for the last parameter.

Problems can occur in a few other places. For example, what if a thread calls **LoadLibrary** to load a new DLL after you call **ReplaceIATEntryInAllMods**? In this case, the newly loaded DLL might have calls to **ExitProcess** that you have not hooked. To solve this problem, you must hook the **LoadLibraryA**, **LoadLibraryW**, **LoadLibraryExA**, and **LoadLibraryExW** functions so that you can trap these calls and call **ReplaceIATEntryInOneMod** for the newly loaded module. However, this is not enough. Imagine that the newly loaded module has link-time dependencies to other DLLs that might also call **ExitProcess**. When a **LoadLibrary*** function is called, Windows first loads these statically linked DLLs without giving you a chance to update their Import Address Table (IAT) corresponding to **ExitProcess**, if any. The solution is simple: instead of just calling **ReplaceIATEntryInOneMod** on the explicitly loaded DLL, we call **ReplaceIATEntryInAllMods** to also update the new implicitly loaded modules.

The last problem has to do with **GetProcAddress**. Say a thread executes this:

```
typedef int (WINAPI *PFNEXITPROCESS)(UINT uExitCode);
PFNEXITPROCESS pfnExitProcess = (PFNEXITPROCESS) GetProcAddress(
   GetModuleHandle("Kernel32"), "ExitProcess");
pfnExitProcess(0);
```

This code tells the system to get the real address of **ExitProcess** in Kernel32.dll and then call that address. If a thread executes this code, your replacement function is not called. To get around this problem, you must also hook the **GetProcAddress** function. If it is called and is about to return the address of a hooked function, you must return the address of the replacement function instead.

The sample application presented in the next section shows how to do API hooking and solves all the **LoadLibrary** and **GetProcAddress** problems as well.

> **Note**   The "Detect and Plug GDI Leaks in Your Code with Two Powerful Tools for Windows XP" MSDN Magazine article at *http://msdn.microsoft.com/msdnmag/issues/03/01/GDILeaks/* explains how to build a more complete two-way communication protocol between such a listener application and the hooked processes based on dedicated threads and memory-mapped files.

The Last MessageBox Info Sample Application

The Last MessageBox Info application (22-LastMsgBoxInfo.exe) demonstrates API hooking. It hooks all calls to the **MessageBox** function contained in User32.dll. To hook this function in all processes, the application performs DLL injection using the Windows hook technique. The source code and resource files for the application and DLL are in the 22-LastMsgBoxInfo and 22-LastMsgBoxInfoLib directories on the companion content Web page.

When you run the application, the following dialog box appears:

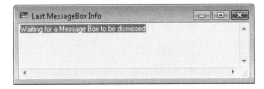

At this point, the application is waiting. Now run any application and cause it to display a message box. For testing purposes, I'm using the 20-DelayLoadApp.exe sample built in Chapter 20. This small C++ application pops up the following kind of message boxes when different delay load scenarios are executed.

When you dismiss this message box, the Last MessageBox Info dialog box looks like this:

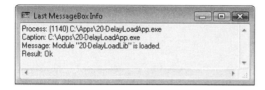

As you can see, the LastMsgBoxInfo application can see exactly how other processes have called the **MessageBox** function. However, you might notice that the first message box is not detected by LastMsgBoxInfo. The reason is simple: the Windows hook used to inject our monitoring code is triggered by the message received after the first message box pops up–too late...

The code for displaying and managing the Last MessageBox Info dialog box is quite simple. The setting up of API hooking is where all the hard work takes place. To make API hooking easier, I created a **CAPIHook** C++ class. The class definition is in APIHook.h, and the class implementation is in APIHook.cpp. The class is easy to use because there are only a few public member functions: a constructor, a destructor, and a function that returns the address of the original function.

To hook a function, you simply create an instance of this C++ class as follows:

```
CAPIHook g_MessageBoxA("User32.dll", "MessageBoxA",
    (PROC) Hook_MessageBoxA, TRUE);

CAPIHook g_MessageBoxW("User32.dll", "MessageBoxW",
    (PROC) Hook_MessageBoxW, TRUE);
```

Notice that I have to hook two functions: **MessageBoxA** and **MessageBoxW**. User32.dll contains both functions. When **MessageBoxA** is called, I want my **Hook_MessageBoxA** to be called instead; when **MessageBoxW** is called, I want my **Hook_MessageBoxW** function called instead.

The constructor of my **CAPIHook** class simply remembers what API you've decided to hook and calls **ReplaceIATEntryInAllMods** to actually perform the hooking.

The next public member function is the destructor. When a **CAPIHook** object goes out of scope, the destructor calls **ReplaceIATEntryInAllMods** to reset the symbol's address back to its original address in every module–the function is no longer hooked.

The third public member returns the address of the original function. This member function is usually called from inside the replacement function in order to call the original function. Here is the code inside the **Hook_MessageBoxA** function:

```
int WINAPI Hook_MessageBoxA(HWND hWnd, PCSTR pszText,
   PCSTR pszCaption, UINT uType) {

   int nResult = ((PFNMESSAGEBOXA)(PROC) g_MessageBoxA)
     (hWnd, pszText, pszCaption, uType);
   SendLastMsgBoxInfo(FALSE, (PVOID) pszCaption, (PVOID) pszText, nResult);
   return(nResult);
}
```

This code refers to the global **g_MessageBoxA CAPIHook** object. Casting this object to a **PROC** data type causes the member function to return the address of the original **MessageBoxA** function inside User32.dll.

If you use this C++ class, that's all there is to hooking and unhooking imported functions. If you examine the code toward the bottom of the CAPIHook.cpp file, you'll notice that the C++ class automatically instantiates **CAPIHook** objects to trap **LoadLibraryA**, **LoadLibraryW**, **Load-LibraryExA**, **LoadLibraryExW**, and **GetProcAddress**. In this way, the **CAPIHook** class automatically takes care of the problems mentioned earlier.

Notice that the module exporting the function you want to hook must be loaded when the **CAPIHook** constructor runs because it is impossible to get the address of the original function otherwise: **GetModuleHandleA** will return **NULL**, and **GetProcAddress** will fail. This is a major limitation because you can't handle the delay-load module case. The optimization provided by delay-load modules is precisely to wait until a delay-load exported function is really called before loading the exporting module.

A possible solution is to use the hooked **LoadLibrary*** functions to detect when a module is exporting an unpatched hooked function and then execute two actions:

1. Hook again the import table of the module already loaded because it is now possible to call **GetProcAddress** and get a pointer to the original implementation of the function to hook. Notice that the name of the function needs to be stored as a class member and set in the constructor.

2. Directly update this hooked function in the Export Address Table of the exporting module as shown by the implementation of the **ReplaceEATEntryInOneMod** function. That way, all new modules calling the hooked function will call our handler.

But what happens if the module exporting the hooked function is unloaded by a call to **Free-Library**? And then reloaded? As you can imagine, a complete implementation is beyond the scope of this chapter, but you now have all the elements in your hands to adapt this solution to your particular problems.

> **Note**   Microsoft Research has published a hooking API called *Detours*, which is documented and downloadable at *http://research.microsoft.com/sn/detours/*.

LastMsgBoxInfo.cpp

```
/*********************************************************************
Notices: Copyright (c) 2008 Jeffrey Richter & Christophe Nasarre
*********************************************************************/


#include "..\CommonFiles\CmnHdr.h"      /* See Appendix A. */
#include <windowsx.h>
#include <tchar.h>
#include "Resource.h"
#include "..\22-LastMsgBoxInfoLib\LastMsgBoxInfoLib.h"


///////////////////////////////////////////////////////////////////////


BOOL Dlg_OnInitDialog(HWND hWnd, HWND hWndFocus, LPARAM lParam) {

   chSETDLGICONS(hWnd, IDI_LASTMSGBOXINFO);
   SetDlgItemText(hWnd, IDC_INFO,
      TEXT("Waiting for a Message Box to be dismissed"));
   return(TRUE);
}


///////////////////////////////////////////////////////////////////////


void Dlg_OnSize(HWND hWnd, UINT state, int cx, int cy) {

   SetWindowPos(GetDlgItem(hWnd, IDC_INFO), NULL,
      0, 0, cx, cy, SWP_NOZORDER);
}


///////////////////////////////////////////////////////////////////////


void Dlg_OnCommand(HWND hWnd, int id, HWND hWndCtl, UINT codeNotify) {

   switch (id) {
      case IDCANCEL:
         EndDialog(hWnd, id);
         break;
   }
}


///////////////////////////////////////////////////////////////////////
```

```
BOOL Dlg_OnCopyData(HWND hWnd, HWND hWndFrom, PCOPYDATASTRUCT pcds) {

   // Some hooked process sent us some message box info, display it
   SetDlgItemTextW(hWnd, IDC_INFO, (PCWSTR) pcds->lpData);
   return(TRUE);
}


///////////////////////////////////////////////////////////////////////////////


INT_PTR WINAPI Dlg_Proc(HWND hWnd, UINT uMsg, WPARAM wParam, LPARAM lParam) {

   switch (uMsg) {
      chHANDLE_DLGMSG(hWnd, WM_INITDIALOG, Dlg_OnInitDialog);
      chHANDLE_DLGMSG(hWnd, WM_SIZE,       Dlg_OnSize);
      chHANDLE_DLGMSG(hWnd, WM_COMMAND,    Dlg_OnCommand);
      chHANDLE_DLGMSG(hWnd, WM_COPYDATA,   Dlg_OnCopyData);
   }
   return(FALSE);
}


///////////////////////////////////////////////////////////////////////////////


int WINAPI _tWinMain(HINSTANCE hInstExe, HINSTANCE, PTSTR pszCmdLine, int) {

   DWORD dwThreadId = 0;
   LastMsgBoxInfo_HookAllApps(TRUE, dwThreadId);
   DialogBox(hInstExe, MAKEINTRESOURCE(IDD_LASTMSGBOXINFO), NULL, Dlg_Proc);
   LastMsgBoxInfo_HookAllApps(FALSE, 0);
   return(0);
}
///////////////////////////// End of File /////////////////////////////////////
```

LastMsgBoxInfoLib.cpp
```
/******************************************************************************
Module:  LastMsgBoxInfoLib.cpp
Notices: Copyright (c) 2008 Jeffrey Richter & Christophe Nasarre
******************************************************************************/


#include "..\CommonFiles\CmnHdr.h"
#include <WindowsX.h>
#include <tchar.h>
#include <stdio.h>
#include "APIHook.h"

#define LASTMSGBOXINFOLIBAPI extern "C" __declspec(dllexport)
#include "LastMsgBoxInfoLib.h"
#include <StrSafe.h>
```

```
//////////////////////////////////////////////////////////////////////////


// Prototypes for the hooked functions
typedef int (WINAPI *PFNMESSAGEBOXA)(HWND hWnd, PCSTR pszText,
   PCSTR pszCaption, UINT uType);

typedef int (WINAPI *PFNMESSAGEBOXW)(HWND hWnd, PCWSTR pszText,
   PCWSTR pszCaption, UINT uType);


// We need to reference these variables before we create them.
extern CAPIHook g_MessageBoxA;
extern CAPIHook g_MessageBoxW;


//////////////////////////////////////////////////////////////////////////


// This function sends the MessageBox info to our main dialog box
void SendLastMsgBoxInfo(BOOL bUnicode,
   PVOID pvCaption, PVOID pvText, int nResult) {

   // Get the pathname of the process displaying the message box
   wchar_t szProcessPathname[MAX_PATH];
   GetModuleFileNameW(NULL, szProcessPathname, MAX_PATH);

   // Convert the return value into a human-readable string
   PCWSTR pszResult = L"(Unknown)";
   switch (nResult) {
      case IDOK:       pszResult = L"Ok";        break;
      case IDCANCEL:   pszResult = L"Cancel";    break;
      case IDABORT:    pszResult = L"Abort";     break;
      case IDRETRY:    pszResult = L"Retry";     break;
      case IDIGNORE:   pszResult = L"Ignore";    break;
      case IDYES:      pszResult = L"Yes";       break;
      case IDNO:       pszResult = L"No";        break;
      case IDCLOSE:    pszResult = L"Close";     break;
      case IDHELP:     pszResult = L"Help";      break;
      case IDTRYAGAIN: pszResult = L"Try Again"; break;
      case IDCONTINUE: pszResult = L"Continue";  break;
   }

   // Construct the string to send to the main dialog box
   wchar_t sz[2048];
   StringCchPrintfW(sz, _countof(sz), bUnicode
      ? L"Process: (%d) %s\r\nCaption: %s\r\nMessage: %s\r\nResult: %s"
      : L"Process: (%d) %s\r\nCaption: %S\r\nMessage: %S\r\nResult: %s",
      GetCurrentProcessId(), szProcessPathname,
      pvCaption, pvText, pszResult);

   // Send the string to the main dialog box
   COPYDATASTRUCT cds = { 0, ((DWORD)wcslen(sz) + 1) * sizeof(wchar_t), sz };
   FORWARD_WM_COPYDATA(FindWindow(NULL, TEXT("Last MessageBox Info")),
      NULL, &cds, SendMessage);
}
```

```
///////////////////////////////////////////////////////////////////////


// This is the MessageBoxW replacement function
int WINAPI Hook_MessageBoxW(HWND hWnd, PCWSTR pszText, LPCWSTR pszCaption,
  UINT uType) {

  // Call the original MessageBoxW function
  int nResult = ((PFNMESSAGEBOXW)(PROC) g_MessageBoxW)
    (hWnd, pszText, pszCaption, uType);

  // Send the information to the main dialog box
  SendLastMsgBoxInfo(TRUE, (PVOID) pszCaption, (PVOID) pszText, nResult);

  // Return the result back to the caller
  return(nResult);
}


///////////////////////////////////////////////////////////////////////


// This is the MessageBoxA replacement function
int WINAPI Hook_MessageBoxA(HWND hWnd, PCSTR pszText, PCSTR pszCaption,
  UINT uType) {

  // Call the original MessageBoxA function
  int nResult = ((PFNMESSAGEBOXA)(PROC) g_MessageBoxA)
    (hWnd, pszText, pszCaption, uType);

  // Send the information to the main dialog box
  SendLastMsgBoxInfo(FALSE, (PVOID) pszCaption, (PVOID) pszText, nResult);

  // Return the result back to the caller
  return(nResult);
}


///////////////////////////////////////////////////////////////////////


// Hook the MessageBoxA and MessageBoxW functions
CAPIHook g_MessageBoxA("User32.dll", "MessageBoxA",
  (PROC) Hook_MessageBoxA);

CAPIHook g_MessageBoxW("User32.dll", "MessageBoxW",
  (PROC) Hook_MessageBoxW);

HHOOK g_hhook = NULL;


///////////////////////////////////////////////////////////////////////
```

```
static LRESULT WINAPI GetMsgProc(int code, WPARAM wParam, LPARAM lParam) {
   return(CallNextHookEx(g_hhook, code, wParam, lParam));
}


///////////////////////////////////////////////////////////////////////////


// Returns the HMODULE that contains the specified memory address
static HMODULE ModuleFromAddress(PVOID pv) {

   MEMORY_BASIC_INFORMATION mbi;
   return((VirtualQuery(pv, &mbi, sizeof(mbi)) != 0)
      ? (HMODULE) mbi.AllocationBase : NULL);
}


///////////////////////////////////////////////////////////////////////////


BOOL WINAPI LastMsgBoxInfo_HookAllApps(BOOL bInstall, DWORD dwThreadId) {

   BOOL bOk;

   if (bInstall) {

      chASSERT(g_hhook == NULL); // Illegal to install twice in a row

      // Install the Windows' hook
      g_hhook = SetWindowsHookEx(WH_GETMESSAGE, GetMsgProc,
         ModuleFromAddress(LastMsgBoxInfo_HookAllApps), dwThreadId);

      bOk = (g_hhook != NULL);
   } else {

      chASSERT(g_hhook != NULL); // Can't uninstall if not installed
      bOk = UnhookWindowsHookEx(g_hhook);
      g_hhook = NULL;
   }

   return(bOk);
}


//////////////////////////// End of File //////////////////////////////////
```

LastMsgBoxInfoLib.h
```
/******************************************************************************
Module:  LastMsgBoxInfoLib.h
Notices: Copyright (c) 2008 Jeffrey Richter & Christophe Nasarre
******************************************************************************/


#ifndef LASTMSGBOXINFOLIBAPI
#define LASTMSGBOXINFOLIBAPI extern "C" __declspec(dllimport)
#endif
```

```
/////////////////////////////////////////////////////////////////////////

LASTMSGBOXINFOLIBAPI BOOL WINAPI LastMsgBoxInfo_HookAllApps(BOOL bInstall,
    DWORD dwThreadId);

/////////////////////////////// End of File ///////////////////////////////
```

APIHook.cpp
```
/*****************************************************************************
Module:  APIHook.cpp
Notices: Copyright (c) 2008 Jeffrey Richter & Christophe Nasarre
*****************************************************************************/


#include "..\CommonFiles\CmnHdr.h"
#include <ImageHlp.h>
#pragma comment(lib, "ImageHlp")

#include "APIHook.h"
#include "..\CommonFiles\Toolhelp.h"
#include <StrSafe.h>


/////////////////////////////////////////////////////////////////////////


// The head of the linked-list of CAPIHook objects
CAPIHook* CAPIHook::sm_pHead = NULL;

// By default, the module containing the CAPIHook() is not hooked
BOOL CAPIHook::ExcludeAPIHookMod = TRUE;


/////////////////////////////////////////////////////////////////////////


CAPIHook::CAPIHook(PSTR pszCalleeModName, PSTR pszFuncName, PROC pfnHook) {

    // Note: the function can be hooked only if the exporting module
    //       is already loaded. A solution could be to store the function
    //       name as a member; then, in the hooked LoadLibrary* handlers, parse
    //       the list of CAPIHook instances, check if pszCalleeModName
    //       is the name of the loaded module to hook its export table, and
    //       re-hook the import tables of all loaded modules.

    m_pNext  = sm_pHead;    // The next node was at the head
    sm_pHead = this;        // This node is now at the head

    // Save information about this hooked function
    m_pszCalleeModName = pszCalleeModName;
    m_pszFuncName      = pszFuncName;
```

```
    m_pfnHook            = pfnHook;
    m_pfnOrig            =
        GetProcAddressRaw(GetModuleHandleA(pszCalleeModName), m_pszFuncName);

    // If function does not exit,... bye bye
    // This happens when the module is not already loaded
    if (m_pfnOrig == NULL)
    {
        wchar_t szPathname[MAX_PATH];
        GetModuleFileNameW(NULL, szPathname, _countof(szPathname));
        wchar_t sz[1024];
        StringCchPrintfW(sz, _countof(sz),
            TEXT("[%4u - %s] impossible to find %S\r\n"),
            GetCurrentProcessId(), szPathname, pszFuncName);
        OutputDebugString(sz);
        return;
    }

#ifdef _DEBUG
    // This section was used for debugging sessions when Explorer died as
    // a folder content was requested
    //
    //static BOOL s_bFirstTime = TRUE;
    //if (s_bFirstTime)
    //{
    //    s_bFirstTime = FALSE;

    //    wchar_t szPathname[MAX_PATH];
    //    GetModuleFileNameW(NULL, szPathname, _countof(szPathname));
    //    wchar_t* pszExeFile = wcsrchr(szPathname, L'\\') + 1;
    //    OutputDebugStringW(L"Injected in ");
    //    OutputDebugStringW(pszExeFile);
    //    if (_wcsicmp(pszExeFile, L"Explorer.EXE") == 0)
    //    {
    //        DebugBreak();
    //    }
    //    OutputDebugStringW(L"\n    --> ");
    //    StringCchPrintfW(szPathname, _countof(szPathname), L"%S", pszFuncName);
    //    OutputDebugStringW(szPathname);
    //    OutputDebugStringW(L"\n");
    //}
#endif


    // Hook this function in all currently loaded modules
    ReplaceIATEntryInAllMods(m_pszCalleeModName, m_pfnOrig, m_pfnHook);
}


/////////////////////////////////////////////////////////////////////////////
```

```
CAPIHook::~CAPIHook() {

   // Unhook this function from all modules
   ReplaceIATEntryInAllMods(m_pszCalleeModName, m_pfnHook, m_pfnOrig);

   // Remove this object from the linked list
   CAPIHook* p = sm_pHead;
   if (p == this) {      // Removing the head node
      sm_pHead = p->m_pNext;
   } else {

      BOOL bFound = FALSE;

      // Walk list from head and fix pointers
      for (; !bFound && (p->m_pNext != NULL); p = p->m_pNext) {
         if (p->m_pNext == this) {
            // Make the node that points to us point to our next node
            p->m_pNext = p->m_pNext->m_pNext;
            bFound = TRUE;
         }
      }
   }
}


///////////////////////////////////////////////////////////////////////////


// NOTE: This function must NOT be inlined
FARPROC CAPIHook::GetProcAddressRaw(HMODULE hmod, PCSTR pszProcName) {

   return(::GetProcAddress(hmod, pszProcName));
}


///////////////////////////////////////////////////////////////////////////


// Returns the HMODULE that contains the specified memory address
static HMODULE ModuleFromAddress(PVOID pv) {

   MEMORY_BASIC_INFORMATION mbi;
   return((VirtualQuery(pv, &mbi, sizeof(mbi)) != 0)
      ? (HMODULE) mbi.AllocationBase : NULL);
}


///////////////////////////////////////////////////////////////////////////
```

```
void CAPIHook::ReplaceIATEntryInAllMods(PCSTR pszCalleeModName,
   PROC pfnCurrent, PROC pfnNew) {

   HMODULE hmodThisMod = ExcludeAPIHookMod
      ? ModuleFromAddress(ReplaceIATEntryInAllMods) : NULL;

   // Get the list of modules in this process
   CToolhelp th(TH32CS_SNAPMODULE, GetCurrentProcessId());

   MODULEENTRY32 me = { sizeof(me) };
   for (BOOL bOk = th.ModuleFirst(&me); bOk; bOk = th.ModuleNext(&me)) {

      // NOTE: We don't hook functions in our own module
      if (me.hModule != hmodThisMod) {

         // Hook this function in this module
         ReplaceIATEntryInOneMod(
            pszCalleeModName, pfnCurrent, pfnNew, me.hModule);
      }
   }
}


///////////////////////////////////////////////////////////////////////////


// Handle unexpected exceptions if the module is unloaded
LONG WINAPI InvalidReadExceptionFilter(PEXCEPTION_POINTERS pep) {

   // handle all unexpected exceptions because we simply don't update
   // any module in that case
   LONG lDisposition = EXCEPTION_EXECUTE_HANDLER;

   // Note: pep->ExceptionRecord->ExceptionCode has 0xc0000005 as a value

   return(lDisposition);
}


void CAPIHook::ReplaceIATEntryInOneMod(PCSTR pszCalleeModName,
   PROC pfnCurrent, PROC pfnNew, HMODULE hmodCaller) {

   // Get the address of the module's import section
   ULONG ulSize;

   // An exception was triggered by Explorer (when browsing the content of
   // a folder) into imagehlp.dll. It looks like one module was unloaded...
   // Maybe some threading problem: the list of modules from Toolhelp might
   // not be accurate if FreeLibrary is called during the enumeration.
   PIMAGE_IMPORT_DESCRIPTOR pImportDesc = NULL;
   __try {
      pImportDesc = (PIMAGE_IMPORT_DESCRIPTOR) ImageDirectoryEntryToData(
         hmodCaller, TRUE, IMAGE_DIRECTORY_ENTRY_IMPORT, &ulSize);
   }
```

```
    __except (InvalidReadExceptionFilter(GetExceptionInformation())) {
        // Nothing to do in here, thread continues to run normally
        // with NULL for pImportDesc
    }

    if (pImportDesc == NULL)
        return;   // This module has no import section or is no longer loaded


    // Find the import descriptor containing references to callee's functions
    for (; pImportDesc->Name; pImportDesc++) {
        PSTR pszModName = (PSTR) ((PBYTE) hmodCaller + pImportDesc->Name);
        if (lstrcmpiA(pszModName, pszCalleeModName) == 0) {

            // Get caller's import address table (IAT) for the callee's functions
            PIMAGE_THUNK_DATA pThunk = (PIMAGE_THUNK_DATA)
                ((PBYTE) hmodCaller + pImportDesc->FirstThunk);

            // Replace current function address with new function address
            for (; pThunk->u1.Function; pThunk++) {

                // Get the address of the function address
                PROC* ppfn = (PROC*) &pThunk->u1.Function;

                // Is this the function we're looking for?
                BOOL bFound = (*ppfn == pfnCurrent);
                if (bFound) {
                    if (!WriteProcessMemory(GetCurrentProcess(), ppfn, &pfnNew,
                        sizeof(pfnNew), NULL) && (ERROR_NOACCESS == GetLastError())) {
                        DWORD dwOldProtect;
                        if (VirtualProtect(ppfn, sizeof(pfnNew), PAGE_WRITECOPY,
                            &dwOldProtect)) {

                            WriteProcessMemory(GetCurrentProcess(), ppfn, &pfnNew,
                                sizeof(pfnNew), NULL);
                            VirtualProtect(ppfn, sizeof(pfnNew), dwOldProtect,
                                &dwOldProtect);
                        }
                    }
                    return;   // We did it, get out
                }
            }
        }
    } // Each import section is parsed until the right entry is found and patched
    }
}


//////////////////////////////////////////////////////////////////////////////


void CAPIHook::ReplaceEATEntryInOneMod(HMODULE hmod, PCSTR pszFunctionName,
    PROC pfnNew) {

    // Get the address of the module's export section
    ULONG ulSize;
```

```
       PIMAGE_EXPORT_DIRECTORY pExportDir = NULL;
       __try {
          pExportDir = (PIMAGE_EXPORT_DIRECTORY) ImageDirectoryEntryToData(
             hmod, TRUE, IMAGE_DIRECTORY_ENTRY_EXPORT, &ulSize);
       }
       __except (InvalidReadExceptionFilter(GetExceptionInformation())) {
          // Nothing to do in here, thread continues to run normally
          // with NULL for pExportDir
       }

       if (pExportDir == NULL)
          return;  // This module has no export section or is unloaded

       PDWORD pdwNamesRvas = (PDWORD) ((PBYTE) hmod + pExportDir->AddressOfNames);
       PWORD pdwNameOrdinals = (PWORD)
          ((PBYTE) hmod + pExportDir->AddressOfNameOrdinals);
       PDWORD pdwFunctionAddresses = (PDWORD)
          ((PBYTE) hmod + pExportDir->AddressOfFunctions);

       // Walk the array of this module's function names
       for (DWORD n = 0; n < pExportDir->NumberOfNames; n++) {
          // Get the function name
          PSTR pszFuncName = (PSTR) ((PBYTE) hmod + pdwNamesRvas[n]);

          // If not the specified function, try the next function
          if (lstrcmpiA(pszFuncName, pszFunctionName) != 0) continue;

          // We found the specified function
          // --> Get this function's ordinal value
          WORD ordinal = pdwNameOrdinals[n];

          // Get the address of this function's address
          PROC* ppfn = (PROC*) &pdwFunctionAddresses[ordinal];

          // Turn the new address into an RVA
          pfnNew = (PROC) ((PBYTE) pfnNew - (PBYTE) hmod);

          // Replace current function address with new function address
          if (!WriteProcessMemory(GetCurrentProcess(), ppfn, &pfnNew,
             sizeof(pfnNew), NULL) && (ERROR_NOACCESS == GetLastError())) {
             DWORD dwOldProtect;
             if (VirtualProtect(ppfn, sizeof(pfnNew), PAGE_WRITECOPY,
                &dwOldProtect)) {

                WriteProcessMemory(GetCurrentProcess(), ppfn, &pfnNew,
                   sizeof(pfnNew), NULL);
                VirtualProtect(ppfn, sizeof(pfnNew), dwOldProtect, &dwOldProtect);
             }
          }
          break;  // We did it, get out
       }
    }
```

///

```
// Hook LoadLibrary functions and GetProcAddress so that hooked functions
// are handled correctly if these functions are called.

CAPIHook CAPIHook::sm_LoadLibraryA  ("Kernel32.dll", "LoadLibraryA",
   (PROC) CAPIHook::LoadLibraryA);

CAPIHook CAPIHook::sm_LoadLibraryW  ("Kernel32.dll", "LoadLibraryW",
   (PROC) CAPIHook::LoadLibraryW);

CAPIHook CAPIHook::sm_LoadLibraryExA("Kernel32.dll", "LoadLibraryExA",
   (PROC) CAPIHook::LoadLibraryExA);

CAPIHook CAPIHook::sm_LoadLibraryExW("Kernel32.dll", "LoadLibraryExW",
   (PROC) CAPIHook::LoadLibraryExW);

CAPIHook CAPIHook::sm_GetProcAddress("Kernel32.dll", "GetProcAddress",
   (PROC) CAPIHook::GetProcAddress);


///////////////////////////////////////////////////////////////////////////////


void CAPIHook::FixupNewlyLoadedModule(HMODULE hmod, DWORD dwFlags) {

   // If a new module is loaded, hook the hooked functions
   if ((hmod != NULL) &&    // Do not hook our own module
       (hmod != ModuleFromAddress(FixupNewlyLoadedModule)) &&
       ((dwFlags & LOAD_LIBRARY_AS_DATAFILE) == 0) &&
       ((dwFlags & LOAD_LIBRARY_AS_DATAFILE_EXCLUSIVE) == 0) &&
       ((dwFlags & LOAD_LIBRARY_AS_IMAGE_RESOURCE) == 0)
       ) {

      for (CAPIHook* p = sm_pHead; p != NULL; p = p->m_pNext) {
         if (p->m_pfnOrig != NULL) {
            ReplaceIATEntryInAllMods(p->m_pszCalleeModName,
               p->m_pfnOrig, p->m_pfnHook);
         } else {
#ifdef _DEBUG
            // We should never end up here
            wchar_t szPathname[MAX_PATH];
            GetModuleFileNameW(NULL, szPathname, _countof(szPathname));
            wchar_t sz[1024];
            StringCchPrintfW(sz, _countof(sz),
               TEXT("[%4u - %s] impossible to find %S\r\n"),
               GetCurrentProcessId(), szPathname, p->m_pszCalleeModName);
            OutputDebugString(sz);
#endif
         }
      }
   }
}


///////////////////////////////////////////////////////////////////////////////
```

```
HMODULE WINAPI CAPIHook::LoadLibraryA(PCSTR pszModulePath) {

   HMODULE hmod = ::LoadLibraryA(pszModulePath);
   FixupNewlyLoadedModule(hmod, 0);
   return(hmod);
}


//////////////////////////////////////////////////////////////////////


HMODULE WINAPI CAPIHook::LoadLibraryW(PCWSTR pszModulePath) {

   HMODULE hmod = ::LoadLibraryW(pszModulePath);
   FixupNewlyLoadedModule(hmod, 0);
   return(hmod);
}


//////////////////////////////////////////////////////////////////////


HMODULE WINAPI CAPIHook::LoadLibraryExA(PCSTR pszModulePath,
   HANDLE hFile, DWORD dwFlags) {

   HMODULE hmod = ::LoadLibraryExA(pszModulePath, hFile, dwFlags);
   FixupNewlyLoadedModule(hmod, dwFlags);
   return(hmod);
}


//////////////////////////////////////////////////////////////////////


HMODULE WINAPI CAPIHook::LoadLibraryExW(PCWSTR pszModulePath,
   HANDLE hFile, DWORD dwFlags) {

   HMODULE hmod = ::LoadLibraryExW(pszModulePath, hFile, dwFlags);
   FixupNewlyLoadedModule(hmod, dwFlags);
   return(hmod);
}


//////////////////////////////////////////////////////////////////////


FARPROC WINAPI CAPIHook::GetProcAddress(HMODULE hmod, PCSTR pszProcName) {

   // Get the true address of the function
   FARPROC pfn = GetProcAddressRaw(hmod, pszProcName);

   // Is it one of the functions that we want hooked?
   CAPIHook* p = sm_pHead;
```

```
    for (; (pfn != NULL) && (p != NULL); p = p->m_pNext) {

       if (pfn == p->m_pfnOrig) {

          // The address to return matches an address we want to hook
          // Return the hook function address instead
          pfn = p->m_pfnHook;
          break;
       }
    }

    return(pfn);
}
//////////////////////////// End of File //////////////////////////////
```

APIHook.h

```
/*****************************************************************************
Module:  APIHook.h
Notices: Copyright (c) 2008 Jeffrey Richter & Christophe Nasarre
*****************************************************************************/


#pragma once


//////////////////////////////////////////////////////////////////////////


class CAPIHook {
public:
   // Hook a function in all modules
   CAPIHook(PSTR pszCalleeModName, PSTR pszFuncName, PROC pfnHook);

   // Unhook a function from all modules
   ~CAPIHook();

   // Returns the original address of the hooked function
   operator PROC() { return(m_pfnOrig); }

   // Hook module w/CAPIHook implementation?
   // I have to make it static because I need to use it
   // in ReplaceIATEntryInAllMods
   static BOOL ExcludeAPIHookMod;


public:
   // Calls the real GetProcAddress
   static FARPROC WINAPI GetProcAddressRaw(HMODULE hmod, PCSTR pszProcName);

private:
   static PVOID sm_pvMaxAppAddr; // Maximum private memory address
   static CAPIHook* sm_pHead;    // Address of first object
```

```
    CAPIHook* m_pNext;              // Address of next  object

    PCSTR m_pszCalleeModName;       // Module containing the function (ANSI)
    PCSTR m_pszFuncName;            // Function name in callee (ANSI)
    PROC  m_pfnOrig;                // Original function address in callee
    PROC  m_pfnHook;                // Hook function address

private:
    // Replaces a symbol's address in a module's import section
    static void WINAPI ReplaceIATEntryInAllMods(PCSTR pszCalleeModName,
        PROC pfnOrig, PROC pfnHook);

    // Replaces a symbol's address in all modules' import sections
    static void WINAPI ReplaceIATEntryTnOneMod(PCSTR pszCalleeModName,
        PROC pfnOrig, PROC pfnHook, HMODULE hmodCaller);

    // Replaces a symbol's address in a module's export sections
    static void ReplaceEATEntryInOneMod(HMODULE hmod, PCSTR pszFunctionName,
        PROC pfnNew);

private:
    // Used when a DLL is newly loaded after hooking a function
    static void    WINAPI FixupNewlyLoadedModule(HMODULE hmod, DWORD dwFlags);

    // Used to trap when DLLs are newly loaded
    static HMODULE WINAPI LoadLibraryA(PCSTR pszModulePath);
    static HMODULE WINAPI LoadLibraryW(PCWSTR pszModulePath);
    static HMODULE WINAPI LoadLibraryExA(PCSTR pszModulePath,
        HANDLE hFile, DWORD dwFlags);
    static HMODULE WINAPI LoadLibraryExW(PCWSTR pszModulePath,
        HANDLE hFile, DWORD dwFlags);

    // Returns address of replacement function if hooked function is requested
    static FARPROC WINAPI GetProcAddress(HMODULE hmod, PCSTR pszProcName);

private:
    // Instantiates hooks on these functions
    static CAPIHook sm_LoadLibraryA;
    static CAPIHook sm_LoadLibraryW;
    static CAPIHook sm_LoadLibraryExA;
    static CAPIHook sm_LoadLibraryExW;
    static CAPIHook sm_GetProcAddress;
};
```

/////////////////////////// End of File ///////////////////////////////

Part V
Structured Exception Handling

Chapter 23
Termination Handlers

Close your eyes for a moment and imagine writing your application as though your code could never fail. That's right—there's always enough memory, no one ever passes you an invalid pointer, and the files you count on always exist. Wouldn't it be a pleasure to write your code if you could make these assumptions? Your code would be so much easier to write, to read, and to understand. No more fussing with **if** statements here and **goto**s there—in each function, you'd just write your code top to bottom.

If this kind of straightforward programming environment seems like a dream to you, you'll love structured exception handling (SEH). The virtue of SEH is that as you write your code, you can focus on getting your task done. If something goes wrong at run time, the system catches it and notifies you of the problem.

With SEH, you can't totally ignore the possibility of an error in your code, but you can separate the main job from the error-handling chores. This division makes it easy to concentrate on the problem at hand and focus on possible errors later.

One of Microsoft's main motivations for adding SEH to Windows was to ease the development of the operating system itself. The developers of the operating system use SEH to make the system more robust. We can use SEH to make our own applications more robust.

The burden of getting SEH to work falls more on the compiler than on the operating system. Your compiler must generate special code when exception blocks are entered into and exited from. The compiler must produce tables of support data structures to handle SEH. The compiler also must supply callback functions that the operating system can call so that exception blocks can be traversed. And the compiler is responsible for preparing stack frames and other internal information that is used and referenced by the operating system. Adding SEH support to a compiler is not an easy task. It shouldn't surprise you that different compiler vendors implement SEH in different ways. Fortunately, we can ignore compiler implementation details and just use the compiler's SEH capabilities.

Differences among compiler implementations could make it difficult to discuss the advantages of SEH in specific ways with specific code examples. However, most compiler vendors follow Microsoft's suggested syntax. The syntax and keywords I use in my examples might differ from those of another company's compiler, but the main SEH concepts are the same. I'll use the Microsoft Visual C++ compiler's syntax throughout this chapter.

> **Note** Don't confuse structured exception handling with C++ exception handling. C++
> exception handling is a different form of exception handling, a form that makes use of the
> C++ keywords **catch** and **throw**. Microsoft's Visual C++ also supports C++ exception han-
> dling and is implemented internally by taking advantage of the structured exception handling
> capabilities already present in the compiler and in Windows operating systems.

SEH really consists of two main capabilities: termination handling and exception handling. We'll discuss termination handlers in this chapter and exception handling in the next chapter.

A termination handler guarantees that a block of code (the termination handler) will be called and executed regardless of how another section of code (the guarded body) is exited. The syntax (using the Microsoft Visual C++ compiler) for a termination handler is as follows:

```
__try {
   // Guarded body
   ...
}
__finally {
   // Termination handler
   ...
}
```

The **__try** and **__finally** keywords delineate the two sections of the termination handler. In the preceding code fragment, the operating system and the compiler work together to guarantee that the **__finally** block code in the termination handler will be executed no matter how the guarded body is exited (except if the process or the thread are terminated by calling **ExitProcess**, **Exit-Thread**, **TerminateProcess**, or **TerminateThread**). Regardless of whether you put a **return**, a **goto**, or even a call to **longjump** in the guarded body, the termination handler will be called. I'll show you several examples demonstrating this.

Understanding Termination Handlers by Example

Because the compiler and the operating system are intimately involved with the execution of your code when you use SEH, I believe that the best way to demonstrate how SEH works is by examining source code samples and discussing the order in which the statements execute in each example.

Therefore, the next few sections show different source code fragments, and the text associated with each fragment explains how the compiler and operating system alter the execution order of your code.

Funcenstein1

To appreciate the ramifications of using termination handlers, let's examine a more concrete coding example:

```
DWORD Funcenstein1() {
   DWORD dwTemp;

   // 1. Do any processing here.
   ...
   __try {
      // 2. Request permission to access
      //    protected data, and then use it.
      WaitForSingleObject(g_hSem, INFINITE);

      g_dwProtectedData = 5;
      dwTemp = g_dwProtectedData;
   }
   __finally {
      // 3. Allow others to use protected data.
      ReleaseSemaphore(g_hSem, 1, NULL);
   }

   // 4. Continue processing.
   return(dwTemp);
}
```

The numbered comments in the preceding code sample indicate the order in which your code will execute. In **Funcenstein1**, using the **try-finally** blocks isn't doing much for you. The code will wait for a semaphore, alter the contents of the protected data, save the new value in the local variable **dwTemp**, release the semaphore, and return the new value to the caller.

Funcenstein2

Now let's modify the function a little and see what happens:

```
DWORD Funcenstein2() {
   DWORD dwTemp;

   // 1. Do any processing here.
   ...
   __try {
      // 2. Request permission to access
      //    protected data, and then use it.
      WaitForSingleObject(g_hSem, INFINITE);

      g_dwProtectedData = 5;
      dwTemp = g_dwProtectedData;

      // Return the new value.
      return(dwTemp);
   }
   __finally {
      // 3. Allow others to use protected data.
      ReleaseSemaphore(g_hSem, 1, NULL);
   }

   // Continue processing--this code
   // will never execute in this version.
   dwTemp = 9;
   return(dwTemp);
}
```

In **Funcenstein2**, a **return** statement has been added to the end of the **try** block. This **return** statement tells the compiler that you want to exit the function and return the contents of the **dwTemp** variable, which now contains the value **5**. However, if this **return** statement had been executed, the thread would not have released the semaphore—and no other thread would ever regain control of the semaphore. As you can imagine, this kind of sequence can become a really big problem because threads waiting for the semaphore might never resume execution.

However, by using the termination handler, you have avoided the premature execution of the **return** statement. When the **return** statement attempts to exit the **try** block, the compiler makes sure that the code in the **finally** block executes first. The code inside the **finally** block is guaranteed to execute before the **return** statement in the **try** block is allowed to exit. In **Funcenstein2**, putting the call to **ReleaseSemaphore** into a termination handler block ensures that the semaphore will always be released. There is no chance for a thread to accidentally retain ownership of the semaphore, which would mean that all other threads waiting for the semaphore would never be scheduled CPU time.

After the code in the **finally** block executes, the function does, in fact, return. Any code appearing below the **finally** block doesn't execute because the function returns in the **try** block. Therefore, this function returns the value **5**, not the value **9**.

You might be asking yourself how the compiler guarantees that the **finally** block executes before the **try** block can be exited. When the compiler examines your source code, it sees that you have coded a **return** statement inside a **try** block. Having seen this, the compiler generates code to save the return value (**5** in our example) in a temporary variable created by the compiler. The compiler then generates code to execute the instructions contained inside the **finally** block; this is called a *local unwind*. More specifically, a local unwind occurs when the system executes the contents of a **finally** block because of the premature exit of code in a **try** block. After the instructions inside the **finally** block execute, the value in the compiler's temporary variable is retrieved and returned from the function.

As you can see, the compiler must generate additional code and the system must perform additional work to pull this whole thing off. On different CPUs, the steps needed for termination handling to work vary. You should avoid writing code that causes premature exits from the **try** block of a termination handler because the performance of your application could be adversely impacted. Later in this chapter, I'll discuss the **__leave** keyword, which can help you avoid writing code that forces local unwinds.

Exception handling is designed to capture exceptions—the exceptions to the rule that you expect to happen infrequently (in our example, the premature **return**). If a situation is the norm, checking for the situation explicitly is much more efficient than relying on the SEH capabilities of the operating system and your compiler to trap common occurrences.

Note that when the flow of control naturally leaves the **try** block and enters the **finally** block (as shown in **Funcenstein1**), the overhead of entering the **finally** block is minimal. On x86 CPUs using Microsoft's compiler, a single machine instruction is executed as execution leaves the **try** block to enter the **finally** block—I doubt that you will even notice this overhead in your application. When the compiler has to generate additional code and the system has to perform additional work, as in **Funcenstein2**, the overhead is much more noticeable.

Funcenstein3

Now let's modify the function again and take a look at what happens:

```
DWORD Funcenstein3() {
   DWORD dwTemp;

   // 1. Do any processing here.
   ...
   __try {
      // 2. Request permission to access
      //    protected data, and then use it.
      WaitForSingleObject(g_hSem, INFINITE);

      g_dwProtectedData = 5;
      dwTemp = g_dwProtectedData;

      // Try to jump over the finally block.
      goto ReturnValue;
   }

   __finally {
      // 3. Allow others to use protected data.
      ReleaseSemaphore(g_hSem, 1, NULL);
   }

   dwTemp = 9;
   // 4. Continue processing.
   ReturnValue:
   return(dwTemp);
}
```

In **Funcenstein3**, when the compiler sees the **goto** statement in the **try** block, it generates a local unwind to execute the contents of the **finally** block first. However, this time, after the code in the **finally** block executes, the code after the **ReturnValue** label is executed because no return occurs in either the **try** or **finally** block. This code causes the function to return a **5**. Again, because you have interrupted the natural flow of control from the **try** block into the **finally** block, you could incur a high performance penalty depending on the CPU your application is running on.

Funcfurter1

Now let's look at another scenario in which termination handling really proves its value. Look at this function:

```
DWORD Funcfurter1() {
   DWORD dwTemp;

   // 1. Do any processing here.
   ...
   __try {
      // 2. Request permission to access
      //    protected data, and then use it.
      WaitForSingleObject(g_hSem, INFINITE);
```

```
      dwTemp = Funcinator(g_dwProtectedData);
   }
   __finally {
      // 3. Allow others to use protected data.
      ReleaseSemaphore(g_hSem, 1, NULL);
   }

   // 4. Continue processing.
   return(dwTemp);
}
```

Now imagine that the **Funcinator** function called in the **try** block contains a bug that causes an invalid memory access. Without SEH, this situation would present the user with the ever-popular "Application has stopped working" dialog box provided by the *Windows Error Reporting* (WER) that will be presented in great detail in Chapter 25, "Unhandled Exceptions, Vectored Exception Handling, and C++ Exceptions." When the user dismissed the error dialog box, the process would be terminated. When the process is terminated (because of an invalid memory access), the semaphore would still be owned and would never be released—any threads in other processes that were waiting for this semaphore would never be scheduled CPU time. But placing the call to **Release-Semaphore** in a **finally** block guarantees that the semaphore gets released even if some other function causes a memory access violation. I have to put a damper on this statement: starting with Windows Vista, you have to explicitly protect your **try**/**finally** to ensure that the **finally** block gets executed when an exception is raised. The necessary explanations are provided in "The SEH Termination Sample Application" on page 673, and the next chapter will dig into the details of the **try**/**except** protection.

However, even in prior versions of Windows, the **finally** blocks are not guaranteed to execute for any exception. For example, in Windows XP, if a stack exhaustion exception occurs in the **try** block, chances are good that the **finally** block is not going to get executed, because the WER code is running inside the faulting process possibly without enough stack left to report an error, so the process would be silently terminated. Similarly, if the exception generated a corruption in the SEH chain, the termination handler will not be executed. Last but not least, if another exception happened in the exception filter, the termination handler will not get executed. The rule of thumb to follow is always minimize the action of the code that runs within **catch** or **finally** blocks; otherwise, the process just terminates and no more **finally** blocks execute. This is why the error reporting in Windows Vista runs in a separate process, as detailed in Chapter 25.

If termination handlers are powerful enough to capture a process while terminating because of an invalid memory access, we should have no trouble believing that they will also capture **setjump** and **longjump** combinations and, of course, simple statements such as **break** and **continue**.

Pop Quiz Time: *FuncaDoodleDoo*

Now for a test. Can you determine what the following function returns?

```
DWORD FuncaDoodleDoo() {
   DWORD dwTemp = 0;

   while (dwTemp < 10) {

      __try {
         if (dwTemp == 2)
            continue;

         if (dwTemp == 3)
            break;
      }
      __finally {
         dwTemp++;
      }

      dwTemp++;
   }

   dwTemp += 10;
   return(dwTemp);
}
```

Let's analyze what the function does step by step. First **dwTemp** is set to **0**. The code in the **try** block executes, but neither of the **if** statements evaluates to **TRUE**. Execution moves naturally to the code in the **finally** block, which increments **dwTemp** to **1**. Then the instruction after the **finally** block increments **dwTemp** again, making it **2**.

When the loop iterates, **dwTemp** is **2** and the **continue** statement in the **try** block will execute. Without a termination handler to force execution of the **finally** block before exit from the **try** block, execution would immediately jump back up to the **while** test, **dwTemp** would not be changed, and we would have started an infinite loop. With a termination handler, the system notes that the **continue** statement causes the flow of control to exit the **try** block prematurely and moves execution to the **finally** block. In the **finally** block, **dwTemp** is incremented to **3**. However, the code after the **finally** block doesn't execute because the flow of control moves back to **continue** and thus to the top of the loop.

Now we are processing the loop's third iteration. This time, the first **if** statement evaluates to **FALSE**, but the second **if** statement evaluates to **TRUE**. The system again catches our attempt to break out of the **try** block and executes the code in the **finally** block first. Now **dwTemp** is incremented to **4**. Because a **break** statement was executed, control resumes after the loop. Thus, the code after the **finally** block and still inside the loop doesn't execute. The code below the loop adds **10** to **dwTemp** for a grand total of **14**—the result of calling this function. It should go without saying that you should never actually write code like **FuncaDoodleDoo**. I placed the **continue** and **break** statements in the middle of the code only to demonstrate the operation of the termination handler.

Although a termination handler will catch most situations in which the **try** block would otherwise be exited prematurely, it can't cause the code in a **finally** block to be executed if the thread or process is terminated. A call to **ExitThread** or **ExitProcess** will immediately terminate the thread or process without executing any of the code in a **finally** block. Also, if your thread or process should die because some application called **TerminateThread** or **TerminateProcess**, the code in a **finally** block again won't execute. Some C run-time functions (such as **abort**) that in turn call **ExitProcess** again preclude the execution of **finally** blocks. You can't do anything to prevent another application from terminating one of your threads or processes, but you can prevent your own premature calls to **ExitThread** and **ExitProcess**.

Funcenstein4

Let's take a look at one more termination-handling scenario:

```
DWORD Funcenstein4() {
   DWORD dwTemp;
   // 1. Do any processing here.
   ...
   __try {
      // 2. Request permission to access
      //    protected data, and then use it.
      WaitForSingleObject(g_hSem, INFINITE);

      g_dwProtectedData = 5;
      dwTemp = g_dwProtectedData;

      // Return the new value.
      return(dwTemp);
   }
   __finally {
      // 3. Allow others to use protected data.
      ReleaseSemaphore(g_hSem, 1, NULL);
      return(103);
   }

   // Continue processing--this code will never execute.
   dwTemp = 9;
   return(dwTemp);
}
```

In **Funcenstein4**, the **try** block will execute and try to return the value of **dwTemp** (**5**) back to **Funcenstein4**'s caller. As noted in the discussion of **Funcenstein2**, trying to return prematurely from a **try** block causes the generation of code that puts the return value into a temporary variable created by the compiler. Then the code inside the **finally** block is executed. Notice that in this variation on **Funcenstein2** I have added a **return** statement to the **finally** block. Will **Funcenstein4** return **5** or **103** to the caller? The answer is **103** because the **return** statement in the **finally** block causes the value **103** to be stored in the same temporary variable in which the value **5** has been stored, overwriting the **5**. When the **finally** block completes execution, the value now in the temporary variable (**103**) is returned from **Funcenstein4** to its caller.

We've seen termination handlers do an effective job of rescuing execution from a premature exit of the **try** block, and we've also seen termination handlers produce an unwanted result because they prevented a premature exit of the **try** block. A good rule of thumb is to avoid any statements that would cause a premature exit of the **try** block part of a termination handler. In fact, it is always best to remove all **return**s, **continue**s, **break**s, **goto**s, and so on from inside both the **try** and **finally** blocks of a termination handler and to put these statements outside the handler. Such a practice will cause the compiler to generate both a smaller amount of code—because it won't have to catch premature exits from the **try** block—and faster code, because it will have fewer instructions to execute in order to perform the local unwind. In addition, your code will be much easier to read and maintain.

Funcarama1

We've pretty much covered the basic syntax and semantics of termination handlers. Now let's look at how a termination handler could be used to simplify a more complicated programming problem. Let's look at a function that doesn't take advantage of termination handlers at all:

```
BOOL Funcarama1() {
   HANDLE hFile = INVALID_HANDLE_VALUE;
   PVOID pvBuf = NULL;
   DWORD dwNumBytesRead;
   BOOL bOk;

   hFile = CreateFile(TEXT("SOMEDATA.DAT"), GENERIC_READ,
      FILE_SHARE_READ, NULL, OPEN_EXISTING, 0, NULL);
   if (hFile == INVALID_HANDLE_VALUE) {
      return(FALSE);
   }

   pvBuf = VirtualAlloc(NULL, 1024, MEM_COMMIT, PAGE_READWRITE);
   if (pvBuf == NULL) {
      CloseHandle(hFile);
      return(FALSE);
   }

   bOk = ReadFile(hFile, pvBuf, 1024, &dwNumBytesRead, NULL);
   if (!bOk || (dwNumBytesRead == 0)) {
      VirtualFree(pvBuf, MEM_RELEASE | MEM_DECOMMIT);
      CloseHandle(hFile);
      return(FALSE);
   }

   // Do some calculation on the data.
   ...
   // Clean up all the resources.
   VirtualFree(pvBuf, MEM_RELEASE | MEM_DECOMMIT);
   CloseHandle(hFile);
   return(TRUE);
}
```

All the error checking in **Funcarama1** makes the function difficult to read, which also makes the function difficult to understand, maintain, and modify.

Funcarama2

Of course, it's possible to rewrite **Funcarama1** so that it is a little cleaner and easier to understand:

```
BOOL Funcarama2() {
   HANDLE hFile = INVALID_HANDLE_VALUE;
   PVOID pvBuf = NULL;
   DWORD dwNumBytesRead;
   BOOL bOk, bSuccess = FALSE;

   hFile = CreateFile(TEXT("SOMEDATA.DAT"), GENERIC_READ,
      FILE_SHARE_READ, NULL, OPEN_EXISTING, 0, NULL);

   if (hFile != INVALID_HANDLE_VALUE) {
      pvBuf = VirtualAlloc(NULL, 1024, MEM_COMMIT, PAGE_READWRITE);
      if (pvBuf != NULL) {
         bOk = ReadFile(hFile, pvBuf, 1024, &dwNumBytesRead, NULL);
         if (bOk && (dwNumBytesRead != 0)) {
            // Do some calculation on the data.
            ...
            bSuccess = TRUE;
         }
         VirtualFree(pvBuf, MEM_RELEASE | MEM_DECOMMIT);
      }
      CloseHandle(hFile);
   }
   return(bSuccess);
}
```

Although easier to understand than **Funcarama1**, **Funcarama2** is still difficult to modify and maintain. Also, the indentation level gets to be pretty extreme as more conditional statements are added; with such a rewrite, you soon end up writing code on the far right of your screen and wrapping statements after every five characters!

Funcarama3

Let's rewrite the first version, **Funcarama1**, to take advantage of an SEH termination handler:

```
DWORD Funcarama3() {

   // IMPORTANT: Initialize all variables to assume failure.
   HANDLE hFile = INVALID_HANDLE_VALUE;
   PVOID pvBuf = NULL;

   __try {
      DWORD dwNumBytesRead;
      BOOL bOk;

      hFile = CreateFile(TEXT("SOMEDATA.DAT"), GENERIC_READ,
         FILE_SHARE_READ, NULL, OPEN_EXISTING, 0, NULL);
      if (hFile == INVALID_HANDLE_VALUE) {
         return(FALSE);
      }
```

```
      pvBuf = VirtualAlloc(NULL, 1024, MEM_COMMIT, PAGE_READWRITE);
      if (pvBuf == NULL) {
         return(FALSE);
      }

      bOk = ReadFile(hFile, pvBuf, 1024, &dwNumBytesRead, NULL);
      if (!bOk || (dwNumBytesRead != 1024)) {
         return(FALSE);
      }

      // Do some calculation on the data.
      ...
   }

   __finally {
      // Clean up all the resources.
      if (pvBuf != NULL)
         VirtualFree(pvBuf, MEM_RELEASE | MEM_DECOMMIT);
      if (hFile != INVALID_HANDLE_VALUE)
         CloseHandle(hFile);
   }
   // Continue processing.
   return(TRUE);
}
```

The real virtue of the **Funcarama3** version is that all of the function's cleanup code is localized in one place and one place only: the **finally** block. If we ever need to add code to this function, we can simply add a single cleanup line in the **finally** block—we won't have to go back to every possible location of failure and add our cleanup line to each failure location.

Funcarama4: The Final Frontier

The real problem with the **Funcarama3** version is the overhead. As I mentioned after the discussion of **Funcenstein4**, you really should avoid putting **return** statements into a **try** block as much as possible.

To help make such avoidance easier, Microsoft added another keyword, **__leave**, to its C/C++ compiler. Here is the **Funcarama4** version, which takes advantage of the **__leave** keyword:

```
DWORD Funcarama4() {

   // IMPORTANT: Initialize all variables to assume failure.
   HANDLE hFile = INVALID_HANDLE_VALUE;
   PVOID pvBuf = NULL;

   // Assume that the function will not execute successfully.
   BOOL bFunctionOk = FALSE;

   __try {
      DWORD dwNumBytesRead;
      BOOL bOk;
```

```
    hFile = CreateFile(TEXT("SOMEDATA.DAT"), GENERIC_READ,
       FILE_SHARE_READ, NULL, OPEN_EXISTING, 0, NULL);
    if (hFile == INVALID_HANDLE_VALUE) {
       __leave;
    }

    pvBuf = VirtualAlloc(NULL, 1024, MEM_COMMIT, PAGE_READWRITE);

    if (pvBuf == NULL) {
       __leave;
    }

    bOk = ReadFile(hFile, pvBuf, 1024, &dwNumBytesRead, NULL);
    if (!bOk || (dwNumBytesRead == 0)) {
       __leave;
    }

    // Do some calculation on the data.
    ...
    // Indicate that the entire function executed successfully.
    bFunctionOk = TRUE;
  }
  __finally {
    // Clean up all the resources.
    if (pvBuf != NULL)
       VirtualFree(pvBuf, MEM_RELEASE | MEM_DECOMMIT);
    if (hFile != INVALID_HANDLE_VALUE)
       CloseHandle(hFile);
  }
  // Continue processing.
  return(bFunctionOk);
}
```

The use of the **__leave** keyword in the **try** block causes a jump to the end of the **try** block. You can think of it as jumping to the **try** block's closing brace. Because the flow of control will exit naturally from the **try** block and enter the **finally** block, no overhead is incurred. However, it was necessary to introduce a new Boolean variable, **bFunctionOk**, to indicate the success or failure of the function. That's a relatively small price to pay.

When designing your functions to take advantage of termination handlers in this way, remember to initialize all of your resource handles to invalid values before entering your **try** block. Then, in the **finally** block, you can check to see which resources have been allocated successfully so that you'll know which ones to free. Another popular method for tracking which resources will need to be freed is to set a flag when a resource allocation is successful. Then the code in the **finally** block can examine the state of the flag to determine whether the resource needs freeing.

Notes About the *finally* Block

So far we have explicitly identified two scenarios that force the **finally** block to be executed:

- Normal flow of control from the **try** block into the **finally** block
- Local unwind: premature exit from the **try** block (**goto, longjump, continue, break, return**, and so on) forcing control to the **finally** block

A third scenario—a *global unwind*—occurred without explicit identification as such in the **Funcfurter1** function we saw on page 663. Inside the **try** block of this function was a call to the **Funcinator** function. Before Windows Vista, if the **Funcinator** function caused a memory access violation, a global unwind caused **Funcfurter1**'s **finally** block to execute. As of Windows Vista, a global unwind is not triggered by default, so the **finally** block is not executed. "The SEH Termination Sample Application" on page 673 gives you a first glance at what triggers a global unwind, and we'll look at global unwinding in greater detail in the next two chapters.

Code in a **finally** block always starts executing as a result of one of these three situations. To determine which of the three possibilities caused the **finally** block to execute, you can call the intrinsic function **AbnormalTermination**:

```
BOOL AbnormalTermination();
```

> **Note**   An *intrinsic function* is a special function recognized by the compiler. The compiler generates the code for the function inline rather than generating code to call the function. For example, **memcpy** is an intrinsic function (if the **/Oi** compiler switch is specified). When the compiler sees a call to **memcpy**, it puts the **memcpy** code directly into the function that called **memcpy** instead of generating a call to the **memcpy** function. This usually has the effect of making your code run faster at the expense of code size.
>
> The intrinsic **AbnormalTermination** function is different from the intrinsic **memcpy** function in that it exists only in an intrinsic form. No C/C++ run-time library contains the **AbnormalTermination** function.

This intrinsic function can be called only from inside a **finally** block, and it returns a Boolean value indicating whether the **try** block associated with the **finally** block was exited prematurely. In other words, if the flow of control leaves the **try** block and naturally enters the **finally** block, **AbnormalTermination** will return **FALSE**. If the flow of control exits the **try** block abnormally—usually because a local unwind has been caused by a **goto, return, break**, or **continue** statement or because a global unwind has been caused by a memory access violation or another exception—a call to **AbnormalTermination** will return **TRUE**. It is impossible to determine whether a **finally** block is executing because of a global unwind or because of a local unwind. This is usually not a problem because you have, of course, avoided writing code that performs local unwinds.

Funcfurter2

Here is **Funcfurter2**, which demonstrates use of the **AbnormalTermination** intrinsic function:

```
DWORD Funcfurter2() {
   DWORD dwTemp;

   // 1. Do any processing here.
   ...
   __try {
      // 2. Request permission to access
      //    protected data, and then use it.
      WaitForSingleObject(g_hSem, INFINITE);

      dwTemp = Funcinator(g_dwProtectedData);
   }
   __finally {
      // 3. Allow others to use protected data.
      ReleaseSemaphore(g_hSem, 1, NULL);

      if (!AbnormalTermination()) {
         // No errors occurred in the try block, and
         // control flowed naturally from try into finally.
         ...
      } else {
         // Something caused an exception, and
         // because there is no code in the try block
         // that would cause a premature exit, we must
         // be executing in the finally block
         // because of a global unwind.

         // If there were a goto in the try block,
         // we wouldn't know how we got here.
         ...
      }
   }

   // 4. Continue processing.
   return(dwTemp);
}
```

Now that you know how to write termination handlers, you'll see that they can be even more useful and important when we look at exception filters and exception handlers in the next chapter. Before we move on, let's review the reasons for using termination handlers:

- They simplify error processing because all cleanup is in one location and is guaranteed to execute.

- They improve program readability.

- They make code easier to maintain.

- They have minimal speed and size overhead if used correctly.

The SEH Termination Sample Application

The SEHTerm application, 23-SEHTerm.exe, demonstrates how termination handlers work. The source code and resource files for the application are in the 23-SEHTerm directory on the companion content Web page.

When you run the application, the primary thread enters a **try** block. Inside this **try** block, the following message box is displayed:

This message box asks whether you want the program to access an invalid byte in memory. (Most applications aren't as considerate as this; they usually just access invalid memory without asking.) Let's examine what happens if you click the No button. In this case, the thread naturally flows out of the **try** block and enters the **finally** block that displays a message box:

Notice, however, that the message box indicates that the **try** block exited normally. When we dismiss this message box, the thread leaves the **finally** block and displays another message box:

Before the application's main thread returns, a final message box pops up to show that no unhandled exception occurred:

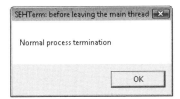

When this message box is dismissed, the process terminates naturally, because **_tWinMain** returns.

OK, now let's run the application again. This time, however, let's click the Yes button so that we do attempt to access invalid memory. When you click Yes, the thread attempts to write a **5** to memory address **NULL**. Writing to address **NULL** always causes an access violation exception. When the thread raises an access violation that is not handled, the system displays the message box shown in Figure 23-1 in Windows XP.

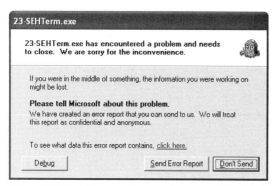

Figure 23-1   Message shown when an unhandled exception occurs in Windows XP

In Windows Vista, by default, the first dialog box that appears is shown in Figure 23-2.

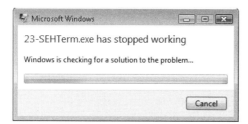

Figure 23-2   First message shown when an unhandled exception occurs in Windows Vista

If the Cancel button is clicked to dismiss the message box, the application silently dies. If the Cancel button is not clicked, another dialog box replaces the previous one, as shown in Figure 23-3.

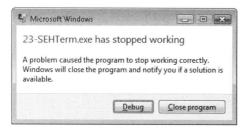

Figure 23-3   Second message shown when an unhandled exception occurs in Windows Vista

If the Debug button is clicked, the system triggers a workflow, detailed in Chapter 25, to start a debugger that will attach to the faulted process.

If you click instead on the Close Program button (in Windows Vista) or the Send Error Report/ Don't Send buttons (in Windows XP), the process will be terminated. However, there is a **finally** block in the source code, so the **finally** block should execute before the process terminates, displaying this message box in Windows XP:

The **finally** block is executing because its associated **try** block exited abnormally. When this message box is dismissed, the process does, in fact, terminate. However, the previous statement is valid only for the versions of Windows prior to Windows Vista, where a **finally** block is executed only if global unwind occurs. As you saw in Chapter 6, "Thread Basics," a thead entry point is protected by a **try/except** construct. For a global unwind to be triggered, the exception filter function called in **__except()** should return **EXCEPTION_EXECUTE_HANDLER**. This is the case for versions of Microsoft Windows prior to Vista. However, in Windows Vista, a major rearchitecture of the unhandled exception has been done to increase the reliability of logging and reporting, as you will see in the Chapter 25. The immediate and visible drawback of these changes is that **EXCEPTION_ CONTINUE_SEARCH** is returned by the wrapping exception filter, so the process is immediately terminated, without allowing your **finally** blocks to execute.

In SEHTerm.exe, the code checks whether the application is running under Windows Vista and, in that case, the following message box gives you the choice whether or not to protect the faulting function within a **try/except**:

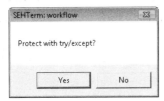

If you click the Yes button, the **try/finally** construct is protected by an exception filter that always returns **EXCEPTION_EXECUTE_HANDLER**. This forces a global unwind to be triggered when an exception is thrown so that the following message box pops up when the **finally** block gets executed:

The code in the **except** block displays this message box before exiting the application main thread with –1 as an error code:

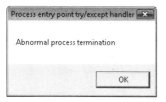

If the No button is clicked instead, when the exception occurs (and if you don't ask for the just-in-time debugging to start), the application is terminated without executing the **finally** block.

```
SEHTerm.cpp
/******************************************************************************
Module:  SEHTerm.cpp
Notices: Copyright (c) 2008 Jeffrey Richter & Christophe Nasarre
******************************************************************************/


#include <windows.h>
#include <tchar.h>


///////////////////////////////////////////////////////////////////////////////


BOOL IsWindowsVista() {

   // Code from Chapter 4
   // Prepare the OSVERSIONINFOEX structure to indicate Windows Vista.
   OSVERSIONINFOEX osver = { 0 };
   osver.dwOSVersionInfoSize = sizeof(osver);
   osver.dwMajorVersion = 6;
   osver.dwMinorVersion = 0;
   osver.dwPlatformId = VER_PLATFORM_WIN32_NT;

   // Prepare the condition mask.
   DWORDLONG dwlConditionMask = 0;  // You MUST initialize this to 0.
   VER_SET_CONDITION(dwlConditionMask, VER_MAJORVERSION, VER_EQUAL);
   VER_SET_CONDITION(dwlConditionMask, VER_MINORVERSION, VER_EQUAL);
   VER_SET_CONDITION(dwlConditionMask, VER_PLATFORMID, VER_EQUAL);

   // Perform the version test.
   if (VerifyVersionInfo(&osver, VER_MAJORVERSION  | VER_MINORVERSION |
      VER_PLATFORMID, dwlConditionMask)) {
      // The host system is Windows Vista exactly.
      return(TRUE);
   } else {
      // The host system is NOT Windows Vista.
      return(FALSE);
   }
}
```

```
void TriggerException() {

   __try {
      int n = MessageBox(NULL, TEXT("Perform invalid memory access?"),
         TEXT("SEHTerm: In try block"), MB_YESNO);

      if (n == IDYES) {
         * (PBYTE) NULL = 5;  // This causes an access violation
      }
   }
   __finally {
      PCTSTR psz = AbnormalTermination()
         ? TEXT("Abnormal termination") : TEXT("Normal termination");
      MessageBox(NULL, psz, TEXT("SEHTerm: In finally block"), MB_OK);
   }

   MessageBox(NULL, TEXT("Normal function termination"),
      TEXT("SEHTerm: After finally block"), MB_OK);
}


int WINAPI _tWinMain(HINSTANCE, HINSTANCE, PTSTR, int) {

   // In Windows Vista, a global unwind occurs if an except filter
   // returns EXCEPTION_EXECUTE_HANDLER. If an unhandled exception
   // occurs, the process is simply terminated and the finally blocks
   // are not exectuted.
   if (IsWindowsVista()) {

      DWORD n = MessageBox(NULL, TEXT("Protect with try/except?"),
         TEXT("SEHTerm: workflow"), MB_YESNO);

      if (n == IDYES) {
         __try {
            TriggerException();
         }
         __except (EXCEPTION_EXECUTE_HANDLER) {
            // But the system dialog will not appear.
            // So, popup a message box.
            MessageBox(NULL, TEXT("Abnormal process termination"),
               TEXT("Process entry point try/except handler"), MB_OK);

            // Exit with a dedicated error code
            return(-1);
         }
      } else {
         TriggerException();
      }
   } else {
      TriggerException();
   }
```

```
    MessageBox(NULL, TEXT("Normal process termination"),
       TEXT("SEHTerm: before leaving the main thread"), MB_OK);

    return(0);
}
```

/////////////////////////////// End of File ///////////////////////////////

Chapter 24
Exception Handlers and Software Exceptions

An exception is an event you don't expect. In a well-written application, you don't expect attempts to access an invalid memory address or divide a value by **0**. Nevertheless, such errors do occur. The CPU is responsible for catching invalid memory accesses and divides by **0**, and it will raise an exception in response to these errors. When the CPU raises an exception, it's known as a *hardware exception*. Later in this chapter, we'll see that the operating system and your applications can raise their own exceptions, known as *software exceptions*.

When a hardware or software exception is raised, the operating system offers your application the opportunity to see what type of exception was raised and allows the application to handle the exception itself. Here is the syntax for an exception handler:

```
__try {
   // Guarded body
   ...
}
__except (exception filter) {
   // Exception handler
   ...
}
```

Notice the **__except** keyword. Whenever you create a **try** block, it must be followed by either a **finally** block or an **except** block. A **try** block can't have both a **finally** block and an **except** block, and a **try** block can't have multiple **finally** or **except** blocks. However, it is possible to nest **try-finally** blocks inside **try-except** blocks and vice versa.

Understanding Exception Filters and Exception Handlers by Example

Unlike termination handlers (discussed in the previous chapter), exception filters and exception handlers are executed directly by the operating system—the compiler has little to do with evaluating exception filters or executing exception handlers. The next several sections illustrate the normal execution of **try-except** blocks, explain how and why the operating system evaluates exception filters, and show the circumstances under which the operating system executes the code inside an exception handler.

Funcmeister1

Here's a more concrete coding example of a **try-except** block:

```
DWORD Funcmeister1() {
   DWORD dwTemp;

   // 1. Do any processing here.
   ...
   __try {
      // 2. Perform some operation.
      dwTemp = 0;
   }
   __except (EXCEPTION_EXECUTE_HANDLER) {
      // Handle an exception; this never executes.
      ...
   }

   // 3. Continue processing.
   return(dwTemp);
}
```

In the **Funcmeister1 try** block, we simply move a **0** into the **dwTemp** variable. This operation will never cause an exception to be raised, so the code inside the **except** block will never execute. Note this difference from **try-finally** behavior. After **dwTemp** is set to **0**, the next instruction to execute is the **return** statement.

Although **return**, **goto**, **continue**, and **break** statements are strongly discouraged in the **try** block of a termination handler, no speed or code-size penalty is associated with using these statements inside the **try** block of an exception handler. Such a statement in the **try** block associated with an **except** block won't incur the overhead of a local unwind.

Funcmeister2

Let's modify the function and see what happens:

```
DWORD Funcmeister2() {
   DWORD dwTemp = 0;

   // 1. Do any processing here.
   ...
   __try {
      // 2. Perform some operation(s).
      dwTemp = 5 / dwTemp;     // Generates an exception
      dwTemp += 10;            // Never executes
   }
   __except ( /* 3. Evaluate filter. */ EXCEPTION_EXECUTE_HANDLER) {
      // 4. Handle an exception.

      MessageBeep(0);
      ...
   }

   // 5. Continue processing.
   return(dwTemp);
}
```

In **Funcmeister2**, an instruction inside the **try** block calls for the attempt to divide **5** by **0**. The CPU will catch this event and raise a hardware exception. When this exception is raised, the system will locate the beginning of the **except** block and evaluate the exception filter expression, an expression that must evaluate to one of the three identifiers shown in Table 24-1, as defined in the Microsoft Windows Excpt.h file.

Table 24-1   Exception Filter Return Values

Identifier	Defined As
EXCEPTION_EXECUTE_HANDLER	1
EXCEPTION_CONTINUE_SEARCH	0
EXCEPTION_CONTINUE_EXECUTION	−1

In the next few sections, we'll discuss how each of these identifiers alters the thread's execution. While reading these sections, you can refer to Figure 24-1, which summarizes how the system processes an exception.

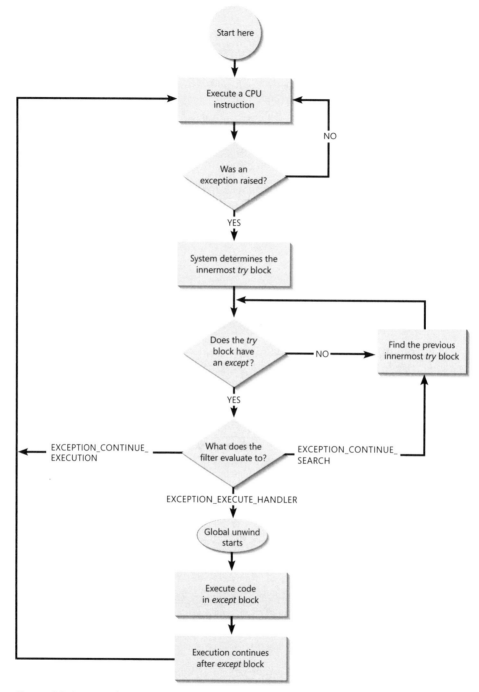

Figure 24-1   How the system processes an exception

EXCEPTION_EXECUTE_HANDLER

In **Funcmeister2**, the exception filter expression evaluates to **EXCEPTION_EXECUTE_HANDLER**. This value basically says to the system, "I recognize the exception. That is, I had a feeling that this exception might occur some time, and I've written some code to deal with it that I'd like to execute now." At this point, the system performs a global unwind (discussed later in this chapter) and then execution jumps to the code inside the **except** block (the exception handler code). After the code in the **except** block has executed, the system considers the exception to be handled and allows your application to continue executing. This mechanism allows Windows applications to trap errors, handle them, and continue running without the user ever knowing that the error happened.

But once the **except** block has executed, where in the code should execution resume? With a little bit of thought, we can easily imagine several possibilities.

The first possibility is for execution to resume after the CPU instruction that generates the exception. In **Funcmeister2**, execution would resume with the instruction that adds **10** to **dwTemp**. This might seem like a reasonable thing to do, but in reality, most programs are written so that they cannot continue executing successfully if one of the earlier instructions fails to execute.

In **Funcmeister2**, the code can continue to execute normally; however, **Funcmeister2** is not the normal situation. Most likely, your code will be structured so that the CPU instructions following the instruction that generates the exception will expect a valid return value. For example, you might have a function that allocates memory, in which case a whole series of instructions will be executed to manipulate that memory. If the memory cannot be allocated, all the lines will fail, making the program generate exceptions repeatedly.

Here is another example of why execution cannot continue after the failed CPU instruction. Let's replace the C statement that generated the exception in **Funcmeister2** with the following line:

```
malloc(5 / dwTemp);
```

For the preceding line, the compiler generates CPU instructions to perform the division, pushes the result on the stack, and calls the **malloc** function. If the division fails, the code can't continue executing properly. The system has to push something on the stack; if it doesn't, the stack gets corrupted.

Fortunately, Microsoft has not made it possible for us to have the system resume execution on the instruction following the instruction that generates the exception. This decision saves us from potential problems like these.

The second possibility is for execution to resume with the instruction that generated the exception. This is an interesting possibility. What if inside the **except** block you had this statement:

```
dwTemp = 2;
```

With this assignment in the **except** block, you could resume execution with the instruction that generated the exception. This time, you would be dividing **5** by **2**, and execution would continue just fine without raising another exception. You can alter something and have the system retry the instruction that generated the exception. However, you should be aware that this technique could result in some subtle behaviors. We'll discuss this technique in "*EXCEPTION_CONTINUE_EXECU-TION*" on page 691.

The third and last possibility is for execution to pick up with the first instruction following the **except** block. This is actually what happens when the exception filter expression evaluates to **EXCEPTION_EXECUTE_HANDLER**. After the code inside the **except** block finishes executing, control resumes at the first instruction after the **except** block.

Some Useful Examples

Let's say that you want to implement a totally robust application that needs to run 24 hours a day, 7 days a week. In today's world, with software so complex and so many variables and factors having an effect on an application's performance, I think that it's impossible to implement a totally robust application without the use of structured exception handling (SEH). Let's look at a simple example: the unsafe C/C++ run-time function **strcpy**:

```
char* strcpy(
   char* strDestination,
   const char* strSource);
```

This is a pretty simple function, huh? How could little old **strcpy** ever cause a process to terminate? Well, if the caller ever passes **NULL** (or any bad address) for either of these parameters, **strcpy** raises an access violation and the whole process is terminated.

Using SEH, it's possible to create a more robust **strcpy** function:

```
char* RobustStrCpy(char* strDestination, const char* strSource) {

   __try {
      strcpy(strDestination, strSource);
   }
   __except (EXCEPTION_EXECUTE_HANDLER) {
      // Nothing to do here
   }

   return(strDestination);
}
```

All this function does is place the call to **strcpy** inside a structured exception-handling frame. If **strcpy** executes successfully, the function just returns. If **strcpy** raises an access violation, the exception filter returns **EXCEPTION_EXECUTE_HANDLER**, causing the thread to execute the handler code. In this function, the handler code does nothing and so again, **RobustStrCpy** just returns to its caller. **RobustStrCpy** will never cause the process to terminate! However, despite the feeling of safety you get from this implementation, it might hide more problems.

Because you don't know how **strcpy** is implemented, you have no idea what types of exceptions could be raised during its execution. The explanation mentioned only the case where the **strDestination** address is **NULL** or invalid. What if the address is valid but the corresponding buffer is not large enough to contain **strSource**? The memory block pointed to by **strDestination** might be part of a larger block whose content will be corrupted by the action of **strcpy**. Maybe the block is not large enough and you still get an access violation exception. However, as you are handling the exception, the process keeps on running—but it's running in a corrupted state that might end up in a crash later that's difficult to understand or in a security issue that could be exploited. The lesson is simple: handle only the exceptions you know how to recover from but without forgetting the other protections to avoid state corruption and security breaches. (Read Chapter 2, "Working with Characters and Strings," for more details about the secured string functions that should be systematically used.)

Let's look at another example. Here's a function that returns the number of space-delimited tokens in a string:

```
int RobustHowManyToken(const char* str) {

   int nHowManyTokens = -1;  // -1 indicates failure
   char* strTemp = NULL;     // Assume failure

   __try {

      // Allocate a temporary buffer
      strTemp = (char*) malloc(strlen(str) + 1);

      // Copy the original string to the temporary buffer
      strcpy(strTemp, str);

      // Get the first token
      char* pszToken = strtok(strTemp, " ");

      // Iterate through all the tokens
      for (; pszToken != NULL; pszToken = strtok(NULL, " "))
         nHowManyTokens++;

      nHowManyTokens++;       // Add 1 since we started at -1
   }
   __except (EXCEPTION_EXECUTE_HANDLER) {
      // Nothing to do here
   }

   // Free the temporary buffer (guaranteed)
   free(strTemp);

   return(nHowManyTokens);
}
```

This function allocates a temporary buffer and copies a string into it. Then the function uses the C/C++ run-time function **strtok** to obtain the tokens within the string. The temporary buffer is necessary because **strtok** modifies the string it's tokenizing.

Thanks to SEH, this deceptively simple function handles all kinds of possibilities. Let's see how this function performs under a few different circumstances.

First, if the caller passes **NULL** (or any bad memory address) to the function, **nHowManyTokens** is initialized to **–1**. The call to **strlen**, inside the **try** block, raises an access violation. The exception filter gets control and passes it to the **except** block, which does nothing. After the **except** block, **free** is called to release the temporary block of memory. However, this memory was never allocated, so we end up calling **free**, passing it **NULL**. ANSI C explicitly states that it is legal to call

free, passing it **NULL**, in which case **free** does nothing—so this is not an error. Finally, the function returns **–1**, indicating failure. Note that the process is not terminated.

Second, the caller might pass a good address to the function but the call to **malloc** (inside the **try** block) can fail and return **NULL**. This will cause the call to **strcpy** to raise an access violation. Again, the exception filter is called, the except **block** executes (which does nothing), **free** is called passing it **NULL** (which does nothing), and **–1** is returned, indicating to the caller that the function failed. Note that the process is not terminated.

Finally, let's assume that the caller passes a good address to the function and the call to **malloc** also succeeds. In this case, the remaining code will also succeed in calculating the number of tokens in the **nHowManyTokens** variable. At the end of the **try** block, the exception filter will not be evaluated, the code in the **except** block will not be executed, the temporary memory buffer will be freed, and **nHowManyTokens** will be returned to the caller.

Using SEH is pretty cool. The **RobustHowManyToken** function demonstrates how to have guaranteed cleanup of a resource without using **try-finally**. Any code that comes after an exception handler is also guaranteed to be executed (assuming that the function does not return from within a **try** block—a practice that should be avoided).

Let's look at one last and particularly useful example of SEH. Here's a function that duplicates a block of memory:

```
PBYTE RobustMemDup(PBYTE pbSrc, size_t cb) {

    PBYTE pbDup = NULL;        // Assume failure

    __try {

        // Allocate a buffer for the duplicate memory block
        pbDup = (PBYTE) malloc(cb);

        memcpy(pbDup, pbSrc, cb);
    }
    __except (EXCEPTION_EXECUTE_HANDLER) {
        free(pbDup);
        pbDup = NULL;
    }

    return(pbDup);
}
```

This function allocates a memory buffer and copies the bytes from the source block into the destination block. Then the function returns the address of the duplicate memory buffer to the caller (or **NULL** if the function fails). The caller is expected to free the buffer when it no longer needs it. This is the first example in which we actually have some code inside the **except** block. Let's see how this function performs under different circumstances:

■ If the caller passes a bad address in the **pbSrc** parameter or if the call to **malloc** fails (returning **NULL**), **memcpy** will raise an access violation. The access violation executes the filter, which passes control to the **except** block. Inside the **except** block, the memory buffer is freed and **pbDup** is set to **NULL** so that the caller will know that the function failed. Again, note that ANSI C allows **free** to be passed **NULL**.

- If the caller passes a good address to the function and if the call to **malloc** is successful, the address of the newly allocated memory block is returned to the caller.

Global Unwinds

When an exception filter evaluates to **EXCEPTION_EXECUTE_HANDLER**, the system must perform a *global unwind*. The global unwind causes all of the outstanding **try-finally** blocks that started executing below the **try-except** block that handles the exception to resume execution. Figure 24-2 shows a flowchart that describes how the system performs a global unwind. Please refer to this figure while I explain the following example.

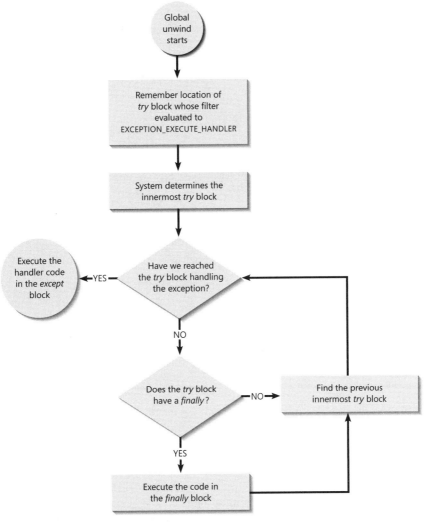

Figure 24-2   How the system performs a global unwind

```
void FuncOStimpy1() {

   // 1. Do any processing here.
   ...
   __try {
      // 2. Call another function.
      FuncORen1();

      // Code here never executes.
   }

   __except ( /* 6. Evaluate filter. */ EXCEPTION_EXECUTE_HANDLER) {
      // 8. After the unwind, the exception handler executes.
      MessageBox(...);
   }

   // 9. Exception handled--continue execution.
   ...
}
void FuncORen1() {
   DWORD dwTemp = 0;

   // 3. Do any processing here.
   ...
   __try {
      // 4. Request permission to access protected data.
      WaitForSingleObject(g_hSem, INFINITE);

      // 5. Modify the data.
      //    An exception is generated here.
      g_dwProtectedData = 5 / dwTemp;
   }
   __finally {
      // 7. Global unwind occurs because filter evaluated
      //    to EXCEPTION_EXECUTE_HANDLER.

      // Allow others to use protected data.
      ReleaseSemaphore(g_hSem, 1, NULL);
   }

   // Continue processing--never executes.
   ...
}
```

Together, **FuncOStimpy1** and **FuncORen1** illustrate the most confusing aspects of SEH. The numbers that begin the comments show the order of execution, but let's hold hands and walk through it together anyway.

FuncOStimpy1 begins execution by entering its **try** block and calling **FuncORen1**. **FuncORen1** starts by entering its own **try** block and waiting to obtain a semaphore. Once it has the semaphore, **FuncORen1** tries to alter the global data variable **g_dwProtectedData**. However, the division by **0** causes an exception to be generated. The system grabs control now and searches for a **try** block matched with an **except** block. Because the **try** block in **Func0Ren1** is matched by a **finally** block, the system searches upward for another **try** block. This time, it finds the **try** block in **Func0Stimpy1**, and it sees that **Func0Stimpy1**'s **try** block is matched by an **except** block.

The system now evaluates the exception filter associated with **Func0Stimpy1**'s **except** block and waits for the return value. When the system sees that the return value is **EXCEPTION_EXECUTE_ HANDLER**, the system begins a global unwind in **Func0Ren1**'s **finally** block. Note that the unwind takes place *before* the system begins execution of the code in **Func0Stimpy1**'s **except** block. For a global unwind, the system starts back at the bottom of all outstanding **try** blocks and searches this time for **try** blocks associated with **finally** blocks. The **finally** block that the system finds here is the one contained inside **Func0Ren1**.

When the system executes the code in **Func0Ren1**'s **finally** block, you can clearly see the power of SEH. Because **Func0Ren1**'s **finally** block releases the semaphore, another thread is allowed to resume execution. If the call to **ReleaseSemaphore** were not contained inside the **finally** block, the semaphore would never be released.

After the code contained in the **finally** block has executed, the system continues walking upward, looking for outstanding **finally** blocks that need to be executed. This example has none. The system stops walking upward when it reaches the **try-except** block that decided to handle the exception. At this point, the global unwind is complete, and the system can execute the code contained inside the **except** block.

That's how structured exception handling works. SEH can be difficult to understand because the system gets quite involved with the execution of your code. No longer does the code flow from top to bottom—the system makes sections of code execute according to its notions of order. This order of execution is complex but predictable, and by following the flowcharts in Figure 24-1 and Figure 24-2, you should be able to use SEH with confidence.

To better understand the order of execution, let's look at what happened from a slightly different perspective. When a filter returns **EXCEPTION_EXECUTE_HANDLER**, the filter is telling the operating system that the thread's instruction pointer should be set to the code inside the **except** block. However, the instruction pointer was inside **Func0Ren1**'s **try** block. From Chapter 23, "Termination Handlers," you'll recall that whenever a thread leaves the **try** portion of a **try-finally** block, the code in the **finally** block is guaranteed to execute. The global unwind is the mechanism that ensures this rule when exceptions are raised.

Caution   Starting with Windows Vista, if there is no **try/except(EXCEPTION_EXECUTE_ HANDLER)** block higher in your code when an exception occurs in an inner **try/finally**, the process is simply terminated, no global unwind occurs, and the inner **finally** blocks are not executed. In previous versions of Windows, a global unwind occurs just before the process is stopped and the **finally** blocks have the chance to be executed. The next chapter provides more details about the workflows related to unhandled exceptions.

Halting Global Unwinds

It's possible to stop the system from completing a global unwind by putting a **return** statement inside a **finally** block. Let's look at the code here:

```
void FuncMonkey() {
   __try {
      FuncFish();
   }
   __except (EXCEPTION_EXECUTE_HANDLER) {
      MessageBeep(0);
   }
   MessageBox(...);
}

void FuncFish() {
   FuncPheasant();
   MessageBox(...);
}

void FuncPheasant() {

   __try {
      strcpy(NULL, NULL);
   }

   __finally {
      return;
   }
}
```

When the **strcpy** function is called in **FuncPheasant**'s **try** block, a memory access violation exception is raised. When this happens, the system starts scanning to see whether any exception filters exist that can handle the exception. The system will find that the exception filter in **FuncMonkey** wants to handle the exception, and the system initiates a global unwind.

The global unwind starts by executing the code inside **FuncPheasant**'s **finally** block. However, this block of code contains a **return** statement. The **return** statement causes the system to stop unwinding, and **FuncPheasant** will actually end up returning to **FuncFish**. **FuncFish** will continue executing and will display a message box on the screen. **FuncFish** will then return to **FuncMonkey**. The code in **FuncMonkey** continues executing by calling **MessageBox**.

Notice that the code inside **FuncMonkey**'s **exception** block never executes the call to **Message-Beep**. The return statement in **FuncPheasant**'s **finally** block causes the system to stop unwinding altogether, and execution continues as though no exception ever happened.

Microsoft deliberately designed SEH to work this way. You might occasionally want to stop unwinding and allow execution to continue. This method allows you to do so, although it usually isn't the sort of thing you want to do. As a rule, avoid putting **return** statements inside **finally** blocks. To help you detect these cases, the C++ compiler generates a C4532 warning:

```
'return' : jump out of __finally block has undefined behavior during termination handling.
```

EXCEPTION_CONTINUE_EXECUTION

Let's take a closer look at the exception filter to see how it evaluates to one of the three exception identifiers defined in Excpt.h. In *"Funcmeister2"* on page 681 the **EXCEPTION_EXECUTE_HANDLER** identifier is hard-coded directly into the filter for simplicity's sake, but you can make the filter call a function that will determine which of the three identifiers should be returned. Here's another code example:

```
TCHAR g_szBuffer[100];

void FunclinRoosevelt1() {
   int x = 0;
   TCHAR *pchBuffer = NULL;

   __try {
      *pchBuffer = TEXT('J');
      x = 5 / x;
   }
   __except (OilFilter1(&pchBuffer)) {
      MessageBox(NULL, TEXT("An exception occurred"), NULL, MB_OK);
   }
   MessageBox(NULL, TEXT("Function completed"), NULL, MB_OK);
}

LONG OilFilter1(TCHAR **ppchBuffer) {
   if (*ppchBuffer == NULL) {
      *ppchBuffer = g_szBuffer;
      return(EXCEPTION_CONTINUE_EXECUTION);
   }
   return(EXCEPTION_EXECUTE_HANDLER);
}
```

We first run into a problem when we try to put a **'J'** into the buffer pointed to by **pchBuffer**. Unfortunately, we didn't initialize **pchBuffer** to point to our global buffer **g_szBuffer**; **pchBuffer** points to **NULL** instead. The CPU will generate an exception and evaluate the exception filter in the **except** block associated with the **try** block in which the exception occurred. In the **except** block, the **OilFilter1** function is passed the address of the **pchBuffer** variable.

When **OilFilter1** gets control, it checks to see whether ***ppchBuffer** is **NULL** and, if it is, sets it to point to the global buffer **g_szBuffer**. The filter then returns **EXCEPTION_CONTINUE_EXECUTION**. When the system sees that the filter evaluated to **EXCEPTION_CONTINUE_EXECUTION**, it jumps back to the instruction that generated the exception and tries to execute it again. This time, the instruction will succeed, and **'J'** will be put into the first byte of **g_szBuffer**.

As the code continues to execute, we run up against the divide by **0** problem in the **try** block. Again the system evaluates the exception filter. This time, **OilFilter1** sees that ***ppchBuffer** is not **NULL** and returns **EXCEPTION_EXECUTE_HANDLER**, which tells the system to execute the **except** block code. This causes a message box to appear with text indicating that an exception occurred.

As you can see, you can do an awful lot of work inside an exception filter. Of course, the filter must return one of the three exception identifiers, but it can also perform any other tasks you want it to. However, keep in mind that the process might be unstable because an exception was raised. So it is advisable to keep the code inside the filter relatively simple. For example, in the case of heap corruptions, trying to run a lot of code inside the filter can lead to hangs or silent process termination.

Use *EXCEPTION_CONTINUE_EXECUTION* with Caution

As it turns out, trying to correct the situation shown in the **FuncIinRoosevelt1** function and having the system continue execution might or might not work—it depends on the target CPU for your application, how your compiler generates instructions for C/C++ statements, and your compiler options.

A compiler might generate two machine instructions for the following C/C++ statement:

```
*pchBuffer = TEXT('J');
```

The machine instructions might look like this:

```
MOV EAX, DWORD PTR[pchBuffer]    // Move the address into a register
MOV WORD PTR[EAX], 'J'           // Move 'J' into the address
```

This second instruction generates the exception. The exception filter would catch the exception, correct the value in **pchBuffer**, and tell the system to re-execute the second CPU instruction. The problem is that the contents of the register wouldn't be changed to reflect the new value loaded into **pchBuffer**, and re-executing the CPU instruction would therefore generate another exception. We'd have an infinite loop!

Continuing execution might be fine if the compiler optimizes the code, but it might fail if the compiler doesn't optimize the code. This can be an incredibly difficult bug to fix, and you will have to examine the assembly language generated for your source code to determine what has gone wrong in your application. The moral of this story is to be *extremely* careful when returning **EXCEPTION_ CONTINUE_EXECUTION** from an exception filter.

In one situation, **EXCEPTION_CONTINUE_EXECUTION** is guaranteed to work every time, all the time: when you are committing storage sparsely to a reserved region. In Chapter 15, "Using Virtual Memory in Your Own Applications," we discussed how to reserve a large address space and then commit storage sparsely to this address space. The VMAlloc sample application demonstrated this. A better way to have written the VMAlloc application would have been to use SEH to commit the storage as necessary instead of calling **VirtualAlloc** all the time.

In Chapter 16, "A Thread's Stack," we talked about thread stacks. In particular, I showed you how the system reserved a 1-MB region of address space for the thread's stack and how the system automatically commits new storage to the stack as the thread needs it. To make this work, the system has internally set up an SEH frame. When your thread attempts to touch stack storage that doesn't exist, an exception is raised. The system's exception filter determines that the exception occurred because of an attempt to touch a stack's reserved address space. The exception filter then calls **VirtualAlloc** internally to commit more storage to your thread's stack, and the filter returns **EXCEPTION_CONTINUE_EXECUTION**. At this point, the CPU instruction that attempted to touch the stack storage will now succeed and the thread continues running.

You can write some incredibly fast-performing and efficient applications when you combine virtual memory techniques with structured exception handling. The Spreadsheet sample application shown in the next chapter demonstrates how to efficiently implement the memory management portions of a spreadsheet application using SEH. This code is also designed to perform extremely fast.

EXCEPTION_CONTINUE_SEARCH

The examples have been pretty tame so far. Let's shake things up a bit by adding a function call:

```
TCHAR g_szBuffer[100];

void FunclinRoosevelt2() {
   TCHAR *pchBuffer = NULL;

   __try {
      FuncAtude2(pchBuffer);
   }
   __except (OilFilter2(&pchBuffer)) {
      MessageBox(...);
   }
}

void FuncAtude2(TCHAR *sz) {
   *sz = TEXT('\0');
}

LONG OilFilter2 (TCHAR **ppchBuffer) {
   if (*ppchBuffer == NULL) {
      *ppchBuffer = g_szBuffer;
      return(EXCEPTION_CONTINUE_EXECUTION);
   }
   return(EXCEPTION_EXECUTE_HANDLER);
}
```

When **FunclinRoosevelt2** executes, it calls **FuncAtude2**, passing it **NULL**. When **FuncAtude2** executes, an exception is raised. Just as before, the system evaluates the exception filter associated with the most recently executing **try** block. In this example, the **try** block inside **FunclinRoosevelt2** is the most recently executing **try** block, so the system calls the **OilFilter2** function to evaluate the exception filter—even though the exception was generated inside the **FuncAtude2** function.

Now let's stir things up a little more by adding another **try-except** block:

```
TCHAR g_szBuffer[100];

void FunclinRoosevelt3() {

   TCHAR *pchBuffer = NULL;

   __try {
      FuncAtude3(pchBuffer);
   }
   __except (OilFilter3(&pchBuffer)) {
      MessageBox(...);
   }
}
```

```
void FuncAtude3(TCHAR *sz) {
   __try {
      *sz = TEXT('\0');
   }
   __except (EXCEPTION_CONTINUE_SEARCH) {
      // This never executes.

      ...
   }
}

LONG OilFilter3(TCHAR **ppchBuffer) {
   if (*ppchBuffer == NULL) {
      *ppchBuffer = g_szBuffer;
      return(EXCEPTION_CONTINUE_EXECUTION);
   }
   return(EXCEPTION_EXECUTE_HANDLER);
}
```

Now when **FuncAtude3** tries to fill address **NULL** with **'\0'**, an exception is still raised but **FuncAtude3**'s exception filter will get executed. **FuncAtude3**'s exception filter is very simple and evaluates to **EXCEPTION_CONTINUE_SEARCH**. This identifier tells the system to walk up to the previous **try** block that's matched with an **except** block and call this previous **try** block's exception filter.

Because **FuncAtude3**'s filter evaluates to **EXCEPTION_CONTINUE_SEARCH**, the system will walk up to the previous **try** block (in **FunclinRoosevelt3**) and evaluate its exception filter, **OilFilter3**. **OilFilter3** will see that **pchBuffer** is **NULL**, will set **pchBuffer** to point to the global buffer, and will then tell the system to resume execution on the instruction that generated the exception. This will allow the code inside **FuncAtude3**'s **try** block to execute; but unfortunately, **FuncAtude3**'s local **sz** variable will not have been changed, and resuming execution on the failed instruction will simply cause another exception to be generated. **OilFilter3** will see that **pchBuffer** is not **NULL** and then return **EXCEPTION_EXECUTE_HANDLER** to tell the system to resume execution in the **except** block. This will allow the code inside **FunclinRoosevelt3**'s **except** block to execute.

You'll notice I said that the system walks up to the most recently executing **try** block that's matched with an **except** block and evaluates its filters. This means that any **try** blocks that are matched with **finally** blocks instead of **except** blocks are skipped by the system while it walks up the chain. The reason for this should be pretty obvious: **finally** blocks don't have exception filters and therefore give the system nothing to evaluate. If **FuncAtude3** in the last example contained a **finally** block instead of its **except** block, the system would have started evaluating exception filters beginning with **FunclinRoosevelt3**'s **OilFilter3**.

Chapter 25 offers more information about **EXCEPTION_CONTINUE_SEARCH**.

GetExceptionCode

Often an exception filter must analyze the situation before it can determine which value to return. For example, your handler might know what to do if a divide by **0** exception occurs, but it might not know how to handle a memory access exception. The exception filter has the responsibility for examining the situation and returning the appropriate value.

This code demonstrates a method for identifying the kind of exception that has occurred:

```
__try {
   x = 0;
   y = 4 / x;  // y is used later so this statement is not optimized away
   ...
}

__except ((GetExceptionCode() == EXCEPTION_INT_DIVIDE_BY_ZERO) ?
   EXCEPTION_EXECUTE_HANDLER : EXCEPTION_CONTINUE_SEARCH) {
   // Handle divide by zero exception.
}
```

The **GetExceptionCode** intrinsic function returns a value identifying the kind of exception that has occurred:

```
DWORD GetExceptionCode();
```

The following list of all predefined exceptions and their meanings is adapted from the Platform SDK documentation. The exception identifiers can be found in the WinBase.h file. I have grouped the exceptions by category.

Memory-Related Exceptions

EXCEPTION_ACCESS_VIOLATION   The thread tried to read from or write to a virtual address for which it doesn't have the appropriate access. This is the most common exception.

EXCEPTION_DATATYPE_MISALIGNMENT   The thread tried to read or write data that is misaligned on hardware that doesn't provide alignment. For example, 16-bit values must be aligned on 2-byte boundaries, 32-bit values on 4-byte boundaries, and so on.

EXCEPTION_ARRAY_BOUNDS_EXCEEDED   The thread tried to access an array element that is out of bounds, and the underlying hardware supports bounds checking.

EXCEPTION_IN_PAGE_ERROR   A page fault couldn't be satisfied because the file system or a device driver returned a read error.

EXCEPTION_GUARD_PAGE   A thread attempted to access a page of memory that has the **PAGE_GUARD** protection attribute. The page is made accessible, and an **EXCEPTION_GUARD_PAGE** exception is raised.

EXCEPTION_STACK_OVERFLOW   The thread has used all of its allotted stack.

EXCEPTION_ILLEGAL_INSTRUCTION   A thread executed an invalid instruction. This exception is defined by the specific CPU architecture; executing an invalid instruction can cause a trap error on different CPUs.

EXCEPTION_PRIV_INSTRUCTION   The thread tried to execute an instruction whose operation is not allowed in the current machine mode.

Exception-Related Exceptions

EXCEPTION_INVALID_DISPOSITION   An exception filter returned a value other than **EXCEPTION_EXECUTE_HANDLER**, **EXCEPTION_CONTINUE_SEARCH**, or **EXCEPTION_CONTINUE_EXECUTION**.

EXCEPTION_NONCONTINUABLE_EXCEPTION   An exception filter returned **EXCEPTION_CONTINUE_EXECUTION** in response to a noncontinuable exception.

Debugging-Related Exceptions

EXCEPTION_BREAKPOINT   A breakpoint was encountered.

EXCEPTION_SINGLE_STEP   A trace trap or other single-instruction mechanism signaled that one instruction has been executed.

EXCEPTION_INVALID_HANDLE   A function was passed an invalid handle.

Integer-Related Exceptions

EXCEPTION_INT_DIVIDE_BY_ZERO   The thread tried to divide an integer value by an integer divisor of **0**.

EXCEPTION_INT_OVERFLOW   The result of an integer operation caused a carry out of the most significant bit of the result.

Floating Point–Related Exceptions

EXCEPTION_FLT_DENORMAL_OPERAND   One of the operands in a floating-point operation is denormal. A denormal value is one that is too small to represent a standard floating-point value.

EXCEPTION_FLT_DIVIDE_BY_ZERO   The thread tried to divide a floating-point value by a floating-point divisor of **0**.

EXCEPTION_FLT_INEXACT_RESULT   The result of a floating-point operation can't be represented exactly as a decimal fraction.

EXCEPTION_FLT_INVALID_OPERATION   This represents any floating-point exception not included in this list.

EXCEPTION_FLT_OVERFLOW   The exponent of a floating-point operation is greater than the magnitude allowed by the corresponding type.

EXCEPTION_FLT_STACK_CHECK   The stack overflowed or underflowed as the result of a floating-point operation.

EXCEPTION_FLT_UNDERFLOW   The exponent of a floating-point operation is less than the magnitude allowed by the type.

The **GetExceptionCode** intrinsic function can be called only in an exception filter (between the parentheses following **__except**) or inside an exception handler. The following code is legal:

```
__try {
    y = 0;
    x = 4 / y;
}

__except (
    ((GetExceptionCode() == EXCEPTION_ACCESS_VIOLATION) ||
     (GetExceptionCode() == EXCEPTION_INT_DIVIDE_BY_ZERO)) ?
    EXCEPTION_EXECUTE_HANDLER : EXCEPTION_CONTINUE_SEARCH) {
```

```
   switch (GetExceptionCode()) {
     case EXCEPTION_ACCESS_VIOLATION:
        // Handle the access violation.
        ...
        break;

     case EXCEPTION_INT_DIVIDE_BY_ZERO:
        // Handle the integer divide by 0.
        ...
        break;
   }
}
```

However, you cannot call **GetExceptionCode** from inside an exception filter function. To help you catch such errors, the compiler will produce a compilation error if you try to compile the following code:

```
__try {
   y = 0;
   x = 4 / y;
}

__except (CoffeeFilter()) {

   // Handle the exception.
   ...
}

LONG CoffeeFilter (void) {
   // Compilation error: illegal call to GetExceptionCode.
   return((GetExceptionCode() == EXCEPTION_ACCESS_VIOLATION) ?
      EXCEPTION_EXECUTE_HANDLER : EXCEPTION_CONTINUE_SEARCH);
}
```

You can get the desired effect by rewriting the code this way:

```
__try {
   y = 0;
   x = 4 / y;
}

__except (CoffeeFilter(GetExceptionCode())) {

   // Handle the exception.
   ...
}

LONG CoffeeFilter (DWORD dwExceptionCode) {
   return((dwExceptionCode == EXCEPTION_ACCESS_VIOLATION) ?
      EXCEPTION_EXECUTE_HANDLER : EXCEPTION_CONTINUE_SEARCH);
}
```

Exception codes follow the rules for error codes as defined inside the WinError.h file. Each **DWORD** is divided as shown in Table 24-2 and detailed in Chapter 1, "Error Handling."

Table 24-2   The Composition of an Error Code

Bits	31–30	29	28	27–16	15–0
Contents	Severity	Microsoft/ customer	Reserved	Facility code	Exception code
Meaning	0=Success 1=Informational 2=Warning 3=Error	0=Microsoft-defined code 1=customer-defined code	Must be 0	The first 256 values are reserved by Microsoft (See Table 24-3.)	Microsoft/ customer-defined code

Currently, Microsoft defines the facility codes shown in Table 24-3.

Table 24-3   Facility Codes

Facility Code	Value	Facility Code	Value
FACILITY_NULL	0	FACILITY_WINDOWS_CE	24
FACILITY_RPC	1	FACILITY_HTTP	25
FACILITY_DISPATCH	2	FACILITY_USERMODE_COMMONLOG	26
FACILITY_STORAGE	3	FACILITY_USERMODE_FILTER_MANAGER	31
FACILITY_ITF	4	FACILITY_BACKGROUNDCOPY	32
FACILITY_WIN32	7	FACILITY_CONFIGURATION	33
FACILITY_WINDOWS	8	FACILITY_STATE_MANAGEMENT	34
FACILITY_SECURITY	9	FACILITY_METADIRECTORY	35
FACILITY_CONTROL	10	FACILITY_WINDOWSUPDATE	36
FACILITY_CERT	11	FACILITY_DIRECTORYSERVICE	37
FACILITY_INTERNET	12	FACILITY_GRAPHICS	38
FACILITY_MEDIASERVER	13	FACILITY_SHELL	39
FACILITY_MSMQ	14	FACILITY_TPM_SERVICES	40
FACILITY_SETUPAPI	15	FACILITY_TPM_SOFTWARE	41
FACILITY_SCARD	16	FACILITY_PLA	48
FACILITY_COMPLUS	17	FACILITY_FVE	49
FACILITY_AAF	18	FACILITY_FWP	50
FACILITY_URT	19	FACILITY_WINRM	51
FACILITY_ACS	20	FACILITY_NDIS	52
FACILITY_DPLAY	21	FACILITY_USERMODE_HYPERVISOR	53
FACILITY_UMI	22	FACILITY_CMI	54
FACILITY_SXS	23	FACILITY_WINDOWS_DEFENDER	80

So here's what we get if we pick apart the **EXCEPTION_ACCESS_VIOLATION** exception code. Looking up **EXCEPTION_ACCESS_VIOLATION** in WinBase.h, we see that it is defined as **STATUS_ACCESS_VIOLATION**, which has a value of **0xC0000005** in WinNT.h:

```
   C    0    0    0    0    0    0    5    (hexadecimal)
1100 0000 0000 0000 0000 0000 0000 0101    (binary)
```

Bits 30 and 31 are both set to **1**, indicating that an access violation is an error (the thread cannot continue running). Bit 29 is **0**, meaning that Microsoft has defined this code. Bit 28 is **0** because it is reserved for future use. Bits 16 through 27 are **0**, indicating **FACILITY_NULL** (an access violation can happen anywhere in the system; it is not an exception that occurs only when using certain facilities). Bits 0 through 15 contain the value **5**, which just means that Microsoft defined an access violation as code **5**.

GetExceptionInformation

When an exception occurs, the operating system pushes the following three structures on the stack of the thread that raised the exception: the **EXCEPTION_RECORD** structure, the **CONTEXT** structure, and the **EXCEPTION_POINTERS** structure.

The **EXCEPTION_RECORD** structure contains CPU-independent information about the raised exception, and the **CONTEXT** structure contains CPU-dependent information about the raised exception. The **EXCEPTION_POINTERS** structure has only two data members that are pointers to the pushed **EXCEPTION_RECORD** and **CONTEXT** data structures:

```
typedef struct _EXCEPTION_POINTERS {
   PEXCEPTION_RECORD ExceptionRecord;
   PCONTEXT ContextRecord;
} EXCEPTION_POINTERS, *PEXCEPTION_POINTERS;
```

To retrieve this information and use it in your own application, you need to call the **GetExceptionInformation** function:

```
PEXCEPTION_POINTERS GetExceptionInformation();
```

This intrinsic function returns a pointer to an **EXCEPTION_POINTERS** structure.

The most important thing to remember about the **GetExceptionInformation** function is that it can be called only in an exception filter—because the **CONTEXT**, **EXCEPTION_RECORD**, and **EXCEPTION_POINTERS** data structures are valid only during the exception filter processing. Once control has been transferred to the exception handler, the data on the stack is destroyed.

Though this situation is rarely necessary, if you need to access the exception information from inside your exception handler block, you must save the **EXCEPTION_RECORD** data structure and/or **CONTEXT** data structure pointed to by the **EXCEPTION_POINTERS** structure in one or more variables that you create. The following code demonstrates how to save both the **EXCEPTION_RECORD** and **CONTEXT** data structures:

```
void FuncSkunk() {
   // Declare variables that we can use to save the exception
   // record and the context if an exception should occur.
   EXCEPTION_RECORD SavedExceptRec;
   CONTEXT SavedContext;
   ...
   __try {
      ...
   }

   __except (
      SavedExceptRec =
         *(GetExceptionInformation())->ExceptionRecord,
      SavedContext =
         *(GetExceptionInformation())->ContextRecord,
      EXCEPTION_EXECUTE_HANDLER) {
```

```
    // We can use the SavedExceptRec and SavedContext
    // variables inside the handler code block.
    switch (SavedExceptRec.ExceptionCode) {
        ...
    }
  }
  ...
}
```

Notice the use of the C/C++ language's comma (**,**) operator in the exception filter. Many programmers aren't used to seeing this operator. It tells the compiler to execute the comma-separated expressions from left to right. When all the expressions have been evaluated, the result of the last (or rightmost) expression is returned.

In **FuncSkunk**, the left expression will execute, causing the **EXCEPTION_RECORD** structure on the stack to be stored in the **SavedExceptRec** local variable. The result of this expression is the value of **SavedExceptRec**. However, this result is discarded and the next expression to the right is evaluated. This second expression causes the **CONTEXT** structure on the stack to be stored in the **SavedContext** local variable. The result of the second expression is **SavedContext**, and again, this expression is discarded as the third expression is evaluated. This is a very simple expression that evaluates to **EXCEPTION_EXECUTE_HANDLER**. The result of this rightmost expression is the result of the entire comma-separated expression.

Because the exception filter evaluated to **EXCEPTION_EXECUTE_HANDLER**, the code inside the **except** block executes. At this point, the **SavedExceptRec** and **SavedContext** variables have been initialized and can be used inside the **except** block. Keep in mind it is important that the **SavedExceptRec** and **SavedContext** variables be declared outside the **try** block.

As you've probably guessed, the **ExceptionRecord** member of the **EXCEPTION_POINTERS** structure points to an **EXCEPTION_RECORD** structure:

```
typedef struct _EXCEPTION_RECORD {
   DWORD ExceptionCode;
   DWORD ExceptionFlags;
   struct _EXCEPTION_RECORD *ExceptionRecord;
   PVOID ExceptionAddress;
   DWORD NumberParameters;
   ULONG_PTR ExceptionInformation[EXCEPTION_MAXIMUM_PARAMETERS];
} EXCEPTION_RECORD;
```

The **EXCEPTION_RECORD** structure contains detailed, CPU-independent information about the exception that has most recently occurred:

- **ExceptionCode** contains the code of the exception. This is the same information that is returned from the **GetExceptionCode** intrinsic function.

- **ExceptionFlags** contains flags about the exception. Currently, the only two values are **0** (which indicates a continuable exception) and **EXCEPTION_NONCONTINUABLE** (which indicates a noncontinuable exception). Any attempt to continue execution after a noncontinuable exception causes an **EXCEPTION_NONCONTINUABLE_EXCEPTION** exception to be raised.

- **ExceptionRecord** points to an **EXCEPTION_RECORD** structure for another unhandled exception. While handling one exception, it is possible to raise another exception. For example, the code in your exception filter could attempt to divide a number by **0**. Exception records can be chained to provide additional information when nested exceptions occur. A nested exception occurs if an exception is generated during the processing of an exception filter. Before Windows Vista, processes are terminated when such a nested exception is unhandled. If there are no unhandled exceptions, this member contains **NULL**.

■ **ExceptionAddress** specifies the address of the CPU instruction that generated the exception.

■ **NumberParameters** specifies the number of parameters (0 through 15) associated with the exception. This is the number of defined elements in the **ExceptionInformation** array. For almost all exceptions, this value will be **0**.

■ **ExceptionInformation** specifies an array of additional arguments that describe the exception. For almost all exceptions, the array elements are undefined.

The last two members of the **EXCEPTION_RECORD** structure, **NumberParameters** and **Exception-Information**, offer the exception filter some additional information about the exception. Currently, only one type of exception offers additional information: **EXCEPTION_ACCESS_VIOLATION**. All other possible exceptions will have the **NumberParameters** member set to **0**. You examine the **NumberParameters** array member to look at the additional information about a generated exception.

For an **EXCEPTION_ACCESS_VIOLATION** exception, **ExceptionInformation[0]** contains a flag that indicates the type of operation that caused the access violation. If this value is **0**, the thread tried to read the inaccessible data. If this value is **1**, the thread tried to write to inaccessible data. **ExceptionInformation[1]** specifies the address of the inaccessible data. When Data Execution Prevention (DEP) detects that a thread tries to run code from a nonexecutable memory page, an exception is raised and **ExceptionInformation[0]** contains **2** for IA-64 and **8** otherwise.

By using these members, you can produce exception filters that offer a significant amount of information about your application. For example, you might write an exception filter like this:

```
__try {
   ...
}
__except (ExpFltr(GetExceptionInformation())) {
   ...
}

LONG ExpFltr (LPEXCEPTION_POINTERS pep) {
   TCHAR szBuf[300], *p;
   PEXCEPTION_RECORD pER = pep->ExceptionRecord;
   DWORD dwExceptionCode = pER->ExceptionCode;

   StringCchPrintf(szBuf, _countof(szBuf), TEXT("Code = %x, Address = %p"),
      dwExceptionCode, pER->ExceptionAddress);

   // Find the end of the string.
   p = _tcschr(szBuf, TEXT('0'));

   // I used a switch statement in case Microsoft adds
   // information for other exception codes in the future.
   switch (dwExceptionCode) {
```

```
      case EXCEPTION_ACCESS_VIOLATION:
         StringCchPrintf(p, _countof(szBuf),
            TEXT("\n--> Attempt to %s data at address %p"),
            pER->ExceptionInformation[0] ? TEXT("write") : TEXT("read"),
            pER->ExceptionInformation[1]);
         break;

      default:
         break;
   }

   MessageBox(NULL, szBuf, TEXT("Exception"), MB_OK | MB_ICONEXCLAMATION);

   return(EXCEPTION_CONTINUE_SEARCH);
}
```

The **ContextRecord** member of the **EXCEPTION_POINTERS** structure points to a **CONTEXT** structure (discussed in Chapter 7, "Thread Scheduling, Priorities, and Affinities"). This structure is platform-dependent—that is, the contents of this structure will differ from one CPU platform to another.

Basically, this structure contains one member for each of the registers available on the CPU. When an exception is raised, you can find out even more information by examining the members of this structure. Unfortunately, realizing the benefit of such a possibility requires you to write platform-dependent code that recognizes the machine it's running on and uses the appropriate **CONTEXT** structure. The best way to handle this is to put **#ifdef**s into your code. The **CONTEXT** structures for the various CPUs supported by Windows are in the WinNT.h file.

Software Exceptions

So far, we have been discussing hardware exceptions in which the CPU catches an event and raises an exception. It is also possible for your code to forcibly raise an exception. This is another way for a function to indicate failure to its caller. Traditionally, functions that can fail return some special value to indicate failure. The caller of the function is supposed to check for this special value and take an alternative course of action. Frequently, the caller has to clean up what it's doing and return its own failure code back to its caller. This propagating of error codes causes your source code to become much more difficult to write and maintain.

An alternative approach is to have functions raise exceptions when they fail. With this approach, the code is much easier to write and maintain. Plus, the code typically performs better without all the error-testing code being executed. In fact, the error-testing code executes only if there is a failure, and this is the exceptional case.

Unfortunately, most developers do not get into the habit of using exceptions for error handling. There are two basic reasons for this. The first reason is that most developers are unfamiliar with SEH. Even if one developer is acquainted with it, other developers might not be. If one developer writes a function that raises an exception but other developers don't write SEH frames to trap the exception, the process will be terminated by the operating system.

The second reason why developers avoid SEH is that it is not portable to other operating systems. Many companies target multiple operating systems and would like to have a single source code base for their products, which is certainly understandable. SEH is a Windows-specific technology.

However, if you decide to return errors via exceptions, I applaud your decision and this section is for you. First, let's look at the Windows heap functions such as **HeapCreate**, **HeapAlloc**, and so on. You'll recall from Chapter 18, "Heaps," that these functions offer developers a choice. Normally when any of the heap functions fail, they return **NULL** to indicate failure. You can, however, pass the **HEAP_GENERATE_EXCEPTIONS** flag to any of these heap functions. If you use this flag and the function fails, the function does not return **NULL**; instead, the function raises a **STATUS_NO_MEMORY** software exception that other parts of your code can catch with an SEH frame.

If you want to take advantage of this exception, you can code your **try** block as though the memory allocation will always succeed; if the allocation fails, you can either handle the exception by using an **except** block or have your function clean up by matching the **try** block with a **finally** block. How convenient!

Your application traps software exceptions exactly the same way that it traps hardware exceptions. In other words, everything I said in the last chapter applies equally well to software exceptions.

What we want to concentrate on in this section is how to have your own functions forcibly raise software exceptions as a method for indicating failure. In fact, you can implement your functions similarly to Microsoft's implementation of the heap functions: have your callers pass a flag that tells your function how it should indicate failures.

Raising a software exception couldn't be easier. You simply call the **RaiseException** function:

```
VOID RaiseException(
   DWORD dwExceptionCode,
   DWORD dwExceptionFlags,
   DWORD nNumberOfArguments,
   CONST ULONG_PTR *pArguments);
```

The first parameter, **dwExceptionCode**, must be a value that identifies the raised exception. The **HeapAlloc** function passes **STATUS_NO_MEMORY** for this parameter. If you define your own exception identifiers, you should follow the same format as the standard Windows error codes as defined in the WinError.h file. Recall that each **DWORD** is divided as shown in Table 24-1 on page 681.

If you create your own exception code, fill out all four fields of the **DWORD**:

- Bits 31 and 30 will contain the severity.
- Bit 29 will be **1**. (**0** is reserved for Microsoft-created exceptions, such as **HeapAlloc**'s **STATUS_NO_MEMORY**.)
- Bit 28 is **0**.
- Bits 27 through 16 will be one of Microsoft's predefined facility codes.
- Bits 15 through 0 will be an arbitrary value that you choose to identify the section of your application that raised the exception.

RaiseException's second parameter, **dwExceptionFlags**, must be either **0** or **EXCEPTION_NON-CONTINUABLE**. Basically, this flag indicates whether it is legal for an exception filter to return **EXCEPTION_CONTINUE_EXECUTION** in response to this raised exception. If you do not pass the

EXCEPTION_NONCONTINUABLE flag to **RaiseException**, the filter can return **EXCEPTION_CONTINUE_EXECUTION**. Normally, this would cause the thread to re-execute the same CPU instruction that raised the software exception. However, Microsoft has done some trickery so that execution continues after the call to the **RaiseException** function.

If you do pass the **EXCEPTION_NONCONTINUABLE** flag to **RaiseException**, you're telling the system that the type of exception you are raising can't be continued. This flag is used internally in the operating system to signal fatal (nonrecoverable) errors. In addition, when **HeapAlloc** raises the **STATUS_NO_MEMORY** software exception, it uses the **EXCEPTION_NONCONTINUABLE** flag to tell the system that this exception cannot be continued. This makes sense: there is no way to force the memory to be allocated and continue running.

If a filter ignores the **EXCEPTION_NONCONTINUABLE** flag and returns **EXCEPTION_CONTINUE_EXECUTION** anyway, the system raises a new exception: **EXCEPTION_NONCONTINUABLE_EXCEPTION**.

It is possible for an exception to be raised while the application is trying to process another exception. This makes sense, of course. While we're at it, let's note that it's also possible for an invalid memory access to occur inside a **finally** block, an exception filter, or an exception handler. When this happens, the system stacks exceptions. Remember the **GetExceptionInformation** function? This function returns the address of an **EXCEPTION_POINTERS** structure. The **ExceptionRecord** member of the **EXCEPTION_POINTERS** structure points to an **EXCEPTION_RECORD** structure that contains another **ExceptionRecord** member. This member is a pointer to another **EXCEPTION_RECORD**, which contains information about the previously raised exception.

Usually the system is processing only one exception at a time, and the **ExceptionRecord** member is **NULL**. However, if during the processing of one exception another exception is raised, the first **EXCEPTION_RECORD** structure contains information about the most recently raised exception and the **ExceptionRecord** member of this first **EXCEPTION_RECORD** structure points to the **EXCEPTION_RECORD** structure for the previously raised exception. If additional exceptions have not been processed completely, you can continue to walk this linked-list of **EXCEPTION_RECORD** structures to determine how to handle the exception.

RaiseException's third and fourth parameters, **nNumberOfArguments** and **pArguments**, are used to pass additional information about the raised exception. Usually, there is no need for additional arguments—you can simply pass **NULL** for the **pArguments** parameter, in which case **RaiseException** ignores the **nNumberOfArguments** parameter. If you do want to pass additional arguments, the **nNumberOfArguments** parameter must indicate the number of elements in the **ULONG_PTR** array pointed to by the **pArguments** parameter. This parameter cannot exceed **EXCEPTION_MAXIMUM_PARAMETERS**, which is defined in WinNT.h as **15**.

During the processing of this exception, you can have an exception filter refer to the **NumberParameters** and **ExceptionInformation** members of the **EXCEPTION_RECORD** structure to examine the information in the **nNumberOfArguments** and **pArguments** parameters.

You might want to generate your own software exceptions in your application for any of several reasons. For example, you might want to send informational messages to the system's event log. Whenever a function in your application sensed some sort of problem, you could call **RaiseException** and have some exception handler further up the call tree look for certain exceptions and either add them to the event log or pop up a message box. You might also want to create software exceptions to signal internal fatal errors in your application.

Chapter 25
Unhandled Exceptions, Vectored Exception Handling, and C++ Exceptions

In the previous chapter, we discussed what happens when a filter returns **EXCEPTION_CONTINUE_SEARCH**. Returning this value tells the system to continue walking up the call tree looking for additional exception filters. But what happens if every filter returns **EXCEPTION_CONTINUE_SEARCH**? In this case, we have what's called an *unhandled exception*.

Microsoft Windows offers the **SetUnhandledExceptionFilter** function, which gives you a last chance to process the exception before Windows declares it as truly being unhandled:

```
PTOP_LEVEL_EXCEPTION_FILTER SetUnhandledExceptionFilter(
   PTOP_LEVEL_EXCEPTION_FILTER pTopLevelExceptionFilter);
```

Your process usually calls this function during initialization. Once this function is called, an unhandled exception occurring in any of your process threads causes the top-level exception filter function you specify (via the **SetUnhandledExceptionFilter** parameter) to be called. The prototype of your filter function must look like this:

```
LONG WINAPI TopLevelUnhandledExceptionFilter(PEXCEPTION_POINTERS pExceptionInfo);
```

In your exception filter, you can perform any processing you desire as long as you return one of the three **EXCEPTION_*** identifiers shown in Table 25-1. Note that the process might be in a corrupt state because of a stack overflow, unreleased thread synchronization primitive, or un-free heap data, so you should keep your processing in the filter function to a bare minimum and avoid any dynamic allocation because the heap might be corrupted.

Whenever you set a new unhandled exception filter, **SetUnhandledExceptionFilter** returns the address of the previously installed exception filter. Notice that if your application is using the C/C++ run-time libraries, before your entry-point function starts to execute, the C/C++ run time installs its own global unhandled exception filter called **__CxxUnhandledExceptionFilter**. This function simply checks that the exception is a C++ exception (more on this in "C++ Exceptions vs. Structured Exceptions" section later in this chapter) and, in this case, ends up executing the **abort** function, which calls the **UnhandledExceptionFilter** function exported by Kernel32.dll.

In older versions of the C/C++ run time, the process was just terminated. The **_set_abort_ behavior** function can be used to configure the error reporting done by **abort**. If the exception is not recognized as a C++ exception, **EXCEPTION_CONTINUE_SEARCH** is returned to let Windows take care of this unhandled exception.

Table 25-1   Top-Level Exception Filter Return Values

Identifier	What Happens
EXCEPTION_EXECUTE_HANDLER	The process simply terminates without any notification to the user. Note that a global unwind is triggered, so the **finally** blocks are executed.
EXCEPTION_CONTINUE_EXECUTION	Execution continues at the instruction that raised the exception. You can modify the exception information referenced by the **PEXCEPTION_POINTERS** parameter. If you don't fix the problem and the same exception occurs again, the process could enter an infinite loop where the same exception triggers again and again.
EXCEPTION_CONTINUE_SEARCH	The exception is really unhandled now. "Inside the *UnhandledExceptionFilter* Function" on the next page describes what happens next.

So, if you call **SetUnhandledExceptionFilter** to install your own global filter, the returned address will be the address of **__CxxUnhandledExceptionFilter**, as you can see through IntelliSense when you debug your code in Microsoft Visual Studio. Otherwise, the default filter is the **UnhandledExceptionFilter** function.

> **Note**   You can simply call **SetUnhandledExceptionFilter** and pass it **NULL** to reset **UnhandledExceptionFilter** as being the global unhandled exception filter.

If your own filter is about to return **EXCEPTION_CONTINUE_SEARCH**, you might be tempted to call the previously installed filter whose address was returned by the **SetUnhandledException-Filter** function. However, this approach is not recommended because you have no idea if one of your third-party components has installed its own unhandled exception filter, which might even be unloaded in the case of a dynamically loaded module. See "Action #3: Notifying Your Globally Set Filter Function" on page 708 for another reason why this should be avoided.

Remember from Chapter 6, "Thread Basics," that every thread truly begins executing with a function inside NTDLL.dll called **BaseThreadStart**:

```
VOID BaseThreadStart(PTHREAD_START_ROUTINE pfnStartAddr, PVOID pvParam) {
   __try {
      ExitThread((pfnStartAddr)(pvParam));
   }
   __except (UnhandledExceptionFilter(GetExceptionInformation())) {
      ExitProcess(GetExceptionCode());
   }
   // NOTE: We never get here
}
```

This function contains a structured exception handling (SEH) frame: it enters a **try** block, and from within the **try** block it calls your thread/application's entry-point function. So, if your thread raises an exception and if all the installed filters return **EXCEPTION_CONTINUE_SEARCH**, the system has provided a special filter function that will be called for you automatically, the same **UnhandledExceptionFilter** function:

```
LONG UnhandledExceptionFilter(PEXCEPTION_POINTERS pExceptionInfo);
```

As a normal exception filter, this function returns one of the three **EXCEPTION_*** identifiers. Table 25-2 shows what happens when each identifier is returned.

Table 25-2   Action of Each UnhandledExceptionFilter Return Value

Identifier	What Happens
EXCEPTION_EXECUTE_HANDLER	A global unwind is triggered, and all pending **finally** blocks are executed. For an unhandled exception, the except handler of **BaseThreadStart** calls **ExitProcess**, so the process silently terminates. Note that the process' exit code will be the exception code.
EXCEPTION_CONTINUE_EXECUTION	Execution continues at the instruction that raised the exception. The first action in the "Inside the *UnhandledExceptionFilter* Function" section shows when this happens.
EXCEPTION_CONTINUE_SEARCH	Either a debugger is already controlling the faulting process or the default debugger will be attached. In both cases, the system notified the debugger about the exception, so you end up at the exact place in your code where the exception occurred. I'll dig into the iterations with the debugger in "Just-in-Time Debugging" on page 713. If no debugger is attached, Windows knows that an unhandled exception occurred in user mode.

> **Note**   In the case of nested exceptions—when an exception occurs in an exception filter—**EXCEPTION_NESTED_CALL** is returned by **UnhandledExceptionFilter**. Before Windows Vista, **UnhandledExceptionFilter** never returned and the process silently terminated.

But a lot of code is executed before one of these values is returned, and it is now time to follow the execution steps inside **UnhandledExceptionFilter**.

Inside the *UnhandledExceptionFilter* Function

The **UnhandledExceptionFilter** function performs five actions (in order) when processing an exception. We will now examine each of these actions in turn. After all of these actions, **UnhandledExceptionFilter** leaves control to *Windows Error Reporting* (WER), as described in "*UnhandledExceptionFilter* and WER Interactions" on page 710.

Action #1: Allowing Write Access to a Resource and Continuing Execution

If an access violation occurred because of the thread attempting to write, **UnhandledException-Filter** checks to see if the thread was attempting to modify a resource in an .exe or DLL module. By default, resources are (and should be) read-only and attempting to modify a resource raises an access violation. However, 16-bit Windows allows resources to be modified, and for backward compatibility this should work in 32-bit and 64-bit Windows as well. To allow this backward compatibility, **UnhandledExceptionFilter** calls **VirtualProtect** to change the protection on the resource's page to **PAGE_READWRITE** and returns **EXCEPTION_CONTINUE_EXECUTION**, allowing the faulted instruction to execute again.

Action #2: Notifying a Debugger of the Unhandled Exception

UnhandledExceptionFilter checks whether the application is currently under the control of a debugger; if it is, **UnhandledExceptionFilter** returns **EXCEPTION_CONTINUE_SEARCH**. At this point, because the exception is not handled, Windows notifies the attached debugger. The debugger receives the **ExceptionInformation** member of the **EXCEPTION_RECORD** structure generated for this exception, and it uses this information to position you at the code instruction that caused the exception to be raised and notify you as to the kind of exception that was raised. Note that your code can use **IsDebuggerPresent** to detect whether or not it is running under the control of a debugger.

Action #3: Notifying Your Globally Set Filter Function

If **SetUnhandledExceptionFilter** has been called to specify a global filter, **UnhandledException-tionFilter** calls this filter function. If the filter function returns **EXCEPTION_EXECUTE_HANDLER** or **EXCEPTION_CONTINUE_EXECUTION**, the **UnhandledExceptionFilter** returns this value to the system. If the unhandled exception filter returns **EXCEPTION_CONTINUE_SEARCH**, processing continues with Action #4. But wait! I've just explained that the C/C++ global unhandled exception filter **__CxxUnhandledExceptionFilter** explicitly calls **UnhandledExceptionFilter**. This kind of infinite series of recursive calls quickly triggers a stack overflow exception that hides the real original exception. This is another reason why you should avoid calling an already-installed global unhandled exception filter. To prevent this recursion, **__CxxUnhandledExceptionFilter** calls **SetUnhandledExceptionFilter(NULL)** just before calling **UnhandledExceptionFilter**.

When a program uses the C/C++ run time, the run time wraps the thread entry point with a **try/except**, where the exception filter calls the C/C++ run time's **_XcpFilter** function. Internally, **_XcpFilter** calls **UnhandledExceptionFilter**, which in turn calls the global filter, if there is any. So, if you have installed a global filter, it will be called when an unhandled exception is seen by **_XcpFilter**. If your filter returns **EXCEPTION_CONTINUE_SEARCH**, the (really) unhandled exception reaches the **BaseThreadStart except** filter and **UnhandledExceptionFilter** is executed again. As a result, your global handler is called a second time.

Action #4: Notifying a Debugger of the Unhandled Exception (Again)

In Action #3, the globally set unhandled exception filter function could invoke a debugger and have the debugger attach to the process containing the thread experiencing an unhandled exception. If the unhandled exception filter now returns **EXCEPTION_CONTINUE_SEARCH**, the debugger is notified (as in Action #2).

Action #5: Silently Terminating the Process

If a thread in the process had called **SetErrorMode** passing the **SEM_NOGPFAULTERRORBOX** flag, **UnhandledExceptionFilter** returns **EXCEPTION_EXECUTE_HANDLER**. In the case of an unhandled exception, returning such a value triggers a global unwind that allows pending **finally** blocks to execute just before the process silently exits. Similarly, if the process is in a job (as shown in Chapter 5, "Jobs") and the job's limit information has the **JOB_OBJECT_LIMIT_DIE_ON_UNHANDLED_EXCEPTION** flag turned on, **UnhandledExceptionFilter** returns **EXCEPTION_EXECUTE_HANDLER** with the same effects.

During these actions, **UnhandledExceptionFilter** works silently, trying to fix the problem that raised the exception, notifying the attached debugger (if any), or simply terminating the application when needed. However, if the exception can't be handled, **EXCEPTION_CONTINUE_SEARCH** is returned and the kernel takes control to notify the user that something wrong happened within the application. Let's detail first the corresponding user interface before going back to what the Windows kernel does when **UnhandledExceptionFilter** returns and how the exception navigates in the system (which is covered in "*UnhandledExceptionFilter* and WER Interactions" on page 710).

Figure 25-1 shows what happens in Windows XP when an exception is passed to **UnhandledExceptionFilter**.

Figure 25-1   Message shown when an unhandled exception occurs in Windows XP

In Windows Vista, two dialog boxes, shown in Figures 25-2 and 25-3, pop up one after the other.

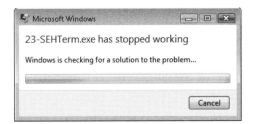

Figure 25-2   First message shown when an unhandled exception occurs in Windows Vista

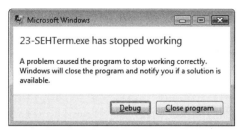

Figure 25-3   Second message shown when an unhandled exception occurs in Windows Vista

You now have the big picture of the workflows that lead to calling **UnhandledExceptionFilter** and what their visible effects are.

UnhandledExceptionFilter and WER Interactions

Figure 25-4 shows how Windows processes an unhandled exception using the Windows Error Reporting infrastructure. Steps 1 and 2 were already discussed in the preceding sections.

Starting with Windows Vista, the **UnhandledExceptionFilter** function no longer sends an error report to Microsoft's servers. Instead, after executing the actions detailed in "Inside the *Unhandled-ExceptionFilter* Function" on page 710, **EXCEPTION_CONTINUE_SEARCH** is simply returned (Step 3 in Figure 25-4). In that case, the kernel detects that the exception is not handled by the user-mode thread (Step 4). Then a notification about the exception is sent to a dedicated service called *WerSvc*.

This notification is done through an undocumented mechanism called *Advanced Local Procedure Call* (ALPC), which blocks the thread execution until the processing done by WerSvc is finished (Step 5). This service spawns the WerFault.exe application via a call to **CreateProcess** (Step 6) and waits for the new process to end. The report construction and its sending (Step 7) are done by the WerFault.exe application. The dialog boxes that allow the user to choose between closing the application or attaching a debugger are also shown in the context of the same WerFault.exe application (Step 8). If the user decides to close the program, **TerminateProcess** is called from WerFault.exe to silently and definitively stop its execution (Step 9). As you can see, the heavy processing is done outside of the faulting application to ensure reliable reporting and behavior.

The interface shown to the user is configured through several registry keys as documented here: *http://msdn2.microsoft.com/en-us/library/bb513638.aspx*. When the **DontShowUI** value under the HKEY_CURRENT_USER\Software\Microsoft\Windows\Windows Error Reporting subkey is set to **1**, no dialog pops up and the report is silently generated before being sent to the Microsoft servers. If you want to let the user choose whether or not a report should be sent to Microsoft when a problem occurs, you can also change the **DefaultConsent DWORD** value under the **Consent** subkey. However, it is recommended to open the WER Console through Problem Reports And Solutions in Control Panel and click the Change Settings link to access the options as shown in Figure 25-5.

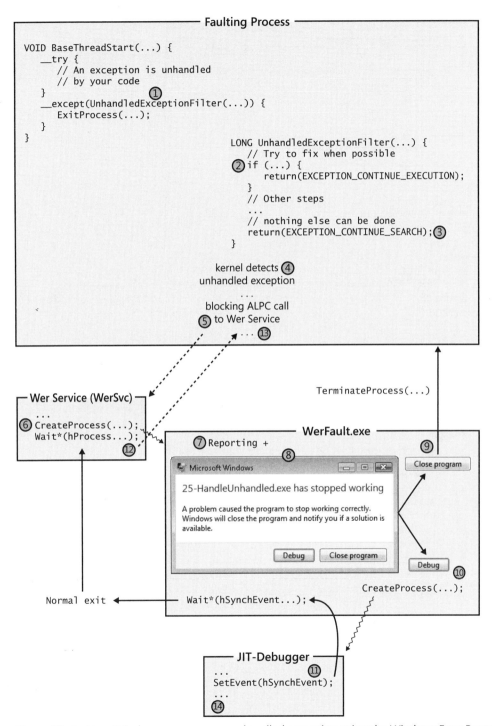

Figure 25-4   How Windows processes an unhandled exception using the Windows Error Reporting infrastructure

Figure 25-5   Allow the user to choose whether or not the problem report should be sent to Microsoft.

When you choose the Ask Me To Check If A Problem Occurs option, WER pops up a new dialog box, which is shown in Figure 25-6 (instead of the usual two shown in Figures 25-2 and 25-3), that provides three choices to the user.

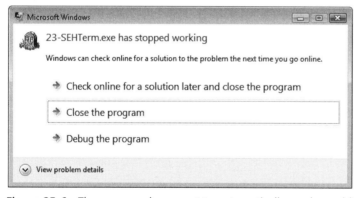

Figure 25-6   The user can choose not to automatically send a problem report to Microsoft.

Even though this option is not recommended on production machines because you don't want to miss any problem, it will save you a lot of time when you are debugging your application because you won't have to wait for the report to be generated and sent. When the machine is not connected to the network, the gained time is even more important because you don't have to wait for WerSvc to time out before popping up the selection dialog box.

In the case of automatic test runs, you don't want to have the WER dialog boxes break and stop the tests. If you set the **ForceQueue** value from the Reporting registry subkey to **1**, WER silently generates a problem report. Once the tests are finished, you can use the WER Console to list the problems and get their associated details, as shown in Figure 26-2 and Figure 26-3 in the next chapter.

It is now time to describe the last feature provided by WER when an unhandled exception occurs: a developer's dream come true called *just-in-time debugging*. If the user chooses to debug the faulting process (Step 10), the WerFault.exe application creates a manual-reset event in the nonsignaled state with its **bInheritHandles** parameter set to **TRUE**. This allows WerFault.exe's child processes, such as the debugger, to inherit the event handle. Then WER locates and launches the default debugger, which attaches itself to the faulting process as explained in "Just-in-Time Debugging" below. With the debugger attached to the process, you can examine the state of global, local, and static variables; set breakpoints; examine the call tree; restart the process; and do anything else you would normally do when you debug a process.

> **Note**   This book concentrates solely on user-mode application development. However, you might find it interesting to know what happens when a thread running in kernel mode raises an unhandled exception. An unhandled exception occurring in the kernel indicates a serious bug that exists in the operating system or (more likely) in a device driver and not in an application.
>
> Because memory in the kernel is now potentially corrupt, it isn't safe for the system to continue running. However, before showing what is typically called "the Blue Screen of Death," the system asks a dedicated device driver called CrashDmp.sys to create a crash dump in the page file. Then the computer's operations are halted. Because the computer's operations are halted, you'll need to reboot it before you can do anything else; any unsaved work is lost. However, when Windows restarts after a crash or a hang, the system checks whether the page file contains a crash dump. In that case, its content is saved and WerFault.exe is spawned to take care of generating a problem report to send to Microsoft servers (if desired). This is what allows you to get the list of Windows problems in the WER Console.

Just-in-Time Debugging

The real boon with just-in-time debugging is that you can handle the failure of your application when it occurs. Under most other operating systems, you must invoke your application through the debugger to debug it. If an exception occurs in a process on one of these other operating systems, you have to terminate the process, start a debugger, and invoke the application–again using the debugger. The problem is that you have to try to reproduce the bug before you can fix it. And who knows what the values of the different variables were when the problem originally occurred? It's much harder to resolve a bug this way. The ability to dynamically attach a debugger to a process as it runs is one of the best features in Windows.

Here's a little more information about how this works. The registry contains the following dedicated key:

```
HKEY_LOCAL_MACHINE\SOFTWARE\Microsoft\Windows NT\CurrentVersion\AeDebug
```

Inside this subkey, there is a data value named **Debugger**, which is typically set to the following value when you install Visual Studio:

```
"C:\Windows\system32\vsjitdebugger.exe" -p %ld -e %ld
```

This line tells the system which program (vsjitdebugger.exe) to run as the debugger. In fact, vsjit-debugger.exe is not a real debugger but rather an application that allows you to select which debugger you want to use through the following dialog box:

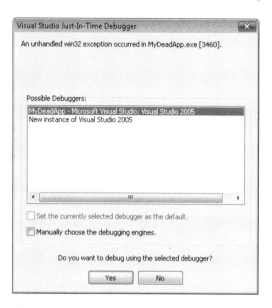

Of course, you can change this to the debugger of your choice. WerFault.exe also passes two parameters on the command line to the debugger. The first parameter is the ID of the process that is to be debugged. The second parameter identifies an inherited handle referring to a manual-reset event that was created in the nonsignaled state by the WerSvc service (Step 6). Notice that the faulting process is also waiting for the ALPC notification to come back from WerSvc. Vendors must implement their debuggers so that they recognize the **-p** and **e** switches as identifying the process ID and the event handle, respectively.

After the process ID and event handle are merged into the string, WerFault.exe executes the debugger by calling **CreateProcess** with its **bInheritHandles** parameter set to **TRUE**, which invokes the debugger process and allows it to inherit the event object's handle. At this point, the debugger process starts running and checks its command-line arguments. If the **-p** switch exists, the debugger grabs the process ID and attaches itself to the process by calling **DebugActiveProcess**:

```
BOOL DebugActiveProcess(DWORD dwProcessID);
```

Once the debugger attaches itself, the operating system informs the debugger of the debuggee's state. For example, the system will tell the debugger how many threads are in the debuggee and which DLLs are loaded in the debuggee's address space. It takes time for the debugger to accumulate all this data as it prepares to debug the process. While all this preparation is going on, the faulting process must wait. The code that has detected the unhandled exception (Step 4) is still waiting for the ALPC notification to come back from the WerSvc service (Step 5). This ALPC itself is blocked on a call to **WaitForSingleObjectEx**, passing the handle of the WerFault.exe process to wait for WER to complete its job. Note that **WaitForSingleObjectEx** is used instead of **WaitForSingleObject** so that the thread can wait in an alertable state. This allows any queued asynchronous procedure calls (APCs) for the thread to be processed.

Note that before Windows Vista, the other threads in the faulting process were not paused, so they might keep on running in a corrupted context and thereby trigger more unhandled exceptions that would be more dramatic because the system would silently kill the process. Even if no other threads crash, the application state might have changed when the report dumps are taken and it would be more difficult to find the root cause of the exception. By default in Windows Vista, if the application is not a service, all the threads of the faulting process are suspended and they don't access any CPU before execution is resumed from WER, to allow the debugger to be notified of the unhandled exception.

After the debugger has fully initialized, it again checks its command line looking for the **-e** switch. If this switch exists, the debugger gets the handle of the event and calls **SetEvent**. The debugger can use the event's handle value directly because the event's handle was created as inheritable by WerFault.exe and was passed to the debugger—spawned as a child process that inherits the same handles—including the synchronization event.

Setting the event (Step 11) lets WerFault.exe know that a debugger has been attached to the faulting application, ready to be notified of the exception. WerFault.exe terminates normally so that the WerSvc service detects that its child process has finished its execution and that it is time to let the ALPC return (Step 12). This allows the debuggee's thread to wake up, and it lets the kernel know that a debugger is now attached and can be notified of the unhandled exception (Step 13). This has the same effect as what happened in Action #3, which was described in "Inside the *Unhandled-ExceptionFilter* Function" on page 710: the debugger then receives a notification about the exception and loads the proper source code file, positioning itself at the instruction that raised the exception (Step 14). Wow, this is all very cool!

By the way, you don't have to wait for an exception before you can debug a process. You can always connect a debugger to any process at any time by running **vsjitdebugger.exe -p** *PID* where *PID* is the ID of the process you want to debug. In fact, the Windows Task Manager makes this easy for you. When viewing the Process tab, you can select a process, click the right mouse button, and choose the Debug menu option. This causes the Task Manager to look at the same registry subkey we just discussed and call **CreateProcess**, passing the ID of the selected process. In this case, the Task Manager passes **0** for the event handle.

> **Tip** The same HKEY_LOCAL_MACHINE\SOFTWARE\Microsoft\Windows NT\CurrentVersion\ AeDebug registry subkey contains another **REG_SZ** data value named **Auto**. This value indicates whether WER should ask the user whether or not the faulting application should be closed or debugged. If **Auto** is set to **1**, WER does not offer any choice to the user and immediately invokes the debugger. This might be the default behavior you want on your developer machine instead of waiting for WER to pop up the two confirmation message boxes—because before being able to start the debugger you always want to debug your application when an unhandled exception occurs.
>
> Sometimes, you might not want to always debug some container applications, such as svchost.exe, when one of the services crashes. In that case, add an **AutoExclusionList** key under the **AeDebug** key and create a **DWORD** value of **1** with the same name as the application you don't want to automatically debug. If you need a more fine-grained way to decide which application should be automatically JIT-debugged, you should leave **Auto** set to **0**, but add a new subkey named **DebugApplications** under HKEY_CURRENT_USER\ SOFTWARE\Microsoft\Windows\Windows Error Reporting. In this subkey, create a **DWORD** value of **1** with the same name as the application to automatically debug when an unhandled exception occurs.

The Spreadsheet Sample Application

It is now time to describe a situation where SEH can be used to control expected exceptions instead of suffering the consequences of unhandled exceptions. The Spreadsheet sample application (25-Spreadsheet.exe) shows how to sparsely commit storage to a reserved address space region using structured exception handling. The source code and resource files for the application are in the 25-Spreadsheet directory on the companion content Web page. When you execute the Spreadsheet sample, the following dialog box appears:

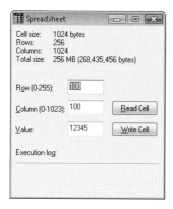

Internally, the application reserved a region for a two-dimensional spreadsheet. The spreadsheet contains 256 rows by 1024 columns, and each cell is 1024 bytes in size. If the application were to commit storage up front for the entire spreadsheet, 268,435,456 bytes (or 256 MB) of storage would be required. To conserve precious storage space, the application reserves a 256-MB region of address space without committing any storage backing this region.

Let's say that the user attempts to place the value 12345 in a cell existing at row 100, column 100 (as shown in the previous dialog box). When the user clicks the Write Cell button, the application code tries to write to that location in the spreadsheet. Of course, this attempted write raises an access violation. However, because I'm using SEH in the application, my exception filter detects the attempted write, displays the "Violation: Attempting to Write" message at the bottom of the dialog box, commits storage for the cell, and has the CPU re-execute the instruction that raised the violation. Because storage has been committed, the value is written to the spreadsheet's cell.

Let's try another experiment. Try to read the value in the cell at row 5, column 20. When you attempt to read from this cell, an access violation is again raised. For an attempted read, the exception filter doesn't commit storage, but it does display the "Violation: Attempting to Read" message in the dialog box. The program gracefully recovers from the failed read by removing the number in the Value field of the dialog box, as shown here:

For our third experiment, try to read the cell value in row 100, column 100. Because storage was committed for this cell, no violation occurs and no exception filter is executed (improving the performance). The dialog box looks like this:

Now for our fourth and last experiment: Try to write the value 54321 into the cell at row 100, column 101. When you attempt this, no violation occurs because this cell is on the same storage page as the cell at (100, 100). We can verify this with the "No violation raised" message at the bottom of the dialog box shown next.

I tend to use virtual memory and SEH quite a bit in my own projects. After a while, I decided to create a templated C++ class, **CVMArray**, which encapsulates all of the hard work. You can find the source code for this C++ class in the VMArray.h file (part of the Spreadsheet sample). You can work with the **CVMArray** class in two ways. First, you can just create an instance of this class passing the maximum number of elements in the array to the constructor. The class automatically sets up a process-wide unhandled exception filter so that whenever any code in any thread accesses a memory address in the virtual memory array, the unhandled exception filter calls *VirtualAlloc* to commit storage for the new element and returns **EXCEPTION_CONTINUE_EXECUTION**. Using the **CVMArray** class in this way allows you to use sparse storage with just a few lines of code, and you don't have to sprinkle SEH frames throughout your source code. The only downside to this approach is that your application can't recover gracefully if for some reason storage cannot be committed when needed.

The second way to use the **CVMArray** class is to derive your own C++ class from it. If you use the derived class, you still get all the benefits of the base class—but now you also get to add features of your own. For example, you can now handle insufficient storage problems more gracefully by overloading the virtual **OnAccessViolation** function. The Spreadsheet sample application shows how a **CVMArray**-derived class can add these features.

```
Spreadsheet.cpp
/**************************************************************************
Module:  Spreadsheet.cpp
Notices: Copyright (c) 2008 Jeffrey Richter & Christophe Nasarre
**************************************************************************/


#include "..\CommonFiles\CmnHdr.h"     /* See Appendix A. */
#include <windowsx.h>
#include <tchar.h>
#include "Resource.h"
#include "VMArray.h"
#include <StrSafe.h>



///////////////////////////////////////////////////////////////////////////
```

```
HWND g_hWnd;    // Global window handle used for SEH reporting

const int g_nNumRows = 256;
const int g_nNumCols = 1024;

// Declare the contents of a single cell in the spreadsheet
typedef struct {
   DWORD dwValue;
   BYTE  bDummy[1020];
} CELL, *PCELL;


// Declare the data type for an entire spreadsheet
typedef CELL SPREADSHEET[g_nNumRows][g_nNumCols];
typedef SPREADSHEET *PSPREADSHEET;


///////////////////////////////////////////////////////////////////////////


// A spreadsheet is a 2-dimensional array of CELLs
class CVMSpreadsheet : public CVMArray<CELL> {
public:
   CVMSpreadsheet() : CVMArray<CELL>(g_nNumRows * g_nNumCols) {}

private:
   LONG OnAccessViolation(PVOID pvAddrTouched, BOOL bAttemptedRead,
      PEXCEPTION_POINTERS pep, BOOL bRetryUntilSuccessful);
};


///////////////////////////////////////////////////////////////////////////


LONG CVMSpreadsheet::OnAccessViolation(PVOID pvAddrTouched, BOOL bAttemptedRead,
   PEXCEPTION_POINTERS pep, BOOL bRetryUntilSuccessful) {

   TCHAR sz[200];
   StringCchPrintf(sz, _countof(sz), TEXT("Violation: Attempting to %s"),
      bAttemptedRead ? TEXT("Read") : TEXT("Write"));
   SetDlgItemText(g_hWnd, IDC_LOG, sz);

   LONG lDisposition = EXCEPTION_EXECUTE_HANDLER;
   if (!bAttemptedRead) {

      // Return whatever the base class says to do
      lDisposition = CVMArray<CELL>::OnAccessViolation(pvAddrTouched,
         bAttemptedRead, pep, bRetryUntilSuccessful);
   }

   return(lDisposition);
}


///////////////////////////////////////////////////////////////////////////
```

```
// This is the global CVMSpreadsheet object
static CVMSpreadsheet g_ssObject;

// Create a global pointer that points to the entire spreadsheet region
SPREADSHEET& g_ss = * (PSPREADSHEET) (PCELL) g_ssObject;


///////////////////////////////////////////////////////////////////////////


BOOL Dlg_OnInitDialog(HWND hWnd, HWND hWndFocus, LPARAM lParam) {

   chSETDLGICONS(hWnd, IDI_SPREADSHEET);

   g_hWnd = hWnd; // Save for SEH reporting

   // Put default values in the dialog box controls
   Edit_LimitText(GetDlgItem(hWnd, IDC_ROW),    3);
   Edit_LimitText(GetDlgItem(hWnd, IDC_COLUMN), 4);
   Edit_LimitText(GetDlgItem(hWnd, IDC_VALUE),  7);
   SetDlgItemInt(hWnd, IDC_ROW,    100,   FALSE);
   SetDlgItemInt(hWnd, IDC_COLUMN, 100,   FALSE);
   SetDlgItemInt(hWnd, IDC_VALUE,  12345, FALSE);
   return(TRUE);
}


///////////////////////////////////////////////////////////////////////////


void Dlg_OnCommand(HWND hWnd, int id, HWND hWndCtl, UINT codeNotify) {

   int nRow, nCol;

   switch (id) {
      case IDCANCEL:
         EndDialog(hWnd, id);
         break;

      case IDC_ROW:
         // User modified the row, update the UI
         nRow = GetDlgItemInt(hWnd, IDC_ROW, NULL, FALSE);
         EnableWindow(GetDlgItem(hWnd, IDC_READCELL),
            chINRANGE(0, nRow, g_nNumRows - 1));
         EnableWindow(GetDlgItem(hWnd, IDC_WRITECELL),
            chINRANGE(0, nRow, g_nNumRows - 1));
         break;

      case IDC_COLUMN:
         // User modified the column, update the UI
         nCol = GetDlgItemInt(hWnd, IDC_COLUMN, NULL, FALSE);
         EnableWindow(GetDlgItem(hWnd, IDC_READCELL),
            chINRANGE(0, nCol, g_nNumCols - 1));
         EnableWindow(GetDlgItem(hWnd, IDC_WRITECELL),
            chINRANGE(0, nCol, g_nNumCols - 1));
         break;
```

```
        case IDC_READCELL:
            // Try to read a value from the user's selected cell
            SetDlgItemText(g_hWnd, IDC_LOG, TEXT("No violation raised"));
            nRow = GetDlgItemInt(hWnd, IDC_ROW, NULL, FALSE);
            nCol = GetDlgItemInt(hWnd, IDC_COLUMN, NULL, FALSE);
            __try {
                SetDlgItemInt(hWnd, IDC_VALUE, g_ss[nRow][nCol].dwValue, FALSE);
            }
            __except (
                g_ssObject.ExceptionFilter(GetExceptionInformation(), FALSE)) {

                // The cell is not backed by storage, the cell contains nothing.
                SetDlgItemText(hWnd, IDC_VALUE, TEXT(""));
            }
            break;

        case IDC_WRITECELL:
            // Try to write a value to the user's selected cell
            SetDlgItemText(g_hWnd, IDC_LOG, TEXT("No violation raised"));
            nRow = GetDlgItemInt(hWnd, IDC_ROW, NULL, FALSE);
            nCol = GetDlgItemInt(hWnd, IDC_COLUMN, NULL, FALSE);

            // If the cell is not backed by storage, an access violation is
            // raised causing storage to automatically be committed.
            g_ss[nRow][nCol].dwValue =
                GetDlgItemInt(hWnd, IDC_VALUE, NULL, FALSE);
            break;
    }
}


///////////////////////////////////////////////////////////////////////////////


INT_PTR WINAPI Dlg_Proc(HWND hWnd, UINT uMsg, WPARAM wParam, LPARAM lParam) {

    switch (uMsg) {
        chHANDLE_DLGMSG(hWnd, WM_INITDIALOG, Dlg_OnInitDialog);
        chHANDLE_DLGMSG(hWnd, WM_COMMAND,    Dlg_OnCommand);
    }
    return(FALSE);
}


///////////////////////////////////////////////////////////////////////////////


int WINAPI _tWinMain(HINSTANCE hInstExe, HINSTANCE, PTSTR, int) {

    DialogBox(hInstExe, MAKEINTRESOURCE(IDD_SPREADSHEET), NULL, Dlg_Proc);
    return(0);
}


///////////////////////////////// End of File ///////////////////////////////////
```

VMArray.h

```
/***************************************************************************
Module:  VMArray.h
Notices: Copyright (c) 2008 Jeffrey Richter & Christophe Nasarre
***************************************************************************/


#pragma once


///////////////////////////////////////////////////////////////////////////


// NOTE: This C++ class is not thread safe. You cannot have multiple threads
// creating and destroying objects of this class at the same time.

// However, once created, multiple threads can access different CVMArray
// objects simultaneously and you can have multiple threads accessing a single
// CVMArray object if you manually synchronize access to the object yourself.


///////////////////////////////////////////////////////////////////////////


template <class TYPE>
class CVMArray {
public:
   // Reserves sparse array of elements
   CVMArray(DWORD dwReserveElements);

   // Frees sparse array of elements
   virtual ~CVMArray();

   // Allows accessing an element in the array
   operator TYPE*()              { return(m_pArray); }
   operator const TYPE*() const { return(m_pArray); }

   // Can be called for fine-tuned handling if commit fails
   LONG ExceptionFilter(PEXCEPTION_POINTERS pep,
      BOOL bRetryUntilSuccessful = FALSE);

protected:
   // Override this to fine-tune handling of access violation
   virtual LONG OnAccessViolation(PVOID pvAddrTouched, BOOL bAttemptedRead,
      PEXCEPTION_POINTERS pep, BOOL bRetryUntilSuccessful);

private:
   static CVMArray* sm_pHead;    // Address of first object
   CVMArray* m_pNext;            // Address of next  object

   TYPE* m_pArray;               // Pointer to reserved region array
   DWORD m_cbReserve;            // Size of reserved region array (in bytes)
```

```
private:
   // Address of previous unhandled exception filter
   static PTOP_LEVEL_EXCEPTION_FILTER sm_pfnUnhandledExceptionFilterPrev;

   // Our global unhandled exception filter for instances of this class
   static LONG WINAPI UnhandledExceptionFilter(PEXCEPTION_POINTERS pep);
};


///////////////////////////////////////////////////////////////////////////


// The head of the linked-list of objects
template <class TYPE>
CVMArray<TYPE>* CVMArray<TYPE>::sm_pHead = NULL;

// Address of previous unhandled exception filter
template <class TYPE>
PTOP_LEVEL_EXCEPTION_FILTER CVMArray<TYPE>::sm_pfnUnhandledExceptionFilterPrev;


///////////////////////////////////////////////////////////////////////////


template <class TYPE>
CVMArray<TYPE>::CVMArray(DWORD dwReserveElements) {

   if (sm_pHead == NULL) {
      // Install our global unhandled exception filter when
      // creating the first instance of the class.
      sm_pfnUnhandledExceptionFilterPrev =
         SetUnhandledExceptionFilter(UnhandledExceptionFilter);
   }

   m_pNext = sm_pHead;  // The next node was at the head
   sm_pHead = this;     // This node is now at the head

   m_cbReserve = sizeof(TYPE) * dwReserveElements;

   // Reserve a region for the entire array
   m_pArray = (TYPE*) VirtualAlloc(NULL, m_cbReserve,
      MEM_RESERVE | MEM_TOP_DOWN, PAGE_READWRITE);
   chASSERT(m_pArray != NULL);
}


///////////////////////////////////////////////////////////////////////////


template <class TYPE>
CVMArray<TYPE>::~CVMArray() {

   // Free the array's region (decommitting all storage within it)
   VirtualFree(m_pArray, 0, MEM_RELEASE);
```

```
      // Remove this object from the linked list
      CVMArray* p = sm_pHead;
      if (p == this) {      // Removing the head node
         sm_pHead = p->m_pNext;
      } else {

         BOOL bFound = FALSE;

         // Walk list from head and fix pointers
         for (; !bFound && (p->m_pNext != NULL); p = p->m_pNext) {
            if (p->m_pNext == this) {
               // Make the node that points to us point to the next node
               p->m_pNext = p->m_pNext->m_pNext;
               break;
            }
         }
         chASSERT(bFound);
      }
   }


   ///////////////////////////////////////////////////////////////////////


   // Default handling of access violations attempts to commit storage
   template <class TYPE>
   LONG CVMArray<TYPE>::OnAccessViolation(PVOID pvAddrTouched,
      BOOL bAttemptedRead, PEXCEPTION_POINTERS pep, BOOL bRetryUntilSuccessful) {

      BOOL bCommittedStorage = FALSE;  // Assume committing storage fails

      do {
         // Attempt to commit storage
         bCommittedStorage = (NULL != VirtualAlloc(pvAddrTouched,
            sizeof(TYPE), MEM_COMMIT, PAGE_READWRITE));

         // If storage could not be committed and we're supposed to keep trying
         // until we succeed, prompt user to free storage
         if (!bCommittedStorage && bRetryUntilSuccessful) {
            MessageBox(NULL,
               TEXT("Please close some other applications and Press OK."),
               TEXT("Insufficient Memory Available"), MB_ICONWARNING | MB_OK);
         }
      } while (!bCommittedStorage && bRetryUntilSuccessful);

      // If storage committed, try again. If not, execute the handler
      return(bCommittedStorage
         ? EXCEPTION_CONTINUE_EXECUTION : EXCEPTION_EXECUTE_HANDLER);
   }


   ///////////////////////////////////////////////////////////////////////
```

```cpp
// The filter associated with a single CVMArray object
template <class TYPE>
LONG CVMArray<TYPE>::ExceptionFilter(PEXCEPTION_POINTERS pep,
   BOOL bRetryUntilSuccessful) {

   // Default to trying another filter (safest thing to do)
   LONG lDisposition = EXCEPTION_CONTINUE_SEARCH;

   // We only fix access violations
   if (pep->ExceptionRecord->ExceptionCode != EXCEPTION_ACCESS_VIOLATION)
      return(lDisposition);

   // Get address of attempted access and get attempted read or write
   PVOID pvAddrTouched = (PVOID) pep->ExceptionRecord->ExceptionInformation[1];
   BOOL bAttemptedRead = (pep->ExceptionRecord->ExceptionInformation[0] == 0);

   // Is attempted access within this VMArray's reserved region?
   if ((m_pArray <= pvAddrTouched) &&
       (pvAddrTouched < ((PBYTE) m_pArray + m_cbReserve))) {

      // Access is in this array; try to fix the problem
      lDisposition = OnAccessViolation(pvAddrTouched, bAttemptedRead,
         pep, bRetryUntilSuccessful);
   }

   return(lDisposition);
}


//////////////////////////////////////////////////////////////////////////////


// The filter associated with all CVMArray objects
template <class TYPE>
LONG WINAPI CVMArray<TYPE>::UnhandledExceptionFilter(PEXCEPTION_POINTERS pep) {

   // Default to trying another filter (safest thing to do)
   LONG lDisposition = EXCEPTION_CONTINUE_SEARCH;

   // We only fix access violations
   if (pep->ExceptionRecord->ExceptionCode == EXCEPTION_ACCESS_VIOLATION) {

      // Walk all the nodes in the linked-list
      for (CVMArray* p = sm_pHead; p != NULL; p = p->m_pNext) {

         // Ask this node if it can fix the problem.
         // NOTE: The problem MUST be fixed or the process will be terminated!
         lDisposition = p->ExceptionFilter(pep, TRUE);

         // If we found the node and it fixed the problem, stop the loop
         if (lDisposition != EXCEPTION_CONTINUE_SEARCH)
            break;
      }
   }
```

```
    // If no node fixed the problem, try the previous exception filter
    if (lDisposition == EXCEPTION_CONTINUE_SEARCH)
        lDisposition = sm_pfnUnhandledExceptionFilterPrev(pep);

    return(lDisposition);
}

/////////////////////////////// End of File ///////////////////////////////
```

Vectored Exception and Continue Handlers

The SEH mechanism presented in Chapters 23 and 24 is a *frame-based* mechanism. That is, as a thread enters into each **try** block (or frame), a node is added to a linked list. If an exception occurs, the system walks the frames in the linked list in order—from the most recently entered **try** block to the **try** block that was entered first by the thread—looking for **catch** handlers. Once a **catch** handler is found, the system walks the linked list again, executing **finally** blocks. When the unwind is complete (or if **try** blocks just exit without raising an exception), the frames are removed from the linked list.

Windows also provides a *vectored exception handling* (VEH) mechanism that works together with SEH. Instead of relying on language-dependent keywords, a program can register functions that are called each time an exception occurs or when an unhandled exception escapes from standard SEH.

The **AddVectoredExceptionHandler** function is responsible for the registration of an *exception handler* that is added into an internal list of functions to call when an exception is triggered in any thread of the process:

```
PVOID AddVectoredExceptionHandler (
    ULONG bFirstInTheList,
    PVECTORED_EXCEPTION_HANDLER pfnHandler);
```

The **pfnHandler** is a pointer to the vectored exception handler. This function must have the following signature:

```
LONG WINAPI ExceptionHandler(struct _EXCEPTION_POINTERS* pExceptionInfo);
```

If the **bFirstInTheList** parameter is **0**, the function passed via the **pfnHandler** parameter is added at the end of the internal list. If the **bFirstInTheList** parameter is non-**0**, the function is added at the beginning of the internal list. When an exception occurs, the functions in the VEH list are called one after the other but before any SEH filter gets called. If the function is able to correct the problem, it should return **EXCEPTION_CONTINUE_EXECUTION** to retry the instruction that caused the exception to be raised in the first place. If a vector handler function returns **EXCEPTION_CONTINUE_EXECUTION**, the SEH filters never even get to process the exception at all. If the handler can't correct the problem, it should return **EXCEPTION_CONTINUE_SEARCH**, allowing other handlers in the list a chance to process the exception. If all the handlers return **EXCEPTION_CONTINUE_SEARCH**, the SEH filter processing begins. Notice that a VEH filter function is not allowed to return **EXCEPTION_EXECUTE_HANDLER**.

A previously-installed VEH exception handler function can be removed from the internal list by calling the following function:

```
ULONG RemoveVectoredExceptionHandler (PVOID pHandler);
```

The **pHandler** parameter identifies a handle to a previously installed function; the handle is returned by the **AddVectoredExceptionHandler** function.

In his "Under the Hood: New Vectored Exception Handling in Windows XP" MSDN Magazine article at http://msdn.microsoft.com/msdnmag/issues/01/09/hood/, *Matt Pietrek describes how vectored exception handlers can be used to implement in-proc API hooking based on breakpoints, which is a different technique than what I presented in Chapter 22, "DLL Injection and API Hooking."*

In addition to being able to handle exceptions before SEH, VEH allows you to be notified after an unhandled exception happens. To receive these notifications, you must register a *continue handler* by calling the following function:

```
PVOID AddVectoredContinueHandler (
   ULONG bFirstInTheList,
   PVECTORED_EXCEPTION_HANDLER pfnHandler);
```

If the **bFirstInTheList** parameter is **0**, the function passed for the **pfnHandler** parameter is added at the end of the internal list of continue handlers. If the **bFirstInTheList** parameter is non-**0**, the function is added at the beginning of the internal list of continue handlers. When an unhandled exception occurs, the continue handler functions in the list are called one after the other. Specifically, the handlers are called after the global unhandled exception filter installed by **SetUnhandledExceptionFilter** returns **EXCEPTION_CONTINUE_SEARCH**. A continue handler function can return **EXCEPTION_CONTINUE_EXECUTION** to halt the execution of the remaining functions in the continue handlers list and to retry the instruction that failed. Or a continue handler can return **EXCEPTION_CONTINUE_SEARCH** to have the remaining handler functions called.

A previously installed continue handler function can be removed from the internal list by calling the following function:

```
ULONG RemoveVectoredContinueHandler (PVOID pHandler);
```

The **pHandler** parameter identifies a handle to a previously installed function; the handle is returned by the **AddVectoredContinueHandler** function.

As you might imagine, continue handler functions are typically used for tracing or diagnostic purposes.

C++ Exceptions vs. Structured Exceptions

Developers frequently ask me whether they should use structured exceptions or C++ exceptions when developing their applications. I'd like to offer an answer in this section.

Let me start by reminding you that SEH is an operating system facility available in any programming language, while C++ EH can be used only when writing C++ code. If you're writing a C++ application, you should use C++ exceptions instead of structured exceptions. The reason is that C++ exceptions are part of the language, and therefore the compiler knows what a C++ class object is. This means that the compiler automatically generates code to call C++ object destructors in order to guarantee object cleanup.

However, you should know that Microsoft's Visual C++ compiler has implemented C++ exception handling using the operating system's structured exception handling. So, when you create a C++ **try** block, the compiler is generating an SEH **__try** block. A C++ **catch** test becomes an SEH exception filter, and the code in the **catch** block becomes the code in the SEH **__except** block. In fact, when you write a C++ **throw** statement, the compiler generates a call to the Windows **RaiseException** function. The variable used in the **throw** statement is passed as an additional argument to **RaiseException**.

The following code fragment will help make all of this a little clearer. The function on the left uses C++ exception handling and the function on the right demonstrates how the C++ compiler generates the equivalent structured exception handling:

```
void ChunkyFunky() {                    void ChunkyFunky() {
   try {                                    __try {
      // Try body                              // Try body
      ...                                      ...
      throw 5;                                 RaiseException(Code=0xE06D7363,
                                                  Flag=EXCEPTION_NONCONTINUABLE,
                                                  Args=5);
   }                                        }
   catch (int x) {                          __except ((ArgType == Integer) ?
                                               EXCEPTION_EXECUTE_HANDLER :
                                               EXCEPTION_CONTINUE_SEARCH) {
      // Catch body                            // Catch body
      ...                                      ...
   }                                        }
   ...                                      ...
}                                        }
```

You'll notice a few interesting details about the code just shown. First, notice that **RaiseException** is called with an exception code of 0xE06D7363. This is the software exception code selected by the Visual C++ team to be used when throwing C++ exceptions. If you use your ASCII skills, you can see that 6D 73 63 stands for "msc."

You'll also notice that the **EXCEPTION_NONCONTINUABLE** flag is always used when a C++ exception is thrown. C++ exceptions can never be re-executed, and it would be an error for a filter diagnosing a C++ exception to return **EXCEPTION_CONTINUE_EXECUTION**. In fact, if you look at the **__except** filter in the function on the right, you'll see that it is only capable of evaluating to **EXCEPTION_ EXECUTE_HANDLER** or **EXCEPTION_CONTINUE_SEARCH**.

The remaining parameters to **RaiseException** are used as the mechanism that actually throws the specified variable. Exactly how the thrown variable information is passed to **RaiseException** is not documented, but it's not too hard to imagine ways that the compiler team could have implemented this.

The last thing I'd like to point out is the **__except** filter. The purpose of this filter is to compare the **throw** variable's data type with the variable type used in the C++ **catch** statement. If the data types are the same, the filter returns **EXCEPTION_EXECUTE_HANDLER**, causing the statements in the

catch block (**__except** block) to execute. If the data types are different, the filter returns **EXCEPTION_CONTINUE_SEARCH**, allowing **catch** filters farther up the call tree to be evaluated.

> **Note** Because C++ exceptions are implemented internally via structured exceptions, you can use both mechanisms in a single application. For example, I love using virtual memory to commit storage when access violations are raised. The C++ language does not support this type of *resumptive exception handling* at all. However, I can use structured exception handling in the parts of my code where I want to take advantage of this and have my own **__except** filter return **EXCEPTION_CONTINUE_EXECUTION**. For all other parts of my code that do not require resumptive exception handling, I'll stick with C++ exception handling.

Exceptions and the Debugger

The Microsoft Visual Studio debugger has fantastic support for debugging exceptions. When a process' thread raises an exception, the operating system immediately notifies a debugger (if a debugger is attached). This notification is called a *first-chance notification*. Normally, the debugger responds to a first-chance notification by telling the thread to search for exception filters. If all the exception filters return **EXCEPTION_CONTINUE_SEARCH**, the operating system notifies the debugger again with a *last-chance notification*. These two notifications exist to give the software developer more control over debugging an exception.

On a per-solution basis, you use the debugger's Exceptions dialog box (shown next) to tell the debugger how to react to first-chance exception notifications.

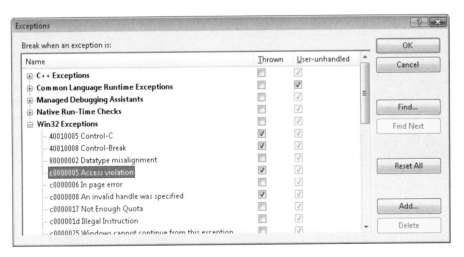

As you can see, the dialog box sorts all the exceptions between categories, among which you find Win32 Exceptions that lists all the system-defined exceptions. Each exception's 32-bit code is shown, followed by a text description and the debugger's action when first-chance notification (Thrown check box) and last-chance notification (User-Unhandled check box) occur. Notice that the latter applies only to common language runtime exceptions. In the dialog box just shown, I have selected the access violation exception and changed its action to stop in the debugger as soon as this exception is thrown . Now, whenever a thread in the debuggee raises an access violation, the debugger receives its first-chance notification and displays a message box similar to the following:

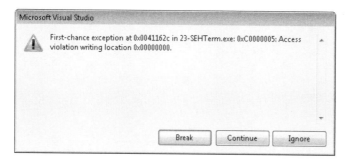

At this point, the thread has *not* had a chance to search for exception filters. I can now place break-points in the code, check variables, or examine the thread's call stack. No exception filters have executed yet; the exception has just occurred. If I now use the debugger to single-step through the code, I am prompted with the following message box:

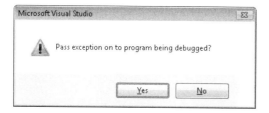

Clicking No tells the debuggee's thread to retry the CPU instruction that failed. For most exceptions, retrying the instruction will just raise the exception again and is not useful. However, for an exception raised with the **RaiseException** function, this tells the thread to continue executing as though the exception was never raised. Continuing in this manner can be particularly useful for debugging C++ programs: it would be as though a C++ **throw** statement never executed. C++ exception handling was discussed in the previous section.

Finally, clicking on Yes allows the debuggee's thread to search for exception filters. If an exception filter is found that returns **EXCEPTION_EXECUTE_HANDLER** or **EXCEPTION_CONTINUE_EXECUTION**, all is well and the thread continues executing its code. However, if all filters return **EXCEPTION_CONTINUE_SEARCH**, the debugger receives a last-chance notification and displays a message box similar to the following:

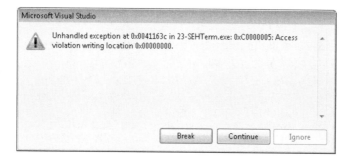

At this point, you must debug the application or terminate it.

I have just shown you what happens if the debugger's action is set to stop as the exception is raised when the Thrown check box is selected. However, for most exceptions, this check box is not selected by default. So, if a thread in the debuggee raises an exception, the debugger receives a first-chance notification. If the check box is not selected, the debugger simply displays a string in the debugger's Output window indicating that it received the notification:

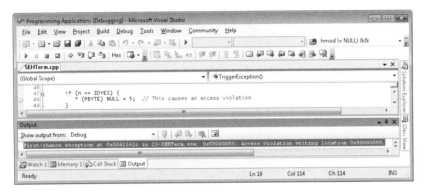

If the Thrown check box is not selected for the access violation exception, the debugger allows the thread to search for exception filters. Only if the exception is not handled will the debugger display the message box shown here:

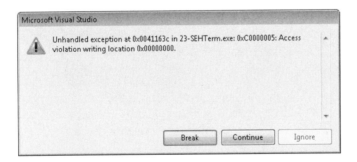

> **Note**   The important point to remember is that first-chance notifications do *not* indicate problems or bugs in the application. In fact, this notification can appear only when your process is being debugged. The debugger is simply reporting that an exception was raised, but if the debugger does not display the message box, a filter handled the exception and the application continues to run just fine. A last-chance notification means that your code has a problem or bug that must be fixed.

As we conclude this chapter, I'd like to point out just one more thing about the debugger's Exceptions dialog box. This dialog box fully supports any software exceptions that you yourself define. All you have to do is click the Add button to pop up the New Exception dialog box, select Win32

Exceptions for the Type, enter a string name for your exception, enter your unique software exception code number, and then click OK to add your exception to the list. The dialog box shown next illustrates how I made the debugger aware of my own software exception:

Chapter 26
Error Reporting and Application Recovery

Chapter 25, "Unhandled Exceptions, Vectored Exception Handling, and C++ Exceptions," discussed how unhandled exceptions and the Windows Error Reporting (WER) mechanism work together so that information about failing applications can be recorded. In this chapter, we take a closer look at these problem reports and how to explicitly use the WER application programming interface (API) in your application. Using the WER API enables you to gain even more insight into your application's failures to improve your chance of finding and fixing bugs, and thereby improve the end user's experience.

The Windows Error Reporting Console

When a process terminates because of an unhandled exception, WER builds a report about the unhandled exception and its execution context.

With the user's consent, this report is sent over a secure channel to Microsoft servers, where it is compared with a database of known application failures. If the database contains a solution for the application failure, the user is notified so that he can take the action or actions necessary to continue his work.

Hardware and software vendors can take advantage of this technology to access reports related to their registered products. Because the same processing also applies to kernel-mode device driver crashes or hangs, a wide spectrum of possible solutions are provided. (Go to *http://www.microsoft.com/whdc/maintain/StartWER.mspx* and the Windows Quality Online Services Web site at *https://winqual.microsoft.com* for more details about this technology and its associated advantages.)

Even if the user does not consent to sending the report to Microsoft's servers, the generated report is still saved on the user's machine. Using the WER console, the user can browse among the problems that have occurred on his machine and examine these reports.

Figure 26-1 shows the Problem Reports And Solutions Control Panel applet (%SystemRoot%\system32\wercon.exe).

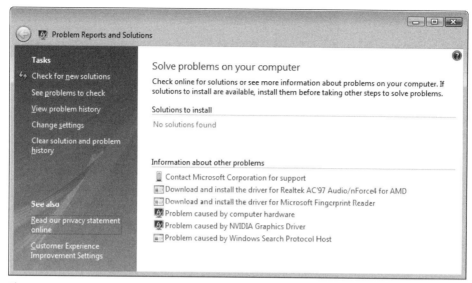

Figure 26-1   The WER console application available from Control Panel

If you click on the View Problem History link on the left, the WER console lists all process crashes or hangs, as shown in Figure 26-2. Other problems, such as drivers not found or system crashes, are also reported.

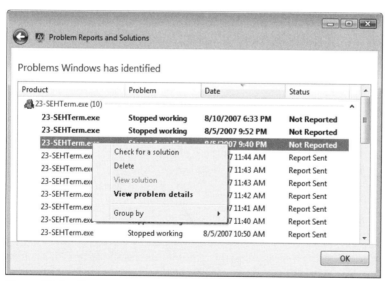

Figure 26-2   The WER console showing each application crash (grouped by Product)

Notice that the Status column points out which problems have been sent to Microsoft and, in bold, which are waiting for submission. When you right-click on a problem, you can check for a solution, delete the problem report, or view the problem details. When you select View Problem Details (or if you double-click on a problem), you see a report similar to that shown in Figure 26-3.

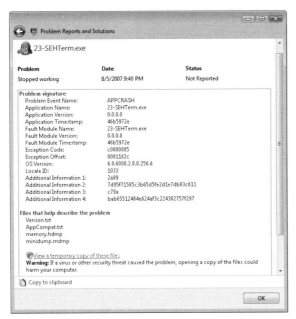

Figure 26-3   The WER console viewing a problem report

The summary screen provides information about the problem, mostly what is available from the **ExceptionInformation** member of the **EXCEPTION_RECORD** structure passed to **UnhandledExceptionFilter**, such as the Exception Code (which Figure 26-3 shows as c0000005 for access violation). These details are cryptic for an end user and are meaningful only for a developer. However, this is not enough to really help you find out what actually happened. Don't worry, the View A Temporary Copy Of These Files link allows you to retrieve the four files listed in Table 26-1 that WER generated when **UnhandledExceptionFilter** was called. By default, these files are available only if the report was not already sent to Microsoft servers. Later in this chapter, we'll see how you can force WER to always keep these files.

The most interesting part of a report is the Memory.hdmp file that can be used to start a post-mortem debug session in your favorite debugger. This allows the debugger to position you at the exact location of the instruction that raised the exception!

> **Note**   In future versions of Windows, the name of the dump files might change to contain the name of the faulting application but keeping the same .hdmp/.mdmp extensions. For example, MyApp.exe.hdmp and MyApp.exe.mdmp would be generated instead of Memory.hdmp and MiniDump.mdmp. Read *Debugging Applications for Microsoft .NET and Microsoft Windows* by John Robbins (Microsoft Press, 2003) to find everything you need to know about minidumps.

Table 26-1   Details of the Four Files Generated by WER

Filename	Description
AppCompat.txt	List of the loaded modules inside the faulting process (in XML format).
Memory.hdmp	User-mode dump of faulting process with stacks, heaps, and handle table. Here are the corresponding flags used to generate this dump file: ``` MiniDumpWithDataSegs | MiniDumpWithProcessThreadData | MiniDumpWithHandleData | MiniDumpWithPrivateReadWriteMemory | MiniDumpWithUnloadedModules | MiniDumpWithFullMemoryInfo ```
MiniDump.mdmp	User-mode minidump of the faulting process. Here are the corresponding flags used to generate this minidump file: ``` MiniDumpWithDataSegs | MiniDumpWithUnloadedModules | MiniDumpWithProcessThreadData ```
Version.txt	Contains the description of the Microsoft Windows installation. ``` Windows NT Version 6.0 Build: 6000 Product (0x6): Windows Vista (TM) Business Edition: Business BuildString: 6000.16386.x86fre.vista_rtm.061101-2205 Flavor: Multiprocessor Free Architecture: X86 LCID: 1033 ```

Programmatic Windows Error Reporting

Exported by kernel32.dll and defined in werapi.h, the following function lets you change a couple of options for your process:

```
HRESULT WerSetFlags(DWORD dwFlags);
```

Table 26-2 lists the four available cumulative options.

Table 26-2   Details of the WerSetFlags Parameter

WER_FAULT_REPORTING_* Options	Description
FLAG_NOHEAP = 1	When a report is generated, it will not contain the heap content. This might be useful to limit the size of reports.
FLAG_DISABLE_THREAD_SUSPENSION = 4	By default, WER suspends all threads in an interactive process so that other threads can't corrupt data further while an application is faulting. This flag tells WER not to suspend the other threads and is potentially a dangerous flag to use.
FLAG_QUEUE = 2	If a critical problem occurs and reporting is turned on, the report is added to the queue on the local machine but not sent to Microsoft.
FLAG_QUEUE_UPLOAD = 8	If a critical problem occurs and reporting is turned on, the report is added to the queue on the local machine and sent to Microsoft.

The real effect of the last two flags—**WER_FAULT_REPORTING_FLAG_QUEUE** and **WER_FAULT_REPORTING_FLAG_QUEUE_UPLOAD**—depends on the current Consent setting, as shown in Figure 25-5 on page 712. If the Consent setting is not the default one recommended to check for a solution, WER generates the reports in both cases; however, a confirmation dialog box for sending it pops up only if **WER_FAULT_REPORTING_FLAG_QUEUE_UPLOAD** is set. The report is not sent if **WER_FAULT_REPORTING_FLAG_QUEUE** is set. An application can't force a report to be uploaded without the consent of the user (or the machine administrator) because this setting always overrides what can be achieved through WER functions.

> **Note**   When a report is generated, it is added to a queue that is local to the machine. If the consent is positive, the report is then uploaded to Microsoft and a trace is archived so that it still appears in the WER console. If the Consent setting is not to send the report and check for solutions, WER provides the necessary dialog boxes to let the user decide what should be done. If the report is not uploaded, it is still kept in the local queue and is visible through the WER console.

If you need to know the current options of a process, call the following function:

```
HRESULT WerGetFlags(HANDLE hProcess, PDWORD pdwFlags);
```

The first parameter, **hProcess**, is the handle of the process you are interested in. This handle must have the **PROCESS_VM_READ** access right enabled. A call to **GetCurrentProcess** returns the handle you need to get the options of the running process.

> **Warning**   If **WerSetFlags** has not been called before **WerGetFlags** is executed, **WER_E_NOT_FOUND** is returned.

Disabling Report Generation and Sending

An application can tell WER not to generate and send a report if it fails. This could certainly be useful while you are in the process of developing and testing your application before you ship or deploy it. To disable report generation and sending, call the following function:

```
HRESULT WerAddExcludedApplication(PCWSTR pwzExeName, BOOL bAllUsers);
```

The **pwzExeName** parameter identifies the filename (or, optionally, the full pathname) of your .exe file (including the extension).

The **bAllUser** parameter indicates whether reporting should be disabled when this application is run by any logged-on user or only for the currently logged-on user. The application must be running under an Administrator account with elevated privileges if passing **TRUE** or an **E_ACCESS-DENIED** error will result. (Read "When Administrator Runs as a Standard User" on page 110 for more details.)

When an unhandled exception occurs in an excluded application, no report gets generated by WER, but WerFault.exe is still launched to offer the choice to the user to debug or close the application, as shown in Figure 26-4.

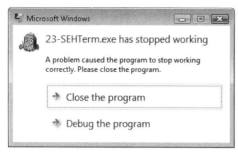

Figure 26-4   The remaining two choices for an excluded application

To enable error reporting for an application, call the **WerRemoveExcludedApplication** function:

```
HRESULT WerRemoveExcludedApplication(PCWSTR pwzExeName, BOOL bAllUsers);
```

> **Note**   Both functions are exported from wer.dll and declared in werapi.h.

Customizing All Problem Reports Within a Process

Sometimes, you might want your application to perform custom error reporting by calling various WER functions. Here are three examples of when you want to take advantage of this:

- You are writing your own unhandled exception filter.
- You want your application to generate a report even though an unhandled exception hasn't occurred.
- You want to add more information to the report.

A simple way to customize all problem reports is to indicate what data blocks or arbitrary files you want added to every problem report generated for your process. To add an arbitrary data block, you simply call

```
HRESULT WerRegisterMemoryBlock(PVOID pvAddress, DWORD dwSize);
```

You pass the address of your memory block for the **pvAddress** parameter and the number of bytes you want saved via the **dwSize** parameter. Now, whenever a problem report is generated, the bytes in this range will be saved in the minidump so that you can examine these bytes with a post-mortem debugger. Note that you can call **WerRegisterMemoryBlock** multiple times to have multiple data blocks saved in the minidump file.

To add an arbitrary file to all problem reports, you simply call

```
HRESULT WerRegisterFile(
    PCWSTR pwzFilename,
    WER_REGISTER_FILE_TYPE regFileType,
    DWORD dwFlags);
```

You pass the pathname of the desired file for the **pwzFilename** parameter. If you don't provide a full pathname, WER looks for the file in the working directory. The **regFileType** parameter takes one of the two values detailed in Table 26-3.

Table 26-3   Type of Files to Add to a Problem Report

regFileType Value	Description
WerRegFileTypeUserDocument = 1	The file is a document potentially containing sensitive user data. By default, the document is not sent to a Microsoft server. However, it is planned in the future to allow a developer to access these files via the Windows Quality Web site.
WerRegFileTypeOther = 2	Any other file.

The **dwFlags** parameter is a bitwise combination of the two values detailed in Table 26-4.

Table 26-4   Flags Associated with an Added File

WER_FILE_* Values for dwFlags	Description
DELETE_WHEN_DONE = 1	Delete the file after the report has been submitted.
ANONYMOUS_DATA = 2	This file does not contain any personal information that could identify the user. If this flag is not set, the first time the Microsoft server asks for this file, a confirmation dialog box pops up to let the user decide whether or not the file should be sent. If the user chooses to upload it, the Consent setting is set to a value of **3** in the registry. Once the consent is set to **3**, files marked as anonymous can be sent without requiring further confirmation from the user.

Now, whenever a problem report is generated, the registered file will be saved in the report. Note that you can call **WerRegisterFile** multiple times to have multiple files saved in the report.

> **Note**   WER allows you to have no more than **WER_MAX_REGISTERED_ENTRIES** (currently defined as 512) entries registered via calls to **WerRegisterMemoryBlock** or **WerRegisterFile**. Note that the **HRESULT** returned when such an error occurs can be mapped to the corresponding Win32 error code through the following operation:
> `if (HRESULT_CODE(hr) == ERROR_INSUFFICIENT_BUFFER)`

I should also point out that you can unregister a data block or file by calling one of these two functions:

```
HRESULT WerUnregisterMemoryBlock(PVOID pvAddress);
HRESULT WerUnregisterFile(PCWSTR pwzFilePath);
```

Creating and Customizing a Problem Report

In this section, I'll discuss how to have your application create its own customized problem report. You can use the functions I present in this section whenever a problem occurs in your application; this includes issues not related to exception handling at all. Also, your application doesn't have to terminate after producing the report. You should consider using Windows Error Reporting instead of adding cryptic information into the Windows Event Log. However, the WER infrastructure does limit the size and number of reports via the registry values shown in Table 26-5. You can find these values under the HKEY_CURRENT_USER\Software\Microsoft\Windows\Windows Error Reporting registry subkey.

Table 26-5 Registry Settings for WER Store

Registry Setting	Description
MaxArchiveCount	Maximum number of files in the archive; between 1 and 5000, with a default value of 1000.
MaxQueueCount	Maximum number of reports in the queue that are stored locally on the machine before being uploaded to the Microsoft servers. The default value is 50, and the value must be between 1 and 500.

> **Note** A trace of the reports sent to Microsoft servers is archived in the current user's AppData\Local\Microsoft\Windows\WER\ReportArchive folder. However, the attached files are not in this folder. The unsent reports are queued in the current user's AppData\Local\Microsoft\Windows\WER\ReportQueue folder. Unfortunately, the API used by the WER console to access these reports is not documented, so you can't enumerate your application's problem reports. Hopefully, this feature will be added in a future version of Windows.

Creating, customizing, and submitting a problem report to WER is performed by calling various functions via this pattern:

1. Call **WerReportCreate** to create a new problem report.

2. Call **WerReportSetParameter** zero or more times to set report parameters.

3. Call **WerReportAddDump** to add a minidump to the report.

4. Call **WerReportAddFile** zero or more times to add arbitrary files (such as user's documents) to the report.

5. Call **WerReportSetUIOption** to modify any strings that might be shown to the user in a consent dialog box when **WerReportSubmit** is called.

6. Call **WerReportSubmit** to submit the report. Based on various flags, Windows might add the report to its queue, prompt the user to send it to the server, and send the report.

7. Call **WerReportCloseHandle** to close the report.

The rest of this section details how each of these steps affects the resulting problem report. While reading the following sections, you might want to refer to the **GenerateWerReport** function (on page 751) that appears in the Customized WER sample application later in this chapter.

After you run this program, open the WER console and select the View Problem History link to get the list of reported problems as shown in Figure 26-5.

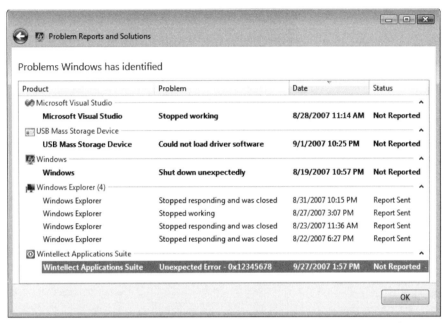

Problem Reports and Solutions

Problems Windows has identified

Product	Problem	Date	Status
Microsoft Visual Studio			^
Microsoft Visual Studio	**Stopped working**	8/28/2007 11:14 AM	**Not Reported**
USB Mass Storage Device			^
USB Mass Storage Device	**Could not load driver software**	9/1/2007 10:25 PM	**Not Reported**
Windows			^
Windows	**Shut down unexpectedly**	8/19/2007 10:57 PM	**Not Reported**
Windows Explorer (4)			^
Windows Explorer	Stopped responding and was closed	8/31/2007 10:15 PM	Report Sent
Windows Explorer	Stopped working	8/27/2007 3:07 PM	Report Sent
Windows Explorer	Stopped responding and was closed	8/23/2007 11:36 AM	Report Sent
Windows Explorer	Stopped responding and was closed	8/22/2007 6:27 PM	Report Sent
Wintellect Applications Suite			^
Wintellect Applications Suite	**Unexpected Error - 0x12345678**	**9/27/2007 1:57 PM**	**Not Reported**

OK

Figure 26-5   The custom entry is sorted by product name in the WER console

Unlike the problem report related to 23-SEHTerm.exe that is listed under a product name identical to the executable name, the problem report for 25-HandleUnhandled.exe appears under the Wintellect Applications Suite product section. The Problem column also presents more detailed information about the problem report than the default "Stopped working" comment.

When you double-click on the report entry to view its details, the result is also customized, as shown in Figure 26-6, with the impact of each **Wer*** function displayed. Compare Figure 26-6 with Figure 26-3 on page 735 to see how the various **Wer*** functions have changed what normally is placed in the report.

The title of the report and the problem label are the same as in the summary list of the WER console. A new Description field is available to provide a high-level definition of the issue, and the corresponding Problem Event Name is now more meaningful than the default APPCRASH string.

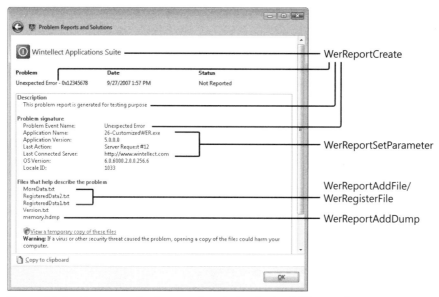

Figure 26-6   The customized report description in the WER console

Creating a Custom Problem Report: *WerReportCreate*

To create a custom report, call **WerReportCreate**, passing it the details of the report:

```
HRESULT WerReportCreate(
    PCWSTR pwzEventType,
    WER_REPORT_TYPE repType,
    PWER_REPORT_INFORMATION pReportInformation,
    HREPORT *phReport);
```

The **pwzEventType** is a Unicode string that appears as the first element of the Problem Signature. Note that if you want the report to be viewable on the Windows Quality Web site (*http://WinQual.Microsoft.com*), the event type has to be registered with Microsoft. (Read the **WerReportCreate** documentation page at *http://msdn2.microsoft.com/en-us/library/bb513625.aspx* in MSDN for more details.)

Important   All **Wer*** functions accept only Unicode strings, and the functions do not have an **A** or **W** suffix.

The **repType** parameter can take one of the values listed in Table 26-6.

Table 26-6   Possible Values of the repType Parameter

repType Value	Description
`WerReportNonCritical` = 0	The report is silently added to the queue and uploaded to Microsoft servers according to the Consent setting.
`WerReportCritical` = 1	The report is added to the local queue with a user-interface (UI) notification, and the application is ended if needed.
`WerReportApplicationCrash` = 2	Same as **WerReportCritical** except that the UI presents the friendly name of the application instead of the executable filename.
`WerReportApplicationHang` = 3	Same as **WerReportApplicationCrash**, but it should be used when a hang or deadlock is detected.

The **pReportInformation** parameter points to a **WER_REPORT_INFORMATION** structure defining several Unicode string fields as listed in Table 26-7.

Table 26-7   WER_REPORT_INFORMATION's String Fields

Field	Description
`wzApplicationName`	Product visible both in the WER console Problem History and close to the application icon in the problem details
`wzApplicationPath`	Not visible locally, but used by the Windows Quality Web site
`wzDescription`	Visible under the Problem Description label
`wzFriendlyEventName`	Problem Event Name entry in the Problem Signature section of the report

Like all **Wer*** functions, **WerReportCreate** returns an **HRESULT** and, if successful, the function returns a handle to a report via the **phReport** parameter.

Setting Report Parameters: *WerReportSetParameter*

After the Problem Event Name and before OS Version and Locale ID, the Problem Signature section of the report shows a set of key/value pairs that you specify by using the following function:

```
HRESULT WerReportSetParameter(
   HREPORT hReport,
   DWORD dwParamID,
   PCWSTR pwzName,
   PCWSTR pwzValue);
```

For the **hReport** parameter, you must pass a handle obtained by first calling **WerReportCreate**. The **dwParamID** parameter indicates which key/value pair you want to set. The function allows you to set up to 10 key/value pairs identified using the macros (defined in werapi.h) **WER_P0** (which has a value of **0**) through **WER_P9** (which has a value of **9**). For the **pwzName** and **pwzValue** parameters, you pass the Unicode strings that you desire.

Note, if you pass an integer value less than **0** or greater than **9**, **WerReportSetParameter** returns **E_INVALIDARG**. Also, you should not skip an ID; that is, if you set **WER_P2**, you must also set **WER_P1** and **WER_P0**. The order in which you set the parameters doesn't matter, but if you skip setting a parameter, the final call to **WerReportSubmit** will fail with an **HRESULT** of 0x8008FF05.

By default, for a noncustomized report, WER sets the parameters shown in Table 26-8.

Table 26-8   Default Parameters for a Problem Report

Parameter ID	Description
1	Name of the faulting application.
2	Version of the faulting application.
3	Time stamp indicating when the application binary was built.
4	Name of the faulting module.
5	Version of the faulting module.
6	Time stamp indicating when the application binary was built.
7	The exception code documenting the type of exception that occurred.
8	Offset in bytes where the fault occurred in the module. This is calculated by getting the Extended Instruction Pointer (EIP) (or equivalent in a non-x86 architecture) of the crash and subtracting from it the load address of the module where the exception occurred.

Adding a Minidump File to the Report: *WerReportAddDump*

When producing a problem report, you add a minidump file to it by calling **WerReportAddDump**:

```
HRESULT WerReportAddDump(
    HREPORT hReport,
    HANDLE hProcess,
    HANDLE hThread,
    WER_DUMP_TYPE dumpType,
    PWER_EXCEPTION_INFORMATION pei,
    PWER_DUMP_CUSTOM_OPTIONS pDumpCustomOptions,
    DWORD dwFlags);
```

The **hReport** parameter indicates the report that the minidump should be added to. The **hProcess** parameter identifies the handle of the process from which the dump will be created. This handle must have been created with the **STANDARD_RIGHTS_READ** and **PROCESS_QUERY_INFORMATION** access rights. Usually, you'll pass a handle obtained by calling **GetCurrentProcess**, which returns a handle that has all process rights.

The **hThread** parameter identifies a thread (within the process identified by **hProcess**). **WerReportAddDump** uses this to walk the thread's call stack. When performing post-mortem debugging, the debugger uses this call stack to position you at the instruction that caused an exception. In addition to saving the call stack, **WerReportAddDump** also needs to know some additional exception information, which you must pass via the **pExceptionParam** parameter as shown by the following code:

```
WER_EXCEPTION_INFORMATION wei;
wei.bClientPointers = FALSE;                // We are in the process where
wei.pExceptionPointers = pExceptionInfo; // pExceptionInfo is valid
```

In this code, **pExceptionInfo** identifies the exception information returned by calling **Get-ExceptionInformation**, and this information is typically passed to an exception filter. Then **&wei** is passed to the **pei** parameter of **WerReportAddDump**. The kind of dump is defined by both the **dumpType** and **pDumpCustomOptions** parameters. (Read the corresponding MSDN documentation for more details.)

For the **dwFlags** parameter, you can either pass **0** or **WER_DUMP_NOHEAP_ONQUEUE**. Normally, a minidump includes heap data. However, the **WER_DUMP_NOHEAP_ONQUEUE** flag tells **WerReport-AddDump** to ignore all the heap data. This flag is useful when you want to conserve disk space, as the heap information will not be placed in the report.

Adding Arbitrary Files to the Report: *WerReportAddFile*

In "Customizing All Problem Reports Within a Process" on page 738, I explained how to add an arbitrary file to all reports generated for a process. However, when producing a custom report, you can add more files (even beyond 512) by calling **WerReportAddFile**:

```
HRESULT WerReportAddFile(
   HREPORT hReport,
   PCWSTR pwzFilename,
   WER_FILE_TYPE addFileType,
   DWORD  dwFileFlags);
```

For the **hReport** parameter, you pass the handle of the report in which you want the **pwzFilename** file to be added. The **addFileType** parameter takes one of the values listed in Table 26-9.

Table 26-9   Types of Files Systematically Added to a Report

File Types	Description
WerFileTypeMicrodump = 1	Custom microdump.
WerFileTypeMinidump = 2	Custom minidump.
WerFileTypeHeapdump = 3	Custom heap dump.
WerFileTypeUserDocument = 4	The file is a document that potentially contains sensitive user data. By default, the document is not sent to a Microsoft server. However, it is planned in the future to allow a developer to access these files from the Windows Quality Web site.
WerFileTypeOther = 5	Any other file.

The **WerFileTypeMicrodump**, **WerFileTypeMinidump**, and **WerFileTypeHeapdump** should not confuse you. When a report is uploaded to a Microsoft server, a fairly complicated discussion is set up and the local machine responds to the server's requests about what files should be sent. In some cases, the server asks for dump files and the local store relies on these three flags to consider custom dumps that your application generated outside the usage of the **WerReportAddDump** function. See the Windows Quality Web site for more details about the communication protocol related to uploading of problem reports. The **dwFileFlags** parameter has the same meaning as it does for the **WerRegisterFile** function, and so Table 26-4 shows the possible flags and their meanings.

Modifying Dialog Box Strings: *WerReportSetUIOption*

If you want to customize the text shown in the consent dialog box that pops up when the report is submitted to WER, you should call the following function:

```
HRESULT WerReportSetUIOption(
   HREPORT hReport,
   WER_REPORT_UI repUITypeID,
   PCWSTR pwzValue);
```

The **hReport** parameter indicates the report whose user interface you want to modify. The **repUITypeID** parameter indicates the user-interface element whose text you want to change, and the **pwzValue** parameter is the Unicode string with the text that you want shown.

You call **WerReportSetUIOption** once for each user-interface element you want to modify. Notice that some labels and buttons are not modifiable. The following screen shots shows some of the text fields that you can modify. For more information, look up the **WerReportSetUIOption** function in the Platform SDK documentation.

Submitting a Problem Report: *WerReportSubmit*

It is now time to submit the problem report by using the following function:

```
HRESULT WerReportSubmit(
   HREPORT hReport,
   WER_CONSENT consent,
   DWORD dwFlags,
   PWER_SUBMIT_RESULT pSubmitResult);
```

The **hReport** parameter is the handle of the report you want to submit. The **consent** parameter takes one of the following three values: **WerConsentNotAsked**, **WerConsentApproved**, or **Wer-ConsentDenied**. As I explained earlier, the decision whether to upload a report is based on the Consent registry setting. However, the user interface shown by WER when a report is submitted varies depending on the value passed for the **consent** parameter. If **WerConsentDenied** is used, the report is not sent. If **WerConsentApproved** is used, the usual notification dialog boxes (shown in Figure 25-2 on page 709 and Figure 25-3 on page 710) appear to the user while the report is generated and sent to Microsoft servers. If **WerConsentNotAsked** is used and the Consent setting is **1** in the registry (which indicates the user should always be prompted before searching for a solution, as shown in Figure 25-5 on page 712), the dialog box shown in Figure 25-6 on page 712 pops up to let the user decide whether the report should be sent to Microsoft and look for a possible solution before closing the application (in addition to offering the usual Debug and Close choices).

The **dwFlags** parameter is a bitmask of values listed in Table 26-10.

Table 26-10   Customization of a Report Submission

WER_SUBMIT_* Values	Description
HONOR_RECOVERY = 1	Show recovery option if this is a critical problem. Read "Automatic Application Restart and Recovery" on page 754 for more details.
HONOR_RESTART = 2	Show application restart option if this is a critical problem. Read "Automatic Application Restart and Recovery" on page 754 for more details.
SHOW_DEBUG = 8	If this flag is not set, the Debug choice is not shown to the user.
NO_CLOSE_UI = 64	The Close choice is not shown to the user.
START_MINIMIZED = 512	The notification dialog box appears as a flashing icon in the Windows taskbar.
QUEUE = 4	Send the report directly to the queue without any visible user interface. If the Consent setting is set to 1 to ask for the user choice, the report is still silently generated but not sent to Microsoft servers.
NO_QUEUE = 128	Do not queue the report.
NO_ARCHIVE = 256	Do not archive the report after uploading it to Microsoft.
OUTOFPROCESS = 32	The report processing is done by another process (wermgr.exe).
OUTOFPROCESS_ASYNC = 1024	The report processing is done by another process (wermgr.exe), and **WerReportSubmit** returns immediately without waiting for the other process to finish its work.
ADD_REGISTERED_DATA = 16	Add registered data to the WER report. Note that if you set this option in conjunction with the out-of-process report generation, the files added by calling **WerRegisterFile** are stored twice in the problem report; this bug will be fixed in a future version of Windows.

The success or failure of the submission is returned as an **HRESULT** by **WerReportSubmit**. However, the exact result is set through the **pSubmitResult** parameter that points to a **WER_SUBMIT_RESULT** variable. Read the MSDN documentation for more details about the possible results. The only case where you should not rely on **pSubmitResult** is when **dwFlags** contains the **WER_SUBMIT_OUTOFPROCESS_ASYNC** flag because **WerReportSubmit** returns before the report processing is finished. As you can imagine, this flag should be used carefully and certainly not in the context of an unhandled exception, because the process would certainly be terminated before the report collection and uploading would be done. You can use it in a nonexception case and when you do not want to block waiting for reporting to finish. The **WER_SUBMIT_OUTOFPROCESS_ASYNC** flag is typically used when a monitoring process detects a problem in another process. For example, the Windows Service Control Manager (SCM) uses this flag to report a hung service process.

Closing a Problem Report: *WerReportCloseHandle*

After the report is submitted, don't forget to pass its handle as the parameter to **WerReportClose-Handle** so that the associated internal data structures will be released:

```
HRESULT WerReportCloseHandle(HREPORT hReportHandle);
```

The Customized WER Sample Application

The Customized WER sample application (26-CustomizedWER.exe) shows how to generate a custom problem report when an unhandled exception is detected. In addition, it provides an implementation that allows **finally** blocks to always execute. Last but not least, instead of using the default consent and displaying WER dialog boxes, a custom user interface is displayed to allow the user to choose between closing the application or debugging it. You can modify this code in your application if you don't want to offer the choice to debug the application by default or you need to localize the dialog boxes in the same language as the application, not as the operating system. The source code and resource files for the application are in the 26-CustomizedWER directory on the companion content Web page.

> **Note** If your application needs to run on versions of Windows prior to Windows Vista, you should use the **ReportFault** function. This function provides far fewer options than the **Wer*** functions detailed in this section. If you are targeting Windows Vista or later, you should avoid the **ReportFault** function.

When you execute the Customized WER sample, the following dialog box appears:

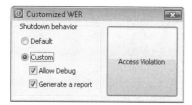

When you click the Access Violation button, the following function is called:

```
void TriggerException() {

    // Trigger an exception wrapped by a finally block
    // that is only executed if a global unwind occurs
    __try {
        TCHAR* p = NULL;
        *p = TEXT('a');
    }
    __finally {
        MessageBox(NULL, TEXT("Finally block is executed"), NULL, MB_OK);
    }
}
```

The **CustomUnhandledExceptionFilter** function is then executed because it is the exception filter of the **try**/**except** block that is protecting the main entry point of the application:

```
int APIENTRY _tWinMain(HINSTANCE hInstExe, HINSTANCE, LPTSTR, int) {

   int iReturn = 0;

   // Disable the automatic JIT-debugger attachment
   // that could have been enabled in CustomUnhandledExceptionFilter
   // in a prior execution of the same application
   EnableAutomaticJITDebug(FALSE);

   // Protect the code with our own exception filter
   __try {
      DialogBox(hInstExe, MAKEINTRESOURCE(IDD_MAINDLG), NULL, Dlg_Proc);
   }
   __except(CustomUnhandledExceptionFilter(GetExceptionInformation())) {
      MessageBox(NULL, TEXT("Bye bye"), NULL, MB_OK);
      ExitProcess(GetExceptionCode());
   }

   return(iReturn);
}
```

The behavior of this filter is driven by the options available in the main window of the application:

```
static BOOL s_bFirstTime = TRUE;

LONG WINAPI CustomUnhandledExceptionFilter(
   struct _EXCEPTION_POINTERS* pExceptionInfo) {

   // When the debugger gets attached and you stop the debugging session,
   // the execution resumes here...
   // So this case is detected and the application exits silently
   if (s_bFirstTime)
      s_bFirstTime = FALSE;
   else
      ExitProcess(pExceptionInfo->ExceptionRecord->ExceptionCode);

   // Check shutdown options
   if (!s_bCustom)
      // Let Windows treat the exception
      return(UnhandledExceptionFilter(pExceptionInfo));

   // Allow global unwind by default
   LONG lReturn = EXCEPTION_EXECUTE_HANDLER;

   // Let the user choose between Debug or Close application
   // except if JIT-debugging was disabled in the options
   int iChoice = IDCANCEL;
   if (s_bAllowJITDebug) {
      iChoice = MessageBox(NULL,
         TEXT("Click RETRY if you want to debug\nClick CANCEL to quit"),
         TEXT("The application must stop"), MB_RETRYCANCEL | MB_ICONHAND);
   }
```

```
   if (iChoice == IDRETRY) {
      // Force JIT-debugging for this application
      EnableAutomaticJITDebug(TRUE);

      // Ask Windows to JIT-attach the default debugger
      lReturn = EXCEPTION_CONTINUE_SEARCH;
   } else {
      // The application will be terminated
      lReturn = EXCEPTION_EXECUTE_HANDLER;

      // But check if we need to generate a problem report first
      if (s_bGenerateReport)
         GenerateWerReport(pExceptionInfo);
   }

   return(lReturn);
}
```

If the Default radio button is selected, the output of **UnhandledExceptionFilter** (the default Windows exception handler) is returned. In that case, the user interface and the problem-reporting processing occur as detailed in the prior sections.

When you select the Custom radio button, two additional options drive the behavior of **Custom-UnhandledExceptionFilter**. If Allow Debug is selected, the following simple dialog box pops up:

If the user clicks Retry, we need to cheat a little to force Windows to start JIT-debugging because returning **EXCEPTION_CONTINUE_SEARCH** is not enough. This simply means that the exception is unhandled and WER starts the default user interface to ask again what to do to the user. The role of **EnableAutomaticJITDebug** is to tell WER that the choice to attach a debugger has already been done.

```
void EnableAutomaticJITDebug(BOOL bAutomaticDebug) {

   // Create the subkey if necessary
   const LPCTSTR szKeyName = TEXT("Software\\Microsoft\\Windows\\" +
      TEXT(Windows Error Reporting\\DebugApplications");
   HKEY hKey = NULL;
   DWORD dwDisposition = 0;
   LSTATUS lResult = ERROR_SUCCESS;
   lResult = RegCreateKeyEx(HKEY_CURRENT_USER, szKeyName, 0, NULL,
      REG_OPTION_NON_VOLATILE, KEY_WRITE, NULL, &hKey, &dwDisposition);
   if (lResult != ERROR_SUCCESS) {
      MessageBox(NULL, TEXT("RegCreateKeyEx failed"),
         TEXT("EnableAutomaticJITDebug"), MB_OK | MB_ICONHAND);
      return;
   }
```

```
// Give the right value to the registry entry
DWORD dwValue = bAutomaticDebug ? 1 : 0;
TCHAR szFullpathName[MAX_PATH];
GetModuleFileName(NULL, szFullpathName, _countof(szFullpathName));
LPTSTR pszExeName = _tcsrchr(szFullpathName, TEXT('\\'));
if (pszExeName != NULL) {
    // Skip the '\'
    pszExeName++;

    // Set the value
    lResult = RegSetValueEx(hKey, pszExeName, 0, REG_DWORD,
        (const BYTE*)&dwValue, sizeof(dwValue));
    if (lResult != ERROR_SUCCESS) {
        MessageBox(NULL, TEXT("RegSetValueEx failed"),
            TEXT("EnableAutomaticJITDebug"), MB_OK | MB_ICONHAND);
        return;
    }
}
}
```

The code is straightforward and takes advantage of the registry setting shown in "Just-in-Time Debugging" on page 713 to force JIT-debugging in Chapter 25. Note that when the application starts, **EnableAutomaticJITDebug** is called with **FALSE** as a parameter to reset the registry value to **0**.

If Allow Debug is selected in the main dialog box, the process is expected to simply end without showing the custom message box. The effect is the same as when the Cancel button is clicked: **EXCEPTION_EXECUTE_HANDLER** is returned, and the global **except** block calls **ExitProcess**. However, before returning **EXCEPTION_EXECUTE_HANDLER**, if Generate A Report has been selected, a WER problem report is manually generated by the following **GenerateWerReport** function that is calling the **WerReport*** functions presented in prior sections of this chapter:

```
LONG GenerateWerReport(struct _EXCEPTION_POINTERS* pExceptionInfo) {

    // Default return value
    LONG lResult = EXCEPTION_CONTINUE_SEARCH;

    // Avoid stack problem because wri is a big structure
    static WER_REPORT_INFORMATION wri = { sizeof(wri) };

    // Set the report details
    StringCchCopyW(wri.wzFriendlyEventName, _countof(wri.wzFriendlyEventName),
        L"Unexpected Error - 0x12345678");
    StringCchCopyW(wri.wzApplicationName, _countof(wri.wzApplicationName),
        L"Wintellect Applications Suite");
    GetModuleFileNameW(NULL, (WCHAR*)&(wri.wzApplicationPath),
        _countof(wri.wzApplicationPath));
    StringCchCopyW(wri.wzDescription, _countof(wri.wzDescription),
        L"This problem report is generated for testing purpose");


    HREPORT hReport = NULL;
```

```
// Create a report and set additional information
__try {                          // instead of the default APPCRASH_EVENT
   HRESULT hr = WerReportCreate(L"Unexpected Error",
      WerReportApplicationCrash, &wri, &hReport);

   if (FAILED(hr)) {
      MessageBox(NULL, TEXT("WerReportCreate failed"),
         TEXT("GenerateWerReport"), MB_OK | MB_ICONHAND);
      return(EXCEPTION_CONTINUE_SEARCH);
   }
   if (hReport == NULL) {
      MessageBox(NULL, TEXT("WerReportCreate failed"),
         TEXT("GenerateWerReport"), MB_OK | MB_ICONHAND);
      return(EXCEPTION_CONTINUE_SEARCH);
   }

   // Set more details important to help fix the problem
   WerReportSetParameter(hReport, WER_P0,
      L"Application Name", L"26-CustomizedWER.exe");
   WerReportSetParameter(hReport, WER_P1,
      L"Application Version", L"5.0.0.0");
   WerReportSetParameter(hReport, WER_P2,
      L"Last Action", L"Server Request #12");
   WerReportSetParameter(hReport, WER_P3,
      L"Last Connected Server", L"http://www.wintellect.com");

   // Add a dump file corresponding to the exception information
   WER_EXCEPTION_INFORMATION wei;
   wei.bClientPointers = FALSE;           // We are in the process where
   wei.pExceptionPointers = pExceptionInfo;  // pExceptionInfo is valid
   hr = WerReportAddDump(
      hReport, GetCurrentProcess(), GetCurrentThread(),
      WerDumpTypeHeapDump, &wei, NULL, 0);
   if (FAILED(hr)) {
      MessageBox(NULL, TEXT("WerReportAddDump failed"),
         TEXT("GenerateWerReport"), MB_OK | MB_ICONHAND);
      return(EXCEPTION_CONTINUE_SEARCH);
   }

   // Let memory blocks be visible from a mini-dump
   s_moreInfo1.dwCode = 0x1;
   s_moreInfo1.dwValue = 0xDEADBEEF;
   s_moreInfo2.dwCode = 0x2;
   s_moreInfo2.dwValue = 0x0BADBEEF;
   hr = WerRegisterMemoryBlock(&s_moreInfo1, sizeof(s_moreInfo1));
   if (hr != S_OK) { // Don't want S_FALSE
      MessageBox(NULL, TEXT("First WerRegisterMemoryBlock failed"),
         TEXT("GenerateWerReport"), MB_OK | MB_ICONHAND);
      return(EXCEPTION_CONTINUE_SEARCH);
   }
   hr = WerRegisterMemoryBlock(&s_moreInfo2, sizeof(s_moreInfo2));
   if (hr != S_OK) { // Don't want S_FALSE
      MessageBox(NULL, TEXT("Second WerRegisterMemoryBlock failed"),
         TEXT("GenerateWerReport"), MB_OK | MB_ICONHAND);
      return(EXCEPTION_CONTINUE_SEARCH);
   }
```

```
// Add more files to this particular report
wchar_t wszFilename[] = L"MoreData.txt";
char textData[] = "Contains more information about the execution \r\n\" +
   "context when the problem occurred. The goal is to \r\n\" +
   "help figure out the root cause of the issue.";
// Note that error checking is removed for readability
HANDLE hFile = CreateFileW(wszFilename, GENERIC_WRITE, 0, NULL,
   CREATE_ALWAYS, FILE_ATTRIBUTE_NORMAL, NULL);
DWORD dwByteWritten = 0;
WriteFile(hFile, (BYTE*)textData, sizeof(textData), &dwByteWritten,
   NULL);
CloseHandle(hFile);
hr = WerReportAddFile(hReport, wszFilename, WerFileTypeOther,
   WER_FILE_ANONYMOUS_DATA);
if (FAILED(hr)) {
   MessageBox(NULL, TEXT("WerReportAddFile failed"),
      TEXT("GenerateWerReport"), MB_OK | MB_ICONHAND);
   return(EXCEPTION_CONTINUE_SEARCH);
}


// It is also possible to use WerRegisterFile
char textRegisteredData[] = "Contains more information about the execution\r\n"+
   "context when the problem occurred. The goal is to \r\n\" +
   "help figure out the root cause of the issue.";
// Note that error checking is removed for readability
hFile = CreateFileW(L"RegisteredData1.txt", GENERIC_WRITE, 0, NULL,
   CREATE_ALWAYS, FILE_ATTRIBUTE_NORMAL, NULL);
dwByteWritten = 0;
WriteFile(hFile, (BYTE*)textRegisteredData, sizeof(textRegisteredData),
   &dwByteWritten, NULL);
CloseHandle(hFile);
hr = WerRegisterFile(L"RegisteredData1.txt", WerRegFileTypeOther,
   WER_FILE_ANONYMOUS_DATA);
if (FAILED(hr)) {
   MessageBox(NULL, TEXT("First WerRegisterFile failed"),
      TEXT("GenerateWerReport"), MB_OK | MB_ICONHAND);
   return(EXCEPTION_CONTINUE_SEARCH);
}
hFile = CreateFileW(L"RegisteredData2.txt", GENERIC_WRITE, 0, NULL,
   CREATE_ALWAYS, FILE_ATTRIBUTE_NORMAL, NULL);
dwByteWritten = 0;
WriteFile(hFile, (BYTE*)textRegisteredData, sizeof(textRegisteredData),
   &dwByteWritten, NULL);
CloseHandle(hFile);
hr = WerRegisterFile(L"RegisteredData2.txt", WerRegFileTypeOther,
   WER_FILE_DELETE_WHEN_DONE);   // File is deleted after WerReportSubmit
if (FAILED(hr)) {
   MessageBox(NULL, TEXT("Second WerRegisterFile failed"),
      TEXT("GenerateWerReport"), MB_OK | MB_ICONHAND);
   return(EXCEPTION_CONTINUE_SEARCH);
}
```

```
    // Submit the report
    WER_SUBMIT_RESULT wsr;
    DWORD submitOptions =
        WER_SUBMIT_QUEUE |
        WER_SUBMIT_OUTOFPROCESS |
        WER_SUBMIT_NO_CLOSE_UI;  // Don't show any UI
    hr = WerReportSubmit(hReport, WerConsentApproved, submitOptions, &wsr);
    if (FAILED(hr)) {
        MessageBox(NULL, TEXT("WerReportSubmit failed"),
            TEXT("GenerateWerReport"), MB_OK | MB_ICONHAND);
        return(EXCEPTION_CONTINUE_SEARCH);
    }

    // The submission was successful, but we might need to check the result
    switch(wsr)
    {
        case WerReportQueued:
        case WerReportUploaded: // To exit the process
            lResult = EXCEPTION_EXECUTE_HANDLER;
            break;

        case WerReportDebug: // To end up in the debugger
            lResult = EXCEPTION_CONTINUE_SEARCH;
            break;

        default: // Let the OS handle the exception
            lResult = EXCEPTION_CONTINUE_SEARCH;
            break;
    }

    // In our case, we always exit the process after the report generation
    lResult = EXCEPTION_EXECUTE_HANDLER;
}
__finally {
    // Don't forget to close the report handle
    if (hReport != NULL) {
        WerReportCloseHandle(hReport);
        hReport = NULL;
    }
}

return(lResult);
}
```

Automatic Application Restart and Recovery

When a critical problem occurs in an application, WER is able to restart the application automatically after its termination. For Windows Vista, it is a quality requirement that most of the applications that ship with Windows Vista (such as Windows Explorer, Internet Explorer, RegEdit, and the games) are restart aware. Even better, WER also allows an application to recover any important data before being terminated.

Automatic Application Restart

A restart-aware application must register itself with WER by calling the following function:

```
HRESULT RegisterApplicationRestart(
    PCWSTR pwzCommandline,
    DWORD dwFlags);
```

The **pwzCommandLine** parameter is a Unicode string identifying the command line that WER should use to restart the application. You should pass **NULL** if the application does not use a special argument to detect a restart. If you pass **0** for the **dwFlags** parameter, the application is always restarted when a critical problem is detected by WER. You can use a bitwise combination of the values, detailed in Table 26-11, to restrict the cases when the application should be restarted.

Table 26-11   Flags to Restrict Application Restart

Flag Value	Description
RESTART_NO_CRASH = 1	Do not restart the application when it crashes.
RESTART_NO_HANG = 2	Do not restart the application when it hangs.
RESTART_NO_PATCH = 4	Do not restart the application after installing an update.
RESTART_NO_REBOOT = 8	Do not restart the application when the system is rebooted as the result of an update of the system.

The last two flag values look strange in the context of exception handling, but the application restart feature is part of a more general API called the Restart Manager. (Read the Restart Manager "Guidelines for Applications" MSDN documentation at *http://msdn2.microsoft.com/en-us/library/ aa373651.aspx* for more details.)

After the **RegisterApplicationRestart** function is called, if the process encounters a critical problem that is handled by WER, the dialog box shown in Figure 26-7 pops up while the application is restarting.

Figure 26-7   The user is notified that the application is restarting

To avoid repeatedly restarting a faulting application, WER verifies that the process has been running for at least 60 seconds before restarting it again.

Note   You call the following function if you want to notify WER that the application should not be restarted:

HRESULT UnregisterApplicationRestart();

Support for Application Recovery

A process can register a callback function that WER will call when the process is terminating abnormally. This callback function can save any data or state information. To register a call function, have your process call the following function:

```
HRESULT RegisterApplicationRecoveryCallback(
   APPLICATION_RECOVERY_CALLBACK pfnRecoveryCallback,
   PVOID pvParameter,
   DWORD dwPingInterval,
   DWORD dwFlags);  // Reserved; pass 0
```

The **pfnRecoveryCallback** parameter must refer to a function that has the following signature:

```
DWORD WINAPI ApplicationRecoveryCallback(PVOID pvParameter);
```

This callback is called by WER with the **pvParameter** parameter you passed when you called **RegisterApplicationRecoveryCallback**. When WER calls your function, the dialog box shown in Figure 26-8 is displayed.

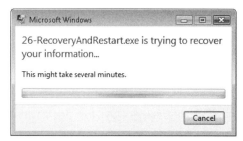

Figure 26-8   The user is notified while the application is preparing for recovery

The **pfnRecoveryCallback** function is supposed to let WER know that it is working by calling the **ApplicationRecoveryInProgress** function at least once every **dwPingInterval** milliseconds. If **ApplicationRecoveryInProgress** is not called in a timely manner, WER terminates the process. The **ApplicationRecoveryInProgress** function takes a pointer to a **BOOL** as a parameter to let you know whether the user has clicked the Cancel button shown in Figure 26-8. When the recovery function is finished, it should call **ApplicationRecoveryFinished** to let WER know whether or not the function completed successfully.

Here is an example of an application recovery callback:

```
DWORD WINAPI ApplicationRecoveryCallback(PVOID pvParameter) {

   DWORD dwReturn = 0;

   BOOL bCancelled = FALSE;
   while (!bCancelled) {

      // Show progress
      ApplicationRecoveryInProgress(&bCancelled);

      // Check for user cancellation
      if (bCancelled) {
         // The user clicked the Cancel button

         // Notify that we have failed to finish the recovery process
         ApplicationRecoveryFinished(FALSE);
      } else {
         // Save the state required for recovery, chunk by chunk

         if (MoreInformationToSave()) {
            // Save a chunk of data in fewer milliseconds than the delay set
            // with the dwPingInterval parameter you passed to
            // RegisterApplicationRecoveryCallback

         } else { // Nothing more to save
            // It is still possible to update the restart command line
            // by calling RegisterApplicationRestart when the name of
            // a recovery file is known, for example.

            // Notify that we have finished the recovery process
            ApplicationRecoveryFinished(TRUE);

            // Set bCancelled to TRUE when finished to exit the loop
            bCancelled = TRUE;
         }
      }
   }

   return(dwReturn);
}
```

Remember that when the callback function runs, the process might be in a corrupted state and the same constraints detailed for an exception filter also apply for this kind of callback.

Part VI
Appendixes

Appendix A
The Build Environment

To build the sample applications in this book, you must deal with compiler and linker switch settings. I have tried to isolate these details from the sample applications by putting almost all of these settings in a single header file, called CmnHdr.h, which is included in all of the sample application source code files.

Because I wasn't able to put all of the settings in this header file, I made some changes to each sample application's project properties. After selecting all projects, I displayed the Properties dialog box and then made the following changes from the Configuration Properties section:

- On the General tab, I set the Output Directory so that all final .exe and .dll files go to a single directory.
- On the C/C++, Code Generation tab, I selected the Multi-Threaded DLL value for the Run-Time Library field.
- On the C/C++ tab, I selected Yes (/Wp64) for the Detect 64-Bit Portability Issues field.

That's it. These are the only settings that I explicitly changed; I accepted the default settings for everything else. Note that I made the changes mentioned for both the Debug and Release builds of each project. I was able to set all other compiler and linker settings in the source code, so these settings will be in effect if you use any of my source code modules in your projects.

The CmnHdr.h Header File

All of the sample programs include the CmnHdr.h header file before any other header file. I wrote CmnHdr.h, shown on page 767, to make my life a little easier. The file contains macros, linker directives, and other code that is common across all the applications. When I want to try something, all I do is modify CmnHdr.h and rebuild all the sample applications. CmnHdr.h is in the root directory on the companion content Web page.

The remainder of this appendix discusses each section of the CmnHdr.h header file. I'll explain the rationale for each section and describe how and why you might want to make changes before rebuilding all the sample applications.

Microsoft Windows Version Build Option

Because some of the sample applications call functions that are new in Microsoft Windows Vista, this section of CmnHdr.h defines the **_WIN32_WINNT** and **WINVER** symbols as follows:

```
// = 0x0600 for VISTA level from sdkddkver.h
#define _WIN32_WINNT _WIN32_WINNT_LONGHORN
#define WINVER       _WIN32_WINNT_LONGHORN
```

I have to do this because the new Windows Vista functions are prototyped in the Windows header files like this:

```
#if (_WIN32_WINNT >= 0x0600)
...

HANDLE
WINAPI
CreateMutexExW(
    LPSECURITY_ATTRIBUTES lpMutexAttributes,
    LPCWSTR lpName,
    DWORD dwFlags,
    DWORD dwDesiredAccess
    );
...

#endif /* _WIN32_WINNT >= 0x0600 */
```

Unless you specifically define **_WIN32_WINNT** as I have (before including Windows.h), the prototypes for the new functions will not be declared and the compiler will generate errors if you attempt to call these functions. Microsoft has protected these functions with the **_WIN32_WINNT** symbol to help ensure that applications you develop can run on multiple versions of Microsoft Windows.

Unicode Build Option

I wrote all the sample applications so that they can be compiled as either Unicode or ANSI. To enforce consistency with Unicode builds, both **UNICODE** and **_UNICODE** symbols are defined in CmnHdr.h. For more information on Unicode, see Chapter 2, "Working with Characters and Strings."

Windows Definitions and Warning Level 4

When I develop software, I always try to ensure that the code compiles free of errors and warnings. I also like to compile at the highest possible warning level so that the compiler does the most work for me and examines even the most minute details of my code. For the Microsoft C/C++ compilers, this means that I built all the sample applications using warning level 4.

Unfortunately, Microsoft's operating systems group doesn't share my sentiments about compiling using warning level 4. As a result, when I set the sample applications to compile at warning level 4, many lines in the Windows header files cause the compiler to generate warnings. Fortunately, these warnings do not represent problems in the code. Most are generated by unconventional uses of the C language that rely on compiler extensions that almost all vendors of Windows-compatible compilers implement.

In this section of CmnHdr.h, I make sure that the warning level is set to 3 and that CmnHdr.h includes the standard Windows.h header file. Once Windows.h is included, I set the warning level to 4 when I compile the rest of the code. At warning level 4, the compiler emits "warnings" for things that I don't consider problems, so I explicitly tell the compiler to ignore certain benign warnings by using the **#pragma warning** directive.

The *pragma message* Helper Macro

When I work on code, I often like to get something working immediately and then make it bullet-proof later. To remind myself that some code needs additional attention, I used to include a line like this:

```
#pragma message("Fix this later")
```

When the compiler compiled this line, it would output a string reminding me that I had some more work to do. This message was not that helpful, however. I decided to find a way for the compiler to output the name of the source code file and the line number that the **pragma** appears on. Not only would I know that I had additional work to do, but I could also locate the surrounding code immediately.

To get this behavior, you have to trick the **pragma message** directive using a series of macros. The result is that you can use the **chMSG** macro like this:

```
#pragma chMSG(Fix this later)
```

When the preceding line is compiled, the compiler produces a line that looks like this:

```
C:\CD\CommonFiles\CmnHdr.h(82):Fix this later
```

Now, using Microsoft Visual Studio, you can double-click on this line in the output window and be automatically positioned at the correct place in the correct file.

As a convenience, the **chMSG** macro does not require quotes to be used around the text string.

The *chINRANGE* Macro

I frequently use this handy macro in my applications. The **chINRANGE** macro checks to see whether a value is between two other values.

The *chBEGINTHREADEX* Macro

All the multithreaded samples in this book use the **_beginthreadex** function, which is in Microsoft's C/C++ run-time library, instead of the operating system's **CreateThread** function. I use this function because the **_beginthreadex** function prepares the new thread so that it can use the C/C++ run-time library functions and because it ensures that the per-thread C/C++ run-time library information is destroyed when the thread returns. (See Chapter 6, "Thread Basics," for more details.) Unfortunately, the **_beginthreadex** function is prototyped as follows:

```
unsigned long __cdecl _beginthreadex(
   void *,
   unsigned,
   unsigned (__stdcall *)(void *),
   void *,
   unsigned,
   unsigned *);
```

Although the parameter values for **_beginthreadex** are identical to the parameter values for the **CreateThread** function, the parameters' data types do not match. Here is the prototype for the **CreateThread** function:

```
typedef DWORD (WINAPI *PTHREAD_START_ROUTINE)(PVOID pvParam);

HANDLE CreateThread(
   PSECURITY_ATTRIBUTES psa,
   SIZE_T cbStackSize,
   PTHREAD_START_ROUTINE pfnStartAddr,
   PVOID pvParam,
   DWORD dwCreateFlags,
   PDWORD pdwThreadId);
```

Microsoft did not use the Windows data types when creating the **_beginthreadex** function's prototype because Microsoft's C/C++ run-time group does not want to have any dependencies on the operating system group. I commend this decision; however, this makes using the **_beginthreadex** function more difficult.

There are really two problems with the way Microsoft prototyped the **_beginthreadex** function. First, some of the data types used for the function do not match the primitive types used by the **CreateThread** function. For example, the Windows data type **DWORD** is defined as follows:

```
typedef unsigned long DWORD;
```

This data type is used for **CreateThread**'s **dwCreateFlags** parameter. The problem is that **_beginthreadex** prototypes these two parameters as **unsigned**, which really means **unsigned int**. The compiler considers an **unsigned int** to be different from an **unsigned long** and generates a warning. Because the **_beginthreadex** function is not a part of the standard C/C++ run-time library and exists only as an alternative to calling the **CreateThread** function, I believe that Microsoft should have prototyped **_beginthreadex** this way so that warnings are not generated:

```
unsigned long __cdecl _beginthreadex(
   void *psa,
   unsigned long cbStackSize,
   unsigned (__stdcall *) (void *pvParam),
   void *pvParam,
   unsigned long dwCreateFlags,
   unsigned long *pdwThreadId);
```

The second problem is just a small variation of the first. The **_beginthreadex** function returns an **unsigned long** representing the handle of the newly created thread. An application typically wants to store this return value in a data variable of type **HANDLE** as follows:

```
HANDLE hThread = _beginthreadex(...);
```

The preceding code causes the compiler to generate another warning. To avoid the compiler warning, you must rewrite the line just shown, introducing a cast as follows:

```
HANDLE hThread = (HANDLE) _beginthreadex(...);
```

Again, this is inconvenient. To make life a little easier, I defined a **chBEGINTHREADEX** macro in CmnHdr.h to perform all of this casting for me:

```
typedef unsigned (__stdcall *PTHREAD_START) (void *);

#define chBEGINTHREADEX(psa, cbStackSize, pfnStartAddr, \
   pvParam, dwCreateFlags, pdwThreadId)                 \
      ((HANDLE)_beginthreadex(                           \
         (void *)        (psa),                          \
         (unsigned)      (cbStackSize),                  \
         (PTHREAD_START) (pfnStartAddr),                 \
         (void *)        (pvParam),                      \
         (unsigned)      (dwCreateFlags),                \
         (unsigned *)    (pdwThreadId)))
```

DebugBreak Improvement for *x*86 Platforms

I sometimes want to force a breakpoint in my code even if the process is not running under a debugger. You can do this in Windows by having a thread call the **DebugBreak** function. This function, which resides in Kernel32.dll, lets you attach a debugger to the process. Once the debugger is attached, the instruction pointer is positioned on the CPU instruction that caused the breakpoint. This instruction is contained in the **DebugBreak** function in Kernel32.dll, so to see my source code I must single-step out of the **DebugBreak** function.

On the *x*86 architecture, you perform a breakpoint by executing an "int 3" CPU instruction. So, on *x*86 platforms, I redefine **DebugBreak** as this inline assembly language instruction. When my **DebugBreak** is executed, I do not call into Kernel32.dll; the breakpoint occurs right in my code and the instruction pointer is positioned to the next C/C++ language statement. This just makes things a little more convenient.

Creating Software Exception Codes

When you work with software exceptions, you must create your own 32-bit exception codes. These codes follow a specific format (discussed in Chapter 24, "Exception Handlers and Software Exceptions"). To make creating these codes easier, I use the **MAKESOFTWAREEXCEPTION** macro.

The *chMB* Macro

The **chMB** macro simply displays a message box. The caption is the full pathname of the executable file for the calling process.

The *chASSERT* and *chVERIFY* Macros

To find potential problems as I developed the sample applications, I sprinkled **chASSERT** macros throughout the code. This macro tests whether the expression identified by **x** is **TRUE** and, if it isn't, displays a message box indicating the file, line, and expression that failed. In release builds of the applications, this macro expands to nothing. The **chVERIFY** macro is almost identical to the **chASSERT** macro except that the expression is evaluated in release builds as well as in debug builds.

The *chHANDLE_DLGMSG* Macro

When you use message crackers with dialog boxes, you should not use the **HANDLE_MSG** macro from Microsoft's WindowsX.h header file because it doesn't return **TRUE** or **FALSE** to indicate whether a message was handled by the dialog box procedure. My **chHANDLE_DLGMSG** macro massages the window message's return value and handles it properly for use in a dialog box procedure.

The *chSETDLGICONS* Macro

Because most of the sample applications use a dialog box as their main window, you must change the dialog box icon manually so that it is displayed correctly on the taskbar, in the task switch window, and in the application's caption itself. The **chSETDLGICONS** macro is always called when dialog boxes receive a **WM_INITDIALOG** message so that the icons are set correctly.

Forcing the Linker to Look for a *(w)WinMain* Entry-Point Function

Some readers of previous editions of this book who added my source code modules to a new Visual Studio project received linker errors when building the project. The problem was that they created a Win32 Console Application project, causing the linker to look for a **(w)main** entry-point function. Because all of the book's sample applications are GUI applications, my source code has a **_tWinMain** entry-point function instead; this is why the linker complained.

My standard reply to readers was that they should delete the project and create a new Win32 project (note that the word "Console" doesn't appear in this project type) with Visual Studio and add my source code files to it. The linker looks for a **(w)WinMain** entry-point function, which I do supply in my code, and the project will build properly.

To reduce the amount of e-mail I get on this issue, I added a **pragma** to CmnHdr.h that forces the linker to look for the **(w)WinMain** entry-point function even if you create a Win32 Console Application project with Visual Studio.

In Chapter 4, "Processes," I go into great detail about what the Visual Studio project types are all about, how the linker chooses which entry-point function to look for, and how to override the linker's default behavior.

Support XP-Theming of the User Interface with *pragma*

Since Windows XP, the system provides glossy-like styles called *themes* for most of the controls you are using to build your application user interface. However, the applications do not support theming by default. An easy way to enable theme support is to provide with your application an XML manifest that requires the binding to the right version of the ComCtl32.dll module, which takes care of repainting the Windows controls the right way. The Microsoft C++ linker provides the **manifestdependency** switch that is set through a **pragma** directive with the right parameters in CmnHdr.h. (Read the "Using Windows XP Visual Styles" page at *http://msdn2.microsoft.com/en-us/library/ms997646.aspx* for more details about theming support.)

CmnHdr.h

```
/*****************************************************************************
Module:  CmnHdr.h
Notices: Copyright (c) 2008 Jeffrey Richter & Christophe Nasarre
Purpose: Common header file containing handy macros and definitions
         used throughout all the applications in the book.
         See Appendix A.
*****************************************************************************/


#pragma once   // Include this header file once per compilation unit


///////////////////////// Windows Version Build Option /////////////////////////


// = 0x0600 for VISTA level from sdkddkver.h
#define _WIN32_WINNT _WIN32_WINNT_LONGHORN
#define WINVER       _WIN32_WINNT_LONGHORN


///////////////////////// Unicode Build Option /////////////////////////


// If we are not compiling for an x86 CPU, we always compile using Unicode.
#ifndef _M_IX86
   #define UNICODE
#endif


// To compile using Unicode on the x86 CPU, uncomment the line below.
#ifndef UNICODE
   #define UNICODE
#endif

// When using Unicode Windows functions, use Unicode C-Runtime functions too.
#ifdef UNICODE
   #ifndef _UNICODE
      #define _UNICODE
   #endif
#endif


///////////////////////// Include Windows Definitions /////////////////////////

#pragma warning(push, 3)
#include <Windows.h>
#pragma warning(pop)
#pragma warning(push, 4)
#include <CommCtrl.h>
#include <process.h>        // For _beginthreadex
```

```
/////////// Verify that the proper header files are being used //////////////


#ifndef FILE_SKIP_COMPLETION_PORT_ON_SUCCESS
#pragma message("You are not using the latest Platform SDK header/library ")
#pragma message("files. This may prevent the project from building correctly.")
#endif


////////////// Allow code to compile cleanly at warning level 4 //////////////


/* nonstandard extension 'single line comment' was used */
#pragma warning(disable:4001)

// unreferenced formal parameter
#pragma warning(disable:4100)

// Note: Creating precompiled header
#pragma warning(disable:4699)

// function not inlined
#pragma warning(disable:4710)

// unreferenced inline function has been removed
#pragma warning(disable:4514)

// assignment operator could not be generated
#pragma warning(disable:4512)


// conversion from 'LONGLONG' to 'ULONGLONG', signed/unsigned mismatch
#pragma warning(disable:4245)

// 'type cast' : conversion from 'LONG' to 'HINSTANCE' of greater size
#pragma warning(disable:4312)

// 'argument' : conversion from 'LPARAM' to 'LONG', possible loss of data
#pragma warning(disable:4244)

// 'wsprintf': name was marked as #pragma deprecated
#pragma warning(disable:4995)

// unary minus operator applied to unsigned type, result still unsigned
#pragma warning(disable:4146)
```

```
///////////////////////// Pragma message helper macro /////////////////////////


/*
When the compiler sees a line like this:
   #pragma chMSG(Fix this later)

it outputs a line like this:

  c:\CD\CmnHdr.h(82):Fix this later

You can easily jump directly to this line and examine the surrounding code.
*/

#define chSTR2(x) #x
#define chSTR(x)  chSTR2(x)
#define chMSG(desc) message(__FILE__ "(" chSTR(__LINE__) "):" #desc)


/////////////////////////// chINRANGE Macro ///////////////////////////////


// This macro returns TRUE if a number is between two others
#define chINRANGE(low, Num, High) (((low) <= (Num)) && ((Num) <= (High)))


/////////////////////////// chSIZEOFSTRING Macro ///////////////////////////


// This macro evaluates to the number of bytes needed by a string.
#define chSIZEOFSTRING(psz)   ((lstrlen(psz) + 1) * sizeof(TCHAR))


///////////////// chROUNDDOWN & chROUNDUP inline functions /////////////////


// This inline function rounds a value down to the nearest multiple
template <class TV, class TM>
inline TV chROUNDDOWN(TV Value, TM Multiple) {
   return((Value / Multiple) * Multiple);
}


// This inline function rounds a value down to the nearest multiple
template <class TV, class TM>
inline TV chROUNDUP(TV Value, TM Multiple) {
   return(chROUNDDOWN(Value, Multiple) +
      (((Value % Multiple) > 0) ? Multiple : 0));
}
```

```
/////////////////////////// chBEGINTHREADEX Macro ///////////////////////////


// This macro function calls the C runtime's _beginthreadex function.
// The C runtime library doesn't want to have any reliance on Windows' data
// types such as HANDLE. This means that a Windows programmer needs to cast
// values when using _beginthreadex. Since this is terribly inconvenient,
// I created this macro to perform the casting.
typedef unsigned (__stdcall *PTHREAD_START) (void *);

#define chBEGINTHREADEX(psa, cbStackSize, pfnStartAddr, \
   pvParam, dwCreateFlags, pdwThreadId)                 \
      ((HANDLE)_beginthreadex(                          \
         (void *)        (psa),                         \
         (unsigned)      (cbStackSize),                 \
         (PTHREAD_START) (pfnStartAddr),                \
         (void *)        (pvParam),                     \
         (unsigned)      (dwCreateFlags),               \
         (unsigned *)    (pdwThreadId)))


////////////////// DebugBreak Improvement for x86 platforms //////////////////


#ifdef _X86_
   #define DebugBreak()    _asm { int 3 }
#endif


/////////////////////////// Software Exception Macro ///////////////////////////


// Useful macro for creating your own software exception codes
#define MAKESOFTWAREEXCEPTION(Severity, Facility, Exception) \
   ((DWORD) ( \
   /* Severity code    */ (Severity      ) |    \
   /* MS(0) or Cust(1) */ (1        << 29) |    \
   /* Reserved(0)      */ (0        << 28) |    \
   /* Facility code    */ (Facility << 16) |    \
   /* Exception code   */ (Exception <<  0)))


/////////////////////////// Quick MessageBox Macro ///////////////////////////


inline void chMB(PCSTR szMsg) {
   char szTitle[MAX_PATH];
   GetModuleFileNameA(NULL, szTitle, _countof(szTitle));
   MessageBoxA(GetActiveWindow(), szMsg, szTitle, MB_OK);
}
```

```
///////////////////////// Assert/Verify Macros /////////////////////////////


inline void chFAIL(PSTR szMsg) {
   chMB(szMsg);
   DebugBreak();
}



// Put up an assertion failure message box.
inline void chASSERTFAIL(LPCSTR file, int line, PCSTR expr) {
   char sz[2*MAX_PATH];
   wsprintfA(sz, "File %s, line %d : %s", file, line, expr);
   chFAIL(sz);
}



// Put up a message box if an assertion fails in a debug build.
#ifdef _DEBUG
   #define chASSERT(x) if (!(x)) chASSERTFAIL(__FILE__, __LINE__, #x)
#else
   #define chASSERT(x)
#endif



// Assert in debug builds, but don't remove the code in retail builds.
#ifdef _DEBUG
   #define chVERIFY(x) chASSERT(x)
#else
   #define chVERIFY(x) (x)
#endif



///////////////////////// chHANDLE_DLGMSG Macro /////////////////////////////


// The normal HANDLE_MSG macro in WindowsX.h does not work properly for dialog
// boxes because DlgProc returns a BOOL instead of an LRESULT (like
// WndProcs). This chHANDLE_DLGMSG macro corrects the problem:
#define chHANDLE_DLGMSG(hWnd, message, fn)              \
   case (message): return (SetDlgMsgResult(hWnd, uMsg,    \
      HANDLE_##message((hWnd), (wParam), (lParam), (fn))))
```

```
//////////////////////// Dialog Box Icon Setting Macro ////////////////////////


// Sets the dialog box icons
inline void chSETDLGICONS(HWND hWnd, int idi) {
   SendMessage(hWnd, WM_SETICON, ICON_BIG,  (LPARAM)
     LoadIcon((HINSTANCE) GetWindowLongPtr(hWnd, GWLP_HINSTANCE),
        MAKEINTRESOURCE(idi)));
   SendMessage(hWnd, WM_SETICON, ICON_SMALL, (LPARAM)
     LoadIcon((HINSTANCE) GetWindowLongPtr(hWnd, GWLP_HINSTANCE),
     MAKEINTRESOURCE(idi)));
}


//////////////////////// Force Windows subsystem ////////////////////////


#pragma comment(linker, "/subsystem:Windows")

// needed for supporting XP/Vista styles.
#pragma comment(linker,"/manifestdependency:\"type='win32'
name='Microsoft.Windows.Common-Controls' version='6.0.0.0' processorArchitecture='x86'
publicKeyToken='6595b64144ccf1df' language='*'\"")


//////////////////////// End of File ////////////////////////
```

Appendix B

Message Crackers, Child Control Macros, and API Macros

By using C/C++ with message crackers to present the sample code in this book, I get to introduce these little-known but useful macros to many people who might not know about them.

Message crackers are in the WindowsX.h file supplied with Microsoft Visual Studio. You usually include this file immediately after the Windows.h file. The WindowsX.h file is nothing more than a bunch of **#define** directives that create a set of macros for you to use. The macros in WindowsX.h are actually divided into three groups: message crackers, child control macros, and application programming interface (API) macros. These macros help you in the following ways:

- They reduce the amount of casting you need to do in an application and make the casting that is required error-free. One of the big problems with programming for Windows in C/C++ has been the amount of casting required. You hardly ever see a call to a Windows function that doesn't require some sort of cast. You should avoid casts because they prevent the compiler from catching potential errors in your code. A cast tells the compiler, "I know I'm passing the wrong type here, but that's OK; I know what I'm doing." When you do a lot of casting, it's easy to make a mistake. The compiler should do as much work as possible to help out.

- They make your code more readable.

- They simplify porting between 32-bit Windows and 64-bit Windows.

- They're easy to understand. (They're just macros, after all.)

- They're easy to incorporate into existing code. You can leave old code alone and immediately use the macros in new code. You don't have to retrofit an entire application.

- You can use them in C and C++ code, although they're not necessary if you're using a C++ class library.

- If you need a feature that the macros don't support, you can easily write your own macros based on the ones in the header file.

- You don't need to reference or remember obscure Windows constructs. For example, many functions in Windows expect a long parameter where the value in the long's high word means one thing and the value in its low word means something else. Before calling these functions, you must construct a long value out of the two individual values. You usually do this by using the MAKELONG macro from WinDef.h. But I can't tell you how many times I've accidentally reversed the two values, causing an incorrect value to be passed to a function. The macros in WindowsX.h come to the rescue.

Message Crackers

Message crackers make it easier to write window procedures. Typically, window procedures are implemented as one huge **switch** statement. In my travels, I've seen window procedure **switch** statements that contained well over 500 lines of code. We all know that implementing window procedures in this way is bad practice, but we do it anyway. I've been known to do it myself on occasion. Message crackers force you to break up your **switch** statements into smaller functions—one function per window message. This makes your code much more manageable.

Another problem with window procedures is that every message has **wParam** and **lParam** parameters, and depending on the message, these parameters have different meanings. In some cases, such as a **WM_COMMAND** message, **wParam** contains two different values. The high word of the **wParam** parameter is the notification code, and the low word is the ID of the control. Or is it the other way around? I always forget. If you use message crackers, you don't have to remember or look up any of this. Message crackers are so named because they crack apart the parameters for any given message. To process the **WM_COMMAND** message, you simply write a function that looks like this:

```c
void Cls_OnCommand(HWND hWnd, int id, HWND hWndCtl,
   UINT codeNotify) {

   switch (id) {

      case ID_SOMELISTBOX:
         if (codeNotify != LBN_SELCHANGE)
         break;

         // Do LBN_SELCHANGE processing.
         break;

      case ID_SOMEBUTTON:
         break;
   ...
```

Look how easy it is! The crackers look at the message's **wParam** and **lParam** parameters, break the parameters apart, and call your function.

To use message crackers, you must make some changes to your window procedure's **switch** statement. Take a look at the window procedure here:

```c
LRESULT WndProc (HWND hWnd, UINT uMsg,
   WPARAM wParam, LPARAM lParam) {

   switch (uMsg) {
      HANDLE_MSG(hWnd, WM_COMMAND, Cls_OnCommand);
      HANDLE_MSG(hWnd, WM_PAINT,   Cls_OnPaint);
      HANDLE_MSG(hWnd, WM_DESTROY, Cls_OnDestroy);
      default:
         return(DefWindowProc(hWnd, uMsg, wParam, lParam));
   }
}
```

The **HANDLE_MSG** macro is defined as follows in WindowsX.h:

```c
#define HANDLE_MSG(hwnd, message, fn) \
   case (message): \
      return HANDLE_##message((hwnd), (wParam), (lParam), (fn))
```

For a **WM_COMMAND** message, the preprocessor expands this line to read as follows:

```
case (WM_COMMAND):
    return HANDLE_WM_COMMAND((hwnd), (wParam), (lParam),
      (Cls_OnCommand));
```

The **HANDLE_WM_*** macros, which are also defined in WindowsX.h, are actually message crackers. They crack the contents of the **wParam** and **lParam** parameters, perform all the necessary casting, and call the appropriate message function, such as the **Cls_OnCommand** function shown earlier. The macro for **HANDLE_WM_COMMAND** is as follows:

```
#define HANDLE_WM_COMMAND(hwnd, wParam, lParam, fn) \
    ( (fn) ((hwnd), (int) (LOWORD(wParam)), (HWND)(lParam),
    (UINT) HIWORD(wParam)), 0L)
```

When the preprocessor expands this macro, the result is a call to the **Cls_OnCommand** function with the contents of the **wParam** and **lParam** parameters broken down into their respective parts and cast appropriately.

Before you use message cracker macros to process a message, you should open the WindowsX.h file and search for the message you want to process. For example, if you search for **WM_COMMAND**, you'll see the part of the file that contains these lines:

```
/* void Cls_OnCommand(HWND hWnd, int id, HWND hWndCtl,
     UINT codeNotify); */
#define HANDLE_WM_COMMAND(hwnd, wParam, lParam, fn) \
   ((fn)((hwnd), (int)(LOWORD(wParam)), (HWND)(lParam), \
   (UINT)HIWORD(wParam)), 0L)
#define FORWARD_WM_COMMAND(hwnd, id, hwndCtl, codeNotify, fn) \
   (void)(fn)((hwnd), WM_COMMAND, \
   MAKEWPARAM((UINT)(id),(UINT)(codeNotify)), \
   (LPARAM)(HWND)(hwndCtl))
```

The first line is a comment that shows you the prototype of the function you have to write. The next line is the **HANDLE_WM_*** macro, which we've already discussed. The last line is a message forwarder. Let's say that during your processing of the **WM_COMMAND** message you want to call the default window procedure to have it do some work for you. This function would look like this:

```
void Cls_OnCommand (HWND hWnd, int id, HWND hWndCtl,
    UINT codeNotify) {

    // Do some normal processing.

    // Do default processing.
    FORWARD_WM_COMMAND(hWnd, id, hwndCtl, codeNotify,
       DefWindowProc);
}
```

The **FORWARD_WM_*** macro takes the cracked message parameters and reconstructs them to their **wParam** and **lParam** equivalents. The macro then calls a function that you supply. In the preceding example, the macro calls the **DefWindowProc** function, but you can just as easily use **SendMessage** or **PostMessage**. In fact, if you want to send (or post) a message to any window in the system, you can use a **FORWARD_WM_*** macro to help combine the individual parameters.

Child Control Macros

The child control macros make it easier to send messages to child controls. They are very similar to the **FORWARD_WM_*** macros. Each macro starts with the type of control you are sending the message to, followed by an underscore and the name of the message. For example, to send an **LB_GETCOUNT** message to a list box, you use the following macro from WindowsX.h:

```
#define ListBox_GetCount(hwndCtl) \
    ((int)(DWORD)SNDMSG((hwndCtl), LB_GETCOUNT, 0, 0L))
```

Let me point out a couple of things about this macro. First, **SNDMSG** is a macro that maps to either **SendMessage** or **AfxSendMessage** in an MFC context. Second, it takes only one parameter, **hwndCtl**, which is the window handle of the list box. Because the **LB_GETCOUNT** message ignores the **wParam** and **lParam** parameters, you don't need to bother with them. The macro passes zeros, as you can see above. Second, when **SendMessage** returns, the result is cast to an **int**, so you don't have to supply your own cast.

The one thing I don't like about the child control macros is that they take the handle of the control window. Most of the time, the controls you need to send messages to are children of a dialog box. So you end up having to call **GetDlgItem** all the time, producing code like this:

```
int n = ListBox_GetCount(GetDlgItem(hDlg, ID_LISTBOX));
```

This code doesn't run any slower than it would if you used **SendDlgItemMessage**, but your application will contain some extra code because of the additional call to **GetDlgItem**. If you need to send several messages to the same control, you might want to call **GetDlgItem** once, save the child window's handle, and then call all the macros you need, as shown in the following code:

```
HWND hWndCtl = GetDlgItem(hDlg, ID_LISTBOX);
int n = ListBox_GetCount(hWndCtl);
ListBox_AddString(hWndCtl, TEXT("Another string"));
...
```

If you design your code in this way, your application will run faster because it won't have to repeatedly call **GetDlgItem**. **GetDlgItem** can be a slow function if your dialog box has many controls and the control you are looking for is toward the end of the z-order.

API Macros

The API macros simplify certain common operations, such as creating a new font, selecting the font into a device context, and saving the handle of the original font. The code looks something like this:

```
HFONT hFontOrig = (HFONT) SelectObject(hDC, (HGDIOBJ) hFontNew);
```

This statement requires two casts to get a warning-free compilation. One of the macros in WindowsX.h was designed for exactly this purpose:

```
#define SelectFont(hdc, hfont) \
    ((HFONT) SelectObject( (hdc), (HGDIOBJ) (HFONT) (hfont)))
```

If you use this macro, the line of code in your program becomes the following:

```
HFONT hFontOrig = SelectFont(hDC, hFontNew);
```

This code is easier to read and is much less error-prone.

Several other API macros in WindowsX.h help with common Windows tasks. I urge you to examine them and use them.

Index

Jeffrey Richter

Jeffrey Richter is a co-founder of Wintellect *(http://www.Wintellect.com/)*, a training, debugging, and consulting company dedicated to helping companies produce better software faster. Jeff has written many books, including *CLR via C#* (Microsoft Press, 2005). Jeff is also a contributing editor for *MSDN Magazine*, where he has written several feature articles and is a columnist. Jeff also speaks at various trade conferences worldwide, including VSLive!, and Microsoft's TechEd and PDC. Jeff has consulted for many companies, including AT&T, DreamWorks, General Electric, Hewlett-Packard, IBM, and Intel. For Microsoft, Jeff's code has shipped in many products including TerraServer, Visual Studio, the .NET Framework, Office, and various versions of Windows. On the personal front, Jeff holds both airplane and helicopter pilot licenses, though he never gets to fly as often as he'd like. He is also a member of the International Brotherhood of Magicians and enjoys showing friends sleight-of-hand card tricks from time to time. Jeff's other hobbies include music, drumming, model railroading, boating, traveling, and the theater. He and his family live in Kirkland, Washington.

Christophe Nasarre

Christophe Nasarre works as a software architect and development lead for Business Objects, a multinational software company that is focused on helping organizations gain better insight into their business, improving decision-making and enterprise performance through business intelligence solutions. He has worked as a technical editor on numerous Addison-Wesley, APress, and Microsoft Press books in addition to writing articles in *MSDN Magazine*.

What do you think of this book?

We want to hear from you!

Do you have a few minutes to participate in a brief online survey?

Microsoft is interested in hearing your feedback so we can continually improve our books and learning resources for you.

To participate in our survey, please visit:

www.microsoft.com/learning/booksurvey/

...and enter this book's ISBN-10 or ISBN-13 number (located above barcode on back cover*). As a thank-you to survey participants in the United States and Canada, each month we'll randomly select five respondents to win one of five $100 gift certificates from a leading online merchant. At the conclusion of the survey, you can enter the drawing by providing your e-mail address, which will be used for prize notification only.

Thanks in advance for your input. Your opinion counts!

* Where to find the ISBN on back cover

ISBN-13: 000-0-0000-0000-0
ISBN-10: 0-0000-0000-0

Example only. Each book has unique ISBN.

Microsoft®
Press

No purchase necessary. Void where prohibited. Open only to residents of the 50 United States (includes District of Columbia) and Canada (void in Quebec). For official rules and entry dates see:

www.microsoft.com/learning/booksurvey/